Frommer's

P9-DTV-421

Paris 2005

POSTCARDS FROM

La Tour Eiffel, stretching 317m (1,056 ft.), shines over the City of Light.
© Hollenbeck Photography.

Even public works can be art works in Paris. The Métro entrance at Port Dauphine is in the Art Nouveau style. © Stephen Studd/Tony Stone Images.

The Basilisque du Sacré-Coeur crowns Montmartre, a neighborhood that offers hidden treasures on its side streets. For a walking tour of the area, see chapter 8, "Strolling Around Paris." © John Elk III Photography.

Pick up a fresh baguette if you're planning a Parisian picnic, and complete your feast with a bottle of wine and a pastry. For the best places to shop for an alfresco lunch, see chapter 9, "Shopping."

Top: © Steven Rothfeld/Tony Stone Images; bottom: © Bill Gallery/Viesti Associates, Inc.

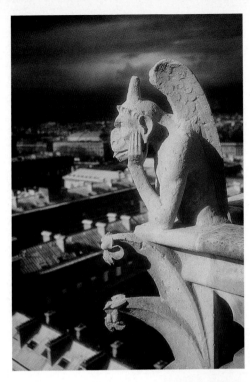

This ugly fellow seems to contemplate the history of Paris from atop the Cathédrale de Notre-Dame. See "Top Attractions" in chapter 7, "Exploring Paris." © Harald Sund/Image Bank.

Paris is filled with museums, from the Louvre to the Musée Picasso, which contains the world's greatest collection of works by the Spanish master. See "The Major Museums," in chapter 7.
© Catherine Karnow Photography.

The parks of Paris, in particular the Jardin des Tuileries, are a favorite spot for young and old to enjoy the city and each others' company. See "Parks & Gardens," in chapter 7.

An hour northwest of Paris is Giverny, where Impressionist Claude Monet captured the beauty and color of his famous water lilies. See "Giverny," in chapter 11, "Side Trips from Paris."
© Robert Holmes Photography.

A bronze Dionysus looks over the great palace of Versailles, home of some of the grandest and most opulent European royal courts. See "Versailles," in chapter 11.
© Robert Holmes Photography.

Light streams through the dazzling rose window at the Cathédral de Notre-Dame.
© John Elk III Photography.

Frommer's

Paris

2005

by Darwin Porter & Danforth Prince

Here's what the critics say about Frommer's:

"Amazingly easy to use. Very portable, very complete."

—*Booklist*

"Detailed, accurate, and easy-to-read information for all price ranges."
—*Glamour Magazine*

"Hotel information is close to encyclopedic."

—*Des Moines Sunday Register*

"Frommer's Guides have a way of giving you a real feel for a place."
—*Knight Ridder Newspapers*

WILEY

Wiley Publishing, Inc.

About the Authors

As a team of veteran travel writers, **Darwin Porter** and **Danforth Prince** have produced numerous titles for Frommer's, including best-selling guides to Italy, France, the Caribbean, England, and Germany. Porter, a former bureau chief of *The Miami Herald*, is also a Hollywood biographer. His most recent releases are *The Secret Life of Humphrey Bogart* and *Katharine the Great*, the latter a close-up of the private life of the late Katharine Hepburn. Prince was formerly employed by the Paris bureau of the *New York Times* and is today the president of Blood Moon Productions and other media-related firms.

Published by:

Wiley Publishing, Inc.

111 River St.
Hoboken, NJ 07030-5774

ISBN 0-7645-6895-7

Editor: Billy Owens
Production Editor: Tammy Ahrens
Cartographer: Nick Trotter
Photo Editor: Richard Fox
Production by Wiley Indianapolis Composition Services

Front cover photo: Seine River towards Eiffel Tower at night
Back cover photo: Montmartre: street with Sacre-Coeur in background

For information on our other products and services or to obtain technical support, please contact our Customer Care Department within the U.S. at 800/762-2974, outside the U.S. at 317/572-3993 or fax 317/572-4002.

Wiley also publishes its books in a variety of electronic formats. Some content that appears in print may not be available in electronic formats.

Manufactured in the United States of America

5   4   3   2   1

Contents

List of Maps

An Invitation to the Reader

In researching this book, we discovered many wonderful places—hotels, restaurants, shops, and more. We're sure you'll find others. Please tell us about them, so we can share the information with your fellow travelers in upcoming editions. If you were disappointed with a recommendation, we'd love to know that, too. Please write to:

Frommer's Paris 2005
Wiley Publishing, Inc. • 111 River St. • Hoboken, NJ 07030-5774

An Additional Note

Please be advised that travel information is subject to change at any time—and this is especially true of prices. We therefore suggest that you write or call ahead for confirmation when making your travel plans. The authors, editors, and publisher cannot be held responsible for the experiences of readers while traveling. Your safety is important to us, however, so we encourage you to stay alert and be aware of your surroundings. Keep a close eye on cameras, purses, and wallets, all favorite targets of thieves and pickpockets.

Frommer's Star Ratings, Icons & Abbreviations

Every hotel, restaurant, and attraction listing in this guide has been ranked for quality, value, service, amenities, and special features using a **star-rating system.** In country, state, and regional guides, we also rate towns and regions to help you narrow down your choices and budget your time accordingly. Hotels and restaurants are rated on a scale of zero (recommended) to three stars (exceptional). Attractions, shopping, nightlife, towns, and regions are rated according to the following scale: zero stars (recommended), one star (highly recommended), two stars (very highly recommended), and three stars (must-see).

In addition to the star-rating system, we also use **seven feature icons** that point you to the great deals, in-the-know advice, and unique experiences that separate travelers from tourists. Throughout the book, look for:

Finds	Special finds—those places only insiders know about
Fun Fact	Fun facts—details that make travelers more informed and their trips more fun
Kids	Best bets for kids and advice for the whole family
Moments	Special moments—those experiences that memories are made of
Overrated	Places or experiences not worth your time or money
Tips	Insider tips—great ways to save time and money
Value	Great values—where to get the best deals

The following **abbreviations** are used for credit cards:

AE	American Express	DISC	Discover	V	Visa
DC	Diners Club	MC	MasterCard		

Frommers.com

Now that you have the guidebook to a great trip, visit our website at **www.frommers.com** for travel information on more than 3,000 destinations. With features updated regularly, we give you instant access to the most current trip-planning information available. At Frommers.com, you'll also find the best prices on airfares, accommodations, and car rentals—and you can even book travel online through our travel booking partners. At Frommers.com, you'll also find the following:

- Online updates to our most popular guidebooks
- Vacation sweepstakes and contest giveaways
- Newsletter highlighting the hottest travel trends
- Online travel message boards with featured travel discussions

What's New in Paris

In a jittery world and with an uncertain economy, Paris remains one of the most visited countries on the planet. Visitors, of course, come to revisit the city's glorious past, as reflected in its art and architecture, but they are also intrigued by Paris's cutting edge in cuisine, style, and fashion. Here are some of the latest developments in an ever-changing City of Light:

ACCOMMODATIONS   Near the Luxembourg Gardens, **Hôtel Luxembourg Parc,** 42 rue de Vaugirad, 6e (℡ **01-53-10-36-50**), has emerged on the scene and been hailed as a small-scale version of the supremely deluxe Hôtel de Crillon. Today one of the most charming hotels on the Left Bank, the inn has been installed in a beautifully restored 17th-century palace. Bedrooms are decorated in one of the Louis periods or else in the style of the Napoleon III era.

Hidden away in the 3rd arrondissement, the restored **Hôtel Bellevue & du Chariot d'Or,** 39 rue de Turbigo (℡ **01-48-87-45-60**), is drawing more and more patrons to the once-neglected Arts et Métiers district north of Pompidou Center. A real bargain for Paris, its good Métro links hook up quickly and conveniently to Paris's major sightseeing attractions.

The Latin Quarter, the district of the Sorbonne, has a restored and most inviting hotel in **La Tour Notre Dame,** 20 rue du Sommerard, 5e (℡ **01-43-54-47-60**). Rising seven floors over a 17th-century vaulted cellar, there is much Rive Gauche charm here and good comfort, even certain romantic touches such as Empire era furnishings.

DINING   One the most famous of French bistros, **Aux Lyonnais,** 32 rue St-Marc, 2e (℡ **01-42-96-65-04**), has come under the culinary baton of a master chef, the fabled Alain Ducasse. His take on the celebrated Lyonnaise cuisine is the best in the city. He has installed a talented young chef, Christophe Saintagne, who offers elegant bistro fare full of flavor.

Hailed as the greatest French chef in Paris of the 1990s, Joël Robuchon has come out of retirement to launch **L'Atelier de Joël Robuchon,** in the Hotel Pont Royal, 5–7 rue de Montalembert, 7e (℡ **01-42-22-56-56**). This is a much simpler brasserie than his elegant citadel of yesterday. But it's nonetheless a chic gastronomic shrine with masterfully prepared fare.

Master chef Alain Ducasse continues to expand his food empire with the opening of **BE,** 73 blvd. de Courcelles, 8e (℡ **01-46-22-20-20**), which is short for **Boulangerie Epicerie,** a sort of upmarket bakery and deli, one of the finest in Paris. It's an ideal place to drop into for the makings of *le grand picnic.* To show the care that goes into running this place, bread is baked at least eight times a day.

In the 18th-century town house of the Marquis de Lafayette, **1728,** 8 rue d'Anjou, 8e (℡ **01-40-17-04-77**), has been installed with its fusion cuisine from both Japan and France. This is a chic rendezvous, beautifully decorated and serving delightful market-fresh offerings.

SIDE TRIPS FROM PARIS As more and more art lovers flock to the little town of Giverny to see the water lilies of Monet, good restaurants continue to open to accommodate them. A recent discovery, **Restaurant Les Fleurs,** 71 rue Sadie-Carnot, Vernon (© **02-32-51-16-80**), is a delight, lying 5km (3 miles) southwest of Monet's museum. Here a disciple of the fabled chef, Alain Ducasse, has forged his own statement with a series of carefully prepared French dishes, both classic and innovative.

SHOPPING Called "the world's smallest department store," **Talmaris,** 61 av. Mozart, 16e (© **01-42-88-20-20**), is the boutique showcase of Alain-Paul Ruzé, who spends months every year traveling the world and looking for "curiosities."

AFTER DARK Currently, one of the hottest and hippest bars on the Left Bank is the aptly named **Bob Cool,** 15 rue des Grands Augustins, 6e (© **01-46-33-33-77**), lying off the fabled rue St-André-des-Arts. Writers and artists, along with patrons in a wide age range, are attracted to this place, which is known for the variety of its recorded music.

The Best of Paris

Discovering the City of Light and making it your own has always been the most compelling reason to visit Paris. If you're a first-timer, everything, of course, will be new to you. If you've been away for a while, expect changes: Taxi drivers may no longer correct your fractured French but address you in English—tantamount to a revolution. More Parisians have a rudimentary knowledge of the language, and France, at least at first glance, seems less xenophobic than in past years. Paris, aware of its role within a united Europe, is an international city. Parisians are attracted to foreign music, videos, and films, especially those from America, even though most French people violently disagree with the political dictates emerging from George Bush's Washington. Security remains tighter than ever in the wake of the September 11, 2001, terrorist attacks. Paris has fully activated its antiterrorist campaign first launched in the mid-1990s when France was the target of a spate of Algerian terrorist attacks.

Expect to see far more police in bulletproof vests at all transport hubs and government buildings, as well as at high-profile sites such as the Eiffel Tower.

Metal detectors at Paris's airports are turned up so high that the zipper on a pair of trousers can trigger an alarm. Often, you have to do a virtual striptease before security will give you the green light.

As Paris and the country itself move deeper into the millennium, there is a fear among the French of a loss of identity. France continues to attract record numbers of immigrants from its former colonies. Many native-born French have expressed concern that the country will lose the battle to keep its language distinct and unadulterated by foreign (particularly American) slang or catchwords (*le weekend* or *le software*). In fact, the rancor of France's collective xenophobia has been increasingly redirected toward the many immigrants seeking better lives in Paris, where the infrastructure has nearly been stretched to its limits.

Though Paris is in flux culturally and socially, it lures travelers for the same reasons it always has. You'll still find classic sights like the Tour Eiffel, Notre-Dame, the Arc de Triomphe, Sacré-Coeur, and all those atmospheric cafes, as well as daring new projects like the Grande Arche de La Défense, the Cité des Sciences et de l'Industrie, the Cité de la Musique, and the Bibliothèque François-Mitterrand. And don't forget the parks, gardens, and squares; the Champs-Elysées and other grand boulevards; the river Seine and its quays. Paris's beauty is still overwhelming, especially at night, when it truly is the City of Light.

1 Frommer's Favorite Paris Experiences

- **Whiling Away an Afternoon in a Parisian Cafe:** The cafe is where passionate meetings of writers, artists, philosophers, thinkers, and revolutionaries once took place—and perhaps still do. Parisians stop by their favorite cafes to meet lovers and friends, to make new ones, or sit in solitude with a newspaper or book. Whether you order a small coffee or the most expensive cognac in the house, nobody will hurry you from this quintessentially Parisian activity. For our recommendations, see "The Top Cafes," in chapter 6, "Where to Dine."

- **Taking Afternoon Tea à la Française:** Drinking tea in London has its charm, but the Parisian *salon de thé* is unique. Skip the cucumber-and-watercress sandwiches and delve into a luscious dessert like the Mont Blanc, a creamy purée of sweetened chestnuts and meringue. The grandest Parisian tea salon is **Angélina,** but you might want to stop by **Berthillon** for one of their scrumptious ice creams. See chapter 6, "Where to Dine," for details.

- **Strolling Along the Seine:** Such painters as Sisley, Turner, and Monet have fallen under the Seine's spell. On its banks, lovers still walk hand in hand, anglers cast their lines, and *bouquinistes* (secondhand-book dealers) peddle their mix of postcards, 100-year-old pornography, and tattered histories of Indochina. *Clochards* (beggars) seek a home for the night under its bridges, and the Bateaux-Mouches (river cruise boats) ply its waters. For a spectacular view of the Louvre, cross the city's first iron bridge, the pont des Arts, one of only four pedestrian bridges. Paris's oldest and most famous bridge is the pont Neuf (New Bridge), from which you have an excellent view of the Palais de Justice and Sainte-Chapelle on Ile de la Cité. For more details on the sights and moments of Paris, see chapter 7, "Exploring Paris."

- **Spending a Day at the Races:** Paris boasts eight tracks for horse racing. The most famous and the classiest is **Hippodrome de Longchamp,** in the Bois de Boulogne, the site of the Prix

de l'Arc de Triomphe and Grand Prix (p. 217). These and other top races are major social events, so you'll have to dress up (buy your outfit on rue du Faubourg St-Honoré). Take the Métro to Porte d'Auteuil, then a bus from there to the track. The racing newspaper *Paris Turf* and weekly entertainment magazines have details about race times.

- **Calling on the Dead:** You don't have to be a ghoul to be thrilled by a visit to Europe's most famous cemetery, **Père-Lachaise** (p. 213). You can pay your respects to the earthly remains of Gertrude Stein and Alice B. Toklas, Oscar Wilde, Yves Montand and Simone Signoret, Edith Piaf, Isadora Duncan, Abélard and Héloïse, Frédéric Chopin, Marcel Proust, Eugène Delacroix, Jim Morrison, and others. The tomb designs are intriguing and often eerie. Laid out in 1803 on a hill in Ménilmontant, the cemetery offers surprises with its bizarre monuments, unexpected views, and ornate sculpture.

- **Discovering Hidden Montmartre:** This is Paris's most touristy area. However, far removed from the area's top draw, Sacré-Coeur, is the neighborhood of the true Montmartrois. Wander the back streets away from the souvenir shops. Arm yourself with a good map and seek out such streets as rue Lepic (refresh yourself at the Lux Bar at no. 12), rue Constance, rue Tholozé (with its view over the Paris rooftops), rue des Abbesses, and rue Germain-Pilon. None of these is famous, but each boasts buildings whose detailing shows the pride and care permeating Paris's architecture. Discover dozens of other streets on your own. At dusk, sit on Sacré-Coeur's top steps and watch as

Paris turns into the City of Light. For a walking tour of Montmartre, see chapter 8, "Strolling Around Paris."

- **Checking Out the Marchés:** A daily Parisian ritual is ambling through one of the open-air markets to buy fresh food—perhaps a properly creamy Camembert or a pumpkin-gold cantaloupe—to be eaten before sundown. You can take part in this time-honored tradition by purchasing the makings for a picnic in a park or even in your room. Like artists, the vendors arrange their wares into a mosaic of vibrant colors: Sanguine, an Italian citrus with juice the color of a brilliant orange sunset; ruby-red peppers; and golden-yellow bananas from Martinique all dazzle the eye. Our favorite market is on rue Montorgueil, beginning at rue Rambuteau, 1e (Métro: Les Halles). During mornings at this grubby little cluster of food stalls, we've spotted some of France's finest chefs stocking up for the day. For more details, see "Food Markets" in chapter 9.

- **Window-Shopping in the Faubourg St-Honoré:** In the 1700s, the wealthiest Parisians resided in the Faubourg St-Honoré; today the quarter is home to stores catering to the rich, particularly on rue du Faubourg St-Honoré and avenue Montaigne. Even if you don't buy anything, it's great to window-shop big names like Hermès, Dior, Laroche, Courrèges, Cardin, and Saint Laurent. If you want to browse in the stores, be sure to dress the part. See chapter 9, "Shopping," for the lowdown on these boutiques.

- **Exploring Ile de la Cité's Flower Market:** A fine finish to any day (Mon–Sat) spent meandering along the Seine is a stroll through the **Marché aux Fleurs,** place Louis-Lépine (p. 259). You can buy rare flowers, the gems of the French Riviera—bouquets that have inspired artists throughout the centuries. Even the most basic hotel room will feel like a luxury suite once you fill it with bunches of carnations, lavender, roses, and tulips. On Sundays, the area is transformed into the **Marché aux Oiseaux,** where you can admire rare birds from around the world.

- **Going Gourmet at Fauchon:** An exotic world of food, **Fauchon** (p. 254) offers more than 20,000 products from around the globe. Everything you never knew you were missing is in aisle after aisle of coffees, spices, pastries, fruits, vegetables, rare Armagnacs, and much more. Take your pick: Tonganese mangoes, Scottish smoked salmon, preserved cocks' combs, Romanian rose-petal jelly, blue-red Indian pomegranates, golden Tunisian dates, larks stuffed with foie gras, dark morels from France's rich soil, Finnish reindeer's tongue, century-old eggs from China, and a Creole punch from Martinique reputed to be the best anywhere.

- **Attending a Free Concert:** Summer brings a Paris joy: free concerts in parks and churches all over the city. Pick up an entertainment weekly for details. Some of the best concerts are held at the **American Church in Paris,** 65 quai d'Orsay, 7e (© **01-40-62-05-00;** Métro: Invalides or Alma-Marceau), which sponsors free concerts from September to June on Sunday at 5pm. You can also attend free concerts at **Eglise St-Merri,** 78 rue St-Martin, 4e (© **01-42-74-59-39;** Métro: Hôtel-de-Ville). These performances are staged based on the availability of the performers, from September to July on Saturday at 9pm and again on Sunday at 4pm. For more concerts, refer to chapter 10, "Paris After Dark."

- **Attending a Ballet or an Opera:** In 1989, the **Opéra Bastille** (p. 267) was inaugurated to compete with the grande dame of the music scene, the **Opéra Garnier** (p. 268), which then was solely for dance and soon closed for renovations. The Garnier reopened a few years ago, and opera has joined dance in the rococo splendor created by Charles Garnier, beneath a controversial ceiling by Chagall. The modern Bastille, France's largest opera house, with curtains by designer Issey Miyake, features opera and symphony performances in four concert halls (its main hall seats 2,700). Whether for a performance of Bizet or Tharp, dress with pomp and circumstance.

- **Watching the Show at the Folies-Bergère:** Often denounced, the campy showcase at the **Folies-Bergère** (p. 270) has been pleasing audiences since 1868, even though classic acts like Maurice Chevalier, Mistinguett, and Josephine Baker (who performed her famous banana dance here) vanished long ago. True, the Tour Eiffel cancan is a bit corny and the show has become less daring, but those ladies in their sequins, feathers, and pom-poms still evoke a Paris of days gone by, immortalized on a Manet canvas. The show, tacky or not, seems to go on forever.

- **Sipping Cocktails at Willi's:** Back in the early 1970s, the first-timer to Paris might have arrived with a copy of Hemingway's *A Moveable Feast* and, taking the author's endorsement to heart, headed for Harry's Bar at "Sank roo doe Noo." Harry's is still around but now draws an older, more conservative clientele. Today's chic younger expats head for **Willi's Wine Bar** (p. 280), where the longhaired young bartenders are mostly English, as are the waitresses, who are dressed in Laura Ashley garb. The place is like an informal club for Brits, Australians, and Yanks, especially in the afternoon. Some 300 wines await your selection.

2 Best Hotel Bets

For full details on the following hotels, see chapter 5, "Where to Stay."

- **Best Boutique Hotel:** In the 6th arrondissement on the Left Bank, **Hotel d'Aubusson,** 33 rue Dauphine (✆ 01-43-29-43-43), is a restored mansion in the heart of St-Germain-de-Prés, a district more famously associated with Literary Bohemia in the post-war era. Graced with original Aubusson tapestries, as befits its name, the hotel was once a grand private residence of a French nobleman in the 17th century. Inside, the hotel is a nugget of Parisian styling and chic, like your own private town house in Paris. See p. 99.

- **Best for Business Travelers:** Corporate types from all over the world converge at the **Hôtel Balzac,** 6 rue Balzac, 8e (✆ **800/ 457-4000** in the U.S. and Canada), a Belle Epoque town house with a good business center, 2 blocks from many of the offices along the Champs-Elysées. Its restaurant serves some of the best food in town and is suitable for entertaining clients. See p. 90.

- **Best for Families:** An affordable Left Bank choice is the **Hôtel de Fleurie,** 32–34 rue Grégoire-de-Tours, 6e (✆ **01-53-73-70-00**), in the heart of St-Germain-des-Prés. The accommodations are thoughtfully appointed, and many connecting rooms with two large beds are perfect for families. Children under 12 stay free with a parent. See p. 100.

- **Best Value:** Not far from the Champs-Elysées, the **Résidence Lord Byron,** 5 rue de Chateaubriand, 8e (☎ 01-43-59-89-98), is a classy little getaway that's far from opulent but is clean and comfortable and worth every euro. See p. 91.

- **Best Location:** Only a 2-minute walk from Paris's most historic and beautiful square, **Hôtel de la Place des Vosges,** 12 rue de Birague, 4e (☎ 01-42-72-60-46), is a little charmer. In a building 350 years old, it is small and inviting, with some decorative touches that evoke the era of Louis XIII. See p. 83.

- **Best View:** Of the 33 rooms at the **Hôtel du Quai Voltaire,** 19 quai Voltaire, 7e (☎ 01-42-61-50-91), 28 open onto views of the Seine. If you stay here, you'll be following in the footsteps of Wilde, Baudelaire, and Wagner. This 17th-century abbey was transformed into a hotel back in 1856 and has been welcoming guests who appreciate its tattered charms ever since. See p. 108.

- **Best for Nostalgia:** If you yearn for a Left Bank "literary" address, make it the **Odéon Hôtel,** 3 rue de l'Odéon, (☎ 01-43-25-90-67), in the heart of the 6th arrondissement, filled with the ghosts of Gide, Hemingway, Fitzgerald, Joyce, and Stein and Toklas. Evoking a Norman country inn, this charming hotel lures guests with its high, crooked ceilings, exposed beams, and memories of yesterday. See p. 101.

- **Best for Stargazing:** The tycoons, hot stars, and hotter mistresses of yesterday—Douglas Fairbanks and Mary Pickford, William Randolph Hearst and Marion Davies—knew where to stay back then. Tom Cruise and his ilk know *the* address in Paris is still the **Hôtel de Crillon,** 10 place de la Concorde, 8e (☎ 800/223-6800 in the U.S. and Canada), once the palace of the duc de Crillon. If you want its grandest suite and have a discriminating taste for the macabre, ask for the Marie Antoinette Apartment—it exhibits Antoinette-style elegance, and its namesake was beheaded practically at the doorstep of this deluxe citadel. See p. 88.

- **Best for Opulence:** Now owned by Mohammed al-Fayed, the **Hôtel Ritz,** 15 place Vendôme, 1e (☎ 800/223-6800 in the U.S. and Canada), has dripped with wealth, luxury, and decadence since César Ritz opened it in 1898. Barbara Hutton, Coco Chanel, and Marcel Proust are just a few names inscribed in its glorious guest book; if you're into romantic tragedy, remember this was where Princess Diana and Dodi al-Fayed had their last meal. You can join the Saudi oil princes, Milanese divas, and movie legends staying here—if you have big bucks. See p. 76.

- **Best-Kept Secret:** Built in 1913 and long in a seedy state, the fully restored **Terrass Hôtel,** 12 rue Joseph-de-Maistre, 18e (☎ 01-46-06-72-85), is now the only four-star choice in Montmartre, an area not known for luxury accommodations. Its rooms take in far-ranging views of the Tour Eiffel, Arc de Triomphe, and Opéra Garnier. See p. 86.

- **Best Historic Hotel:** Inaugurated by Napoleon III in 1855, the **Hôtel du Louvre,** place André-Malraux, 1e (☎ 800/888-4747 in the U.S. and Canada), was once described by a French journalist as "a palace of the people, rising adjacent to the palace of kings." Today, the hotel offers luxurious accommodations and panoramic views down avenue de l'Opéra. See p. 73.

- **Best for Romance:** Until the 1970s, **L'Hôtel,** 13 rue des Beaux Arts, 6e (© **01-44-41-99-00**), was a fleabag filled with drunks and addicts (in 1900, Oscar Wilde died here penniless). Millions of francs of renovations later, the rooms that were once cramped and claustrophobic are now ravishingly romantic, wrought like small jewel boxes. See p. 99.
- **Most Trendy Hotel:** A converted town house, the **Hôtel Costes,** 239 rue St-Honoré, 1e (© **01-42-44-50-50**), evokes the imperial

heyday of Napoleon III. Fashion headliners especially like it— Costes is the choice of many a model, as the Paris offices of *Harper's Bazaar* are close at hand. If you're into swags, patterned fabrics, jewel-tone colors, and lavish accessories, this can be your Gilded Age address. See p. 73.

- **Best Service:** Though you can't fault the flawless decor of the **Plaza Athénée,** 25 av. Montaigne, 8e (© **866/732-1106** in the U.S. and Canada), billionaires check in because they get the royal treatment from the jaded but indulgent and ever-so-polite staff. In an upscale neighborhood between the Seine and the Champs-Elysées, the Plaza Athénée offers service that's impeccable. See p. 88.

3 Best Dining Bets

For full listings of the following restaurants, see chapter 6, "Where to Dine."

- **Best Chef:** Proud owner of five Michelin stars, **Alain Ducasse,** at the Restaurant Plaza Athénée, 25 av. Montaigne, 8e (© **01-53-67-66-65**), has taken Paris by storm, dividing his time between his restaurant here and the one in Monte Carlo. He combines produce from every French region in a cuisine that's contemporary but not quite new, embracing the Mediterranean without abandoning France. See p. 137.
- **Best Haute Cuisine Restaurant:** Named for a 14th-century chef who wrote one of the oldest known books on French cookery, **Taillevent,** 15 rue Lamennais, 8e (© **01-44-95-15-01**), occupies a 19th-century town house off the Champs-Elysées. Though its owner likes to keep about 60% of the crowd French, you should still try

for a reservation at Paris's most outstanding all-around restaurant. See p. 137.

- **Best Newcomer:** In the restored town house of the Marquis de Lafayette, **1728,** 8 rue d'Anjou, 8e (© **01-40-17-04-77**), is a real discovery—and a delight. In an elegant setting, it offers a delectable fusion cuisine of both Japanese and French dishes. You can buy not only the food here but the modern paintings off the walls. See p. 139.
- **Best Modern French Cuisine:** A temple of gastronomy is found at **Carré des Feuillants,** 14 rue de Castiglione, 1e (© **01-42-86-82-82**), near place Vendôme and the Tuileries. Alain Dutournier is one of the leading chefs of France, and he restored this 17th-century convent, turning it into a citadel of refined cuisine and mouthwatering specialties. See p. 117.

- **Best Provençal Cuisine:** With Michelin's coveted two stars, **Les Elysées du Vernet,** 25 rue Vernet, 8e (℃ **01-44-31-98-98**), hosts *tout Paris* (all of Paris) and the media. Montpellier-born chef Alain Solivérès has emerged as one of the greatest in Paris, challenging some big-name chefs. His Provençal cookery is the freshest and among the best in the whole country. See p. 137.

- **Best Old-Fashioned Bistro:** Established in 1931 and bouncing back from a period of decline, **Allard,** 41 rue St-André-des-Arts, 6e (℃ **01-43-26-48-23**), is better than ever, from its zinc bar to its repertoire of French classics— escargots, frogs' legs, foie gras, *boeuf à la mode* (marinated beef), and cassoulet. This is a good bet for real Left Bank bistro ambience. See p. 152.

- **Best Rising Chef:** In the residential 17th arrondissement, chef Jacques Fassat is luring *tout Paris* to **La Braisière,** 54 rue Cardinet, 17e (℃ **01-47-63-40-37**), with his take on the succulent cuisine of southwest France. In 2004 Fassat won his first Michelin star, and if our last visit was an indication of things to come, there may be other stars in his future. See p. 145.

- **Best View:** A penthouse restaurant, **La Tour d'Argent,** 15–17 quai de la Tournelle, 5e (℃ **01-43-54-23-31**), is owned by ex-playboy Claude Terrail, who pays part of Notre-Dame's electric bill to illuminate the cathedral at night for his diners' pleasure. Dining here is a theatrical event. See p. 146.

- **Best Provincial Restaurant:** The cuisine of the Auvergne in central France is showcased at **Bath's,** 9 rue de la Trémoille, 8e (℃ **01-40-70-01-09**). In a cozy, elegant setting, you can dine on the best dishes of this province, including ravioli stuffed with Cantal cheese, and filet of beef with lentils. See p. 138.

- **Best for Stargazing:** No, it's not Taillevent or even Alain Ducasse. On the see-and-be-seen circuit, the star is still the **Buddha Bar,** 8 rue Boissy d'Anglas, 8e (℃ **01-53-05-90-00**). The crowd doesn't come for the cuisine, though its fusion of French and Pacific Rim is exceedingly well executed. If you don't want to eat, stop by the hip, lacquered bar across from the dining room. See p. 134.

- **Worst-Kept Secret:** In the heart of the Latin Quarter, **Perraudin,** 157 rue St-Jacques, 5e (℃ **01-46-33-15-75**), duplicates the allure of an early-1900s bistro. You get the feeling Emile Zola could walk in any minute. It offers great food and great value, and an old-fashioned dining experience that's rapidly disappearing from the city. See p. 150.

- **Best Brasserie:** Head for the Left Bank and the **Brasserie Balzar,** 49 rue des Ecoles, 5e (℃ **01-43-54-13-67**), which opened in 1898. If you dine on the familiar French food here, you'll be following in the footsteps of Sartre and Camus and others. You can even have a complete dinner in the middle of the afternoon. See p. 147.

- **Best Seafood:** The fattest lobsters and prawns in the Rungis market emerge on platters at **Goumard,** 9 rue Duphot, 1e (℃ **01-42-60-36-07**), so chic that even the toilets are historic monuments. Nothing interferes with the taste of the sea: You'd have to fly to the Riviera to find a better bouillabaisse. See p. 120.

- **Best *Cuisine Bourgeoise* (Comfort Food):** If Joyce, Verlaine, Valéry, and Hemingway rose from the grave today and strode into the **Crémerie-Restaurant Polidor,** 41 rue Monsieur-le-Prince, 6e (℃ **01-43-26-95-34**), not only would they not notice any differences, not even on the menu, but they could ask for their napkins, which are locked in a cabinet in back with their names on them. See p. 154.

• **Best Atmosphere:** A favorite of Colette and Cocteau, the world-famous **Le Grand Véfour,** 17 rue de Beaujolais, 1e (℃ **01-42-96-56-27**), at the Palais-Royal, has an interior classified as a historic monument. Incidentally, it serves some of the most refined cuisine in Paris. See p. 117.

• **Best Lyonnais Cuisine:** Lyon is hailed as France's gastronomic capital, and the best place in Paris to introduce yourself to its cuisine is **Aux Lyonnais,** 32 rue St-Marc, 2e (℃ **01-42-96-65-04**). This *fin-de-siècle* bistro turns out the dishes for which Lyon is famous, from perfect pike dumplings to Lyonnais sausages—all washed down, of course, with Beaujolais. See p. 123.

• **Best Kosher Food:** If corned beef, pastrami, herring, and dill pickles thrill you, head to **rue des Rosiers** in the 4th arrondissement (Métro: St-Paul). John Russel wrote that rue des Rosiers is the "last sanctuary of certain ways of life; what you see there in miniature is Warsaw before the ghetto was razed." North African overtones reflect the long-ago arrival of Jews from Morocco, Tunisia, and Algeria. The best time to go is Sunday morning: You can wander the streets eating as you go—apple strudel, Jewish rye bread, pickled lemons, smoked salmon, and *merguez,* a spicy smoked sausage from Algeria. Many spots offer sit-down meals, like **Chez Jo Goldenberg,** 7 rue des Rosiers, 4e (℃ **01-48-87-20-16**), where the *carpe farcie* (stuffed carp) is outstanding and beef goulash a fine runner-up. See p. 129.

• **Best American Cuisine:** A Yankee outpost in Les Halles, **Joe Allen,** 30 rue Pierre-Lescot, 1e (℃ **01-42-36-70-13**), serves the finest burgers in Paris. Desserts include New York cheesecake, pecan pie made with pecans imported from the United States, and an inspired cultural fusion of American brownies made with French chocolate. See p. 121.

• **Best Vegetarian Cuisine:** One of the best-known veggie restaurants in the Marais is **Le Marais,** 54 rue Ste-Croix-de-la-Bretonnerie, 4e (℃ **01-48-87-48-71**). Choose from the array of soups and salads, or have a mushroom tart or a *galette* (a flat pastry) of wheat with raw vegetables. In this rustic 17th-century setting, you can expect flavorful, wholesome, and generous meals. See p. 129.

• **Best Wine Cellar:** At the elegant **Lasserre,** 17 av. Franklin D. Roosevelt, 8e (℃ **01-43-59-53-43**), you'll find not only wonderful food but also one of the great wine cellars of France, with some 160,000 bottles. See p. 136.

• **Best for Cheese:** Cheese is king at **Androuët sur le Pouce,** 49 rue St-Roch, 1e (℃ **01-42-97-57-39**). Many cheese lovers opt for a bottle of wine, a green salad, and all-you-can-eat choices from the most sophisticated *dégustation de fromages* (cheese-sampling menu) in the world. See p. 123.

• **Best Late-Night Dining:** There's no place better in Paris to get a good meal at 3am than **Au Pied de Cochon,** 6 rue Coquillière, 1e (℃ **01-40-13-77-00**). Though everyone lauds its grilled pig's feet with béarnaise sauce, few have noticed you can also find some of the freshest oysters in town here. See p. 120.

- **Best Champagne Julep:** While you wait for a table at **Closerie** des Lilas, 171 bd. du Montparnasse, 6e (℃ **01-40-51-34-50**), savor the best champagne julep in the world at the bar. See p. 152.

4 The Best Cafes

For full details on the following cafes, turn to chapter 6, "Where to Dine."

- **Most Evocative Left Bank Cafe:** Old bohemia still lives at the battered but artistic Quartier Latin cafe, **La Palette,** 43 rue de Seine, 6e (℃ **01-43-26-68-15**), where patrons still down the same Ricard and Pernod they did back in the 1930s. See p. 164.

- **Most Historical Cafe:** Fans of French history flock to **Le Procope,** 13 rue de l'Ancienne-Comédie, 6e (℃ **01-40-46-79-00**), where such luminaries as Voltaire, Oscar Wilde, and Napoleon used to hang out. The ground floor is outfitted like an antique library. See p. 164.

- **Most Legendary Hangout:** Once a gathering place for French intellectuals, **Les Deux Magots,** 6 place St-Germain-des-Prés, 6e (℃ **01-45-48-55-25**), is still going strong, with tourists now sitting at tables where Gore Vidal and James Baldwin once did. See p. 165.

- **Most Nostalgic Cafe:** In the wake of the worldwide success of the low budget film *Amélie,* **Café des Deux Moulins,** 15 rue Lepic, 18e (℃ **01-42-54-90-50**), where Amélie worked as a waitress in the film, is luring droves of "cult visitors" to its 1950s precincts. Its musty atmosphere of unisex toilets and antique lace curtains is

---

Tips **The Best Websites for Paris**

Surf these recommended websites for information on the City of Light:

- **Bonjour Paris, www.bparis.com**, is one of the most comprehensive and fun sites about life in Paris, written from an American-expatriate point of view. You can also subscribe to a regular e-newsletter.

- **Paris Digest, www.parisdigest.com**, is an independent site containing articles that link to restaurants, hotels, museums, monuments, parks, and activities. It includes city history and tips for getting around.

- **Paris Pages, www.paris.org**, offers a wealth of information on Paris for a widespread audience. The lodging reviews are organized by area and by the nearby monuments. The guide includes an event calendar, shop listings, a map of attractions with details about each, and photo tours.

- **Paris Tourist Office, www.paris-touristoffice.com**, offers information on city events arranged by week, month, favorites, and year, plus the closest Métro stops for museums, lodgings, restaurants, and nightlife. You can tour parks and gardens and discover Paris's trendy districts.

the most evocative place in Montmartre for a glass of Côtes du Rhône, or whatever. See p. 165.

- **Most Quintessential Paris Left Bank Cafe:** Vying with Deux Magots (see above), **Café de Flore,** 172 bd. St-Germain, 6e (© **01-45-48-55-26**), basks in its memories of its famous visitors, who included Camus, Picasso, and Apollinaire. Even though tourists now take up the tables here, Café de Flore still pulls off a Left Bank aura. See p. 162.

2

A Traveler's Guide to Paris's Art & Architecture

by Reid Bramblett

Paris is one of the artistic capitals of Europe. For centuries the city has produced, and been home to, countless artists and artistic movements. This chapter will help you find the best examples of each period in the city's museums and architecture.

1 Art 101

GOTHIC (1100–1400)

Almost all artistic expression in medieval France was church-related. Paris retains almost no art from the Classical or Romanesque eras, but much remains from the medieval Gothic era, when artists created sculpture and stained glass for churches.

Because Mass was in Latin, many images were used to communicate the Bible's most important lessons to the mostly illiterate populace. **Bas reliefs** (sculpture that projects slightly from a flat surface) were used to illustrate key tales that inspired faith in God and fear of sin (last judgments were favorites). These reliefs were wrapped around column capitals, festooned onto facades, and fitted into the **tympanum** (the arched spaces above doorways; the complete door, tympanum, arch, and supporting pillars assemblage is the **portal**).

The French were also becoming masters of **stained glass.** Many painterly conventions began in this era on windowpanes, or as elaborate doodles in the margins of **illuminated manuscripts,** which developed into altarpieces of the colorful **International Gothic** style.

In both Gothic painting and sculpture, figures tend to be highly stylized, flowing, and rhythmic. The figures' features and gestures are exaggerated for symbolic or emotional emphasis.

Outstanding examples include:

- **Cathédrale de Chartres** (1194–1220). A day trip from Paris, Cathédrale de Chartres boasts magnificent sculpture and some of the best stained glass in Europe.
- **Cathédrale de Notre-Dame** (1163–1250). The Gothic high points of this cathedral are the sculpture on the facade, an interior choir screen lined with deep-relief carvings, and three rose windows filled with stained glass.
- **Sainte-Chapelle** (1240–50). The finest stained glass in the world adorns this tiny chapel.

- **The Lady and the Unicorn Tapestries** (1499–1514). These famed tapestries shine brightly as a final statement of medieval sensibilities while borrowing some burgeoning Renaissance conventions. Find them in the **Musée de Cluny.**

THE RENAISSANCE (1400–1600)

Renaissance means "rebirth," in this case the return of classical ideals originating in Greece and Rome. Humanist thinkers rediscovered the wisdom of the ancients, while artists strove for greater naturalism, using newly developed techniques such as linear perspective to achieve new heights of realism. Famous practitioners of the style include **Michelangelo** (1475–1564) and **Leonardo da Vinci** (1452–1519). **Mannerism,** the late 16th-century branch of the High Renaissance, took Michelangelo's bright color palate and twisting figures to extremes and exhausted the movement.

Aside from collecting Italian art, the French had little to do with the Renaissance, which started in Italy and was quickly picked up in Germany and the Low Countries. France owes many of its early Renaissance treasures to **François I,** who imported art (paintings by Raphael and Titian) and artists (Leonardo da Vinci). Henri II's Florentine wife, **Catherine de Médicis,** also collected 16th-century Italian masterpieces.

Significant artists and examples to look for in Paris include:

- **Italian Artists.** Many works by Italy's finest reside in the **Louvre,** including paintings by **Giotto, Fra' Angelico,** and **Veronese;** sculptures by Michelangelo; and a handful of works by Leonardo da Vinci, who moved to a Loire Valley château for the last 3 years of his life and whose *Mona Lisa* (1503–05), perhaps the world's most famous painting, hangs here.
- **The School of Fontainebleau.** This group of artists working on the **Palais de Fontainebleau** outside Paris from 1530 to 1560 were imported Italian mannerists who combined painting, stucco, sculpture, and woodwork to decorate the château's Galerie François I. They included **Niccolò dell'Abbate, Benvenuto Cellini, Primaticcio,** and **Rosso Fiorentino.** (If you don't make it out to Fontainebleau, check out Cellini's sculpture *Diana of Fontainebleau* [1543–44] in the Louvre.)

THE BAROQUE (1600–1800)

The 17th-century **baroque style** is hard to pin down. In some ways it was a result of the Catholic Counter-Reformation, reaffirming spirituality in a simplified, monumental, and religious version of Renaissance ideals. In other ways it delved even deeper into classical modes and a kind of super-realism based on using peasants as models and the exaggerated *chiaroscuro* (interplay or contrast of light and dark) of Italian painter Caravaggio.

Some view those two movements as extensions of Renaissance experiments, and find the true baroque in later compositions—all explosions of dynamic fury, movement, color, and figures—that are well balanced, but in such cluttered abundance as to appear untamed. **Rococo** is this later baroque art gone awry, frothy, and chaotic.

Significant practitioners of the baroque with examples in the **Louvre** include:

- **Nicolas Poussin** (1594–1665). The most classical French painter, Poussin created mythological scenes that presaged the Romantic Movement. His balance and predilection to paint from nature influenced French Impressionists such as Cézanne.

- **Antoine Watteau** (1684–1721). Watteau indulged in the wild, untamed complexity of the rococo. Cruise the Louvre for his colorful, theatrical works. He began the short-lived *fête galante* style that featured china-doll figures against stylized landscapes of woodlands or ballrooms.
- **François Boucher** (1703–70). Louis XV's rococo court painter, Boucher studied Watteau and produced lots of decorative landscapes and genre works.
- **Jean-Honoré Fragonard** (1732–1806). Boucher's student and the master of rococo, Fragonard painted an overindulgence of pink-cheeked, genteel lovers frolicking against billowing treescapes. The Louvre hangs his famous *The Bathers.*

NEOCLASSICAL & ROMANTIC (1770–1890)

As the baroque got excessive, the rococo got cute, and the somber Counter-Reformation got serious about the limits on religious art, several artists looked for relief to the ancients. Viewing new excavations of Greek and Roman sites (Pompeii and Paestum) and statuary became integral parts of the Grand Tour through Italy, while the Enlightenment (and growing Revolutionary) interest in Greek democracy beat an intellectual path to the distant past. This gave rise to a **neoclassical** artistic style that emphasized symmetry, austerity, clean lines, and classical themes, such as depictions of events from history or mythology.

The **romantics,** on the other hand, felt both the ancients and the Renaissance had gotten it wrong and that the Middle Ages was the place to be. They idealized romantic tales of chivalry and held a deep respect for nature, human rights, and the nobility of peasantry, and a suspicion of progress. Their paintings were heroic, historic, and (melo)dramatic, and quested for beauty.

Some great artists and movements of the era, all with examples in the **Louvre,** include:

- **Jacques-Louis David** (1748–1825). David dropped the baroque after a year of study in Rome exposed him to neoclassicism, which he brought back to Paris and displayed in such paintings as *The Oath of the Horatii* (1784) and *Coronation of Napoléon and Josephine* (1805–08).
- **Jean Ingres** (1780–1867). Trained with David, Ingres become a defender of the neoclassicists and the Royal French Academy, and opposed the romantics. His *Grand Odalisque* (1814) hangs in the Louvre.
- **Theodore Géricault** (1791–1824). One of the great early romantics, Géricault produced the large, dramatic history painting *The Raft of the Medusa* (1819), which served as a model for the movement.
- **Eugène Delacroix** (1798–1863). His *Liberty Leading the People* (1830) was painted in the romantic style, but the artist was also experimenting with color and brushstroke.
- **The Barbizon School.** This school of landscape painters, founded in the 1830s by **Théodore Rousseau** (1812–67), painted directly from nature at Barbizon near Paris. **Jean François Millet** (1814–75) preferred classical scenes and local peasants; his works are at the **Musée d'Orsay. Jean Baptiste Camille Corot** (1796–1875), the third Barbizon great, was a sort of idealistic proto-Impressionist.

IMPRESSIONISM (1870–1920)

Formal, rigid neoclassicism and idealized romanticism rankled some late 19th-century artists interested in painting directly from nature. Seeking to capture the *impression* light made reflecting off objects, they adopted a free, open style;

deceptively loose compositions; swift, visible brushwork; and often light colors. For subject matter, they turned away from the classical themes of previous styles to landscapes and scenes of modern life. Unless specified below, you'll find some of the best examples of their works in the **Musée d'Orsay.**

Impressionist greats include:

- **Edouard Manet** (1832–83). His groundbreaking *Picnic on the Grass* (1863) and *Olympia* (1863) weren't Impressionism proper, but they helped inspire the movement with their harsh realism, visible brushstrokes, and thick outlines.
- **Claude Monet** (1840–1926). The Impressionist movement officially began with an 1874 exhibition in which Monet exhibited his loose, Turner-inspired *Impression, Sunrise* (1874), now in the **Musée Marmottan,** which one critic picked to lambaste the whole exhibition, deriding it all as "Impressionist." Far from being insulted, the antiestablishment artists in the show adopted the word for their exhibits, held through the 1880s.
- **Pierre-Auguste Renoir** (1841–1919). Originally, Renoir was a porcelain painter, which helps explain his figures' ivory skin and chubby pink cheeks.
- **Edgar Degas** (1834–1917). Degas was an accomplished painter, sculptor, and draughtsman—his pastels of dancers and bathers are particularly memorable.
- **Auguste Rodin** (1840–1917). The greatest Impressionist-era sculptor, Rodin crafted remarkably expressive bronzes, refusing to idealize the human figure as had his neoclassical predecessors. The **Musée Rodin,** his former Paris studio, contains, among other works, his *Burghers of Calais* (1886), *The Kiss* (1886–98), and *The Thinker* (1880).

POST-IMPRESSIONISM (1880–1930)

Few experimental French artists of the late 19th century were technically Impressionists, though many were friends with those in the movement. The smaller movements or styles are usually lumped together as "post-Impressionist."

Again, you'll find the best examples of their works at the **Musée d'Orsay,** though you'll find pieces by Matisse, Chagall, and the cubists, including Picasso, in the **Centre Pompidou.** Important post-Impressionists include:

- **Paul Cézanne** (1839–1906). He adopted the short brushstrokes, love of landscape, and light color palate of his Impressionist friends, but Cézanne was more formal and deliberate in his style. He sought to give his art monumentality and permanence, even if the subjects were simple still lifes, portraits, or landscapes.
- **Paul Gauguin** (1848–1903). Gauguin could never settle himself or his work, trying Brittany first, where he developed **synthetism** (black outlines around solid colors), and later hopping around the South Pacific, where he was inspired by local styles and colors.
- **Georges Seurat** (1859–91), **Paul Signac** (1863–1935), and **Camille Jacob Pissarro** (1830–1903). Together these artists developed **divisionism** and its more formal cousin, **pointillism.** Rather than mixing, say, yellow and blue paint together to make green, they applied tiny dots of yellow and blue right next to each other so that the viewer's eye mixes them together to make green.
- **Henri de Toulouse-Lautrec** (1864–1901). Most famous for his work with thinned-down oils, Toulouse-Lautrec created paintings and posters of wispy, fluid lines anticipating Art Nouveau and often depicting the bohemian life of Paris's dance halls and cafes. In Montmartre you can still visit the **Moulin Rouge,** the cabaret he immortalized on canvas.

- **Vincent van Gogh** (1853–90) spent most of his tortured artistic career in France. He combined divisionism, synthetism, and a touch of Japanese influence, and painted with thick, short strokes. Never particularly accepted by any artistic circle, he is the most popular painter in the world today (his paintings fetch record sums at auction, and he sells more postcards and posters than any other artist), even though he sold only one painting in his short life.

- **Henri Matisse** (1869–1954). He took a hint from synthetism and added wild colors and strong patterns to create **fauvism** (a critic described those who used the style as *fauves,* meaning "wild beasts"). Matisse continued exploring these themes, even when most artists were turning to cubism. When his health failed, he began assembling brightly colored collages of paper cutouts.

- **Pablo Picasso** (1881–1973). Along with **Georges Braque** (1882–1963), this Barcelona-born artist painted objects from all points of view at once, rather than use optical tricks like perspective to fool viewers into seeing three dimensions. The fractured result was **cubism** and was expanded upon by the likes of **Fernand Léger** (1881–1955) and **Juan Gris** (1887–1927), while Picasso moved on to other styles. You can see all of his periods at the **Musée Picasso** in the Marais.

2 Architecture 101

While each architectural era has its distinctive features, there are some elements, general floor plans, and terms common to many.

From the Romanesque period on, most **churches** consist either of a single wide **aisle,** or a wide central **nave** flanked by two narrow aisles. A row of **columns,** or square stacks of masonry called **piers,** connected by **arches,** separates the aisles from the nave.

This main nave/aisle assemblage is usually crossed by a perpendicular corridor called a **transept** near the far, east end of the church so that the floor plan looks like a Latin cross (shaped like a lowercase "t"). At the east end sits the holy **altar.** This is usually on a raised dais and in the entrance to—or, especially later, just in front of—the large **chapel** formed by the shorter, far end of the cross. If this large, main chapel is rounded off on the end, it is called an **apse;** it is often elongated and filled with the stalls of the **choir.** Some churches, especially after the Renaissance when mathematical proportion became important, were built on a Greek cross plan, each axis the same length, like a giant "+."

It's worth pointing out that very few buildings (especially churches) were built in one particular style. These massive, expensive structures often took centuries to complete, during which time tastes would change and plans would be altered.

Church Floor Plan

ANCIENT ROMAN (B.C. 125–450 A.D.)

France was Rome's first transalpine conquest, and the legions of Julius Caesar quickly subdued the Celtic tribes across France, converting it into Roman Gaul and importing Roman building concepts.

IDENTIFIABLE FEATURES
- **The load-bearing arch.**
- **The use of concrete and brick.**

BEST EXAMPLES
- **Parvis Archaeological Excavations.** The Romanized village of Lutèce, later renamed after its native *Parisii* tribe of Celtic Gauls, is partially excavated under place du Parvis in front of Notre-Dame.
- **Musée de Cluny.** This medieval monastery was built on top of a **Roman baths complex,** remnants of which are still visible on the grounds outside and in the huge preserved *frigidarium* (the cold-water bath) that is now a room of the museum. The museum itself also contains ancient statuary.

ROMANESQUE (800–1100)

Romanesque architects concentrated on building large churches with wide aisles to accommodate the population that came to hear Mass and worship at the altars of various saints. The Romanesque took its inspiration from ancient Rome (hence the name). Early Christians in Italy had adapted the basilica (ancient Roman lawcourt buildings) to become churches. Few examples of the Romanesque remain in Paris, however, with most churches having been rebuilt in later eras.

IDENTIFIABLE FEATURES
- **Rounded arches.** These load-bearing architectural devices allowed the architects to open up wide naves and spaces, channeling all the weight of the stone walls and ceiling across the curve of the arch and down into the ground via the columns or pilasters.
- **Thick walls, infrequent and small windows, and huge piers.** These were necessary to support the weight of all that masonry, giving Romanesque churches a dark, somber, mysterious, and often oppressive feeling.
- **Apse.** This rounded space behind the altar in many Romanesque churches opens up the holiest, east end of the church.
- **Radiating chapels.** These smaller chapels began to sprout off the east end of the church, especially later in the Romanesque period, often in the form of a fan of minichapels radiating off the apse.
- **Ambulatory.** This curving corridor separates the altar and choir area from the ring of smaller, radiating chapels. This, too, was a convention of the later Romanesque and carried into the Gothic.

BEST EXAMPLES
- **St-Germain-des-Prés.** The overall building is Romanesque, including the fine sculpted column capitals near the entrance of the left aisle; only the far left corner is original, the others are copies. By the time builders got to creating the choir, the early Gothic was on—note the pointy arches. Over the (early Renaissance) portal is a Romanesque carving of the *Last Judgment.*
- **St-Julien-le-Pauvre.** This small church has a general Romanesque plan overwritten by later Gothic embellishments, including the facade.

GOTHIC (1100–1500)

By the 12th century, engineering developments freed church architecture from the heavy, thick walls of Romanesque structures and allowed ceilings to soar, walls to thin, and windows to proliferate.

Instead of dark, somber, relatively unadorned Romanesque interiors that forced the eyes of the faithful toward the altar, the Gothic interior enticed the churchgoers' gaze upward to high ceilings filled with light. The priests still conducted Mass in Latin, but now peasants could "read" the stories told in pictures in the stained-glass windows.

The squat, brooding exteriors of the Romanesque fortresses of God were replaced by graceful buttresses and spires that soared above town centers.

IDENTIFIABLE FEATURES

- **Pointed arches.** The most significant development of the Gothic era was the discovery that pointed arches could carry far more weight than rounded ones.
- **Cross vaults.** Instead of being flat, the square patch of ceiling between four columns arches up to a point in the center, creating four sail shapes, sort of like the underside of a pyramid. The "X" separating these four sails is often reinforced with ridges called **ribbing.** As the Gothic progressed, four-sided cross vaults became six- or eight-sided as architects played with the angles.

Cross Vault

- **Flying buttresses.** These free-standing exterior pillars connected by graceful, thin arms of stone help channel the weight of the building and its roof out and down into the ground. To help counter the cross forces involved in this engineering sleight of hand, the piers of buttresses were often topped by heavy pinnacles, which took the form of minispires or statues.
- **Spires.** These pinnacles of masonry seem to defy gravity and reach toward heaven itself.
- **Gargoyles.** Disguised as wide-mouthed creatures, gargoyles are actually drain spouts.
- **Tracery.** These lacy spider webs of carved stone grace the pointy ends of windows and sometimes the spans of ceiling vaults.
- **Stained glass.** Because pointy arches can carry more weight than rounded ones, windows could be larger and more numerous. They were often filled with Bible stories and symbolism writ in the colorful patterns of stained glass.

Flying Buttress

Cross Section of Gothic Church

- **Rose windows.** Huge circular windows filled with tracery and "petals" of stained glass, rose windows often appear as the centerpiece of facades and, in some larger churches, at the ends of transepts as well.

- **Ambulatory.** The Gothic made much greater use of this corridor of space wrapping behind the apse and often around a **choir** (the boxed-off area, usually behind the altar, where the choir sat and sang).
- **Choir screen.** Serving as the inner wall of the ambulatory and the outer wall of the choir section, choir screens are often decorated with carvings or serve as tombs.

BEST EXAMPLES
- **Basilique St-Denis** (1140–44). Today you'll find the world's first Gothic cathedral in a Paris suburb.
- **Cathédrale de Chartres** (1194–1220). This Gothic masterpiece boasts good statuary, a soaring spire, and some 150 glorious stained-glass windows.
- **Cathédrale de Notre-Dame** (1163–1250). This famous cathedral possesses pinnacled flying buttresses, a trio of France's best rose windows, good portal carvings, a choir screen of deeply carved reliefs, and spiffy gargoyles (though many of those are actually 19th-century neo-Gothic).

Cathédrale de Chartres

RENAISSANCE (1500–1630)
In architecture, as in painting, the Renaissance came from Italy and was only slowly Frenchified. And, as in painting, its rules stressed proportion, order, classical inspiration, and precision to create unified, balanced structures.

IDENTIFIABLE FEATURES
- **Proportion and symmetry.** Other than a close eye to these Renaissance ideals, little specifically identifies buildings of this period.
- **Steeply pitched roofs.** Many roofs are of pale stone with dark gray tiles. This feature is a throwback to medieval sensibilities, but because almost no medieval mansions survive in Paris, the buildings that *do* sport steep roofs tend to be Renaissance.
- **Dormer windows.** These tend to be tall and made of stone, which differentiates them from the less extravagant, wooden ones of later periods.

BEST EXAMPLES
- **Hôtel Carnavalet** (1544). This Renaissance mansion is the only 16th-century hotel left in Paris. It contains the **Musée Carnavalet,** a museum devoted to the history of Paris and the French Revolution.
- **Place des Vosges.** This square is lined by Renaissance mansions rising above a lovely arcaded corridor that wraps all the way around.

CLASSICISM & ROCOCO (1630–1800)
While Italy and Germany embraced the opulent baroque, France took the fundamentals of Renaissance **classicism** even further, becoming more imitative of

ancient models—this represents a change from the Renaissance preference to find inspiration in the classic era.

During the reign of Louis XIV, art and architecture were subservient to political ends. Buildings were grandiose and severely ordered on the Versailles model. Opulence was saved for interior decoration, which increasingly (especially 1715–50, after the death of Louis XIV) became an excessively detailed and self-indulgent **rococo** (*rocaille* in French). Externally, this later style is only noticeable by a greater elegance and delicacy.

Rococo tastes didn't last long, though, and soon a **neoclassical** movement was raising structures, such as Paris's **Panthéon** (1758), even more strictly based on ancient models than the earlier classicism was.

IDENTIFIABLE FEATURES

- **Symmetrical, rectangular structures.** French classicism concentrated on horizontal and vertical lines and simple proportions.
- **Classical throwbacks.** Classicism was favored for the very fact that it brought back such elements as classical orders (Doric, Ionic, and Corinthian) and projecting central sections topped by triangular pediments.

Corinthian Order   Ionic Order   Doric Order

Classical Orders

- **Mansard roofs.** A defining feature and true French trademark developed by **François Mansart** (1598–1666) in the early 15th century, a mansard roof has a double slope, the lower being longer and steeper than the upper.
- **Dormer windows.** Unlike the larger Renaissance ones flanked by showy stone scrolls, later dormers tended to be lower, less extravagant, and wooden.
- *Oeil-de-bouef* **windows.** These small, round "ox-eye" windows poke out of the roof's slope.
- **Excessive detail.** Rococo interior decoration is often asymmetrical and abstract with shell-like forms and many C- and S-curves. Naturalistic flowers and trees are sometimes playfully introduced.

Mansard Roof

BEST EXAMPLES

- **Palais du Louvre** (1650–70). A collaborative classical masterpiece, the Louvre was designed as a palace. **Le Vau** (1612–70) was its chief architect, along with collaborators **François Mansart** (1598–1666), the interior decorator **Charles Le Brun** (1619–90), and the unparalleled landscape gardener **André Le Nôtre** (1613–1700). The structure subsequently had several purposes (see chapter 7 for the complete history) before becoming a museum.
- **Versailles** (1669–85). Versailles is France's—indeed, Europe's—grandest palace, the Divine Monarchy writ as a statement of fussily decorative, politically charged classical architecture, though the interior was redecorated in more flamboyant styles. The chief architects of its complete overhaul under Louis XIV were the oft-used team (see Palais du Louvre, above) of Le Vau, Mansart, Le Brun, and Le Nôtre. Mansart's grand-nephew (and Louis XIV's chief architect) **Jules Hardouin-Mansart** (1646–1708) took over after Le Vau's death, changing much of the exterior look. The **Clock Room** is a good example of rococo interior decoration.

Versailles

- **Panthéon** (1758). This Left Bank monument is a perfect example of the strict neoclassical style.

THE 19TH CENTURY

Architectural styles in 19th-century Paris were eclectic, beginning in a severe classical mode and ending with an identity crisis torn between Industrial Age technology and Art Nouveau organic. The "Identifiable Features" section explores the main facets of competing styles during this turbulent century.

IDENTIFIABLE FEATURES

- **First Empire.** Elegant, neoclassical furnishings—distinguished by strong lines often accented with a simple curve—became the rage during Napoleon's reign.
- **Second Empire.** Napoleon III's reign saw the eclectic Second Empire reinterpret classicism in an ornate, dramatic mode. Urban planning was the architectural rage, and Paris became a city of wide boulevards courtesy of **Baron Georges-Eugène Haussmann** (1809–91), commissioned by Napoleon III in 1852 to redesign the city. Paris owes much of its remarkably unified look to Haussmann, who drew his beloved thoroughfares directly across the city, tearing down existing structures along the way. He lined the boulevards with simple, six-story apartment blocks, like elongated 18th-century town houses with continuous balconies wrapping around the third and sixth floors and mansard roofs with dormer windows.

- **Third Republic.** Expositions in 1878, 1889, and 1900 were the catalysts for constructing huge glass-and-steel structures that showed off modern techniques and the engineering prowess of the Industrial Revolution. This produced such Parisian monuments as the Tour Eiffel and Sacré-Coeur.
- **Art Nouveau.** These architects and decorators rebelled against the Third Republic era of mass production by stressing the uniqueness of craft. They created asymmetrical, curvaceous designs based on organic inspiration (plants and flowers) in such mediums as wrought iron, stained glass, tile, and hand-painted wallpaper.

BEST EXAMPLES

- **Palais de Fontainebleau.** Napoleon spent his imperial decade (1804–14) refurbishing his quarters in this palace in First Empire style.
- **Arc de Triomphe** (1836). Napoleon's oversize imitation of a Roman triumphal arch is the ultimate paean to the classical era. The arch presides over **L'Etoile,** an intersection of 12 wide boulevards laid out by Baron Haussmann in the Second Empire.
- **Tour Eiffel** (1889). Under the Third Republic, the French wanted to show

Tour Eiffel

how far they had come in the 100 years since the Revolution. They hired **Gustave Eiffel** (1832–1923) to slap together the world's tallest structure, a temporary 320m (1,050-ft.) tower made of riveted steel girders. Everyone agreed it was tall; most thought it was ugly and completely lacking in aesthetics. Its usefulness as a radio transmitter saved Eiffel's tower from being torn down.
- **Métro station entrances.** Art Nouveau was less an architectural mode than a decorative movement. You can still find some of the original Art Nouveau Métro entrances designed by **Hector Guimard** (1867–1942). A recently renovated entrance is at the Porte Dauphine station on the No. 2 line.

THE 20TH CENTURY

France commissioned some ambitious architectural projects in the last century, most of them the *grand projets* of the late François Mitterrand. The majority were considered controversial or even offensive when completed. Only slowly have structures such as the Centre Pompidou or Louvre's glass pyramids become accepted. Over time, a lucky few may even become as beloved as the once-despised Tour Eiffel.

IDENTIFIABLE FEATURES

Other than a concerted effort to be unique, break convention, and look stunningly modern, nothing communally identifies France's recent architecture.

BEST EXAMPLES

- **Centre Pompidou** (1977). Brit Richard Rogers (b. 1933) and Italian Renzo Piano (b. 1937) turned architecture inside out—literally—to craft Paris's eye-popping modern-art museum. Exposed pipes, steel supports, and plastic-tube escalators wrap around the exterior.

Centre Pompidou

- **Louvre's glass pyramids** (1989). Chinese-American architect I. M. Pei (b. 1917) was called in to cap the Louvre's new underground entrance with these pyramids in the center of the Palais du Louvre's 17th-century courtyard.
- **Opéra Bastille** (1989). In 1989, Paris's opera company moved into this curvaceous, dark glass mound of space designed by Canadian Carlos Ott. Unfortunately, the acoustics have been lambasted.

3

Planning Your Trip to Paris

This chapter provides the nuts-and-bolts details you need before setting off for Paris—everything from information sources to money matters to the major airlines and how to save money on your flight.

1 Visitor Information

TOURIST OFFICES

Your best source of information is the **French Government Tourist Office,** which you can reach at the following addresses:

IN THE UNITED STATES 444 Madison Ave., 16th Floor, New York, NY 10022 (© **212/838-7800;** fax 212/838-7855); 676 N. Michigan Ave., Suite 3214, Chicago, IL 60611 (© **312/751-7800;** fax 312/337-6339); 9454 Wilshire Blvd., Suite 715, Beverly Hills, CA 90212 (© **310/271-6665;** fax 310/276-2835). To request additional information call **Info France** at © **410/286-8310.**

IN CANADA Maison de la France/French Government Tourist Office, 1981 av. McGill College, Suite 490, Montreal, H3A 2W9 (© **514/876-9881;** fax 514/845-4868).

IN THE UNITED KINGDOM Maison de la France/French Government Tourist Office, 178 Piccadilly, London, W1J 9AL (© and fax **020/7943-6594**).

IN AUSTRALIA French Tourist Bureau, 25 Bligh St., Sydney, NSW 2000 (© **02/9231-5244;** fax 02/9221-8682).

WEBSITES

The French Government Tourist Office's home on the Internet is at **www.franceguide.com**, or **www.francetourism.com**.

For general information, see "Planning Your Trip Online" later in this chapter. For more Paris-related websites, see "The Best Websites for Paris" box on p. 11.

2 Entry Requirements & Customs

ENTRY REQUIREMENTS

All non-French nationals need a **valid passport** to enter France (check its expiration date). The French government no longer requires visas for **U.S. citizens,** provided they're staying less than 90 days. For longer stays, they must apply for a long-term visa, residence card, or temporary-stay visa. Each requires proof of income or a viable means of support in France and

a legitimate purpose for remaining in the country. Applications are available from the **Consulate Section of the French Embassy,** 4101 Reservoir Rd. NW, Washington, DC 20007 (© **202/944-6000**), or from the **Visa Section of the French Consulate,** 934 Fifth Ave., New York, NY 10021 (© **212/606-3680**). Visas are required for students planning to study in France even if the stay is less than 90 days.

Destination Paris: Red-Alert Checklist

- If you purchased traveler's checks, have you recorded the check numbers, and stored the documentation separately from the checks?
- Did you stop the newspaper and mail delivery, and leave a set of keys with someone reliable?
- Did you pack your camera and an extra set of camera batteries, and purchase enough film? If you packed film in your checked baggage, did you invest in protective pouches to shield film from airport X-rays?
- Do you have a safe, accessible place to store money?
- Did you bring your ID cards that could entitle you to discounts, such as AAA and AARP cards, student IDs, and so on?
- Did you bring emergency drug prescriptions and extra glasses and/or contact lenses?
- Did you find out your daily ATM withdrawal limit?
- Do you have your credit card pin numbers? Is there a daily withdrawal limit on credit card cash advances?
- If you have an E-ticket, do you have documentation?
- Did you leave a copy of your itinerary with someone at home?
- Do you have the measurements for those people you plan to buy clothes for on your trip?
- Do you have the address and phone number of your country's embassy with you?

Citizens of Australia, Canada, New Zealand, Switzerland, Japan, and European Union countries do not need visas.

If your passport is lost or stolen, go to your consulate as soon as possible for a replacement.

For information on how to get a passport, and for an up-to-date country-by-country listings of passport requirements around the world, go to the website of the U.S. State Department at **http://travel.state.gov**.

CUSTOMS
WHAT YOU CAN BRING INTO FRANCE Customs restrictions differ for citizens of European Union (EU) countries and non-EU countries.

For Non-EU Nationals You can bring in, duty-free, 200 cigarettes, 100 cigarillos, 50 cigars, or 250 grams of smoking tobacco. You can also bring in 2 liters of wine and either 1 liter of alcohol over 22 proof or 2 liters of alcohol under 22 proof. In addition, you can bring in 60cc (2 oz.) of perfume, a quarter liter of eau de toilette, 250cc (8.5 oz.) of coffee, and 200 grams of tea. Visitors 15 and over may bring in other goods totaling 175€ ($201); the allowance for those 14 and under is 90€ ($104). (Customs officials tend to be lenient about general merchandise, realizing the limits are unrealistically low.)

For EU Citizens Visitors from European Union countries can bring into France any amount of goods as long as they're intended for their personal use—not for resale.

WHAT YOU CAN TAKE HOME FROM PARIS
Returning **U.S. citizens** who have been away for at least 48 hours are allowed to bring back, once every 30 days, $800 worth of merchandise

duty-free. You'll be charged a flat rate of 4% duty on the next $1,000 worth of purchases. Be sure to have your receipts handy. On mailed gifts, the duty-free limit is $200. With some exceptions, you cannot bring fresh fruits and vegetables into the United States. For specifics on what you can bring back, download the invaluable free pamphlet *Know Before You Go* online at **www.customs.gov**. Or contact the **U.S. Customs Service,** 1300 Pennsylvania Ave., NW, Washington, DC 20229 (© **202/354-1000**) and request the pamphlet.

For a clear summary of **Canadian** rules, write for the booklet *I Declare,* issued by the **Canada Customs and Revenue Agency** (© **800/461-9999** in Canada, or 204/983-3500; www.ccra-adrc.gc.ca). Canada allows its citizens a C$750 exemption, and you're allowed to bring back duty-free one carton of cigarettes, 2.2 pounds of tobacco, 40 imperial ounces of liquor, and 50 cigars. In addition, you're allowed to mail gifts to Canada valued at less than C$60 a day, provided they're unsolicited and don't contain alcohol or tobacco (write on the package "Unsolicited gift, under $60 value"). All valuables should be declared on the Y-38 form before departure from Canada, including serial numbers of valuables you already own, such as expensive foreign cameras. *Note:* The C$750 exemption can only be used once a year and only after an absence of 7 days.

Citizens of the U.K. who are **returning from a European Union (EU) country** will go through a separate Customs Exit (called the "Blue Exit") especially for EU travelers. In essence, there is no limit on what you can bring back from an EU country, as long as the items are for personal use (this includes gifts) and you have already paid the necessary duty and tax. However, customs law sets out guidance levels. If you bring in more than these levels, you may be asked to prove that the goods are for your own use. Guidance levels on goods bought in the EU for your own use are 3,200 cigarettes, 200 cigars, 400 cigarillos, 3 kilograms of smoking tobacco, 10 liters of spirits, 90 liters of wine, 20 liters of fortified wine (such as port or sherry), and 110 liters of beer.

For more information, contact HM Customs & Excise at © **020/8929-0152,** or consult their website at www.hmce.gov.uk.

The duty-free allowance in **Australia** is A$400 or, for those under 18, A$200. Citizens can bring in 250 cigarettes or 250 grams of loose tobacco, and 1,125 liters of alcohol. If you're returning with valuables you already own, such as foreign-made cameras, you should file form B263. A helpful brochure available from Australian consulates or Customs offices is *Know Before You Go*. For more information, call the **Australian Customs Service** at © **02/6275-666,** or log on to www.customs.gov.au.

(*Tips* Passport

Allow plenty of time before your trip to apply for a passport; processing normally takes 3 weeks but can take longer during busy periods (especially spring). And keep in mind that if you need a passport in a hurry, you'll pay a higher processing fee. When traveling, safeguard your passport in an inconspicuous, inaccessible place like a money belt and keep a copy of the critical pages with your passport number in a separate place. If you lose your passport, visit the nearest consulate of your native country as soon as possible for a replacement.

The duty-free allowance for **New Zealand** is NZ$700. Citizens over 17 can bring in 200 cigarettes, 50 cigars, or 250 grams of tobacco (or a mixture of all three if their combined weight doesn't exceed 250g); plus 4.5 liters of wine and beer, or 1.125 milliliters of liquor. New Zealand currency does not carry import or export restrictions. Fill out a certificate of export, listing the valuables you are taking out of the country; that way, you can bring them back without paying duty. Most questions are answered in a free pamphlet available at New Zealand consulates and Customs offices: *New Zealand Customs Guide for Travellers, Notice no. 4.* For more information, contact **New Zealand Customs,** The Customhouse, 17–21 Whitmore St., Box 2218, Wellington (② **04/473-6099** or 0800/428-786 in New Zealand; www.customs.govt.nz).

3 Money

CURRENCY

The **euro,** the new single European currency, became the official currency of France and 11 other participating countries on January 1, 1999.

The euro didn't go into general circulation until January 1, 2002. The old currency, the French franc, disappeared into history on March 1, 2002, replaced by the euro, which is officially abbreviated as "EUR," or €. Exchange rates of participating countries are locked into a common currency fluctuating against the dollar.

For more details on the euro, check out **www.europa.eu.int/euro**.

FOREIGN CURRENCIES VS. THE U.S. DOLLAR

Conversion ratios between the U.S. dollar and other currencies fluctuate, and their differences could affect the relative costs of your holiday. The figures reflected in the currency chart below were valid at the time of this writing, but they might not be valid by the time of your departure. This chart would be useful for conversions of small amounts of money, but if you're planning on any major transactions, check for more updated rates prior to making any serious commitments.

It's a good idea to exchange at least some money—just enough to cover airport incidentals and transportation to your hotel—before you leave home, so you can avoid lines at airport ATMs (automated teller machines). You can exchange money at your local American Express or Thomas Cook office or your bank. If you're far away from a bank with currency-exchange services, American Express offers traveler's checks and foreign currency, though with a $15 order fee and additional shipping costs, at www.american express.com or ② **800/223-7373.**

ATMS

The easiest and best way to get cash away from home is from an ATM. The **Cirrus** (② 800/424-7787; www.mastercard.com) and **PLUS** (② **800/843-7587**; www.visa.com) networks span the globe; look at the back of your bank card to see which network you're on, then call or check online for

---

Tips **Small Change**

When you change money, ask for some small bills or loose change. Petty cash will come in handy for tipping and public transportation. Consider keeping the change separate from your larger bills, so that it's readily accessible and you'll be less of a target for theft.

The Euro, the U.S. Dollar & the British Pound

For American Readers Since the euro's inception, the U.S. dollar and the euro have traded on par (i.e., $1 approximately equals 1€). But as this book went to press, the euro continued to gain strength against the dollar. In converting prices to U.S. dollars, we used a conversion rate of 1€ = $1.15. For up-to-the minute exchange rates between the euro and the dollar, check the currency converter website **www.xe.com/ucc**.

For British Readers At this writing, £1 = approximately $1.65, and at approximately the same rate vis-à-vis the euro. These were the rates of exchange used to calculate the values in the table below.

Euro €	US$	UK£	Euro €	US$	UK£
1.00	1.15	0.60	75.00	6.25	45.00
2.00	2.30	1.20	100.00	115.00	60.00
3.00	3.45	1.80	125.00	143.75	75.00
4.00	4.60	2.40	150.00	172.50	90.00
5.00	5.75	3.00	175.00	201.25	105.00
6.00	6.90	3.60	200.00	230.00	120.00
7.00	8.05	4.20	225.00	258.75	135.00
8.00	9.20	4.80	250.00	287.50	150.00
9.00	10.35	5.40	275.00	316.25	165.00
10.00	11.50	6.00	300.00	345.00	180.00
15.00	17.25	9.00	350.00	402.50	210.00
20.00	23.00	12.00	400.00	460.00	240.00
25.00	28.75	15.00	500.00	575.00	300.00
50.00	57.50	30.00	1000.00	1150.00	600.00

ATM locations at your destination. Be sure you know your personal identification number (PIN) before you leave home and be sure to find out your daily withdrawal limit before you depart. Also keep in mind that many banks impose a fee every time a card is used at a different bank's ATM, and that fee can be higher for international transactions (up to $5 or more) than for domestic ones (where they're rarely more than $1.50). On top of this, the bank from which you withdraw cash may charge its own fee. To compare banks' ATM fees within the U.S., use www.bankrate.com. For international withdrawal fees, ask your bank.

You can also get cash advances on your credit card at an ATM. Keep in mind that credit card companies try to protect themselves from theft by limiting the funds someone can withdraw outside their home country, so call your credit card company before you leave home.

TRAVELER'S CHECKS

Traveler's checks are something of an anachronism from the days before the ATM made cash accessible at any time. Traveler's checks used to be the only sound alternative to traveling with dangerously large amounts of cash. They were as reliable as currency, but, unlike cash, could be replaced if lost or stolen.

These days, traveler's checks are less necessary because most cities have

24-hour ATMs that allow you to withdraw small amounts of cash as needed. However, keep in mind that you will likely be charged an ATM withdrawal fee if the bank is not your own, so if you're withdrawing money every day, you might be better off with traveler's checks—provided that you don't mind showing identification every time you want to cash one.

You can get traveler's checks at almost any bank. **American Express** offers denominations of $20, $50, $100, $500, and (for cardholders only) $1,000. You'll pay a service charge ranging from 1% to 4%. You can also get American Express traveler's checks over the phone by calling ℰ **800/221-7282;** Amex gold and platinum cardholders who use this number are exempt from the 1% fee. **Visa** offers traveler's checks at Citibank locations nationwide, as well as at several other banks. The service charge ranges between 1.5% and 2%; checks come in denominations of $20, $50, $100, $500, and $1,000. Call ℰ **800/732-1322** for information. AAA members can obtain Visa checks without a fee at most AAA offices or by calling ℰ **866/339-3378. MasterCard** also offers traveler's checks. Call ℰ **800/223-9920** for a location near you.

Foreign currency traveler's checks are useful if you're traveling to one country, or to the euro zone; they're accepted at locations such as bed-and-breakfasts where dollar checks may not be, and they minimize the amount of math you have to do at your destination. **American Express** offers checks in Australian dollars, Canadian dollars, British pounds, euros, and Japanese yen. **Visa** checks come in Australian, Canadian, British, and euro versions; **MasterCard** offers those four plus yen and South African rands.

CREDIT CARDS

Credit cards are a safe way to carry money, they provide a convenient record of all your expenses, and they generally offer good exchange rates. You can also withdraw cash advances from your credit cards at banks or ATMs, provided you know your PIN. If you've forgotten yours, or didn't even know you had one, call the number on the back of your credit card and ask the bank to send it to you. It usually takes 5 to 7 business days, though some banks will provide the number over the phone if you tell them your mother's maiden name or some other personal information. Your credit card company will likely charge a commission (1% or 2%) on every foreign purchase you make, but don't sweat this small stuff; for most purchases, you'll still get the best deal with credit cards when you factor in things like ATM fees and higher traveler's check exchange rates.

⌒ **Tips Dear Visa: I'm Off to the Marais!**

Some credit card companies recommend that you notify them of any impending trip abroad so that they don't become suspicious when the card is used numerous times in a foreign destination and block your charges. Even if you don't call your credit card company in advance, you can always use the card's toll-free emergency number if a charge is refused—a good reason to carry the phone number with you. But perhaps the most important lesson here is to carry more than one card with you on your trip; a card might not work for any number of reasons, so having a backup is the smart way to go.

Tips **Quick ID**

Tie a colorful ribbon or piece of yarn around your luggage handle, or slap a distinctive sticker on the side of your bag. This makes it less likely that someone will mistakenly appropriate it. And if your luggage gets lost, it will be easier to find.

4 When to Go

In August, Parisians traditionally leave for their annual holiday and the city serves visitors on a skeleton staff. July has also become a popular vacation month, with many restaurateurs taking a holiday then.

Hotels, especially first class and deluxe, are easy to come by in July and August. Budget hotels, on the other hand, are likely to be full during these months of student invasion. You might also try to avoid late September and the first 2 weeks in October, when the annual auto show attracts thousands of enthusiasts.

THE WEATHER: APRIL IN PARIS?

Balmy weather in Paris has prompted more popular songs and love ballads than weather conditions in any other city. But the weather here is actually quite fickle. Rain is more common than snow throughout the winter, prompting longtime residents to complain about the occasional bone-chilling dampness.

In recent years, Paris has had about 15 snow days a year, and there are only a few oppressively hot days (over 86°F, or 30°C) in summer. What will most likely chill a Parisian heart, however, are the winds that sweep along the city's boulevards, channeled by bordering buildings. Other than the occasional winds and rain (which add an undeniable drama to many of the city's panoramas), Paris offers some of the most pleasant weather of any capital in Europe, with an average temperature of 53°F (12°C).

Paris's Average Daytime Temperature & Rainfall

	Jan	Feb	Mar	Apr	May	June	July	Aug	Sept	Oct	Nov	Dec
Temp. (°F)	38	39	46	51	58	64	66	66	61	53	45	40
Temp. (°C)	3	4	8	11	14	18	19	19	16	12	7	4
Rainfall (in.)	3.2	2.9	2.4	2.7	3.2	3.5	3.3	3.7	3.3	3.0	3.5	3.1

HOLIDAYS

Holidays in France are known as *jours fériés*. Shops and banks are closed, as well as many (but not all) restaurants and museums. Major holidays include January 1 (New Year's Day), Easter, Ascension Day (40 days after Easter), Pentecost (seventh Sun after Easter), May 1 (May Day), May 8 (VE Day), July 14 (Bastille Day), August 15 (Assumption of the Virgin Mary), November 1 (All Saints' Day), November 11 (Armistice Day), and December 25 (Christmas).

PARIS CALENDAR OF EVENTS

Check the Paris Tourist Office website at **www.paris-touristoffice.com** and other websites listed in "The Best Websites for Paris" in chapter 1 for up-to-the-minute details on these and other events.

January

International Ready-to-Wear Fashion Shows (Salon International de Prêt-à-Porter), Parc des Expositions (Hall #7), 15e. Hundreds of designers, from the giants to the unknown, unveil their visions (hallucinations?) of what you will be wearing in 6 months. The event in the Porte de Versailles convention facilities is geared to wholesalers, retailers, buyers, journalists, and industry professionals, but for the 18€ to 25€ ($21–$29) entrance fee, the rules are usually bent for the merely fashion-conscious. Much more exclusive are the *défilés* (fashion shows) at the headquarters of houses like Lagerfeld, Lanvin, Courrèges, and Valentino. For details, call © **01-44-94-70-00;** www.pretparis.com. End of January.

February

Special Exhibitions, Special Concerts: During Paris's grayest month, look for a splash of expositions and concerts designed to perk up the city. Concerts and theaters spring up at such diverse sites as the **Cité de la Musique,** 221 av. Jean-Jaurès, 19e (© 01-44-84-45-00; Métro: Porte-de-Pantin); the **Théâtre des Champs-Elysées,** 15 av. Montaigne, 8e (© 01-49-52-50-50; Métro: Alma-Marceau); and the **Maison de Radio-France,** 116 av. du Président-Kennedy, 16e (© 01-56-40-15-16; Métro: Passy-Ranelagh). Also look for openings of new operas at the **Opéra Bastille,** 2 place de la Bastille, 4e (© 01-40-01-17-89; Métro: Bastille); operas and dance at the **Opéra Garnier,** place de l'Opéra, 9e (© 01-40-01-17-89); and concerts at the **Auditorium du Louvre,** 1e (© 01-40-20-51-51; Métro: Musée du Louvre), and the **Salle Cortot,** 78 rue Cardinet, 17e (© 01-47-63-80-16; Métro: Malesherbes). A copy of *Pariscope* or *L'Officiel des Spectacles,* available at most newsstands, is the best info source.

March

Foire du Trône, Bois de Vincennes, 12e. A mammoth amusement park that its fans call France's largest country fair, the Foire du Trône originated in 957, when merchants met with farmers to exchange grain and wine. This high-tech continuation of that tradition, held on the lawns of the Pelouse de Reuilly, has a Ferris wheel, carousels, acrobats, fire eaters, and diversions that seem like a Gallic Coney Island. It's open Sunday from noon to 1am, Monday to Thursday from 2pm to midnight, and Friday and Saturday from 2pm to 1am. Call © **01-46-27-52-29.** End of March to end of May.

April

International Marathon of Paris. Beginning on the Champs-Elysées at 9am, runners take over Paris's boulevards in a race that draws competitors from around the world. Depending on their speed and endurance, participants arrive at the finishing point on avenue Foch, 16e, beginning about 2½ hours later. For details, call © **01-41-33-15-68;** www.parismarathon.com. Early April.

Les Grandes Eaux Musicales, Versailles. These musical events are intended to re-create the atmosphere of the ancient regime. The fountains around the palace are turned on, with special emphasis on the Neptune Fountain, which sits squarely in front of the best view of the château. You can promenade in the garden and listen to the music of French composers (Couperin, Charpentier, and Lully) and others (Mozart or Haydn) whose careers thrived during the years of the palace's construction. The music is recorded, but the vistas are monumental, and no other option exists wherein the music, the fountains, and the architectural vistas of the world's grandest château all operate in unison. The events occur every Saturday and Sunday from 11:15am till noon and 2:30pm till 5pm, between April and early October. For details, call ℂ **01-30-83-78-00.**

May

VE Day (in French: *Jour de l'Armistice*), citywide. The celebration commemorating the capitulation of the Nazis on May 7, 1945, lasts 4 days in Paris, with a parade along the Champs-Elysées and additional ceremonies in Reims. Pro-American sentiments are probably higher during this festival than at any other time of year. May 5 to May 8.

Grand Steeplechase de Paris, Auteuil and Longchamp racetracks, Bois de Boulogne. In this equestrian event, obstacle courses at both Auteuil and Longchamps racetracks are laid out that incorporate hurdles and crossings over streams. The result is a rougher, more rustic counterpoint to the flatbed races conducted at Chantilly (see below). For details call ℂ **01-49-10-20-30** or click on www.france-galop.com. May 20, 2005.

French Open Tennis Championship, Stade Roland-Garros, 16e. The Open features 10 days of Grand Slam men's and women's tennis, with European and South American players traditionally dominating on the hot, dusty red courts. For details, call ℂ **01-47-43-48-00.** May 23 to June 5, 2005.

June

Fête de St-Denis, St-Denis. This series presents a month of artfully contrived music in the burial place of the French kings, a grim early Gothic monument in this industrialized northern suburb. For details, call ℂ **01-48-13-06-07;** www.festival-saint-denis.fr. Early June to July.

Prix du Jockey Club & Prix Diane-Hermès, Hippodrome de Chantilly. Thoroughbreds from as far away as Kentucky and Brunei, as well as mounts sponsored by Europe's old and new fortunes, compete in a very civil competition broadcast around France and talked about in horse circles around the world. On race days, as many as 30 trains depart from Paris's Gare du Nord for Chantilly, where they're met by free shuttle buses to the track. For details on this and all other equine events in this calendar, call ℂ **01-49-10-20-30;** www.france-galop.com. First week of June (Jockey Club) and second week of June (Prix Diane-Hermès).

Paris Air Show, Le Bourget. This is where France's military-industrial complex shows off enough high-tech hardware to make anyone think twice about invading La Patrie. Fans, competitors, and industrial spies mob the airport's exhibition halls for a taste of what Gallic technocrats have wrought. For details, call ℂ **01-53-23-33-33;** www.salon-du-bourget.fr. Mid-June.

Fête de la Musique, citywide. This celebration at the summer solstice is the only day that noise laws don't apply in Paris. Musicians and wannabes pour into the streets, where you can make music with anything, even if it means banging two garbage cans together or driving around blowing your car horn (illegal otherwise). You might hear anything from Russians playing balalaikas to Cubans playing mambo rhythms. There are musical parties in virtually all the open spaces, with more organized concerts at place de la Bastille and place de la République, and in La Villette and the Latin Quarter. For details, call ℓ **01-40-03-94-70;** www.fete delamusique.culture.fr. Mid-June.

Festival Musique en l'Ile. A series of concerts, most including dignified masses composed from the 17th to the late 19th centuries, are presented at the Church St-Louis-en-l'Ile and the Church St-Germain-des-Prés. For more information, call La Toison d'Art at ℓ **01-44-62-00-55;** www.toisondart.com. Late June to late August.

La Course des Garçons de Café, throughout the city. Although it has diminished somewhat in importance in Paris since the postwar years when it was much more visible, there's no more amusing race in Paris. Balancing heavy trays, the *garçons* (both waiters and waitresses) line up in front of the Hôtel de Ville in the 4th arrondissement, then race for 8km (5 miles) through the streets, ending back at the Hôtel de Ville. Some obviously don't make it. A Sunday in the last week of June or first week of July.

La Villette Jazz Festival, La Villette. This homage to the art of jazz incorporates 50 concerts in churches, auditoriums, and concert halls in all neighborhoods of this Paris suburb. Past festivals have welcomed Herbie Hancock, Shirley Horn, Michel Portal, and other artists from around the world. For details, call ℓ **08-03-30-63-06.** Late June to early July.

Gay Pride Parade, place de la République to place de la Bastille. A week of expositions and parties climaxes in a parade patterned after those in New York and San Francisco. It's followed by a dance at the Palais de Bercy, a convention hall/sports arena. For more information about gay pride and any other aspect of gay, lesbian, and transgendered life in and around

Paris, contact Lesbian and Gay Pride, Ile de France, 3 rue Keller, BP 255, 75524 Paris Cedex 11. For information about the parade, call or fax ℓ **01-53-01-47-01.** Late June.

July

Tour de France. This is Europe's most visible, highly contested, and overabundantly televised bicycle race. Crews of wind tunnel–tested athletes speed along an itinerary tracing the six sides of the French "hexagon," detouring deep into the Massif Central and across the Swiss Alps. The race is decided at a finish line drawn across the Champs-Elysées. For details, call ℓ **01-41-33-15-00;** www.letour.fr. Month of July.

Bastille Day, citywide. This celebration of the 1789 storming of the Bastille is the birth date of modern France, and festivities reach their peak in Paris with street fairs, pageants, fireworks, and feasts. The day begins with a parade down the Champs-Elysées and ends with fireworks in Montmartre. Wherever you are, before the end of the day you'll hear Piaf warbling "La Foule" ("The Crowd"), the song that celebrated her passion for the stranger she met and later lost in a crowd on Bastille Day, and lots of people singing "La Marseillaise." July 14, 2005.

Fête Chopin, Orangerie du Parc de Bagatelle, Versailles. Hear all the Chopin you want at these piano recitals from the works of the Polish exile who lived most of his life in Paris. For details, call ℓ **01-45-01-51-85.** Early July.

Paris Quartier d'Eté, Latin Quarter. For 4 weeks the Arènes de Lutèce or the Sorbonne's Cour d'Honneur host pop orchestral concerts. The dozen or so concerts are grander than the outdoor setting would imply and include performances by the Orchestre de Paris, Orchestre National de France, and Baroque Orchestra of the European Union. On the fringes you can find plays, jazz, and parades in the Tuileries. For details, call © **01-44-94-98-00** or fax 01-44-94-98-01; www.quartierdete.com. Mid-July to mid-August.

September

International Ready-to-Wear Fashion Shows (Salon International de Prêt-à-Porter), Parc des Expositions, 15e. More of what took place at the fashion shows in January (see above), with an emphasis on what *le beau monde* (the rich and the beautiful) will be wearing next spring. For details, call **01-44-94-70-00.** Early September.

Biennale des Antiquaires, Carrousel du Louvre, 99 rue de Rivoli, 1e. Antiques dealers and lovers from all over gather at this gilded event in even-numbered years. Precious furnishings and objets d'art are displayed in the underground exhibit halls linked to the Louvre, or perhaps in the Grand Palais once it's restored. For details, call © **01-44-51-74-74;** www.biennaledes antiquaires.com. Usually third week in September. Next event 2006.

Fête d'Automne (Autumn Festival), citywide. Paris welcomes the return of its residents from their August holidays with an ongoing and eclectic festival of modern music, ballet, theater, and modern art. Venues include art galleries, churches, concert halls, auditoriums, and parks throughout Paris. There's an emphasis on experimental works, which the festival's promoters scatter judiciously between more traditional productions. Depending on the event, tickets cost from 15€ to 73€ ($17–$84). For details, contact the **Fête d'Automne,** 156 rue de

Rivoli, 75001 Paris (© **01-53-45-17-00;** fax 01-53-45-17-01; www.festival-automne.com). Mid-September to late December.

Paris Auto Show, Parc des Expositions, 15e. Glitzy attendees and lots of hype attend this showcase for European car design. The show takes place in even-numbered years near the Porte de Versailles. In addition, a permanent exhibit on French auto design at the Cité des Sciences et de l'Industrie is upgraded and enriched during October. For details, call © **01-56-88-22-40;** www.mondial-automobile.com. Late September to mid October.

October

Prix de l'Arc de Triomphe, Hippodrome de Longchamp, 16e. France's answer to England's Ascot is the country's most prestigious horse race, culminating the equine season in Europe. For details, call © **01-49-10-20-30;** www.france-galop.com. Early October.

November

Armistice Day, citywide. The signing of the controversial document that ended World War I is celebrated with a military parade from the Arc de Triomphe to the Hôtel des Invalides. November 11.

Fête d'Art Sacré (Festival of Sacred Art). A series of classical concerts is held in five of the oldest churches of Paris. For details, call © **01-44-70-64-10.** Mid-November to mid-December.

Release of the Beaujolais Nouveau, citywide. Parisians eagerly await the yearly release of the first new Beaujolais, that fruity wine from Burgundy. Signs are posted in bistros, wine bars, and cafes—these places report their heaviest patronage of the year during this celebration of the grape. Third Thursday in November.

December

Le Salon Nautique de Paris (Boat Fair), Parc des Expositions, 15e. This is Europe's most visible exposition of what's afloat and of interest to wholesalers, retailers, boat owners (or wannabes), and anyone involved in the business of waterborne holidaymaking. For details, call © **01-41-90-47-22,** or check on the Web at www.salonnautiqueparis.com. Ten days in early December.

Fête de St-Sylvestre (New Year's Eve), citywide. It's most boisterously celebrated in the Latin Quarter around the Sorbonne. At midnight, the city explodes. Strangers kiss strangers, and boulevard St-Michel and the Champs-Elysées become virtual pedestrian malls. December 31.

5 Travel Insurance

Since France is far from home for most of us, and a number of things could go wrong—lost luggage, trip cancellation, a medical emergency—consider the following types of insurance.

Check your existing insurance policies and credit card coverage before you buy travel insurance. You may already be covered for lost luggage, cancelled tickets, or medical expenses. The cost of travel insurance varies widely, depending on the cost and length of your trip, your age, health, and the type of trip you're taking.

TRIP-CANCELLATION INSURANCE Trip-cancellation insurance helps you get your money back if you have to back out of a trip, if you have to go home early, or if your travel supplier goes bankrupt. Allowed reasons for cancellation can range from sickness to natural disasters to the State Department declaring your destination unsafe for travel. In this unstable world, trip-cancellation insurance is a good buy if you're getting tickets well in advance—who knows what the state of your airline (or of the world) will be in 9 months? Insurance policy details vary, so read the fine print—and especially make sure that your airline or cruise line is on the list of carriers covered in case of bankruptcy. For information, contact one of the following insurers: **Access America** (© 866/807-3982; www.accessamerica.com); **Travel Guard International**

(© 800/826-4919; www.travelguard.com); **Travel Insured International** (© 800/243-3174; www.travelinsured.com); and **Travelex Insurance Services** (© 888/457-4602; www.travelex-insurance.com).

MEDICAL INSURANCE Most health insurance policies cover you if you get sick away from home—but check, particularly if you're insured by an HMO. With the exception of certain HMOs and Medicare/Medicaid, your medical insurance should cover medical treatment—even hospital care—overseas. However, most out-of-country hospitals make you pay your bills upfront, and send you a refund after you've returned home and filed the necessary paperwork. And in a worst-case scenario, there's the high cost of emergency evacuation. If you require additional medical insurance, try **MEDEX International** (© 888/MEDEX-00 or 410/453-6300; www.medexassist.com) or **Travel Assistance International** (© 800/821-2828; www.travelassistance.com).

LOST-LUGGAGE INSURANCE On international flights (including U.S. portions of international trips), baggage is limited to approximately $9.10 per pound, up to approximately $635 per checked bag. If you plan to check items more valuable than the standard liability, see if your valuables are covered by your homeowner's policy, get baggage insurance as part of your comprehensive travel-insurance package, or buy Travel Guard's "Bag-Trak" product (see above). Don't buy insurance at the airport, as it's usually overpriced. Be sure to take any valuables or irreplaceable items with you in your carry-on luggage, as many valuables (including books, money, and electronics) aren't covered by airline policies.

If your luggage is lost, immediately file a lost-luggage claim at the airport, detailing the luggage contents. For most airlines, you must report delayed, damaged, or lost baggage within 4 hours of arrival. The airlines are required to deliver luggage, once found, directly to your house or destination free.

6 Health & Safety

STAYING HEALTHY

In general, Paris is a "safe" destination, although problems can and do occur anywhere. You don't need shots; most foodstuff is safe and the water in Paris is potable. If you're concerned, order bottled water. It is easy to get a prescription filled in French towns and cities, and nearly all places contain English-speaking doctors at hospitals with well-trained medical staffs, which are found throughout France.

In other words, France is part of the civilized world.

The vegetarian can go into almost any restaurant in Paris, even those specializing in meat and fish, and order a heaping plate of fresh vegetables.

Regarding the outbreaks of mad cow disease, the World Health Organization recently reported that the current risk in the United Kingdom appears to be extremely small, perhaps about "1 case per billion" servings. They also reported that in France, "this risk, if it exists at all, would be perhaps even less than in the United Kingdom."

Nonetheless, France is leery of U.K. beef despite the "all clear" signals coming from the EU. France even flaunted EU laws and banned U.K. beef.

WHAT TO DO IF YOU GET SICK AWAY FROM HOME

In most cases, your existing health plan will provide the coverage you need. But double-check; you may want to buy **travel medical insurance** instead. (See the section on insurance, above.) Bring your insurance ID card with you when you travel.

If you suffer from a chronic illness, consult your doctor before your departure. For conditions like epilepsy, diabetes, or heart problems, wear a **MedicAlert Identification Tag** (© 800/825-3785; www.medicalert. org), which will immediately alert doctors to your condition and give them access to your records through MedicAlert's 24-hour hotline.

Pack **prescription medications** in your carry-on luggage, and carry prescription medications in their original containers, with pharmacy labels—otherwise they won't make it through airport security. Also bring along copies of your prescriptions in case you lose your pills or run out. Don't forget an extra pair of contact lenses or prescription glasses. Carry the generic name of prescription medicines, in case a local pharmacist is unfamiliar with the brand name.

Contact the **International Association for Medical Assistance to Travelers (IAMAT)** (© 716/754-4883; www.iamat.org) for tips on travel and health concerns in the countries you're visiting, and lists of local, English-speaking doctors. The United States **Centers for Disease Control and Prevention** (© 800/311-3435; www. cdc.gov) provides up-to-date information on necessary vaccines and health hazards by region or country. Any foreign consulate can provide a list of area doctors who speak English. If you get sick, consider asking your hotel concierge to recommend a local doctor—even his or her own. You can also try the emergency room at a local hospital; many have walk-in clinics for emergency cases that are not life-threatening. You may not get immediate attention, but you won't pay the high price of an emergency room visit.

STAYING SAFE
The most common menace in Paris is the plague of pickpockets and roving gangs of Gypsy children who surround you, distract you, and steal your purse or wallet. Never leave valuables in a car, and never travel with your car unlocked. A U.S. State Department travel advisory warns that every car (whether parked, stopped at a traffic light, or moving) can be a potential target for armed robbery. In these uncertain times, it is prudent to check the U.S. State Department's travel advisories at http://travel.state.gov/travel_warnings.html.

The government of France maintains a national antiterrorism plan; in times of heightened security concerns, the government mobilizes police and armed forces and installs them at airports, train and Métro stations, and high-profile locations such as schools, embassies, and government installations.

In recent years, Paris has experienced political assassinations and random bombings. One U.S. citizen was injured in these attacks, but none has been killed. All passengers on subways and trains are urged to be aware of their surroundings and to report any unattended baggage to the nearest authority.

Violent civil disorder is rare in France. In the past, however, student demonstrations, labor protests, or other routine demonstrations have turned into violent confrontations between demonstrators and police. Americans are advised to avoid street demonstrations.

Gangs of thieves operate on the rail link from Charles de Gaulle Airport to downtown Paris by preying on jet-lagged, luggage-burdened tourists. Often, one thief distracts the tourist with a question about directions while an accomplice takes a momentarily unguarded backpack, briefcase, or purse. Thieves also time their thefts to coincide with train stops so that they may quickly exit the car. Travelers may wish to consider traveling from the airport to the city by bus or taxi.

There have been a number of violent armed robberies, including knife attacks, in the vicinity of the Eiffel Tower late at night.

Thieves on motorcycles have been known to reach into moving cars by opening the car door or reaching through an open window to steal purses and other bags visible inside. Those traveling by car in Paris should remember to keep windows closed and doors locked.

The No. 1 subway line, which runs by many major tourist attractions (including the Grand Arch at La Defense, Arc de Triomphe, Champs Elysées, Concorde, Louvre, and Bastille), is the site of many thefts. Pickpockets are especially active on this Métro line during the summer months. Gare du Nord train station, where the express trains from the airport arrive in Paris, is also a high-risk area for pickpocketing and theft.

Many thefts occur at the major department stores (Galeries Lafeyette, Printemps, and Samarataine), where tourists often leave wallets, passports, and credit cards on cashier counters during transactions.

In hotels, thieves frequent lobbies and breakfast rooms, and take advantage of a minute of inattention to snatch jackets, purses, and backpacks. Also, while many hotels do have safety latches that allow guests to secure their rooms while they are inside, this feature is not as universal as it is in the United States. If no chain or latch is present, a chair placed up against the door is usually an effective obstacle to surreptitious entry during the night.

In restaurants, many Americans have reported that women's purses placed on the floor under the table at the feet of the diner are stolen during the meal.

7 Specialized Travel Resources

TRAVELERS WITH DISABILITIES

Facilities in Paris for travelers with disabilities are certainly better than you'll find in most cities. Nearly all modern hotels in France now have rooms designed especially for persons with disabilities. Older hotels, unless renovated, may not provide important features like elevators, special toilet facilities, or ramps for wheelchair accessibility. Depending on your needs, it's best to contact each hotel directly and make your needs known before you arrive.

Most high-speed trains in France can deal with wheelchairs, and guide dogs ride free. Older trains have compartments for wheelchair boarding. On the Paris Métro, persons with disabilities can sit in wider seats. Some stations don't have escalators or elevators, however, and this may present problems.

The **Association des Paralysés de France,** 17 bd. Auguste-Blanqui, 75013 Paris (℗ **01-40-78-69-00;** www.apf.asso.fr), is an organization that provides documentation, moral support, and travel ideas for individuals who use wheelchairs.

Organizations that offer assistance to travelers with disabilities include the **MossRehab Hospital** (℗ **800/ CALLMOSS;** www.mossresourcenet. org), which provides a library of accessible-travel resources online; the **Society for Accessible Travel and Hospitality** (℗ **212/447-7284;** www. sath.org; annual membership fees: $45 adults, $30 seniors and students), which offers a wealth of travel resources for all types of disabilities and informed recommendations on

destinations, access guides, travel agents, tour operators, vehicle rentals, and companion services; and the **American Foundation for the Blind** (℗ **800/232-5463;** www.afb.org), which provides information on traveling with Seeing Eye dogs.

For more information specifically targeted to travelers with disabilities, the community website **iCan** (www. icanonline.net/channels/travel/index. cfm) has destination guides and several regular columns on accessible travel. Also check out the quarterly magazine *Emerging Horizons* ($15 per yr., $20 outside the U.S.; www. emerginghorizons.com); and *Open World Magazine,* published by the Society for Accessible Travel and Hospitality (see above; subscription: $18 per year, $35 outside the U.S.).

FOR BRITISH TRAVELERS

The **Royal Association for Disability and Rehabilitation** (RADAR), Unit 12, City Forum, 250 City Rd., London EC1V 8AF (℗ **020/7250-3222;** www.radar.org.uk), publishes three holiday "fact packs" for £2 each or £5 for all three. The first provides general information, including tips for planning and booking a holiday, obtaining insurance, and handling finances; the second outlines transportation available when going abroad and equipment for rent; the third deals with specialized accommodations. Another good resource is **Holiday Care Service,** 7th floor, Sunley House, 4 Bedford Park, Croydon, Surrey CR0 2AP (℗ **0845/124-9971;** www.holiday care.org.uk), a national charity advising on accessible accommodations for the elderly and persons with disabilities. Annual membership costs £37.

GAYS & LESBIANS

France is one of the world's most tolerant countries toward gays and lesbians, and no special laws discriminate against them. "Gay Paree" boasts a large gay population, with dozens of gay clubs, restaurants, organizations, and services.

Ecoute Gay, 7 place du Commerce, 75015 Paris (© 08-10-81-10-57) is a hot line designed for the counseling of persons with gay-related problems and issues. The phone is staffed every Monday to Friday from 6 to 10pm by volunteers, some not as helpful as others. Also helpful is La Maison des Femmes, 163 rue de Charenton, 12e (© 01-43-43-41-13; Métro: Charonne), offering information about Paris for lesbians and bisexual women, and sometimes sponsoring informal dinners and get-togethers. Call anytime for a recorded announcement that gives the hours that someone will be available for that particular week.

Lesbian or bisexual women might also like to pick up a copy of *Lesbia,* if only to check out the ads. These and other publications are available at Paris's largest gay bookstore, Les Mots à la Bouche, 6 rue Ste-Croix-de-la-Bretonnerie, 4e (© 01-42-78-88-30). Hours are Monday to Saturday from 11am to 11pm and Sunday from 2 to 8pm. Both French- and English-language publications are available.

The International Gay & Lesbian Travel Association (IGLTA) (© 800/448-8550 or 954/776-2626; www.iglta.org) is the trade association for the gay and lesbian travel industry, and offers an online directory of gay- and lesbian-friendly travel businesses; go to their website and click on "Members."

Many agencies offer tours and travel itineraries specifically for gay and lesbian travelers. Now, Voyager (© 800/255-6951; www.nowvoyager.com) is a well-known San Francisco–based gay-owned and -operated travel service. Olivia Cruises & Resorts (© 800/631-6277 or 510/655-0364; www.olivia.com) charters entire resorts and ships for exclusive lesbian vacations and offers smaller group experiences for both gay and lesbian travelers.

Above and Beyond Tours (© 800/397-2681; www.abovebeyondtours.com) is the exclusive gay and lesbian tour operator for United Airlines.

The following travel guides are available at most travel bookstores and gay and lesbian bookstores, or you can order them from Giovanni's Room bookstore, 1145 Pine St., Philadelphia, PA 19107 (© 215/923-2960; www.giovannisroom.com):

Frommer's Gay & Lesbian Europe, an excellent travel resource; *Out and About* (© 800/929-2268 or 415/644-8044; www.outandabout.com), which offers guidebooks and a newsletter 10 times a year packed with solid information on the global gay and lesbian scene; *Spartacus International Gay Guide* and *Odysseus,* both good, annual English-language guidebooks focused on gay men; the *Damron* guides, with separate, annual books for gay men and lesbians; and *Gay Travel A to Z: The World of Gay & Lesbian Travel Options at Your Fingertips,* by Marianne Ferrari (Ferrari Publications; Box 35575, Phoenix, AZ 85069), a very good gay and lesbian guidebook series.

SENIOR TRAVEL

Mention the fact that you're a senior citizen when you make your travel reservations. In most cities, people over the age of 60 qualify for reduced admission to theaters, museums, and other attractions, as well as discounted fares on public transportation.

Members of AARP (formerly known as the American Association of

Retired Persons), 601 E St. NW, Washington, DC 20049 (© **800/ 424-3410** or 202/434-2277; www. aarp.org), get discounts on hotels, air-fares, and car rentals. AARP offers members a wide range of benefits, including *AARP: The Magazine* and a monthly newsletter. Anyone over 50 can join.

Many reliable agencies and organizations target the 50-plus market. **Elderhostel** (© **877/426-8056;** www. elderhostel.org) arranges study programs for those aged 55 and over (and a spouse or companion of any age) in the U.S. and in more than 80 countries around the world. Most courses last 5 to 7 days in the U.S. (2–4 weeks abroad), and many include airfare, accommodations in university dormitories or modest inns, meals, and tuition. **ElderTreks** (© **800/741-7956;** www.eldertreks.com) offers small-group tours to off-the-beaten-path or adventure-travel locations, restricted to travelers 50 and older.

Recommended publications offering travel resources and discounts for seniors include the quarterly magazine *Travel 50 & Beyond* (www.travel50 andbeyond.com); *Travel Unlimited: Uncommon Adventures for the Mature Traveler* (Avalon); *101 Tips for Mature Travelers,* available from Grand Circle Travel (© **800/221-2610** or 617/350-7500; www.gct. com); *The 50+ Traveler's Guidebook* (St. Martin's Press); and *Unbelievably Good Deals and Great Adventures*

*That You Absolut...
You're Over 50*

STUDENT TRAV...

If you're planning to tra... U.S., you'd be wise to arm... with an **International Student ...tity Card (ISIC),** which offers su... stantial savings on rail passes, plane tickets, and entrance fees. It also provides you with basic health and life insurance and a 24-hour help line. The card is available for $22 from **STA Travel** (© **800/781-4040,** www. statravel.com), the biggest student travel agency in the world. If you're no longer a student but are still under 26, you can get an **International Youth Travel Card (IYTC)** for the same price from the same people, which entitles you to some discounts (but not on museum admissions). *Note:* In 2002, STA Travel bought competitors **Council Travel** and **USIT Campus** after they went bankrupt. STA still operates some offices under the Council name.

Travel CUTS (© **800/667-2887** or 416/614-2887; www.travelcuts. com) offers similar services for both Canadians and U.S. residents. Irish students should turn to **USIT** (© **01/ 602-1600;** www.usitnow.ie).

The **Hanging Out Guides** (www.frommers.com/hangingout), published by Wiley Publishing, Inc., is the top travel series for today's students, covering everything from adrenaline sports to the hottest club and music scenes.

8 Planning Your Trip Online

SURFING FOR AIRFARES

The "big three" online travel agencies, **Expedia** (www.expedia.com), **Travelocity** (www.travelocity.com), and **Orbitz** (www.orbitz.com), sell most of the air tickets bought on the Internet. (Canadian travelers should try expedia. ca and travelocity.ca; U.K. residents can go for expedia.co.uk and opodo.co.uk.)

Each has different business deals with the airlines and may offer different fares on the same flights, so it's wise to shop around. Expedia and Travelocity will also send you **e-mail notification** when a cheap fare becomes available to your favorite destination. Of the smaller travel agency websites, **Side-Step** (www.sidestep.com) has gotten best reviews from Frommer's authors. It's a browser add-on that purports to "search 140 sites at once," but in reality only beats competitors' fares as often as other sites do.

Also remember to check **airline websites,** especially those for low-fare carriers. Even with major airlines, you can often shave a few bucks from a fare by booking directly through the airline and avoiding a travel agency's transaction fee. But you'll get these discounts only by **booking online:** Most airlines now offer online-only fares that even their phone agents know nothing about. For the websites of airlines that fly to and from your destination, go to "Getting There," below.

Great **last-minute deals** are available through free weekly e-mail services provided directly by the airlines. Most of these are announced on Tuesday or Wednesday and must be purchased online. Most are only valid for travel that weekend, but some can be booked weeks or months in advance. Sign up for weekly e-mail alerts at airline websites or check megasites that compile comprehensive lists of last-minute specials, such as **Smarter Living** (smarter living.com). For last-minute trips,

Lastminute.com often has better deals than the major-label sites.

For much more about airfares and savvy air-travel tips and advice, pick up a copy of *Frommer's Fly Safe, Fly Smart* (Wiley Publishing, Inc.).

SURFING FOR HOTELS

Of the "big three" sites, **Expedia** (www.expedia.com) may be the best choice, thanks to its long list of special deals. **Travelocity** (www.travelocity. com) runs a close second. Hotel specialist sites **hotels.com** and **hoteldiscounts.com** are also reliable. An excellent free program, **TravelAxe** (www.travelaxe.net), can help you search multiple hotel sites at once, even ones you may never have heard of.

SURFING FOR RENTAL CARS

For booking rental cars online, the best deals are usually found at rental-car company websites, although all the major online travel agencies also offer rental-car reservations services. **Priceline.com** and **Hotwire.com** work well for rental cars, too; the only "mystery" is which major rental company you get, and for most travelers the difference between **Hertz** (www.hertz. com), **Avis** (www.avis.com), and **Budget** (www.budget.com) is negligible.

Frommers.com: The Complete Travel Resource

For an excellent travel-planning resource, we highly recommend Frommers.com (www.frommers.com). We're a little biased, of course, but we guarantee that you'll find the travel tips, reviews, monthly vacation giveaways, and online-booking capabilities thoroughly indispensable. Among the special features are our popular **Message Boards,** where Frommer's readers post queries and share advice (sometimes even our authors show up to answer questions); free **Newsletters,** for the latest travel bargains and insider travel secrets; and our **Destinations Section,** where you'll get expert travel tips, hotel and dining recommendations, and advice on the sights to see for more than 3,000 destinations around the globe. When your research is done, the **Online Reservations System** (www.frommers.com/book_a_trip) takes you to Frommer's preferred online partners for booking your vacation at affordable prices.

INTERNET ACCESS AWAY FROM HOME

Travelers have any number of ways to check their e-mail and access the Internet on the road. Of course, using your own laptop—or even a PDA (personal digital assistant) or electronic organizer with a modem—gives you the most flexibility. But even if you don't have a computer, you can still access your e-mail and even your office computer from cybercafes.

WITHOUT YOUR OWN COMPUTER

It's hard nowadays to find a city that *doesn't* have a few cybercafes. Although there's no definitive directory for cybercafes—these are independent businesses, after all—three places to start looking are **www.cybercaptive. com**, **www.netcafeguide.com**, and **www.cybercafe.com**.

Most major airports now have **Internet kiosks** scattered throughout their gates. These kiosks, which you'll also see in shopping malls, hotel lobbies, and tourist information offices around the world, give you basic Web access for a per-minute fee that's usually higher than cybercafe prices. The kiosks' clunkiness and high price means they should be avoided whenever possible.

To retrieve your e-mail, ask your **Internet Service Provider (ISP)** if it has a Web-based interface tied to your existing e-mail account. If your ISP doesn't have such an interface, you can use the free **mail2web** service (www. mail2web.com) to view and reply to your home e-mail. For more flexibility, you may want to open a free, Web-based e-mail account with **Yahoo! Mail** (mail.yahoo.com). Microsoft's **Hotmail** (www.hotmail.com) is another popular option, but Hotmail has severe spam problems. Your home ISP may be able to forward your e-mail to the Web-based account automatically.

Most business-class hotels throughout the world offer dataports for laptop modems, and a few thousand hotels in the U.S. and Europe, including Paris, now offer high-speed Internet access using an Ethernet network cable. You'll have to bring your own cables either way, so call your hotel in advance to find out what the options are.

USING A CELLPHONE
OUTSIDE THE U.S.

The three letters that define much of the world's **wireless capabilities** are GSM (Global System for Mobiles), a big, seamless network that makes for easy cross-border cellphone use throughout Europe and dozens of other countries worldwide. In the U.S., T-Mobile, AT&T Wireless, and Cingular use this quasi-universal system; in Canada, Microcell and some Rogers customers are GSM, and all Europeans and most Australians use GSM.

If your cellphone is on a GSM system, and you have a world-capable phone such as many (but not all) Sony Ericsson, Motorola, or Samsung models, you can make and receive calls across civilized areas on much of the globe, from Andorra to Uganda. Just call your wireless operator and ask for "international roaming" to be activated on your account. Unfortunately, per-minute charges can be high—usually $1 to $1.50 in western Europe.

World-phone owners can bring down their per-minute charges with a bit of trickery. Call up your cellular operator and say you'll be going abroad for several months and want to "unlock" your phone to use it with a local provider. Usually, they'll oblige. Then, in your destination country, pick up a cheap, prepaid phone chip at a mobile phone store and slip it into your phone. (Show your phone to the salesperson, as not all phones work on all networks.) You'll get a local phone number in your destination eteran travelers usually carry some essential items to make their trips easier. Following is a selection of online tools to bookmark and use.

- **Visa ATM Locator** (www.visa.com), for locations of PLUS ATMs worldwide, or **MasterCard ATM Locator** (www.mastercard.com), for locations of Cirrus ATMs worldwide.
- **Foreign Languages for Travelers** (www.travlang.com). Learn basic terms in more than 70 languages and click on any underlined phrase to hear what it sounds like.
- **Intellicast** (www.intellicast.com) and **Weather.com** (www.weather.com). Gives weather forecasts for all 50 states and for cities around the world, including Paris.
- **Mapquest** (www.mapquest.com). This mapping site lets you choose a specific address or destination, and in seconds, it will return a map and detailed directions.
- **Universal Currency Converter** (www.xe.com/ucc). See what your dollar or pound is worth in more than 100 other countries.

country—and much, much lower calling rates.

Two good wireless rental companies are **InTouch USA** (© 800/872-7626; www.intouchglobal.com) and **Road-Post** (www.roadpost.com; © 888/290-1606 or 905/272-5665). Give them your itinerary, and they'll tell you what wireless products you need. InTouch will also, for free, advise you on whether your existing phone will work overseas; simply call © 703/222-7161 between 9am and 4pm EST, or go to www.intouchglobal.com/travel.htm.

10 Getting There

BY PLANE

High season on most airlines' routes to Paris is usually June to the beginning of September. This is the most expensive and most crowded time to travel. **Shoulder season** is April to May, early September to October, and December 15 to December 24. **Low season** is November 1 to December 14 and December 25 to March 31.

THE MAJOR AIRLINES

FROM NORTH AMERICA One of the best choices for travelers in the southeastern United States and Midwest is **Delta Airlines** (© 800/241-4141; www.delta.com). Delta flies direct to Paris from Atlanta, which is a hub for frequent flights from cities like New Orleans, Phoenix, Columbia (South Carolina), and Nashville. Delta also operates daily nonstop flights to Paris from Cincinnati and New York.

Another good option is **Continental Airlines** (© 800/525-0280; www.continental.com), serving the Northeast and much of the Southwest through its busy hubs in Newark (New Jersey) and Houston. From both cities, Continental provides nonstop flights to Paris.

The French flag carrier, **Air France** (© 800/237-2747; www.airfrance.com), offers daily or several-times-a-week flights to Paris from Newark; Washington, D.C.; Miami; Chicago;

New York; Houston; San Francisco; Los Angeles; Boston; Cincinnati; Atlanta; Montreal; Toronto; and Mexico City.

American Airlines (℃ 800/433-7300; www.aa.com) provides daily nonstop flights to Paris from Dallas/Fort Worth, Chicago, Miami, Boston, and New York.

US Airways (℃ 800/428-4322; www.usairways.com) offers daily nonstop service from Philadelphia to Paris.

If you'd like to see London before traveling on to Paris, there are dozens of **British Airways** (℃ 800/AIRWAYS**;** www.britishairways.com) flights from North American cities to London. You can fly first from, say, New York to London, and then take the BA shuttle flight to Paris following a holiday in England.

Canadians usually choose **Air Canada** (℃ 888/247-2262 from the U.S. and Canada; www.aircanada.ca) for flights to Paris from Toronto and Montreal. Nonstop flights from Montreal and Toronto depart every evening. Two of the nonstop flights from Toronto are shared with Air France and feature Air France aircraft.

FROM THE UNITED KINGDOM
From London, **Air France** (℃ 0845/084-5111; www.airfrance.com) and **British Airways** (℃ 0870/850-9850 in the U.K.; www.britishairways.com) fly frequently to Paris, offering up to 17 flights daily from Heathrow. **Aer Lingus** (℃ 866/IRISH-AIR; www.aerlingus.com) has frequent direct flights from Dublin to Paris

throughout the day. Many commercial travelers also use regular flights from the London City Airport in the Docklands. There are also direct flights to Paris from major cities such as Manchester, Edinburgh, and Southampton. For more information, contact Air France, British Airways, or **British Midland** (℃ 0870/607-0555; www.flybmi.com).

FROM AUSTRALIA Getting to Paris from Australia is rather difficult, because **Air France** (℃ 02-92-44-21-00; www.airfrance.com) has discontinued all direct flights to and from that country, requiring transfers through, among others, Singapore, with ongoing service to and from Sydney provided by Qantas. Consequently, on virtually any route, and with any airline you take, you have to change planes at least once en route. **British Airways** (℃ 02-89-04-88-00; www.britishairways.com) flies daily from both Sydney and Melbourne to London in time for any of several connecting flights to Paris. **Qantas** (℃ 13-13-13-68-46; www.qantas.com.au) can route passengers from Australia into London, where plentiful connections exist for the hop across the Channel.

GETTING THROUGH THE AIRPORT

With the federalization of airport security, security procedures at U.S. airports are more stable and consistent than ever. Generally, you'll be fine if you arrive **2 hours** before an international flight; if you show up late, tell

---

⟨Fun Fact **Sample Flying Times**

The flying time to Paris from New York is about 7 hours; from Chicago, 9 hours; from Los Angeles, 11 hours; from Atlanta, about 8 hours; from Washington, D.C., about 7½ hours; from London, about 1 hour; from Edinburgh, 2 hours; from Dublin, 2 hours; from Sydney, 21½ hours; and from Auckland, 23¼ hours.

an airline employee and he or she will probably whisk you to the front of the line.

Bring a **current, government-issued photo ID** such as a driver's license, and if you've got an E-ticket, print out the **official confirmation page;** you'll need to show your confirmation at the security checkpoint, and your ID at the ticket counter or the gate. (Children under 18 do not need photo IDs for domestic flights, but the adults checking in with them need them.)

Speed up security by **not wearing metal objects** such as big belt buckles or clanky earrings. If you've got metallic body parts, a note from your doctor can prevent a long chat with the security screeners. Keep in mind that only **ticketed passengers** are allowed past security, except for folks escorting disabled passengers or children.

Federalization has stabilized **what you can carry on** and **what you can't.** The general rule is that sharp things are out, nail clippers are okay, and food and beverages must be passed through the X-ray machine—but that security screeners can't make you drink from your coffee cup. Bring food in your carry-on rather than checking it, as explosive-detection machines used on checked luggage have been known to mistake food (especially chocolate, for some reason) for bombs. Travelers in the U.S. are allowed one carry-on bag, plus a "personal item" such as a purse, briefcase, or laptop bag. Carry-on hoarders can stuff all sorts of things into a laptop bag; as long as it has a laptop in it, it's still considered a personal item. The Transportation Security Administration (TSA) has issued a list of restricted items; check its website (www.tsa.gov/public/index.jsp) for details.

The TSA is also recommending that you **not lock your checked luggage** so screeners can search it by hand if necessary. The agency says to use plastic "zip ties" instead, which can be bought at hardware stores and can be easily cut off.

GETTING INTO TOWN FROM THE AIRPORT
Paris Airports

Paris has two international airports: **Orly** (✆ **01-49-75-15-15**), 14km (8½ miles) south of the city, and **Charles de Gaulle (Roissy)** (✆ 01-48-62-22-80), 23km (14 miles) northeast. A 13€ ($15) Air France shuttle operates between the two every 30 minutes, taking 50 to 75 minutes. For information on either airport go to www.adp.fr.

CHARLES DE GAULLE AIRPORT (ROISSY) At Charles de Gaulle, foreign carriers use Aérogare 1 and Air France uses Aérogare 2. From Aérogare 1, take a walkway to the passport checkpoint and the Customs area. A **shuttle bus** *(navette)* links the terminals.

The free shuttle bus connecting Aérogare 1 with Aérogare 2 also transports passengers to the Roissy rail station, from which fast **RER trains** (Line B) leave every 15 minutes daily between 5am to midnight for such Métro stations as Gare du Nord, Châtelet, Luxembourg, Port Royal, and Denfert-Rochereau. A typical RER fare from Roissy to any point in central Paris is 13€ ($15) in first class or 8€ ($9.20) in second.

You can also take either of two Air France shuttle buses, both of which depart from Roissy for points within central Paris. Line 2 departs at 12-minute intervals every day between 5:45am and 11pm, charging 10€ ($12) each way for the 40-minute transit to the place de l'Etoile, with a stop en route at Porte Maillot. Line 4 departs at 30-minute intervals every day between 7am and 9:30pm, charging 12€ ($14) for the 50-minute trip to the Gare Montparnasse, making an intermediate stop at the Gare de Lyon

Value Airport Shuttle

A commuter service is provided by **PariShuttle,** 103 rue Villiers de l'Isle Adam, 75020 Paris (*©* **01-43-90-91-91;** fax 01-53-39-13-13; www. parishuttle.com). Before collecting your baggage at the airport, you can call their toll-free number (*©* **08-00-69-96-99**) and make your way later to the arranged meeting point. You can also call and reserve by phone before your arrival in Paris. PariShuttle will take you to your desired address in Paris, and service in the eight-seat minivans is 7 days a week. The cost is 25€ ($29) per person or 15€ ($17) per person if more than one person is traveling together.

en route. From any of those points within central Paris, Métro lines can carry you on to virtually any other point within the city.

Another option, the **Roissybus** (*©* **01-48-04-18-24**), departs from a point near the corner of the rue Scribe and place de l'Opéra every 15 minutes from 5:45am to 11pm. The cost for the 50-minute ride is 8€ ($9.20).

Taxis from Roissy into the city run about 40€ ($46) on the meter. At night (8pm–7am) fares are about 40% higher. Long queues of both taxis and passengers form outside each of the airport's terminals in a surprisingly orderly fashion.

ORLY AIRPORT   Orly has two terminals: Orly Sud (south) for international flights and Orly Ouest (west) for domestic flights. A free shuttle bus links them together.

Air France buses leave from exit E of Orly Ouest and from exit K, Platform 5, of Orly Sud every 12 minutes from 5:45am to 11pm for Gare des Invalides in central Paris at a cost of 8.50€ ($9.80) one-way. Other buses depart for place Denfert-Rochereau in the south of Paris at a cost of 6.20€ ($7.15).

An alternative method for reaching central Paris involves taking a **monorail** (Orly Val) to the RER station of Anthony, then the RER train into downtown Paris. The Orly Val makes stops at the north and south terminals,

and continues at 8-minute intervals for the 10-minute ride to the Anthony RER station. At Anthony, you'll board an RER train (Line B) for the 30-minute ride into the city. The cost of the Orly Val monorail plus the RER (Line B) transit into Paris is 9€ ($10), a fare that might seem a bit high, but which offsets the horrendous construction costs of a monorail that sails above the congested roadways encircling the airport.

A **taxi** from Orly to the center of Paris costs about 35€ ($40), more at night and on weekends. Returning to the airport, **buses** to Orly leave from the Invalides terminal to either Orly Sud or Orly Ouest every 15 minutes, taking about 30 minutes.

Caution: Don't take a meterless taxi from Orly Sud or Orly Ouest—it's much safer (and usually cheaper) to hire a metered cab from the taxi queues, which are under the scrutiny of a police officer.

FLYING FOR LESS: TIPS FOR GETTING THE BEST AIRFARE

Passengers sharing the same airplane cabin rarely pay the same fare. Travelers who need to purchase tickets at the last minute, change their itinerary at a moment's notice, or fly one-way often get stuck paying the premium rate. Here are some ways to keep your airfare costs down.

- Passengers who can book their ticket **long in advance,** who can **stay over Saturday night,** or who **fly midweek** or **at less-trafficked hours** will pay a fraction of the full fare. If your schedule is flexible, say so, and ask if you can secure a cheaper fare by changing your flight plans.

- You can also save on airfares by keeping an eye out in local newspapers for **promotional specials** or **fare wars,** when airlines lower prices on their most popular routes. You rarely see fare wars offered for peak travel times, but if you can travel in the off-months, you may snag a bargain.

- Search **the Internet** for cheap fares (see "Planning Your Trip Online" earlier in this chapter).

- **Consolidators,** also known as bucket shops, are great sources for international tickets, although they usually can't beat the Internet on fares within North America. Start by looking in Sunday newspaper travel sections; U.S. travelers should focus on the *New York Times, Los Angeles Times,* and *Miami Herald.* For less-developed destinations, small travel agents who cater to immigrant communities in large cities often have the best deals. *Beware:* Bucket shop tickets are usually nonrefundable or rigged with stiff cancellation penalties, often as high as 50% to 75% of the ticket price, and some put you on charter airlines with questionable safety records.

- One of the best agencies for trips to France is **Nouvelles Frontieres,** whose American subsidiary is **New Frontiers USA** (✆ **800/ 366-6387;** fax 212/779-1007; www.newfrontiers.com). It maintains that it can "beat published prices by 20% to 30%." Because of the company's massive buying power in Paris, rates in hotels from budget to first class can be slashed considerably. Value-packed travel packages, low-cost airfares across the Atlantic, and reduced car rental rates continue to make New Frontiers a major player in the Paris-bound market.

- Several reliable consolidators are worldwide and available on the Net. **STA Travel** (www.statravel. com) is now the world's leader in student travel, thanks to its purchase of Council Travel. It also offers good fares for travelers of all ages. **Flights.com** (www.flights. com) started in Europe and has excellent fares worldwide, but particularly to that continent. It also has "local" websites in 12 countries. **Air Tickets Direct** (✆ **800/ 778-3447;** www.airticketsdirect. com) is based in Montreal and leverages the currently weak Canadian dollar for low fares.

- Join **frequent-flier clubs.** Accrue enough miles, and you'll be rewarded with free flights and elite status. It's free, and you'll get the best choice of seats, faster response to phone inquiries, and prompter service if your luggage is stolen, your flight is canceled or delayed, or if you want to change your seat. You don't need to fly to build frequent-flier miles—**frequent-flier credit cards** can provide thousands of miles for doing your everyday shopping.

BY CAR

Driving in Paris is definitely not recommended. Parking is difficult, traffic is dense, and networks of one-way streets make navigation, even with the best of maps, a problem. If you do drive, remember that Paris is encircled by a ring road called the *périphérique.* Always obtain detailed directions to your destination, including the name of the exit on the périphérique you're looking for (exits aren't numbered).

Avoid rush hours. Few hotels, except the luxury ones, have garages, but the staff will usually be able to direct you to one nearby.

The **major highways** into Paris are the A1 from the north (Great Britain and Benelux); A13 from Rouen, Normandy, and northwest France; A10 from Bordeaux, the Pyrenees, France's southwest, and Spain; A6 from Lyon, the French Alps, the Riviera, and Italy; and A4 from Metz, Nancy, and Strasbourg in eastern France.

BY TRAIN

If you're already in Europe, you might decide to travel to Paris by train, especially if you have a **Eurailpass.** Rail passes or individual rail tickets within Europe are available at most travel agencies, at any office of **Rail Europe** (② **877/272-RAIL;** www.raileurope. com), or at **Eurostar** (② **800/ EUROSTAR** in the U.S., 0870/584-8848 in London, 01-55-31-54-54 in Paris; www.eurostar.com).

There are six major train stations in Paris: **Gare d'Austerlitz,** 55 quai d'Austerlitz, 13e (serving the southwest, with trains from the Loire Valley, the Bordeaux country, and the Pyrenees); **Gare de l'Est,** place du 11 Novembre 1918, 10e (serving the east, with trains from Strasbourg, Nancy, Reims, and beyond to Zurich, Basel, Luxembourg, and Austria); **Gare de Lyon,** 20 bd. Diderot, 12e (serving the southeast with trains from the Côte d'Azur and Provence to Geneva, Lausanne, and Italy); **Gare Montparnasse,** 17 bd. Vaugirard, 15e (serving the west, with trains from Brittany); **Gare du Nord,** 18 rue de Dunkerque, 15e (serving the north, with trains from Holland, Denmark, Belgium, and Germany); and **Gare St-Lazare,** 13 rue d'Amsterdam, 8e (serving the northwest, with trains from Normandy).

For general train information and to make reservations, call Rail Europe at ② **08-36-35-35-39** daily from 7am to 8pm. Buses operate between rail stations. Each of these stations has a Métro stop, making the whole city easily accessible. Taxis are also available at designated stands at every station. Look for the sign that says TETE DE STATION. Be alert in train stations, especially at night.

BY BUS

Bus travel to Paris is available from London and many other cities on the Continent. In the early 1990s, the French government established strong incentives for long-haul buses not to drive into the center of Paris, so the arrival/departure point for Europe's largest bus operator, **Eurolines France,** is a 35-minute Métro ride from central Paris, at the terminus of Métro line 3 (Gallieni), in the eastern suburb of Bagnolet. Despite this inconvenience, many people prefer bus travel. Eurolines France is at 28 av. du Général-de-Gaulle, 93541 Bagnolet (② **01-49-72-51-58**).

Long-haul buses are equipped with toilets, and they stop at mealtimes for rest and refreshment. The price of a round-trip ticket between Paris and London (a 7-hr. trip) is 55€ to 72€ ($63–$83) for passengers 26 or over, and 55€ to 65€ ($63–$75) for passengers under 26.

Because Eurolines doesn't have a U.S.-based sales agent, most people wait until they reach Europe to buy their tickets. Any European travel agent can arrange these purchases. If you're traveling to Paris from London, contact **Eurolines (U.K.) Ltd.,** 52 Grosvenor Gardens, Victoria, London SW1 (② **020/7730-8235;** www.euro lines.co.uk), for information or credit card sales.

BY FERRY FROM ENGLAND

Despite competition from the Chunnel, services aboard ferries and hydrofoils operate day and night in all seasons, with the exception of last-minute cancellations during storms. Many channel crossings are timed to coincide with the arrival/departure of major trains (especially those between London and Paris); trains let you off a short walk from the piers. Most ferries carry cars, trucks, and massive amounts of freight, but some hydrofoils take passengers only. The major routes include at least 12 trips a day between Dover or Folkestone and Calais or Boulogne. Hovercraft and hydrofoils make the trip from Dover to Calais, the shortest distance across the Channel, in 40 minutes during good weather; the slower-moving ferries might take several hours, depending on weather and tides. If you're bringing a car, it's important to make reservations, as space below decks is usually crowded. Timetables can vary depending on the weather and many other factors.

The leading operator of ferries across the Channel is **P&O Ferries** (call Rail Europe for reservations at ℂ **877/272-RAIL** in North America or 0870/520-2020 in England; www.poferries.com). It operates car and passenger ferries between Portsmouth, England, and Cherbourg, France (three departures a day; 4¼ hr. each way during daylight hours, 7 hr. each way at night); between Portsmouth and Le Havre, France (three a day; 5½ hr. each way). The most popular routes are between Dover and Calais, France (25 sailings a day; 75 min. each way), which costs £10 ($16) one-way for adults; children under 4 go free.

The shortest and most popular route is between Calais and Dover. **Hoverspeed** operates at least 12 hovercraft crossings daily; the trip takes 35 minutes. It also runs a SeaCat (a catamaran propelled by jet engines) that takes longer, just under 1 hour, between Dover and Calais. For reservations and information, call Hoverspeed (ℂ **800/677-8585** in North America or 0870/240-8070 in England; www.hoverspeed.com). Typical one-way fares are £27 ($43) per person.

If you plan to transport a rental car between England and France, check in advance with the rental company about license and insurance requirements and additional drop-off charges. And be aware that many car-rental companies, for insurance reasons, forbid transport of one of their vehicles over the water between England and France. Transport of a car each way begins at £128 ($205).

UNDER THE CHANNEL

One of the great engineering feats of our time, the $15 billion Channel Tunnel (Chunnel) opened in 1994, and the **Eurostar Express** now has daily service from London to both Paris and Brussels. The 50km (31-mile) journey takes 35 minutes, though actual time spent in the Chunnel is only 19 minutes. Stores selling duty-free goods, restaurants, service stations, and bilingual staffs are available to travelers on both sides of the Channel.

Eurostar tickets are available through **Rail Europe** (ℂ **877/272-RAIL;** www.raileurope.com). In Great Britain, make reservations for Eurostar at ℂ **0870/530-0003;** in the United States, call ℂ **800/EUROSTAR.** Chunnel train traffic is roughly competitive with air travel, if you calculate door-to-door travel time. Trains leave from London's Waterloo Station and arrive in Paris at the Gare du Nord.

The tunnel also accommodates passenger cars, charter buses, taxis, and motorcycles, transporting them under the Channel from Folkestone, England, to Calais, France. It operates 24 hours a day, running every 15 minutes during peak travel times and at least once an hour at night. You can buy tickets at the tollbooth at the tunnel's entrance. With **Le Shuttle** (ℂ **0870/535-3535;** www.eurotunnel.com), gone are the days of weather-related delays, seasickness, and advance reservations.

Before they board Le Shuttle, motorists stop at a tollbooth and pass through British and French immigration at the same time. Then they drive onto a 1km-long (½ mile) train and travel through the tunnel. During the ride, motorists stay in air-conditioned carriages, remaining inside their cars or stepping outside to stretch their legs. When the trip is completed, they simply drive off. Total travel time is about an hour. Once on French soil, British drivers must remember to drive on the right-hand side of the road.

11 Tours: Packages, Escorted & Special Interest

Before you start your search for the lowest airfare, you may want to consider booking your flight as part of a travel package. Package tours are not the same thing as escorted tours. Package tours are simply a way to buy the airfare, accommodations, and other elements of your trip (such as car rentals, airport transfers, and sometimes even activities) at the same time and often at discounted prices—kind of like one-stop shopping. Packages are sold in bulk to tour operators—who resell them to the public at a cost that usually undercuts standard rates.

One good source of package deals is the airlines themselves. Most major airlines offer air/land packages, including **American Airlines Vacations** (© 800/321-2121; www.aavacations. com), **Delta Vacations** (© 800/221-6666; www.deltavacations.com), and **Continental Airlines Vacations** (© 800/301-3800; www.coolvacations. com). Several big **online travel agencies**—Expedia, Travelocity, Orbitz, Site59, and Lastminute.com—also do a brisk business in packages. If you're unsure about the pedigree of a smaller packager, check with the Better Business Bureau in the city where the company is based, or go online at www. bbb.org. If a packager won't tell you where it's based, don't fly with them.

The French Experience, 370 Lexington Ave., Room 511, New York, NY 10017 (© **800/283-7262** or 212/986-3800; fax 212/986-3808; www.frenchexperience.com), offers inexpensive tickets to Paris on most scheduled airlines and arranges tours and stays in various types and categories of country inns, hotels, private châteaux, and B&Bs. In addition, it takes reservations for about 38 small hotels in Paris and arranges short-term apartment rentals in the city or farmhouse rentals in the countryside, and offers all-inclusive packages in Paris and prearranged package tours of various regions of France. Tours can be adapted to suit individual needs.

ESCORTED TOURS The two largest tour operators conducting escorted tours of France and Europe are **Globus/Cosmos** (© **800/338-7092;** www.globusandcosmos.com) and **Trafalgar** (© **800/854-0103;** www.trafalgartours.com). Both companies have first-class tours that run about $100 a day and budget tours for even less. The differences are mainly in hotel location and the number of activities. There's little difference in the companies' services, so choose your tour based on the itinerary and preferred date of departure. Brochures are available at travel agencies, and all tours must be booked through travel agents.

FINDING A SPECIALTY PACKAGE What about special-interest tours? For a city as diverse and popular as Paris, there are only a few specialty tours.

One outfit that coordinates hotel stays with major musical events, usually within at least one (and often both) of the city's opera houses, is **Dailey-Thorp Travel,** P.O. Box 670, Big Horn, WY 82833 (© **800/998-4677** or 307/673-1555; fax 307/674-7474; www.daileythorp.com). Stays in Paris last between 3 and 7 days and, in many cases, are tied in with opera performances in other cities (usually London, Berlin, or Milan) as well. Expect accommodations in deluxe hotels such as the Grand, the Louvre, or the Scribe, and a staff that has made arrangements for all the nuts-and-bolts of your arrival in, and artistic exposure to, Paris.

Die-hard tennis fans set their calendars by the events that transpire each year in Paris's Roland-Garros stadium at the French Open. If you're unsure about how to match the dates of your visit with tennis tournaments that will be watched around the world, consider the California-based company that specializes in this issue: **Advantage Tennis Tours,** 33 White Sail Drive,

Suite 100, Laguna Niguel, CA 92677 (© **800/341-8687;** www.advantage tennistours.com).

Packages usually include either 5 or 6 nights of hotel accommodations in Paris, 2 or 3 days on Center Court, the organizational skills of a bilingual hostess, and a chance to meet and mingle, at any of at least one catered lunch, with tennis fans of many different nationalities. There will even be an opportunity to grab a racquet and play some tennis on your own, in between bouts of sightseeing. Rates, per person, without airfare, begin at $2,795, double occupancy, depending on your choice of hotel and the duration of your visit.

12 Recommended Reading

There are numerous books on all aspects of French history and society—ranging from the very general, such as the section on France in the *Encyclopedia Americana,* International Edition (Grolier, 1989), which presents an excellent illustrated overview of the French people and their way of life, to the very specific, such as Judi Culbertson and Tom Randall's *Permanent Parisians: An Illustrated Guide to the Cemeteries of Paris* (Chelsea Green, 1986), which depicts the lives of famous French and expatriates who are buried in Paris.

HISTORY In addition to the encyclopedia reference above, a broad overview of French history can be found in other encyclopedias and general history books. One very good one is *History of France,* by Guillaume de Bertier de Savigny and David H. Pinkney (Forum Press, 1983), a comprehensive history with illustrations and plenty of obscure but interesting facts.

Two books that present French life and society in the 17th century are Warren Lewis's *The Splendid Century* (William Morrow, 1978) and Madame de Sévigne's *Selected Letters,* edited by

Leonard W. Tancock (Penguin, 1982), which contains imaginative and witty letters written to her daughter during the reign of Louis XIV.

Simon Schama's *Citizens* (Alfred A. Knopf, 1989) is "a magnificent and electrifyingly new history of the French Revolution"—long, but enjoyable.

Moving into the 20th century, *Pleasure of the Belle Epoque: Entertainment and Festivity in Turn-of-the-Century France,* by Charles Rearick (Yale University Press, 1985), depicts public diversions in the changing and troubled times of the Third Republic. *Paris Was Yesterday, 1925–1939* (Harcourt Brace Jovanovich, 1988) is a fascinating collection of excerpts from Janet Flanner's "Letters from Paris" column of the *New Yorker.* Larry Collins and Dominique Lapierre have written a popular history of the liberation of Paris in 1944 called *Is Paris Burning?* (Warner Books, 1991).

Finally, two unusual approaches to French history are Rudolph Chleminski's *The French at Table* (William Morrow, 1985), a funny and honest history of why the French know how to eat better than anyone and how they go about it, and *Paris: A Century of Change, 1878–1978,* by Normal Evenson (Yale University Press, 1979), a notable study of the urban development of Paris.

TRAVEL   Since 1323 some 10,000 books have been devoted to exploring Paris. One of the latest is *Paris: Capital of the World,* by Patrice Higonnet (Harvard University, 2002). This book takes a fresh, social, cultural, and political look at this City of Lights. Higonnet even explores Paris as "the capital of sex," and in contrast the "capital of art." The gang's all here from Balzac to Zola.

Showing a greater fondness for gossip is Alistair Horne in his *Seven Pages of Paris* (Alfred A. Knopf, 2002). From the Roman founding up to the student riots of 1968, this is one of the most amusing books on Paris we've ever read. Horne is not a timid writer. He calls the Palais de Chaillot fascistic and hideous, the Pompidou Center a horror. We even learn that a woman once jumped off the Eiffel tower, bounced off the roof of a parked car, and survived. In *The Flâneur, A Stroll Through the Paradoxes of Paris* (Bloomsbury, 2001), Edmund White wants the reader to experience Paris as Parisians do. Hard to translate exactly, *a flâneur* is someone who strolls, loafs, or idles. With White, you can circumnavigate Paris as whim dictates.

BIOGRAPHY   You can get a more intimate look at history through biographies of historical figures. The best book yet on the architect who changed the face of Paris is *Haussmann: His Life and Times and the Making of Modern Paris,* by Patrick Camiller (Ivan R. Dee, 2002). Hugh Ross Williamson brings to life Catherine de Médici in his *Catherine de Medici* (Viking Press, 1973) by combining text and magnificent illustrations from the art of the 16th century. This queen of France was the dominant personality during her nation's religious wars and mother of three kings of France, a queen of Spain, and a queen of Navarre.

Representing a very different era are *A Moveable Feast* (Collier Books, 1987), Ernest Hemingway's recollections of Paris during the 1920s, and Morley Callaghan's *That Summer in Paris: Memories of Tangled Friendships with Hemingway, Fitzgerald and Some Others* (1963), an anecdotal account of the same period. Another interesting read is *The Autobiography of Alice B. Toklas,* by Gertrude Stein (Vintage Books, 1990). It's not only the account of 30 years in Paris, but also the autobiography of Gertrude Stein.

Simone de Beauvoir, by Deirdre Bair (Summit Books, 1990), was described by one critic as " . . . a biography 'à l'Americaine'—that is to say, long, with all the warts of its subject unsparingly described." The story of the great feminist intellectual was based in part on tape-recorded conversations and unpublished letters.

Colette: A Life, by Herbert R. Lottman (Little, Brown, 1991), is a painstakingly researched biography of the celebrated French writer and her fascinating life—which included not only writing novels and appearing in cabarets but also dabbling in lesbianism and perhaps even collaborating with the enemy during the Nazi occupation.

THE ARTS   Much of France's beauty can be found in its art. Three books that approach France from this perspective are *The History of Impressionism,* by John Rewald (Museum of Modern Art, 1973), which is a collection of writings about and quotations from the artists, illuminating this period in art; *The French Through Their Films,* by Robin Buss (Ungar, 1988), an exploration of more than 100 widely circulated films; and *The Studios of Paris: The Capital of Art in the Late Nineteenth Century,* by John Milner (Yale University Press, 1988). In the last, Milner presents the dynamic forces that made Paris one of the most complex centers of the art world in the early modern era.

Nightlife of Paris: The Art of Toulouse-Lautrec, by Patrick O'Connor (Universe, 1992), is an enchanting 80-page book with anecdotes about the hedonistic luminaries of Belle Epoque Paris, with paintings, sketches, and lithographs by the artist.

Olympia: Paris in the Age of Manet, by Otto Friedrich (Harper-Collins, 1992), takes its inspiration from the celebrated artwork in the Musée d'Orsay in Paris. From here the book takes off on an anecdote-rich, gossipy chain of historical associations, tracing the rise of the Impressionist school of modern painting, but incorporating social commentary, too, such as the pattern of prostitution and venereal disease in 19th-century France.

FICTION   The *Chanson de Roland,* edited by F. Whitehead (2nd ed.; Basil Blackwell, 1942), written between the 11th and 14th centuries, is the earliest and most celebrated of the "songs of heroic exploits." *The Misanthrope* and *Tartuffe* (Harcourt, Brace and World, 1965) are two masterful satires on the frivolity of the 17th century by the great comic dramatist Molière. François-Marie Arouet Voltaire's *Candide* (Bantam Classics, 1981) is a classic satire attacking the philosophy of optimism and the abuses of the ancient regime.

A few of the masterpieces of the 19th century are *Madame Bovary,* by Gustave Flaubert (Random House, 1982), in which the carefully wrought characters, setting, and plot attest to Flaubert's genius in presenting the tragedy of Emma Bovary; Victor Hugo's *Les Misérables* (Modern Library, 1983), a classic tale of social oppression and human courage set in the era of Napoleon I; and *Selected Stories* by the master of short stories, Guy de Maupassant (New American Library, 1984).

Honoré de Balzac's *La comédie humaine* (Centre d'Exportation du Livre, Francais, 1999/Original 1831) depicts life in France from the fall of Napoleon to 1848. Henry James's *The Ambassadors* (Penguin USA, 1987/ Original 1903) and *The American* (Oxford University Press, 1999/Original 1877) both take place in Paris. *The Vagabond* (Farrar Straus & Giroux, 2001/Original 1978), by Colette, evokes the life of a French music-hall performer.

Tropic of Cancer (Grove Press, 1989/Original 1934) is the semiautobiographical story of Henry Miller's years in Paris. One of France's leading thinkers, Jean-Paul Sartre, shows individuals struggling against their freedom in *No Exit and Three Other Plays* (Vintage Books 1989/Original 1956).

4

Getting to Know
the City of Light

Ernest Hemingway called the many splendors of Paris a "moveable feast" and wrote, "There is never any ending to Paris, and the memory of each person who has lived in it differs from that of any other." It's this aura of personal discovery that has always been the most compelling reason to come to Paris. Perhaps that's why France has been called *le deuxième pays de tout le monde* (everybody's second country).

The Seine not only divides Paris into the Right Bank and the Left Bank but seems to split the city into two vastly different sections and ways of life. Depending on your time, interest, and budget, you may quickly decide which section of Paris suits you best.

The old clichés about the Left Bank being for poor, struggling artists and the Right Bank being for the well-heeled were broken down long ago. The very heart of the Left Bank, including the areas around Odéon and St-Germain-des-Prés, are as chic as

anything on the Right Bank—and just as expensive.

The history of Paris repeats itself. In the old days, Montmartre was the artists' quarter until prices and tourism drove these "bohemians" to less expensive *quartiers* such as Montparnasse. But Montparnasse long ago became gold-plated real estate.

So where does the struggling artist go today? Not to the central core of the Right or Left Bank, but farther afield. First, it was the Marais, until that district, too, saw rents spiral and the average visitor carrying a gold American Express card. Now, it's farther east, into the 11th arrondissement, a blue-collar neighborhood between the Marais, Ménilmontant, and République. The heartbeat of this area is rue Oberkampf. If you'd like to see this newly gentrified area before it, too, changes forever, refer to the box "A Bar Crawl in Trendy Ménilmontant," in chapter 10, "Paris After Dark."

1 Essentials

VISITOR INFORMATION

The **Paris Convention and Visitors Bureau** has a number of offices scattered throughout the city, the main headquarters being 25–27 rue des Pyramides, 1e (Métro: Palais Royal/Musée du Louvre). It's open April to October daily 9am to 8pm; off-season daily 11am to 6pm. Branch offices include **Opéra-Grands Magasins,** 11 rue Scribe, 9e (Métro: Opéra), open Monday to Saturday 9am to 6:30pm; **Gare de Lyon,** 20 bd. Diderot, 12e (Métro: Gare de Lyon), open Monday to Saturday 8am to 6pm; **Gare du Nord,** 10e (Métro: Gare du Nord), open daily 12:30 to 8pm; **Montmartre Tourist Office,** 18 rue de Dunkerque, 10e (Métro: Abbesses), daily 10am to 7pm. For information over the phone, call ✆ **08-92-68-30-00,** which costs .34€ (40¢) per minute. The website can be accessed at **www.paris-touristoffice.com**. The branches will make hotel reservations. The

---

⌒ **Tips**   **Country & City Telephone Codes**

The country code for France is **33**. The city code for Paris (as well as for all cities in the Ile de France region) is **1**; use this code if you're calling from outside France. If you're calling Paris from within Paris or from anywhere else in France, use 01, which is now built into all phone numbers in the Ile de France, making them 10 digits long.

---

service charge is free for hostels; 2€ ($2.30) for one-star hotels; 4€ ($4.60) for two-star hotels; and 6€ ($6.90) for three-star hotels. Stars refer to government ratings, rather than those used in this guide. Offices are very busy in summer, so you'll have to wait in line.

CITY LAYOUT

Paris is surprisingly compact. Occupying 1,119 sq. km (436 sq. miles), it's home to more than 10 million people. The city is divided into 20 municipal wards called **arrondissements,** each with its own mayor, city hall, police station, and central post office. Some even have remnants of market squares.

The river Seine divides Paris into the *Rive Droite* (**Right Bank**) to the north and the *Rive Gauche* (**Left Bank**) to the south. These designations make sense when you stand on a bridge and face downstream; watching the water flow out toward the sea, to your right is the north bank, to your left the south. Thirty-two bridges link the banks of the Seine, some providing access to the two small islands at the heart of the city, **Ile de la Cité,** the city's birthplace and site of Notre-Dame, and **Ile St-Louis,** a moat-guarded oasis of sober 17th-century mansions. These islands can cause some confusion to walkers who think they've just crossed a bridge from one bank to the other, only to find themselves caught up in an almost medieval maze of narrow streets and old buildings.

As part of Napoleon III's massive urban redevelopment project, Baron Georges-Eugène Haussmann forever changed the look of Paris between 1860 and 1870 by creating the legendary **boulevards:** St-Michel, St-Germain, Haussmann, Malesherbes, Sébastopol, Magenta, Voltaire, and Strasbourg.

The "main street" on the Right Bank is the **Champs-Elysées,** beginning at the Arc de Triomphe and running to place de la Concorde. Haussmann also created avenue de l'Opéra (as well as the Opéra), and the 12 avenues that radiate starlike from the Arc de Triomphe, giving it its original name, place de *l'Etoile* (star); it was renamed place Charles de Gaulle following the general's death and is often referred to as **place Charles de Gaulle–Etoile.**

Haussmann also cleared Ile de la Cité of its medieval buildings, transforming it into a showcase for Notre-Dame. Finally, he laid out two elegant parks on the western and southeastern fringes of the city: the **Bois de Boulogne** and **Bois de Vincennes.**

FINDING AN ADDRESS

The key to finding any address in Paris is looking for the arrondissement number, rendered either as a number followed by "e" (1e, 2e, and so on) or more formally as part of the postal code (the last two digits indicate the arrondissement—75007 indicates the 7th arrondissement, 75017 the 17th). Numbers on buildings running parallel to the Seine usually follow the course of the river—east to west. On north-south streets, numbering begins at the river.

If you're staying more than 2 or 3 days, buy one of the inexpensive little books that include the *plan de Paris* by arrondissement, available at all major newsstands and bookshops. If you can find it, the forest-green "Paris Classique l'Indispensable" is a thorough, well-indexed, and accurate guide to the city and its suburbs. Most map guides provide you with a Métro map, a foldout map of the city, and indexed maps of each arrondissement, with all streets listed and keyed. We've given you a head start by including a **full-color foldout map** at the back of this guide.

ARRONDISSEMENTS IN BRIEF

Each of Paris's 20 arrondissements possesses a unique style and flavor. You'll want to decide which district appeals most to you and then try to find accommodations there. Later on, try to visit as many areas as you can so you get the full taste of Paris.

1ST ARRONDISSEMENT (MUSEE DU LOUVRE/LES HALLES) "I never knew what a palace was until I had a glimpse of the Louvre," wrote Nathaniel Hawthorne. Perhaps the world's greatest art museum, the **Louvre,** a former royal residence, still lures visitors to the 1st arrondissement. Walk through the **Jardin des Tuileries,** Paris's most formal garden (laid out by Le Nôtre, gardener to Louis XIV). Pause to take in the classic beauty of **place Vendôme,** the opulent home of the Hôtel Ritz. Zola's "belly of Paris" (Les Halles) is no longer the food-and-meat market of Paris (traders moved to the new, more accessible suburb of Rungis); today the **Forum des Halles** is a center of shopping, entertainment, and culture.

2ND ARRONDISSEMENT (LA BOURSE) Home to the **Bourse** (stock exchange), this Right Bank district lies between the Grands Boulevards and rue Etienne-Marcel. From Monday to Friday, brokers play the market until it's time to break for lunch, when the movers and shakers of French capitalism channel their hysteria into the area restaurants. Much of the eastern end of the arrondissement **(Le Sentier)** is devoted to wholesale outlets of the Paris garment district, where thousands of garments are sold (usually in bulk) to buyers

from clothing stores throughout Europe. "Everything that exists elsewhere exists in Paris," wrote Victor Hugo in *Les Misérables,* and this district provides ample evidence of that.

3RD ARRONDISSEMENT (LE MARAIS) This district embraces much of Le Marais (the swamp), one of the best-loved Right Bank neighborhoods. (It extends into the 4th as well.) After decades of decay, Le Marais recently made a comeback, though it may never again enjoy the prosperity of its 17th-century aristocratic heyday; today it contains Paris's **gay neighborhood,** with lots of gay/lesbian restaurants, bars, and stores, as well as the remains of the old Jewish quarter, centered on **rue des Rosiers.** Two of the chief attractions are the **Musée Picasso,** a kind of pirate's ransom of painting and sculpture the Picasso estate had to turn over to the French government in lieu of the artist's astronomical death duties, and the **Musée Carnavalet,** which brings to life the history of Paris from prehistoric times to the present.

4TH ARRONDISSEMENT (ILE DE LA CITE/ILE ST-LOUIS & BEAUBOURG) It seems as if the 4th has it all: Notre-Dame on Ile de la Cité, Ile St-Louis and its aristocratic town houses, courtyards, and antiques shops. **Ile St-Louis,** a

Paris Arrondissements

Railway

st-Ouen **St-Denis** ↑ **To Roissy/Charles-de-Gaulle Airport**
PORTE DE   **PORTE DE** **PORTE**Aubervilliers **PORTE DE**
CLIGNANCOURT **LA CHAPELLE D'AUBERVILLIERS** **LA VILLETTE**

. Ney
bd. **bd. Macdonald**
bd. Ornano
rue de la Chapelle **Cité des Sciences**
8e **et de l'Industrie**
rue de Flandre *Canal de l'Ourcq*

MONTMARTRE bd. Barbès **LA VILLETTE**
rue Riquet
place Max Dormoy **PORTE DE**
† bd. de la Chapelle St-Martin **PANTIN**
Sacré-Cœur *Bassin de la Villette*
bd. de av. Jean Jaurès **Le Pré St-Gervais**
Rochechouart **Gare** **19e**
du
Nord rue du Faubourg *PARC DE*
9e **Gare** *BUTTES-*
de l'Est *CHAUMONT* **PORTE**
e La Fayette bd. de **DES LILAS**
bd. de Magenta Villette
2e **10e** bd. de la **BELLEVILLE**
rue du Faubourg Villette
du Temple bd. de
pl. de la République Belleville bd. de Ménilmontant **MÉNILMONTANT**
BOURSE rue de Turbigo
av. de la République **20e**
e bd. de Sébastopol **3e** bd. Beaumarchais *CIMETIÈRE* **PORTE DE**
Les rue Rambuteau *DU PÈRE-* **BAGNOLET**
ouvre **Halles** bd. Voltaire *LACHAISE*
ai du Louvre rue de Rivoli **Centre**
Ile de la Cité **Pompidou** **MARAIS**
ainte-Chapelle **Hôtel** bd. R. Lenoir **11e** bd. Voltaire **PORTE DE**
de Ville **pl. des** av. Philippe **MONTREUIL**
Vosges **BASTILLE** bd. Voltaire Auguste
Ile St-Louis **pl. de la**
Notre-Dame **Bastille** rue de Faubourg St-Antoine **PORTE DE**
St-Michel **Opéra** **VINCENNES**
Sorbonne **4e** **Bastille** **pl. de la** Cours de Vincennes
LATIN av. Ledru-Rollin **Nation**
IN **QUARTER** av. **PORTE DE**
EM- bd. Diderot Daumesnil **ST-MANDÉ**
RG ■**Panthéon** *JARDIN* **Gare**
DES **Gare** **de Lyon**
5e *PLANTES* **d'Austerlitz**
av. des Gobelins *Seine* bd. de Bercy **pl. Félix** **PORTE**
bd. **Eboué** **DORÉE**
bd. St-Marcel **Bibliothèque** ■**Parc**
d. Arago bd. de l'Hôpital **National** quai de Bercy **12e** **Zoologique**
d. Blanqui bd. Auriol **de France** quai de la Gare **PORTE DE**
pl. d'Italie **CHARENTON** *BOIS DE VINCENNES*
' d'Alésia **13e** av. de Choisy **PORTE DE**
av. d'Italie **BERCY**
ARC DE av. d'Ivry bd. Masséna **Charenton**
NTSOURIS bd. Kellerman
Cité **Ivry-Sur-Seine**
versitaire **PORTE**
D'IVRY
PORTE **PORTE**
DE GENTILLY **D'ITALIE**
6A **Gentilly**
o Orly)

former cow pasture and dueling ground, is home to dozens of 17th-century mansions and 6,000 lucky Louisiens, its permanent residents. Seek out **Ile de la Cité**'s two Gothic churches, **Sainte-Chapelle** and **Notre-Dame,** a majestic structure that, according to poet e. e. cummings, "doesn't budge an inch for all the idiocies of this world." You'll find France's finest bird and flower markets along with the nation's law courts, which Balzac described as a "cathedral of chicanery." It was here that Marie Antoinette was sentenced to death in 1793. The 4th is also home to the freshly renovated **Centre Pompidou,** one of the top three attractions in France. After all this pomp and glory, you can retreat to **place des Vosges,** a square of perfect harmony and beauty where Victor Hugo lived from 1832 to 1848 and penned many of his famous masterpieces. (His house is now a museum—see p. 208.)

5TH ARRONDISSEMENT (QUARTIER LATIN) The Latin Quarter is the intellectual heart and soul of Paris. Bookstores, schools, churches, clubs, student dives, Roman ruins, publishing houses, and expensive boutiques characterize the district. Discussions of Artaud or Molière over cups of coffee may be more rare than in the past, but they aren't out of place. Beginning with the founding of the **Sorbonne** in 1253, the quarter was called Latin because students and professors spoke the language. You'll follow in the footsteps of Descartes, Verlaine, Camus, Sartre, James Thurber, Elliot Paul, and Hemingway as you explore. Changing times have brought Greek, Moroccan, and Vietnamese immigrants, among others, offering everything from couscous to fiery-hot spring rolls and souvlaki. The 5th borders the Seine, and you'll want to stroll along quai de Montebello, inspecting the inventories of the *bouquinistes* (secondhand-book dealers), who sell everything from antique Daumier prints to yellowing copies of Balzac's *Père Goriot,* in the shadow of Notre-Dame. The 5th also has the **Panthéon,** built by Louis XV after he recovered from gout and wanted to do something nice for St. Geneviève, Paris's patron saint. It's the resting place of Rousseau, Gambetta, Zola, Braille, Hugo, Voltaire, and Jean Moulin, the World War II Resistance leader whom the Gestapo tortured to death.

6TH ARRONDISSEMENT (ST-GERMAIN/LUXEMBOURG) This is the heartland of Paris publishing and, for some, the most colorful Left Bank quarter, where waves of young artists still emerge from the Ecole des Beaux-Arts. The secret of the district lies in discovering its narrow streets, hidden squares, and magnificent gardens. To be really authentic, stroll with an unwrapped loaf of sourdough bread from the wood-fired ovens of **Poilâne** at 8 rue du Cherche-Midi. Everywhere you turn, you'll encounter historic and literary associations, nowhere more so than on **rue Jacob.** At no. 7, Racine lived with his uncle as a teenager; Richard Wagner resided at no. 14 from 1841 to 1842; Ingres lived at no. 27 (now it's the office of the French publishing house Editions du Seuil); and Hemingway once occupied a tiny upstairs room at no. 44. The 6th takes in the **Jardin du Luxembourg,** a 24-hectare (59-acre) playground where Isadora Duncan went dancing in the predawn hours and a destitute Ernest Hemingway went looking for pigeons for lunch, carrying them in a baby carriage back to his humble flat for cooking.

7TH ARRONDISSEMENT (EIF-FEL TOWER/MUSEE D'OR-SAY) Paris's most famous symbol, **la Tour Eiffel,** dominates Paris and especially the 7th, a Left Bank district of residences and offices. The tower is one of the most recognizable landmarks in the world, despite the fact that many Parisians (especially its nearest neighbors) hated it when it was unveiled in 1889. Many of Paris's most imposing monuments are in the 7th, like the **Hôtel des Invalides,** which contains Napoleon's Tomb and the Musée de l'Armée, and the **Musée d'Orsay,** the world's premier showcase of 19th-century French art and culture, housed in the old Gare d'Orsay. But there's much hidden charm here as well. **Rue du Bac** was home to the swashbuckling heroes of Dumas's *The Three Musketeers* and to James McNeill Whistler, who moved to no. 110 after selling *Mother.* Auguste Rodin lived at what's now the **Musée Rodin,** 77 rue de Varenne, until his death in 1917.

8TH ARRONDISSEMENT (CHAMPS-ELYSEES/ MADELEINE) The showcase of the 8th is the **Champs-Elysées,** stretching from the **Arc de Triomphe** to the Egyptian obelisk on **place de la Concorde.** By the 1980s, the Champs-Elysées had become a garish strip, with too much traffic, fast-food joints, and panhandlers. In the 1990s, Jacques Chirac, then the Gaullist mayor, launched a cleanup, broadening the sidewalks and planting new trees. Now you'll find fashion houses, elegant hotels, restaurants, and shops. Everything in the 8th is the city's best, grandest, and most impressive: It has the best restaurant **(Taillevent),** the sexiest strip joint **(Crazy Horse Saloon),** the most splendid square **(place de la Concorde),** the best rooftop cafe **(La Samaritaine),**

the grandest hotel (the **Crillon**), the most impressive arch **(Arc de Triomphe),** the most expensive residential street **(avenue Montaigne),** the world's oldest subway station **(Franklin-D.-Roosevelt),** and the most ancient monument (the 3,300-year-old **Obelisk of Luxor**).

9TH ARRONDISSEMENT (OPERA GARNIER/PIGALLE) From the Quartier de l'Opéra to the strip joints of Pigalle (the infamous "Pig Alley" of World War II GIs), the 9th endures, even if fashion prefers other addresses. Over the decades, the 9th has been celebrated in literature and song for the music halls that brought gaiety to the city. The building at 17 bd. de la Madeleine was where Marie Duplessis, who gained fame as the heroine Marguerite Gautier in Alexandre Dumas the younger's *La Dame aux camellias,* died. (Greta Garbo played her in the film *Camille.*) **Place Pigalle** has nightclubs but is no longer home to cafe La Nouvelle Athènes, where Degas, Pissarro, and Manet used to meet. Other attractions include the **Folies-Bergère,** where cancan dancers have been high-kicking since 1868. It is the rococo **Opéra Garnier** (home of the Phantom) that made the 9th the last hurrah of Second Empire opulence. Renoir hated it, but generations later, Chagall did the ceilings. Pavlova danced *Swan Lake* here, and Nijinsky took the night off to go cruising.

10TH ARRONDISSEMENT (GARE DU NORD/GARE DE L'EST) The **Gare du Nord** and **Gare de l'Est,** along with porno houses and dreary commercial zones, make the 10th one of the least desirable arrondissements for living, dining, or sightseeing. We try to avoid it, except for two longtime favorite restaurants: **Brasserie**

Flo (☎ **01-47-70-13-59**), 7 cour des Petites-Ecuries, best known for its formidable *choucroute,* a heap of sauerkraut garnished with everything; and **Julien** (☎ **01-47-70-12-06**), 16 rue du Faubourg St-Denis, called the poor man's Maxim's for its Belle Epoque interiors and moderate prices.

11TH ARRONDISSEMENT (OPERA BASTILLE) For many years, this quarter seemed to sink lower and lower into decay, overcrowded by working-class immigrants from the far reaches of the former Empire. The opening of the **Opéra Bastille,** however, has given the 11th new hope and new life. The facility, called the "people's opera house," stands on the landmark place de la Bastille, where on July 14, 1789, 633 Parisians stormed the fortress and seized the ammunition depot, as the French Revolution swept across the city. Over the years, the prison held Voltaire, the Marquis de Sade, and the mysterious "Man in the Iron Mask." The area between the Marais, Ménilmontant, and République is now being called "blue-collar chic," as the *artistes* of Paris have been driven from the costlier sections of the Marais and can now be found walking the gritty sidewalks of rue Oberkampf. Hip Parisians in search of a more cutting-edge experience are now found living and working among the decaying 19th-century apartments and the 1960s public housing with graffiti-splattered walls.

12TH ARRONDISSEMENT (BOIS DE VINCENNES/GARE DE LYON) Very few out-of-towners came here until a French chef opened a restaurant called **Au Trou Gascon** (p. 133). The 12th's major attraction remains the **Bois de Vincennes,** sprawling on the eastern periphery of Paris. This park is a longtime favorite of French families,

who enjoy its zoos and museums, its royal châteaux and boating lakes, and its **Parc Floral de Paris,** a celebrated flower garden boasting springtime rhododendrons and autumn dahlias. Venture into the dreary **Gare de Lyon** for **Le Train Bleu** (☎ **01-43-43-09-06**), in the Gare de Lyon, 12e, a restaurant whose ceiling frescoes and Art Nouveau decor are national artistic treasures; the food's good, too. The 12th, once a depressing urban wasteland, has been singled out for budgetary resuscitation and is beginning to sport new housing, shops, gardens, and restaurants. Many will occupy the site of the former Reuilly rail tracks.

13TH ARRONDISSEMENT (GARE D'AUSTERLITZ) Centered around the grimy **Gare d'Austerlitz,** the 13th might have its devotees, but we've yet to meet one. British snobs who flitted in and out of the train station were among the first of the district's foreign visitors and wrote the 13th off as a dreary working-class counterpart of London's East End. The 13th is also home to Paris's **Chinatown,** stretching for 13 square blocks around the Tolbiac Métro stop. It emerged out of the refugee crisis at the end of the Vietnam War, taking over a neighborhood that had held mostly Arab-speaking peoples. Today, recognizing overcrowding in the district, the Paris civic authorities are imposing new, not particularly welcome, restrictions on population densities.

14TH ARRONDISSEMENT (MONTPARNASSE) The northern end of this large arrondissement is devoted to **Montparnasse,** home of the "lost generation" and stamping ground of Stein, Toklas, Hemingway, and other American expats of the 1920s. After World War II, it ceased to be the center of intellectual life, but the memory lingers in its cafes. One of the monuments that sets the tone of the neighborhood is **Rodin's statue of Balzac** at the junction of boulevards Montparnasse and Raspail. At this corner are some of the world's most famous **literary cafes**, including La Rotonde, Le Select, La Dôme, and La Coupole. Though Gertrude Stein avoided them (she loathed cafes), other American expatriates, including Hemingway and Fitzgerald, had no qualms about enjoying a drink here (or quite a few of them, for that matter). Stein stayed at home (27 rue de Fleurus) with Alice B. Toklas, collecting paintings, including those of Picasso, and entertaining the likes of Max Jacob, Apollinaire, T. S. Eliot, and Matisse.

15TH ARRONDISSEMENT (GARE MONTPARNASSE/ INSTITUT PASTEUR) This is a mostly residential district beginning at **Gare Montparnasse** and stretching to the Seine. In size and population, it's the largest quarter of Paris but draws few tourists and has few attractions, except for the **Parc des Expositions,** the **Cimetière du Montparnasse,** and the **Institut Pasteur.** In the early 20th century, many artists—like Chagall, Léger, and Modigliani—lived here in a shared atelier known as "The Beehive."

16TH ARRONDISSEMENT (TROCADERO/BOIS DE BOULOGNE) Originally the village of Passy, where Benjamin Franklin lived during most of his time in Paris, this district is still reminiscent of Proust's world. Highlights include the **Bois de Boulogne;** the **Jardin du Trocadéro;** the **Maison de Balzac;** the **Musée Guimet** (famous for its Asian collections); and the **Cimetière de Passy,** resting place of Manet, Talleyrand, Giraudoux, and Debussy. One of the largest arrondissements, it's known today for its well-heeled

bourgeoisie, its upscale rents, and some rather posh (and, according to its critics, rather smug) residential boulevards. The arrondissement also has the best vantage point to view the Eiffel Tower: **place du Trocadéro.**

17TH ARRONDISSEMENT (PARC MONCEAU/PLACE CLICHY) Flanking the northern periphery of Paris, the 17th incorporates neighborhoods of bourgeois respectability (in its west end) and less affluent neighborhoods in its east end. It boasts two of the great restaurants of Paris, **Guy Savoy** and **Michel Rostang** (see chapter 6, "Where to Dine").

18TH ARRONDISSEMENT (MONTMARTRE) The 18th is the most famous outer quarter of Paris, containing **Montmartre,** the **Moulin Rouge, Sacré-Coeur,** and ultratouristy **place du Tertre.** Utrillo was its native son, Renoir lived here, and Toulouse-Lautrec adopted the area as his own. The most famous enclave of artists in Paris's history, the **Bateau-Lavoir** of Picasso fame, gathered here. Max Jacob, Matisse, and Braque were all frequent visitors. Today, place Blanche is known for its prostitutes, and Montmartre is filled with honky-tonks, souvenir shops, and terrible restaurants. You can still find pockets of quiet beauty, though. The city's most famous flea market, the **Marché aux Puces de Clignancourt,** is another landmark.

19TH ARRONDISSEMENT (LA VILLETTE) Today, visitors come to what was once the village of La Villette to see the angular **Cité des Sciences et de l'Industrie,** a spectacular science museum and park built on a site that for years was devoted to the city's slaughterhouses. Mostly residential, and not at all upscale, the district is one of the most ethnically diverse in Paris, the home of people from all parts of the former Empire. A highlight is **Les Buttes Chaumont,** a park where kids can enjoy puppet shows and donkey rides.

20TH ARRONDISSEMENT (PERE-LACHAISE CEMETERY)

The 20th's greatest landmark is **Père-Lachaise Cemetery,** the resting place of Edith Piaf, Marcel Proust, Oscar Wilde, Isadora Duncan, Sarah Bernhardt, Gertrude Stein and Alice B. Toklas, Colette, Jim Morrison, and many others. Otherwise, the 20th arrondissement is a dreary and sometimes volatile melting pot comprising residents from France's former colonies. Though nostalgia buffs sometimes head here to visit Piaf's former neighborhood, **Ménilmontant-Belleville,** it has been almost totally bulldozed and rebuilt since the bad old days when she grew up here.

2 Getting Around

Paris is a city for strollers who enjoy rambling through unexpected alleyways and squares. Only when you're dead tired and can't walk another step, or have to go all the way across town in a hurry, should you consider using the Métro, a swift but dull means of urban transport.

BY METRO & RER

A century old, the **Paris Métro** (℡ **08-92-68-77-14**) will soon become one of the most modern and efficient in the world. Recently some 200 of the system's nearly 300 stations were refurbished. The Métro is the easiest and most efficient way to get around Paris. Most stations display a map of the system at the entrance. Within Paris, you can transfer between the subway and the RER regional trains for no additional cost. To make sure you catch the right train, find your destination, and then visually follow the line it's on to the end of the route and note its name. This is the sign you look for in the stations and the name you'll see on the train. Transfer stations are known as *correspondances* (note that some require long walks—Châtelet–Les Halles is the most notorious).

Few trips will require more than one transfer. Some stations have maps with push-button indicators that'll help you plot your route by lighting up when you press the button for your destination. A ride on the urban lines costs 2€ ($2.30) to any point within the 20 arrondissements of Paris, as well as to many of its nearby suburbs. A bulk purchase of 10 tickets (bound together into what the French refer to as a *carnet*) costs 10€ ($12). Métro fares to outlying suburbs on the Sceaux, the Noissy-St-Léger, and St-Germain-en-Laye lines cost more and are sold on an individual basis depending on the distance you travel. At the entrance to the Métro station, insert your ticket into the turnstile and pass through. Take the ticket back, because it may be checked by uniformed police officers when you leave the subway. There are also occasional ticket checks on the trains, platforms, and passageways. If you're changing trains, get out and determine which direction (final destination) on the next line you want, then follow the bright orange CORRESPONDANCE signs until you reach the proper platform. Don't follow a SORTIE sign, which means "exit." If you exit, you'll have to pay another fare to resume your journey.

The Paris Métro runs daily from 5:30am to 1:15am, at which time all underground trains reach their final terminus at the end of each of their respective lines. Be alert that the last train may pass through central Paris as much as an hour before that time. The subways are reasonably safe at any hour, but beware of pickpockets.

Value **Discount Transit Passes**

The **Paris-Visite** (✆ **01-38-78-20-20**) is valid for 1, 2, 3, or 5 days on pub-lic transport, including the Métro, buses, and RER trains. The funicular ride to Montmartre is included. Its cost ranges from 17€ ($20) for 1 day to 37€ ($43) for 5 days. Get it at RATP (Régie Autonome des Transports Parisiens) offices, the tourist office, and Métro stations.

Another discount pass is **Carte Mobilis,** which allows unlimited travel on all bus, subway, and RER lines during a 1-day period for 6€ to 12€ ($6.90–$14), depending on the zone. Ask for it at any Métro station.

Most economical, for anyone who arrives in Paris early in the week, is a **Carte Orange.** Sold at large Métro stations, it allows 1 week of unlimited Métro or bus transit within central Paris for 14€ ($16). They're valid from any Monday to the following Sunday, and are sold only on Mondays, Tuesdays, and Wednesdays. You'll have to submit a passport-sized photo.

BY BUS

Bus travel is much slower than the subway. Most buses run from 7am to 8:30pm (a few run until 12:30am, and 10 operate during the early morning hours). Ser-vice is limited on Sundays and holidays. Bus and Métro fares are the same and you can use the same carnet tickets on both. At certain stops, signs list the des-tinations and numbers of the buses serving that point. Destinations are usually listed north to south and east to west. Most stops along the way are also posted on the sides of the buses. To catch a bus, wait in line at the bus stop. Signal the driver to stop the bus and board.

Most bus rides (including any that begin and end within Paris's 20 arrondisse-ments and nearby suburbs) require one ticket. For bus travel to some of the more distant suburbs, an additional ticket might be required. If you intend to use the buses a lot, pick up an **RATP bus map** at its offices at place de la Madeleine, 8e (Métro: Madeleine), or 54 quai de la Rapée, 12e (Métro: Gare de Lyon), or at any tourist office. For details on bus and Métro routes, call ✆ **08-92-68-77-14.**

The same entity that maintains Paris's network of Métros and buses, the **RATP,** has initiated a motorized mode of transport designed as a means of appreciating the city's visual grandeur. Known as the **Balabus,** it's a fleet of big-windowed orange-and-white motor coaches whose major drawback is their lim-ited hours—they run only on Sunday and national holidays from noon to 9pm, April to September. The coaches travel in both directions between the Gare de Lyon and the Grande Arche de La Défense, encompassing some of the city's most monumental vistas and making regular stops. Presentation of two Métro tickets, each priced at 2.60€ ($3), or a valid Carte Mobilis or Paris-Visite pass (see the box above) will take you along the entire route. You'll recognize the bus and the route it follows by the "Bb" symbol on each bus's side and on signs posted beside the route it follows.

BY CAR

Don't even think about driving in Paris. The streets are narrow, with confusing one-way designations, and parking is next to impossible. Besides, most visitors don't have the ruthlessness required to survive in Parisian traffic. Think about renting a car only if you plan to explore the Ile de France and beyond.

You can rent cars from locally based agencies like **Autorent,** 98 rue de la Convention, 15e (✆ **01-45-54-22-45;** Métro: Boucicaut), or from **Rent-a-Car,** 62 bd. Malesherbes, 8e (✆ **01-45-22-28-28;** Métro: Gare St-Lazare). **Budget** (✆ **800/472-3325** in the U.S. and Canada; www.budget.com) maintains locations in Paris at Gare du Nord, Gare du Lyon, and Gare du Montparnasse. **Hertz** (✆ **800/654-3001** in the U.S. and Canada; www.hertz.com) has about 15 locations in Paris, including offices at the airports and the main office at 27 place St-Ferdinand, 17e (✆ **01-45-74-97-39;** Métro: Argentine). Ask about promotional discounts. **Avis** (✆ **800/331-2112** in the U.S. and Canada; www.avis.com) has offices at both airports, and a headquarters at 5 rue Bixio, 7e (✆ **01-44-18-10-50;** Métro: Ecole Militaire), near the Eiffel Tower. **National** (✆ **800/227-7368** in the U.S. and Canada; www.nationalcar.com) is represented in Paris by **National Citer,** whose largest office is at 165 bis rue de Vaugirard, 15e (✆ **01-42-79-06-11;** Métro: Pasteur). It has offices at both airports as well.

BY TAXI

Taxi drivers are organized into an effective lobby to keep their number limited to around 15,000, and it's nearly impossible to get one at rush hour. You can hail regular cabs on the street when their signs read LIBRE. Taxis are easier to find at the many stands near Métro stations.

The flag drops at 4.25€ ($4.90), and from 7am to 7pm you pay 1€ ($1.15) per kilometer. From 7pm to 7am, you pay 1.20€ ($1.40) per kilometer. On airport trips, you're not required to pay for the driver's empty return ride.

You're allowed several pieces of luggage free if they're transported inside and are less than 5 kilograms (11 lb.). Heavier suitcases carried in the trunk cost 1€ to 1.50€ ($1.15–$1.75) apiece. Tip 12% to 15%—the latter usually elicits a *merci*. For radio cabs, call **Les Taxis Bleus** (✆ **08-25-16-10-10**) or **Taxi G7** (✆ **01-47-39-47-39**)—note that you'll be charged from the point where the taxi begins the drive to pick you up.

BY BICYCLE

To bike through the streets and parks of Paris, perhaps with a baguette tucked under your arm, might've been a fantasy of yours since you saw your first Maurice Chevalier film. In recent years, the city has added many miles of right-hand lanes designated for cyclists as well as hundreds of bike racks. (When these aren't available, many Parisians simply chain their bikes to fences or lampposts.) Cycling is especially popular in the larger parks and gardens.

Paris-Vélos, 2 rue du Fer-à-Moulin, 5e (✆ **01-43-37-59-22;** Métro: Censier-Daubenton), rents bicycles by the day, weekend, or week, charging 14€ to 18€ ($16–$21) per weekday, 30€ to 33€ ($35–$38) Saturday and Sunday, and 64€ ($74) per week. You must leave a 300€ ($345) deposit. It's open Monday to Saturday from 10am to 12:30pm and 2 to 7pm, and Sunday 10am to 6pm.

BY BOAT

From April to mid-October, the **Batobus** (✆ **01-44-11-33-99**), a series of 150-passenger ferries with big windows for viewing the riverfronts, operates at 15- to 25-minute intervals daily from 10am to 7pm (until 9pm during June, July, and Aug). Boats chug along between the quays at the base of the Eiffel Tower and the quays at the base of the Louvre, stopping at the Musée d'Orsay, St-Germain-des-Prés, Notre-Dame, the Hôtel de Ville, and what the management refers to as the Champs-Elysées, but which is actually a stop at the base of the Pont Alexandre-III. Transit between any two stops costs 2.50€ ($2.90).

FAST FACTS: Paris

American Express With a Paris office at 11 rue Scribe, 9e (✆ **01-47-14-50-00**; Métro: Opéra, Chaussée-d'Antin, or Havre-Caumartin; RER: Auber), Amex is quite busy. It's open Monday through Friday from 9am to 6pm; the bank is also open Saturday from 8am to 5:30pm, but the mail pick-up window is closed.

Babysitters The best selection of English-speaking sitters is found at **Kid Services** (✆ **08-20-00-02-30**).

Banks Banks in Paris are open Monday to Friday from 9am to 4:30pm. A few are open on Saturday. Ask at your hotel for the location of the bank nearest you. Shops and most hotels will cash your traveler's checks, but not at the advantageous rate a bank or foreign-exchange office will give you, so if you don't have access to your funds through an ATM, make sure you've allowed enough funds for *le weekend.*

Business Hours Opening hours in France are erratic, as befits a nation of individualists. Most museums close 1 day a week (often Tues) and national holidays; hours tend to be from 9:30am to 5pm. Some museums, particularly the smaller ones, close for lunch from noon to 2pm. Most museums are open Saturday, but many close Sunday morning and reopen in the afternoon (see chapter 7 for specific times). Generally, **offices** are open Monday to Friday from 9am to 5pm, but don't count on it—always call first. **Large stores** are open from 9 or 9:30am (often 10am) to 6 or 7pm without a break for lunch. Some **shops,** particularly those operated by non-native French owners, open at 8am and close at 8 or 9pm. In some **small stores,** the lunch break can last 3 hours, beginning at 1pm.

Currency Exchange For the best exchange rate, cash your traveler's checks at banks or foreign-exchange offices, not at shops and hotels. Most post offices will change traveler's checks or convert currency. Currency exchanges are also found at Paris airports and train stations and along most of the major boulevards. A small commission is charged.

Some exchange places charge favorable rates to lure you into their stores. For example, **Paris Vision,** 214 rue de Rivoli, 1e (✆ **01-42-60-31-25**; Métro: Tuileries), maintains a minibank in the back of a travel agency, open daily from 6:30am to 8:30pm. Its rates are only a fraction less favorable than those offered for very large blocks of money as listed by the Paris stock exchange.

Dentists For emergency dental service, call **S.O.S. Dentaire,** 87 bd. du Port-Royal, 13e (✆ **01-43-37-51-00**; Métro: Port-Royal), Monday through Friday from 8pm to midnight and Saturday and Sunday from 9:30am to midnight. You can also call or visit the **American Hospital,** 63 bd. Victor-Hugo, in the suburb of Neuilly-sur-Seine outside Paris (✆ **01-46-41-25-25**; Métro: Pont-de-Levallois or Pont-de-Neuilly; Bus: 82).

Drugstores After regular hours, ask at your hotel where the nearest 24-hour *pharmacie* is. You'll also find the address posted on the doors or windows of other drugstores in the neighborhood. One all-night drugstore is the **Pharmacie Derhy,** in La Galerie Les Champs, 84 av. des Champs-Elysées, 8e (© **01-45-62-02-41;** Métro: George-V).

Electricity In general, expect 200 volts AC (60 cycles), though you'll encounter 110 and 115 volts in some older establishments. Adapters are needed to fit sockets. Many hotels have two-pin (in some cases, three-pin) sockets for electric razors. It's best to ask at your hotel before plugging in any electrical appliance.

Embassies & Consulates If you have a passport, immigration, legal, or other problem, contact your consulate. Call before you go, as they often keep odd hours and observe both French and home-country holidays. The Embassy of the **United States,** at 2 av. Gabriel, 8e (© **01-43-12-47-08;** Métro: Concorde), is open Monday through Friday from 9am to 6pm. Passports are issued at its consulate at 2 rue St-Florentin (© **01-43-12-22-22;** Métro: Concorde). The Embassy of **Canada** is at 35 av. Montaigne, 8e (© **01-44-43-29-00;** Métro: Franklin-D.-Roosevelt or Alma-Marceau), open Monday through Friday from 9am to noon and 2 to 5pm. The Embassy of the **United Kingdom** is at 35 rue Faubourg St-Honore, 8e (© **01-44-51-31-00;** Métro: Concorde or Madeleine), open Monday through Friday from 9:30am to 1pm and 2:30 to 5pm. The consulate is at 18 bis rue d'Anjou, 8e (© **01-44-51-31-02;** Métro: Concorde or Madeleine), open Monday through Friday from 9am to noon and 2 to 5pm. The Embassy of **Ireland** is at 4 rue Rude, 16e (© **01-44-17-67-00;** Métro: Etoile), open Monday through Friday from 9:30am to noon and 2:30 to 5:30pm. The Embassy of **Australia** is at 4 rue Jean-Rey, 15e (© **01-40-59-33-00;** Métro: Bir-Hakeim), open Monday through Friday from 9:15am to noon and 2:30 to 4:30pm. The embassy of **New Zealand** is at 7 ter rue Léonard-de-Vinci, 16e (© **01-45-00-24-11;** Métro: Victor Hugo), open Monday through Friday from 9am to 1pm and 2:30 to 6pm.

Emergencies For the police, call © **17;** to report a fire, call © **18.** For an ambulance, call the fire department at © **01-45-78-74-52;** a fire vehicle rushes patients to the nearest emergency room. For **S.A.M.U.,** an independently operated, privately owned ambulance company, call © **15.**

Hospitals Open Monday to Saturday from 8am to 7pm, **Central Médical Europe,** 44 rue d'Amsterdam, 9e (© **01-42-81-93-33;** Métro: Liège or St-Lazare), maintains contacts with medical and dental practitioners in all fields. Appointments are recommended. Another choice is the **American Hospital of Paris,** 63 bd. Victor-Hugo, Neuilly (© **01-46-41-25-25;** Métro: Pont de Levallois or Pont de Neuilly; Bus: 82), which operates 24-hour medical and dental services. An additional clinic is the **Centre Figuier,** 2 rue du Figuier, 4e (© **01-49-96-62-70;** Métro: St-Paul). Call before visiting.

Internet Access To surf the Net or check your e-mail, try **Le Rendez-vous Toyota,** 79 av. des Champs-Elysées, 8e (© **01-56-89-29-79;** www.lerendez-voustoyota.com; Métro: George-V), open Tuesday to Thursday from 10:30am to 8pm, Friday and Saturday from 10:30am to midnight, and Sunday from noon to 8pm.

Liquor Laws Supermarkets, grocery stores, and cafes sell alcoholic beverages. The legal drinking age is 16, but persons under that age can be served alcohol in a bar or restaurant if accompanied by a parent or legal guardian. Wine and liquor are sold every day of the week, year-round. Hours of cafes vary. Some open at 6am, serving drinks to 3am; others are open 24 hours. Bars and nightclubs may stay open as late as they wish.

The Breathalyzer test is used in France, and a motorist is considered "legally intoxicated" with .5 grams of alcohol per liter of blood (the more liberal U.S. law is 1g per liter). If convicted, a motorist faces a stiff fine and a possible prison term of 2 months to 2 years. If bodily injury results, sentences can range from 2 years to life.

Mail/Post Offices Most post offices in Paris are open Monday to Friday from 8am to 7pm and Saturday from 8am to noon. The **main post office** (PTT) for Paris is at 52 rue du Louvre, 75001 Paris (② **01-40-28-76-00;** Métro: Louvre). It's open 24 hours a day for the sale of stamps, phone calls, and sending faxes and telegrams, with limited hours (Mon–Fri 8am–7pm and Sat 8am–noon) for services like the sale of money orders. Stamps can usually be purchased at your hotel reception desk and at cafes with red TABAC signs. You can send faxes at the main post office in each arrondissement.

Airmail letters cost .90€ ($1.05). You can have mail sent to you *poste restante* (general delivery) at the main post office for a small fee. Take an ID, such as a passport, to pick up mail. American Express (see above) offers a *poste restante* service, but you may be asked to show an American Express card or traveler's checks.

Newspapers & Magazines English-language newspapers are available at nearly every kiosk. Published Monday to Saturday, the *International Herald-Tribune* is the most popular paper with visiting Americans and Canadians; the *Guardian* provides a British point of view. For those who read in French, the leading domestic newspapers are *Le Monde, Le Figaro,* and *Libération;* the top magazines are *L'Express, Le Point,* and *Le Nouvel Observateur.* Kiosks are generally open daily from 8am to 9pm.

Police Call ② **17** for emergencies. The principal *Préfecture* (police station) is at 9 bd. du Palais, 4e (② **01-53-71-53-73;** Métro: Cité).

Restrooms If you're in dire need, duck into a cafe or brasserie to use the toilet. It's customary to make some small purchase if you do so. In the street, the domed self-cleaning lavatories are a decent option if you have small change; Métro stations and underground garages usually have public lavatories, but the degree of cleanliness varies.

Safety In Paris, be especially aware of child pickpockets. They roam the capital, preying on tourists around attractions like the Louvre, Eiffel Tower, and Notre-Dame, and they also often strike in the Métro, sometimes blocking a victim from the escalator. A band of these young thieves can clean your pockets even while you try to fend them off. Their method is to get very close to a target, ask for a handout (sometimes), and deftly help themselves to your money or passport.

Although public safety is not as much a problem in Paris as it is in large American cities, concerns are growing. Robbery at gun- or knifepoint is uncommon, but not unknown. Be careful.

Telephone Public phones are found in cafes, restaurants, Métro stations, post offices, airports, and train stations, and occasionally on the streets. Finding a coin-operated telephone in France is an arduous task. A simpler and more widely accepted method of payment is the *télécarte,* a prepaid calling card available at kiosks, post offices, and Métro stations and costing 7.45€ to 15€ ($8.55–$17) for 50 and 120 units, respectively. A local call costs one unit, which provides you with 6 to 18 minutes of conversation, depending on the rate. Avoid making calls from your hotel, which might double or triple the charges.

To call **long distance within France,** dial the 10-digit number (9-digit in some cases outside Paris) of the person or place you're calling. To make a **direct international call,** first dial 00, listen for the tone, then slowly dial the country code, the area code, and the local number. The country code for the **U.S.** and **Canada** is 1; **Great Britain,** 44; **Ireland,** 353; **Australia,** 61; **New Zealand,** 64; and **South Africa,** 27.

An easy and relatively inexpensive way to call home is **USA Direct/AT&T World Connect.** From within France, dial any of the following numbers: (℡ **0800/99-00-11,** -10-11, -11-11, or -12-11). Then follow the prompt, which will ask you to punch in the number of either your AT&T credit card or a MasterCard or Visa. Along with the U.S., the countries participating in the system—referred to as World Connect—include **Canada,** the **United Kingdom, Ireland, Australia,** and **New Zealand.** By punching in the number of the party you want in any of these countries, you'll avoid the surcharges imposed by the hotel operator. An AT&T operator is available to help should complications arise during the process.

Time France is usually 6 hours ahead of Eastern Standard Time and 9 hours ahead of Pacific Standard Time in the United States. French daylight savings time lasts from around April to September, when clocks are set 1 hour ahead of the standard time.

Tipping By law, all bills show *service compris,* which means the tip is included; additional gratuities are customarily given as follows: For **hotel staff,** tip the porter 1.05€ to 1.50€ ($1.20–$1.75) per item of baggage, and 1.50€ ($1.75) per day for the chambermaid. You're not obligated to tip the concierge, doorman, or anyone else unless you use his or her services. In **cafes** and **restaurants,** waiter service is usually included, though you can leave some small change, if you like. Tip **taxi drivers** 12% to 15% of the amount on the meter. In **theaters** and **restaurants,** give cloakroom attendants at least .75€ (85¢) per item. Give **restroom attendants** in nightclubs and such places about .30€ (35¢). Tip the **hairdresser** about 15%, and don't forget to tip the person who gives you a shampoo or a manicure 1.50€ ($1.75). For **guides** for group visits to museums and monuments, .75€ to 1.50€ (85¢–$1.75) is a reasonable tip.

Water Drinking water is generally safe, though some who are unused to it have gotten diarrhea. If you ask for water in a restaurant, it'll be bottled water (for which you'll pay), unless you specifically request tap water (*l'eau du robinet*).

5

Where to Stay

Paris boasts some 2,000 hotels—with about 80,000 rooms—spread across its 20 arrondissements. They range from the Ritz and the Crillon to dives so repellent even George Orwell, author of *Down and Out in Paris and London,* wouldn't have considered checking in. (Of course, you won't find those in this guide!) We've included deluxe places for those who can afford to live like the Sultan of Brunei, as well as a wide range of moderate and inexpensive choices for the rest of us.

Most visitors, at least those from North America, come to Paris in July and August. Many French are on vacation, and trade fairs and conventions come to a halt, so there are usually plenty of rooms, even though these months have traditionally been the peak season for European travel. In most hotels, February is as busy as April or September because of the volume of business travelers and the numbers of tourists taking advantage of off-season discounts.

Because hot weather rarely lasts long in Paris, few hotels, except the deluxe ones, provide air-conditioning. If you're trapped in a garret on a hot summer night, you'll have to sweat it out. You can open your window to get cooler air, but open windows admit noise pollution. To avoid this, request a room in back when reserving.

READING THE GOVERNMENT RATINGS

The French government grades hotels with a star system, ranging from one star for a simple inn to four stars for a deluxe hotel. Moderately priced hotels usually get two or three stars. This system is based on a complex formula of room sizes, facilities, plumbing, elevators, dining options, renovations, and so on. In one-star hotels, the bathrooms are often shared, the facilities are extremely limited (such as no elevator), the rooms may not have phones or TVs, and breakfast is often the only meal served. In two- or three-star hotels, there are usually elevators, and rooms will likely have baths, phones, and TVs. In four-star hotels, you'll get all the amenities plus facilities and services like room service, 24-hour concierges, elevators, and perhaps even health clubs.

However, the system is a bit misleading. For tax reasons, a four-star hotel might elect to have a three-star rating, which, with the hotel's permission, is granted by the government. The government won't add a star where it's not merited, but will remove one at the hotel's request.

WHICH BANK IS FOR YOU?

The river dividing Paris geographically and culturally demands you make a choice. Are you more **Left Bank,** wanting a room in the heart of St-Germain, where Jean-Paul Sartre and Simone de Beauvoir once spent the night? Or are you more **Right Bank,** preferring sumptuous quarters like those at the Crillon, where Tom Cruise once slept? Would you rather look for that special old curio in a dusty shop on the Left Bank's rue Jacob, or inspect the latest Lagerfeld or

Dior couture on the Right Bank's avenue Montaigne? Each of Paris's neighborhoods has its own flavor, and your experiences and memories of Paris will likely be formed by where you choose to stay.

If you desire chic surroundings, choose a Right Bank hotel. That puts you near the most elegant shops and within walking distance of major sights like the Arc de Triomphe, place de la Concorde, the Jardin des Tuileries, the Opéra Garnier, and the Louvre. The best Right Bank hotels are near the Arc de Triomphe in the 8th arrondissement, though many first-class lodgings cluster near the Trocadéro and Bois du Boulogne in the 16th, or near the Palais des Congrès in the 17th. If you'd like to be near place Vendôme, try for a hotel in the 1st. Also popular are the increasingly fashionable Marais and Bastille in the 3rd, 4th, and 11th arrondissements, and Les Halles/Beaubourg, home of the Centre Pompidou and Les Halles shopping mall, in the 1st.

If you want less formality and tiny bohemian streets, head for the Left Bank, where prices are traditionally lower. Hotels that cater to students are found in the 5th and 6th arrondissements, the 5th being known as the Latin Quarter. These areas, with their literary overtones, boast the Sorbonne, the Panthéon, the Jardin du Luxembourg, cafe life, bookstores, and publishing houses. The 6th arrondissement provides a touch of avant-garde St-Germain.

BEST HOTEL BETS
See chapter 1 for a list of our hotel favorites—the best newcomer, the best view, and more.

A Room in Paris

If you want to stay somewhere more intimate (and in some cases, more restrictive) than a hotel, consider booking a room within a private home. A California-based agency promoting upmarket B&B accommodations in Paris is **European B&B**, 437 J St., Suite 210, San Diego, CA 92101 (© **800/872-2632** in the U.S.; fax 619/531-1686; www.paris bandb.com). In Paris, contact their affiliate, **Alcôve & Agapes,** 8 bus rue Coysevox, 75018 Paris (© **01-44-85-06-05;** fax 01-44-85-06-14).

These organizations act as intermediaries between travelers who seek rooms in private homes and Parisians who wish to welcome visitors. Most hosts speak at least some English, range in age from 30 to 75, and have at least some points of view about entertainment and dining options within the neighborhood. Available options include individual bedrooms, usually within large, old-fashioned private apartments, as well as "unhosted" accommodations where the apartment is otherwise empty and without the benefit (or restrictions) of a live-in host.

Rates for occupancy by either one or two persons, with breakfast included, range from 95€ to 195€ ($109–$224) per unit, depending on the apartment, the neighborhood, the setup, and the plumbing. In cases where a client occupies an unhosted apartment, the refrigerators will be stocked with up to 3 days' breakfast supplies, and are replenished at regular intervals if your stay exceeds 3 days.

1 On the Right Bank

We'll begin with the most centrally located arrondissements on the Right Bank, then work our way through the more outlying neighborhoods and to the area around the Arc de Triomphe.

1ST ARRONDISSEMENT
VERY EXPENSIVE

Hôtel Costes ★★★   Fashion types gravitate toward this hotel for its grand style and location close to the headquarters of some of Paris's most upscale shops. It is one of the shining stars of Paris. The town house–style premises were a *maison bourgeoise* (upper-middle-class home) for generations. In 1996, it was adorned with jewel-toned colors, swagged curtains, and Napoleon III accessories. Now it evokes the rich days of the Gilded Age, especially the guest rooms. Some are small, but cozy and ornate, with one or two large beds, CD players, and fax machines. Bathrooms are large with shower-tub combinations. The suites are spacious with sitting areas and theme designs such as "Moroccan nights." For ultimate luxury, ask for one of the duplex units with split-level layouts.

239 rue St-Honoré, 75001 Paris. ✆ **01-42-44-50-50.** Fax 01-42-44-50-01. 82 units. 400€–700€ ($460–$805) double; from 1,400€ ($1,610) suite. AE, DC, MC, V. Métro: Tuileries or Concorde. **Amenities:** Restaurant; bar; pool; gym; car rental; 24-hr. room service; in-room massage; babysitting; laundry service/dry cleaning; rooms for those with limited mobility. *In room:* A/C, TV, fax, dataport, minibar, hair dryer, safe.

Hôtel de Vendôme ★★   This jewel box was the former embassy of Texas when that state was a nation. The hotel opened in 1998 and stands at one of the world's most prestigious addresses. It is comparable to the Costes, but with a less flashy clientele. Though the guest rooms are moderate in size, they're opulent and designed in classic Second Empire style with luxurious beds; well-upholstered, hand-carved furnishings; and first-rate bathrooms with tub-and-shower combinations. Suites have generous space and such extras as blackout draperies and quadruple glazing. The security is fantastic, with TV intercoms. This new version of the hotel replaces a lackluster one that stood here for a century, and its facade and roof are classified as historic monuments by the French government.

1 place Vendôme, 75001 Paris. ✆ **01-55-04-55-00.** Fax 01-49-27-97-89. www.hoteldevendome.com. 29 units. 440€–620€ ($506–$713) double; 840€–1,210€ ($966–$1,391) suite. AE, DC, MC, V. Métro: Concorde or Opéra. **Amenities:** Restaurant; piano bar; 24-hr. room service; massage; babysitting; laundry service/dry cleaning; nonsmoking rooms; rooms for those with limited mobility. *In room:* A/C, TV, dataport, minibar, hair dryer, safe.

Hôtel du Louvre ★   When Napoleon III inaugurated the hotel in 1855, it was described as "a palace of the people, rising adjacent to the palace of kings." In 1897, Camille Pissarro moved into a room with a view that inspired many of his landscapes. Its decor features marble, bronze, and gilt. The guest rooms are filled with souvenirs of the Belle Epoque along with elegant fabrics, carpeting, double-glazed windows, comfortable beds, and wood furniture. Suites provide greater dimensions and better exposures, as well as such upgrades as antiques, trouser presses, and robes. All rooms have well-maintained bathrooms with a choice of tub or shower.

Place André-Malraux, 75001 Paris. ✆ **800/888-4747** in the U.S. and Canada, or 01-44-58-38-38. Fax 01-44-58-38-01. www.hoteldulouvre.com. 177 units. 450€–500€ ($517–$575) double; 700€–1,800€ ($805–$2,070) suite. Ask about off-season discounts. AE, DC, MC, V. Parking 18€ ($21). Métro: Palais Royal or Louvre-Rivoli. **Amenities:** Restaurant; bar; pool; gym; business center; 24-hr. room service; in-room massage; babysitting; laundry service/dry cleaning; nonsmoking rooms; rooms for those with limited mobility. *In room:* A/C, TV, dataport, minibar, hair dryer, safe.

Where to Stay on the Right Bank (1–4, 9–12 & 18e)

Axial Beaubourg **33**
Concorde St-Lazare **5**
Golden Tulip Opéra de Noailles **6**
Hôtel Bonséjour **1**
Hôtel Britannique **36**
Hôtel Caron de Beaumarchais **31**
Hôtel Chopin **4**

Hôtel Costes **11**
Hôtel de la Place des Vosges **23**
Hôtel de la Tour d'Auvergne **3**
Hôtel de Lutéce **28**
Hôtel des Chevaliers **22**
Hôtel des Deux-Iles **29**
Hôtel de Vendôme **10**

Hôtel du Bourg Tibourg **32**
Hôtel du Jeu de Paume **30**
Hôtel du Louvre **14**
Hôtel du 7e Art **26**
Hôtel Ermitage **2**
Hôtel Langlois **5**
Hôtel Pavillion Bastille **25**

Hôtel Regina **13**
Hôtel Ritz **8**
Hôtel Royal Saint-Honoré **9**
Hôtel Saintonge **19**
Hôtel St-Louis **27**
Hôtel Saint-Merry **34**
Hôtel Victories Opéra **17**

Le Petit Châtelet **35**
Libertel Croix de Malte **21**
Nouvel Hôtel **24**
Park Hyatt Vendôme **7**
Relais de Louvre **16**
Résidence Alhambra **20**
Terrass Hôtel **2**
Timhôtel Le Louvre **15**

Tips **Cafe & a Croissant?**

Hotel breakfasts are fairly uniform and include your choice of coffee, tea, or hot chocolate; a freshly baked croissant and roll; and limited quantities of butter and jam or jelly. It can be at your door moments after you call for it and is served at almost any hour. (When we mention breakfast charges in our listings, we refer to continental breakfasts only.) Breakfasts with eggs, bacon, ham, or other items must be ordered from the a la carte menu. For a charge, larger hotels serve the full or "English" breakfast, but smaller hotels typically serve only the continental variety.

Hôtel Meurice ★★★   After a renovation, this landmark is better than ever, lying between the place de la Concorde and the Grand Louvre, facing the Tuileries Gardens. Since the 1800s, it has welcomed the royal and the rich and even the radical. The mad genius Salvador Dalí made the Meurice his headquarters. The mosaic floors, plaster ceilings, hand-carved moldings, and Art Nouveau glass roof atop the Winter Garden look like new. Each room is individually decorated with period pieces, fine carpets, Italian and French fabrics, marbles, and modern features like fax and Internet access. Our favorites and the least expensive are the sixth-floor rooms. Some have painted ceilings of puffy clouds and blue skies along with canopied beds. Suites are among the most lavish in France. Beds are sumptuous, furnished in luxurious fabrics; and the bathrooms are well managed, with shower-and-tub combinations.

228 rue de Rivoli, 75001 Paris. © 01-44-58-10-10. Fax 01-44-58-10-15. www.meuricehotel.com. 160 units. 650€–760€ ($748–$874) double; from 1,250€ ($1,438) suite. AE, DC, MC, V. Parking 20€ ($23). Métro: Tuileries or Concorde. **Amenities:** 2 restaurants; bar; gym; full-service spa; 24-hr. room service; massage; babysitting; laundry service/dry cleaning; winter garden; nonsmoking rooms; rooms for those with limited mobility. *In room:* A/C, TV, fax, dataport, minibar, hair dryer, safe.

Hôtel Regina ★   Restored to its old-fashioned grandeur, Hôtel Regina is adjacent to rue de Rivoli's equestrian statue of Joan of Arc opposite the Louvre. Since 1999, the management has poured millions into a full-fledged renovation, retaining the patina of the Art Nouveau interior and making historically appropriate improvements. The guest rooms are richly decorated and spacious; those overlooking the Tuileries enjoy panoramic views as far away as the Eiffel Tower. The bathrooms, each with tub and shower, are midsize to large, many with stained-glass windows. The public areas contain every period of Louis furniture imaginable, Oriental carpets, 18th-century paintings, and bowls of flowers. Fountains play in a flagstone-covered courtyard. There are more grace notes in this hotel than at its closest competitor, Hôtel du Louvre.

2 place des Pyramides, 75001 Paris. © 01-42-60-31-10. Fax 01-40-15-95-16. www.regina-hotel.com. 120 units. 390€–440€ ($449–$506) double; 535€–824€ ($615–$948) suite. AE, DC, MC, V. Parking 10€ ($12). Métro: Pyramides or Tuileries. **Amenities:** 2 restaurants; bar; 24-hr. room service; massage; babysitting; laundry service/dry cleaning; nonsmoking rooms. *In room:* A/C, TV, dataport, minibar, hair dryer, iron/board, safe.

Hôtel Ritz ★★★   The Ritz is Europe's greatest hotel, an enduring symbol of elegance on one of Paris's most beautiful and historic squares. César Ritz, the "little shepherd boy from Niederwald," converted the Hôtel de Lazun into a luxury hotel in 1898. With the help of the culinary master Escoffier, he made the Ritz a miracle of luxury. In 1979, the Ritz family sold the hotel to Mohammed al Fayed, who refurbished it and added a cooking school. Two town houses were annexed, joined by an arcade lined with display cases representing

125 of Paris's leading boutiques. The public salons are furnished with museum-caliber antiques. Each guest room is uniquely decorated, most with Louis XIV or XV reproductions; all have fine rugs, marble fireplaces, tapestries, brass beds, and more. The spacious bathrooms are the city's most luxurious, with deluxe toiletries, sumptuous tubs, scales, private phones, cords to summon maids and valets, robes, full-length and makeup mirrors, and dual basins. Ever since Edward VII got stuck in a too-narrow bathtub with his lover of the evening, the tubs at the Ritz have been deep and big.

15 place Vendôme, 75001 Paris. (C) **800/223-6800** in the U.S. and Canada, or 01-43-16-30-30. Fax 01-43-16-36-68. www.ritzparis.com. 175 units. 590€–750€ ($679–$863) double; from 1,180€ ($1,357) suite. AE, DC, MC, V. Parking 44€ ($51). Métro: Opéra, Concorde, or Madeleine. **Amenities:** 2 restaurants; 3 bars; indoor pool; health club; sauna; 24-hr. room service; in-room massage; babysitting; laundry service/dry cleaning; nonsmoking rooms; rooms for those with limited mobility. *In room:* A/C, TV, dataport, minibar, hair dryer, iron/board, safe.

EXPENSIVE

Hôtel Royal Saint-Honoré ★★   This recently renovated, government-rated four-star hotel enjoys one of the most fashionable locations in Paris, lying between place Vendôme and the Tuileries. Although its facade dates from 1830, it has been practically rebuilt inside and turned into an oasis of charm. The *fashionistas* and the glitterati check into the tony Hôtel Costes nearby, while the Royal Saint-Honoré attracts a more conservative (read, less rich) clientele. At the doorstep are famous shops like Chanel, Hermès, Lanvin, Guerlin, and Cartier. After its latest overhaul, the hotel is imbued with luxurious contemporary styling with impressive redwood English furnishings, Louis XVI–styled paneling in the breakfast room, and an on-site cafe that is also a chic bar. Bedrooms are midsize to spacious, with Louis XVI–style or Directoire wood pieces, botanical prints on the walls, and color-coordinated upholsteries and fabrics. The tubs are a bit narrow, but the appointments are first-rate.

221 rue St-Honoré, 75001 Paris. (C) **01-42-60-32-79**. Fax 01-42-60-47-44. www.hotel-royal-st-honore.com. 72 units. 220€–400€ ($253–$460) double; 350€–490€ ($403–$564) suite. Rates include breakfast. AE, DC, MC, V. Métro: Tuileries. **Amenities:** Restaurant; bar; limited room service; babysitting; laundry service/dry cleaning; nonsmoking rooms; rooms for those with limited mobility. *In room:* A/C, TV, dataport, minibar, hair dryer, safe.

MODERATE

Hôtel Britannique *Value*   Conservatively modern and plush, this is a much-renovated 19th-century hotel near Les Halles and Notre-Dame. The place is not only British in name, but seems to have cultivated an English graciousness. The guest rooms are small, but immaculate and soundproof, with comfortable beds and well-maintained bathrooms with shower-tub combinations. A satellite receiver gets U.S. and U.K. television shows. The reading room is a cozy retreat.

20 av. Victoria, 75001 Paris. (C) **01-42-33-74-59**. Fax 01-42-33-82-65. www.hotel-britannic.com. 39 units. 157€–180€ ($181–$207) double; 280€ ($322) suite. AE, DC, MC, V. Parking 20€ ($23). Métro: Châtelet. **Amenities:** Limited room service; laundry service/dry cleaning. *In room:* A/C, TV, dataport, minibar, hair dryer, safe.

Hôtel Burgundy ★ *Value*   The Burgundy is one of the best values in this expensive area. The frequently renovated mansion began as two adjacent town houses in the 1830s, one a pension where Baudelaire wrote poetry in the 1860s, the other a bordello. The houses were linked by British-born managers who insisted on using the English name. Renovated in 1992, with improvements in 2001, the hotel hosts many North and South Americans and features conservatively decorated rooms, each with a bathroom with full tub and shower.

8 rue Duphot, 75001 Paris. ℂ **01-42-60-34-12.** Fax 01-47-03-95-20. www.burgundyhotel.com. 89 units. 165€–195€ ($190–$224) double; 300€ ($345) suite. AE, DC, MC, V. Métro: Madeleine or Concorde. **Amenities:** Restaurant; bar; limited room service; babysitting; laundry service/dry cleaning. *In room:* TV, dataport, minibar, hair dryer.

Le Relais du Louvre   One of the neighborhood's most up-to-date hotels, Relais du Louvre overlooks the neoclassical colonnade at the eastern end of the Louvre. Between 1800 and 1941, its upper floors contained the printing presses that recorded the goings-on in Paris's House of Representatives. Its street level held the Café Momus, favored by Voltaire, Hugo, and intellectuals of the day, and where Puccini set one of the pivotal scenes of *La Bohème*. Bedrooms are out-fitted in monochromatic schemes of blue, yellow, or soft reds, usually with copies of Directoire-style (French 1830s) furniture. All units have shower-tub combos except for four of the simplest and smallest singles, which have only a shower. Many rooms are a bit small, but others contain roomy sitting areas.

19 rue des Prêtres-St-Germain-l'Auxerrois, 75001 Paris. ℂ **01-40-41-96-42.** Fax 01-40-41-96-44. www. relaisdulouvre.com. 21 units. 145€–180€ ($167–$207) double; 205€–244€ ($236–$281) suite. AE, DC, MC, V. Parking 14€ ($16). Métro: Louvre or Pont Neuf. **Amenities:** Limited room service (24-hr. room service for drinks); babysitting; laundry service/dry cleaning; nonsmoking rooms. *In room:* A/C, TV, dataport, minibar, hair dryer, safe.

INEXPENSIVE

Le Petit Châtelet ★ *Value*   Small, unpretentious, and inexpensive, this hotel has a difficult-to-detect front entrance (it's tucked within a cluster of more highly visible restaurants), a clientele that includes lots of musicians playing at the nearby jazz clubs; and a warm-toned decorative scheme loosely inspired by India, Southeast Asia, and Africa. Bedrooms are small, a bit battered, and art-fully accessorized with musical instruments and framed paintings, in some cases originals. Bathrooms are compact, with showers but not bathtubs, and tile work. There's no elevator, so be prepared to climb as many as six flights of stairs. The largest room, and the only one with its own private terrace, is on the top floor. All of the rooms in this hotel that don't have private bathrooms are designated as singles. Accommodations facing the street can be noisy, but double-glazed windows keep out most of the noise, except during the heat of midsummer, when you might have to leave the windows open.

9 rue St-Denis, 75001 Paris. ℂ **01-42-33-32-31.** Fax 01-42-33-32-45. 15 units. 70€ ($81) double. AE, MC, V. Métro: Châtelet. **Amenities:** Restaurant (dinner only); bar; nonsmoking rooms. *In room:* A/C, TV, dataport.

Prince Albert *Value*   A government-rated two-star hotel, this undiscovered hotel enjoys a great location near the place Vendôme and the Louvre area. It is a century and a half old but has been brought completely up-to-date and has a cer-tain charm—all at an affordable price. Built in the 1820s, the rooms are still evocative of 19th-century Paris with their high ceilings. The furnishings, how-ever, are modern and comfortable. About two-thirds of the bedrooms contain showers, the rest bathtubs. Accommodations reveal that a decorator has come by, one fond of the color schemes of pink or green—sometimes with flowery fabrics.

5 rue Saint-Hyacinthe, 75001 Paris. ℂ **01-42-61-58-36.** Fax 01-42-60-04-06. www.hotelprincealbert.com. 30 units. 109€–120€ ($125–$138) double. MC, V. Métro: Tuileries. *In room:* A/C (in some), TV, dataport, mini-bar, hair dryer, safe.

Timhôtel Le Louvre *Kids*   This hotel and its sibling, the Timhôtel Palais-Royal, are mirror images, at least inside; they're part of a new breed of two-star family-friendly hotels cropping up in France. These Timhôtels share the same manager and temperament. Though the rooms at the Palais-Royal branch are a

---

Tips **Splish, Splash—Taking a Bath**

Throughout the hotels in this chapter, expect the bathrooms in very expensive and expensive hotels to be a bit larger than normal, with fine toiletries, plush towels, and perhaps bathrobes. The bathrooms in moderate and inexpensive hotels tend to be cramped but still acceptable, with towels that are less plush than those at expensive places.

Be aware that some hotels offer tub-shower combinations; some offer shower stalls, and some offer a mix. If this is important to you, request your preference when reserving. Almost all hotels, except the inexpensive ones, include hair dryers in the bathrooms.

---

bit larger than the ones here, this branch is so close to the Louvre it's almost irresistible. The ambience is modern, with monochromatic rooms and wall-to-wall carpeting upgraded in 1998. Each unit's bathroom comes with a tub and shower.

4 rue Croix des Petits-Champs, 75001 Paris. ☎ **01-42-60-34-86.** Fax 01-42-60-10-39. www.timhotel.fr. 56 units. 125€–150€ ($144–$173) double. Children under 12 stay free in parent's room. AE, DC, MC, V. Métro: Palais Royal. **Amenities:** Limited room service; babysitting; laundry service/dry cleaning; nonsmoking rooms; rooms for those with limited mobility. *In room:* A/C, TV, dataport.

2ND ARRONDISSEMENT
VERY EXPENSIVE

Park Hyatt Vendôme ★★★   American interior designer Ed Tuttle took five separate Haussmann-era buildings and wove them into a seamless whole to create this citadel of 21st-century luxury living. High ceilings, colonnades, and interior courtyards speak of the buildings' former lives, but other than the facades, all is completely modern inside—not just contemporary but luxe modern. The third Hyatt in Paris, this palace enjoys the greatest and most prestigious location in "Ritz Hotel country." Graced with modern art, this place is filled with elegant fabrics, huge mirrors, walk-in closets, mahogany doors, and Jim Thompson silk. Bedrooms and bathrooms are spacious and state of the art, with elegant furnishings and glamorous bathrooms with "rain showers," plus a separate tub.

3–5 rue de la Paix, 75002 Paris. ☎ **01-58-71-12-24.** Fax 01-58-71-12-35. www.paris.vendome.hyatt.com. 177 units. 410€–600€ ($472–$690) double; 600€–790€ ($690–$909) suite. AE, DC, MC, V. Métro: Tuileries or Opéra. **Amenities:** Restaurant; bar; lounge with fireplace; health club; spa; 24-hr. room service; babysitting; laundry service/dry cleaning. *In room:* A/C, TV, dataport, minibar, hair dryer, safe.

EXPENSIVE

Hôtel Victoires Opéra ★   Head to this little charmer in the fashion district if you want a reasonably priced place convenient to Les Halles and the Pompidou as well as to the Marais, with its shops and gay and straight restaurants. It's a classically decorated hotel, evoking the era of Louis Philippe. Renovations in 2001 included the addition of a private bathroom to every room. The rooms are comfortable, but rather small in most cases, except for the junior suites. All come with a tub-shower combination. Skip the hotel breakfast (which costs extra) and cross the street to Stohrer at no. 51, one of Paris's most historic patisseries, founded in 1730 by the *pâtissier* to Louis XV (see "In Pursuit of the Perfect Parisian Pastry" in chapter 6).

56 rue Montorgueil, 75002 Paris. ☎ **01-42-36-41-08.** Fax 01-45-08-08-79. www.hotelvictoiresopera.com. 24 units. 244€–275€ ($281–$316) double; 335€ ($385) junior suite. AE, DC, MC, V. Métro: Les Halles. **Amenities:** 24-hr. room service; babysitting; laundry service/dry cleaning; nonsmoking rooms; rooms for those with limited mobility. *In room:* A/C, TV, dataport, minibar, safe.

MODERATE

Golden Tulip Opéra de Noailles   If you're looking for a postmodern hotel in the style of Putman and Starck, book here. Proprietor Martine Falck has turned this old-fashioned place in a great location into a refined Art Deco choice with bold colors and cutting-edge style, yet the prices remain reasonable. The guest rooms come in various shapes and sizes, but all are comfortable and have a tub-and-shower combo. A favorite is no. 601, which has its own terrace.

9 rue de la Michodière, 75002 Paris. (℃) 800/344-1212 in the U.S., or 01-47-42-92-90. Fax 01-49-24-92-71. www.hoteldenoailles.com. 61 units. 190€–250€ ($219–$288) double. AE, DC, MC, V. Métro: 4 Septembre or Opéra. RER: Opéra. **Amenities:** Bar; health club; sauna; limited room service (8–10:30am); massage; babysitting; laundry service/dry cleaning. *In room:* A/C, TV, dataport, minibar, hair dryer, safe.

3RD ARRONDISSEMENT

INEXPENSIVE

Hôtel Bellevue & du Chariot d'Or   Originally built in 1860 as part of the majestic redevelopment of central Paris by Baron Haussmann, this hotel offers a grand facade and inexpensive, relatively comfortable and cozy but very simple bedrooms that are priced as a distinct bargain within its neighborhood. The hotel has become more desirable because of its location in the once-neglected Arts et Métiers district north of the Pompidou Center. The second part of its name—"Chariot d'Or" (Golden Carriage)—derives from the medieval custom of placing brides-to-be (along with their dowries) into a flower-draped ceremonial carriage, to carry them across what at the time was a courtyard near the entrance to the Church of St-Martin des Champs, which still stands within a 2-minute walk from the hotel. During the occupation of Paris during World War II, the site was commandeered as a garrison for rank-and-file Nazi troops. Expect a polite and well-spoken reception staff, a rather grand entrance hallway, and very comfortable bedrooms into which have been added touches of warmth.

39 rue de Turbigo, 75003 Paris. (℃) 01-48-87-45-60. Fax 01-48-87-95-04. www.hotelbellevue75.com. 59 units. 60€ ($69) double. AE, DC, MC, V. Métro: Châtelet–Les Halles or Réaumur-Sebastopol. **Amenities:** Bar; babysitting; rooms for those with limited mobility. *In room:* TV, dataport, safe.

Hôtel des Chevaliers   Half a block from the place des Vosges, this hotel occupies a corner building whose 17th-century vestiges have been elevated into high art. These include the remnants of a well in the cellar, a stone barrel vault covering the breakfast area, and Louis XIII accessories that will remind you of the hotel's origins. Each guest room is comfortable and well maintained, and all bathrooms come with both tub and shower. Units on the top floor have exposed ceiling beams. Some are larger than others, with an extra bed making them suitable for those traveling with a child or for three people on the road together.

30 rue de Turenne, 75003 Paris. (℃) 01-42-72-73-47. Fax 01-42-72-54-10. www.hoteldeschevaliers.com. 24 units. 116€–145€ ($133–$167) double; 160€ ($184) triple. Parking 20€ ($23). Métro: Chemin Vert or St-Paul. **Amenities:** Bar; limited room service; laundry service/dry cleaning; rooms for those with limited mobility. *In room:* A/C, TV, dataport, minibar, hair dryer, safe.

Hôtel Saintonge ★ *Finds*   Its rooms are small but there's a coziness about this hotel that you might appreciate, especially if you're attracted to beamed ceilings, patches of exposed and very old masonry, and charmingly claustrophobic upstairs hallways. It rises seven stories above a quiet neighborhood in the Marais, one of the many structures that functioned as private houses in the 17th century, and which have been converted to hotels or private apartments. Breakfast is served beneath the vaulted ceiling of what used to be a cellar-level storage area; the lobby boasts hand-hewn beams and a tile floor, and bedrooms have tall windows or, if they're on the building's uppermost floor, angled ceilings that evoke the feeling of an artist's studio in a garret. There are few amenities in this hotel other than the breakfast room, but considering the wealth of museums and architecture in the surrounding neighborhood, no one seems to care. Bathrooms are sheathed in tile, most only with shower.

16 rue Saintonge, 75003 Paris. © 01-42-77-91-13. Fax 01-48-87-76-41. www.hotelmarais.com. 23 units. 115€ ($132) double; 170€ ($196) suite. AE, DC, MC, V. Métro: Filles du Calvaire or République. **Amenities:** Limited room service; babysitting; nonsmoking rooms; rooms for those with limited mobility. *In room:* TV, dataport, minibar, hair dryer, safe.

4TH ARRONDISSEMENT
EXPENSIVE

Hôtel du Bourg Tibourg ★ *Finds*   This is a coveted address right in the heart of the Marais. Jacques Garcia, the designer of one of Paris's most famous hotels, Hôtel Costes, also designed this little charmer. Hotels with far less style can cost twice as much, so this is a real discovery. Known to many visitors in the old days as the Hôtel Rivoli-Notre-Dame, the restored hotel occupies a landmark position in a historic neighborhood, close to many mansions and cobbled streets. Notre-Dame and Ile St-Louis are within walking distance. You can order breakfast in an attractive dining room under a 17th-century vaulted ceiling. Bedrooms are small to midsize, each comfortably and attractively furnished.

19 rue du Bourg-Tibourg, 75004 Paris. © **01-42-78-47-39.** Fax 01-40-29-07-00. www.hoteldubourg tibourg.com. 30 units. 200€–250€ ($230–$288) double; 350€ ($403) suite. AE, MC, V. Métro: Hôtel-de-Ville. **Amenities:** Lounge; babysitting; laundry service/dry cleaning; 1 room for those with limited mobility. *In room:* A/C, TV, dataport, minibar, hair dryer, safe.

Hôtel du Jeu de Paume ★   This hotel is small scale and charming, with a layout that includes a pair of 17th-century town houses accessible via a timbered passageway from the street outside. The rooms are a bit larger than those within some of the nearby competitors. Originally, the hotel was a "clubhouse" used by members of the court of Louis XIII, who amused themselves with *Les jeux de paume* (an early form of tennis) nearby. Public areas are outfitted in a simple version of Art Deco. Bedrooms, some under a wooden-beamed ceiling, are freshly decorated with sleek contemporary styling, each with elegant materials such as oak floors and fine craftsmanship. All contain well-maintained private bathrooms with tub-and-shower combinations. The most luxurious way to live here is in one of the five duplexes or two junior suites, each individually decorated and opening onto an indoor courtyard.

54 rue St-Louis en l'Ile, 75004 Paris. © **01-43-26-14-18.** Fax 01-40-46-02-76. www.jeudepaumehotel.com. 30 units. 215€–285€ ($247–$328) double; 465€ ($535) suite. AE, DC, MC, V. Métro: Pont Marie. **Amenities:** Bar; gym; sauna; limited room service; babysitting; laundry service/dry cleaning. *In room:* TV, dataport, minibar, hair dryer, safe.

MODERATE

Axial Beaubourg ★ *Finds*   Fashionistas flock to this restored hotel in the Marais, which is one of the cutting-edge places to stay in Paris. The location is convenient to the Centre Pompidou, Notre-Dame, the Louvre, and the Picasso Museum. The building has been in the family of Veronique Turmel since 1918. In 2002, she decided to completely convert the interior while retaining the facade. She hired Jean-Philippe Nuel, who kept many of the original architectural features, including exposed beams, old stones, and hardwood floors. He created a medieval look graced with *wenge*-wood furnishings, white walls, and bronzed sconces—old-world charm in a tasteful and refined setting. The midsize bedrooms are completely up-to-date with beautiful and comfortable furnishings, along with impressive bathrooms with tub and shower. The so-called breakfast "cave" is actually a charming room with slip-covered chairs and sea-grass matting.

11 rue du Temple, 75004 Paris. ℂ **01-42-72-72-22.** Fax 01-42-72-03-53. www.axialbeaubourg.com. 39 units. 155€–200€ ($178–$230) double. AE, DC, MC, V. Métro: Hôtel-de-Ville. **Amenities:** Lounge for drinks; limited room service; laundry service/dry cleaning; nonsmoking rooms. *In room:* A/C, TV, dataport, minibar, hair dryer, safe.

Hôtel Caron de Beaumarchais *Value* Built in the 18th century, this good-value choice features floors of artfully worn gray stone, antique reproductions, and elaborate fabrics based on antique patterns. Hotelier Alain Bigeard intends his primrose-colored guest rooms to evoke the taste of the French gentry in the 18th century when the Marais was the scene of high-society dances or even duels. Most rooms retain their original ceiling beams. The smallest units overlook the interior courtyard, and the top-floor rooms are tiny but have panoramic balcony views across the Right Bank. All but two of the bedrooms have a tub-shower combination.

12 rue Vieille-du-Temple, 75004 Paris. ℂ **01-42-72-34-12.** Fax 01-42-72-34-63. www.caronde beaumarchais.com. 19 units. 120€–152€ ($138–$175) double. AE, MC, V. Métro: St-Paul or Hôtel-de-Ville. **Amenities:** Babysitting. *In room:* A/C, TV, dataport, minibar, hair dryer.

Hôtel de Lutèce This hotel feels like a country house in Brittany. The lounge, with its old fireplace, is furnished with antiques and contemporary paintings. Each of the guest rooms boasts antiques, adding to a refined atmosphere that attracts celebrities like the duke and duchess of Bedford. Each unit comes with either tub or shower. The suites, larger than the doubles, of course, are often like doubles with extended sitting areas. Each is tastefully furnished, with an antique or two. The hotel is comparable in style and amenities to the Deux-Iles (see below), under the same ownership.

65 rue St-Louis-en-l'Ile, 75004 Paris. ℂ **01-43-26-23-52.** Fax 01-43-29-60-25. www.hotel-ile-saintlouis.com. 23 units. 150€ ($173) double; 165€ ($190) triple. AE, MC, V. Métro: Pont Marie or Cité. **Amenities:** Laundry service/dry cleaning; rooms for those with limited mobility. *In room:* A/C, TV, dataport, hair dryer, safe.

Kids **Family-Friendly Hotels**

Hôtel de Fleurie (p. 100) In the heart of St-Germain-des-Prés, this has long been a Left Bank family favorite. The hotel is known for its *chambres familiales*—two connecting rooms with a pair of large beds in each room. Children under 12 stay free with a parent.

Hôtel du Ministère (p. 90) For the family on a budget that doesn't mind cramped quarters, the Ministère is one of the best bets in this expensive area near the Champs-Elysées.

Résidence Lord Byron (p. 91) The Byron is not only a good value and an unusually family-oriented place for the swanky 8th arrondissement, but is only a short walk from many major monuments.

Timhôtel Le Louvre (p. 78) This is an especially convenient choice because it offers some rooms with four beds for the price of a double. And the location near the Louvre is irresistible.

Hôtel des Deux-Iles ⭐ This hotel is housed in a restored 18th-century town house. The decor is elaborate, with bamboo and reed furniture and French provincial touches. This is an unpretentious but charming choice with a great location. The guest rooms are on the small side, but the beds are very comfortable and the bathrooms are well maintained with shower units. A garden of plants and flowers off the lobby leads to a basement breakfast room with a fireplace.

59 rue St-Louis-en-l'Ile, 75004 Paris. ✆ **01-43-26-13-35.** Fax 01-43-29-60-25. www.2iles.com. 17 units. 150€–158€ ($173–$182) double. AE, MC, V. Métro: Pont Marie. **Amenities:** Limited room service; laundry service/dry cleaning; nonsmoking rooms. *In room:* A/C, TV, hair dryer, safe.

Hôtel Saint-Louis ⭐ *(Value)* Proprietors Guy and Andrée Record maintain a charming family atmosphere at this antique-filled hotel in a 17th-century town house. Despite a renovation completed in 1998, it represents an incredible value considering its prime location on Ile St-Louis. Expect cozy, slightly cramped rooms, each with a small private bathroom containing a shower-tub combination. With mansard roofs and old-fashioned moldings, the top-floor units sport tiny balconies with sweeping views. The breakfast room is in the cellar, with 17th-century stone vaulting.

75 rue St-Louis-en-l'Ile, 75004 Paris. ✆ **01-46-34-04-80.** Fax 01-46-34-02-13. www.hotelsaintlouis.com. 19 units. 130€–210€ ($150–$242) double. MC, V. Métro: Pont Marie or St-Michel-Notre-Dame. **Amenities:** Limited room service; babysitting. *In room:* TV, dataport, minibar, hair dryer, safe.

Hôtel Saint-Merry ⭐ *(Finds)* The rebirth of this once-notorious brothel as a charming upscale hotel is an example of how the area has been gentrified. It contains only a dozen rooms, each relatively small, but accented with neo-Gothic detail, exposed stone, 18th-century ceiling beams, and lots of quirky architecture. Suites, much larger than doubles, have upgraded furnishings and more comfort. All units contain tiled bathrooms with shower-tub combinations. According to the staff, the clientele here is about 50% gay males; the other half is straight and involved in the arts scene in the surrounding neighborhood. Before it became a bordello, it was conceived as the presbytery of the nearby Church of Saint-Merry.

78 rue de la Verrerie, 75004 Paris. ✆ **01-42-78-14-15.** Fax 01-40-29-06-82. www.hotelmarais.com. 12 units. 130€–230€ ($150–$265) double; 335€ ($385) suite. MC, V. Métro: Hôtel-de-Ville or Châtelet. **Amenities:** Breakfast lounge; limited room service; babysitting; laundry service/dry cleaning. *In room:* TV (in some), minibar (in some), hair dryer, safe.

INEXPENSIVE

Hôtel de la Place des Vosges ⭐ *(Value)* Built about 350 years ago, during the same era as the construction of the majestic square it's named for (a 2-min. walk away), this is a well-managed, small-scale property with reasonable prices and lots of charm. The structure was once used as a stable for the mules of Henri IV. Many of the small guest rooms have beamed ceilings, tiled bathrooms (with tub or shower), small TVs hanging from the ceiling, and a sense of cozy, well-ordered efficiency. The most desirable and expensive accommodation is top-floor room no. 60, overlooking the rooftops of Paris, with a luxurious private bathroom. There are patches of chiseled stone at various parts of the hotel—a nice, decorative touch.

12 rue de Birague, 75004 Paris. ✆ **01-42-72-60-46.** Fax 01-42-72-02-64. 16 units. 120€–140€ ($138–$161) double. AE, MC, V. Métro: Bastille. **Amenities:** Limited room service; nonsmoking rooms; elevator. *In room:* TV, dataport, minibar, hair dryer, safe.

Hôtel du 7e Art The structure that contains this place is one of many 17th-century buildings in this neighborhood classified as historic monuments. Don't expect grand luxury: Bedrooms are cramped but clean, and outfitted with the simplest of furniture. Each has white walls, and some—including those under the sloping mansard-style roof—have exposed ceiling beams. All have small bathrooms with either a tub or shower. The "7th Art" is a French term for film-making; images from the cinema decorate the otherwise black-and-white interior of both the public areas and bedrooms of this hotel. Look for stills of Charlie Chaplain, Laurel and Hardy, and more, within the framework of a building that, until only 15 years ago, functioned as a flophouse residential hotel. There's a lobby bar and a breakfast room, but there's no elevator and it's a five-story building.

20 rue St-Paul, 75004 Paris. ✆ 01-44-54-85-00. Fax 01-42-77-69-10. 23 units. 75€–130€ ($86–$150) double. AE, DC, MC, V. Métro: St-Paul. **Amenities:** Bar; health club; laundromat. *In room:* TV, dataport, hair dryer, safe.

9TH ARRONDISSEMENT
MODERATE
Hôtel de la Tour d'Auvergne   Here's a good bet for those who want to be near the Opéra or the Gare du Nord. This building was erected before Baron Haussmann reconfigured Paris's avenues around 1870. Later, Modigliani rented a room for 6 months, and Victor Hugo and Auguste Rodin lived on this street. The interior has been modernized into a glossy internationalism. The guest rooms are meticulously coordinated, yet the small decorative canopies over the headboards make them feel cluttered. Though the views over the back courtyard are uninspired, some guests prefer the quiet of the rear rooms. Every year, five rooms are renovated, and each unit comes with a tub-shower combination.

10 rue de la Tour d'Auvergne, 75009 Paris. ✆ 01-48-78-61-60. Fax 01-49-95-99-00. www.hotel-tour-auvergne-opera-paris.federal-hotel.com. 24 units. 130€–145€ ($150–$167) double. AE, DC, MC, V. Métro: Cadet. **Amenities:** Bar; limited room service; babysitting; nonsmoking rooms. *In room:* TV, dataport, minibar, hair dryer.

Hôtel Langlois   This hotel used to be known as Hôtel des Croises, but when it was used as a setting for the Jonathan Demme film *The Truth About Charlie,* the hotel owners changed the name to match the one used in the film. It's a well-proportioned, restored town house with a main stairwell and spacious landing. In an old-fashioned Parisian touch, there's an antique wrought-iron elevator running up the center of the building. The rooms are well proportioned, but not overly large; those in the front get the most light. Units in the rear are darker but quieter. Rooms with their aura of *Ecole de Nancy* (a florid Art Nouveau style) have well-chosen antiques, tasteful rugs and fabrics, even an occasional fireplace. Bathrooms are modernized with tub and shower. We suggest avoiding the upper floors in summer; there's no air-conditioning and the heat is often stifling.

63 rue St-Lazare, 75009 Paris. ✆ 01-48-74-78-24. Fax 01-49-95-04-43. www.hotel-langlois.com. 27 units. 89€–99€ ($103–$114) double; 132€ ($152) triple. AE, DC, MC, V. Métro: Trinité. **Amenities:** Breakfast room; 24-hr. room service. *In room:* TV, dataport, minibar, hair dryer.

INEXPENSIVE
Hôtel Chopin *Value*   Enter this intimate, offbeat hotel through a passageway that includes a toy store, a bookstore, the exit from the Musée Grevin, and the architectural trappings of its original construction in 1846. Just off the Grands Boulevards, this old-fashioned hotel evokes the charm of yesteryear. In honor of its namesake, the Chopin features a piano in its reception area. The inviting lobby welcomes you behind its 1850s facade of elegant woodwork and Victorian-era glass. In the style of Paris of long ago, the comfortably furnished bedrooms open onto a glass-topped arcade instead of the hysterically busy street, so

> **Value Good, Clean Rooms for Around $50 a Night**
>
> Largely unnoticed by U.S. visitors—as yet—a French Revolution is quietly taking place. Some two dozen modern, amenity-packed hotels have sprouted up in Paris under the **Ibis Hotel** banner. These cookie-cutter properties have become the McDonald's of French budget lodgings. Operated by Accor Hotels (✆ **800/221-4542**), they have attractive but tiny rooms and offer simple but comfortable decors that are cost-efficient albeit without any particular antique or glamorous trappings. If you stay at Motel 6 and Red Roof Inns in the United States, it's a comparable experience. You can book a room at an Ibis for the price of two martinis at the George V.

they are rather tranquil. We prefer the bedrooms on the top floor as they are larger and quieter, with views over the rooftops of Paris. The least expensive bedrooms lie behind the elevator bank and get less light. An elevator leads to the bedrooms, which are much nicer than the less desirable and often small and dark bathrooms.

10 bd. Montmartre or 46 passage Jouffroy, 75009 Paris. ✆ 01-47-70-58-10. Fax 01-42-47-00-70. 36 units. 73€–84€ ($84–$97) double. Métro: Grands-Boulevards. *In room:* TV, hair dryer, safe.

11TH ARRONDISSEMENT
INEXPENSIVE

Libertel Croix de Malte   A member of a nationwide chain of government-rated two-star hotels, this is a well-maintained choice. The hotel consists of buildings of two and three floors, one of which is accessible through a shared breakfast room. There's a landscaped courtyard in back with access to a lobby bar. The cozy guest rooms contain brightly painted modern furniture accented with vivid green, blue, and pink patterns that flash back to the 1960s. About half of the units contain tubs; the rest are equipped with showers.

5 rue de Malte, 75011 Paris. ✆ 01-48-05-09-36. Fax 01-43-57-02-54. www.libertel-hotels.com. 29 units. 102€–127€ ($117–$146) double. AE, DC, MC, V. Métro: Oberkampf. **Amenities:** Bar; limited room service (breakfast); babysitting; laundry service/dry cleaning. *In room:* TV, dataport, hair dryer, minibar.

Résidence Alhambra   Named for the famous cabaret/vaudeville theater that once stood nearby, the Alhambra dates from the 1800s. A radical renovation in 2000 gave the hotel its fine contemporary format. In the rear garden, its two-story chalet offers eight additional guest rooms. The small accommodations are bland but comfortable, each in a dull pastel scheme that includes white and ocher. Ten private bathrooms contain a tub-and-shower combo, the rest showers.

13 rue de Malte, 75011 Paris. ✆ 01-47-00-35-52. Fax 01-43-57-98-75. www.hotelalhambra.fr. 58 units. 67€ ($77) double; 103€ ($118) triple. AE, DC, MC, V. Métro: Oberkampf. **Amenities:** Garden. *In room:* TV, dataport.

12TH ARRONDISSEMENT
MODERATE

Hôtel Pavillon Bastille   This is a bold, innovative hotel in a town house across from the Opéra Bastille, a block south of place de la Bastille. A 17th-century fountain graces the courtyard. The guest rooms have twin or double beds, partially mirrored walls, and contemporary built-in furniture. Each unit comes with a tub-shower combo.

65 rue de Lyon, 75012 Paris. ℭ 01-43-43-65-65. Fax 01-43-43-96-52. www.paris-pavillonbastille.com. 25 units. 130€ ($150) double; 213€ ($245) suite. AE, DC, MC, V. Métro: Bastille. **Amenities:** 24-hr. room service; babysitting; laundry service/dry cleaning; nonsmoking rooms. *In room:* A/C, TV, dataport, minibar, hair dryer, safe.

INEXPENSIVE

Le Nouvel Hôtel This hotel evokes the French provinces more than urban Paris. Surrounded by greenery in a neighborhood rarely visited by tourists, the Nouvel conjures a day when parts of Paris still seemed like small country towns. The most attractive spot is the inside courtyard, site of warm-weather breakfasts. Winding halls lead to small guest rooms overlooking the courtyard or, less appealingly, the street. Each contains flowered fabrics and old-fashioned furniture, but only three have tub baths; the rest are equipped with showers.

24 av. du Bel-Air, 75012 Paris. ℭ 01-43-43-01-81. Fax 01-43-44-64-13. www.nouvel-hotel-paris.com. 28 units. 68€–78€ ($78–$90) double. AE, DC, MC, V. Métro: Nation. **Amenities:** Nonsmoking rooms. *In room:* TV, dataport.

18TH ARRONDISSEMENT
EXPENSIVE

Terrass Hôtel ★★ *Finds* Built in 1913, this is the only government-rated four-star hotel on the Butte Montmartre. In an area filled with some of Paris's seediest hotels, this place is easily in a class of its own. Its main advantage is its location amid Montmartre's bohemian atmosphere (or what's left of it). Staffed by English-speaking employees, it has a large marble-floored lobby ringed with blond-oak paneling and accented with 18th-century antiques and valuable paintings. The guest rooms are high ceilinged and well upholstered, often featuring views. All the bathrooms are well maintained, each with a shower and about half with both a shower and tub.

12 rue Joseph-de-Maistre, 75018 Paris. ℭ 01-46-06-72-85. Fax 01-42-52-29-11. www.terrass-hotel.com. 100 units. 244€–270€ ($281–$311) double; 326€ ($375) suite. Rates include breakfast. AE, DC, MC, V. Métro: Place de Clichy or Blanche. **Amenities:** 2 restaurants; bar; sauna; limited room service (7am–11pm); babysitting; laundry service/dry cleaning; nonsmoking rooms; rooms for those with limited mobility. *In room:* A/C, TV, dataport, minibar, coffeemaker, hair dryer, safe.

INEXPENSIVE

Hôtel Bonséjour *Value* One of the cheapest hotels in Montmartre boasts turn-of-the-century rooms and furnishings, and dimensions larger than those you might find within the more contemporary (and more plush) hotels nearby. Built around 1918, the hotel has six floors and no elevator, so if your room is on top, be prepared for some climbing. Expect old-fashioned furniture, including large-scale armoires in lieu of closets, communal showers on one of the building's lower floors and a communal WC on each of the stair landings, creaky but congenial dowdiness, and a friendly reception. The most desirable rooms, partly because of their small private terraces, include nos. 14, 23, 33, 43, and 53.

11 rue Burq, 75018 Paris. ℭ 01-42-54-22-53. Fax 01-42-54-25-92. 34 units, none with toilet, all with sink, 9 with shower. 32€ ($37) double; 38€–40€ ($44–$46) double with shower. No credit cards. Métro: Abbesses. **Amenities:** Limited room service. *In room:* TV.

Hôtel Ermitage Built in 1870 of chiseled limestone in the Napoleon III style, this hotel's facade evokes a perfectly proportioned small villa. It's set in a calm area, a brief uphill stroll from Sacré-Coeur. Views extend over Paris, and there's a garden in the back courtyard. The small guest rooms are like those in a countryside *auberge* (inn), with exposed ceiling beams, flowered wallpaper, and casement windows opening onto the garden or a street seemingly airlifted from the provinces. All the bedrooms come with small tubs and showers.

24 rue Lamarck, 75018 Paris. © **01-42-64-79-22.** Fax 01-42-64-10-33. 12 units. 86€ ($99) double. Rates include breakfast. No credit cards. Métro: Lamarck-Caulaincourt. **Amenities:** Limited room service; babysitting; garden.

8TH ARRONDISSEMENT
VERY EXPENSIVE

Concorde St-Lazare 🐤   Across from the St-Lazare rail station, this hotel—the area's best—first greeted visitors flocking to the Universal Exposition of 1889. In 2000 each of the guest rooms was elevated to modern standards of comfort and redecorated. Many rooms (medium-size to quite large) have high ceilings, especially those on the lower floors, which also have double-glazed windows to cut down on the noise. The beds are plush and comfortable, and bathrooms come with tub-and-shower combos.

108 rue St-Lazare, 75008 Paris. © **800/888-4747** in the U.S. outside New York State and Canada, 0800/02-89-880 in London, or 01-40-08-44-44. Fax 01-42-93-01-20. www.concordestlazare-paris.com. 266 units. 360€–450€ ($414–$518) double; from 685€ ($788) suite. AE, DC, MC, V. Parking 23€ ($26). Métro: St-Lazare. **Amenities:** Restaurant; bar; cafe; 24-hr. room service; babysitting; laundry service/dry cleaning; nonsmoking rooms. *In room:* A/C, TV, dataport, minibar, hair dryer, safe.

Four Seasons Hotel George V 🐤🐤🐤   In its latest reincarnation, with all its glitz and glamour, this hotel is one of the best in the world. And the George V's history is as gilt-edged as they come. It opened in 1928 in honor of George V of England. During the liberation of Paris, it housed Dwight D. Eisenhower. After its acquisition by Saudi Prince Al Waleed and a 2-year renovation, it was reopened under the banner of Toronto-based Four Seasons. The guest rooms are about as close as you'll come to residency in a well-upholstered private home where teams of decorators have lavished vast amounts of attention and money. The beds rival those at the Ritz and Meurice in comfort. It's deluxe all the way. The renovation reduced the number of units from 300 to 245, which now come in three sizes. The largest are magnificent; the smallest are, in the words of a spokesperson, *"très agreeable."* Each unit comes with a large bathroom with a shower-tub combination. Security is tight—a fact appreciated by sometimes notorious guests.

31 av. George V, 75008 Paris. © **800/332-3442** in the U.S. or Canada, or 01-49-52-70-00. Fax 01-49-52-70-10. www.fourseasons.com. 245 units. 670€–890€ ($771–$1,024) double; from 1,250€ ($1,438) suite. AE, DC, MC, V. Parking 40€ ($46) Métro: George-V. **Amenities:** Restaurant; bar; indoor pool; fitness center; spa; sauna; 24-hr. room service; babysitting; laundry service/dry cleaning; nonsmoking rooms; rooms for those with limited mobility. *In room:* A/C, TV, dataport, minibar, hair dryer, safe.

Hôtel Bristol 🐤🐤🐤   This palace is near the Palais d'Elysée (home of the French president), on the shopping street parallel to the Champs-Elysées. In terms of style and glamour, here's how the lineup reads in Paris: (1) Ritz, (2) Plaza Athénée, (3) Bristol, and (4) George V. The 18th-century Parisian facade has a glass-and-wrought-iron entryway, where uniformed English-speaking attendants greet you. Hippolyte Jammet founded the Bristol in 1924, installing many antiques and Louis XV and XVI furnishings. The guest rooms are opulent, with antiques or well-made reproductions, inlaid wood, bronze, crystal, Oriental carpets, and original oil paintings. Each room is freshened every 3 years, and each comes with a luxurious bathroom with tub-and-shower combo. Personalized old-world service is rigidly maintained here—some guests find it forbidding, others absolutely adore it.

112 rue du Faubourg St-Honoré, 75008 Paris. © **01-53-43-43-00.** Fax 01-53-43-43-01. www.lebristolparis. com. 170 units. 630€–670€ ($725–$771) double; from 1,100€ ($1,265) suite. AE, DC, MC, V. Free parking. Métro: Miromesnil. **Amenities:** Restaurant; bar; indoor pool; fitness room; spa; sauna/hamman; 24-hr. room service; babysitting; laundry service/dry cleaning; nonsmoking rooms. *In room:* A/C, TV, dataport, minibar, hair dryer, safe.

Hôtel de Crillon ★★★   The Crillon, one of Europe's grand hotels, sits across from the U.S. Embassy. Although some international CEOs and diplomats treat it as a shrine, those seeking less pomposity might prefer the Plaza Athénée or the Ritz. The 200-plus-year-old building, once the palace of the duc de Crillon, is now owned by Jean Taittinger, of the champagne family. The salons boast 17th- and 18th-century tapestries, gilt-and-brocade furniture, chandeliers, fine sculpture, and Louis XVI chests and chairs. The guest rooms are luxurious. Some are spectacular, like the Leonard Bernstein Suite, which has one of the maestro's pianos and one of the grandest views of any hotel room in Paris. The marble bathrooms offer deluxe toiletries, dual sinks, shower-tub combinations, and robes. The furniture, including the beds, offers grand comfort. The boudoir luxury was overseen by Sonia Rykiel doing her take on Louis XV and Madame Pompadour.

10 place de la Concorde, 75008 Paris. ✆ **800/223-6800** in the U.S. and Canada, or 01-44-71-15-00. Fax 01-44-71-15-02. www.crillon.com. 147 units. 575€–655€ ($661–$753) double; from 1,400€ ($1,610) suite. AE, DC, MC, V. Free parking. Métro: Concorde. **Amenities:** 2 restaurants; bar; tearoom; gym; 24-hr. room service; babysitting; laundry service/dry cleaning; nonsmoking rooms. *In room:* A/C, TV, dataport, minibar, hair dryer, safe.

Hôtel Pershing Hall ★★★   Set on a hyper-stylish street that parallels the Avenue Montaigne, this hotel was created when a late 19th-century town house was radically altered by one of France's most celebrated modern designers, Andrée Putnam. Admittedly, she had fascinating raw materials: The five-story town house was built in 1890 by the Comte de Paris—at the time the heir apparent to the French monarchy had it been fully restored—as a home for his mistress. During World War I, it was transformed into the Paris headquarters of American General John Pershing. Today, the walls of the soaring courtyard are draped in lush tropical plants from Southeast Asia that thrive in the microclimate of the courtyard. Inside, don't expect an homage to the imperial days of the French monarchy, as all appointments have been replaced in favor of the warm but artfully spartan and rectilinear style favored by the woman who designed the original decors of Air France's Concorde. There's a lavish use of quarried stone, tile, mosaics, and hardwoods, a subtle color scheme of warm beiges and grays, bead curtains, bathtubs with claw-and-ball feet, and comfortable, subtly contemporary furniture.

49 rue Pierre Charron, 75008 Paris. ✆ **01-58-36-58-00.** Fax 01-58-36-58-01. www.pershing-hall.com. 26 units. 330€–390€ ($380–$449) double; 850€–1,000€ ($978–$1,150) suite. AE, DC, MC, V. Métro: Georges V. **Amenities:** Restaurant; bar; health club; sauna; 24-hr. room service; babysitting; laundry/dry cleaning; courtyard terrace; nonsmoking rooms; rooms for those with limited mobility. *In room:* A/C, TV, dataport, minibar, hair dryer, safe.

Plaza Athénée ★★★   The Plaza Athénée, an 1889 Art Nouveau marvel, is a landmark of discretion and style. In the 8th, only the Bristol can compare. About half the celebrities visiting Paris have been pampered here; in the old days, Mata Hari used to frequent the place. Superbly decorated subdivisions within the hotel include the **Bar Montaigne,** whose audaciously designed countertops are crafted from crystal that's lit from beneath. It's been described as an enormous iceberg that self-illuminates when you touch it. The **Salon Gobelins** (with tapestries against rich paneling) and the **Salon Marie Antoinette,** a richly paneled and grand room, are two public rooms that add to the ambience of this lavish hotel. There's also a calm, quiet interior courtyard draped with vines and dotted with geraniums. The quietest guest rooms overlook a courtyard with awnings and parasol-shaded tables; they have ample closet space, and their large

Au Palais de Chaillot **12**
Best Western Hôtel Regent's
  Garden **2**
Four Seasons Hôtel
  George V **13**
Galileo Hôtel **9**
Hôtel Balzac **7**
Hôtel Bristol **5**
Hôtel de Crillon **16**
Hôtel de Palma **3**
Hôtel du Ministère **17**
Hôtel Flaubert **1**
Hôtel Meurice **15**
Hôtel Opal **19**
Hôtel Pershing Hall **8**
Hôtel Queen Mary **20**
Hôtel Sofitel Trocadero
  Dokhans **11**
Hotel Trocadéro La Tour **10**
Hyatt Regency
  Paris-Madeleine **18**
Le Méridien Etoile **4**
Plaza Athénée **14**
Résidence Lord Byron **6**

tiled bathrooms contain double basins. Some rooms overlooking avenue Montaigne have views of the Eiffel Tower.

25 av. Montaigne, 75008 Paris. © **866/732-1106** in the U.S. and Canada, or 01-53-67-66-65. Fax 01-53-67-66-66. www.plaza-athenee-paris.com. 188 units. 680€–740€ ($782–$851) double; from 870€ ($1,000) junior suite. AE, DC, MC, V. Parking 23€ ($26). Métro: Franklin-D.-Roosevelt or Alma-Marceau. **Amenities:** 2 restaurants; bar; health club; sauna/*hamman;* 24-hr. room service; massage; babysitting; laundry service/dry cleaning; nonsmoking rooms; rooms for those with limited mobility. *In room:* A/C, TV, dataport, minibar, hair dryer, iron/board, safe.

EXPENSIVE

Hôtel Balzac ✹✹✹ If the Crillon and the Ritz are Rolls-Royces, then the Balzac is a Bentley, boasting a well-trained formal staff. Elegant and discreet, it opened in 1986 in a Belle Epoque mansion, then was redecorated in 1994 by English designer Nina Campbell. Most of the guest rooms are medium to spacious, with modern furniture, double-glazed windows, mirrored closets, and king-size beds. Most rooms have shower-tub bathroom combos; six just have showers.

6 rue Balzac, 75008 Paris. © **800/457-4000** in the U.S. and Canada, or 01-44-35-18-00. Fax 01-44-35-18-05. 70 units. 380€–460€ ($437–$529) double; from 490€ ($563) suite. AE, DC, MC, V. Parking 23€ ($26). Métro: George-V. **Amenities:** Bar; 24-hr. room service; babysitting; laundry service/dry cleaning; nonsmoking rooms. *In room:* A/C, TV, dataport, minibar, hair dryer.

Hyatt Regency Paris-Madeleine ✹✹ In the heart of the financial district, this is Paris's latest luxury hotel and represents Hyatt's first venture into the heart of the French capital. This is our top recommendation for those visiting Paris on business, as rooms are designed not only for rest but for work—large writing desks, three phones, modem sockets, voice mail, individual fax machines—you name it. As you enter, the hotel evokes a noble, romantic private home with a lavish use of quality materials such as sycamore wood. Bedrooms are spacious with large beds and luxurious, tiled bathrooms with tubs and showers. Some of the units boast exceptional views over the rooftops of Paris.

24 bd. Malesherbes, 75008 Paris. © **01-55-27-12-34.** Fax 01-55-27-12-35. www.paris.madeleine.hyatt. com. 86 units. 350€–410€ ($402–$472) double; 700€–1,000€ ($805–$1,150) suite. AE, DC, MC, V. Free parking. Métro: Madeleine. **Amenities:** 2 restaurants; bar; fitness center; 24-hr. business center; salon; 24-hr. room service; massage; babysitting; laundry service/dry cleaning; nonsmoking rooms; rooms for those with limited mobility. *In room:* A/C, TV, dataport, minibar, hair dryer, iron/board, safe.

MODERATE

Galileo Hôtel ✹ *Finds* This is one of the 8th's most charming hotels, run by Roland and Elisabeth Buffat, who have won friends from all over with their Hôtel des Deux-Iles (p. 83) and Hôtel de Lutèce on St-Louis-en-l'Ile (p. 82). A short walk from the Champ-Elysées, the town house is the epitome of French elegance and charm. The rooms are medium-size and a study in understated taste, decorated in cocoa and beige. Bathrooms are beautifully kept with either a tub or shower. The most spacious are room nos. 100, 200, 501, and 502, with a glass-covered veranda you can use even in winter. For this neighborhood, the prices are moderate.

54 rue Galilée, 75008 Paris. © 01-47-20-66-06. Fax 01-47-20-67-17. 27 units. 153€ ($176) double. AE, DC, MC, V. Parking 23€ ($26). Métro: Charles de Gaulle–Etoile or George-V. **Amenities:** Limited room service; laundry service/dry cleaning; rooms for those with limited mobility. *In room:* A/C, TV, dataport, minibar, hair dryer.

Hôtel du Ministère ✹ *Kids* The Ministère is a winning choice near the Champs-Elysées, though it's far from being Paris's cheapest budget hotel. The guest rooms are on the small side, but comfortable and well maintained; many have oak beams and fine furnishings. Try to avoid a room on the top floor, as you'll be too cramped. Each unit's bathroom is equipped with a tub-shower combo. Junior suites are only slightly larger than the regular doubles. But because the doubles are a bit small, you may want to pay extra for this added living space.

31 rue de Surène, 75008 Paris. © **01-42-66-21-43.** Fax 01-42-66-96-04. www.ministerehotel.com. 28 units. 120€–199€ ($138–$229) double. AE, MC, V. Métro: Madeleine. **Amenities:** Bar; limited room service; laundry service/dry cleaning; nonsmoking rooms; rooms for those with limited mobility. *In room:* A/C, TV, dataport, minibar, hair dryer, iron/board, safe.

Hôtel Opal *Finds*   This rejuvenated hotel, built around 1900, is a real find behind La Madeleine church and near the Opéra Garnier. The guest rooms are somewhat tight but very clean and comfortable, and many of them are air-conditioned. Those on the top floor are reached by a narrow staircase; some have skylights. Most rooms have twin brass beds, and all of them come with a tub-and-shower combo. Reception will make arrangements for parking at a nearby garage.

19 rue Tronchet, 75008 Paris. © **01-42-65-77-97.** Fax 01-49-24-06-58. www.hotelopal.com. 34 units. 150€–195€ ($173–$224) double. Extra bed 15€ ($17). AE, DC, V. Métro: Madeleine. **Amenities:** Bar; limited room service (breakfast); babysitting; laundry service/dry cleaning. *In room:* A/C, TV, dataport, minibar, hair dryer, safe.

Hôtel Queen Mary *✦*   Meticulously renovated inside and out, this early-1900s hotel is graced with an iron-and-glass canopy, wrought iron, and the kind of detailing normally reserved for more expensive hotels. The public rooms have touches of greenery and reproductions of antiques; guest rooms contain upholstered headboards, comfortable beds, and mahogany furnishings, plus a carafe of sherry. All units were renovated in 1998, and most come with a tub-shower combination (five have shower only). Suites are slightly more spacious than the regular doubles but meticulously maintained and beautifully furnished.

9 rue Greffulhe, 75008 Paris. © **01-42-66-40-50.** Fax 01-42-66-94-92. www.hotelqueenmary.com. 36 units. 149€–179€ ($171–$206) double; 239€ ($275) suite. AE, DC, MC, V. Métro: Madeleine or Havre-Caumartin. **Amenities:** Bar; business center; limited room service; nonsmoking rooms; rooms for those with limited mobility. *In room:* A/C, TV, dataport, minibar, hair dryer, safe.

Résidence Lord Byron *Kids*   Off the Champs-Elysées on a curving street of handsome buildings, the Lord Byron may not be as grand as other hotels in the neighborhood, but it's more affordable. Unassuming and a bit staid, it's exactly what repeat guests want—a sense of luxury, solitude, and understatement; it's a fine choice for families. Beds are old-fashioned and bathrooms are well kept with mainly shower units. Families often book the suites because of the larger living space. You can eat breakfast in the dining room or in the shaded inner garden.

5 rue de Chateaubriand, 75008 Paris. © **01-43-59-89-98.** Fax 01-42-89-46-04. www.escapade-paris.com. 31 units. 152€–169€ ($175–$195) double; 243€ ($279) suite. AE, DC, MC, V. Parking 20€ ($23). Métro: George-V. RER: Etoile. **Amenities:** Limited room service; babysitting; laundry service/dry cleaning. *In room:* A/C, TV, dataport, minibar, hair dryer, safe.

16TH ARRONDISSEMENT
VERY EXPENSIVE

Hôtel Sofitel Trocadéro Dokhan's *✦✦*   Except for the porters walking through its public areas carrying luggage, you might suspect that this well-accessorized hotel was a private home. It's housed within a stately 19th-century Haussmann-styled building vaguely inspired by Palladio, and contains accessories like antique paneling, Regency-era armchairs, chandeliers, and a pervasive sense of upper-bourgeois taste. Each bedroom has a different decorative style, with antiques or good reproductions, lots of personalized touches, triple-glazed windows, and beautifully maintained bathrooms with shower-tub combinations. Beds are often antique reproductions with maximum comfort. Suites have larger living space and spacious bathrooms with such extras as makeup mirrors and luxe toiletries.

117 rue Lauriston, 75116 Paris. © **01-53-65-66-99.** Fax 01-53-65-66-88. www.sofitel.com. 45 units. 400€–480€ ($460–$552) double; 820€ ($943) suite. AE, DC, MC, V. Parking 20€ ($23). Métro: Trocadéro. **Amenities:** Restaurant (lunch only); champagne bar; babysitting; laundry service/dry cleaning; nonsmoking rooms. *In room:* A/C, TV, fax, minibar, hair dryer, safe.

MODERATE

Hotel Trocadéro La Tour ★ *Finds*   Originally built in the late 19th century, this eight-story building is a well-maintained, well-managed hotel with comfortable, well-accessorized bedrooms and a location that's near the best viewing platform for the Eiffel Tower (place de Trocadéro) in Paris. The hotel is one of subdued elegance and refined comfort, filled with grace notes such as a lobby that evokes a library, a bar wainscoted in mahogany for teatime, and a tree-filled courtyard. The rather spacious bedrooms are each outfitted with a slightly different floor plan and color scheme, usually a coordinated palette of pale pastels. Each of the bathrooms has marble or tile trim and a shower-tub combination. The staff is kindly, albeit overworked and a bit harassed.

5 bis rue Massenet, 75116 Paris. © **01-45-24-43-03.** Fax 01-45-24-41-39. www.hotel-la-tour.com. 41 units. 129€–155€ ($148–$178) double; 220€ ($253) suite. AE, DC, MC, V. Métro: La Muette or Passy. **Amenities:** Bar; babysitting; laundry service/dry cleaning; nonsmoking rooms. *In room:* A/C, TV, minibar, hair dryer, safe.

INEXPENSIVE

Au Palais de Chaillot Hôtel   When Thierry and Cyrille Pien, brothers trained in the States, opened this hotel, budget travelers flocked here. Located between the Champ-Elysées and Trocadéro, the town house was restored from top to bottom and the result is a contemporary yet informal variation on Parisian chic. The guest rooms come in various shapes and sizes and are furnished with a light touch, with bright colors and wicker. Room nos. 61, 62, and 63 afford partial views of the Eiffel Tower. Each comes with a neatly tiled, shower-only bathroom.

35 av. Raymond-Poincaré, 75016 Paris. © **01-53-70-09-09.** Fax 01-53-70-09-08. www.chaillotel.com. 28 units. 115€–135€ ($132–$155) double; 135€ ($155) triple. AE, DC, MC, V. Métro: Victor Hugo or Trocadéro. **Amenities:** Limited room service; laundry service. *In room:* AC, TV, dataport, minibar, hair dryer, safe.

17TH ARRONDISSEMENT
EXPENSIVE

Le Méridien Etoile   This hotel made records as the largest in Paris when it was built in 1972. Rising nine stories above a rather dull residential and commercial neighborhood at the northwestern fringe of Paris, near the exposition halls at Porte Maillot, it's the flagship of the Méridien chain. Rooms are contemporary looking, not overly large, and standardized, reflecting a bland but completely acceptable international taste. Rooms on the hotel's uppermost two floors are a bit plusher than rooms on the lower floors, and feature a more personalized approach, including a separate breakfast and bar-lounge, separate check-in facilities, and a separate concierge. Expect a lot of corporate bustle at this megahotel, a hardworking staff, and occasional touches of charm that help overcome the hotel's sense of anonymity. *Hint:* The enormous size of this hotel, and the ongoing efforts of the sales and marketing staff to keep its occupancy levels high, lead to promotional rates that can be much as 50% less than the official rates quoted below. Thanks to a business-oriented clientele, the demand is lower on weekends, so be sure to ask for discounts if you're staying on a Friday, Saturday, or Sunday night.

81 bd. Gouviion Saint-Cyr, 75017 Paris. ℂ **01-40-68-34-34**. Fax 01-40-68-31-31. www.lemeridien-etoile. com. 1,025 units. 180€–450€ ($207–$518) double; from 700€ ($805) suite. Rates include breakfast. AE, DC, MC, V. Parking 20€ ($23). Métro: Porte Maillot. **Amenities:** 2 restaurants; bar; jazz club/nightclub; car rental; business center; news agent and gift shop; 24-hr. room service; babysitting; laundry service/dry cleaning; nonsmoking rooms; currency exchange; rooms for those with limited mobility. *In room:* A/C, TV, dataport, minibar, hair dryer, safe.

MODERATE

Best Western Hôtel Regent's Garden ★   Near the convention center (Palais des Congrés) and the Arc de Triomphe, the Regent's Garden boasts a proud heritage: Napoleon III built this château for his physician. The interior resembles a classically decorated country house. Fluted columns mark the entryway, which leads to a mix of furniture in the lobby. The guest rooms have flower prints on the walls, traditional French furniture, and tall soundproof windows, plus neatly organized private bathrooms with both a tub and shower. There's a garden with ivy-covered walls and umbrella-shaded tables—a perfect place to meet other guests.

6 rue Pierre-Demours, 75017 Paris. ℂ **800/528-1234** in the U.S., or 01-45-74-07-30. Fax 01-40-55-01-42. www.hotel-paris-garden.com. 39 units. 135€–249€ ($155–$286) double. AE, DC, MC, V. Parking 11€ ($13). Métro: Ternes or Charles de Gaulle–Etoile. **Amenities:** Limited room service; babysitting; nonsmoking rooms; garden. *In room:* A/C, TV, dataport, minibar, hair dryer, safe.

INEXPENSIVE

Hôtel de Palma ★ *(Finds)*   Although it's off-the-beaten track for most visitors, some patrons like the quiet residential neighborhood that surrounds this hotel, and there is quick access by Métro to other parts of Paris. The location is also only a 15-minute walk to the Air France/Roissy bus stops. Built at the beginning of the 20th century expressly as a hotel, this seven-story structure totters on the borderline between a government-rated two-star hotel and a three-star hotel, with very reasonable prices for a hostelry in that category. The lobby, with its rattan chairs and prints of animals from the savannah, has a vaguely African colonial aura. The bedrooms, with their warm, sunny colors, evoke Provence. About two-thirds of the rooms contain showers, the other one-third tubs; there are no shower-tub combos. Only the bedrooms on the sixth floor are air-conditioned. In honor of the hotel's namesake, the breakfast room is adorned with potted palms.

46 rue Brunel, 75017 Paris. ℂ **01-45-74-74-51**. Fax 01-45-74-40-90. www.hotelpalma-paris.com. 37 units. 95€–110€ ($109–$127) double. AE, MC, V. Métro: Argentine. RER: Neuilly–Porte Maillot. **Amenities:** Bar; laundry service; nonsmoking rooms; rooms for those with limited mobility. *In room:* A/C (in some), TV, dataport, hair dryer.

Hôtel Flaubert   For an inexpensive retreat in the 17th, this is as good as it gets. The staff long ago became accustomed to handling the problems their international guests might have. Terra-cotta tiles and bentwood furniture in the public areas make for an efficient if not lushly comfortable setting for breakfast. Though the climbing plants in the courtyard overshadow the guest rooms, the accommodations are appealing and, particularly those beneath the mansard's eaves, cozy. In 2000, management added about a dozen new rooms, thanks to the acquisition and refurbishment of a building next door. Throughout, rooms are modern, relatively small-scale, and comfortable. About half of the private bathrooms contain tubs, the others showers.

19 rue Rennequin, 75017 Paris. ℂ **01-46-22-44-35**. Fax 01-43-80-32-34. www.hotelflaubert.com. 49 units. 109€ ($125) double. AE, DC, MC, V. Métro: Ternes. **Amenities:** Limited room service (breakfast); garden. *In room:* TV, hair dryer.

2 On the Left Bank

We'll begin with the most centrally located arrondissements on the Left Bank, then work our way through the more outlying neighborhoods and to the area near the Eiffel Tower.

5TH ARRONDISSEMENT
MODERATE

Grand Hôtel Saint-Michel   Built in the 19th century, this hotel is larger and more businesslike than many town house–style inns nearby. It basks in the reflected glow of Brazilian dissident Georges Amado, whose memoirs recorded his 2-year sojourn in one of the rooms. In 1997, the hotel completed a renovation and moved from two- to three-star status. The public areas are tasteful, with portraits and rich upholsteries. All but four rooms have tub-shower combinations. The improvements enlarged some rooms, lowering their ceilings and adding amenities, but retained old-fashioned touches like wrought-iron balconies (on the fifth floor). Triple rooms have an extra bed and are suitable for families. Others have only shower, toilet, and sink. Sixth-floor rooms offer views over the rooftops.

19 rue Cujas, 75005 Paris. ℰ **01-46-33-33-02.** Fax 01-40-46-96-33. www.grand-hotel-st-michel.com. 46 units. 130€–170€ ($150–$196) double; 220€ ($253) triple. AE, DC, MC, V. Métro: Cluny–La Sorbonne. RER: Luxembourg or St-Michel. **Amenities:** Bar; limited room service (breakfast only); babysitting; laundry service/dry cleaning; nonsmoking rooms; rooms for those with limited mobility. *In room:* A/C, TV, dataport, minibar, hair dryer, safe.

Hôtel Abbatial Saint-Germain   The origins of this hotel run deep: Interior renovations have revealed such 17th-century touches as dovecotes and oak beams. In the early 1990s, a restoration made the public areas appealing and brought the small bedrooms, furnished in faux Louis XVI, up to modern standards. Bedrooms were again restored in 2001 and 2002. All the beds are fitted with immaculate linens. All windows are double-glazed, and the fifth- and sixth-floor units enjoy views over Notre-Dame. The neatly kept bathrooms are equipped with showers.

46 bd. St-Germain, 75005 Paris. ℰ **01-46-34-02-12.** Fax 01-43-25-47-73. www.abbatial.com. 43 units. 127€–150€ ($146–$173) double. AE, MC, V. Parking 19€ ($22). Métro: Cluny–La Sorbonne. **Amenities:** Limited room service; babysitting; laundry service/dry cleaning; nonsmoking rooms. *In room:* A/C, TV, dataport, minibar, hair dryer, safe.

Hôtel Agora St-Germain   One of the neighborhood's best moderately priced choices, this hotel occupies a building constructed in the early 1600s, probably to house a group of guardsmen protecting the brother of the king at his lodgings nearby. It's in the heart of artistic/historic Paris and offers compact, soundproof guest rooms that are not particularly fashionably furnished. All but seven of the bedrooms have tub-shower combos; the rest have only showers.

42 rue des Bernardins, 75005 Paris. ℰ **01-46-34-13-00.** Fax 01-46-34-75-05. www.sahuc-hotels.com/agora. 39 units. 134€–150€ ($154–$173) double. AE, DC, MC, V. Parking 20€ ($23). Métro: Maubert-Mutualité. **Amenities:** Limited room service (8am–noon); laundry service/dry cleaning. *In room:* A/C, TV, dataport, minibar, hair dryer, safe.

Hôtel des Jardins du Luxembourg   Built during Baron Haussmann's 19th-century overhaul of Paris, this hotel boasts an imposing facade of honey-colored stone accented with ornate iron balconies. The interior is outfitted in strong, clean lines, often with groupings of Art Deco furnishings. The high-ceilinged guest rooms, some with Provençal tiles and ornate moldings, are well maintained, the size ranging from small to medium. Best of all, they overlook a quiet dead-end alley, ensuring relatively peaceful nights. Some have balconies over-looking the rooftops. In 2000, the carpeting was replaced in all the bedrooms. Each unit comes with a neat, tidily arranged bathroom with a combined tub and shower.

5 impasse Royer-Collard, 75005 Paris. ℂ **01-40-46-08-88.** Fax 01-40-46-02-28. http://monsite.wanadoo.fr./ jardinslux. 25 units. 139€–149€ ($160–$171) double. AE, DC, MC, V. Parking 15€ ($17). Métro: Cluny–La Sorbonne. RER: Luxembourg. **Amenities:** Bar; sauna; limited room service; babysitting; laundry/dry cleaning; nonsmoking rooms; rooms for those with limited mobility. *In room:* A/C, TV, dataport, minibar, hair dryer, safe.

Hôtel Sully Saint-Germain ⭐

With its medieval-style decoration and its numerous and beautiful antiques, this is a winning choice with a bit of charm. A government-rated three-star hotel, it captures much of the spirit of the Quartier Latin in the St-Germain-des-Prés area in the heart of the Left Bank. At your doorstep are some of Paris's major attractions, including Notre-Dame, Cluny Abbey, the banks of the Seine, and even the Louvre and Orsay museums. The public rooms are not overly adorned, but are furnished with taste and comfort. The midsize bedrooms, with brass beds set against stone walls, are handsomely furnished and comfortable. They're not grand, but are imbued with Parisian charm.

31 rue des Ecoles, 75005 Paris. ℂ **01-43-26-56-02.** Fax 01-43-29-74-42. www.hotel-paris-sully.com. 61 units. 150€ ($173) double; 220€ ($253) triple. AE, DC, MC, V. Métro: Maubert-Mutualité. **Amenities:** Bar; fitness room; Jacuzzi; sauna/*hamman;* limited room service; laundry service/dry cleaning; nonsmoking rooms. *In room:* A/C, TV, dataport, minibar, hair dryer, safe.

La Tour Notre Dame ⭐

In the heart of the Sorbonne district, this restored Latin Quarter hotel rises seven floors over a 17th-century vaulted cellar where breakfast is served. A hotel of Rive Gauche character, it is ideally situated for Left Bank living, lying between St-German-des-Prés and the cathedral of Notre-Dame, opposite the Sorbonne and the Cluny Museum. Bedrooms, many with exposed beams, have been given a decorator's touch and are adorned with certain romantic accents, although the busy decor in a few rooms may be a bit off-putting to some. Liberty prints and Empire-era furniture decorate many of the bedrooms, which are beautifully maintained. Sixty percent of the bathrooms contain a shower, the rest bathtubs.

20 rue du Sommerard, 75005 Paris. ℂ **01-43-54-47-60.** Fax 01-43-26-42-34. www.tour-notre-dame.com. 48 units. 129€–169€ ($148–$194) double. AE, DC, MC, V. Métro: Cluny–Sorbonne. RER: Saint-Michel or Notre-Dame. **Amenities:** Bar; laundry service. *In room:* TV, minibar, hair dryer, safe.

Libertel Quartier Latin

Between the Sorbonne and the Musée de Cluny, this hotel captures the flavor of the Paris literati better than any other in Paris. It was conceived by Didier Gomez, who calls the decor "contemporary with cultural references." That means walls stenciled with passages from Victor Hugo or photographs of Colette or André Gide. Even the breakfast room is stocked with bookshelves and its ceiling inscribed with quotes from Baudelaire. Bibliomania continues in the lobby, which is filled with floor-to-ceiling bookcases. Bedrooms are comfortably and tastefully decorated in blue and white, with such delicacies as linen curtains along with fine wood furnishings, plus white-tiled bathrooms that are large and equipped with tub or shower. In all, this is a "novel" hotel and ideal for bookworms.

9 rue des Ecoles, 75005 Paris. ℂ **01-44-27-06-45.** Fax 01-43-25-36-70. www.libertel-hotels.com. 29 units. 149€–176€ ($171–$202) double. AE, MC, V. Métro: Cardinal Lemoine. **Amenities:** Limited room service; babysitting; laundry service/dry cleaning; nonsmoking rooms; rooms for those with limited mobility. *In room:* A/C, TV, dataport, minibar, hair dryer, safe.

Where to Stay on the Left Bank (5–6 & 13–14e)

INEXPENSIVE

Familia-Hôtel As the name implies, this is a hotel that has been family-run for decades. Many personal touches make the place unique. The walls of 14 rooms are graced with finely executed sepia-colored frescoes of Parisian scenes. Eight units have restored stone walls, and seven boast balconies with delightful views over the Latin Quarter. Half of the bathrooms come with tubs as well as showers. Thanks to a dynamic family ownership that likes to keep this place up and running, the bedrooms are renovated as often as needed to maintain a high level of comfort.

Apollon Montparnasse **2**
Best Western Aramis
   Saint-Germain **3**
Familia-Hôtel **32**
Grand Hôtel St-Michel **22**
Hôtel Abbatial St-Germain **30**
Hôtel Agora St-Germain **29**
Hôtel Bel-Ami **8**
Hôtel Clément **15**
Hôtel d'Aubusson **12**
Hôtel Delavigne **19**
Hôtel des Deux Continents **10**
Hôtel des Grandes Ecoles **31**
Hôtel des Jardins du
   Luxembourg **21**
Hôtel du Globe **16**
Hôtel du Parc-Montsouris **1**
Hôtel du Pas-de-Calais **6**
Hôtel du Vert Galant **35**
Hôtel La Manufacture **34**
Hôtel Le Sainte-Beuve **4**
Hôtel Louis II **17**
Hôtel Luxembourg Parc **5**
Hôtel Moderne St-Germain **28**
Hôtel Observatorie-
   Luxembourg **20**
Hôtel Résidence
   St-Christophe **33**
Hôtel St-Germain-des-Prés **7**
Hôtel Sully Saint-Germain **26**
La Tour Notre Dame **24**
La Villa **9**
Le Home Latin Hôtel **27**
L'Hôtel **11**
Libertel Quartier Latin **23**
Minerve Hôtel **25**
Odéon-Hôtel **18**
Regent's Hôtel **6**
Relais Christine **13**
Résidence des Arts **14**

11 rue des Ecoles, 75005 Paris. ✆ **01-43-54-55-27.** Fax 01-43-29-61-77. www.hotel-paris-familia.com. 30 units. 79€–109€ ($91–$125) double. AE, DC, MC, V. Métro: Jussieu or Maubert-Mutualité. **Amenities:** Car-rental desk; limited room service; nonsmoking rooms; rooms for those with limited mobility. *In room:* TV, minibar, hair dryer.

Home Latin Hôtel *(Value)* This is one of Paris's most famous budget hotels, known since the 1970s for its simple lodgings and lying only a 2-minute walk from the Luxembourg Gardens. The functional rooms were renovated in 1999; some have small balconies overlooking the street. Those facing the courtyard are quieter than those on the street. The elevator only goes to the fifth floor, but to make up for the stair climb, the sixth floor's *chambres mansardées* (attic rooms) offer a romantic location under the eaves and panoramic views. Forty-seven units come with a shower only; the rest have a tub-shower combo.

15–17 rue du Sommerard, 75005 Paris. ✆ 01-43-26-25-21. Fax 01-43-29-87-04. www.homelatinhotel.com. 54 units. 91€ ($105) double; 115€ ($132) triple; 131€ ($151) quad. AE, DC, MC, V. Métro: St-Michel or Maubert-Mutualité. **Amenities:** Breakfast lounge. *In room:* TV, hair dryer.

Hôtel des Grandes Ecoles (Value)   Few other hotels in the neighborhood offer so much low-key charm at such reasonable prices. It's composed of a trio of high-ceilinged buildings, interconnected via a sheltered courtyard where in warm weather singing birds provide a worthy substitute for the TVs deliberately missing from the rooms. Accommodations, as reflected by the price, range from snug, cozy doubles to more spacious chambers. All units were renovated in 2001, and the small bathrooms with showers were also spruced up. Each room is comfortable, but with a lot of luggage the very smallest would be cramped. The room decor is old-fashioned, with feminine touches such as Laura Ashley–inspired flowered upholsteries and ruffles. Many offer views of a garden whose trellises and flowerbeds evoke the countryside.

75 rue de Cardinal-Lemoine, 75005 Paris. ✆ 01-43-26-79-23. Fax 01-43-25-28-15. www.hotel-grandes-ecoles. com. 51 units. 100€–125€ ($115–$144) double. MC, V. Parking 30€ ($35). Métro: Cardinal Lemoine or Monge. **Amenities:** Limited room service; babysitting; garden; nonsmoking rooms; rooms for those with limited mobility. *In room:* Dataport, hair dryer.

Hôtel Moderne Saint-Germain ★   In the heart of the Latin Quarter, between the Pantheon and Saint-Michel, the Hôtel Moderne is better than ever since it ended the 20th century with a complete overhaul. Though the rooms are small, this is still one of the neighborhood's better three-star hotels. Its charming owner, Mme Gibon, welcomes guests to her spotless accommodations. In the units fronting rue des Ecoles, double-glazed windows hush the traffic. About half of the bathrooms have a tub as well as a shower. Guests can use the sauna and Jacuzzi at the Hôtel Sully next door.

33 rue des Ecoles, 75005 Paris. ✆ 01-43-54-37-78. Fax 01-43-29-91-31. www.hotel-paris-stgermain.com. 45 units. 90€–145€ ($104–$167) double; 150€–200€ ($173–$230) triple. AE, DC, MC, V. Parking 25€ ($29). Métro: Maubert-Mutualité. **Amenities:** Bar; limited room service; laundry service/dry cleaning; nonsmoking rooms. *In room:* A/C, TV, dataport, minibar, hair dryer.

Hôtel-Résidence Saint-Christophe   This hotel, in one of the Latin Quarter's undiscovered areas, offers a gracious English-speaking staff. It was created in 1987 when an older hotel was connected to a butcher shop. All the small- to medium-size rooms were renovated in 1998, with Louis XV–style furniture and carpeting. Half of the bathrooms have tubs in addition to showers.

17 rue Lacépède, 75005 Paris. ✆ 01-43-31-81-54. Fax 01-43-31-12-54. www.charm-hotel-paris.com. 31 units. 100€–125€ ($115–$144) double. AE, DC, MC, V. Métro: Place Monge. **Amenities:** Limited room service; nonsmoking rooms. *In room:* TV, dataport, minibar, hair dryer.

Minerve Hôtel   This is a well-managed, government-rated two-star hotel in the heart of the Latin Quarter, with good-size, comfortable rooms and a staff with a sense of humor. Bedrooms have contemporary-looking mahogany furniture and walls covered in fabric. Try for one of 10 rooms with balconies where you can look out over the street life of Paris, and in some cases enjoy a view of Notre-Dame. Depending on your room assignment, bathrooms range in dimension from cramped to midsize, each with a tub-and-shower combo. If there's no space at the Minerve, a staff member will arrange an equivalent (and equivalently priced) lodging in its sibling, the Familia, next door (see description above).

13 rue des Ecoles, 75005 Paris. © **01-43-26-26-04.** Fax 01-44-07-01-96. www.hotel-paris-minerve.com. 54 units. 96€–129€ ($110–$149) double. AE, MC, V. Métro: Cardinal Lemoine. **Amenities:** Limited room service; 1 room for those with limited mobility. *In room:* A/C, TV, dataport, hair dryer.

6TH ARRONDISSEMENT
VERY EXPENSIVE

Hotel Bel-Ami ★ *Finds*   Until around 2 years ago, this was a simple government-rated three-star hotel that was known by a different name (L'Alliance St-Germain). Beginning in 2002, the hotel was restored, floor by floor, to this four-star hotel, designed to appeal to fashion-conscious patrons, in the heart of the Left Bank cafe district. Its name translates as "handsome (male) friend." You'll get the feeling that this is an arts-conscious hotel whose minimalist public areas were built only after months of careful design by a team of trend-following architects. Expect color schemes of lilac walls, acid-green sofas, copper-colored tiles, bleached ash, and industrial-style lighting fixtures. Bedrooms contain a palette of earth tones, such as pistachio ice or pumpkin pie, and an almost aggressively minimalist, even Cubist, design. Bathrooms are artfully spartan, usually with shower-tub combinations. The hip and well-meaning staff sometimes gets overwhelmed by the ego-driven needs of the hotel's demanding clientele.

7–11 rue St. Benoît, 75006 Paris. © **01-42-61-53-53.** Fax 01-49-27-09-33. www.hotel-bel-ami.com. 115 units. 260€–380€ ($299–$437) double; 490€ ($564) suite. AE, DC, MC, V. Métro: St-Germain-des-Prés. **Amenities:** Snack bar; bar; espresso bar; limited room service; laundry service/dry cleaning; computer workstations with Internet access (in the lobby). *In room:* TV, dataport, minibar, safe.

Hôtel d'Aubusson ★★★   This mansion in the heart of St-Germain-des-Prés was the site of the city's first literary salon. Fully restored, it is today one of the best of the luxe boutique hotels of Paris. It's graced with original Aubusson tapestries. Lying 2 blocks south of Pont Neuf and the Seine, the hotel has taken over a former private residence from the 1600s, to which is attached a 1950s building. It opens onto a beautiful courtyard. You enter a grand hall under a beamed ceiling with a baronial fireplace and furnishings in the style of Louis XV. There are also a number of smaller, more intimate lounges. The bedrooms are midsize to large, each attractively and comfortably furnished, often in a Directoire style. Antiques are often placed in front of the original stone walls. For the most traditional flair, ask for one of the rooms on the top two floors. The best units are labeled deluxe, and these are quite large and graced with canopied beds.

33 rue Dauphine, Paris 75006. © **01-43-29-43-43.** Fax 01-43-29-12-62. www.hoteldaubusson.com. 50 units. 260€–410€ ($299–$472) double. AE, MC, V. Parking: 25€ ($29). Métro: Odéon. **Amenities:** Bar; cafe; limited room service; babysitting; laundry service/dry cleaning; nonsmoking rooms; rooms for those with limited mobility. *In room:* A/C, TV, dataport, minibar, hair dryer, safe.

L'Hôtel ★   Ranking just a notch below the Relais Christine, this is one of the Left Bank's most charming boutique hotels. It was once a 19th-century fleabag whose major distinction was that Oscar Wilde died here. But today's guests aren't anywhere near poverty row. The guest rooms vary in size, style, and price, from small to deluxe, but all have nonworking fireplaces and fabric-covered walls. One spacious room contains the furnishings and memorabilia of stage star Mistinguett. Her pedestal bed is in the middle of the room, surrounded by mirrors, as she liked to see how she looked at all times. In 2000, aesthetic superstar Jacques Garcia redecorated this hotel and he retained its Victorian-baroque sense, but outfitted each room differently. Expect to be lodged amid themes that reflect China, Russia, Japan, India, or high-camp Victorian. The Cardinal room is all scarlet, the *Viollet-le-Duc* room is neo-Gothic, and the room where Wilde died is stately looking, Victorian, respectful, and nostalgia-laden. They installed a small swimming pool and *hamman* (steam bath) in the cellar, renovated the bar (see chapter 10, "Paris After Dark"), and revitalized the restaurant. About half the bathrooms are small, tubless nooks. All the sumptuous beds have tasteful fabrics and crisp linens.

13 rue des Beaux-Arts, 75006 Paris. ℂ **01-44-41-99-00.** Fax 01-43-25-64-81. www.l-hotel.com. 20 units. 248€–721€ ($285–$829) double; from 721€ ($829) suite. AE, DC, MC, V. Métro: St-Germain-des-Prés. **Amenities:** Restaurant; bar; indoor pool; steam room; limited room service; babysitting; laundry service/dry cleaning. *In room:* A/C, TV, dataport, minibar, hair dryer, safe.

Relais Christine ★★   This hotel welcomes you into what was a 16th-century Augustinian cloister. Enter from a cobblestone street into a symmetrical courtyard and find an elegant reception area with sculpture and Renaissance antiques. Each room is uniquely decorated with wooden beams and Louis XIII-style furnishings; the rooms come in a range of styles and shapes, and some are among the Left Bank's largest, with extras like mirrored closets, plush carpets, thermostats, and some balconies facing the courtyard. The least attractive rooms are those in the interior. Each comes with a tub and shower. Bed configurations vary but all are on the soft side, offering comfort with quality linens.

3 rue Christine, 75006 Paris. ℂ **01-40-51-60-80.** Fax 01-40-51-60-81. www.relais-christine.com. 51 units. 335€–430€ ($385–$495) double; 480€–730€ ($552–$840) duplex or suite. AE, DC, MC, V. Free parking. Métro: Odéon or St-Michel. **Amenities:** Honor bar in lobby; gym; 24-hr. room service; massage; babysitting; laundry service/dry cleaning; nonsmoking rooms. *In room:* A/C, TV, dataport, minibar, hair dryer, iron/board, safe.

EXPENSIVE

Hôtel de Fleurie ★ *Kids*   Off boulevard St-Germain on a colorful little street, the Fleurie is one of the best of the "new" old hotels; its statuary-studded facade recaptures a 17th-century elegance, and the stone walls have been exposed in the salon. All the bedrooms have been recently renovated. Many have elaborate draperies and antique reproductions. Some of the rooms have tub-and-shower combinations, others a full bathroom except for a tub (shower stalls instead). Because some of the rooms are larger than others and contain an extra bed for one or two children, the hotel has long been a family favorite.

32–34 rue Grégoire-de-Tours, 75006 Paris. ℂ **01-53-73-70-00.** Fax 01-53-73-70-20. www.hotel-de-fleurie.tm.fr. 29 units. 165€–185€ ($190–$213) double; 290€–325€ ($334–$374) family room. Children 12 and under stay free in parent's room. AE, DC, MC, V. Métro: Odéon or Mabillon. **Amenities:** Bar; car rental; limited room service (breakfast only); babysitting; laundry service/dry cleaning; rooms for those with limited mobility. *In room:* A/C, TV, dataport, minibar, hair dryer, safe.

Hôtel de l'Abbaye ★   This boutique hotel—a convent in the early 18th century—is one of the district's most charming. Its brightly colored rooms have traditional furniture, plus touches of sophisticated flair. In front is a small garden and in back a verdant courtyard with a fountain, raised flowerbeds, and masses of ivy and climbing vines. If you don't mind the expense, one of the most charming rooms has a terrace overlooking the upper floors of neighboring buildings. Bedrooms come with tiled, full bathrooms. Suites are generous in size and full of Left Bank charm, often with antique reproductions.

10 rue Cassette, 75006 Paris. ℂ **01-45-44-38-11.** Fax 01-45-48-07-86. www.hotel-abbaye.com. 46 units. 190€–283€ ($219–$325) double; 390€–438€ ($449–$504) suite. Rates include breakfast. AE, MC, V. Métro: St-Sulpice. **Amenities:** Bar; limited room service; laundry service/dry cleaning; garden. *In room:* A/C, TV, dataport, minibar, hair dryer, safe.

Hôtel Le Sainte-Beuve ★ *Finds*   Lying off the tree-lined boulevard Raspail, this Montparnasse choice is close to the "Lost Generation" cafes made famous

in the pages of Ernest Hemingway's *The Sun Also Rises*. The famous English decorator, David Hicks, had a hand in the stylish decor. If you stay here, you're just
3 minutes from the Luxembourg gardens. You enter a small reception area opening into a Georgian parlor with plush sofas, armchairs, and columns, even a
marble fireplace for those nippy Paris nights. Bedrooms are often furnished in
part with antiques but have all the modern comforts. Some come with small sitting rooms; all have marble bathrooms equipped with everything from deluxe
toiletries to makeup mirrors. The cheaper rooms are small. If you can afford it,
ask for one of the deluxe units, which also have love seats and safes.

9 rue Ste-Beuve, 75006 Paris. © 01-45-48-20-07. Fax 01-45-48-67-52. www.hotel-sainte-beuve.fr. 22 units.
130€–230€ ($150–$265) double; 325€ ($374) suite. AE, DC, MC, V. Métro: Notre-Dame-des-Champs.
Amenities: Bar; limited room service; babysitting; laundry service/dry cleaning. *In room:* A/C, TV, dataport,
minibar, hair dryer, safe.

Hôtel Luxembourg Parc ★★   Near the Luxembourg Gardens for those
lovely strolls, this elegant bastion of fine living has been called a small scale version of the swank Hôtel de Crillon. In one of the Left Bank's most charming and
historic districts, a 17th-century palace has been beautifully restored and decorated. The bedrooms are decorated in the styles of Louis XV, Louis XVI, and
Napoleon III. The bar is an elegant rendezvous point, and the library is relaxing. Bathrooms are generous in size, and units contain such thoughtful touches
as bathrobes and plenty of hangers. The around-the-clock room service is actually takeout from nearby restaurants. The breakfast room on the ground floor
overlooks the Luxembourg Gardens.

42 rue de Vaugirad, 75006 Paris. © 01-53-10-36-50. Fax 01-53-10-36-59. www.luxembourg-paris-hotel.
com. 23 units. 200€–475€ ($230–$546) double. AE, DC, MC, V. Métro: Luxembourg. **Amenities:** Restaurant;
bar; fitness center; 24-hr. room service; laundry service; units for those with limited mobility. *In room:* A/C, TV,
dataport, minibar, hair dryer, safe.

La Villa ★   This hotel's facade resembles those of many of the other buildings
in the neighborhood. Inside, however, the decor is a minimalist ultramodern
creation rejecting all traditional French aesthetics. The public areas and guest
rooms contain Bauhaus-like furniture; the lobby's angular lines are softened with
bouquets of leaves and flowers. Most unusual are the baths, whose stainless steel
and pink, black, or beige marble are decidedly postmodern. Everything was renovated in 2000, and all but four units contain a complete tub and shower.

29 rue Jacob, 75006 Paris. © 01-43-26-60-00. Fax 01-46-34-63-63. www.villa-saintgermain.com. 31 units.
240€ ($276) double; 440€ ($506) suite. AE, DC, MC, V. Métro: St-Germain-des-Prés. **Amenities:** Bar; limited
room service; babysitting; rooms for those with limited mobility. *In room:* A/C, TV, dataport, minibar, hair dryer,
safe.

Odéon Hôtel ★   Reminiscent of a modernized Norman country inn, the
Odéon offers rustic touches like exposed beams, stone walls, high ceilings, and
tapestries mixed with contemporary fabrics, mirrored ceilings, and black leather
furnishings. Near the Théâtre de l'Odéon and boulevard St-Germain, the
Odéon stands on the first paved street in Paris (1779). By the 20th century, this
area began attracting such writers as Gertrude Stein and her coterie. The guest
rooms are small to medium but charming, and each comes with a combo tub
and shower. The beds are excellent, with reading lamps and bedside controls.

3 rue de l'Odéon, 75006 Paris. © 01-43-25-90-67. Fax 01-43-25-55-98. www.odeonhotel.fr. 33 units.
160€–270€ ($184–$311) double. AE, DC, MC, V. Métro: Odéon. **Amenities:** Bar; limited room service;
babysitting; laundry service/dry cleaning; nonsmoking rooms. *In room:* A/C, TV, dataport, hair dryer, safe.

MODERATE

Best Western Aramis Saint-Germain Between St-Germain-des-Prés and Montparnasse, this is a recently renovated hotel that is attractively modernized and gracefully comfortable. Individually decorated bedrooms are midsize and furnished in a sleek, modern fashion, each with a private tiled bathroom with tub and shower. Nine of the bedrooms also contain a private Jacuzzi, and rooms are also soundproofed. The English-speaking staff is helpful.

124 rue de Rennes, 75006 Paris. ℘ **800/528-1234** in the U.S., or 01-45-48-03-75. Fax 01-45-44-99-29. www.hotel-aramis.com. 42 units. 95€–190€ ($109–$219) double; 160€–220€ ($184–$253) triple. Rooms with Jacuzzi 15€ ($17) extra. AE, DC, MC, V. Métro: Rennes or Sainte Placido. **Amenities:** Private bar; babysitting; laundry service/dry cleaning. *In room:* A/C, TV, dataport, minibar, coffeemaker, hair dryer, safe.

Hôtel des Deux Continents Built from three interconnected historic buildings, each between three and six stories high, this hotel is a reliable choice with a sense of Latin Quarter style. The carefully coordinated guest rooms range from small to medium size and include reproductions of antique furnishings and soundproof upholstered walls. Each is equipped with a neatly tiled shower bathroom, a third of which also offer tubs.

25 rue Jacob, 75006 Paris. ℘ **01-43-26-72-46.** Fax 01-43-25-67-80. www.2continents-hotel.com. 41 units. 145€–158€ ($167–$182) double; 193€ ($222) triple. MC, V. Métro: St-Germain-des-Prés. *In room:* A/C, TV, dataport, hair dryer.

Hôtel du Pas-de-Calais The Pas-de-Calais goes back to the 17th century. Its elegant facade, with wooden doors, has been retained. Novelist Chateaubriand lived here from 1811 to 1814, but its most famous guest was Jean-Paul Sartre, who struggled with the play *Les Mains Sales* (Dirty Hands) in room no. 41. The hotel is a bit weak on style, but as one longtime guest confided, despite the updates, "We still stay here for the memories." Inner rooms surround a courtyard with two garden tables and several trellises. Each bathroom has a tub and shower.

59 rue des Sts-Pères, 75006 Paris. ℘ **01-45-48-78-74.** Fax 01-45-44-94-57. 40 units. 150€–214€ ($173–$246) double; 275€ ($316) suite. AE, DC, MC, V. Parking 20€ ($23). Métro: St-Germain-des-Prés or Sèvres-Babylone. **Amenities:** Bar; limited room service; babysitting; laundry service/dry cleaning; nonsmoking rooms; rooms for those with limited mobility. *In room:* A/C, TV, hair dryer, safe.

Hôtel Louis II In an 18th-century building, this hotel offers guest rooms decorated in rustic French tones. Afternoon drinks and morning coffee are served in the reception salon, where gilt-framed mirrors, fresh flowers, and antiques radiate a provincial aura, like something out of Proust. The generally small, soundproof rooms with exposed beams and lace bedding complete the impression. Many visitors ask for the romantic attic rooms. In 2000, the hotel's public and private spaces were upgraded into cozy, nostalgically decorated areas that evoke the charm of a 19th-century private home, replete with flowered fabrics and a sense of the cozy country life. About half of the rooms contain bathtubs, the rest showers.

2 rue St-Sulpice, 75006 Paris. ℘ **01-46-33-13-80.** Fax 01-46-33-17-29. www.hotel-louis2.com. 22 units. 120€–135€ ($138–$155) double; 185€–230€ ($213–$265) triple. AE, DC, MC, V. Métro: Odéon. **Amenities:** Limited room service; laundry service/dry cleaning. *In room:* A/C (in some), TV, dataport, minibar, hair dryer, safe.

Hôtel St-Germain-des-Prés Most of this hotel's attraction comes from its location in the Latin Quarter, behind a well-known Left Bank street. Janet Flanner, the legendary 1920s *New Yorker* correspondent, lived here for a while. Renovated in 1999, the guest rooms are small but charming, with antique ceiling beams and safes; air-conditioning is available in most. The public areas are severely elegant. Most of the bathrooms contain tubs, and all come with showers.

36 rue Bonaparte, 75006 Paris. © **01-43-26-00-19.** Fax 01-40-46-83-63. 30 units. 160€–255€ ($184–$293) double; 310€ ($357) suite. Rates include breakfast. AE, MC, V. Métro: St-Germain-des-Prés. **Amenities:** Room service (breakfast only); babysitting; laundry service/dry cleaning. *In room:* A/C, TV, dataport, minibar, hair dryer, safe.

Résidence des Arts ⭐   A converted 1550 residence, this winner is filled with handsomely decorated suites, studios, and apartments in the heart of the Latin Quarter. The structure was an apartment building until the mid-1990s, and two additional floors were added when it opened for business in 1998. Regular doubles are rented with shower-only bathrooms. Each suite and apartment offers a large sitting room with a hide-a-bed, and a separate bedroom with a king-size bed. Suites and apartments have full bathrooms with tubs and showers, and each apartment comes with a kitchenette. The furnishings are tasteful and comfortable, and the service first-rate. A bistro and restaurant are connected to the hotel.

14 rue Git-le-Coeur, 75006 Paris. © **01-55-42-71-11.** Fax 01-55-42-71-00. www.arts-residence-paris.com. 11 units. 180€ ($207) double; 280€ ($322) suite for 2–4; 285€–320€ ($328–$368) apt for 2–4; 380€–420€ ($437–$483) apt for 4–6. AE, MC, V. Métro: St-Michel. **Amenities:** Restaurant; bar; 24-hr. room service; babysitting; laundry service/dry cleaning; nonsmoking rooms. *In room:* A/C, TV, dataport, minibar, hair dryer, safe.

INEXPENSIVE

Hôtel Delavigne   Despite modernization, you still get a sense of the building's 18th-century origins, next to the Luxembourg Gardens. The public areas feature a rustic use of chiseled stone, some of it original. The high-ceilinged guest rooms are tasteful, sometimes with wooden furniture, often with upholstered headboards, and sometimes with Spanish-style wrought iron. All of the bathrooms except four have both a tub and shower.

1 rue Casimir-Delavigne, 75006 Paris. © **01-43-29-31-50.** Fax 01-43-29-78-56. www.hoteldelavigne.com. 34 units. 85€–130€ ($98–$150) double; 130€–145€ ($150–$167) triple. MC, V. Métro: Odéon. **Amenities:** Limited room service; babysitting; laundry service/dry cleaning. *In room:* TV, dataport, hair dryer, safe.

Hôtel du Globe   This 17th-century building is on an evocative street; inside you'll find most of the original stonework and dozens of original timbers and beams. There's no elevator (and a very narrow antique staircase) and no breakfast area (trays are brought to your room). Each guest room is decorated with old-fashioned flair. The rooms with tubs are almost twice as large as those with shower stalls. The largest and most desirable are nos. 1, 12 (with a baldachin-style bed), 14, 15, and 16. The room without a bathroom is a single that goes for 50€ ($58).

15 rue des Quatre-Vents, 75006 Paris. © **01-46-26-35-50.** Fax 01-46-33-62-69. 15 units. 70€–105€ ($81–$121) double. MC, V. Closed Aug. Métro: Mabillon, Odéon, or St-Sulpice. **Amenities:** Limited room service. *In room:* TV.

Hôtel Le Clément   This hotel sits on a narrow street within sight of the towers of St-Sulpice church. The building dates to the 1700s, but was renovated several years ago. Guest rooms are comfortably furnished but often small, although in 2000 some walls in the smaller rooms were knocked down, creating larger units. Most of the bathrooms contain tubs; two have shower-only bathrooms.

6 rue Clément, 75006 Paris. © **01-43-26-53-60.** Fax 01-44-07-06-83. www.hotel-clement.com. 28 units. 117€–127€ ($135–$146) double; 127€–145€ ($146–$167) suite. AE, DC, V. Métro: Mabillon. **Amenities:** Bar; limited room service. *In room:* A/C, TV, hair dryer, safe.

Regent's Hôtel *Value*   In the heart of St-Germain-des-Prés, this is a smart Left Bank address. You'll find it in a neighborhood of tony boutiques and fashionable hair salons, and just a short walk over to the Jardin du Luxembourg, where Hemingway strolled as a poor struggling artist looking for a pigeon to kill for his dinner. This is a high-quality choice at reasonable prices, considering its location. Inside, carved-wood headboards, fluffy yellow bedspreads, and flower boxes in the windows evoke sunny Provence. We prefer the rooms on the top floor with their slender balconies overlooking Paris rooftops. All the furnishings are comfortable, and the bathrooms with tub and shower are completely restored. Some rooms open onto a secluded courtyard where breakfast is served if the weather behaves. A few rooms are big enough to accommodate a family of four.

44 rue Madame, 75006 Paris. (C) 01-45-48-02-81. Fax 01-45-44-85-73. www.france-hotel-guide.com. 34 units. 80€–110€ ($92–$127) double. AE, MC, V. Métro: Rennes or St-Sulpice. **Amenities:** Limited room service; rooms for those with limited mobility. *In room:* TV, dataport, hair dryer.

13TH ARRONDISSEMENT
MODERATE

Hôtel La Manufacture (★) (Finds) If you don't mind its offbeat 13th arrondissement location, this undiscovered hotel with good rooms and decent prices lying on a small street near place d'Italie is a real find. It is only 10 minutes by Métro from the stations at Montparnasse and Gare de Lyon. Small to midsize bedrooms are decorated in printed fabrics and soothing pastels, and the large bathrooms are spotlessly maintained, each with a shower. The most desirable room is no. 74 because of its distant views of the Eiffel Tower. This restored 19th-century building has a wrought-iron door and is graced with iron lamps, wicker chairs, oak floors, and bright paintings. It contains a number of old-fashioned armoires called *chapeau de gendarme* (police hat). The staff is one of the most helpful we've discovered in our tours of Paris's small hotels. Each day the staff serves a different set of pastries.

8 rue Philippe de Champagne (av. des Gobelins), 75013 Paris. (C) 01-45-35-45-25. Fax 01-45-35-45-40. www.hotel-la-manufacture.com. 57 units. 139€ ($160) double; 217€–239€ ($250–$275) suite. AE, DC, MC, V. Métro: Place d'Italie. **Amenities:** Bar; breakfast room; limited room service; babysitting; laundry service/dry cleaning; nonsmoking rooms. *In room:* A/C, TV, dataport, hair dryer, iron/board.

INEXPENSIVE

Hôtel du Vert Galant—Verdant climbing plants and shrubs make this hotel feel like an *auberge* deep in the French countryside. The smallish guest rooms have tiled or carpeted floors, unfussy furniture, and (in most cases) views of the garden or the public park across the street. All bathrooms have showers and nearly three-fourths of them also contain tubs. One of the place's best aspects is the Basque inn next door, the Auberge Etchegorry, sharing the same management; hotel guests receive a discount.

41 rue Croulebarbe, 75013 Paris. (C) 01-44-08-83-50. Fax 01-44-08-83-69. 15 units. 90€ ($104) double. AE, DC, MC, V. Parking 10€ ($12). Métro: Corvisart or Gobelins. **Amenities:** Restaurant; limited room service; laundry service/dry cleaning. *In room:* TV, dataport, minibar, hair dryer, safe.

14TH ARRONDISSEMENT
INEXPENSIVE

Apollon Montparnasse This privately owned hotel lies in Montparnasse, former home of such Left Bank residents as Gertrude Stein and Alice B. Toklas. Since opening, the hotel has established a reputation for its good rates and very comfortable bedrooms, which are midsize and furnished with flower spreads and draperies, each with a well-maintained bathroom with tub or shower.

91 rue de l'Ouest, 75014 Paris. (C) 01-43-95-62-00. Fax 01-43-95-62-10. www.apollon-montparnasse.com. 33 units. 79€–84€ ($91–$97) double; 99€ ($114) triple. AE, DC, MC, V. Métro: Pernety. **Amenities:** Breakfast lounge; limited room service. *In room:* TV, dataport, minibar, hair dryer, safe.

Hôtel du Parc-Montsouris   The residential neighborhood is far removed from central Paris's bustle, the staff is a bit absent-minded, and the decor doesn't pretend to be stylish, but the prices are reasonable enough that this government-rated two-star hotel (a simple structure built in the 1930s) attracts loyal repeat guests; they might be parents of students studying at the nearby Cité Universitaire or provincial clothiers attending fashion shows at the nearby Porte de Versailles. The guest rooms are low-key and quiet, each renovated in the late 1990s. Singles and doubles are small, but the triples are spacious, the suites even more so. Bathrooms contain tubs and showers, except for the seven with showers only.

4 rue du Parc de Montsouris, 75014 Paris. © **01-45-89-09-72.** Fax 01-45-80-92-72. www.hotel-parc-montsouris.com. 35 units. 70€ ($81) double; 79€ ($91) triple; 96€ ($110) suite. AE, MC, V. Métro: Porte d'Orléans. RER: Cité-Universitaire. **Amenities:** Limited room service; laundry service/dry cleaning. *In room:* TV, dataport.

7TH ARRONDISSEMENT
VERY EXPENSIVE

Hôtel Montalembert ★★   Unusually elegant for the Left Bank, the Montalembert dates from 1926 when it was built in the beaux arts style. Its beige, cream, and gold decor borrows elements of Bauhaus and postmodern design. The guest rooms are spacious, except for some standard doubles, which are small unless you're a very thin model. Frette linens decorate roomy beds topped with cabana-stripe duvets crowning deluxe French mattresses. The bathrooms are luxurious with deep tubs, Cascais marble, and tall pivoting mirrors.

3 rue de Montalembert, 75007 Paris. © **800/786-6397** in the U.S. and Canada, or 01-45-49-68-68. Fax 01-45-49-69-49. www.montalembert.com. 56 units. 340€–430€ ($391–$495) double; 560€–750€ ($644–$863) suite. AE, DC, MC, V. Parking 25€ ($29). Métro: Rue du Bac. **Amenities:** Restaurant; bar; privileges at nearby health club; 24-hr. room service; laundry service/dry cleaning. *In room:* A/C, TV, dataport, minibar, hair dryer, safe.

EXPENSIVE

Bourgogne & Montana   Across from the Palais Bourbon and just 2 blocks from the Seine, this boutique hotel resides in the same tony neighborhood as fashion designer Karl Lagerfeld and the former prime minister, Lionel Jospin. It is only a short walk to the landmark place du Palais-Bourbon and the boulevard St-Germain. A six-floor hotel, the building itself dates from 1791. Many of the bedrooms open onto the Grand Palais or the Assemblée Nationale, and from some windows you can see all the way down to the place de la Concorde. A cage elevator from 1924 takes visitors to the accommodations, which are midsize for the most part, although some are small and have no view whatsoever. Each room is individually decorated, often with Empire or Empire reproductions, and all contain tiled bathrooms, which, though small, are equipped with bathtubs and showers. The lounge is also small, but there's a marble-topped bar. Rollet Pradier, one of the city's best *patisseries*, lies just across the street.

3 rue de Bourgogne, 75007 Paris. © **01-45-51-20-22.** Fax 01-45-56-11-98. www.bourgogne-montana.com. 32 units. 160€–200€ ($184–$230) double; 230€–305€ ($265–$351) suite. Rates include breakfast. AE, DC, MC, V. Métro: Invalides. **Amenities:** Bar; limited room service; babysitting; laundry service/dry cleaning. *In room:* A/C, TV, dataport, minibar, hair dryer.

Hôtel de l'Académie ★★   The exterior walls and old ceiling beams are all that remain of this 18th-century residence of the duc de Rohan's private guards. Other than its Renaissance origins and associations with the duc de Rohan, this place is locally famous for having housed poet and novelist Antonio Machado, "the Victor Hugo of Spain," between 1909 and 1914. In 1999, the hotel was completely renovated to include an elegant reception area. The up-to-date guest rooms have a lush Ile-de-France decor and views over the neighborhood's 18th- and 19th-century buildings. By American standards the rooms are small, but they're average for Paris. All but eight bathrooms have full tub-shower combos.

32 rue des Sts-Pères, 75007 Paris. © 800/246-0041 in the U.S. and Canada, or 01-45-49-80-00. Fax 01-45-44-75-24. www.academiehotel.com. 33 units. 199€–229€ ($229–$263) double; 299€–458€ ($344–$527) suite. AE, DC, MC, V. Parking 23€ ($26). Métro: St-Germain-des-Prés. **Amenities:** Limited room service (7am–11pm); babysitting; laundry service/dry cleaning; nonsmoking rooms. *In room:* A/C, TV, dataport, minibar, hair dryer, safe.

Hôtel de l'Université ✪   Long favored by well-heeled parents of North American students studying in Paris, this 300-year-old, antiques-filled town house enjoys a location in a discreetly upscale neighborhood. Room no. 54 is a favorite, containing a rattan bed and period pieces. Another charmer is room no. 35, which has a fireplace and opens onto a courtyard with a fountain. The most expensive unit has a small terrace overlooking the surrounding rooftops. Each unit comes with a well-maintained bathroom equipped with a shower-tub combination. Beds have plush comfort and discreet French styling. You'll sleep well here.

22 rue de l'Université, 75007 Paris. © 01-42-61-09-39. Fax 01-42-60-40-84. www.hoteluniversite.com. 27 units. 160€–205€ ($184–$236) double. AE, DC, MC, V. Métro: St-Germain-des-Prés. **Amenities:** Limited room service. *In room:* A/C, TV, dataport, minibar, hair dryer, safe.

Hôtel Le Tourville ✪   This is a well-managed, personalized town house between the Eiffel Tower and Les Invalides. It originated in the 1930s as a hotel, and was revitalized much later into the charmer of today. Bedrooms offer original art, antique furnishings or reproductions, and wooden furniture covered in modern, sometimes bold, upholsteries. Four of the rooms, including the suite, have private terraces. Beds are queens or twins, each of which was recently renewed. About half of the well-maintained bathrooms have shower-tub combinations. The staff is well trained, with the kind of personalities that make you want to linger at the reception desk. Breakfast is the only meal served, but you can get a drink in the lobby.

16 av. de Tourville, 75007 Paris. © 01-47-05-62-62. Fax 01-47-05-43-90. www.hoteltourville.com. 30 units. 150€–310€ ($173–$357) double; 310€ ($357) suite. AE, DC, MC, V. Métro: Ecole Militaire. **Amenities:** Bar; limited room service; massage; laundry service/dry cleaning; nonsmoking rooms; rooms for those with limited mobility. *In room:* A/C, TV, dataport, hair dryer.

Hôtel Verneuil ✪ *Finds*   Small-scale and personal, this hotel, in the words of a recent critic, "combines modernist sympathies with nostalgia for *la vieille France* (old-fashioned France)." Within what was built in the 1600s as a town house, it offers a creative and intimate jumble of charm and coziness. Expect a mixture of antique and contemporary furniture, lots of books, and, in the bedrooms, *trompe l'oeil* ceilings, antique beams, quilts, and walls covered in fabric that comes in a rainbow of colors. The well-kept bathrooms come with shower-tub combinations.

8 rue de Verneuil,.75007 Paris. © 01-42-60-82-14. Fax 01-42-61-40-38. www.hotelverneuil.com. 26 units. 145€–190€ ($167–$219) double. AE, DC, MC, V. Métro: St-Germain-des-Prés. **Amenities:** Bar; limited room service; babysitting; laundry service/dry cleaning. *In room:* A/C (in some), TV, dataport, minibar, hair dryer, safe.

MODERATE

Best Western Hôtel Derby Eiffel   Upgraded in 2001, this hotel faces the Ecole Militaire and contains airy public areas. Our favorite is a glass-roofed conservatory in back, filled year-round with plants and used as a breakfast area. The soundproof and modern guest rooms employ thick fabrics and soothing neutral

Best Western Hôtel Derby Eiffel **5**
Bourgogne & Montana **7**
Grand Hôtel L'Eveque **3**
Hôtel à l' Eiffel Rive Gauche **2**
Hôtel de l'Académie **11**
Hôtel de l'Université **10**
Hôtel de Nevers **13**
Hôtel du Palais Bourbon **6**
Hôtel du Quai-Voltaire **9**
Hôtel Le Tourville **4**
Hôtel Lindbergh **14**
Hôtel Montalembert **12**
Hôtel Saint-Dominique **1**
Hôtel Verneuil **8**

colors. Most front-facing rooms offer views of the Eiffel Tower. In 1998, enormous sums were spent upgrading the rooms and bathrooms and improving the hotel's interior aesthetics. All bathrooms have showers and half tubs.

5 av. Duquesne, 75007 Paris. **℗** **800/528-1234** in the U.S. and Canada, or 01-47-05-12-05. Fax 01-47-05-43-43. 43 units. 135€–180€ ($155–$207) double; 165€–196€ ($190–$225) triple; 190€–229€ ($219–$263) suite. AE, DC, MC, V. Métro: Ecole Militaire. **Amenities:** Limited room service; babysitting; laundry service/dry cleaning; nonsmoking rooms. *In room:* A/C, TV, dataport, minibar, hair dryer, safe.

INEXPENSIVE

Grand Hôtel L'Eveque   Built in the 1930s, this hotel draws lots of English-speaking guests, many of whom appreciate its proximity to the Eiffel Tower. The pastel-colored guest rooms retain an Art Deco inspiration, just enough space to be comfortable, and double-insulated windows overlooking a courtyard in back or the street in front. Suites are only slightly larger than double rooms, and are no better than the standard. The small bathrooms contain shower units.

29 rue Cler, 75007 Paris. **℗** **01-47-05-49-15.** Fax 01-45-50-49-36. www.hotel-leveque.com. 50 units. 86€–106€ ($99–$122) double. AE, MC, V. Métro: Ecole Militaire. *In room:* A/C, TV, dataport, hair dryer, safe.

Hôtel à l'Eiffel Rive Gauche   The charm of this family-owned and run intimate hotel derives from a very small on-site team and the sense that you've entered a distinctive universe that's very closely linked to the upscale residential neighborhood that surrounds you. Originally built around 1900, the hotel retains such original touches as the black-and-white, checkerboard-patterned floor tiles from the 1930s. Bedrooms are outfitted in tones of off-white and dark Bordeaux, with vaguely French Empire themes scattered with some angular furniture from the 1960s and 1970s. The hotel lies on a tranquil street in the heart of the so-called "Triangle" (Eiffel, Invalides, and Champs-Elysées).

6 rue du Gros Caillou, 75007 Paris. **℗** **01-45-51-24-56.** Fax 01-45-51-11-77. www.hotel-eiffel.com. 29 units. 79€–95€ ($91–$109) double. MC, V. Métro: Ecole-Militaire. **Amenities:** Laundry service. *In room:* TV, dataport, hair dryer.

Hôtel de Nevers   This is one of the neighborhood's most historic choices—it was a convent from 1627 to 1790. In 2000, many aspects were upgraded and renovated. The building is *classé*, meaning any restoration must respect the original architecture. That precludes an elevator, so you'll have to use the beautiful wrought-iron staircase. The cozy, pleasant guest rooms contain a mix of antique and reproduction furniture. Room nos. 10 and 11 are especially sought after for their terraces overlooking a corner of rue du Bac or a rear courtyard. About half of the units have shower-tub combination bathrooms.

83 rue du Bac, 75007 Paris. **℗** **01-45-44-61-30.** Fax 01-42-22-29-47. 11 units. 70€–83€ ($81–$95) double. No credit cards. Métro: Rue du Bac. **Amenities:** Limited room service. *In room:* TV, dataport, minibar, hair dryer.

Hôtel du Palais Bourbon   The solid stone walls of this 18th-century building aren't as grand as those of the embassies and stately homes nearby. But don't be put off by the tight entranceway and rather dark halls: Though the guest rooms on the upper floors are larger, all the rooms are pleasantly decorated, with carefully crafted built-in furniture. Each bathroom contains both a tub and a shower.

49 rue de Bourgogne, 75007 Paris. **℗** **01-44-11-30-70.** Fax 01-45-55-20-21. www.hotel-palais-bourbon.com. 30 units. 120€ ($138) double; 140€ ($161) triple; 155€ ($178) quad. Rate includes breakfast. MC, V. Métro: Varenne. **Amenities:** Limited room service (7–10am); nonsmoking rooms. *In room:* A/C, TV, dataport, minibar, hair dryer, safe.

Hôtel du Quai Voltaire   Built in the 1600s as an abbey, then transformed into a hotel in 1856, the Quai Voltaire is best known for its illustrious guests, like Wilde, Richard Wagner, and Baudelaire, who occupied room nos. 47, 55, and 56, respectively. Camille Pissarro painted Le Pont Royal from the window of his fourth-floor room. Many guest rooms in this modest inn have been renovated; most overlook the bookstalls and boats of the Seine. Each unit comes with a tub-and-shower bathroom, except for five that have a shower only.

19 quai Voltaire, 75007 Paris. ℭ **01-42-61-50-91**. Fax 01-42-61-62-26. www.quaivoltaire.fr. 33 units. 118€–125€ ($136–$144) double. AE, DC, MC, V. Parking 20€ ($23) nearby. Métro: Musée d'Orsay or Rue du Bac. **Amenities:** Bar; limited room service; laundry service. *In room:* TV, hair dryer.

Hôtel Lindbergh   A 5-minute walk from St-Germain-des-Prés, this hotel offers streamlined, simple guest rooms. About two-thirds of the bathrooms contain tubs as well as showers. Breakfast is the only meal served, but the staff will point out good restaurants nearby—an inexpensive bistro, Le Cigale, is quite close.

5 rue Chomel, 75007 Paris. ℭ **01-45-48-35-53**. Fax 01-45-49-31-48. www.hotellindbergh.com. 26 units. 95€–108€ ($109–$124) double; 132€–146€ ($152–$168) triple; 142€–156€ ($163–$180) quad. AE, DC, MC, V. Parking 27€ ($31). Métro: Sèvres-Babylone or St-Sulpice. **Amenities:** Limited room service; laundry service/dry cleaning; 1 room for those with limited mobility. *In room:* TV, dataport, hair dryer.

Hôtel Saint-Dominique   Part of this place's charm derives from its division into three buildings connected through an open-air courtyard. The most visible of these was an 18th-century convent—you can still see its ceiling beams and structural timbers in the reception area. The guest rooms aren't large, but each is warm and simply decorated. About a third of the bathrooms have full shower-tub combinations; the remaining have only showers.

62 rue St-Dominique, 75007 Paris. ℭ **01-47-05-51-44**. Fax 01-47-05-81-28. www.hotelstdominique.com. 34 units. 105€–119€ ($121–$137) double. AE, MC, V. Métro: Latour-Maubourg or Invalides. **Amenities:** Limited room service. *In room:* TV, dataport, minibar, hair dryer, safe.

3 Near the Airports

ORLY
MODERATE

Hilton Paris Orly Airport ★   Boxy and bland, the Hilton at Orly is a well-maintained business hotel that's especially convenient. Incoming planes can't penetrate the guest rooms' sound barriers, giving you a decent shot at a night's sleep. (Unlike the 24-hr. Charles de Gaulle Airport, Orly is closed to arriving flights from midnight to 6am.) The rooms are standard for a chain hotel; each was renovated in the late 1990s, with a tub-and-shower combination.

Aéroport Orly, 267 Orly Sud, 94544 Orly Aerogare Cedex. ℭ **800/445-8667** in the U.S. and Canada, or 01-45-12-45-12. Fax 01-45-12-45-00. www.hilton.com. 352 units. 130€–160€ ($150–$184) double; 200€ ($230) suite. AE, DC, MC, V. Parking 90€ ($104). Free shuttle bus between hotel and both Orly terminals. **Amenities:** Restaurant; bar; nearby tennis court; fitness center; sauna; 24-hr. room service; babysitting; laundry service/dry cleaning; nonsmoking rooms; rooms for those with limited mobility. *In room:* A/C, TV, dataport, hair dryer.

INEXPENSIVE

Kyriad Air Plus   Also boxy and contemporary looking, and interconnected with Orly by frequent 10-minute complimentary shuttle-bus rides, this 1990s hotel offers standard bedrooms. Each is comfortable, insulated against noises from the nearby airport, and a bit larger than you might expect. Each unit comes with a neatly tiled bathroom with tub and shower.

58 voie Nouvelle (near the Parc Georges Mélliès), 94544 Orly. ℭ **01-41-80-75-75**. Fax 01-41-80-12-12. airplus@ club-internet.fr. 72 units. 60€–68€ ($69–$78) double. AE, MC, V. Free parking. Transit to and from airport by complimentary shuttle bus. **Amenities:** Restaurant; limited room service (12:30–2:30pm and 7:30–10:30pm); nonsmoking rooms; rooms for those with limited mobility. *In room:* A/C, TV, coffeemaker, hair dryer.

CHARLES DE GAULLE

EXPENSIVE

Hôtel Sofitel Paris Aéroport CDG ★   Many travelers pass happily through this bustling, somewhat anonymous member of the French chain. It employs a multilingual staff accustomed to accommodating constantly arriving and departing international business travelers. The conservative guest rooms are soundproof havens against the all-night roar of jets. Suites are larger and have more comfort, although they are not especially elegant and are more of the chain format. Each unit comes with a tiled bathroom with tub and shower.

Aéroport Charles de Gaulle, Zone Central, B.P. 20248, 95713 Roissy. © **800/221-4542** in the U.S. and Canada, or 01-49-19-29-29. Fax 01-49-19-29-28. www.accor.com. 350 units. 290€–555€ ($334–$638) double; from 950€ ($1,093) suite. AE, DC, MC, V. Parking 25€ ($29). Free shuttles to and from airport. **Amenities:** Restaurant; bar; business center; 24-hr. room service; laundry service/dry cleaning; nonsmoking rooms; rooms for those with limited mobility. *In room:* A/C, TV, dataport, minibar, hair dryer, safe.

Hyatt Regency Paris–Charles de Gaulle ★   Adjacent to the Charles de Gaulle Airport, this is one of the latest Hyatts to open in Europe. Lying only a 25-minute drive from Disneyland Paris, and a half an hour from the attractions of central Paris, the Roissy property was designed by the renowned architect, Helmut Jahn. He created a stunning five-story structure of sleek design and tech-smart features. This is the first hotel of this size to be built in Paris since 1975, and as airport hotels go, the cutting-edge architecture puts it in a class by itself. The builder allowed natural glass to flow into the hotel, with a spectacular glass atrium overlooking the lobby. Jet-lagged passengers find ultimate comfort in the elegantly furnished and soundproof guest rooms, which meld American convenience with European elegance. The state-of-the-art bathrooms contain separate showers and tubs.

351 av. du Bois de la Pie, 95912 Roissy. © **01-48-17-12-34.** Fax 01-48-17-17-17. www.paris.hyatt.com. 388 units. 339€ ($390) double; 1,039€ ($1,195) suite. AE, DC, MC, V. RER1 train to airport, then Hyatt shuttle. **Amenities:** Restaurant; bar; indoor pool; 2 tennis courts; fitness center; nearby jogging track; sauna; 24-hr. room service; babysitting; laundry service/dry cleaning. *In room:* A/C, TV, dataport, minibar, hair dryer, safe.

INEXPENSIVE

Hôtel Campanile de Roissy   This hotel is less expensive than most other lodgings near the airport. Its cement-and-glass design is barely masked by a thin overlay of cheerful-looking and rustic artifacts, but generally, this is an efficiently decorated and not particularly stylish place to stay, with a well-meaning but overworked staff. Each unit comes with a small, shower-only bathroom.

Parc de Roissy, 95700 Val-d'Oise. © **01-34-29-80-40.** Fax 01-34-29-80-39. 260 units. 65€–120€ ($75–$138) double. AE, DC, MC, V. Shuttle van to and from Roissy 5€ ($5.75). **Amenities:** Restaurant; bar; laundry service/dry cleaning; nonsmoking rooms; rooms for those with limited mobility. *In room:* TV, dataport, hair dryer.

Where to Dine

Welcome to the city that prides itself on being the world's culinary capital. Only in Paris can you turn onto the nearest little crooked side street, enter the first nondescript bistro you see, sit down at a bare, wobbly table, order from an illegibly hand-scrawled menu, and get a truly memorable meal.

See chapter 1 for a list of our favorites—the best chef, the best view, the best old-fashioned bistro, and more.

1 Food for Thought

WHAT'S COOKING IN FRANCE   Once you arrive in Paris, you'll find that the word "French," although used frequently, isn't very helpful in describing cuisine. "French" covers such a broad scope that it doesn't prepare you for the offerings of the specialty chefs. Even the Parisians themselves might ask, "What *type* of French cooking?"

Sometimes a chef will include regional specialties, classic dishes, and even modern cuisine all on one menu. In that case, such a restaurant is truly "French." Other chefs prefer a more narrow focus and feature the cooking of one region or one style—classic or modern. Still others prefer to strike a middle ground between classic and modern; they're called "creative."

Regional cuisine showcases the diversity of the provinces of France, from Alsace on the German border to the Basque country at the frontier of Spain. The climate has a lot to do with this diversified offering—olive oil, garlic, and tomatoes from Provence in the south to oysters and saltwater fish from Brittany. Every region is known for special dishes—Burgundy for its escargots plucked off the grape vines; Périgord for its truffles and foie gras; Normandy for its soft, rich cheeses, Calvados, and cream sauces; and Alsace for its sauerkraut and wines. Today, one or more restaurants in Paris represent almost every region of France. You can go on a complete culinary tour of the country without leaving the city.

Few chefs today use the expression **"nouvelle cuisine,"** now called "modern." This cooking style, which burst upon us in the early 1970s, is now old hat (or should we say old *toque?*). It was a rebellion against the fats, butter, and sauces of haute cuisine, and used reductions of foodstuff to create flavor along with vegetable purées and lighter ingredients. Portions were reduced. Diners were shocked to see a piece of *boeuf* (beef) the size of an egg on their plate under a slice of fresh kiwi. Created in the name of innovation, many of these dishes were successful, while others, such as asparagus ice cream, were dismal failures.

From nouvelle cuisine grew *cuisine improvisée,* which is creative cookery based on the freshest ingredients available. Chefs make their selections at the morning market and then rush back to their kitchen to create spontaneously, often while dictating the menu of the day to an assistant who rushes it into print.

But fans of the great chef Escoffier can rest assured. Modern hasn't replaced **classic cuisine,** and France is still awash in béchamel and ablaze with cognac.

Haute gastronomie is alive and thriving at restaurants not only in Paris but throughout France. This richly extravagant fare is often lethal in price as it makes use of expensive ingredients, including fatted ducks, lobster, truffles, and plenty of butter and cream, plus sauces that consume endless time in their preparation. Breaking from Escoffier, many chefs today have forged ahead with a **"new classic cuisine,"** where they have taken classic dishes and branded them with their own distinctive style and flavor, often reducing the calories.

PARIS'S RANGE OF RESTAURANTS   Paris boasts a surplus of restaurants and cafes. Ultraexpensive **temples of gastronomy** include Alain Ducasse, L'Astor, Taillevent, Pierre Gagnaire, Lasserre, Jacques Cagna, Le Grand Véfour, and La Tour d'Argent. Savvy diners confine their trips to luxe places for special occasions. An array of other choices awaits, including simpler restaurants dispensing cuisines from every province of France and from former colonies like Morocco and Algeria.

Paris has hundreds of restaurants serving exotic **international fare,** reflecting the changing complexion of Paris itself and the city's increasing appreciation for food from other cultures. Your most memorable meal in Paris may turn out to be Vietnamese or West African.

You'll also find hundreds of bistros, brasseries, and cafes. In modern times their designations and roles have become almost meaningless. Traditionally, a **bistro** was a small restaurant, often with Mom at the cash register and Pop in the kitchen. Menus are most often handwritten or mimeographed, and the selection of dishes tends to be small. They can be chic and elegant, sometimes heavily Mediterranean, and often dispensing gutsy fare, including the *pot-au-feu* (beef simmered with vegetables) the chef's grandmother prepared for him as a kid.

French for "brewery," most **brasseries** have an Alsatian connection, and that means lots of beer, although Alsatian wines are also featured. They are almost always brightly lit and open 24 hours. Both snacks and full meals are available. The Alsatian establishments serve sauerkraut with an array of pork products.

The **cafe** is a French institution. Not just places for an aperitif, a café au lait, or a croissant, many serve rib-sticking fare as well, certainly entrecôte with french fries but often classics like *blanquette de veau* (veal in white sauce). For more cafe lore, see section 5, "The Top Cafes," later in this chapter.

More attention in the late 1990s focused on the **wine bar,** a host of which we recommend in chapter 10, "Paris After Dark." Originally, wine bars concentrated on their lists of wines, featuring many esoteric choices and ignoring the food except for some charcuterie (cold cuts) and cheeses. Today, you're likely to be offered various daily specials, from homemade foie gras to *boeuf à la mode* (marinated beef braised with red wine and served with vegetables).

Paris prices may seem extravagant to visitors from other parts of the world, particularly those who don't live in big cities, but there has been an emergence of moderately priced **informal restaurants** here, and we recommend several.

Although they're not as fashionable as they were, still around are **baby bistros,** reasonably priced spinoffs from deluxe restaurants where you can get a taste of a famous chef's cuisine without breaking the bank. We cover the best of them.

Tips   Mystifying Menu?

If you need help distinguishing a *boeuf à la mode* from a *crème brûlée,* turn to the glossary in appendix B.

Tips Dining Savoir-Faire

- Three-star dining remains quite expensive, with appetizers sometimes priced at 44€ ($50) and dinners easily costing from 174€ ($200) per person in the top dining rooms of celebrated chefs. But you can get around that high price tag in many places by **dining at lunch** (when prices are always cheaper) or ordering a prix fixe meal at lunch or dinner.
- The **prix fixe (fixed-price) menu** or *le menu* is a set meal that the chef prepares that day. It is most often fresh and promptly served and represents a greater bargain than dining a la carte. Of course, it's limited, so you'll have to like the choices provided. Sometimes there are one to three menus, beginning with the less expensive and going up for a more elaborate meal. A lot depends on your pocketbook and appetite.
- In France, **lunch** (as well as dinner) tends to be a full-course meal with meat, vegetables, salad, bread, cheese, dessert, wine, and coffee. It may be difficult to find a restaurant that serves the type of light lunch North Americans usually eat. Cafes, however, offer sandwiches, soup, and salads in a relaxed setting.
- Average visitors head for the old-fashioned family-run **bistro**, and we've ferreted out the best ones. In today's Paris, tradition and nostalgia, along with affordable prices, make these bistros busier than ever, especially because so many are being forced out of existence due to rising rents.
- **Coffee** in France is served after the meal and carries an extra charge. The French consider it barbaric to drink coffee during the meal and, unless you order it with milk *(au lait)*, it'll be served black. In more conscientious places, it's prepared as the traditional *café filtre*, a slow but rewarding java draw.
- In years gone by, no man would consider dining out, even at the neighborhood bistro, without a suit and tie, and no woman would be seen without a smart dress or suit. That **dress code** is more relaxed now, except in first-class and luxe establishments. Relaxed doesn't mean sloppy jeans and jogging attire, however. Parisians still value style, even when dressing informally.
- Sometimes service is added to your tab—usually 12% to 15%. If not, look for the words *service non compris* on your bill. That means that the cost of service was not added, and you'll be expected to leave a **tip.**

2 Restaurants by Cuisine

ALGERIAN

Au Clair de Lune (2e, $, p. 124)
Wally Le Saharien (9e, $$, p. 130)

ALSATIAN

Bofinger ✿ (4e, $$, p. 127)
Brasserie Flo ✿ (10e, $$, p. 131)
Jenny (3e, $, p. 125)

Key to Abbreviations: $$$$ = Very Expensive $$$ = Expensive $$ = Moderate $ = Inexpensive

AMERICAN
Joe Allen ✤ (1e, $$, p. 121)

ASIAN
Cabaret (1e, $$, p. 120)
Kambodia (16e, $, p. 144)
Le Pré Verre ✤ (5e, $$, p. 148)

AUVERGNAT
Bath's (8e, $$$, p. 138)
Chez Savy ✤ (8e, $, p. 141)
L'Ambassade d'Auvergne ✤ (3e, $, p. 126)

BASQUE
Au Bascou ✤ (3e, $, p. 125)
Auberge Etchegorry (13e, $$, p. 155)
Chez l'Ami Jean (7e, $, p. 160)

BRETON
Chez Michel (10e, $$, p. 131)

BURGUNDIAN
Chez Pauline ✤ (1e, $$$, p. 117)

CAFES
Brasserie Lipp (6e, $$$, p. 162)
Café Beaubourg (4e, $$, p. 163)
Café de Flore ✤✤ (6e, $$$, p. 162)
Café de la Musique (19e, $$, p. 163)
Café de l'Industrie (11e, $, p. 165)
Cafe des Deux Moulins (18e, $, p. 165)
Fouquet's ✤ (8e, $$$, p. 162)
La Belle Hortense (4e, $$, p. 163)
La Coupole ✤ (14e, $$, p. 163)
La Palette ✤✤ (6e, $$, p. 164)
La Rotonde (6e, $$, p. 164)
Le Procope ✤✤ (6e, $$, p. 164)
Le Rouquet ✤ (7e, $, p. 165)
Les Deux Magots ✤✤ (6e, $$, p. 165)

CAMBODIAN
Kambodia (16e, $, p. 144)

CANTONESE
Chez Vong ✤ (1e, $$, p. 121)
China Club ✤ (12e, $$, p.134)

CENTRAL EUROPEAN
Chez Jo Goldenberg ✤ (4e, $, p. 129)
La Cagouille ✤ (14e, $$, p. 155)

CHINESE
China Club ✤ (12e, $$, p. 134)
Le Canton (6e, $, p. 155)

CORSICAN
Chez la Vieille ✤ (1e, $$, p. 121)

FRENCH (MODERN)
Alcazar Bar & Restaurant ✤ (6e, $$, p. 152)
Bofinger ✤ (4e, $$, p. 127)
Buddha Bar ✤ (8e, $$$$, p. 134)
Cabaret (1e, $$, p. 120)
Carré des Feuillants ✤✤✤ (1e, $$$$, p. 117)
Chez Diane (6e, $, p. 154)
Chez Jean ✤ (9e, $$, p. 129)
Jacques Cagna ✤✤✤ (6e, $$$$, p. 151)
L'Ambroisie ✤✤✤ (4e, $$$$, p. 126)
L'Angle du Faubourg ✤✤ (8e, $$$, p. 138)
L'Arpège ✤✤✤ (7e, $$$$, p. 156)
L'Atelier de Joël Robuchon ✤✤ (7e, $$$, p. 156)
Lasserre ✤✤✤ (8e, $$$$, p. 136)
L'Astor ✤✤✤ (8e, $$$$, p. 136)
L'Astrance ✤✤✤ (16e, $$$, p. 142)
Le Chamarré ✤✤✤ (7e, $$$, p. 158)
Le Violon d'Ingres ✤✤✤ (7e, $$$, p. 160)
Marty ✤ (5e, $$, p. 150)
Michel Rostang ✤✤✤ (17e, $$$$, p. 145)
Pierre Gagnaire ✤✤✤ (8e, $$$$, p. 137)
Restaurant Plaza Athénée (Alain Ducasse) ✤✤✤ (8e, $$$$, p. 137)
1728 ✤ (8e, $$$, p. 139)
Shozan ✤ (8e, $$$, p. 139)
Taillevent ✤✤✤ (8e, $$$$, p. 137)
Ze Kitchen Galerie ✤ (6e, $$, p. 153)

FRENCH (TRADITIONAL)
Allard ✤ (6e, $$, p. 152)
Angélina ✤✤ (1e, $, p. 122)
A Sousceyrac ✤ (11e, $$, p. 132)
Au Clair de Lune (2e, $, p. 124)

Au Gourmet de l'Ile ✦ (4e, $,
    p. 128)
Au Pied de Cochon ✦✦ (1e, $$,
    p. 120)
Au Pied de Fouet (7e, $, p. 160)
Aux Charpentiers (6e, $, p. 154)
Aux Lyonnais ✦ (2e, $$, p. 123)
Bath's (8e, $$$, p. 138)
Benoit ✦ (4e, $$$, p. 126)
Bofinger ✦ (4e, $$, p. 127)
Brasserie Balzar ✦ (5e, $$, p. 147)
C'amelot ✦ (11e, $$, p. 132)
Cave de l'Os à Moelle (15e, $$,
    p. 161)
Chartier (9e, $, p. 131)
Chez André (8e, $$, p. 140)
Chez Diane (6e, $, p. 154)
Chez Georges (2e, $$, p. 124)
Chez Georges (17e, $$, p. 145)
Chez Gramond ✦ (6e, $$, p. 152)
Chez Jean ✦ (9e, $$, p. 129)
Chez la Vieille ✦ (1e, $$, p. 121)
Chez Pauline ✦ (1e, $$$, p. 117)
Closerie des Lilas ✦ (6e, $$$,
    p. 152)
Crémerie-Restaurant Polidor ✦
    (6e, $, p. 154)
Guy Savoy ✦✦✦ (17e, $$$$,
    p. 145)
Hiramatsu ✦ (4e, $$$, p. 127)
Jacques Cagna ✦✦✦ (6e, $$$$,
    p. 151)
Jamin ✦✦✦ (16e, $$$$, p. 142)
La Butte Chaillot ✦ (16e, $$,
    p. 144)
La Cagouille ✦ (14e, $$, p. 155)
Ladurée ✦ (8e, $$, p. 140)
La Grille (10e, $$, p. 131)
La Maison Blanche ✦✦ (8e, $$$,
    p. 138)
L'Ambassade d'Auvergne ✦ (3e, $,
    p. 126)
L'Ambroisie ✦✦✦ (4e, $$$$,
    p. 126)
L'Ami Louis ✦ (3e, $$$, p. 124)
L'Angle du Faubourg ✦✦ (8e, $$$,
    p. 138)
La Petite Chaise (7e, $$, p. 160)
La Petite Hostellerie ✦ (5e, $,
    p. 150)
La Poule au Pot (1e, $$, p. 122)

La Rôtisserie d'en Face ✦ (6e, $$,
    p. 153)
Lasserre ✦✦✦ (8e, $$$$, p. 136)
La Tour d'Argent ✦✦✦ (5e, $$$$,
    p. 146)
L'Ebauchoir ✦ (12e, $, p. 134)
Le Bistro de l'Etoile ✦ (16e, $$,
    p. 144)
Le Grand Véfour ✦✦✦ (1e, $$$$,
    p. 117)
Le Pamphlet ✦ (3e, $$, p. 125)
Le Petit Marguery (13e, $$, p. 155)
Le Petit Pontoise ✦ (5e, $$,
    p. 147)
Le Pré Verre ✦ (5e, $$, p. 148)
Les Gourmets des Ternes (8e, $$,
    p. 141)
Le Square Trousseau (12e, $$,
    p. 134)
Le Vaudeville (2e, $$, p. 124)
Le Vieux Bistro ✦ (4e, $$, p. 128)
Le Violon d'Ingres ✦✦✦ (7e, $$$,
    p. 160)
Michel Rostang ✦✦✦ (17e, $$$$,
    p. 145)
Perraudin (5e, $$, p. 150)
Restaurant Caïus ✦ (17e, $$,
    p. 146)
Restaurant Plaza Athénée (Alain
    Ducasse) ✦✦✦ (8e, $$$$,
    p. 137)
Taillevent ✦✦✦ (8e, $$$$, p. 137)

FUSION
Market ✦ (8e, $$, p. 141)

GASCONY
Au Trou Gascon ✦✦✦ (12e, $$$,
    p. 133)

INDIAN
Yugaraj (6e, $$, p. 153)

INTERNATIONAL
Georges ✦ (4e, $$, p. 128)
Le Fumoir ✦ (1e, $$, p. 122)
Spoon, Food & Wine ✦ (8e, $$$,
    p. 140)
Ze Kitchen Galerie ✦ (6e, $$,
    p. 153)

ITALIAN
Il Cortile ✦✦ (1e, $$, p. 121)

JAPANESE
Isami (4e, $$$, p. 127)
1728 ✿ (8e, $$$, p. 139)
Shozan ✿ (8e, $$$, p. 139)

JEWISH
Chez Jo Goldenberg ✿ (4e, $,
p. 129)

LATE NIGHT
Au Pied de Cochon ✿✿ (1e, $$,
p. 120)
La Poule au Pot (1e, $$, p. 122)
Le Vaudeville (2e, $$, p. 124)

LEBANESE
Al Dar (5e, $$, p. 147)

LOIRE VALLEY (ANJOU)
Au Petit Riche ✿ (9e, $$, p. 129)

LYONNAIS
Aux Lyonnais ✿ (2e, $$, p. 123)

MAURITIEN
Le Chamarré ✿✿✿ (7e, $$$, p. 158)

MEDITERRANEAN
Il Cortile ✿✿ (1e, $$, p. 121)

MOROCCAN
Mansouria (11e, $$, p. 133)

ORGANIC
Le Grain de Folie (18e, $, p. 134)

PACIFIC RIM
Buddha Bar ✿ (8e, $$$$, p. 134)

POITEVINE
Le Petit Marguery (13e, $$, p. 155)

PROVENÇAL
Chez Janou (3e, $, p. 125)
La Bastide Odéon ✿ (6e, $, p. 154)

La Maison Blanche ✿✿ (8e, $$$,
p. 138)
Les Elysées du Vernet ✿✿✿ (8e,
$$$$, p. 137)

SEAFOOD
59 Poincaré ✿ (16e, $$$, p. 142)
Goumard ✿✿✿ (1e, $$$, p. 120)
La Cagouille ✿ (14e, $$, p. 155)
La Grille (10e, $$, p. 131)
Le Marais (4e, $, p. 129)

SENEGALESE
Le Manguier (11e, $, p. 133)
Paris-Dakar (10e, $, p. 132)

SEYCHELLE ISLANDS
Coco de Mer ✿ (5e, $, p. 150)

SOUTHWESTERN FRENCH
Chez l'Ami Jean (7e, $, p. 160)
La Braisière ✿✿ (17e, $$, p. 145)
La Fermette du Sud-Ouest ✿
(1e, $, p. 122)
La Régalade (14e, $$, p. 156)
Le Pamphlet ✿ (3e, $$, p. 125)
Restaurant d'Hélène/Salon d'Hélène
✿✿✿ (6e, $$$$, p. 151)

STEAK
59 Poincaré ✿ (16e, $$$, p. 142)

TEA
Angélina ✿✿ (1e, $, p. 122)

THAI
Blue Elephant ✿ (11e, $$$, p. 132)

VEGETARIAN
Le Grain de Folie (18e, $, p. 134)
Le Marais (4e, $, p. 129)

VIETNAMESE
Kim Anh (15e, $$, p. 161)
Le Canton (6e, $, p. 155)

Tips Don't Leave Home Without Them

No matter how long you stay in Paris, we suggest you indulge in at least one break-the-bank French meal at a fabulous restaurant. It will be a memory you'll treasure long after you've recovered from paying the tab. However, to get a table at one of these places, *you must reserve far in advance*—at least a day or two ahead, sometimes even a few weeks or months ahead! We suggest you look over these listings, and call for reservations before you leave or at least as soon as you get into town.

3 On the Right Bank

We'll begin with the most centrally located arrondissements on the Right Bank, then work our way through the more outlying neighborhoods and to the area around the Arc de Triomphe.

1ST ARRONDISSEMENT
VERY EXPENSIVE

Carré des Feuillants ★★★ MODERN FRENCH   This is a bastion of perfection, an enclave of haute gastronomy between the place Vendôme and the Tuileries. When chef Alain Dutournier turned this 17th-century convent into a restaurant, it was an overnight success. The interior is like an early-1900s bourgeois house with several salons opening onto a sky-lit courtyard, across from a glass-enclosed kitchen. You'll find a sophisticated reinterpretation of cuisine from France's southwest, using seasonally fresh ingredients and lots of know-how. Examples are roasted veal kidneys cooked in their own fat; or grilled wood pigeon with chutney and polenta. Lighter dishes are scallops wrapped in parsley-infused puff pastry served with cabbage and truffles, and mullet-studded risotto with lettuce. For dessert, try the pistachio cream cake with candied tangerines.

14 rue de Castiglione (near place Vendôme and the Tuileries), 1e. ✆ **01-42-86-82-82.** Fax 01-42-86-07-71. Reservations required far in advance. Main courses 54€–55€ ($62–$63); prix fixe lunch 140€ ($161). AE, DC, MC, V. Mon–Fri noon–2:30pm and 7:30–10pm. Closed Aug. Métro: Tuileries, Concorde, Opéra, or Madeleine.

Le Grand Véfour ★★★ TRADITIONAL FRENCH   This is the all-time winner: a great chef; the most beautiful restaurant decor in Paris; and a history-infused citadel of classic French cuisine. This restaurant has been around since the reign of Louis XV. Napoleon, Danton, Hugo, Colette, and Cocteau have dined here—as the brass plaques on the tables testify—and it's still a gastronomic experience. Guy Martin, chef for the past decade, bases many dishes on recipes from the French Alps. He prepares such heavenly dishes as filet of lamb cooked with sweet muscat wine and carved into rib sections and served with the smoked essence of its own juice. Other specialties are noisettes of lamb with star anise, Breton lobster, and a cabbage sorbet in dark-chocolate sauce. The desserts are often grand, like the *gourmandises au chocolat* (medley of chocolate), served with chocolate sorbet.

17 rue de Beaujolais, 1e. ✆ **01-42-96-56-27.** Fax 01-42-86-80-71. Reservations required far in advance. Main courses 65€–76€ ($75–$87); prix fixe lunch 75€ ($86), dinner 230€ ($265). AE, DC, MC, V. Mon–Fri 12:30–2pm; Mon–Thurs 8–9:15pm. Closed Aug. Métro: Louvre-Palais Royal or Pyramide.

EXPENSIVE

Chez Pauline ★ Finds BURGUNDIAN/FRENCH   Fans say this *bistrot de luxe* is a less expensive, less majestic version of Le Grand Véfour. The early-1900s setting is grand enough to impress a business client and lighthearted enough to attract a roster of VIPs. You'll be ushered to a table on one of two levels, amid polished mirrors, red leather banquettes, and memorabilia of long-ago Paris. The emphasis is on the cuisine of central France, especially Burgundy, shown by the liberal use of wines in favorites like cassoulet of Burgundian snails with bacon and tomatoes, *boeuf bourguignon* (braised beef in red-wine sauce) with tagliatelle, terrine of parslied ham, and salmon steak with green peppercorns. Also wonderful is the roasted Bresse chicken with dauphinois potatoes. Dessert may include a *clafoutis* (pastry) of apricots and raspberries sautéed in sugar as

Where to Dine on the Right Bank (1–4, 9–12 & 18–19e)

Androuët sur le Pouce **14**	Blue Elephant **42**
Angélina **18**	Bofinger **37**
A Sousceyrac **44**	Brasserie Flo **5**
Au Bascou **32**	Cabaret **19**
Au Clair de Lune **25**	Café Beaubourg **28**
Au Gourmet de l'Île **53**	Café de la Musique **36**
Au Petit Riche **7**	Cafe de l'Industrie **43**
Au Pied de Cochon **24**	C'Amelot **41**
Au Trou Gascon **54**	Carré des Feuillants **17**
Aux Lyonnais **9**	Chartier **8**
Benoit **34**	Chez Georges **11**

Chez Janou **40**	China Club **45**
Chez Jean **6**	Georges **30**
Chez Jo Goldenberg **48**	Goumard **16**
Chez La Vielle **21**	Hiramatsa **52**
Chez Michel **2**	Il Cortile **15**
Chez Pauline **13**	Isami **51**
Chez Vong **26**	Jenny **38**

Métro Stop M
RER Stop R
Railway —

Joe Allen **27**
L'Ambassade
  d'Auvergne **31**
L'Ambroisie **47**
L'Ami Louis **33**
La Belle Hortense **49**
La Fermette du
  Sud-Ouest **23**

La Grille **4**
La Poule au Pot **22**
Le Fumoir **20**
Le Grain de Folie **1**
Le Grand Véfour **12**
Le Manguier **46**
Le Marais **29**

Le Pamphlet **39**
Le Square Trousseau **44**
Le Vaudeville **10**
Le Vieux Bistro **50**
Paris-Dakar **35**
Wally Le Saharien **3**

well as caramelized rice pudding. Owner/chef André Genin is an author of children's books, some on the value and techniques of French cuisine.

5 rue Villedo, 1e. © **01-42-96-20-70.** Reservations recommended. Main courses 25€–50€ ($29–$58); prix fixe lunch 35€ ($40). AE, DC, V. Mon–Fri 12:15–2:30pm and 7:15–10:30pm; Sat 7:15–10:30pm. Closed Sat–Sun May to late Aug. Métro: Pyramide.

Goumard ✸✸✸ SEAFOOD   Opened in 1872, this landmark is one of Paris's leading seafood restaurants. It's so devoted to the fine art of preparing fish that other food is banned from the menu (the staff will verbally present a limited roster of meat dishes). The decor consists of a collection of Lalique crystal fish in artificial aquariums. Even more unusual are the men's and women's restrooms, classified as historic monuments; the commodes were designed by the Art Nouveau master cabinetmaker Majorelle in the early 1900s. Much of the seafood is flown in from Brittany daily. Examples are a *craquant* (crisp-cooked) crayfish in its own herb salad, lobster soup with coconut, and a grilled turbot salad on a bed of artichokes with tarragon. In all these dishes, nothing (no excess butter, spices, or salt) is allowed to interfere with the natural flavor of the sea. Be prepared for some unusual food—the staff will help translate the menu items for you.

9 rue Duphot, 1e. © **01-42-60-36-07.** Fax 01-42-60-04-54. www.goumard.com. Reservations required far in advance. Main courses 29€–75€ ($33–$86); prix fixe menu 40€ ($46). AE, DC, MC, V. Daily noon–2:30pm and 7:30–10:30pm. Closed 2 weeks in Aug. Métro: Madeleine or Concorde.

MODERATE

Au Pied de Cochon ✸✸ TRADITIONAL FRENCH/LATE NIGHT   Their famous onion soup and namesake specialty (grilled pig's feet with béarnaise sauce) still lure visitors, and where else in Paris can you get such a good meal at 3am? Two other specialties are the *tentation* (temptation) platter, including grilled pig's tail, pig's snout, and half a pig's foot with béarnaise and *pommes frites* (french fries), and *andouillette* (chitterling sausages) with béarnaise. Two flavorful but less unusual dishes are a *jarret* (shin) of pork, caramelized in honey and served on a bed of sauerkraut, and grilled pork ribs with sage sauce. On the street outside, you can buy some of the freshest oysters in town. The attendants will give you slices of lemon and you can down them on the spot.

6 rue Coquillière, 1e. © **01-40-13-77-00.** Reservations recommended for lunch and dinner hours. Main courses 15€–29€ ($17–$33). AE, DC, V. Daily 24 hr. Métro: Les Halles.

Cabaret MODERN FRENCH/ASIAN   You'll either admire this restaurant for its sense of cutting-edge glamour, or become irritated with its inflated sense of grandeur, its artfully vague lack of organization, and in some cases, its genuinely silly sense of chichi. Depending on when you arrive, your meal will be served either on the street level or within the cellar, where a well-publicized team of hot designers (including Jacques Garcia and Ora-Ito) have installed a postmodern decor that's coy, minimalist, and thought provoking. An "African-looking" bar is accessorized with tribal motifs, and replicas of beds are scattered across the lounge-disco area. Recommended dishes include crab claws with a sweet-and-sour sauce; fried slices of foie gras with green asparagus tips; pasta shells with Parmesan cream sauce; and T-bone of veal with a ginger-flavored lime sauce.

Night owls with a sense of humor may enjoy dining here late, then descending into the club area for dancing and people-watching on the phosphorescent day-glo floor. There's a cover charge of 20€ ($23) on Friday and Saturday after 11:30pm.

2 place du Palais-Royal, 1e. © **01-58-62-56-25.** Reservations recommended. Main courses 15€–30€ ($17–$35). AE, MC, V. Restaurant Mon–Sat 8–10:45pm. Club daily 11:30pm–5 or 6am. Métro: Palais-Royal.

Travel Tip: He who finds the best hotel deal has more to spend on facials involving knobbly vegetables.

Hello, the Roaming Gnome here. I've been nabbed from the garden and taken round the world. The people who took me are so terribly clever. They find the best offerings on Travelocity. For very little cha-ching. And that means I get to be pampered and exfoliated till I'm pink as a bunny's doodah.

Plan your vacation

- flights, hotels, car rentals
- cruises & vacation packages
- destination guides
- fare alerts
- go to yahoo.com, click travel

Chez la Vieille ★ *Finds* TRADITIONAL FRENCH/CORSICAN   Except on Thursday night when a clientele of mostly local residents is likely to drop in for dinner, Chez la Vieille only serves lunch. Amid a crush of local office workers and visitors to the nearby Louvre, you'll be served the first course and your dessert from a trolley, and wait for the staff to bring you your main course directly from the kitchen. This method evokes a large communal meal in a private home, or perhaps a boarding house. Starters change with the season and the mood of the staff, and include homemade terrines (there's one made from wild boar), stuffed cabbages and tomatoes, and more. Main courses might include *pot-au-feu* (beef stew with carrots), or perhaps braised calf's liver. Walls are plastered with the photos of aspiring actors, singers, and *photo-modèles* who have enjoyed meals here.

1 rue Bailleul, 1e. ✆ **01-42-60-15-78.** Reservations recommended. Main courses 16€–25€ ($18–$29); prix fixe lunch 26€ ($30). AE, MC, V. Mon–Fri noon–2:30pm; Thurs 7:30–9pm. Closed Aug. Métro: Louvre-Rivoli.

Chez Vong ★ CANTONESE   This is the kind of Les Halles restaurant you head for when you've had your fill of grand cuisine and pretensions. The decor is a soothing mix of greens and browns, steeped in a Chinese-colonial ambience that evokes early 1900s Shanghai. Menu items feature shrimp and scallops served as spicy as you like, including a superhot version with garlic and red peppers; "joyous beef" with pepper sauce; chicken in puff pastry with ginger; and an array of fish dishes. The whims of fashion have decreed this one of the restaurants of the moment, so it's full of folks from the worlds of entertainment and the arts.

10 rue de la Grande-Truanderie, 1e. ✆ **01-40-26-09-36.** Reservations recommended. Main courses 25€–30€ ($29–$35); prix fixe lunch Mon–Fri 50€ ($58). AE, DC, MC, V. Mon–Sat noon–2:30pm and 7pm–midnight. Métro: Etienne-Marcel or Les Halles.

Il Cortile ★★ ITALIAN/MEDITERRANEAN   Flanking the verdant courtyard of a small hotel, this much-talked-about restaurant serves the best Italian food in Paris. In warm weather, tables are set up in an enclosed patio—a luxury in this congested neighborhood. The cuisine is fresh, inventive, and seasonal. Dishes are from throughout Italy, with emphasis on the north. Look for items like farfalle pasta with squid ink and fresh shellfish and an award-winning guinea fowl (spit-roasted and served with artfully shaped slices of the bird's gizzard, heart, and liver, it comes with polenta). The service is flawless: The Italian-speaking staff is diplomatic and good-humored. If you want to see what's cooking, ask for a seat in the dining room with a view of the rotisserie, where hens and guinea fowl slowly spin.

In the Hôtel Castille, 37 rue Cambon, 1e. ✆ **01-44-58-45-67.** Reservations recommended. Main courses 17€–35€ ($20–$40); prix fixe menu 40€ ($46). AE, DC, DISC, MC, V. Mon–Fri noon–2:30pm and 7:30–10:30pm. Métro: Concorde or Madeleine.

Joe Allen ★ *Kids* AMERICAN   The first American restaurant in Les Halles is aging well. Joe Allen long ago invaded the place with his hamburger. Though the New York restaurateur admits "it's a silly idea," it works, and it's Paris's best burger. While listening to the jukebox, you can order black-bean soup, chili, sirloin steak, ribs, or apple pie. Joe Allen is getting more sophisticated, catering to modern tastes with dishes like grilled salmon with coconut rice and sun-dried tomatoes. His saloon is the only place in Paris serving New York cheesecake and real pecan pie, and thanks to French chocolate, he feels his brownies are better than in the States. Giving them tough competition are the California chocolate-mousse pie and strawberries Romanoff. If you haven't made a reservation for dinner, expect a wait of at least 30 minutes at the New York Bar.

30 rue Pierre-Lescot, 1e. ✆ **01-42-36-70-13.** Reservations recommended for dinner. Main courses 12€–20€ ($14–$23); prix fixe menu 23€ ($26). AE, MC, V. Daily noon–12:30am. Métro: Etienne-Marcel.

La Poule au Pot TRADITIONAL FRENCH/LATE NIGHT This bistro welcomes late-night carousers and showbiz personalities looking for a meal after a performance. (Past aficionados have included the Rolling Stones, Prince, Dustin Hoffman, Johnny Hallyday, and French pop star Patrick Bruel.) The decor is authentically Art Deco, the ambience nurturing. Time-tested and savory menu items include a salad of warm goat cheese on toast, onion soup, pan-fried stingray with capers, Burgundy-style snails, country pâté on a bed of onion marmalade, and a succulent version of the restaurant's namesake, chicken in a pot with slices of pâté and fresh vegetables (in summer, it can be served cold, on a bed of lettuce, with vinaigrette sauce).

9 rue Vauvilliers, 1e. ℂ **01-42-36-32-96.** Reservations recommended. Main courses 20€–33€ ($23–$38); prix fixe menu 30€ ($35). MC, V. Tues–Sun 7pm–5am. Métro: Louvre or Les Halles.

Le Fumoir ⭐ INTERNATIONAL This upscale brasserie is set in an antique building a few steps from the Louvre. It's one of the most fashionable places in Paris for a bite or drink. You can order salads, pastries, and drinks at off-hours, and platters of more substantial food at mealtimes. Examples are codfish with onions and herbs, rack of veal simmered in its own juices with tarragon, calves' liver with onions, and herring in mustard-flavored cream sauce.

6 rue de l'Amiral-Coligny, 1e. ℂ **01-42-92-00-24.** Reservations recommended. Main courses 14€–27€ ($16–$31). Salads, pastries, and snacks daily 11am–2pm; full menu daily noon–3pm and 7–11:30pm. AE, V. Métro: Louvre-Rivoli.

INEXPENSIVE

Angélina ⭐⭐ TEA/TRADITIONAL FRENCH In the high-rent area near the Inter-Continental, this *salon de thé* (tea salon) combines fashion-industry glitter and bourgeois respectability. The carpets are plush, the ceilings high, and the accessories have the right amount of patina. This place has no equal when it comes to viewing the lionesses of haute couture over tea and sandwiches. The slightly snooty waitresses bear silver trays with pastries, drinks, and tea or coffee to marble-topped tables. Lunch usually offers a salad and a *plat du jour* like *salade gourmande* with foie gras and smoked breast of duck on a bed of fresh salad greens. The specialty, designed to go well with tea, is the Mont Blanc, a combination of chestnut cream and meringue.

226 rue de Rivoli, 1e. ℂ **01-42-60-82-00.** Reservations accepted for lunch, not for teatime. Pot of tea for 1 5.85€–6€ ($6.75–$6.90); sandwiches and salads 5.90€–11€ ($6.80–$13); main courses 12€–15€ ($14–$17). AE, MC, V. Daily 9am–7pm; lunch served 11:45am–3pm. Métro: Tuileries or Concorde.

La Fermette du Sud-Ouest ⭐ SOUTHWESTERN FRENCH This restaurant, which occupies the site of a 1500s convent, is in the heart of one of Paris's oldest neighborhoods. After the Revolution, the convent was converted into a coaching inn, preserving the original stonework and massive beams. La Fermette prepares rich, savory stews and confits celebrating agrarian France, serving them on the ground floor and on a mezzanine resembling a choir loft. Menu items include an age-old but ever-popular magret of duckling with flap mushrooms, *andouillette* (chitterling sausages), and a sometimes startling array of *cochonailles* (pork products and byproducts) you probably need to be French to appreciate. Cassoulet and *pot-au-feu* (beef stew) are enduring specialties.

31 rue Coquillière, 1e. ℂ **01-42-36-73-55.** Reservations recommended. Main courses 15€–22€ ($17–$25); prix fixe lunch 16€ ($18); set menu 25€ ($29). MC, V. Mon–Sat noon–2pm and 7:30–10pm. Métro: Les Halles.

Moments Le Grand Fromage

Cheese is king at **Androuët sur le Pouce** ★★, 49 rue St-Roch, 1e (© **01-42-97-57-39**), where a tradition that began in 1909 has evolved into a *bar à fromage* (cheese bar) that's the modern-day evolution of one of the most famous purveyors of cheese in the world. Gone are the formal meals and dining rituals that used to prevail at Androuët. Today, the venue is more basic, quicker, and more tuned to the demands on the modern Parisian's time. As such, it has met with approval from the French-speaking public. The menu is simple, consisting of either *tartines* (open-faced sandwiches) or cheese platters. Tartines, priced at from 15€ to 20€ ($17–$23), include your choice of any kind of cheese and/or a medley of smoked or marinated fish or meats. If you opt for a platter, you'll select from offerings presented on a half-dozen cheese boards, whose categories are organized into such classifications as goat cheeses, triple crèmes, and so on. If you select a portion of five different cheeses from the platters, it will cost 12€ ($14); seven cheeses cost 15€ ($17), 11 cheeses cost 23€ ($26); and 15 different cheeses (recommended only for serious cheese lovers who won't mind some degree of indigestion) cost 28€ ($32). Ultrafresh bread and green salads are the only accompaniment for your tartines and cheese platters. There's also a staggering assortment of French wines. It's open Monday to Friday from noon to 2:30pm and 7 to 9:45pm.

Although this organization maintains a total of 10 branches within greater Paris, the most centrally located of the other branches is **Androuët sur le Pouce**, 23 rue des Acacias, 17e (© **01-40-68-00-12**; Métro: Argentine). Charging the same prices and using the same system as the larger branch described above, it's open Monday to Friday from noon to 2:30pm and from 7 to 9:30pm.

Don't expect a full-fledged shop selling cheeses at either of the branches, since the organization's shops are usually separate entities located within walking distance of an Androuët sur le Pouce outlet. The chain's largest sales outlet is Androuët, 23 rue du Villiers, 17e (© **01-47-64-39-20**; Métro: Villiers).

2ND ARRONDISSEMENT
MODERATE

Aux Lyonnais ★ LYONNAIS/FRENCH   After a meal here, you'll know why Lyon is called the gastronomic capital of France. There is no better Lyonnaise bistro in Paris than this time-mellowed place. It's grown ever better, now that the world-class chef, Alain Ducasse, has taken it over and installed young Christophe Saintagne as head chef. He trained under Ducasse at the swank Plaza Athénée. The menu is based on his shopping that morning for the freshest produce in the market. Whatever he serves is offered against an 1890s bistro backdrop of potted palms, etched glass, and globe lamps. Inventiveness and a solid technique are reflected by such dishes as parslied calf's liver, pike dumplings (the best in Paris), skate meunière, and a peppery *coq au vin* (chicken stewed in wine) with crème fraîche macaroni. Foie gras is a starter, or else you can opt for a charcuterie platter. The best for last: a heaven-sent Cointreau soufflé.

32 rue St-Marc, 2e. ✆ **01-42-96-65-04.** Reservations required. 3-course prix fixe menu 18€–32€ ($21–$37). AE, DC, MC, V. Tues–Fri noon–2pm; Tues–Sat 7:30–11:30pm. Métro: Grands-Boulevards.

Chez Georges TRADITIONAL FRENCH   This bistro was opened in 1964 near La Bourse (stock exchange), and is run by three generations of the same family. At lunch it's packed with stock exchange members. The owners serve *la cuisine bourgeoise* (comfort food). Waiters bring around bowls of appetizers, like celery rémoulade, to get you started. You can follow with sweetbreads with morels, duck breast with cèpe mushrooms, cassoulet, or *pot-au-feu* (beef simmered with vegetables). A delight is sole filet with a sauce made from Pouilly wine and crème fraîche. Beaujolais goes great with this hearty food.

1 rue du Mail, 2e. ✆ **01-42-60-07-11.** Reservations required. Main courses 25€–27€ ($29–$31). AE, MC, V. Mon–Sat noon–2pm and 7–9:45pm. Closed 3 weeks in Aug. Métro: Bourse.

Le Vaudeville TRADITIONAL FRENCH/LATE NIGHT   Adjacent to La Bourse (stock exchange), this bistro retains its marble walls and Art Deco carvings from 1918. In summer, tables dot a terrace amid banks of geraniums. The place is boisterous and informal, often welcoming groups of six or eight diners at a time. A bar near the entrance provides a perch if your reservation is delayed. The roster of platters includes snails in garlic butter, shellfish, smoked salmon, sauerkraut, and grilled meats. Three dishes reign as enduring favorites: fresh grilled codfish with mashed potatoes and truffle juice, fresh escalope of warm foie gras with grapes or raspberries, and grilled salmon in a crayfish sauce. The prix fixe menu is a good deal.

29 rue Vivienne, 2e. ✆ **01-40-20-04-62.** Reservations recommended in the evenings. Main courses 11€–24€ ($13–$27); prix fixe lunch 23€ ($26), dinner 33€ ($38). AE, DC, MC, V. Daily noon–3pm and 7pm–1am. Métro: Bourse.

INEXPENSIVE

Au Clair de Lune ALGERIAN/FRENCH   This neighborhood staple has flourished in the heart of Paris's garment district since the 1930s, when Algeria was a distinct part of the French-speaking world. You'll dine in a long, narrow room whose walls are hung with Berber carpets, and whose patrons are likely to include shop workers from the nearby wholesale clothiers. On the menu is always the Algerian staple of couscous, as well as an array of daily specials such as veal stew, shoulder or rack of lamb, and roast chicken. The portions are large, so come hungry. The wines are from throughout France and North Africa.

13 rue Française, 2e. ✆ **01-42-33-59-10.** Main courses 9€–14€ ($10–$16). MC, V. Daily noon–2:30pm and 7:30–11pm. Métro: Etienne-Marcel or Les Halles.

3RD ARRONDISSEMENT
EXPENSIVE

L'Ami Louis ★ TRADITIONAL FRENCH   L'Ami Louis is in one of central Paris's least fashionable neighborhoods, far removed from the part of the Marais that has become chic, and its facade has seen better days. It was one of Paris's most famous brasseries in the 1930s, thanks to its excellent food served in copious portions and its old-fashioned decor. Its traditions, even the hostile waiters, are fervently maintained today. Amid a "brown gravy" decor (the walls retain a smoky patina), dishes like grilled veal kidneys, roasted suckling lamb, pheasant, venison, confit of duckling, and endless slices of foie gras are served on marble-topped tables. Though some say the ingredients aren't as good as they were in the restaurant's heyday, the sauces are as thick as they were between the wars. Don't save room for dessert, which isn't very good.

32 rue du Vertbois, 3e. © **01-48-87-77-48.** Reservations required far in advance. Main courses 39€–65€ ($45–$75). MC, V. Wed–Sun noon–1:30pm and 8–11pm. Closed July 19–Aug 25. Métro: Temple.

MODERATE

Le Pamphlet ⭐ *Value* TRADITIONAL FRENCH/SOUTHWESTERN FRENCH This is the kind of rustic, country-comfortable inn where Parisians book a table at least 48 hours in advance, and then schedule the event in their appointment books as a kind of midweek break from urban life. Part of the charm here involves discussing the political theories of strong-willed and gruffly charming owner and chef, Alain Carrère. (In the 18th century, a "pamphlet" was a journalistic tract condemning some aspect of French politics. Mr. Carrère's "pamphlet" is, in his own words, an ongoing dislike of most French politicians.) The menu changes several times a week. Your meal might begin with rillettes (a rough-textured terrine) of rabbit with crayfish or a thick cream of crabmeat soup garnished with baby peas. Recommended main courses include a rack of Pyrenean lamb served with *croustillant* (a crisp pastry) enriched with Rocamadour goat cheese, or braised sea bass with carrots, leeks, and a shrimp-flavored cream sauce. We think this place is a lot of fun, and if you can handle its eccentricities, you may agree.

38 rue Debelleyme, 3e. © **01-42-72-39-24.** Reservations required, usually 48 hr. in advance. Prix fixe menu 30€–45€ ($35–$52). MC, V. Tues–Fri noon–2:30pm and Mon–Sat 7:30–11pm. Closed 1st 2 weeks of Jan and 2 weeks in mid-Aug. Métro: Filles du Calvaire.

INEXPENSIVE

Au Bascou ⭐ *Finds* BASQUE The succulent cuisine of France's "deep southwest" is the specialty here, where art objects and oil paintings celebrate the beauty of the region, and hanging clusters of pimentos add spice to the air. For a ray of sunshine in your life, try the *piperade basquaise,* a spicy omelet loaded with peppers and onions; pimentos stuffed with a purée of codfish; and an *axoa* of veal (shoulder of calf served with a pimento-and-pepper-based green sauce). Also noteworthy is the thick-sliced filet of cod served with a confit of tomatoes.

38 rue Réaumur, 3e. © **01-42-72-69-25.** Reservations recommended. Main courses 15€ ($17). AE, MC, V. Tues–Fri noon–2pm and 8–10:30pm. Closed Aug. Métro: Arts-et-Métiers.

Chez Janou PROVENÇAL On one of the 17th-century streets behind place des Vosges, this bistro operates from a pair of cramped but cozy dining rooms filled with memorabilia from Provence. The service is brusque and sometimes hectic. But the food is like a visit to your French grandmother's kitchen, where she'll regale you with dishes like shrimp with pastis sauce, *brouillade des pleurotes* (baked eggs with oyster mushrooms), spinach salad with goat cheese, fondue of ratatouille, gratin of mussels, and a simple but savory magret of duck with rosemary. You can enjoy these specialties on a covered terrace.

2 rue Roger-Verlomme, 3e. © **01-42-72-28-41.** Reservations recommended. Main courses 13€–18€ ($15–$21); 2-course prix fixe menu 13€ ($15). No credit cards. Daily noon–3pm and 7:30pm–midnight. Métro: Chemin-Vert.

Jenny *Value* ALSATIAN One of the city's most famous and popular Alsatian restaurants was established in 1930 by members of the Jenny family, who commissioned one of the noteworthy craftsmen of the era, Spindler, to create marquetry panels for the sheathing of the walls. Today, little has changed since its inauguration, except for the fact that the clientele is a lot more contemporary-looking than in the old days. Up to 220 diners can fit into this nostalgia-laden setting, where Alsatian *Gemütlichkeit* prevails. An ongoing specialty is the *choucroute* (sauerkraut) *de chez Jenny,* which is piled high with sausages, tender pork knuckles, and slices of ham. Also available are oysters, onion soup, grilled meats, and grilled fish. Any of these taste wonderful accompanied by one of the Alsatian wines (especially Rieslings) that fill the wine list.

39 bd. du Temple, 3e. ℂ 01-44-54-39-00. Reservations recommended. Main courses 17€–28€ ($20–$32); prix fixe menu 17€–24€ ($20–$28). AE, DC, MC, V. Daily noon–midnight. Métro: République.

L'Ambassade d'Auvergne ✹ AUVERGNAT/FRENCH   You enter this rustic tavern through a bar with heavy oak beams, hanging hams, and ceramic plates. This favorite showcases the culinary generosity of France's most isolated region, the Auvergne, whose pork products are widely celebrated. Try a chicory salad with apples and pieces of country ham; pork braised with cabbage, turnips, and white beans; or grilled tripe sausages with mashed potatoes and cantal cheese with garlic. Nonpork specialties are pan-fried duck liver with gingerbread, perch steamed in verbena tea, and roasted rack of lamb with wild mushrooms. Dessert might be a poached pear with crispy almonds and caramel sauce.

22 rue de Grenier St-Lazare, 3e. ℂ 01-42-72-31-22. Reservations recommended. Main courses 16€–19€ ($18–$22); prix fixe menu 27€ ($31). AE, MC, V. Daily noon–2pm and 7:30–10:30pm. Métro: Rambuteau.

4TH ARRONDISSEMENT
VERY EXPENSIVE
L'Ambroisie ✹✹✹ MODERN & TRADITIONAL FRENCH   One of Paris's most talented chefs, Bernard Pacaud draws attention with his vivid flavors and culinary skill. Expect culinary perfection but a cool reception at this 17th-century town house, whose decor resembles an Italian palazzo. Pacaud's tables are nearly always filled with diners who come back again and again to see where his imagination will take him next. The dishes change seasonally and may include fricassee of Breton lobster with chestnuts, served with a purée of pumpkin; turbot braised with endive, served with a julienne of black truffles; or one of our favorite dishes in all Paris, *poulard de Bresse demi-deuil homage à la Mè Brazier* (chicken roasted with black truffles and truffled vegetables in a style invented by a Lyonnais matron after World War II). An award-winning dessert is the *tarte fine sablée* (a delicate small biscuit) served with bitter chocolate and vanilla-flavored ice cream.

9 place des Vosges, 4e. ℂ 01-42-78-51-45. Reservations required far in advance. Main courses 70€–130€ ($81–$150). AE, MC, V. Tues–Sat noon–1:30pm and 8–9:30pm. Métro: St-Paul or Chèmin Vert.

EXPENSIVE
Benoit ✹ TRADITIONAL FRENCH   There's something traditional and weighty about this historical monument; every mayor in Paris has dined here since the restaurant was founded in 1912 by the grandfather of the present owner. He's one of the last *bistrotiers* who purchases Beaujolais in casks and bottles it in his own cellars. The setting is theatrical, and the service can be attentive or arrogant, depending on a delicate chemistry that only longtime fans of this place understand. Prices are higher than you'd expect for bistro fare, but all seems part of the self-satisfied norm here, and clients keep coming back for more. Cuisine is full of flavor, and satisfying, based on time-tested classics. Traditional crowd-pleasers include salmon that's both marinated and smoked; snails served in their shells with garlic butter; and cassoulet, a white bean–and–pork dish that's fabulous on a cold day. A dessert that earns raves is the *Sainte-Eve,* pears layered with macaroon-flavored cream enclosed in puff pastry.

20 rue St-Martin, 4e. ℂ 01-42-72-25-76. Reservations required. Main courses 50€–120€ ($58–$138); prix fixe lunch 38€ ($44). AE. Daily noon–2pm and 8–10pm. Métro: Hôtel-de-Ville.

Hiramatsu *Finds* TRADITIONAL FRENCH   Other than the fact that the chef (Hiroyuki Hiramatsu) and most of his staff are Japanese, the only other Asian-derived ritual at this restaurant involves a hot and wet towel that guests are given at the debut of their meals, in the Japanese style. Other than that, the food, the decor, and the dining rituals here are unabashedly French, with a subtle and well-deserved perception that this is the finest interpretation of the French aesthetic by a Japanese staff anywhere in the world. The decor is culturally neutral, with only 20 seats in a contemporary-looking dining room outfitted in tones of blonde-brown and pale gray, in an antique building on the Ile St-Louis. The menu changes frequently, but whatever you order is artfully presented on arrangements of beauty and style. A good example is strips of pink-colored pigeon with foie gras, served on a double-decker platter; hot broth is poured over the upper of the two plates, cooking the julienned vegetables and foie gras. (A staff member will remove the upper plate when you've finished with it, thereby creating a "two in one" appetizer.) Heavenly main courses include filets of steamed sea bass served with a fricassee of flap mushrooms and red-wine sauce; and saddle of roasted venison in puff pastry with a vanilla and walnut gnocchi and a purée of celeriac and green apples.

7 quai de Bourbon, 4e. © 01-56-81-08-80. Reservations required. Main courses 48€–80€ ($55–$92); prix fixe menus 95€–130€ ($109–$150). AE, DC, MC, V. Tues–Sat 12:30–1:30pm and 8–9:30pm. Métro: Pont-Marie.

Isami JAPANESE   Dining here is guaranteed to evoke a sense of cultural dislocation—the staff is mostly from Japan, and few speak much French or English. That, however, is part of the place's allure for its loyal customers, many of whom work in the arts. The staff will tell you that only authentic Japanese versions of sushi and sashimi are served, with absolutely none of what they call California/Japanese cuisine and almost no cooked food of any kind. Begin a meal with miso soup or some pickled vegetables, as a prelude for the wide array of fish (tuna, salmon, whitefish, fluke, snapper, bluefish, oysters, clams, shrimp, and more) that form this restaurant's backbone. Lingering isn't encouraged.

4 quai d'Orléans, 4e. © 01-40-46-06-97. Reservations recommended. Meals 31€–34€ ($36–$39). MC, V. Tues–Sat noon–2pm and 7:30–10pm. Métro: Pont Marie.

MODERATE

Bofinger *★* ALSATIAN/MODERN & TRADITIONAL FRENCH Opened in the 1860s, Bofinger is the oldest Alsatian brasserie in town and one of the best. It's a Belle Epoque dining palace, resplendent with brass and stained glass. Weather permitting, you can dine on an outdoor terrace. Affiliated with La Coupole, Julien, and Brasserie Flo, the restaurant has updated its menu, retaining the most popular of its traditional dishes, like sauerkraut and sole

---

Moments **Taking an Ice Cream Break at Berthillon**

A landmark on Ile St-Louis after 3 dozen years in business, the *salon de thé* **Berthillon** *★★★*, 31 rue St-Louis-en-l'Ile, 4e (© 01-43-54-31-61; Métro: Pont Marie), offers the world's best selection of ice creams. Try gingerbread, bitter-chocolate mousse, rhubarb, melon, kumquat, black currant, or any fresh fruit in season—there are more than 50 flavors and nothing artificial. Parisians flock here in such numbers that gendarmes have been called out to direct the traffic of ice cream aficionados. It's open Wednesday to Sunday from 10am to 8pm.

meunière. Recent additions include roasted leg of lamb with a fondant of artichoke hearts and a purée of parsley, grilled turbot with fennel, and stingray with chives and burnt-butter sauce. Shellfish, including fresh oysters and lobster, is almost always available in season.

5–7 rue de la Bastille, 4e. ✆ 01-42-72-87-82. Reservations recommended. Main courses 15€–35€ ($17–$40). AE, DC, MC, V. Mon–Fri noon–3pm and 6:30pm–1am; Sat–Sun noon–1am. Métro: Bastille.

Georges ★ INTERNATIONAL   The Centre Pompidou is again in the spotlight; all of artsy Paris is talking about this place. Georges is in a large space on the top floor of Paris's most comprehensive arts complex, with views through bay windows over most of the city. The decor is minimalist and postmodern, with lots of brushed aluminum and stainless steel. Tables are made from sandblasted glass, lit from below, and accessorized with hypermodern cutlery. Menu items are mostly Continental, with hints of Asia. Some combinations come as a surprise—macaroni with lobster, for example. Others seem exotic, including roasted ostrich steak. Aside from these dishes, some of the best items on the menu are the roasted scallops with lemon butter and a tuna steak spiced up with coriander. There's also a luscious version of sole meunière. (May that dish never go out of style!) To get here, head for the exterior elevator to the left of the Pompidou's main entrance. Tell the guard you have a reservation; otherwise, you might not be allowed up.

On the 6th floor of the Centre Georges Pompidou, 19 rue Beaubourg, 4e. ✆ 01-44-78-47-99. Reservations imperative for dinner, recommended for lunch. Main courses 13€–39€ ($15–$45). AE, DC, MC, V. Wed–Mon noon–2am. Métro: Châtelet or Rambuteau.

Le Vieux Bistro ★ *Finds* TRADITIONAL FRENCH   This is one of the last old-fashioned bistros in the heart of Paris. Few other restaurants offer so close-up, and so forbidding, a view of the massive walls of Paris's largest cathedral; it's visible through lacy curtains from the windows of the front dining room. To reach it, you'll bypass a dozen souvenir stands, then settle into one of the two old-time dining rooms. The cuisine, which is a bit heavy, evokes the French staples you're served along little back roads deep in the heart of France. The specialty is *boeuf bourguignon* (beef simmered in red-wine sauce), and in winter lots of game dishes. You can order snails with garlic butter, filet mignon with Roquefort sauce, veal filets, and a classic dessert, *tarte tatin* (studded with apples and sugar, drenched with Calvados, and capped with fresh cream).

14 rue du Cloître-Notre-Dame, 4e. ✆ 01-43-54-18-95. Main courses 20€–28€ ($23–$32). MC, V. Daily noon–2pm and 7:30–11pm. Métro: Cité.

INEXPENSIVE

Au Gourmet de l'Ile ★ *Value* TRADITIONAL FRENCH   Locals swear by the cuisine at Au Gourmet de l'Ile, whose fixed-price meals are among Paris's best bargains. The setting is beautiful, with a beamed ceiling, walls from the 1400s, and candlelit tables. In the window is a sign emblazoned with AAAAA, which, roughly translated, stands for the Amiable Association of Amateurs of the Authentic Andouillette. Their chitterling sausages are soul food to the French. Popular and tasty too is *la charbonnée de l'Ile,* a savory pork with onions, and stuffed mussels in shallot butter. The fixed-price menu includes a choice of 15 appetizers, 15 main courses, salad or cheese, and 15 desserts.

42 rue St-Louis-en-l'Ile, 4e. ✆ 01-43-26-79-27. Reservations required. Main courses 17€–22€ ($19–$25); prix fixe menu 33€ ($38). MC, V. Wed–Sun noon–2pm and 7–10:30pm. Métro: Pont Marie.

Chez Jo Goldenberg ⭐ JEWISH/CENTRAL EUROPEAN   This is the best-known restaurant on the "Street of the Rose Bushes." Albert Goldenberg, the doyen of Jewish restaurateurs in Paris, moved to choicer surroundings (69 av. de Wagram, 17e), but his brother, Joseph, has remained. Dining is on two levels, one for nonsmokers. Look for the collection of samovars, the fantail pigeon in a wicker cage, and the paintings. The *carpe farcie* (stuffed carp) is a preferred selection, but the beef goulash is also good. We like the eggplant moussaka and the pastrami. The menu offers Israeli wines, but M. Goldenberg admits they're not as good as French wines. Live Yiddish music is presented every night beginning at 9pm, and special menus are offered during Jewish holidays—reservations are a must.

7 rue des Rosiers, 4e. ☎ **01-48-87-20-16.** Reservations required. Main courses 13€–18€ ($15–$21). AE, MC, V. Daily 11am–midnight. Métro: St-Paul.

Le Marais VEGETARIAN/SEAFOOD   Housed in a 17th-century building whose stonework forms part of the earthy decor, this is one of the best-known vegetarian restaurants in Le Marais. The owners serve a limited array of (strictly organic) wine, and smoking is forbidden. Flavorful meals are healthfully prepared and come in generous portions. Choose from a variety of soups and salads; a *galette* (a flat pastry) of wheat served with raw vegetables and mushroom tarts; or a country plate composed of fried mushrooms and potatoes, garlic, and goat cheese, served with a salad. There is a wide choice of fish dishes, so it's not strictly vegetarian.

54 rue Ste-Croix-de-la-Bretonnerie, 4e. ☎ **01-48-87-48-71.** Main courses 12€–14€ ($14–$16); prix fixe menus 20€ ($23). MC, V. Mon–Sat noon–midnight. Métro: Hôtel de Ville. RER: Châtelet–Les Halles.

9TH ARRONDISSEMENT

Like its counterparts from Hong Kong to Reykjavík, the **Hard Rock Cafe,** 14 bd. Montmartre, 9e (☎ **01-53-24-60-00;** Métro: Grands Boulevards or Richelieu-Drouot), offers musical memorabilia as well as musical selections from 35 years of rock. The crowd appreciates the juicy steaks, hamburgers, veggie burgers, salads, and heaping platters of informal French-inspired food. It's open Monday to Thursday from noon to 1am and Friday to Sunday from noon to 2am.

MODERATE

Au Petit Riche ⭐ LOIRE VALLEY (ANJOU)   No, that's not Flaubert or Balzac walking through the door. But should they miraculously come back, the decor of old Paris with the original gas lamps and time-mellowed paneling would make them feel at home. When it opened in 1865, this bistro was the food outlet for the Café Riche next door; today, it offers yesterday's grandeur and simple, well-prepared food. You'll be ushered to one of five areas crafted for maximum intimacy, with red banquettes, ceilings painted with allegorical themes, and accents of brass and frosted glass. The wine list favors Loire Valley vintages that go well with such dishes as *rillettes* and *rillons* (potted fish or meat, especially pork) in Vouvray wine aspic, poached fish with buttery white-wine sauce, old-fashioned blanquette of chicken, and seasonal game dishes like *civet* (a wild hare) or rabbit.

25 rue Le Peletier, 9e. ☎ **01-47-70-68-68.** Reservations recommended. Main courses 14€–24€ ($16–$28); prix fixe lunch 23€ ($26), dinner 29€ ($33). AE, DC, MC, V. Mon–Sat noon–2:15pm and 7pm–midnight. Métro: Le Peletier or Richelieu-Drouot.

Chez Jean ⭐ MODERN & TRADITIONAL FRENCH   The crowd is young, the food is good, and the vintage brassiere aura of the 1950s makes you think that American expatriate novelist James Baldwin will arrive any minute.

Moments A Parisian *Pique-nique*

One of the best ways to save money while still enjoying Parisian cuisine is to picnic. Go to a *fromagerie* for cheese; to a *boulangerie* for a baguette; to a charcuterie for pâté, sausage, or salad; and to a patisserie for luscious pastries. Add a bottle of Côtes du Rhone—it goes well with picnics—and you'll have the makings of a delightful, typically French meal you can take to the nearest park or along the banks of the Seine. Pretend you're in Manet's *Déjeuner sur l'herbe* and enjoy! (Don't forget the corkscrew!)

The best spot for a picnic is a cozy nook along the **Seine.** Another great place for picnics (also boating, walks, and jogging) is the **Bois de Boulogne** (Métro: Porte Maillot), covering some 2,000 acres at the western edge of Paris. At night it becomes a twilight zone of sex and drugs, but it's lovely during the day. (See chapter 7 for more on the Bois de Boulogne.) Even though they're in a state of restoration, the splendid gardens of **Versailles** offer another fine picnic spot. You can also enjoy your meal on the grass on a day trip to the cathedral city of **Chartres.** Go to bucolic **Parc André Gagon,** a 5-minute walk northwest of the fabled cathedral.

There's been a brasserie on this site since around 1900. Amid well-oiled, pine-wood panels and polished copper, you can choose from some of grandmother's favorites as well as more modern dishes. The owner, Jean-Frederic Guidoni, worked for years in the kitchens of Taillevent, one of Paris's best restaurants, but he has brought his own innovative touch here. The dishes are sometimes simple, sometimes complex, rarely mannered, and never pointless. For starters, try frogs' legs sautéed with fresh basil followed by a main course such as roast lamb with a puree of chickpeas or braised pork on a bed of shredded carrots, apricots, and a confit of lemons. Our most recent dessert was an inspired brownie of praline-laced chocolate with a Clementine-flavored sorbet with "perfumed juices." The menu attracts fans who consider the food more sophisticated than that served at other brasseries. (The chefs gained their experience in upscale restaurants.)

8 rue St-Lazare, 9e. ✆ 01-48-78-62-73. Reservations recommended far in advance. Main courses 25€–34€ ($29–$39); prix fixe menu 33€ ($38). AE, MC, V. Mon–Fri noon–2:30pm and 7:30–10:30pm. Métro: Notre-Dame de Lorette, Opéra, or Cadet.

Wally Le Saharien ALGERIAN Head to this dining room—lined with desert photos and tribal artifacts crafted from ceramics, wood, and weavings—for an insight into the spicy, slow-cooked cuisine that fueled the colonial expansion of France into North Africa. The fixed-price dinner menu begins with a trio of starters: a spicy soup, stuffed and grilled sardines, and a savory *pastilla* (baked with herbs and a touch of honey) of pigeon in puff pastry. This can be followed by any of several kinds of couscous or a *méchouia* (slow-cooked tart) of lamb dusted with an optional coating of sugar, according to your taste. *Merguez,* the cumin-laden spicy sausage of the North African world, factors importantly into any meal, as does homemade (usually honey-infused) pastries. End your meal with traditional mint-flavored tea.

36 rue Rodier, 9e. ✆ 01-42-85-51-90. Reservations recommended. A la carte main courses (available only at lunch) 26€ ($30); prix fixe dinner 40€ ($46). MC, V. Tues–Sat noon–2pm and 7–10pm. Métro: Anvers.

INEXPENSIVE

Chartier TRADITIONAL FRENCH Opened in 1896, this unpretentious *fin-de-siècle* restaurant is now an official historic monument featuring a whimsical mural with trees, a flowering staircase, and an early depiction of an airplane (it was painted in 1929 by an artist who traded his work for food). The menu follows brasserie-style traditions, including items you might not dare to eat—boiled veal's head, tripe, tongue, sweetbreads, lamb's brains, chitterling sausages—as well as some old-time tempters. The waiter will steer you through dishes like *boeuf bourguignon* (braised beef in red-wine sauce), *pot-au-feu* (combining beef, turnips, cabbage, and carrots), *pavé* (a thick slice) of rump steak, and at least five kinds of fish. The prices are low, even for a three-course meal, a fact that as many as 320 diners appreciate at a time.

7 rue de Faubourg Montmartre, 9e. ℂ 01-47-70-86-29. Main courses 9.50€–18€ ($11–$21). MC, V. Daily 11:30am–3pm and 6–10pm. Métro: Grands Boulevards.

10TH ARRONDISSEMENT
MODERATE

Brasserie Flo ★ ALSATIAN This remote restaurant is hard to find, but once you arrive (after walking through passageway after passageway), you'll see that *fin-de-siècle* Paris lives on. The restaurant opened in 1860 and has changed its decor very little since. The specialty is *la formidable choucroute* (a mound of sauerkraut with boiled ham, bacon, and sausage) for two. The onion soup and sole meunière are always good, as are the warm foie gras and guinea hen with lentils. Look for the *plats du jour,* ranging from roast pigeon to veal fricassee with sorrel, and a filet of beef with foie gras.

7 cour des Petites-Ecuries, 10e. ℂ 01-47-70-13-59. Reservations recommended. Main courses 16€–24€ ($18–$28); prix fixe lunch 23€ ($26), dinner 33€ ($38). AE, DC, MC, V. Daily noon–3pm and 7pm–1am. Métro: Château d'Eau or Strasbourg-St-Denis.

Chez Michel BRETON Adapting to the tastes and income of its loyal crowd, this restaurant near the Gare du Nord serves generous portions of well-prepared Breton dishes. In a pair of dining rooms accented with exposed wood, you'll enjoy the fruits of the fields and seacoast, densely flavored and traditional; they include veal chops fried in butter and served with gratin of potatoes enriched with calf's foot gelatin, and codfish filets served on beds of tomatoes and onions and a tapenade of black olives. Other regional choices include a Celtic stew (*kig ha farz* in Breton dialect) made from stewed veal and pork, and served with grilled lard, herbs, and baby vegetables; and *les craquelins de Saint Mâlo* (small Breton-style tarts) stuffed with aromatic goat cheese. The appropriate conclusion to a meal is a snifter of Calvados, the apple-based brandy of the French coast.

10 rue de Belzunce, 10e. ℂ 01-44-53-06-20. Reservations recommended. Prix fixe menu 30€ ($35). MC, V. Tues–Fri noon–2pm; Mon–Fri 7pm–midnight. Métro: Gare du Nord.

La Grille (Value TRADITIONAL FRENCH/SEAFOOD Few other moderate restaurants are as hotly pursued by Parisians as this nine-table holdover from another age. For at least a century after the French Revolution, fishermen from Dieppe used this place as a springboard for carousing and cabaret watching after delivering their fish to Les Halles market. Since the late 1960s the charming, outspoken M. and Mme Cullere have run this restaurant. They have become distinctive, albeit slightly eccentric, neighborhood fixtures. The Holy Grail at La Grille is an entire turbot prepared tableside with an emulsified white-butter sauce. Other recommended dishes are seafood terrine, *boeuf bourguignon* (braised beef in red-wine sauce), and marinated sardine filets. The high-calorie, high-satisfaction desserts include chocolate mousse and vanilla custard. (The restaurant name derives from the 200-year-old wrought-iron grills in front, classified as national treasures and among the best examples of their kind in Paris.)

80 rue du Faubourg-Poissonnière, 10e. (℃) **01-47-70-89-73**. Reservations required. Main courses 16€–32€ ($18–$37). AE, MC, V. Mon–Fri noon–2:30pm and 7pm–midnight. Métro: Poissonnière.

INEXPENSIVE

Paris-Dakar SENEGALESE   Named after the rally that carries vehicles across the world's toughest terrain, this restaurant celebrates the culinary traditions of France's former colonies in West Africa. After a warm welcome, you can sample such Senegalese dishes as *poulet yassa* (chicken braised with limes and onions), *maffé* (beef fried with peanuts, onions, and spice), and the national dish, *thiebkou-diene* (fish sautéed with rice, fresh vegetables, and fiery chiles). A Senegalese version of the Arab-derived *méchoui* (roasted rack of lamb) is served, as is *le capitaine,* a fish that flourishes off the coast of West Africa, with a lime-and-sweet-onion sauce. If you're adventurous, ask for a glass of the palm wine, fermented from coconuts in a style common in West Africa.

95 rue du Faubourg St-Martin, 10e. (℃) **01-42-08-16-64**. Reservations recommended. Main courses 12€–17€ ($14–$20); prix fixe 25€–30€ ($29–$35). AE, MC, V. Tues–Thurs and Sat–Sun noon–3pm; Tues–Sun 7pm–1am. Métro: Gare de l'Est.

11TH ARRONDISSEMENT
EXPENSIVE

Blue Elephant ⚡ THAI   At this branch of a chain of Thai restaurants, the decor evokes the jungles of Southeast Asia, interspersed with Thai sculptures and paintings. The menu items are succulent, infused with lemon grass, curries, and the aromas that make Thai cuisine distinctive. Examples are a salad made with *pomelo,* a Thai fruit larger and tarter than a grapefruit, studded with shrimp and herbs; salmon soufflé served in banana leaves; and grilled fish with passion fruit.

43 rue de la Roquette, 11e. (℃) **01-47-00-42-00**. Reservations recommended far in advance. Main courses 22€–27€ ($25–$31); prix fixe menu 44€ ($51). AE, DC, MC, V. Mon–Fri noon–2:30pm; Mon–Sat 7pm–midnight. Métro: Bastille.

MODERATE

A Sousceyrac ★ TRADITIONAL FRENCH   Its name is derived from a village (in the Lotte region of southwestern France) that has always been associated with rich cuisine, traditional values, and literature. (*Le Dejeuner de Sousceyrac,* by Pere Benoit, was a best-selling ode to French nostalgia in the 1970s.) You can capture some of that feeling at this charmer, whose decor and menu have changed little since 1925. Even the nicotine stains in the paneling might have been made by previous clients such as former French president Mitterand and the current holder of the office, Jacques Chirac. Classic menu examples include slices of velvety foie gras; mousse of grouse; and roasted rabbit *a la royale,* cooked in a blend of red wine, a puréed medley of its innards, and its own blood. Dishes like this demand accompaniment by a strong red wine, of which the restaurant lists many.

85 rue Faidherbe, 11e. (℃) **01-43-71-65-30**. Reservations recommended. Main courses 18€–28€ ($21–$32); prix fixe menus 23€–28€ ($26–$32). V. Tues–Sat noon–2pm and 8–10:15pm. Closed Aug and 1 week in Mar. Métro: Charonnes.

C'amelot ★ *(Finds)* TRADITIONAL FRENCH   A meal at this restaurant, tucked away in the 11th arrondissement, is like dining in the French countryside. Under wooden beams and held up by old stonewalls, the three dining rooms are decorated with country crockery. Patrons dine at bare wooden tables, using kitchen towels as napkins. Both modernists and upholders of French culinary tradition find a happy home here. Everything is served by a capable staff sensitive to your needs and orders. The fixed-price lunch and dinner menus are changed every day. Appetizers often begin with a tureen of soup from which you help yourself. Count yourself lucky if it's the well-flavored pumpkin with tasty homemade croutons. Delicate red mullet often comes with eggplant "caviar" and a fresh arugula salad, the fish enhanced by a sprinkling of basil juice. Meat and poultry dishes are also savory. Since dining here we've become addicted to fennel ice cream.

50 rue Amelot, 11e. ℭ **01-43-55-54-04.** Reservations required. Prix fixe lunch 16€–23€ ($18–$26); prix fixe dinner 32€ ($37). AE, V. Mon–Sat noon–2pm and 7–10pm. Métro: Chemin Vert.

Mansouria MOROCCAN   One of Paris's most charming Moroccan restaurants occupies a much-restored building midway between place de la Bastille and place de la Nation. The minimalist decor combines futuristic architecture with bare sand-colored walls, accented only with sets of antique doors and portals from the sub-Sahara. Look for seven kinds of couscous, including versions with chicken; beef brochettes; or lamb, onions, and almonds. *Tagines* are succulent dishes of chicken or fish prepared with aromatic herbs and slow cooked in clay pots that are carried to your table.

11 rue Faidherbe, 11e. ℭ **01-43-71-00-16.** Reservations recommended. Main courses 16€–24€ ($18–$28); prix fixe 29€–44€ ($33–$51). V. Wed–Sat noon–2pm; Mon–Sat 7:30–11pm. Métro: Faidherbe-Chaligny.

INEXPENSIVE

Le Manguier SENEGALESE   Many of the patrons who dine here don't know much about Senegalese cuisine, but thanks to a charming welcome and live music presenting African jazz at its most compelling, they tend to come back. The decor evokes a West African fishing village. You can order zesty fare like roast chicken marinated with lime and served with onions; smoked shark meat; and the national dish, *thiebkoudiene* (a blend of fish, rice, and fresh vegetables). The medley is perked up with a selection of fiery sauces you apply yourself. The drinks of choice are beer, a rum-based cocktail called *Le Dakar,* and wine.

67 av. Parmentier, 11e. ℭ **01-48-07-03-27.** Reservations recommended. Main courses 10€–18€ ($12–$21). AE, MC, V. Mon–Sat noon–3pm and 7pm–1am. Métro: Parmentier.

12TH ARRONDISSEMENT
EXPENSIVE

Au Trou Gascon ★★★ GASCONY   One of Paris's most acclaimed chefs, Alain Dutournier, lures fashionable palates to an unchic area. He launched his career in southwest France's Gascony region. His parents mortgaged their inn to allow Dutournier to open an early-1900s bistro in a little known part of the 12th. Word spread of a savant in the kitchen who practiced authentic *cuisine moderne.* His wife, Nicole, is the welcoming hostess, and the wine steward has distinguished himself for his exciting cave containing several little-known wines along with a fabulous collection of Armagnacs. You can start with duck foie gras cooked in a terrine or Gascony-cured ham. The best main courses include fresh tuna with braised cabbage, a superb cassoulet, and chicken from the Chalosse region of Landes, which Dutournier roasts and serves in its own drippings.

40 rue Taine, 12e. ℭ **01-43-44-34-26.** Reservations required far in advance. Main courses 28€–35€ ($32–$40); prix fixe lunch 36€ ($41). AE, DC, MC, V. Mon–Fri noon–2pm, 7:30–10:30pm. Closed Aug. Métro: Daumesnil.

MODERATE

China Club ★ CHINESE/CANTONESE Evoking 1930s Hong Kong, this favorite is still going strong, still laughing at upstart new Asian restaurants, and still serving some of the best Asian cuisine in Paris. The food is mainly Cantonese, prepared with flair. The menu is vast, with plenty of choices. Nearly everything is good, especially the sautéed shrimp and calamari, Shanghai chicken, and red rice sautéed with vegetables. Before dinner, you might want to enjoy a drink in the upstairs smoking lounge. Downstairs, the Sing Song club has live music, including something called Sino-French jazz on Thursdays, Fridays, and Saturdays.

50 rue de Charenton, 12e. ☏ 01-43-43-82-02. Main courses 13€–29€ ($15–$33); prix fixe dinner 28€ ($32); prix fixe Sun dinner 18€ ($21). AE, MC, V. Sun–Thurs 7pm–2am; Fri–Sat 7pm–3am. Closed July 20 and Aug 20. Métro: Bastille.

Le Square Trousseau TRADITIONAL FRENCH This bistro serves traditional food in a setting that evokes the best of turn-of-the-20th-century France. Within a 1905 decor accented with etched glass, tiles, and banquettes, you can enjoy dishes that include *pot-au-feu* (beef stew), sole meunière, sweetbreads, calf's liver, and *steak au poivre* (pepper steak). A habitué told us that she comes here for "comfort food," including terrines and tarts like those her mother used to prepare. But she notes many innovations in the menu, which she calls "winds of change." Among these are some delicious risottos.

1 rue Antoine-Vollon, 12e. ☏ 01-43-43-06-00. Reservations recommended. Main courses 18€–27€ ($21–$31); prix fixe lunch 21€–24€ ($24–$28). AE, MC, V. Tues–Sat noon–2:30pm and 8–11:30pm. Métro: Ledru-Rollin.

INEXPENSIVE

L'Ebauchoir ★ *Finds* TRADITIONAL FRENCH Tucked into a neighborhood rarely visited by foreigners and featuring a 1950s decor so out it's in, this bistro attracts carpenters, plumbers, and electricians, as well as an occasional journalist and screenwriter. With buffed aluminum trim and plaster-and-stucco walls tinted dark orange-yellow and blue, the place might remind you of a factory canteen. You can order surprisingly generous and well-prepared stuffed sardines, snapper filet with olive oil and garlic, crabmeat soup, fried calf's liver with coriander and honey, and rack of lamb combined with saddle of lamb.

43 rue de Cîteaux, 12e. ☏ 01-43-42-49-31. Reservations recommended for dinner. Main courses 20€–30€ ($23–$35); prix fixe lunch 13€ ($15). AE, MC, V. Mon–Sat noon–2:30pm and 8–11pm. Métro: Faidherbe-Chaligny.

18TH ARRONDISSEMENT
INEXPENSIVE

Le Grain de Folie ORGANIC/VEGETARIAN Simple and wholesome, the cuisine at this vegetarian restaurant is inspired by France, Greece, California, Turkey, and India. The menu includes an array of theme salads, cereals, tarts, terrines, and casseroles. Dessert selections might include an old-fashioned tart or a fruit salad. The decor includes potted plants and exposed stone. You can choose one of an array of wines or a frothy glass of vegetable juice to accompany your meal. This place may be a bit difficult to find, but it's worth the search.

24 rue de la Vieuville, 18e. ☏ 01-42-58-15-57. Reservations recommended. Main courses 10€–12€ ($12–$14); prix fixe menus 12€–16€ ($14–$18). No credit cards. Mon–Sat 12:30–2:30pm and 7:30–11pm; Sun 11:30am–11pm. Métro: Abbesses.

8TH ARRONDISSEMENT
VERY EXPENSIVE

Buddha Bar ★ MODERN FRENCH/PACIFIC RIM This place remains Paris's restaurant of the moment, even though it's been around for a while. A location near the Champs-Elysées and place de la Concorde, and an allegiance

Where to Dine on the Right Bank (8 & 16–17e)

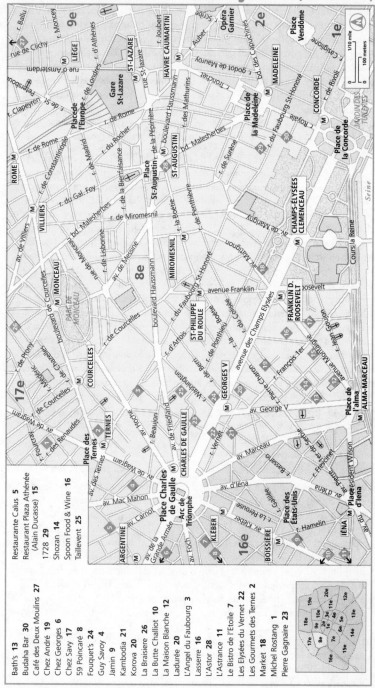

Restaurante Caïus 5
Restaurant Plaza Athénée
(Alain Ducasse) 15
1728 29
Shozan 14
Spoon Food & Wine 16
Taillevent 25

Bath's 13
Budaha Bar 30
Café des Deux Moulins 27
Chez André 19
Chez Georges 6
Chez Savy 17
59 Poincaré 8
Fouquet's 24
Guy Savoy 4
Jamin 9
Kambodia 21
Korova 20
La Braisière 26
La Butte Chaillot 10
La Maison Blanche 12
Ladurée 20
L'Angel du Faubourg 3
Lasserre 16
L'Astor 28
L'Astrance 11
Le Bistro de l'Etoile 7
Les Elysées du Vernet 22
Les Gourmets des Ternes 2
Market 18
Michel Rostang 1
Pierre Gagnaire 23

135

to a fusion of French, Asian, and Californian cuisines, attract trendy diners devoted to the whims of fashion. The vast dining room is presided over by a giant Buddha, and the culinary theme combines Japanese sashimi, Vietnamese spring rolls, lacquered duck, sautéed shrimp with black-bean sauce, grilled chicken skewers with orange sauce, sweet-and-sour spareribs, and crackling squab *à l'orange.* There are two sittings for dinner: 7 to 9pm and 10:30pm to 12:30am. Many come here just for a drink in the carefully lacquered bar, upstairs from the street-level dining room.

8 rue Boissy d'Anglas, 8e. ⓒ **01-53-05-90-00.** Reservations required far in advance. Main courses 70€–80€ ($81–$92). AE, MC, V. Mon–Fri noon–3pm; daily 7pm–12:30am. Métro: Concorde.

Lasserre ⭐⭐⭐ MODERN & TRADITIONAL FRENCH   It's so old it's new again. This elegant restaurant was a bistro before World War II and has since become a legend. The main salon stretches two stories high, with a mezzanine on each side. Tall silk-draped arched windows frame tables set with fine porcelain, gold-edged crystal glasses, and silver candelabras. The ceiling is painted with white clouds and a cerulean sky, but in good weather the staff slides back the roof to reveal the real sky. The faces of Audrey Hepburn, Maria Callas, and Marlene Dietrich have given way to young British royals and statuesque models from Brazil. A spectacular chef, Jean-Louis Nomicos, is a master of taste and texture, and he's brought renewed life to this swank citadel. The appetizers are among Paris's finest, including truffle salad; grilled foie gras of duckling served with a confit of green apples; Chablis-flavored belon oysters; and a hyper-upscale version of macaroni with foie gras and truffles. The signature main course is poached sole filets *Club de la Casserole,* in puff pastry with asparagus tips and asparagus-flavored cream sauce; also wonderful are the veal kidneys flambé; pigeon André Malraux; and roast duckling with an orange sauce. For dessert, and evocative of the new menu, the chef serves roasted baby pineapples in passion fruit juice with coconut sorbet. The wine cellar, with some 160,000 bottles, is one of the city's most remarkable.

17 av. Franklin D. Roosevelt, 8e. ⓒ **01-43-59-53-43.** Fax 01-45-63-72-23. Reservations required far in advance. Main courses 66€–75€ ($76–$86); prix fixe 185€ ($213). AE, MC, V. Thurs–Fri 12:15–2pm; Mon–Sat 7:30–10pm. Closed Aug. Métro: Franklin-D.-Roosevelt.

L'Astor ⭐⭐⭐ MODERN FRENCH   The setting is a tawny-colored enclave beneath an etched-glass Art Deco ceiling, with luxurious touches inspired by the 1930s. Since great French chef Joël Robuchon's departure, there have been a series of young chefs who have filled in. The newest is very talented Christophe Dié, who took over in February of 2003. Time will tell whether Mr. Dié will influence the menu with creative ideas of his own, but until then, this restaurant perpetuates the Robuchon legend with an almost slavish devotion to Robuchon's time-tested specialties. Examples include caramelized sea urchins in aspic with fennel-flavored cream sauce, eggplant-stuffed cannelloni with tuna filets and olive oil, and crisp-fried crayfish served with basil. There is also a selection of dishes revived from the Escoffier-inspired tenets of grand 19th-century cuisine, including spit-roasted Bresse chicken in cream sauce with baby vegetables; *merlan Colbert,* consisting of deep-fried filets of whiting in an herb-flavored butter sauce; and (during the autumn game season) *lièvre la royale du Senateur Couteaux,* wild hare cooked in a mixture of red wine and its own blood, named for a famed 19th-century gastronome.

In the Hôtel Astor, 11 rue d'Astorg, 8e. ⓒ **01-53-05-05-20.** Fax 01-53-05-05-30. Reservations required far in advance, especially for lunch. Main courses 60€–70€ ($69–$81); prix fixe menu 55€–98€ ($63–$113). AE, DC, MC, V. Mon–Fri noon–2pm and 7:30–10pm. Closed Aug. Métro: St-Augustin or Madeleine.

Les Elysées du Vernet ✶✶✶ PROVENÇAL   This restaurant is a gastro-nomic wonder. It has one of the neighborhood's most panoramic glass ceilings, a gray-and-green translucent dome designed by the architect (Gustav Eiffel) who conceived the famous tower. Chef Eric Brifford keeps the crowds lined up. Menu items focus on Provençal models and change every 2 months, based on whatever is fresh. A recent sampling of perfectly prepared, imaginative dishes included a shoulder of French lamb with a thick sauce of fruit compote and aro-matic herbs, or else a braised "blue" Atlantic lobster with fresh rosemary and an accompaniment of ravioli stuffed with fish roe and a charlotte of red peppers. There's also a melt-in-your-mouth version of apple charlotte, and even a black-truffle ice cream, a dish that traditionalists consider far-fetched. Candles illumi-nate the place and during the dinner hour, there's a pianist, whose music reverberates off the dome.

In the Hôtel Vernet, 25 rue Vernet, 8e. (✆) 01-44-31-98-98. Reservations required. Main courses 42€–78€ ($48–$90); *menu gastronomique* 128€ ($147). AE, DC, MC, V. Mon 7:30–10pm; Tues–Fri 12:30–2pm and 7:30–10pm. Métro: George-V.

Pierre Gagnaire ✶✶✶ MODERN FRENCH   If you're able to get a reser-vation, it's worth the effort. The menus are seasonal to take advantage of France's rich bounty; owner Pierre Gagnaire demands perfection, and the chef has a daz-zling way of flavors and textures. Stellar examples are crayfish cooked tempura style with thin-sliced flash-seared vegetables and sweet-and-sour sauce; and turbot cooked in a bag and served with fennel and Provençal lemons. Chicken with truffles is part of a two-tiered service—first the breast in a wine-based aspic, second the thighs chopped into roughly textured pieces. For dessert, try the chocolate soufflé served with a frozen parfait and pistachios.

6 rue Balzac, 8e. (✆) 01-58-36-12-50. Fax 01-58-36-12-51. Reservations are imperative and difficult to get. Main courses 65€–120€ ($75–$138); prix fixe lunch 90€ ($104), dinner 195€ ($225). AE, DC, MC, V. Mon–Fri noon–1:30pm and 7:30–10pm; Sun 7:30–10pm. Métro: George-V.

Restaurant Plaza Athénée (Alain Ducasse) ✶✶✶ MODERN & TRADI-TIONAL FRENCH   Few other chefs have catapulted to international fame as quickly as Alain Ducasse. The most recent setting for his cuisine is in a world-renowned hotel, the Plaza Athénée. There's a lot of marketing and glitter involved, but what you'll find is a lobby-level hideaway that top-notch decora-tor Patrick Jouin transformed with layers of pearl-gray paint and yards of translucent organdy. The five-star Michelin chef divides his time between Paris and Monaco, though he insists he doesn't repeat himself in either of his famous eateries. He seeds his dishes with produce from every corner of France—rare local vegetables, fish from the coasts, and dishes incorporating cardoons, turnips, celery, turbot, cuttlefish, and Bresse fowl. His French cuisine is con-temporary and Mediterranean, yet not new. Though many dishes are light, Ducasse isn't afraid of lard, as he proves by his thick, oozing slabs of pork grilled to a crisp. The wine list is superb, with some selections deriving from the best vintages of France, Germany, Switzerland, Spain, California, and Italy.

In the Hotel Plaza Athénée, 25 av. Montaigne, 8e. (✆) 01-53-67-66-65 or 01-53-67-65-00. Fax 01-53-67-66-66. Reservations required 6–8 weeks in advance. Main courses 70€–105€ ($81–$121); prix fixe menus 190€–300€ ($219–$345). AE, DC, MC, V. Thurs–Fri noon–2pm; Mon–Fri 8–10:30pm. Closed mid-July to Aug 29 and Dec 17–31. Métro: Alma-Marceau.

Taillevent ✶✶✶ MODERN & TRADITIONAL FRENCH   This is the Parisian *ne plus ultra* of gastronomy. Taillevent opened in 1946 and has climbed steadily in excellence; today it ranks as Paris's outstanding all-around restaurant, challenged only by Lucas-Carton and Pierre Gagnaire. It's in a grand 19th-century town house off the Champs-Elysées, with paneled rooms and crystal chandeliers. The place is small, as the owner wishes, since it permits him to give personal attention to every facet of the operation and maintain a discreet atmosphere. You might begin with a *boudin* (sausage) of Breton lobster a la Nage, cream of watercress soup with Sevruga caviar, or duck liver with spice bread and ginger. Main courses include red snapper with black olives, Scottish salmon cooked in sea salt with a sauce of olive oil and lemons, and cassolette of crayfish. Dessert might be a *nougatine glacé* with pears. The wine list is among the best in Paris.

15 rue Lamennais, 8e. ② **01-44-95-15-01.** Fax 01-42-25-95-18. Reservations required 4–6 weeks in advance. Main courses 34€–90€ ($39–$104); *menu dégustation* (tasting menu) 130€ ($150). AE, DC, MC, V. Mon–Fri noon–2:30pm and 7–10pm. Closed Aug. Métro: George-V.

EXPENSIVE

Bath's AUVERGNAT/TRADITIONAL FRENCH   The rocky and agrarian region of central France known as L'Auvergne has never been considered particularly chic. This restaurant, however, more than any other Auvergnat restaurant in Paris, manages to transform the region's provincial image into something that's cozy but elegant. The setting is a well-upholstered, ocher-colored dining room where menu items are divided between the pork-based culinary specialties of the Auvergne and lighter dishes from the rest of France. The finest examples include ravioli stuffed with a pungent Cantal cheese from the Auvergne; cream of lentil soup studded with foie gras "bonbons"; filet of beef from Salers (a part of the Auvergne) served with lentils; roasted veal served with morel-studded macaroni; and something that's absolutely not native to the Auvergne, a cassoulet (stew pot) of lobster. Jean-Yves Bath, the owner and chef, earned a Michelin star just a few months after the place opened in 1999.

9 rue de la Trémoille, 8e. ② **01-40-70-01-09.** Reservations required. Main courses 18€–44€ ($21–$51); prix fixe lunch 30€ ($35), dinner 70€ ($81). AE, DC, MC, V. Mon–Fri noon–2:30pm and 7:30–10:30pm. Closed Aug. Métro: Alma-Marceau.

La Maison Blanche ★★ TRADITIONAL FRENCH/PROVENÇAL Jacques and his twin brother Lauren Pourcel were two of the most famous chefs in the southerly province of Languedoc before deciding to head north to Paris a few years ago. The setting would be the envy of any restaurant in the world: Positioned on the uppermost (fifth) floor of the Art Deco–style Theatre des Champs-Elysees, it contains a contemporary, all-white decor, sweeping views across the Seine, and two dining rooms. Clientele tends to be rich, non-French, and a bit pretentious, but in light of the brilliant food and the sublime setting, who cares? The menu changes with the inspiration of the chefs and the seasons, but stellar examples include filet of grilled sole with a citrus sauce; rack of roasted lamb with sesame seeds; and filet of partridge cooked on the bone with caramelized turnips and Szechuan-style spicy peppers, with a syrup of licorice-flavored blackberries drippled on.

15 Ave. Montaigne, 8e. ② **01-47-23-55-99.** Reservations required. Main courses 39€–71€ ($45–$82); prix fixe lunch, with wine 75€ ($86). AE, DC, MC, V. Mon–Fri noon–1:45pm; daily 8–10:45pm. Métro: Alma-Marceau.

L'Angle du Faubourg ★★ MODERN & TRADITIONAL FRENCH Throughout the 1980s and early 1990s, a reservation at the Restaurant Taillevent was sought after by diplomats, billionaires, and demimondains from around Europe. In 2001, the owner and chef, Mr. Vrinat, opened a cost-conscious bistro that capitalized on Taillevent's reputation, but at much lower prices. Lunches here tend to be efficient, relatively quick, and businesslike, while dinners are more

---

Finds **The Best Food Shopping in Paris**

Master chef Alain Ducasse continues to expand his empire with the opening of **BE,** 73 blvd. de Courcelles, 8e ((C) **01-46-22-20-20;** Métro: Courcelles). Short for Boulangerie Epicerie, BE is part bakery and part upmarket deli. As a baker, Eric Kayser is famous in Paris, and he sells some 400 products from all over the globe, including 10 varieties of French bread baked fresh at least eight times a day. You can stop off here for the makings of a picnic, costing about 20€ to 25€ ($23–$29) per person, depending on your selection. There are only 10 seats. If a table is free, grab it. You can eat an array of freshly made salads for 6.50€ to 9€ ($7.50–$10); delicious homemade soups at 4€ ($4.60), and some of the best and most delectable sandwiches in Paris, costing from 4€ to 8.50€ ($4.60–$9.80). Of course, if you want some walnut oil from the Dordogne or some lavender honey from Moustiers-Ste-Marie, that is standing on the shelves as well. Open Monday to Saturday 8am to 9pm.

---

leisurely, even romantic. Expect an ultramodern dining room in tones of soft red and pink, additional seating in the cellar, and a menu that simplifies the lofty culinary ideas of Taillevent. The best examples include cream of beet soup; marinated salmon; a risotto whose ingredients change weekly (during our visit, it was studded with braised radicchio); and a grilled, low-fat version of *daurade* (bream or porgy), served with a sweet-and-sour sauce, appreciated by the many diet-conscious *photo-modèles* who stop in between bouts of shopping. Dessert might be an old-fashioned rice pudding.

195 rue du Faubourg St-Honoré, 8e. (C) **01-40-74-20-20.** Reservations required. Main courses 18€–28€ ($21–$32); prix fixe menu 35€–60€ ($40–$69). AE, DC, MC, V. Mon–Fri noon–2:30pm and 7–10:30pm. Métro: Terme.

1728 ⭐ *Finds* MODERN FRENCH/JAPANESE An 18th-century town house, just off Faubourg-St-Honoré where the Marquis de Lafayette lived, has been turned into this chic rendezvous. The decor is sumptuous just like it was in the 1700s, with paintings on the wall—each for sale—and low marble dining tables and chairs. Call the place what you like—upmarket tea salon or cafe. Its chef, Gao Lin, hails from China, and he's brought a fusion of French and Japanese dishes to his menu. Start with the tuna tartare, or even a well-stuffed club sandwich at lunch. The tiger shrimp is savory and is scented with malt whisky. For a main course, one of the most delightful offerings is steamed sea bass, flavored with ginger, and served with snow peas and zucchini. Other fine selections include filet of sole with a saffron-laced sauce and filet of beef in a sauce made of Chinese truffles. The pastries are supplied from the famous Pierre Hermé bakeries. Many visit in the afternoon just for tea and pastries.

8 rue d'Anjou, 8e. (C) **01-40-17-04-77.** Reservations recommended for main meals. Main courses 30€–40€ ($35–$46). AE, MC, V. Mon–Fri 12:30–3pm; Mon–Sat 8:30–11pm. Closed 3 weeks in Aug. Métro: Concorde.

Shozan ⭐ MODERN FRENCH/JAPANESE East and West form a perfect synthesis in this Franco-Japanese alliance. It's not for the traditionalist, but trendy Parisians enjoy the new flavors. The classic foie gras appears as foie gras sushi with sansho pepper, and the roast lamb comes with a green-tea crust. The roast tuna with buckwheat seed and the scampi concoction are delectable. A chef's specialty is lobster with white-sesame sauce spiked with sweet sake.

Famous interior designer Christian Liaigre created the stunning setting, dominated by wood and leather.

11 rue de la Trémoille, 8e. (C) **01-47-23-37-32.** Reservations recommended far in advance. Main courses 19€–38€ ($22–$44); prix fixe lunch 17€–30€ ($19–$34), dinner 68€–69€ ($78–$79). AE, DC, MC, V. Mon–Fri noon–2:30pm; Mon–Sat 7–10:30pm. Closed last week of July and 1st week of Aug. Métro: Alma-Marceau.

Spoon, Food & Wine ★ INTERNATIONAL   This hyper-modern venture of star chef Alain Ducasse is hailed as a "restaurant for the millennium" and condemned by some as surreal and a bit absurd. Despite that, there can be a wait of 2 weeks for a dinner reservation, and the sense that this upscale but relatively affordable restaurant might be the least pretentious and most hip of any of Ducasse's ventures. The somewhat claustrophobic dining room evokes a blend of Parisian and Californian references, and the cuisine—whose menu changes every 2 months—roams the world. Examples include grilled tuna steak with satay sauce; deliberately undercooked grilled squid (part of it will evoke a sushi dish) with curry sauce; and roasted pigeon with an Italian *dolce-forte* (sweet-and-sour) sauce. Vegetarians appreciate stir-fried dishes where you can mix and match up to 15 ingredients. Pastas come with a selection of three sauces, including a three-tomato marmalade. Desserts feature Parisian versions of such U.S.-inspired dishes as cheesecake and doughnuts drenched with bitter chocolate.

In the Hôtel Marignan-Elysée, 14 rue Marignan, 8e. (C) **01-40-76-34-44.** Reservations recommended 2 weeks in advance. Main courses 25€–40€ ($29–$46). Mon–Fri noon–2pm and 7–11pm. AE, DC, V. Métro: Franklin-D.-Roosevelt.

MODERATE

Chez André TRADITIONAL FRENCH   Chez André is one of the neighborhood's favorite bistros with an ambience that evokes France of the 1950s and a clientele that includes everyday folk as well as some of the most prosperous residents of this extremely upscale neighborhood. Outside, a discreet red awning stretches over an array of shellfish on ice; inside, an Art Nouveau decor includes etched glass and masses of flowers. This has been a landmark on rue Marbeuf since 1937. It remains as it was when it was founded (an agreement was made with the original owners). The old-style cuisine on the menu includes pâté of thrush, Roquefort in puff pastry, grilled veal kidneys, roast rack of lamb, a *potage du jour,* fresh shellfish, and on Fridays, bouillabaisse. There are several reasonably priced wines offered as well. For variety, some locals opt for the *plat du jour.* The dessert choices may be *baba au rhum* (rum cake with raisins), chocolate cake, or a daily pastry.

12 rue Marbeuf (at rue Clément-Marot), 8e. (C) **01-47-20-59-57.** Reservations recommended. Main courses 16€–32€ ($18–$37); prix fixe menu 34€ ($39). AE, DC, MC, V. Daily noon–1am. Métro: Franklin-D.-Roosevelt.

Ladurée ★ TRADITIONAL FRENCH   Ladurée, acclaimed since 1862 as one of Paris's grand cafes (located near La Madeleine), is now on the Champs-Elysées, adding a touch of class to the neighborhood. This offshoot caters to an international set wearing everything from Givenchy to Gap. Expect a stylish, somewhat chaotic venue that changes from tearoom to full-fledged restaurant at least twice during the course of any day. The Belle Epoque setting is ideal for sampling Ladurée's macaroons—not the coconut version familiar to Americans but two almond meringue cookies, flavored with vanilla, coffee, strawberry, pistachio, or another flavor, held together with butter cream. The menu of talented chefs is constantly adjusted to take advantage of the freshest ingredients. It may include a crisp and tender pork filet with potato-and-parsley purée, and marinated red mullet on a salad of cold ratatouille. If you're looking for a pick-me-up to accompany your tea, consider a *plaisir sucre,* a chocolate confection decorated with spun sugar. The only downside: Service isn't always efficient.

75 av. des Champs-Elysées, 8e. (C) **01-40-75-08-75.** Reservations required for restaurant, not for cafe. Main courses 23€–28€ ($26–$32); pastries from 8€ ($9.20). AE, DC, MC, V. Daily 7:30am–1am. Métro: George-V.

Les Gourmets des Ternes *Value* TRADITIONAL FRENCH   Les Gourmets des Ternes caters to hordes who appreciate its affordable prices and lack of pretension. Despite the brusque service, diners have included the mayor of Atlanta (who wrote the bistro a thank-you letter), Sean Penn, Jack Nicholson, and Oliver Stone, as well as hundreds of folks from this neighborhood. Thriving in this spot since 1892, the place retains an early-1900s paneled decor, with some additions from the 1950s, including Bordeaux-colored banquettes, mirrors, wooden panels, touches of brass, and paper tablecloths. There's an outdoor terrace as well. The finely grilled signature dishes include rib steak with marrow sauce and fries; country pâtés and sausages; sole, turbot, and monkfish; sautéed sea scallops; filet of beef; and satisfying desserts like peach Melba and *baba au rhum* (rum cake with raisins).

87 bd. de Courcelles, 8e. (C) **01-42-27-43-04.** Prix fixe menu 40€ ($46). AE, MC, V. Mon–Fri noon–2:30pm and 7–10pm. Métro: Ternes.

Market ★ FUSION   The creative force here is Alsatian Jean-Georges Vongerichten, whose restaurants in New York, Hong Kong, London, and Las Vegas are classified by local critics as both megahip and top tier. The Paris gemstone in the Vongerichten empire holds 140 diners in a richly paneled postmodern decor, designed by decorating mogul Christian Liaigre, dotted with carved masks from Oceania (Polynesia) and Borneo, and with art objects on loan from the Paris branch of Christie's auction house. Menu items might remind you of the fare you'd find in a superhip Los Angeles restaurant. Examples include a pizza with black truffles and fontina cheese; foie gras with a purée of quince, corn pancakes, and wild cranberries; or crabmeat salad with mango. Main courses might feature *daurade* (bream or porgy) baked in a salt crust; a faux-filet with exotic mushrooms; or a "black plate" for two diners, loaded high with shellfish and their garnishes. There's a lavish assortment of oysters, clams, and shellfish, and a wine list that most oenophiles consider extremely interesting.

15 av. Matignon, 8e. (C) **01-56-43-40-90.** Reservations required. Prix fixe lunch 32€ ($37); pizzas 12€–27€ ($13–$31); main courses 22€–39€ ($25–$45). AE, MC, V. Daily noon–3pm and 7–11:30pm; Sat–Sun brunch 10am–6pm. Métro: Champs-Elysées–Clémenceau.

INEXPENSIVE

Chez Savy ★ *Value* AUVERGNAT   Set within one of Paris's most stratospherically expensive neighborhoods, this old-time brasserie has prices that, in comparison to those charged by many of its nearby competitors, seem particularly modest. Founded in 1923, and with an old-fashioned bistro decor (mirrors, brass hardware, polished paneling, banquettes) that hasn't changed much since the Jazz Age, it has a pair of long and narrow dining rooms, the first of which is known as *le wagon* (the dining car) by some of its clients. Come here for the kind of hearty, flavorful food that your great-grandmother (had she been from the Avergne) would have prepared for a holiday meal around 1910. Sauces here are likely to have been enriched with bone marrow; pork chitterlings are laboriously processed into earthy versions of *andouillettes;* and accompaniments to a main course might include a *petit farçou,* a thick crepe enriched with such green leafy vegetables as chard, spinach, and leeks. Lamb here is superb, especially the slow-cooked haunches, cooked with rosemary until the meat is literally falling off the bone. Wines are strong and heady, cheeses (Cantal, Roquefort, and others) are fresh from farms in central France and appropriately satisfying.

23 rue Bayard, 8e. ⓒ 01-47-23-46-98. Reservations recommended. Main courses 22€–28€ ($25–$32); prix fixe lunch 20€–24€ ($22–$27), dinner 27€ ($31). AE, MC, V. Mon–Fri noon–2:30pm and 7:30–11pm. Closed Aug. Métro: Franklin-D.-Roosevelt.

16TH ARRONDISSEMENT
VERY EXPENSIVE

Jamin ★★★ TRADITIONAL FRENCH   This is where Paris's great chef of the 1980s, Joël Robuchon, made his mark. Now Robuchon's longtime second in command, Benoit Guichard, is in charge, inspired by his master but an imaginative chef in his own right. Guichard has chosen pale-green panels and pink banquettes as a backdrop to his brief but well-chosen menu. Lunches can be simple, though each dish, like a beautifully seasoned salmon tartare, is done to perfection. Classic technique and an homage to tradition characterize the cuisine, with offerings like filet of sole with an oyster-studded cream sauce, and pigeon sausage with foie gras, pistachios, and *mâche* lettuce. A particularly earthy dish celebrates various parts of the sow that are usually rejected, blending the tail and cheeks on a platter with walnuts and fresh herbs. Finish with a *tarte tatin* (caramelized apple pie).

32 rue de Longchamp, 16e. ⓒ 01-45-53-00-07. Fax 01-45-53-00-15. Reservations required far in advance. Main courses 45€–79€ ($52–$91); prix fixe lunch 50€ ($58), dinner 95€–130€ ($109–$150). AE, DC, MC, V. Mon–Fri 12:30–2pm and 7:45–9:45pm. Métro: Trocadéro.

EXPENSIVE

59 Poincaré ★ SEAFOOD/STEAK   Not another Alain Ducasse restaurant! The French emperor of gastronomy keeps expanding his empire. This so-called "concept" restaurant comes as a surprise with its limited but top-quality ingredients. It's in the same town house where Ducasse launched himself into three-star Michelin history with his truffle-tasting menu.

Some critics have called this a refined version of an American steakhouse. Beef is carefully selected from controlled breeds in the country, and it's slowly spit-roasted for such dishes as rib of beef with an onion-flavored sweet-and-sour juice. The french fries are cut by hand, and there's also a fresh, crisp salad to go with your meal. Vegetables are featured in 20 different dishes, including on a skewer, and seasonal fruits range from cherries to wild strawberries or both red and green pears. Dessert fanciers have a choice of classical Parisian pastries such as éclairs or strawberry tarts. The profiteroles with a hot chocolate sauce are unbeatable in Paris.

Le-Parc-Sofitel-Demeure-Hotel, 59 av. Raymond-Poincaré, 16e. ⓒ 01-47-27-59-59. Reservations required. Main courses 15€–55€ ($17–$63); prix fixe dinner 90€–115€ ($104–$132). AE, DC, MC, V. Tues–Fri noon–2pm; Tues–Sat 7–11pm. Métro: Victor-Hugo or Trocadéro.

L'Astrance ★★★ MODERN FRENCH   It's small, it's charming, and shortly after its debut in 2000, it exploded into the Parisian consciousness with more fanfare and praise than anyone can remember. Its creative flair derives from the partnership of two former employees (some say "disciples") of megachef Alain Passard, scion of L'Arpège, an ultraglam restaurant in the 7th arrondissement. The perfectly mannered Christophe Rohat, supervising the dining room, is the more visible of the two; but Pascal Barbot, the chef creating the food that emerges from the kitchens, has become a true culinary force. Expect a crisply

Kids Family-Friendly Restaurants

Meals at Paris's grand restaurants are rarely suitable for young children. Nevertheless, many parents drag their kids along, often to the
annoyance of other diners. You may have to make some compromises,
such as dining earlier than most Parisians. **Hotel dining rooms** can be
another good choice for family dining. They usually have children's
menus or at least one or two *plats du jour* cooked for children, like
spaghetti with meat sauce.

If you take your child to a **moderate** or an **inexpensive restaurant,**
ask if they will serve a child's plate. If not, order a *plat du jour* or *plat
garni* (a garnished main-course platter), which will be suitable for most
children, particularly if a dessert is to follow. Most **cafes** welcome children during the day and early evening. At a cafe, children seem to like
the sandwiches (try a *croque monsieur,* or toasted ham and cheese), the
omelets, and the *pommes frites* (french fries). Though this chapter lists
a number of cafes (see "The Top Cafes" later in this chapter), one that
appeals to children is **La Samaritaine,** 75 rue de Rivoli, 1e (✆ **01-40-41-
20-20;** Métro: Pont Neuf). The snack bar below doesn't have a
panoramic view, but the fifth-floor restaurant does. You can take
children to the top and order ice cream at teatime daily from 3 to 5pm.
The snack bar is open Monday to Wednesday from 9:30am to 7pm;
Thursday from 9:30am to 9pm; and Saturday from 9:30am to 8pm.

Les Drug Stores, 149 bd. St-Germain-des-Prés, 6e, and at Publicis
Champs-Elysées, 133 av. des Champs-Elysées, 8e—like American drug
stores but with sections for upscale gift items and food service—also
welcome children, especially in the early evening, as do most **tea-
rooms,** and you can tide the kids over with pastries and ice cream if
dinner will be late. You could also try a **picnic** in the park or one of the
many fast-food chains, like **Pizza Hut** and **McDonald's,** all over the city.

Androuët sur le Pouce (p. 123)   If your kids love cheese, they'll get the
fill of a lifetime here, where cheese is part of all the dishes. Especially
delectable is the ravioli stuffed with goat cheese.

Chicago Pizza Pie Factory, 5 rue Berri, 8e (✆ **01-45-62-50-23)**   There
are no frogs' legs or snails to gross out little minds and stomachs at the
Chicago Pizza Pie Factory, just the City of Light's best pizza followed by
a kid-pleasing cheesecake.

Crémerie-Restaurant Polidor (p. 154)   One of the most popular restaurants on the Left Bank, this reasonably priced dining room is so family
friendly it calls its food *cuisine familiale.* This might be the best place
to introduce your child to bistro food.

Hard Rock Cafe (p. 129)   At the Paris branch of this chain, good old
American burgers and more are served against a background of rock
memorabilia and loud rock music.

Joe Allen (p. 121)   This American restaurant in Les Halles delivers
everything from chili to chocolate-mousse pie to the best hamburgers
in Paris.

contemporary dining room. The menu, wherein flavors practically jump off the plates, might include an unusual form of "ravioli," wherein thin slices of avocado encase a filling of seasoned crabmeat, all of it accompanied by salted almonds and a splash of almond oil. A mussel salad is enriched with cumin, chervil, and carrots, and buckwheat blinis come layered with a confit of shallots and a cupful of oyster-based "cappuchino."

4 rue Beethoven, 16e. ℂ 01-40-50-84-40. Reservations required 3 or 4 weeks in advance. Main courses 24€–38€ ($28–$44). AE, DC, MC, V. Wed–Sun 12:30–2:30pm; Tues–Sun 8–11:30pm. Closed 3 weeks in Aug. Métro: Trocadéro.

MODERATE

La Butte Chaillot ★ *Value* TRADITIONAL FRENCH   This baby bistro showcases culinary high priest Guy Savoy and draws a crowd from the affluent neighborhood's corporate offices. Diners congregate in posh but congested areas. Menu items change weekly (sometimes daily) and betray a strange sense of mass production not unlike that found in a luxury cruise liner's dining room. Examples are a sophisticated medley of terrines; a "low-fat" version of chunky mushroom soup; a salad of snails and herbed potatoes; succulent rack of lamb; and roasted rabbit with sage and a compote of onions, bacon, and mushrooms. A starkly contemporary stainless-steel staircase leads to extra seating in the cellar.

110 bis av. Kléber, 16e. ℂ 01-47-27-88-88. Reservations recommended. Main courses 20€–25€ ($23–$29); prix fixe menus 50€–70€ ($58–$81). AE, DC, MC, V. Sun–Fri noon–2:30pm; daily 7pm–midnight. Métro: Trocadéro.

Le Bistro de l'Etoile ★ *Value* TRADITIONAL FRENCH   This is the more interesting of the two baby bistros, both with the same name, clustered around place Charles de Gaulle–Etoile. They serve affordable versions of the grand cuisine featured in Guy Savoy's nearby three-star restaurant (see below). The setting is a warmly contemporary dining room in shades of butterscotch and caramel. Menu items include sautéed sea scallops; a rack of lamb *au jus* (cooked in its own juices); codfish studded with lard and prepared with a coconut-lime sauce; Lyon sausages with sauerkraut and pistachios; and red-snapper filets with caramelized endive and exotic mushrooms. A particularly interesting sampler combines three of Savoy's creations on a platter—a cup of lentil cream soup with a slice of fried foie gras, a fondant of celery, and a pan-fried slice of foie gras. Expect some odd terms on the dessert menu, which only a professional chef can fully describe: An example is spice bread baked in the fashion of *pain perdu* (lost bread) garnished with banana sorbet and pineapple sauce.

19 rue Lauriston, 16e. ℂ 01-40-67-11-16. Reservations recommended. Main courses 19€–26€ ($21–$29); prix fixe lunch 21€–26€ ($24–$30), dinner 35€ ($40). AE, DC, MC, V. Mon–Fri noon–2:30pm; daily 7:30pm–midnight. Métro: Kléber.

INEXPENSIVE

Kambodia ASIAN/CAMBODIAN   The waiters, all dressed in black cotton tunics, will welcome you to this excellent eatery that serves some of the best and most flavorful Asian dishes in Paris. The basement atmosphere has been called "Zen-like," but the service is welcoming and it's a good choice for a romantic dinner not far from the Champs-Elysées. Two of our favorite dishes include a superb seafood *pot-au-feu* (stew) and chicken roasted with honey and lemon. One Cambodian dish that's a delight is ginger fish wrapped in a banana leaf.

15 rue de Bassano, 16e. ℂ 01-47-23-31-80. Reservations required. Main courses 15€–22€ ($17–$25); prix fixe lunch 18€–23€ ($21–$26). AE, MC, V. Mon–Fri noon–2:30pm; Mon–Sat 7:30–10:30pm. Closed Aug. Métro: George-V.

17TH ARRONDISSEMENT
VERY EXPENSIVE

Guy Savoy ★★★ TRADITIONAL FRENCH   One of the hottest chefs in Europe, Guy Savoy serves the kind of food he likes to eat, prepared with consummate skill. We think he has a slight edge over his rival, Michel Rostang (see below), though Ducasse, at least in media coverage, surpasses them both. Although the food is superb and meals comprise as many as nine courses, the portions are small; you won't necessarily be satiated at the end. The menu changes with the seasons, but may include a cream soup of lentils and crayfish, duckling foie gras with aspic and gray salt; or sea bass grilled in a salt shell and served with a sauce of sweet herbs. If you come in the right season, you may have a chance to order game like mallard and venison. Savoy is fascinated with mushrooms and has been known to serve a dozen types, especially in autumn. An example includes a delectable pan-fried combination of mussels and wild mushrooms.

18 rue Troyon, 17e. ℂ **01-43-80-40-61.** Fax 01-46-22-43-09. Reservations required 1 month in advance. Main courses 72€–160€ ($83–$184); *menu dégustation* (tasting menu) 200€–250€ ($230–$288). AE, DC, MC, V. Tues–Fri noon–2pm; Tues–Sat 7:30–10:30pm. Métro: Charles de Gaulle–Etoile or Ternes.

Michel Rostang ★★★ MODERN & TRADITIONAL FRENCH   Michel Rostang is one of Paris's most creative chefs, the fifth generation of a distinguished French "cooking family." His restaurant contains four dining rooms paneled in mahogany, cherry-, or pearwood; some have frosted Lalique crystal panels. Changing every 2 months, the menu offers modern improvements on *la cuisine bourgeoise* (comfort food). Truffles are the dish of choice in midwinter, and you'll find racks of suckling lamb from the salt marshes of France's western seacoasts in spring; in game season, look for preparations of pheasant and venison. Year-round staples are quail eggs with a coque of sea urchins, fricassee of sole, and Bresse chicken with mushroom purée and a salad composed of the chicken's thighs.

20 rue Rennequin, 17e. ℂ **01-47-63-40-77.** Fax 01-47-63-82-75. Reservations required far in advance. Main courses 39€–68€ ($45–$78); prix fixe lunch 65€ ($75), dinner 175€–230€ ($201–$265). AE, DC, MC, V. Tues–Fri 12:30–2:30pm; Mon–Sat 8:30–10:30pm. Closed 3 weeks in Aug. Métro: Ternes.

MODERATE

Chez Georges TRADITIONAL FRENCH   Not to be confused with a bistro of the same name in the 2nd arrondissement, this is a worthy choice. It has flourished since 1926, despite an obscure location. The setting has changed little— cheerfully harassed waiters barge through a dining room sheathed with old-fashioned paneling and etched glass, and savory odors emerge from the hysterically busy kitchen. Two enduring specialties are leg of lamb with white kidney beans, and standing rib roast with herbs (especially thyme) in its own juices and a gratin of potatoes. Preceding these might be Baltic herring in cream sauce, cheese ravioli, cabbage soup, or a wide selection of sausages and pork products that taste best when eaten with bread, butter, and sour pickles. The adventurous French love the calf's head and the braised veal trotters, both served cold in vinaigrette.

273 bd. Pereire, 17e. ℂ **01-45-74-31-00.** Reservations recommended. Main courses 18€–28€ ($20–$32). MC, V. Daily noon–2:30pm and 7pm–midnight. Métro: Porte Maillot.

La Braisière ★★ *Finds* SOUTHWESTERN FRENCH   In this very residential arrondissement, Jacques Fassat is all the rage, winning his first Michelin star in 2004. Born in the Pyrenees, he brings the savory cuisine of the southwest to this 40-seat restaurant whose entrance is dominated by an enormous vase of flowers in a Medici-inspired Renaissance vase. The decor is cozy, warm, and

> **Tips** **Can You Dine Badly in Paris?**
>
> The answer is an emphatic yes. Our mailbox fills with complaints from readers who've encountered haughty service and paid outrageous prices for swill. Often these complaints are about restaurants catering to tourists. Avoid them by following our suggestions or looking in non-touristy areas for new discoveries. If you ask Parisians for recommendations, specify that you're looking for restaurants where *they'd* dine, not where they think you, as a tourist, would dine.

intimate, the restaurant evoking upscale chic in one of the French provinces. From the first bite, we fell in love with Fassat's savory, ambitious cuisine, with its contrast in texture and flavor. Nothing is finer for a starter than his signature appetizer of lobster ceviche with a red-wine jelly. Fiery red peppers from the Southwest and crunchy, diced cucumbers evoke gazpacho, and they're served like scoops of ice cream. You can also delight in the foie gras, before going on to one of the beautifully prepared and seasoned fish dishes such as red tuna served with onions and braised endive. The lamb from the Pyrenees is among the best we've ever had, and it comes with eggplant-filled ravioli flavored with cumin. The dessert specialty, familiar to residents of Gascony, is *tortière,* made with a light phyllo pastry stretched over stewed prunes flavored with Armagnac and cinnamon. It's garnished with what must be the world's best fig ice cream.

54 rue Cardinet, 17e. ⓒ **01-47-63-40-37.** Reservations required. Main courses 23€–25€ ($26–$29). Prix fixe lunch 30€ ($35). AE, DC, MC, V. Mon–Sat noon–3pm and 7:30–10pm. Closed Aug. Métro: Malesherbes.

Restaurant Caïus ✦ *Value* TRADITIONAL FRENCH   The chic place is popular for business lunches and dinners, also drawing residents and shoppers from the neighborhood. It's ringed with wood paneling and banquettes. The new owner, Jean-Marc Notelet, has brought renewed vigor to the kitchen. His cuisine, however, remains traditionally French, as before, and is based on spices and a judicious use of pepper. The dining room is a showcase for the chef's enticing cuisine, which is based on authentically flavor-filled local foodstuffs. We were recently intrigued by his rooster from the Somme Valley. This was served with *topinébours,* a rare type of potato whose origins are found in medieval France—very esoteric. Among other masterful offerings were dorado braised with Belgian endives and root vegetables, and a confit of beef with fava beans and aged vinegar along with celery whipped into almond milk.

6 rue d'Armaillé, 17e. ⓒ **01-42-27-19-20.** Reservations recommended. Main courses 19€–23€ ($22–$26); prix fixe menu 23€ ($26). AE, DC, MC, V. Mon–Fri noon–2:30pm; Mon–Sat 7:30–10:30pm. Métro: Charles de Gaulle–Etoile or Argentine.

4 On the Left Bank

We'll begin with the most centrally located arrondissements on the Left Bank, then work our way through the more outlying neighborhoods and to the area near the Eiffel Tower.

5TH ARRONDISSEMENT
VERY EXPENSIVE

La Tour d'Argent ✦✦✦ TRADITIONAL FRENCH   This penthouse restaurant, a national institution, serves up a panoramic view over the Seine and Notre-Dame. Although its reputation as the best in Paris has been eclipsed, dining here remains an unsurpassed event. A restaurant of some sort has stood on this site since 1582: Mme de Sévigné refers to a cafe here in her letters, and Dumas used it in one of his novels. The fame of La Tour d'Argent spread during its ownership by Frédéric Delair, who started the practice of issuing certificates to diners who ordered *caneton* (pressed duckling). The birds are numbered: The first was served to Edward VII in 1890, and now they're over one million! Under the sharp eye of owner Claude Terrail, the cooking is superb and the service impeccable. A good part of the menu is devoted to duck, but the kitchen knows how to prepare other dishes. Start with the pheasant consommé or pike-perch quenelles André Terrail; follow with the foie gras or filet of sole cardinal with shrimp sauce.

15–17 quai de la Tournelle, 5e. © 01-43-54-23-31. Fax 01-44-07-12-04. Reservations required far in advance. Main courses 60€–70€ ($69–$81); prix fixe lunch 70€ ($81). AE, DC, MC, V. Tues 7:30–9pm; Wed–Sun noon–1:15pm and 7:30–9pm. Métro: St-Michel or Pont Marie.

MODERATE

Al Dar LEBANESE   This well-respected restaurant works hard to popularize the savory cuisine of Lebanon. Within a modern decor whose colors might remind you of the arid scrublands of the Middle East, you'll dine on dishes like tabbouleh, a refreshing combination of finely chopped parsley, mint, milk, tomatoes, onions, lemon juice, olive oil, and salt; baba ghanouj, pulverized and seasoned eggplant; and hummus, pulverized chickpeas with herbs. These can be followed with savory roasted chicken; tender minced lamb with mint, cumin, and Mediterranean herbs; and any of several delectable tangines and couscous.

8 rue Frédéric-Sauton, 5e. © 01-43-25-17-15. Reservations recommended. Main courses 14€–17€ ($16–$20); prix fixe lunch 20€–27€ ($23–$31), dinner 35€–51€ ($40–$59). AE, MC, V. Daily noon–3pm and 7pm–12:30am. Métro: Maubert-Mutualité.

Brasserie Balzar ★ TRADITIONAL FRENCH   Opened in 1898, Brasserie Balzar is battered but cheerful, with some of Paris's most colorful waiters. The menu makes almost no concessions to modern cuisine; it includes onion soup, pepper steak, sole meunière, sauerkraut with ham and sausage, pigs' feet, and fried calves' liver served without garnish. Be warned that if you want just coffee or a drink, you probably won't get a table at meal hours. But the staff will be happy to serve you if you want to have dinner in the mid-afternoon, accustomed as they are to the odd hours of their many patrons. Former guests have included both Sartre and Camus (who often got in arguments), James Thurber, countless professors from the nearby Sorbonne, and numerous English and American journalists.

49 rue des Ecoles, 5e. © 01-43-54-13-67. Reservations strongly recommended. Main courses 15€–25€ ($17–$28). AE, MC, V. Daily noon–11:45pm. Métro: Odéon or Cluny–La Sorbonne.

Le Petit Pontoise ★ *Finds* TRADITIONAL FRENCH   Lying on a little-visited Left Bank side street, off Quai de la Tournelle, this restaurant is often frequented by both professors and students from the Sorbonne. It's tiny but the portions are big and generous. The clientele—often made up of regulars—is pampered with comfort food. Fine ingredients and a technique honed to perfection have made this a citadel of fine dining. You could take your grandmother here, even your great-grandmother, and she would likely be pleased with the seared scallops in the garlicky tomato sauce or the fresh chicken cooked in wine and mushrooms. Tender, well-flavored duckling comes with foie gras, and you can also take delight in the stew of pig cheeks and fresh vegetables. This dish comes in an iron casserole. Look for the day's specialties posted on a blackboard.

9 rue de Pontoise, 5e. © 01-43-29-25-20. Main courses 13€–24€ ($14–$28). AE, MC, V. Daily noon–2pm and 7–10pm. Métro: Maubert-Mutualité.

Where to Dine on the Left Bank (5–6 & 13–14e)

Le Pré Verre ⚑ *Value* TRADITIONAL FRENCH/ASIAN   Around the corner from the Sorbonne in the heart of the Latin Quarter comes a refreshing restaurant where you can get seriously good food—all for an affordable price. Even if this is not an earth-shattering gastronomic experience, it is solid and reliable, with good cooking and market-fresh ingredients. The Delacourcelle brothers are firmly based in the French tradition, but they had added innovative modern twists by giving extra spicing to the food, many of the flavorings inspired by Asia. In a welcoming, relaxed, and convivial atmosphere, tables are placed so close together it's as if you're dining with the people rubbing elbows

Al Dar **25**
Alcazar Bar & Restaurant **14**
Allard **16**
Auberge Etchegorry **31**
Aux Charpentiers **9**
Brasserie Balzar **23**
Brasserie Lipp **11**
Café de Flore **10**
Chez Diane **6**
Chez Gramond **4**
Closerie des Lilas **32**
Coco de Mer **28**
Crémerie-Restaurant
  Polidor **8**
Jacques Cagna **20**
La Bastide Odéon **7**
La Cagouille **1**
La Coupole **3**
La Palette **17**
La Petite Hostellerie **22**
La Régalade **1**
La Rôtisserie d'en Face **19**
La Rotonde **2**
La Tour d'Argent **27**
Le Canton **12**
Le Petit Marguery **30**
Le Petit Pontoise **26**
Le Pré Verre **24**
Le Procope **15**
Les Deux Magots **13**
Marty **29**
Perraudin **33**
Restaurant D'Hélène/
  Salon D'Hélène **5**
Yugaraj **18**
Ze Kitchen Galerie **21**

with you, which you are, of course. For something bourgeois, dig into the well-flavored terrines for starters. One of these—and the most delectable—is made with layers of foie gras and mashed potatoes. *Tete de veau* (head of veal) is sprightly seasoned with Thai spices, and one of the best specialties is milk-fed piglet which has been given added zest by a sprinkling of star anise and cinnamon. The fork-tender lamb shanks are one of the best examples of the comfort cuisine served here. For dessert? Why not roasted figs with olives and ice cream?

8 rue Thenard, 5e. ✆ **01-43-54-59-47**. Reservations required. Main courses at lunch 12€–25€ ($14–29), at dinner 15€–25€ ($17–$29). MC, V. Tues–Sat noon–2pm and 7:30–10pm. Closed Aug. Métro: Maubert-Mutualité.

Marty ★ *Finds* MODERN FRENCH   Charming, with a stone-trimmed decor that's authentic to the era (1913) it was established, this restaurant has been "discovered" by new generations of restaurant-goers. Named after its founders, Étienne and Marthe Marty, its fame now extends beyond the 5th arrondissement. Service is attentive, and there are lots of Jazz Age murals on the walls. Food is savory, satisfying, and unfussy. If someone opts to seat you on one of the hide-away tables on the mezzanine, don't resist, because views from here sweep over the entire human comedy unfolding above and below you. Begin your meal with a tartare of sea bream flavored with anise and lime; lobster ravioli with sherry vinegar; or fresh oysters. Continue with a supreme of guinea fowl with a vegetable moussaka, a platter that combines grilled squid with grilled strips of red mullet; or perhaps a brochette of hake and salmon, served with a mustard-flavored olive tapenade. Dessert might include a soup of red fruits with orange-flavored liqueur.

20 av. des Gobelins, 5e. (¢ **01-43-31-39-51.** Main courses 19€–27€ ($22–$31); prix fixe menu 36€ ($42). AE, DC, MC, V. Daily noon–midnight. Métro: Gobelins.

Perraudin TRADITIONAL FRENCH   Everything about this place—decor, cuisine, price, and service—attempts to duplicate an early-1900s bistro. This one was built in 1870 as an outlet for coal and wine. It evolved into the wood-paneled bistro you see today, where little has changed since Zola was buried in the Panthéon nearby. The walls look like they've been marinated in tea; the marble-topped tables, mirrors, and vaudeville posters have been here forever. Reservations aren't made in advance: Diners usually drink a glass of kir at the zinc-topped bar as they wait. (Tables turn over quickly.) The menu includes roast leg of lamb with dauphinois potatoes, *boeuf bourguignon* (braised beef in red-wine sauce), and grilled salmon with sage sauce. The onion tart, pumpkin soup, or terrine are all good appetizers.

157 rue St-Jacques, 5e. (¢ **01-46-33-15-75.** Main courses 15€–23€ ($17–$26); prix fixe lunch 18€ ($21), dinner 28€ ($32). DC, MC, V. Mon–Fri noon–2:15pm and 7–10pm. Closed 3 weeks in Aug. Métro: Cluny–La Sorbonne. RER: Luxembourg.

INEXPENSIVE

Coco de Mer ★ *Finds* SEYCHELLE ISLANDS   The theme of this restaurant tugs at the emotions of the Parisians who have spent their holidays on the beaches of the Seychelles in the Indian Ocean. It contains several dining rooms, one of which is outfitted like a beach, with a sand-covered floor, replicas of palm trees, and a scattering of conch shells. Menu items feature such exotic dishes as tartare of tuna flavored with ginger, olive oil, salt, and pepper; and smoked swordfish, served as a carpaccio or in thin slices with mango mousse and a spicy sauce. Main courses focus on fish, including *boirzoes* (a species of red snapper) imported from the Seychelles. Dessert might be a *crème de banana gratinée*.

34 bd. St-Marcel, 5e. (¢ **01-47-07-06-64.** Reservations recommended. Main courses 14€–20€ ($16–$23); prix fixe menus 23€–30€ ($26–$35). AE, DC, MC, V. Tues–Sat noon–3pm; Mon–Sat 7:30pm–midnight. Métro: Les Gobelins or St-Marcel.

La Petite Hostellerie ★ *Value* TRADITIONAL FRENCH   This 1902 restaurant offers a ground-floor dining room that's usually crowded and a larger upstairs one with 18th-century woodwork. People come for the cozy ambience and decor, French country cooking, polite service, and excellent prices. The fixed-price dinner might feature favorites like *boeuf bourguignon* (braised beef in red-wine sauce), or duckling *à l'orange*. Start with onion soup or stuffed mussels and finish with cheese, or peach Melba.

You can find a large variety of street food sold everywhere from the Latin Quarter to outside the *grands magasins* (department stores) on the Right Bank. Sandwiches, crepes, frites, and (in cold weather) roasted chestnuts are just a few of the items available. The crepes are especially good—freshly made and filled with your choice of ingredients: cheese, ham, egg (or a combination of these); chocolate and nuts; apricot jam; or some other treat.

35 rue de la Harpe (a side street north of bd. St-Germain, just east of bd. St-Michel), 5e. ℭ **01-43-54-47-12.** All main courses 9.90€ ($11); prix fixe menu 14€–20€ ($16–$22). DC, MC, V. Tues–Sun noon–2pm and 6:30–11pm. Closed 2 weeks in Feb and 3 weeks in Aug. Métro: St-Michel or Cluny–La Sorbonne.

6TH ARRONDISSEMENT
VERY EXPENSIVE

Jacques Cagna ✦✦✦ MODERN & TRADITIONAL FRENCH   St-Germain knows no finer dining than at Jacques Cagna, a sophisticated restaurant in a 17th-century town house with massive timbers, burnished paneling, and 17th-century Dutch paintings. Jacques Cagna is one of the best classically trained chefs in Paris, though he has become a half apostle to *cuisine moderne.* This is evident in his delectable carpaccio of pearly sea bream with caviar-lavished *céleric rémoulade* (celery root in mayonnaise with capers, parsley, gherkins, spring onions, chervil, chopped tarragon, and anchovy essence). Also sublime are the carpaccio of dorado; roasted crayfish with fresh herbs; fried foie gras of duckling served with caramelized fruits of the season (in winter, that usually means pears and quince); standing roast of veal with a lime-and-ginger sauce; and line-caught sea bass roasted with baby vegetables and fresh herbs.

14 rue des Grands-Augustins, 6e. ℭ **01-43-26-49-39.** Fax 01-43-54-54-48. Reservations required in advance. Main courses 32€–72€ ($37–$83); prix fixe 40€–85€ ($46–$98) at lunch, 85€ ($98) at dinner. AE, DC, MC, V. Tues–Fri noon–2pm; Mon–Sat 7:30–10:30pm. Closed 3 weeks in Aug. Métro: St-Michel or Odéon.

Restaurant d'Hélène/Salon d'Hélène ✦✦✦ SOUTHWESTERN FRENCH   Hélène d'Arroze is the most famous female chef in Paris, a Basque-born *wunderkind* whose southwestern French cuisine is a superb modern take on a classic. Be very clear before you enter this restaurant about what it is that you want: The upstairs dining room (Le Restaurant d'Hélène, where tables are round and outfitted with elaborate napery) is more formal, expensive, and sedate than the bistro (Le Salon d'Hélène). In both areas expect a pop-influenced decor of bright colors and relatively slow service. Upstairs, menus are artfully composed and presented as part of fixed-price meals that contain, among others, a confit of foie gras with grilled apples; a salad of white beans and clams; and roast wild duck stuffed with foie gras and truffles. On street level, food focuses on an array of *plats du jour* (such as skate Grenobloise with lemon and capers) and tapas, two or three of which can be combined to create a meal. Tapas might include raw marinated tuna with Basque-derived red-pepper sauce, or cannelloni gratinéed with Basque sheep's milk cheese and smoked Basque ham.

4 rue d'Assas, 6e. ℭ **01-42-22-00-11.** Reservations required. In restaurant: prix fixe menus 150€–195€ ($173–$225). In salon: prix fixe lunch 61€ ($70); tapas 7€–15€ ($8–$17). AE, MC, V. Tues–Sat 12:30–2:15pm and 7:30–10pm. Métro: Sèvres-Babylone.

EXPENSIVE

Closerie des Lilas ✪ TRADITIONAL FRENCH   Opened in 1847, the Closerie was a social and culinary magnet for the avant-garde. The famous people who have sat in the "Pleasure Garden of the Lilacs" include Gertrude Stein and Alice B. Toklas, Ingrés, Henry James, Chateaubriand, Picasso, Hemingway, Apollinaire, Lenin and Trotsky (at the chess board), Whistler, and others. Today, the crowd may include a sprinkling of stars and the starstruck. The place resounds with the sometimes rather loud sounds of a jazz pianist, making the interior seem more claustrophobic than it is. It can be tough to get a seat in what's called the *bâteau* (boat) section, but you can make the wait more enjoyable by ordering the world's best champagne julep at the bar. It's also possible to have just coffee or a drink at the bar, though the food is better than ever. Try the veal kidneys with mustard, veal ribs in cider sauce, steak tartare, pike-perch quenelles, or filet of beef with a green-peppercorn sauce.

171 bd. du Montparnasse, 6e. ℂ 01-40-51-34-50. Reservations recommended far in advance (for restaurant only). Restaurant main courses 35€–45€ ($40–$52); brasserie main courses 19€–24€ ($22–$28). AE, DC, V. Restaurant daily noon–3pm and 7:30–11:30pm; brasserie daily 11:30am–1am. Métro: Port Royal or Vavin.

MODERATE

Alcazar Bar & Restaurant ✪ MODERN FRENCH   Paris's most high-profile *brasserie de luxe* is this high-tech place funded by British restaurateur Sir Terence Conran. It features an all-white futuristic decor in a street-level dining room and a busy upstairs bar. The menu includes rack of veal sautéed with wild mushrooms; roasted rack of lamb with thyme; Charolais duckling with honey and spices; sashimi and sushi with lime; monkfish with saffron in puff pastry; and shellfish and oysters from the waters of Brittany. The wines are as stylish and diverse as you'd expect, and the trendy crowd tends to wear a lot of black.

62 rue Mazarine, 6e. ℂ 01-53-10-19-99. Reservations recommended. Main courses 15€–30€ ($17–$35); prix fixe lunch 16€–26€ ($18–$30). AE, DC, MC, V. Daily noon–3pm and 7pm–1am. Métro: Odéon.

Allard ✪ TRADITIONAL FRENCH   Long missing from this guide, this old-time bistro, opened in 1931, is back and as good as ever following a long decline. It was once the leading bistro, although today the competition is too great to reclaim that reputation. The front room's zinc bar has been a haven preferred by many celebrities over the years, including Mme Pompidou and actor Alain Delon. All the old Allard specialties are still offered, with quality ingredients deftly handled by the kitchen. Try the snails, foie gras, veal stew, or frogs' legs. We head here on Mondays for the cassoulet Toulousian (casserole of white beans and goose and other meats) and on Saturdays for the *coq au vin* (chicken stewed in wine). The cassoulet remains one of the Left Bank's best. For dessert, we vote for the *tarte tatin* (caramelized apple pie).

41 rue St-André-des-Arts, 6e. ℂ 01-43-26-48-23. Reservations required. Main courses 19€–35€ ($21–$40); prix fixe lunch 23€–31€ ($26–$35), dinner 35€ ($40). AE, DC, MC, V. Mon–Sat noon–3pm and 7:30–11pm. Métro: St-Michel or Odéon.

Chez Gramond ✪ *Finds* TRADITIONAL FRENCH   Aficionados of the way France used to be seek out this place, and if you're looking for the kind of cuisine that used to satisfy the *grands intellectuels* of the Latin Quarter in the 1960s, you might find it appealing. It seats only 20 people, each of whom is treated to the savoir-faire of Auvergne-born Jean-Claude Gramond and his charming wife, Jeannine. Listed in purple ink that's duplicated on an old-time mimeograph machine, the menu items may include a marinade of mushrooms with coriander; a *navarin* (rich stew) of lamb with scotch beans; roasted grouse with figs;

scallops cooked with white wine, leeks, and shallots; partridge (this is increasingly rare and expensive) served with an *émincé* (shredded mixture) of cabbage; sautéed pheasant with a Calvados-flavored cream sauce; and two different preparations of rabbit, one of which is a *civet* (a wild hare) served Alsatian-style, with noodles and a sauce made from a mixture of red wine and the rabbit's own blood. Try the soufflé Grand Marnier for dessert. The wine list is carefully balanced with lots of fine bottles from the 1970s and 1980s, and fairly priced.

5 rue de Fleurus, 6e. ✆ 01-42-22-28-89. Reservations recommended. Main courses 24€–35€ ($28–$40). MC, V. Mon–Sat noon–2:30pm and 7–10:30pm. Closed in Aug. Métro: Notre-Dame des Champs.

La Rôtisserie d'en Face ✮ *Value* TRADITIONAL FRENCH This is Paris's most frequented baby bistro, operated by Jacques Cagna, whose expensive restaurant (see above) is across the street. The informal place features a postmodern decor with high-tech lighting and black lacquered chairs. The simply prepared food is very good and employs high-quality ingredients. It includes several types of ravioli, pâté of duckling *en croûte* (in a pastry) with foie gras, *friture d'éperlans* (tiny fried freshwater fish), and smoked Scottish salmon with spinach. Cagna's Barbary duckling in red-wine sauce is incomparable.

2 rue Christine, 6e. ✆ 01-43-26-40-98. Reservations recommended. Main courses 22€–35€ ($25–$40); prix fixe lunch 17€–27€ ($20–$31), dinner 39€ ($45). AE, DC, MC, V. Mon–Fri noon–2:30pm; Mon–Sat 7–11pm. Métro: Odéon or Pont-Neuf.

Yugaraj INDIAN On two floors of an old Latin Quarter building, Yugaraj serves flavorful food based on the recipes of northern and (to a lesser degree) southern India. In recently renovated rooms done in vivid shades of ochre, with a formally dressed staff and lots of intricately carved Kashmiri panels and statues, you can sample the spicy, aromatic tandoori dishes that are all the rage in France. Seafood specialties are usually made with warm-water fish imported from the Seychelles, including *thiof, capitaine,* and *bourgeois,* prepared as they would be in Calcutta, with tomatoes, onions, cumin, coriander, ginger, and garlic. Curried lamb with coriander is a particular favorite. And chicken dishes are made with one of the best types of poultry in France from the region around Bresse.

14 rue Dauphine, 6e. ✆ 01-43-26-44-91. Reservations recommended. Main courses 26€–30€ ($30–$34); prix fixe lunch 23€–29€ ($26–$33), dinner 32€–39€ ($37–$45). AE, DC, MC, V. Tues–Wed and Fri–Sat noon–2:15pm; Tues–Sun 7–10pm. Métro: Pont-Neuf or Odeon.

Ze Kitchen Galerie ✮ *Finds* MODERN FRENCH/INTERNATIONAL The owner and head chef of this restaurant was trained in the lofty plateau of haute Parisian gastronomy under the directive of culinary czar Guy Savoy. Since William Ledeuil established the place in 2001, he's attracted the likes of First Lady Laura Bush, who dined here in the spring of 2002, accompanied by a daunting staff of security guards. If you opt for a meal here, the venue will be less intimidating. The setting is a loft space within an antique building, with an open-to-view "showcase"-style kitchen, and a color scheme of bold, primary colors (especially reds and greens). And if you feel a strong attraction to one of the paintings on display, most of them are for sale, because the place doubles as an art gallery. Menu items, like the paintings, change about every 5 weeks, but regardless of the time of your arrival, appetizers are subdivided into pastas, soups, and fish; and main courses are divided into meats and fish that are usually grilled *a la plancha* (on an iron skillet). The best examples include platters of oysters, mussels, and sea urchins served with an herb sauce and *crostini* (toasted bread slathered in garlic butter), or grilled shoulder of wild boar with tamarind sauce. Desserts are modern and unusual; an imaginative example is a pumpkin beignet with corn-flavored ice cream, roasted fruit, apples, ginger, and vanilla sauce.

4 rue des Grands-Augustins, 6e. ⓒ **01-44-32-00-32**. Reservations recommended. Main courses 21€–25€ ($25–$29); prix fixe lunches, with wine, 21€–32€ ($24–$37). AE, DC, MC, V. Métro: St-Michel.

INEXPENSIVE

Aux Charpentiers TRADITIONAL FRENCH   This old bistro, which opened more than 130 years ago, attracts those seeking the Left Bank Paris of yesteryear. It was once the rendezvous spot of the master carpenters, whose guild was next door. Nowadays, it's where young men take their dates. Though the food isn't imaginative, it's well prepared in the best tradition of *la cuisine bourgeoise* (comfort food)—hearty and not effete. Appetizers include pâté of duck and rabbit terrine. Recommended as a main course is the roast duck with olives. The *plats du jour* recall French home cooking: salt pork with lentils, *pot-au-feu* (stew), and stuffed cabbage. The wine list has a selection of Bordeaux, including Château Gaussens.

10 rue Mabillon, 6e. ⓒ **01-43-26-30-05**. Reservations required. Main courses 15€–24€ ($17–$28); prix fixe lunch 19€ ($22), dinner 25€ ($29). AE, DC, MC, V. Daily noon–3pm and 7–11:30pm. Métro: St-Germain-des-Prés or Mabillon.

Chez Diane MODERN & TRADITIONAL FRENCH   Come here for restaurant food at bistro prices. Designed to accommodate only 40 diners, this place is illuminated by Venetian glass chandeliers and paved with old-fashioned floor tiles. The deep ochres and terra cottas are redolent of Provence's landscapes and villas. The offerings change with the seasons and the owners' inspirations. Recently, we enjoyed sweetbreads in flap mushroom sauce, minced salmon terrine with peppercorns, and a light-textured modern adaptation of *hachis Parmentier,* a meatloaf lightened with parsley, chopped onions, and herbs. To finish, we recommend the *charlotte au fromage blanc,* a cheesecake with blueberry sauce.

25 rue Servandoni, 6e. ⓒ **01-46-33-12-06**. Reservations recommended for groups of 4 or more. Main courses 18€–22€ ($21–$25); prix fixe menu 26€ ($29). MC, V. Mon–Fri noon–2pm; Mon–Sat 8–11:30pm. Métro: St-Sulpice.

Crémerie-Restaurant Polidor ★ *Kids* TRADITIONAL FRENCH Crémerie Polidor is the most traditional bistro in the Odéon area, serving *cuisine familiale.* Its name dates from the early 1900s, when it specialized in frosted cream desserts, but the restaurant can trace its history back to 1845. The Crémerie was André Gide's favorite, and Joyce, Hemingway, Valéry, Artaud, and Kerouac also dined here. The place is still frequented by students and artists, who head for the rear. Peer beyond the lace curtains and brass hat racks to see drawers where repeat customers lock up their cloth napkins. Overworked but smiling waitresses serve the 19th-century cuisine. Try the pumpkin soup followed by *boeuf bourguignon* (braised beef in red-wine sauce), Basque-style chicken, or *blanquette de veau* (veal stew). For dessert, get a chocolate, raspberry, or lemon tart—the best in all Paris.

41 rue Monsieur-le-Prince, 6e. ⓒ **01-43-26-95-34**. Main courses 8€–15€ ($9.20–$17); prix fixe lunch (Mon–Fri) 9€ ($10), dinner 18€–26€ ($21–$30). No credit cards. Daily noon–2:30pm and 7pm–12:30am; Sun 7–11pm. Métro: Odéon.

La Bastide Odéon ★ *Finds* PROVENÇAL   The sunny climes of Provence come through in the pale yellow walls, oak tables, and bouquets of wheat and dried roses. Chef Gilles Ajuelos prepares a market-based cuisine. His simplest first courses are the most satisfying, like pumpkin soup with oysters and mussels, and eggplant-stuffed roasted rabbit with olive toast and balsamic vinegar. Main courses include duckling with pepper sauce and exotica like lamb's feet and giblets. A winning dessert is the almond pie with prune and Armagnac ice cream.

7 rue Corneille, 6e. ℂ **01-43-26-03-65.** Reservations recommended. All courses 19€ ($22). AE, MC, V. Tues–Sat 12:30–2pm and 7:30–10:30pm. Métro: Odéon. RER: Luxembourg.

Le Canton *finds* CHINESE/VIETNAMESE   The cuisine is exotic, especially the Vietnamese dishes, and the setting relaxing and evocative of Asia. Best of all, the food is affordable and better than that served at the nearby fast-food joints. Begin with any of the versions of *nem* (Vietnamese ravioli) stuffed with shrimp and vegetables. Main courses include salt-and-pepper shrimp, Szechuan-style chicken, and the best-selling shrimp quick-fried with black soy beans, garlic, peppers, and onions. The soups are wonderful. The chefs use lots of basil, and its aroma permeates the two dining rooms.

5 rue Gozlin, 6e. ℂ **01-43-26-51-86.** Reservations recommended. Main courses 5€–13€ ($5.75–$15); prix fixe lunch 14€ ($16), dinner 17€ ($19). MC, V. Mon–Sat noon–2:30pm and 7–10:30pm. Métro: St-Germain-des-Prés.

13TH ARRONDISSEMENT
MODERATE

Auberge Etchegorry BASQUE   Its windows overlook a verdant patch of lawn that's so green you might for a moment imagine you've entered a rustic countryside inn. Dark paneling, deep colors, hanging hams and pigtails of garlic, and lacy curtains emulate the Basque country, the corner of southwestern France adjacent to Spain. Victor Hugo and Chateaubriand ate here in centuries past. The cramped tables are a drawback, but not much of one in this rich atmosphere. The menu includes a roster of specialties like cassoulet, magret of duckling, beef filet with peppercorns, a peppery omelet known as *piperades,* cocottes of mussels, and terrines or pan-fried slices of foie gras.

41 rue Croulebarbe, 6e. ℂ **01-44-08-83-51.** Reservations recommended. All courses 15€ ($18); prix fixe menus 24€–37€ ($28–$42). AE, MC, V. Tues–Sat noon–2:30pm and 7:30–10:30pm. Métro: Gobelins or Corvisart.

Le Petit Marguery TRADITIONAL FRENCH/POITEVINE   This place feels like a turn-of-the-20th-century bistro, with antique floor tiles, banquettes, etched glass, vested waiters, and a color scheme of dark rose. Menu items are firmly based in old-fashioned French traditions, especially those from the Poitou region of west-central France, with emphasis on game dishes in autumn and fresh produce in summer. The finest examples include slices of wild duck breast, dusted with white pepper and strewn over mounds of shredded cabbage; a sautée of wild mushrooms; a *petit salé* (family-style stew) of duckling that's served with braised cabbage and garlic-flavored cream sauce; roasted suckling lamb from the Pyrenees; homemade ravioli stuffed with sea scallops on a bed of shellfish sauce; and a variety of homemade terrines (including an excellent version from blood sausage). There are also two very fine dishes, classics from *la cuisine bourgeoise* (comfort food) of the late 19th century: *lièvre à la royale* and *coq à la Pictavienne,* whereby a hare *(lièvre)* or rooster *(coq)* are deboned, marinated, roasted, and served in a sauce that combines red wine, some of the animal's blood, and foie gras. The restaurant's specialty dessert is a soufflé with Grand Marnier.

9 bd. du Port-Royal, 6e. ℂ **01-43-31-58-59.** Reservations recommended. 3-course lunch 25€–34€ ($29–$39); 3-course dinner 34€ ($39). AE, DC, MC, V. Tues–Sat noon–2pm and 7:30–10pm. Métro: Gobelins.

14TH ARRONDISSEMENT
MODERATE

La Cagouille ⭐ *finds* CENTRAL EUROPEAN/TRADITIONAL FRENCH/ SEAFOOD   Don't expect to find meat at this temple of seafood—burly and genteel chef and co-owner Gérard Allamandou refuses to feature it on his menu. Everything about La Cagouille testifies to a modern version of the culinary arts of La Charente, the flat sandy district hugging the Atlantic south of Bordeaux. In a trio of simple oak-sheathed dining rooms with marble-topped tables, you'll sample seafood prepared as simply and naturally as possible, with no fancy sauces or elaborate cooking techniques. Allamandou's preferred fish is red mullet, which might appear sautéed in a bland oil or baked in rock salt. The name of the place derives from the regional symbol of La Charente: the sea snail, whose preparation is elevated to a fine culinary art. Look for a vast assemblage of all-French, mostly white wines and at least 150 cognacs. During the summer there's a partially concealed terrace for outside dining.

10–12 place Constantin-Brancusi (opposite 23 rue de l'Ouest), 14e. ℂ 01-43-22-09-01. Reservations recommended. Main courses 19€–34€ ($21–$39); prix fixe menu 23€–39€ ($26–$45). AE, MC, V. Daily noon–2:30pm and 7:30–10:30pm. Métro: Gaîté.

La Régalade SOUTHWESTERN FRENCH   The setting is a bistro with banquettes the color of aged Bordeaux wine, congenially harried service, and unexpectedly good food. The prix fixe presents a choice of at least 10 starters, 10 main courses, and about a dozen fresh desserts or selections from a cheese tray. The inspiration is Yves Camdeborde's, known for his training at the Hôtel de Crillon. The menu changes weekly (sometimes daily) according to the availability of the ingredients, but examples that particularly impressed us include cream of walnut soup that's poured over a flan of foie gras; roasted Pyrenean lamb served with thyme and a confit of roasted garlic; filet of wild boar with a red-wine sauce; and an always-popular platter of fried goose liver served on toasted slices of spice bread.

49 av. Jean-Moulin, 14e. ℂ 01-45-45-68-58. Reservations recommended. Prix fixe menu 35€ ($40). V. Tues–Fri noon–2pm; Mon–Fri 7–11pm. Closed mid-July to mid-Aug. Métro: Alésia.

7TH ARRONDISSEMENT
VERY EXPENSIVE
L'Arpège ★★★ MODERN FRENCH   L'Arpège is best known for Alain Passard's specialties—no restaurant in the 7th serves better food. Amid a modern decor of etched glass, burnished steel, monochromatic oil paintings, and pearwood paneling, you can enjoy specialties like a couscous of vegetables and shellfish; lobster braised in the yellow wine of the Jura; pigeon roasted with almonds and honey-flavored mead; and carpaccio of crayfish with a caviar-flavored cream sauce. While Passard is loathe to include red meat on his menus, it does appear from time to time, in dishes of Japan-derived Kobe beef; and venison during late autumn and early winter. But he focuses on fish, shellfish, poultry, and—his current passion—vegetables. These, he elevates to levels unequalled by any other chef in Paris. The signature dessert is a candied tomato stuffed with 12 kinds of dried and fresh fruit, served with anise-flavored ice cream.

84 rue de Varenne, 7e. ℂ 01-47-05-09-06. Fax 01-44-18-98-39. Reservations required far in advance. Main courses 74€–200€ ($85–$230); *menu dégustation* (tasting menu) 320€ ($368). AE, DC, MC, V. Mon–Fri 12:30–2:30pm and 8–10pm. Métro: Varenne.

EXPENSIVE
L'Atelier de Joël Robuchon ★★ MODERN FRENCH   Upon his retirement in the mid-'90s, Joël Robuchon was hailed as the greatest chef in France. His mashed potatoes alone were a masterpiece—acclaimed as the world's greatest. His specialties were heralded around the world. Well, he's back. But not quite as grandly as before. His new restaurant is in a government-rated four-star

Where to Dine on the Left Bank (7 & 15e)

Au pied de Fouet **6**
Cave del'Os à Molle **1**
Chez L'Ami Jean **3**
Kim Anh **1**
L'Arpège **5**
L'Atelier de Joël Robuchon **9**
La Petite Chaise **7**
Le Chamarré **4**
Le Rouquet **8**
Le Violon d'Ingres **2**

157

In Pursuit of the Perfect Parisian Pastry

Could it be true, as rumor has it, that more eggs, sugar, cream, and butter per capita are consumed in Paris than in any other city? From a modern-day Proust sampling a madeleine to a child munching a *pain au chocolat* (chocolate-filled croissant), everyone in Paris seems to be looking for two things: the perfect lover and the perfect pastry, not necessarily in that order. As a Parisian food critic once said, "A day without a pastry is a day in hell!"

Who'd think of beginning a morning in Paris without a **croissant** or two—freshly baked, flaky, and light, and made with real butter, preferably from Norman cows. The Greeks may have invented pastry making, but the French perfected it. Some French pastries have made a greater impact than others. The croissant and the *brioche,* a yeasty sweet breakfast bread, are baked around the world today, as is the fabled *éclair au chocolat* (chocolate éclair), a pastry filled with whipped cream or pastry cream and topped with chocolate. Another pastry you should sample on its home turf is the **Napolitain**—layers of cake flour and almonds alternating with fruit purée. (Don't confuse this term with *Neapolitan,* meaning sweets and cakes made with layers of two or more colors, each layer flavored differently.) Very much in vogue is the *mille-feuille* ("thousand leaves"), made by arranging thin layers of flaky pastry on top of each other, along with layers of cream or fruit purée or jam; the American version is the napoleon.

Here are some of our favorite patisseries: **Stohrer,** 51 rue Montorgueil, 2e (© **01-42-33-38-20;** Métro: Sentier or Les Halles), has been going strong ever since it was opened by Louis XV's pastry chef in 1730. A pastry always associated with this place is *puits d'amour* (well of love), which consists of caramelized puff pastry filled with vanilla ice cream.

hotel and serves all day and into the early morning. The chic enclave is built around an open kitchen. Robuchon has hired and trained a team of master chefs. The restaurant has a sleek red- and black-lacquered finish and is dimly lit. Each dish is masterfully prepared but not as elaborate as those memorable dishes from the golden age of 1996. Seated at a dining bar wrapped around the open kitchen, you can enjoy, among other delights, sushi, which can be consumed with a basket of sourdough bread or a crusty baguette. The menu is ever changing but you might start with a pumpkin-and-cauliflower soup with smoky bacon or a divine chicken-liver terrine. Among the sublime main courses is caramelized quail glazed with a shallot-perfumed sauce, or a buttery and tender platter of langoustines in a pastry pate. Duckling comes both roasted and braised and flavored with spices such as ginger, nutmeg, and cinnamon. The fish and shellfish are shipped fresh from Brittany.

In the Hotel Pont Royal, 5–7 rue de Montalembert, 7e. © **01-42-22-56-56.** Reservations required. Main courses 15€–50€ ($17–$58); prix fixe menu 80€ ($92). AE, DC, MC, V. Daily 11am–2am.

Le Chamarré ★★★ *Finds* MODERN FRENCH/MAURITIEN   Come here for the kind of food that appeals to your brain as much as it does to your palate.

Available at any time is one of the most luscious desserts in Paris, *baba au rhum,* or its even richer cousin, *un Ali Baba,* which also incorporates cream-based rum-and-raisin filling. Stohrer boasts an interior decor classified as a national historic treasure, with frescoes of damsels in 18th-century costume bearing flowers and (what else?) pastries.

Opened in 1862, a few steps from La Madeleine, **Ladurée Royale,** 16 rue Royale, 8e (✆ **01-42-60-21-79;** Métro: Concorde or Madeleine), is Paris's dowager tearoom. Its pastry chefs are known for the **macaron,** a pastry for which this place is celebrated. Karl Lagerfeld comes here and raves about them, as did the late ambassador Pamela Harriman. This isn't the sticky coconut-version macaroon known to many, but two almond meringue cookies, flavored with chocolate, vanilla, pistachio, coffee, or other flavor, stuck together with butter cream. You may also want to try one of Hermé's latest creations—**Le Faubourg,** a lusciously dense chocolate cake with layers of caramel and apricots.

In business since Napoleon was in power, **Dalloyau,** 101 rue du Faubourg St-Honoré, 8e (✆ **01-42-99-90-00;** Métro: St-Philippe du Roule), has a name instantly recognizable throughout Paris; it supplies pastries to the Elysée Palace (the French White House) and many Rothschild mansions nearby. Its specialties are **Le Dalloyau,** praline cake filled with almond meringue that's marvelously light-textured, and **un Opéra,** composed of an almond-flavored biscuit layered with butter cream, chocolate, coffee, and cashews. Unlike Stohrer, Dalloyau has a tearoom (open daily 8am–7:30pm) one floor above street level, where ladies who lunch can drop in for a slice of pastry that Dalloyau warns is "too fragile to transport, or to mail, over long distances."

Founded in 2002, it immediately shot onto the Parisian consciousness, thanks to the happy memories many Europeans have of their holidays on the island of Mauritius (adjacent to Madagascar in the Indian Ocean), and thanks to the inspired cuisine of a pair of French and Mauritien chefs. The restaurant's name translates as "nuances of color," something you'll find in the dark beige and chocolate-colored decor, and definitely something you'll find in the cuisine. On chairs upholstered in a yummy shade of cinnamon-chocolate leather, amid lots of gold velvet upholsteries, you'll enjoy French cuisine that's subtly affected by the heat, aromas, and flavors of Mauritius. Try the chicken studded with black truffles and herbs; line-caught sea bass served with an emulsion of limes and a confit of leeks with banana leaves; Auvergnat flap mushrooms prepared with eggplant caviar and linden-leaf tea; and French-derived grilled slices of suckling veal with fried mushroom and walnut oil. Desserts are unusual, composed from ingredients you might not associate with desserts, like sliced and fried eggplant with sweetened vanilla sauce and laurel-flavored ice cream.

13 bd. de la Tour-Maubourg, 7e. ✆ 01-47-05-50-18. Reservations required. Main courses 28€–46€ ($32–$53); prix fixe lunch 28€–40€ ($32–$46), dinner 80€–100€ ($92–$115). AE, DC, MC, V. Mon–Fri noon–2:30pm and 7:30–10pm; Sat 7:30–10:30pm. Closed Aug. Métro: Invalides.

Le Violon d'Ingres ★★★ MODERN & TRADITIONAL FRENCH   This restaurant is Paris's *pièce de résistance.* Chef/owner Christian Constant is "the new Robuchon." Those fortunate enough to dine in Violon's warm atmosphere rave about the artistic dishes. They range from pan-fried foie gras with gingerbread and spinach salad to more elegant main courses like lobster ravioli with crushed vine-ripened tomatoes; roasted veal in a light and creamy milk sauce served with tender spring vegetables; and even a selection from the rotisserie, like spit-roasted leg of lamb rubbed with fresh garlic and thyme. A well-chosen selection of wine is offered. The service is charming and discreet.

135 rue St-Dominique, 7e. 𝄞 **01-45-55-15-05.** Fax 01-45-55-48-42. Reservations required at least 4–5 days in advance. Main courses 40€–46€ ($46–$53); *menu dégustation* (tasting menu) 110€ ($127). AE, MC, V. Tues–Sat noon–2:30pm and 7–10:30pm.

MODERATE

La Petite Chaise TRADITIONAL FRENCH   This is Paris's oldest restaurant, opened as an inn in 1680 by the baron de la Chaise at the edge of what was a hunting preserve. (According to lore, the baron used the upstairs bedrooms for afternoon dalliances, between fox and pheasant hunts.) Very Parisian, the "Little Chair" invites you into a world of cramped but attractive tables, old wood paneling, and ornate wall sconces. A vigorous chef has brought renewed taste and flavor to this longtime favorite, and the four-course prix fixe menu offers a large choice of dishes in each category. Examples are magret of duck with a sweet-and-sour sauce; a seasonal variation of *pot-au-feu* (stew) whose ingredients change with the seasons; and grilled sea bass on a bed of fennel with a light butter sauce.

36–38 rue de Grenelle, 7e. 𝄞 **01-42-22-13-35.** Reservations recommended. Prix fixe menu 24€–29€ ($28–$33). V. Daily noon–2pm and 7–11pm. Métro: Sèvres-Babylone or Rue du Bac.

INEXPENSIVE

Au Pied de Fouet TRADITIONAL FRENCH   This is one of the neighborhood's oldest and most reasonably priced restaurants. In the 1700s it was a stopover for carriages en route to Paris, offering wine, food, and stables. Don't expect a leisurely or attentive meal: Food and drink will disappear quickly from your table, under the gaze of others waiting their turn. The dishes are solid and unpretentious and include *blanquette de veau* (veal stew), chicken in vinegar sauce (a house specialty), *petit salé* (a savory family-style stew made from pork and vegetables and served with lentils), and filet of sea wolf or filet of codfish.

45 rue de Babylone, 7e. 𝄞 **01-47-05-12-27.** Main courses 6.90€–11€ ($7.95–$13). No credit cards. Mon–Sat noon–2:30pm; Mon–Fri 7–9:30pm. Closed Aug. Métro: Vaneau.

Chez l'Ami Jean BASQUE/SOUTHWESTERN FRENCH   This restaurant was opened by a Basque nationalist in 1931, and fans claim its Basque cuisine and setting are the most authentic on the Left Bank. Decorative details include wood panels; memorabilia from *pelote* (a Basque game like jai alai), rugby, and soccer; and red-and-white woven tablecloths like the ones sold in Bayonne. Dishes include Bayonne ham; herb-laden Béarn-influenced vegetable soups; confit of duck with small sautéed potatoes; and fine slices of veal with fresh herbs, onions, red peppers, and a light tomato sauce. In springtime, look for a specialty rarely available elsewhere: *saumon de l'Adour* (Adour salmon) with béarnaise sauce.

27 rue Malar, 7e. 𝄞 **01-47-05-86-89.** Reservations recommended. Main courses 14€–22€ ($16–$25); 3-course Basque menu 28€ ($32). MC, V. Tues–Sat noon–2pm and 7pm–midnight. Métro: Invalides.

15TH ARRONDISSEMENT
MODERATE

Cave de l'Os à Moelle *Finds* TRADITIONAL FRENCH   This restaurant contains three large tables, where guests are seated family-style next to strangers, whom they often end up toasting with one or more glasses of wine before the end of the meal. There's only one option here: a *grand-mère* (grandmother; implying old fashioned) prix fixe menu with bowls of soup and platters of pâté, rillettes, and cheese. Main-course and dessert selections are plunked down on a corner buffet, and guests serve themselves until they're full. Anticipate country-style beef stews, blood-sausage terrine, tiny shellfish with freshly made mayonnaise, and a vast array of desserts. Wines are numerous and cheap—the restaurant sells glasses and bottles of wine at rates substantially less than what's available at other competitors. Overall, the experience is satisfying and jolly. Management encourages guests to come either at 7:30 or 9:30pm, as part of a carefully controlled access.

181 rue de Lourmel, 15e. C 01-45-57-28-28. Reservations recommended. Prix fixe menu 25€ ($29). MC, V. Tues–Sun noon–2:30pm; Tues–Sat 7:30–9:30pm. Métro: Lourmel.

Kim Anh VIETNAMESE   This is one of the best addresses in Paris for the savory, spicy cuisine of its former colony. It's a bit lost down in the 15th, but many Parisian foodies journey here anyway. The cuisine includes the sharp, spicy, sour, and succulent flavors of Vietnam, as prepared in pork, chicken, fish, and beef dishes, many of them excellent. Waiters are very patient in explaining various dishes to newcomers. We are especially fond of the caramelized langoustines and most definitely the stuffed crabs and steamed pork ravioli.

51 av. Emile Zola, 15e. C 01-45-79-40-96. Reservations recommended. Main courses 20€–40€ ($23–$46); prix fixe menu 34€ ($39). AE, MC, V. Tues–Sun 7–11pm. Métro: Charles-Michels.

5 The Top Cafes

As surely everyone knows, the cafe is a Parisian institution. Parisians use them as combination club/tavern/snack bars, almost as extensions of their living rooms. They're spots where you can sit alone reading your newspaper, doing your homework, or writing your memoirs; meet a friend or lover; nibble at a hard-boiled egg; or drink yourself into oblivion. At cafes you meet your dates to go on to a show or to stay and talk. Above all, cafes are for people-watching.

Their single common denominator is the encouragement of leisurely sitting. Regardless of whether you have one small coffee or the house's most expensive cognac, nobody will badger, pressure, or hurry you. If you wish to sit there until the place closes, that's your affair. Cafes keep flexible hours depending on the season, the traffic, and the part of town they're in. Nearly all stay open until 1 or 2am, and a few are open all night.

Coffee, of course, is the chief drink. It comes black in a small cup, unless you specifically order it *au lait* (with milk). *Thé* (tea, pronounced *tay*) is also fairly popular but is generally not of a high quality. If you prefer beer, we advise you to pay a bit more for the imported German, Dutch, or Danish brands, which are much better than the local brew. If you insist on a French beer, at least order it *á pression* (draft), which is superior. There's also a vast variety of fruit drinks, as well as Coca-Cola, which can be rather expensive. French chocolate drinks— either hot or iced—are absolutely superb and on par with the finest Dutch brands. They're made from ground chocolate, not a chemical compound.

Now just a few words on cafe etiquette: You don't pay when you get your order—only when you intend to leave. Payment indicates you've had all you want. *Service compris* means the tip is included in your bill, so it isn't necessary to tip extra; still, most people leave an extra euro or so. You'll hear the locals call for the *"garçon,"* but as a foreigner it would be more polite to say *"monsieur."* All waitresses, on the other hand, are addressed as *"mademoiselle,"* regardless of age or marital status. In the smaller cafes, you may have to share your table. In that case, even if you haven't exchanged a word with your table companion, when you leave it's customary to bid him or her *au revoir.*

For the locations of these cafes, see the corresponding arrondissement maps earlier in this chapter.

EXPENSIVE

Brasserie Lipp   This is a Left Bank institution. On the day of Paris's liberation in 1944, late owner Roger Cazes welcomed Hemingway as the first man to drop in for a drink. Then, as now, famous people often drop by for beer, wine, and conversation. Since its acquisition a few years ago by members of the Bertrand Group (the force behind Paris's St. James Club), the mechanics whereby you can obtain a table in this cultural monument are a lot easier, and a lot less arbitrary, than when Cazes granted or denied a table in his joint based basically on whether or not he considered you worthy. Reservations are accepted today, and usually respected, for dining tables, but not cafe tables. The specialty is *choucroute garni,* Paris's best—you get not only sauerkraut but also a thick layer of ham and braised pork, which you can wash down with the house Riesling (an Alsatian white wine) or beer. Even if you don't go inside, you can sit at a sidewalk table to enjoy a cognac and people-watch.

151 bd. St-Germain, 6e. ☎ 01-45-48-53-91. Main courses 16€–17€ ($18–$20); full meals with a modest wine average 50€ ($58); café au lait 3€ ($3.45). AE, DC, MC, V. Daily 11am–2am; restaurant service 12:15pm–12:45am. Métro: St-Germain-des-Prés.

Café de Flore ★★   It's the most famous cafe in the world, still fighting to maintain a Left Bank aura despite hordes of visitors from around the world. Sartre—the granddaddy of existentialism, a key figure in the Resistance, and a renowned cafe-sitter—often came here during World War II. Wearing a leather jacket and beret, he sat and wrote his trilogy, *Les Chemins de la Liberté* (The Roads to Freedom). Camus, Picasso, and Apollinaire also frequented the Flore. The cafe is still going strong, though the famous patrons have moved on and tourists have taken up all the tables. The menu offers omelets, salads, club sandwiches, and more. The place is especially popular on Sunday mornings.

172 bd. St-Germain, 6e. ☎ 01-45-48-55-26. Café espresso 4€ ($4.60); glass of beer 7.50€ ($8.65); snacks from 16€ ($18). AE, DC, MC, V. Daily 7:30am–1:30am. Métro: St-Germain-des-Prés.

Fouquet's ★   For people-watching, this is definitely on the see-and-be-seen circuit. Fouquet's has been collecting anecdotes and a patina since it was founded in 1901. A celebrity favorite, it has attracted Chaplin, Chevalier, Dietrich, Churchill, Roosevelt, and Jackie Onassis. The premier cafe on the Champs-Elysées sits behind a barricade of potted flowers at the edge of the sidewalk. Today, it's owned by the well-managed hotel and dining conglomerate, Lucien Barrière. You can choose a table in the sunshine or retreat to the glassed-in elegance of the leather banquettes and rattan furniture of the grillroom. Though this is a full-fledged restaurant, with a beautiful formal dining room on the second floor, most visitors come by just for a glass of wine, coffee, or sandwich.

99 av. des Champs-Elysées, 8e. ☎ 01-47-23-50-00. Glass of wine from 8€ ($9.20); sandwiches 9.50€–14€ ($11–$16); main courses 28€–48€ ($32–$55); prix fixe lunch 54€ ($62), dinner 78€ ($90). AE, MC, V. Daily 8am–2am. Restaurant daily noon–3pm and 7pm–midnight; bar 9am–2am. Métro: George V.

MODERATE

Café Beaubourg   Next to the all-pedestrian plaza of the Centre Pompidou, this is a trendy cafe with soaring concrete columns and a minimalist decor. Many of the regulars work in the neighborhood's eclectic shops and galleries. You can order salads, omelets, grilled steak, chicken *cordon bleu,* pastries, and daily platters. In warm weather, tables are set up on the sprawling outdoor terrace, providing an appropriate niche for watching the young and the restless go by.

100 rue St-Martin, 4e. ⓒ **01-48-87-63-96.** Glass of wine 4€–9€ ($4.60–$10); beer 5€ ($5.75); American breakfast 23€ ($26); sandwiches and platters 7€–20€ ($8–$23). AE, DC, MC, V. Sun–Thurs 8am–1am; Fri–Sat 8am–2am. Métro: Rambuteau or Hôtel-de-Ville.

Café de la Musique   This cafe's location in one of the grandest of Mitterrand's *grands travaux* guarantees a crowd passionately devoted to music; the recorded sounds that play in the background are likely to be more diverse and more eclectic than those in any other cafe in Paris. The red-and-green velour setting might remind you of a modern opera house, with windows overlooking nearby place de la Fontaine. Although it originated in the late 1990s as a cafe serving light platters, sandwiches, and drinks, its cuisine became dramatically more sophisticated in 2002, the year it was taken over by culinary legend and nightlife impresario Alain Poudou. The menu was inspired by the cuisine within one of Paris's trendiest hotels, the Costes, and is likely to include lobster-studded risotto, roasted rack of lamb with thyme, very fresh salads of the type you'd find in Italy, brochettes of shrimp with spinach, and sliced baked salmon in a white wine–cream sauce. As the evening progresses, this place takes on more of the ambience of a hip nightclub, when DJs spin some kind of music most nights, and with an especially dense concentration of urbanized, young hipsters appearing on Friday and Saturday nights.

> **Value   Did You Know?**
>
> You'll pay substantially less in a cafe if you stand at the counter rather than sit at a table, because there's no service charge.

In the Cité de la Musique, place Fontaine Aux Lions, 213 av. Jean-Jaurès, 19e. ⓒ **01-48-03-15-91.** Main courses 15€–26€ ($17–$30). Daily 8am–2am; restaurant daily 8am–1am. Métro: Porte de Pantin.

La Belle Hortense   This is the most literary cafe in a neighborhood (the Marais) that's loaded with literary antecedents and references. It contains an erudite and accessible staff; an inventory of French literary classics as well as modern tomes about art, psychoanalysis, history, and culture; and two high-ceilinged, 19th-century rooms little changed since the days of Baudelaire and Balzac. Prominently positioned near the entrance is a zinc-covered bar that sells glasses of wine. If you're fluent in French, you might be interested in attending a reading, a book signing, or a lecture. Some kind of public gathering, conducted only in rapid, colloquial French, is scheduled every Tuesday, Wednesday, and Thursday, usually at 8pm. One particularly intriguing and ongoing lecture series involves three trained actors, each reading sequential passages from a book.

31 rue Vieille du Temple, 4e. ⓒ **01-48-04-71-60.** Glass of wine 3.50€–6€ ($4–$6.90); coffee 1.30€ ($1.50); snacks from 12€ ($14). MC, V. Daily 5pm–2am. Métro: Hôtel de Ville or St-Paul.

La Coupole ★   Born in 1927 and once a leading center of artistic life, La Coupole is now the epitome of the grand Paris brasserie in Montparnasse. Former patrons included Josephine Baker, Henry Miller, Dalí, Calder, Hemingway, Fitzgerald, and Picasso. At one of its sidewalk tables, you can sit and watch the passing scene and order a coffee or a cognac VSOP. The food is quite good, despite the fact that the dining room resembles an enormous rail-station wait-ing room. Try main dishes like sole meunière, cassoulet, fresh oysters, shellfish, grilled lobster with flambéed whisky sauce, and some of the best pepper steak in Paris. The waiters are as rude and inattentive as ever, and aficionados of the place wouldn't have it any other way.

102 bd. du Montparnasse, 14e. ℰ **01-43-20-14-20.** Breakfast buffet 13€ ($15); main courses 14€–19€ ($16–$22); prix fixe lunch 23€–33€ ($26–$38), dinner 33€ ($38). AE, DC, MC, V. Daily 8:30am–1am (break-fast buffet Mon–Fri 8:30–10:30am). Métro: Vavin.

La Palette ★★   The staff here defiantly maintains old-fashioned Parisian tra-ditions that haven't changed much since the days of Picasso and Braque—the same drinks (Ricard and Pernod, among others) are still popular. A bustle of comings and goings makes La Palette an insider's version of a battered, artisti-cally evocative Quartier Latin cafe. The interior, inhabited by amiably crotchety waiters, consists of tiled murals, installed around 1935, advertising the virtues of a brand of liqueur that's no longer manufactured. If you happen to drop in dur-ing mealtime, you'll have a limited selection of salads and *croque monsieur* (toasted ham and cheese), plus one *plat de jour* per day, always priced at 11€ ($13), which may include roast beef, lamb stew, fish, and gigot of lamb. The food is well prepared, and the dish of the day is usually announced as a kind of surprise to the joint's devoted fans.

43 rue de Seine, 6e. ℰ **01-43-26-68-15.** Sandwiches, omelets, and *plats de jour* 6€–12€ ($6.90–$14). MC, V. Cafe and bar Mon–Sat 8am–2am; restaurant Mon–Sat 11:30am–3pm. Métro: Mabillion or St-Germain-des-Prés.

La Rotonde   Once patronized by Hemingway, the original Rotonde faded into history but is immortalized in the pages of *The Sun Also Rises*, in which Papa wrote, "No matter what cafe in Montparnasse you ask a taxi driver to bring you to from the right bank of the river, they always take you to the Rotonde." Lavishly upgraded, its reincarnation has a paneled Art Deco elegance and shares the site with a cinema. The menu includes hearty fare like pepper steak with *pommes frites* (french fries), shellfish in season, a superb and genuinely succulent version of sole meunière, and sea-bass filets with herb-flavored lemon sauce.

105 bd. du Montparnasse, 6e. ℰ **01-43-26-48-26.** Glass of wine from 4€ ($4.60); prix fixe lunch 15€ ($17); main course 19€–38€ ($22–$44). AE, MC, V. Cafe daily 7:15am–1am; food service daily noon–1am. Métro: Vavin.

Le Procope ★★   To fans of French history, this is the holy grail of Parisian cafes. Opened in 1686, it occupies a three-story town house categorized as a historic monument. Inside, nine salons and dining rooms, each of whose 300-year-old walls have been carefully preserved and painted a deep red, are available for languorous afternoon coffee breaks or well-presented meals. Menu items include platters of shellfish, onion soup au gratin, *coq au vin* (chicken stewed in wine), duck breast in honey sauce, and grilled versions of various meats and fish. Every day between 3 and 7pm, the place makes itself available to sightseers who come to look but not necessarily eat and drink at the site that welcomed such movers and shakers as Diderot, Voltaire, George Sand, Victor Hugo, and Oscar Wilde. Of special charm is the ground-floor room outfitted like an antique library.

13 rue de l'Ancienne-Comédie, 6e. ℰ **01-40-46-79-00.** Reservations recommended. Coffee 2.80€ ($3.20); glass of beer 4.70€ ($5.40); main courses 17€–44€ ($20–$51). AE, DC, MC, V. Daily noon–midnight. Métro: Odéon.

Les Deux Magots ★★   This legendary hangout for the sophisticated residents of St-Germain-des-Prés becomes a tourist favorite in summer. Visitors monopolize the few sidewalk tables as the waiters rush about, seemingly oblivious to anyone's needs. Regulars from around the neighborhood reclaim it in the off-season. Les Deux Magots was once a gathering place of the intellectual elite, like Sartre, de Beauvoir, and Giraudoux. Inside are the two large statues of *magots* (Confucian wise men) that give the cafe its name. The crystal chandeliers are too brightly lit, but the regulars are used to the glare. After all, some of them even read their daily papers here. You can order salads, pastries, ice cream, or one of the daily specials; the fresh fish is usually a good bet.

6 place St-Germain-des-Prés, 6e. ℗ **01-45-48-55-25.** Café au lait 4.50€ ($5.20); whiskey soda 11€–15€ ($12–$17); *plats du jour* 16€–22€ ($18–$25). AE, DC, V. Daily 7:30am–1:30am. Métro: St-Germain-des-Prés.

INEXPENSIVE

Café de l'Industrie   This place is so old it's new again. Founded pre–World War II, it received a vital new lease on life after the opening of the nearby Opéra Bastille. Today its three dining rooms boast a decor evoking aspects of both the Tropics and faux-baroque Europe, with green plants and lots of original oil paintings by long-term patrons. Known for decanting obscure vintages from the Touraine and the region around Beaujolais and Bordeaux, it appeals to photographers and lesser-known characters in French-speaking showbiz. If you're hungry, consider any of the generous *plats du jour* like leeks steeped in vinaigrette, minced chicken with tarragon, *boeuf bourguignon* (braised beef in red-wine sauce), fried haddock, and tagliatelle with salmon, chives, and cream sauce.

16 rue St-Sabin, 11e. ℗ **01-47-00-13-53.** Main courses 8€–25€ ($9.20–$29). MC, V. Daily 10am–2am. Métro: Bastille or Breguier-Sabin.

Café des Deux Moulins   *Amélie* was a quirky low-budget film that was nominated for five Oscars and was seen by more than 25 million people around the world following its release in 2001. The film was set in Montmartre, and the cafe featured in the film has developed into a mandatory stopping-off place for the constantly arriving "cult of *Amélie*." In the film Amélie worked as a waitress at the Café des Deux Moulins. The musty atmosphere with its 1950s decor, mustard-colored ceiling, and lace curtains has been preserved, even the wall lamps and unisex toilet. The menu remains much the same as it always was—escalopes of veal in a cream sauce, beef filets, calf's liver, green frisée salad with bacon bits and warm goat cheese, and pig's brains with lentils. The kitchen serves hamburgers, but with an egg on top. Of course, the classic dish is a demi-Camembert with a glass of Côtes du Rhône.

15 rue Lepic, 18e. ℗ **01-42-54-90-50.** Main courses 8.90€–15€ ($10–$17). AE, DISC, MC, V. Mon–Fri 7am–2am; Sat 7:30am–2am; Sun 9am–2am. Métro: Blanche.

Le Rouquet ★ *Finds*   Despite its conventional food, Le Rouquet enjoys an enviable cachet and sense of chic, partly because it competes on a less flamboyant scale with the nearby Café de Flore and Les Deux Magots and partly because the decor hasn't changed since a 1954 remodeling. Less than 60 yards from St-Germain church, you can sit for as long as you want, watching a crowd of stylish Italians and Americans performing shopping and people-watching rituals barely altered since Le Rouquet's founding in 1922.

188 bd. St-Germain, 7e. ℗ **01-45-48-06-93.** Café au lait 2.20€ ($2.55) counter, 3.80€ ($4.35) at table; *plats du jour* 12€ ($14). MC, V. Mon–Sat 7am–9pm. Métro: St-Germain-des-Prés.

7

Exploring Paris

Paris is a city where taking in the street life—shopping, strolling, and hanging out—should claim as much of your time as sightseeing in churches or museums. Having a picnic in the Bois de Boulogne, taking a sunrise amble along the Seine, spending an afternoon at a flea market—Paris bewitches you with these kinds of experiences. For all the Louvre's beauty, you'll probably remember the Latin Quarter's crooked alleyways better than the 370th oil painting of your visit.

1 Sightseeing Suggestions for the First-Timer

The following suggested itineraries will allow first-time visitors to experience Paris's highlights in only a few days.

IF YOU HAVE 1 DAY   Get up early and begin your day with some live theater by walking the streets around your hotel. Find a cafe and order a Parisian breakfast of coffee and croissants. If you're a museum and monument junkie and don't dare return home without seeing the "musts," the top two museums are the **Musée du Louvre** and **Musée d'Orsay,** and the top three monuments are the **Tour Eiffel, Arc de Triomphe,** and **Notre-Dame** (which you can see later in the day). If it's a toss-up between the Louvre and the d'Orsay, we'd choose the Louvre because it holds a greater variety of works. Among the monuments, we'd make it the Tour Eiffel for the panoramic view of the city.

If your day is too short to visit museums or wait in line for the tower, we suggest you spend your time strolling the streets. **Ile St-Louis** is the most elegant place for a walk. After exploring this island and its mansions, wander through such Left Bank districts as **St-Germain-des-Prés** and the area around **place St-Michel,** the heart of the student quarter. As the sun sets, head for **Notre-Dame,** standing along the banks of the Seine. This is a good place to watch the shadows fall over Paris as the lights come on for the night. Afterward, walk along the Seine, where vendors sell books and souvenir prints. Promise yourself a return visit and have dinner in the Left Bank bistro of your choice.

IF YOU HAVE 2 DAYS   Follow the above for day 1, except now you can fit in on day 2 more of the top five sights. Day 1 covered a lot of the Left Bank, so if you want to explore the Right Bank, begin at the **Arc de Triomphe** and stroll down the **Champs-Elysées,** Paris's main boulevard, until you reach the Egyptian obelisk at **place de la Concorde,** where some of France's most notable figures lost their heads on the guillotine. Place de la Concorde affords terrific views of **La Madeleine,** the **Palais Bourbon,** the **Arc de Triomphe,** and the **Musée du Louvre.** Nearby **place Vendôme** is worth a visit, as it represents the Right Bank at its most elegant, with the Hôtel Ritz and Paris's top jewelry stores. Now we suggest a rest stop in the **Jardin de Tuileries,** west and adjacent to the Louvre. After a bistro lunch, walk in the **Marais** for a contrast to monumental Paris. Our favorite stroll is along **rue des Rosiers,** the heart of the Jewish community. Don't miss **place des Vosges.** After a rest, select a restaurant in **Montparnasse,** following in Hemingway's footsteps. This area is far livelier at night.

IF YOU HAVE 3 DAYS   Spend days 1 and 2 as above. As you've already seen the Left Bank and the Right Bank, this day should be about your special interests. You might target the **Centre Pompidou** and the **Musée Carnavalet,** Paris's history museum. If you're a Monet fan, you might head for the **Musée Marmottan–Claude Monet.** Or perhaps you'd rather wander the sculpture garden of the **Musée Rodin.** If you select the **Musée Picasso,** you can use part of the morning to explore a few of the Marais's art galleries. After lunch, spend the afternoon on **Ile de la Cité,** where you'll get not only to see Notre-Dame again but also to visit the **Conciergerie,** where Marie Antoinette and others were held captive before they were beheaded. And you certainly can't miss the stunning stained glass of **Sainte-Chapelle** in the Palais de Justice. After dinner, if your energy holds, you can sample Paris's nightlife—whatever you fancy: the dancers at the **Lido** or the **Folies-Bergère,** or a smoky Left Bank jazz club, or a frenzied dance club. If you'd like to just sit and have a drink, Paris has some of the most elegant hotel bars in the world—try the **Crillon** or the **Plaza Athénée.**

IF YOU HAVE 4 DAYS   For your first 3 days, follow the above. On day 4, head to **Versailles,** 21km (13 miles) south of Paris, the greatest attraction in the Ile de France. When Louis XIV decided to move to the suburbs, he created a spectacle unlike anything the world had ever seen. Most of the palace remains intact, in all its opulence and glitter. A full day here almost feels like too little time. After you return to Paris for the night, take a good rest and spend the evening wandering around the Left Bank's **Latin Quarter,** enjoying the student cafes and bars and selecting your bistro of choice for the evening. Two of the livelier streets for wandering are rue de la Huchette and rue Monsieur-le-Prince.

IF YOU HAVE 5 DAYS   Spend days 1 to 4 as above. On day 5, devote at least a morning to **Montmartre,** the community formerly known for its artists atop the highest of Paris's seven hills. Though the starving artists who made it the embodiment of *la vie de bohème* (Bohemian life) are long gone, there's much to enchant, especially if you wander the back streets and avoid place du Tertre. Away from the tacky shops and sleazy clubs, you'll see picture-postcard lanes and staircases known to Picasso, Toulouse-Lautrec, and Utrillo. It's virtually mandatory to visit **Sacré-Coeur,** for the view if nothing else. If it's your last night in Paris, let your own interests take over. Lovers traditionally spend it clasping hands in a walk along the Seine; less goo-goo-eyed visitors can still find a full agenda. Try an evening at **Willi's Wine Bar,** with more than 250 vintages and good food. For a nightcap, we always head for the **Hemingway Bar** at the Ritz, where Garbo, Coward, and Fitzgerald once lifted their glasses. If that's too elegant, head for **Closerie des Lilas** in the 6th arrondissement, where you can rub shoulders with the movers and shakers of the film and fashion industries.

2 Attractions by Arrondissement

For the locations of these sights, see the **"Top Paris Attractions"** map on p. 170 and the individual **arrondissement maps** that follow.

THE RIGHT BANK
1ST ARRONDISSEMENT

Jardin des Tuileries ★★ (p. 209)
Jardin du Carrousel (p. 209)
Les Halles ★ (p. 220)
Musée des Arts Décoratifs ★
(p. 196)
Musée du Louvre ★★★ (p. 185)
Palais Royal ★★ (p. 207)
Place Vendôme (p. 166)
St-Eustache ★★ (p. 202)
St-Germain l'Auxerrois ★★ (p. 203)

3RD ARRONDISSEMENT

Hôtel de Clisson (p. 199)
Hôtel de Rohan (p. 199)
Hôtel le Pelletier de St-Fargeau
(p. 192)
Musée Carnavalet-Histoire
de Paris ★★ (p. 192)
Musée Cognacq-Jay ★ (p. 196)
Musée d'Art et Histoire du
Judaisme ★★ (p. 198)
Musée de la Chasse (p. 200)
Musée de l'Histoire de France ★
(p. 199)
Musée Picasso ★★ (p. 194)

4TH ARRONDISSEMENT

Atelier Brancusi ★ (p. 191)
Cathédrale de Notre-Dame ★★★
(p. 180)
Centre Pompidou ★★★ (p. 191)
Hôtel de Lauzun (p. 218)
Hôtel de Ville ★ (p. 206)
Hôtel Dieu (p. 218)
Hôtel Lambert (p. 220)
Maison de Victor Hugo ★ (p. 208)
No. 9 quai d'Anjou (p. 220)
Place des Vosges (p. 167)
Pont Neuf (p. 218)
Rue des Rosiers (p. 166)
Sainte-Chapelle ★★★ (p. 188)
Square du Vert Galant (p. 218)
St-Louis-en-l'Ile (p. 220)

8TH ARRONDISSEMENT

American Cathedral of the Holy
Trinity (p. 201)
Arc de Triomphe ★★★ (p. 166)
Champs-Elysées (p. 166)
La Madeleine ★★ (p. 201)
Musée Jacquemart-André ★★
(p. 192)

Musée Nissim de Camondo ★
(p. 197)
Parc Monceau ★ (p. 211)
Place de la Concorde (p. 166)

9TH ARRONDISSEMENT

Musée Grévin ★ (p. 225)
Paris-Story (p. 199)

11TH ARRONDISSEMENT

Musée Edith Piaf (p. 197)
Villa Calte (p. 197)

12TH ARRONDISSEMENT

Musée des Arts d'Afrique et
d'Océanie (p. 196)
Parc Zoologique de Paris (p. 226)

16TH ARRONDISSEMENT

Bois de Boulogne ★★ (p. 210)
Cimetière de Passy (p. 212)
Hippodrome d'Auteuil (p. 217)
Hippodrome de Longchamp ★★★
(p. 217)
Jardin d'Acclimatation ★ (p. 225)
Maison de Balzac (p. 208)
Musée d'Art Moderne de la Ville
de Paris (p. 196)
Musée de la Marine ★★ (p. 224)
Musée des Enfants (p. 196)
Musée du Vin (p. 201)
Musée Marmottan–Claude
Monet ★★ (p. 192)
Musée National des Arts
Asiatiques–Guimet ★★ (p. 197)

18TH ARRONDISSEMENT

Basilique du Sacré-Coeur ★★
(p. 179)
Cimetière de Montmartre ★
(p. 212)
Cimetière St-Vincent (p. 213)
Musée de l'Erotisme (p. 200)

19TH ARRONDISSEMENT

Cité des Sciences et de
l'Industrie ★★ (p. 224)
La Géode (p. 224)
Musée de la Musique (p. 196)
Parc de La Villette (p. 224)

20TH ARRONDISSEMENT

Cimetière du Père-Lachaise ★★★
(p. 213)

THE LEFT BANK
5TH ARRONDISSEMENT

6TH ARRONDISSEMENT

7TH ARRONDISSEMENT

13TH ARRONDISSEMENT

14TH ARRONDISSEMENT

15TH ARRONDISSEMENT

3 The Top Attractions: From the Arc de Triomphe to the Tour Eiffel

Arc de Triomphe ✶✶✶   At the western end of the Champs-Elysées, the Arc de Triomphe suggests an ancient Roman arch, only it's larger. Actually, it's the biggest triumphal arch in the world, about 49m (161 ft.) high and 44m (144 ft.) wide. To reach it, *don't try to cross the square,* Paris's busiest traffic hub. With a dozen streets radiating from the "Star," the roundabout has been called by one writer "vehicular roulette with more balls than numbers" (death is certain!). Take the underground passage and live a little longer.

Commissioned by Napoleon in 1806 to commemorate the victories of his Grand Armée, the arch wasn't ready for the entrance of his empress, Marie-Louise, in 1810 (he'd divorced Josephine because she couldn't provide him an heir). It wasn't completed until 1836, under the reign of Louis-Philippe. Four years later, Napoleon's remains, brought from St. Helena, passed under the arch on their journey to his tomb at the Hôtel des Invalides. Since that time it has become the focal point for state funerals. It's also the site of the tomb of the Unknown Soldier, in whose honor an eternal flame burns.

Top Paris Attractions

*Top attractions are listed here; for more
attractions in each neighborhood, please
see neighborhood maps.*

Attractions in the 1st Arrondissement

bd. de Sébastopol

rue St-Denis

r. Pierre Lescot

ÉTIENNE MARCEL

CHÂTELET

bd. du Palais

quai de la Mégisserie

ÎLE DE LA CITÉ

q. des Orfèvres

q. des Grands Augustins

r. Etienne Marcel

rue de Turbigo

r. Rambuteau

LES HALLES

r. des Halles

rue du Pont Neuf

rue des Bourdonnais

r. du Jour

r. Coquillère

r.J.J. Rousseau

rue Berger

r. du Roule

r. St-Honoré

r. de l'Arbre

pont Neuf

Seine

quai de Conti

rue du Louvre

r. Hérold

r. du Bouloi

r. J.J. Rousseau

r. de Col-Driant

LOUVRE-RIVOLI

rue de Rivoli

PONT NEUF

pont des Arts

quai Malaquais

r. Croix des Petits Champs

r. des Bons Enfants

quai du Louvre

quai Voltaire

r. des Sts-Pères

rue de la Banque

1e

rue de Valois

JARDIN DU PALAIS ROYAL

MUSÉE DU LOUVRE-PALAIS ROYAL

pont du Carrousel

6e

rue des Petits Champs

r. de Montpensier

place du Carrousel

r. de Richelieu

r. Thérèse

r. Molière

r. de l'Échelle

PYRAMIDES

JARDIN DU CARROUSEL

pont Royal

2e

rue du Quatre Septembre

rue St-Augustin

Casanova

av. de l'Opéra

r. des Pyramides

rue St-Roch

av. Gen. Lemonnier

quai Anatole France

pont Solférino

Seine

rue Danielle

r. de la Sourdière

TUILERIES

place de l'Opéra

OPÉRA

rue de la Paix

Daunou

rue Danielle

Thabor

rue de Rivoli

JARDIN DES TUILERIES

quai des Tuileries

8e

r. des Capucines

r. Cambon

place Vendôme

rue de Castiglione

rue du Mont

bd. St-Germain

MADELEINE

rue Royale

rue St-Honoré

CONCORDE

pont de la Concorde

place de la Concorde

M Métro

1/5 Mi

0.2 Km

Arc de Triomphe du Carrousel **6**
Cour Napoléon & I. M. Pei Pyramid **8**
Forum des Halles **15**
Fragonard Musée du Parfum **1**
Jardin du Palais Royal **11**
Jardin des Tuileries **4**
Jardin du Carrousel **5**
Les Halles **16**
Musée des Arts Décoratifs **7**
Musée du Louvre **12**
Palais Royal **10**
Place de la Concorde **3**
Place du Palais Royal **11**
Place Vendôme **2**
St-Eustache **14**
St-Germain l'Auxerrois **13**

0   1/4 Mi
0   0.25 Km

BONNE NOUVELLE
Ⓜ bd. de Bonne

STRASBOURG ST-DENIS

10e

RÉPUBLIQUE
Ⓜ

rue Réaumur

place de la République

av. de la République

Oberkampf

2e

RÉAUMUR SÉBASTOPOL
Ⓜ

ÉTIENNE MARCEL

rue de Turbigo

TEMPLE

ARTS ET MÉTIERS
Ⓜ

sq. du Temple

3e

rue de Bretagne

FILLES DU CALVAIRE
Ⓜ

ST-SÉBASTIEN FROISSART
Ⓜ

RICHARD LENOIR
Ⓜ

RAMBUTEAU
Ⓜ

r. Rambuteau

rue des Archives

⑥

⑤

rue Aubry le Boucher

⑧ ⑨ ⑩

rue Vieille du Temple

⑦

rue des Francs

rue Elzévir

⑫

BRÉGUET SABIN

Sq. Bréguet Sabin
Ⓜ

CHÂTELET

place de l'Hôtel de Ville

HÔTEL DE VILLE
④

Princess Garden

⑪

de Rosiers

Bourgeois

⑬

place des Vosges sq. Louis XIII

CHEMIN VERT
Ⓜ

11e

quai de Gesvres
quai de la Corse

②

③

pont d'Arcole

ÎLE DE LA CITÉ

rue de Rivoli

4e

⑮ ⑭

ST-PAUL

rue St-Antoine

place du Parvis Notre Dame

①

sq. Jean XXIII

PONT MARIE

l'Hôtel de Ville

quai des Célestins

place de la Bastille

rue de Lappe

rue du Faubourg

12e

BASTILLE
Ⓜ

⑰ ⑱ ⑯

ÎLE ST-LOUIS

SULLY MORLAND
Ⓜ

Bibliothèque de l'Arsenal

pont de Plaisance de Paris

rue de Lyon

bd. St-Germain

5e

Seine

quai Henri IV

Ⓜ **Métro**

17e 18e 19e
8e 9e 10e
2e 3e 20e
16e 1e 4e 11e
7e
15e 6e 5e 12e
14e 13e

Attractions in the 5th–6th Arrondissements

Arènes de Lutèce **17**
Institut de France **1**
Jardin du Luxembourg **7**
Mosquée de Paris **16**
Musée de l'Institut du Monde Arabe **18**
Musée National d'Histoire Naturelle
 (Museum of Natural History) **15**
Musée National du Moyen Age/Thermes
 de Cluny (Musée de Cluny) **11**
Musée National Eugène Delacroix **3**
Musée Zadkine **6**
Palais du Luxembourg **8**
Panthéon **12**
Roman Baths **11**
Rue de la Huchette **10**
Rue Monsieur-le-Prince **9**
Rue Visconti **2**
St-Etienne-du-Mont **13**
St-Germain-des-Prés **4**
St-Sulpice **5**
Val-de-Grâce **14**

Hôtel des Invalides/Napoléon's Tomb **4**

Les Egouts (Sewers of Paris) **2**

Musée d'Orsay **7**

Musée de l'Armée **3**

Musée des Plans-Reliefs **4**

Musée Rodin **5**

Palais Bourbon/ Assemblée Nationale **6**

Tour Eiffel **1**

Attractions in the 8th Arrondissement

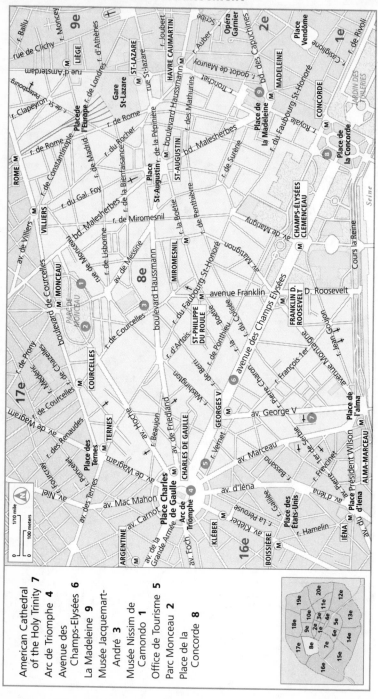

American Cathedral
of the Holy Trinity **7**
Arc de Triomphe **4**
Avenue des
Champs-Elysées **6**
La Madeleine **9**
Musée Jacquemart-
André **3**
Musée Nissim de
Camondo **1**
Office de Tourisme **5**
Parc Monceau **2**
Place de la
Concorde **8**

Attractions in the 16th Arrondissement

Arc de Triomphe **9**
Bois de Boulogne **1**
Cimetière de Passy **5**
Maison de Balzac **3**
Musée d'Art Moderne de la Ville de Paris **7**
Musée de la Marine **6**
Musée des Enfants **7**
Musée du Vin **4**
Musée Marmottan–
 Claude Monet **2**
Musée National des Arts
 Asiatiques–Guimet **8**

Attractions in the 18th Arrondissement

Basilique du Sacré-Coeur **8**
Cimetière de Montmartre **3**
Cimetière St-Vincent **5**
Espace Dali Montmartre **7**
Moulin de la Galette **4**
Moulin Rouge **2**
Musée de l'Erotisme **1**
Musée de Vieux Montmartre **6**

The greatest state funeral was Victor Hugo's in 1885; his coffin was placed under the arch, and much of Paris came to pay tribute. Another notable funeral was in 1929 for Ferdinand Foch, commander of the Allied forces in World War I. The arch has been the centerpiece of some of France's proudest moments and some of its most humiliating defeats, notably in 1871 and 1940. The memory of German troops marching under the arch is still painful to the French. Who can forget the 1940 newsreel of the Frenchman standing on the Champs-Elysées, weeping as the Nazi storm troopers goose-stepped through Paris? The arch's happiest moment occurred in 1944, when the liberation-of-Paris parade passed beneath it. That same year, Eisenhower paid a visit to the tomb of the Unknown Soldier, a new tradition among leaders of state and important figures. After Charles de Gaulle's death, the French government (despite protests from anti-Gaullists) voted to change the name of this site from place de l'Etoile to place Charles de Gaulle. Nowadays it's often known as place Charles de Gaulle–Etoile.

Of the sculptures on the monument, the best known is Rude's *Marseillaise,* or *The Departure of the Volunteers.* J. P. Cortot's *Triumph of Napoléon in 1810* and Etex's *Resistance of 1814* and *Peace of 1815* also adorn the facade. The monument is engraved with the names of hundreds of generals (those underlined died in battle) who commanded French troops in Napoleonic victories.

You can take an elevator or climb the stairway to the top, where there's an exhibition hall with lithographs and photos depicting the arch throughout its history, as well as an observation deck with a fantastic view.

Place Charles de Gaulle–Etoile, 8e. ✆ 01-55-37-73-77. www.monum.fr. Admission 7€ ($8.05) adults, 4.50€ ($5.20) ages 18–25, free for 17 and under. Apr–Sept daily 10am–11pm; Oct–Mar daily 10am–10:30pm. Métro: Charles de Gaulle–Etoile. Bus: 22, 30, 31, 52, 73, or 92.

Basilique du Sacré-Coeur ★★

Sacré-Coeur is one of Paris's most characteristic landmarks and has been the subject of much controversy. One Parisian called it "a lunatic's confectionery dream." An offended Zola declared it "the basilica of the ridiculous." Sacré-Coeur has had warm supporters as well, including poet Max Jacob and artist Maurice Utrillo. Utrillo never tired of drawing and painting it, and he and Jacob came here regularly to pray. Atop the *butte* (hill) in Montmartre, its multiple gleaming white domes and *campanile* (bell tower) loom over Paris like a 12th-century Byzantine church. But it's not that old. After France's 1870 defeat by the Prussians, the basilica was planned as a votive offering to cure France's misfortunes. Rich and poor alike contributed money to build it. Construction began in 1876, and though the church wasn't consecrated until 1919, perpetual prayers of adoration have been made here day and night since 1885. The interior is brilliantly decorated with mosaics: Look for the striking Christ on the ceiling and the mural of his Passion at the back of the altar. The stained-glass windows were shattered during the struggle for Paris

Tips **Best City View**

From the observation deck of the Arc de Triomphe, you can see up the Champs-Elysées and such landmarks as the Louvre, the Eiffel Tower, Sacré-Coeur, and La Défense. Although we don't want to get into any arguments about this, we think the view of Paris from this perspective is the grandest in the entire city.

in 1944 but have been well replaced. The crypt contains what some of the devout believe is Christ's sacred heart—hence, the name of the church.

Insider's tip: Although the view from the Arc de Triomphe is the greatest panorama of Paris, we also want to endorse the view from the gallery around the inner dome of Sacré-Coeur. On a clear day your eyes take in a sweep of Paris extending for 48km (30 miles) into the Ile de France. You can also walk around the inner dome, an attraction even better than the interior of Sacré-Coeur itself.

Place St-Pierre, 18e. 🕐 01-53-41-89-00. www.paris.org/Monuments/Sacre.Coeur. Free admission to basilica; joint ticket to dome and crypt 5€ ($5.75). Basilica open daily 6am–11pm; dome and crypt daily 9am–6pm. Métro: Abbesses; take the elevator to the surface and follow the signs to the *funiculaire*, which goes up to the church for the price of a Métro ticket.

Cathédrale de Notre-Dame ★★★   Notre-Dame is the heart of Paris and even of the country itself: Distances from the city to all parts of France are calculated from a spot at the far end of place du Parvis, in front of the cathedral, where a circular bronze plaque marks **Kilomètre Zéro.**

The cathedral's setting on the banks of the Seine has always been memorable. Founded in the 12th century by Maurice de Sully, bishop of Paris, Notre-Dame has grown over the years, changing as Paris has changed, often falling victim to whims of taste. Its flying buttresses (the external side supports, giving the massive interior a sense of weightlessness) were rebuilt in 1330. Though many disagree, we feel Notre-Dame is more interesting outside than in, and you'll want to walk all around it to fully appreciate this "vast symphony of stone." Better yet, cross over the pont au Double to the Left Bank and view it from the quay.

The histories of Paris and Notre-Dame are inseparable. Many prayed here before going off to fight in the Crusades. The revolutionaries who destroyed the Galerie des Rois and converted the building into a secular temple didn't spare "Our Lady of Paris." Later, Napoleon crowned himself emperor here, yanking the crown out of Pius VII's hands and placing it on his own head before crowning his Josephine empress (see David's *Coronation of Napoléon* in the Louvre). But carelessness, vandalism, embellishments, and wars of religion had already demolished much of the previously existing structure.

The cathedral was once scheduled for demolition, but, because of the popularity of Victor Hugo's *Hunchback of Notre-Dame* and the revival of interest in the Gothic period, a movement mushroomed to restore the cathedral to its original glory. The task was completed under Viollet-le-Duc, an architectural genius. The houses of old Paris used to crowd in on Notre-Dame, but during his redesign of the city, Baron Haussmann ordered them torn down to show the cathedral to its best advantage from the parvis. This is the best vantage for seeing the three sculpted 13th-century portals (the Virgin, the Last Judgment, and St. Anne).

(*Moments*   **A Nighttime Walk & an "Abomination"**

When Viollet-le-Duc designed the flying buttresses of the cathedral of Notre-Dame, they were denounced as "horrendous," "a blight of Paris," and an "abomination." Now they're a reason to go walking at night after a meal in a bistro. On the Ile de la Cité, wander through the garden in the rear of the cathedral. Near the Square Jean XXIII, cross the pont de l'Archevêche and walk along quai de Montebello along the Left Bank of the Seine for a wonderful perspective, especially when the *bateaux-mouches* (river cruise boats) light up the buttresses as they pass along.

On the left, the **Portal of the Virgin** depicts the signs of the zodiac and the coronation of the Virgin, an association found in dozens of medieval churches. The restored central **Portal of the Last Judgment** depicts three levels: the first shows Vices and Virtues; the second, Christ and his Apostles; and above that, Christ in triumph after the Resurrection. The portal is a close illustration of the Gospel according to Matthew. Over it is the remarkable **west rose window** ★★, 9.5m (31 ft.) wide, forming a showcase for a statue of the Virgin and Child. On the far right is the **Portal of St. Anne,** depicting scenes like the Virgin enthroned with Child; it's Notre-Dame's best-preserved and most perfect piece of sculpture. Equally interesting (though often missed) is the **Portal of the Cloisters** (around on the left), with its dour-faced 13th-century Virgin, a survivor among the figures that originally adorned the facade. (Alas, the Child she's holding has been decapitated.) Finally, on the Seine side of Notre-Dame, the **Portal of St. Stephen** traces that saint's martyrdom.

Frommer's Favorite Paris Experiences

Strolling Along the Seine. Lovers still walk hand in hand alongside it, and vendors on its banks still peddle everything from postcards to 100-year-old pornography. Some energetic types walk the full 11km (7-mile) stretch of the river, but you may want to confine your stroll to central Paris, passing the Louvre, Notre-Dame, and pont Neuf.

Window-Shopping Along the Faubourg St-Honoré. In the 1700s, this was home to the wealthiest of Parisians; today, it's home to the stores that cater to them. Even if you don't buy anything, you'll enjoy some great window-shopping with all the big names, like Hermès, Larouche, Lacroix, Lanvin, Courrèges, Cardin, St-Laurent, and Lagerfeld.

Enjoying an Afternoon of Cafe-Sitting. The Parisian cafe is an integral part of the city's life. Even if it means skipping a museum, spend some time at a cafe. Whether you have a coffee or the most expensive cognac in the house, nobody will hurry you, and you can see how the French really live. See our recommendations in chapter 6.

Taking Afternoon Tea à la Française. Get down to the business of rich, luscious desserts like Mont Blanc, that creamy purée of sweetened chestnuts. Try it at the grandest Parisian tea salon: Angélina, 226 rue de Rivoli, 1e (© **01-42-60-82-00**); see p. 122. A close rival is the Salon de Thé Bernardaud, 9–11 rue Royale, 8e (© **01-42-66-22-55**; Métro: Concorde), run by the Limoges-based manufacturer of fine porcelain. Teatime here is unique: A staff member presents you with five porcelain patterns and you choose the one in which you'd like your tea served.

Attending an Opera or a Ballet. In 1989, the acoustically perfect Opéra Bastille was inaugurated to compete with the grande dame Opéra

If possible, come to see Notre-Dame at sunset. Inside, of the three giant medallions warming the austere cathedral, the **north rose window** ★★ in the transept, from the mid-13th century, is best. The main body of the church is typically Gothic, with slender, graceful columns. In the **choir,** a stone-carved screen from the early 14th century depicts such biblical scenes as the Last Supper. Near the altar stands the 14th-century *Virgin and Child* ★, highly venerated among Paris's faithful. In the **treasury** are displayed vestments and gold objects, including crowns. Exhibited are a cross presented to Haile Selassie, former emperor of Ethiopia, and a reliquary given by Napoleon. Notre-Dame is especially proud of its relic of the True Cross and the Crown of Thorns.

To visit the **gargoyles** ★★ immortalized by Hugo, you have to scale steps leading to the twin **towers** rising to a height of 68m (223 ft.). Once there, you can inspect devils (some giving you the raspberry), hobgoblins, and birds of prey. Look carefully and you may see hunchback Quasimodo with Esmerelda.

Approached through a garden behind Notre-Dame is the **Mémorial des Martyrs Français de la Déportation de 1945 (Deportation Memorial),** out on the tip of Ile de la Cité. Here, birds chirp and the Seine flows gently by, but the memories are far from pleasant. The memorial commemorates the French citizens who were deported to concentration camps during World War II. Carved into stone are these blood-red words (in French): "Forgive, but don't

Garnier, then reserved for dance only and eventually closed for renovations. Now the Garnier has reopened, and opera has returned to its rococo splendor. A night here will take you back to the Second Empire, beneath a ceiling by Chagall. Whether for a performance of Bizet or Tharp, check out these two major Paris landmarks. Dress with pomp and circumstance.

Discovering Hidden Montmartre. This is the most touristy part of Paris. But far removed from the area's top draw, Sacré-Coeur, another neighborhood unfolds—the true Montmartre. Wander on any of the back streets away from the souvenir shops. Arm yourself with a good map and seek out streets like rue Lepic (refresh yourself at the Lux Bar at no. 12), rue Constance, rue Tholozé (with its view over the rooftops of Paris), rue des Abbesses, and rue Germain-Pilon. None of these is famous, none is crowded with hordes of visitors, but each is flanked with buildings whose detailing shows the pride and care that permeates Paris's architecture.

Checking Out the Marchés. A daily Parisian ritual is ambling through one of the open-air markets to purchase fresh food to be consumed that day—some ripe and creamy Camembert or a pumpkin-gold cantaloupe. You can gather supplies for a picnic in one of the city's parks. The vendors arrange their wares into a mosaic of vibrant colors. Sanguine, an Italian citrus whose juice is the color of an orange sunset; ruby-red peppers; and golden yellow bananas from Martinique all dazzle the eye. Our favorite is on rue Montorgeuil, beginning at rue Rambuteau, 1e (Métro: Les-Halles). See chapter 9 for other markets to check out.

forget." The memorial is open Monday to Friday from 8:30am to 9:45pm and Saturday and Sunday from 9am to 9:45pm. Admission is free.

6 place du parvis Notre-Dame, 4e. © 01-42-34-56-10. www.paris.org/Monuments/NDame. Free admission to cathedral; towers 6.10€ ($7) adults, 4.10€ ($4.70) ages 18–25 and seniors, free for children under 18; treasury 3€ ($3.45) adults, 2€ ($2.30) ages 12–25 and seniors, 1€ ($1.15) ages 5–11, free for children under 5. Cathedral open year-round daily 8am–6:45pm. Towers and crypt Apr–Sept daily 9:30am–6pm; Oct–Mar daily 10am–5:15pm. Museum Sat–Sun 2–5pm. Treasury Mon–Sat 9:30am–6pm, Sun 2–6pm. Métro: Cité or St-Michel. RER: St-Michel.

Hôtel des Invalides/Napoleon's Tomb ★★★   In 1670, the Sun King decided to build this "hotel" to house disabled soldiers. It wasn't an entirely benevolent gesture considering the men had been injured, crippled, or blinded while fighting his battles. When the building was finally completed (Louis XIV had long been dead), a gilded dome by Jules Hardouin-Mansart crowned it and its corridors stretched for miles. The best way to approach the Invalides is by crossing over the Right Bank via the early-1900s pont Alexander-III and entering the cobblestone forecourt, where a display of massive cannons makes a formidable welcome.

Before rushing on to Napoleon's Tomb, you may want to visit the world's greatest military museum, the **Musée de l'Armée.** In 1794, a French inspector started collecting weapons, uniforms, and equipment, and with the accumulation of war material over time, the museum has become a documentary of man's self-destruction. Viking swords, Burgundian battle axes, 14th-century blunderbusses, Balkan *khandjars,* American Browning machine guns, war pitchforks, salamander-engraved Renaissance serpentines, a 1528 Griffon, musketoons, grenadiers . . . if it can kill, it's enshrined here. As a sardonic touch, there's even the wooden leg of General Daumesnil, the governor of Vincennes who lost his leg in the battle of Wagram. Oblivious to the irony of committing a crime against a place that documents man's evil nature, the Nazis looted the museum in 1940.

Among the outstanding acquisitions are suits of armor worn by the kings and dignitaries of France, including Louis XIV. The best are in the new Arsenal. The most famous one, the "armor suit of the lion," was made for François I. Henri II ordered his suit engraved with the monogram of his mistress, Diane de Poitiers, and (perhaps reluctantly) that of his wife, Catherine de Médicis. Particularly fine are the showcases of swords and the World War I mementos, including those of American and Canadian soldiers—seek out the Armistice Bugle, which sounded the cease-fire on November 7, 1918, before the general cease-fire on November 11. The west wing's Salle Orientale has arms of the Eastern world, including Asia and the Mideast Muslim countries, from the 16th century to the 19th century. Turkish armor (look for Bajazet's helmet) and weaponry, and Chinese and Japanese armor and swords are on display.

Then there's that little Corsican who became France's greatest soldier. Here you can see the death mask Antommarchi made of him, as well as an oil by Delaroche, painted at the time of Napoleon's first banishment (Apr 1814) and depicting him as he probably looked, paunch and all. The First Empire exhibit displays Napoleon's field bed with his tent; in the room devoted to the Restoration, the 100 Days, and Waterloo, you can see his bedroom as it was at the time of his death on St. Helena. The Turenne Salon contains other souvenirs, like the hat Napoleon wore at Eylau, the sword from his Austerlitz victory, and his "Flag of Farewell," which he kissed before departing for Elba.

You can gain access to the **Musée des Plans-Reliefs** through the west wing. This collection shows French towns and monuments done in scale models (the model of Strasbourg fills an entire room) as well as models of military fortifications since the days of the great Vauban.

A walk across the Cour d'Honneur (Court of Honor) delivers you to the **Eglise du Dôme,** designed by Hardouin-Mansart for Louis XIV. The architect began work on the church in 1677, though he died before its completion. The dome is the second-tallest monument in Paris (the Tour Eiffel is the tallest, of course). The hearse used at the emperor's funeral on May 9, 1821, is in the Napoleon Chapel.

To accommodate **Napoleon's Tomb** ★★★, the architect Visconti had to redesign the church's high altar in 1842. First buried on St. Helena, Napoleon's remains were exhumed and brought to Paris in 1840 on the orders of Louis-Philippe, who demanded the English return the emperor to French soil. The remains were locked inside six coffins in this tomb made of red Finnish porphyry, with a green granite base. Surrounding it are a dozen Amazon-like figures representing Napoleon's victories. Almost lampooning the smallness of the man, everything is done on a gargantuan scale. In his coronation robes, the statue of Napoleon stands 2.5m (8¼ ft.) high. The grave of the "King of Rome," his son by second wife Marie-Louise, lies at his feet. Surrounding Napoleon's Tomb are those of his brother Joseph Bonaparte; the great Vauban, who built many of

France's fortifications; World War I Allied commander Foch; and the vicomte de Turenne, the republic's first grenadier (actually, only his heart is entombed here).

Place des Invalides, 7e. ℂ 01-44-42-37-72. Admission to Musée de l'Armée, Napoléon's Tomb, and Musée des Plans-Reliefs 7€ ($8.05) adults, 5€ ($5.75) students, free for children 18 and under. Oct–Mar daily 10am–5pm; Apr–May and Sept daily 10am–6pm; June–Aug daily 10am–7pm. Closed Jan 1, May 1, Nov 1, and Dec 25. Métro: Latour-Maubourg, Varenne, or Invalides.

Musée du Louvre ★★★ The Louvre is the world's largest palace and museum. As a palace, it leaves us cold, except for the **Cour Carrée.** As a museum, it's one of the greatest art collections ever. To enter, pass through I. M. Pei's controversial 21m (69-ft.) **glass pyramid** ★—a startling though effective contrast of ultramodern against the palace's classical lines. Commissioned by the late president François Mitterrand and completed in 1989, it allows sunlight to shine on an underground reception area with a complex of shops and restaurants. Ticket machines relieve the long lines of yesteryear.

People on one of those "Paris-in-a-day" tours try to break track records to get a glimpse of the Louvre's two most famous ladies: the beguiling **Mona Lisa** and the armless **Venus de Milo** ★★★. The herd then dashes on a 5-minute stampede in pursuit of **Winged Victory** ★★★, the headless statue discovered at Samothrace and dating from about 200 B.C. In defiance of the assembly-line theory of art, we head instead for David's **Coronation of Napoleon,** showing Napoleon poised with the crown aloft as Josephine kneels before him, just across from his **Portrait of Madame Récamier** ★, depicting Napoleon's opponent at age 23; she reclines on her sofa agelessly in the style of classical antiquity.

Then a big question looms: Which of the rest of the 30,000 works on display would you like to see?

Between the Seine and rue de Rivoli, the Palais du Louvre suffers from an embarrassment of riches, stretching for almost a kilometer (half a mile). In the days of Charles V, it was a fortress, but François I, a patron of Leonardo da Vinci, had it torn down and rebuilt as a royal residence. Less than a month after Marie Antoinette's head and body parted company, the Revolutionary Committee decided the king's collection of paintings and sculpture should be opened to the public. At the lowest point in its history, in the 18th century, the Louvre was home for anybody who wanted to set up housekeeping. Laundry hung in the windows, corners were pigpens, and families built fires to cook their meals in winter. Napoleon ended all that, chasing out the squatters and restoring the palace. In fact, he chose the Louvre as the site of his wedding to Marie-Louise.

So where did all these paintings come from? The kings of France, notably François I and Louis XIV, acquired many of them, and others were willed to or purchased by the state. Many contributed by Napoleon were taken from reluctant donors: The church was one especially heavy and unwilling giver. Much of Napoleon's plunder had to be returned, though France hasn't yet seen its way clear to giving back all the booty.

The collections are divided into seven departments: Egyptian Antiquities; Oriental Antiquities; Greek, Etruscan, and Roman Antiquities; Sculpture; Painting; Decorative Arts; and Graphic Arts. A number of galleries, devoted to Italian paintings, Roman glass and bronzes, Oriental antiquities, and Egyptian antiquities, were opened in 1997 and 1998. If you don't have to do Paris in a day, you might want to visit several times, concentrating on different collections or schools of painting. Those with little time should take a guided tour.

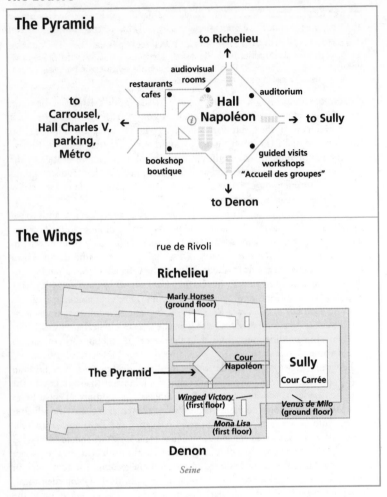

The Pyramid

to Richelieu

audiovisual rooms

restaurants cafes

Hall Napoléon

auditorium

to Carrousel, Hall Charles V, parking, Métro

ⓘ

to Sully

bookshop boutique

guided visits workshops "Accueil des groupes"

to Denon

The Wings

rue de Rivoli

Richelieu

Marly Horses (ground floor)

The Pyramid →

Cour Napoléon

Sully

Cour Carrée

Winged Victory (first floor)

Mona Lisa (first floor)

Venus de Milo **(ground floor)**

Denon

Seine

Acquired by François I to hang above his bathtub, Leonardo's ***La Gioconda (Mona Lisa)*** ★★★ has been the source of legend for centuries. Note the guard and bulletproof glass: The world's most famous painting was stolen in 1911 and found in Florence in 1913. At first, both the poet Guillaume Apollinaire and Picasso were suspected, but it was discovered in the possession of a former Louvre employee, who'd apparently carried it out under his overcoat. Two centuries after its arrival at the Louvre, the *Mona Lisa* in 2003 was assigned a new gallery of her own. Less well known (but to us even more enchanting) are Leonardo's ***Virgin and Child with St. Anne*** ★ and the ***Virgin of the Rocks.***

After paying your respects to the "smiling one," allow time to see some French works stretching from the Richelieu wing through the entire **Sully wing** and even overflowing into the **Denon wing.** It's all here: Watteau's ***Gilles*** with the mysterious boy in a clown suit staring at you; Fragonard's and Boucher's rococo renderings of the aristocracy; and the greatest masterpieces of David, including his stellar 1785 ***The Oath of the Horatii*** and the vast and vivid ***Coronation of***

THE TOP ATTRACTIONS   187

> ### Tips Some Louvre Tips
>
> The long lines outside the Louvre's pyramid entrance are notorious, but there are some tricks for avoiding them:
>
> - Order tickets by phone at ℰ **08-03-80-88-03,** paying with a credit card, then pick them up at any FNAC store (p. 261). This gives you direct entry through the Passage Richelieu, 93 rue de Rivoli.
> - Enter via the underground shopping mall, the Carrousel du Louvre, at 99 rue de Rivoli.
> - Enter directly from the Palais Royal–Musée du Louvre Métro station.
> - Buy Le Carte Musées et Monuments (Museums and Monuments Pass), allowing direct entry through the priority entrance at the Passage Richelieu, 93 rue de Rivoli. For details on the pass, see "The Major Museums" later in this chapter.

Napoleon. Only Florence's Uffizi rivals the Denon wing for its Italian Renaissance collection—everything from Raphael's *Portrait of Balthazar Castiglione* to Titian's *Man with a Glove.* Veronese's gigantic *Wedding Feast at Cana* ★, a romp of Viennese high society in the 1500s, occupies an entire wall (that's Paolo himself playing the cello).

Of the Greek and Roman antiquities, the most notable collections, aside from the *Venus de Milo* and *Winged Victory,* are fragments of a **Parthenon frieze** (in the Denon wing). In Renaissance sculpture, you'll see Michelangelo's *Esclaves (Slaves),* originally intended for the tomb of Julius II but sold into other bondage. The Denon wing houses masterpieces like Ingres's *The Turkish Bath;* the **Botticelli frescoes** from the Villa Lemmi; Raphael's *La Belle Jardinière;* and Titian's *Open Air Concert.* The Sully wing is also filled with old masters, like Boucher's *Diana Resting After Her Bath* and Fragonard's *Bathers.*

The **Richelieu wing** ★★★ reopened in 1993 after lying empty for years. Now with an additional 69,000 sq. m (743,000 sq. ft.) of exhibition space, it houses northern European and French paintings, along with decorative arts, sculpture, Oriental antiquities (a rich collection of Islamic art), and the Napoleon III salons. One of its galleries displays 21 works Rubens painted in a space of only 2 years for Marie de Médicis's Palais de Luxembourg. The masterpieces here include Dürer's *Self-Portrait,* Van Dyck's *Portrait of Charles I of England,* and Holbein the Younger's *Portrait of Erasmus of Rotterdam.*

When you get tired, consider a pick-me-up at **Café Marly** in the Cour Napoléon. This cafe overlooks the glass pyramid and offers coffees, pastries (by Paris's legendary pastry-maker, Lenôtre), salads, sandwiches, and simple platters.

34–36 quai du Louvre, 1e. Main entrance in the glass pyramid, Cour Napoléon. ℰ **01-40-20-53-17,** or 01-40-20-51-51 for recorded message, or 08-92-68-46-94 for advance credit card sales. www.louvre.fr. Admission 8.50€ ($9.80). On Sun, free for children 17 and under; free for all ages first Sun of every month. Mon and Wed 9am–9:30pm (Mon short tour only); Thurs–Sun 9am–6pm (parts of the museum begin to close at 5:30pm). 1½-hr. English-language tours leave Mon and Wed–Sat at various times for 3.50€ ($4.05); free for children 12 and under with museum ticket. Métro: Palais Royal–Musée du Louvre.

Musée d'Orsay ★★★   Architects created one of the world's great museums from an old rail station, the neoclassical Gare d'Orsay, across the Seine from the Louvre and the Tuileries. Don't skip the Louvre, of course, but come here even if you have to miss all the other art museums in town. The Orsay boasts an astounding collection devoted to the watershed years 1848 to 1914, with a treasure trove by the big names plus all the lesser-known groups (the symbolists, pointillists, nabis, realists, and late romantics). The 80 galleries also include Belle Epoque furniture, photographs, objets d'art, and architectural models. There's even a cinema showing classic films.

A monument to the Industrial Revolution, the Orsay is covered by an arching glass roof allowing in floods of light. It displays works ranging from the creations of academic and historic painters like Ingres to romanticists like Delacroix, to neorealists like Courbet and Daumier. The Impressionists and post-Impressionists, including Manet, Monet, Cézanne, van Gogh, and Renoir, share space with the fauves, Matisse, the cubists, and the expressionists in a setting once used by Orson Welles to film a nightmarish scene in *The Trial,* based on Kafka's unfinished novel. You'll find Millet's sunny wheat fields, Barbizon landscapes, Corot's mists, and Tahitian Gauguins all in the same hall.

But it's the Impressionists who draw the crowds. When the nose-in-the-air Louvre chose not to display their works, a great rival was born. Led by Manet, Renoir, and Monet, the Impressionists shunned ecclesiastical and mythological set pieces for a light-bathed Seine, faint figures strolling in the Tuileries, pale-faced women in hazy bars, and even vulgar rail stations like the Gare St-Lazare. And the Impressionists were the first to paint that most characteristic feature of Parisian life: the sidewalk cafe, especially in the artists' quarter of Montmartre.

The most famous painting from this era is Manet's 1863 **Déjeuner sur l'herbe (Picnic on the Grass),** whose forest setting with a nude woman and two fully clothed men sent shock waves through respectable society when it was first exhibited. Two years later, Manet's **Olympia** created another scandal by depicting a woman lounging on her bed and wearing nothing but a flower in her hair and high-heeled shoes; she's attended by an African maid in the background. Zola called Manet "a man among eunuchs."

One of Renoir's most joyous paintings is here: the **Moulin de la Galette** (1876). Degas is represented by his paintings of racehorses and dancers; his 1876 cafe scene, **Absinthe,** remains one of his most reproduced works. Paris-born Monet was fascinated by the effect changing light had on Rouen Cathédrale, and its stone bubbles to life in a series of five paintings—our favorite is **Rouen Cathédrale: Full Sunlight.** Another celebrated work is by an American, Whistler's **Arrangement in Grey and Black: Portrait of the Painter's Mother,** better known as **Whistler's Mother.** It's said this painting heralded modern art, though many critics denounced it at the time because of its funereal overtones. Whistler was content to claim he'd made "Mummy just as nice as possible."

1 rue de Bellechasse or 62 rue de Lille, 7e. 🕐 **01-40-49-48-14.** www.musee-orsay.fr. Admission 7€ ($8.05) adults, 5€ ($5.75) ages 18–24 and seniors, free for children 17 and under. Tues–Wed and Fri–Sat 10am–6pm; Thurs 10am–9:45pm (June 20–Sept 20 9am–6pm); Sun 9am–6:30pm. Métro: Solférino. RER: Musée d'Orsay.

Sainte-Chapelle ★★★   Countless writers have called this tiny chapel a jewel box. Yet that hardly suffices. Nor will it do to call it "a light show." Go when the sun is shining and you'll need no one else's words to describe the remarkable effects of natural light on Sainte-Chapelle. You approach the church through the Cour de la Sainte-Chapelle of the Palais de Justice. If it weren't for the chapel's 74m (243-ft.) spire, the law courts here would almost swallow it up.

Begun in 1246, the bi-level chapel was built to house relics of the True Cross, including the Crown of Thorns acquired by St. Louis (the Crusader king, Louis

IX) from the emperor of Constantinople. (In those days, cathedrals throughout Europe were busy acquiring relics for their treasuries, regardless of their authenticity. It was a seller's, perhaps a sucker's, market.) Louis IX is said to have paid heavily for his relics, raising the money through unscrupulous means. He died of the plague on a crusade and was canonized in 1297.

You enter through the *chapelle basse* (lower chapel), used by the palace servants; it's supported by flying buttresses and ornamented with fleur-de-lis designs. The king and his courtiers used the *chapelle haute* (upper chapel), one of the greatest achievements of Gothic art; you reach it by ascending a narrow spiral staircase. Viewed on a bright day, the 15 stained-glass windows seem to glow with Chartres blue and with reds that have inspired the saying "wine the color of Sainte-Chapelle's windows." The walls consist almost entirely of the glass, 612 sq. m (6,588 sq. ft.) of it, which had to be removed for safekeeping during the Revolution and again during both world wars. In their Old and New Testament designs are embodied the hopes and dreams (and the pretensions) of the kings who ordered their construction. The 1,134 scenes depict the Christian story from the Garden of Eden through the Apocalypse; you read them from bottom to top and from left to right. The great rose window depicts the Apocalypse.

Sainte-Chapelle stages **concerts** in summer, with tickets at 19€ to 25€ ($22–$29). Call ☎ **01-42-77-65-65** from 11am to 6pm daily for details.

Palais de Justice, 4 bd. du Palais, 4e. ☎ 01-53-73-78-50. www.monum.fr. Free admission. Apr–Sept daily 9:30am–6:30pm; Oct–Mar daily 10am–5pm. Métro: Cité, St-Michel, or Châtelet–Les Halles. RER: St-Michel.

Tour Eiffel ★★★   This is without doubt one of the most recognizable structures in the world. Weighing 7,000 tons but exerting about the same pressure on the ground as an average-size person sitting in a chair, the wrought-iron tower wasn't meant to be permanent. Gustave-Alexandre Eiffel, the French engineer whose fame rested mainly on his iron bridges, built it for the 1889 Universal Exhibition. (Eiffel also designed the framework for the Statue of Liberty.) Praised by some and denounced by others (some called it a "giraffe," the "world's greatest lamppost," or the "iron monster"), the tower created as much controversy in the 1880s as I. M. Pei's glass pyramid at the Louvre did in the 1980s. What saved it from demolition was the advent of radio—as the tallest structure in Europe, it made a perfect spot to place a radio antenna (now a TV antenna).

The tower, including its TV antenna, is 317m (1,040 ft.) high. On a clear day you can see it from 65km (40 miles) away. An open-framework construction, the tower unlocked the almost unlimited possibilities of steel construction, paving the way for skyscrapers. Skeptics said it couldn't be built, and Eiffel actually wanted to make it soar higher. For years it remained the tallest man-made structure on earth, until skyscrapers like the Empire State Building surpassed it.

Value **Tour Eiffel Bargain**

The least expensive way to see the Tour Eiffel is to walk up the first two floors at a cost of 3.20€ ($3.70). That way you also avoid the long lines waiting for the elevator—although the views are less spectacular from this platform. If you dine at the tower's own **Altitude 95** (☎ **01-45-55-20-04**), an Eiffel restaurant on the first floor, management allows patrons to cut to the head of the line.

Tips   **Time Out at the Tower**

To see Tour Eiffel best, don't sprint—approach it gradually. We suggest taking the Métro to the Trocadéro stop and walking from the Palais de Chaillot to the Seine to get the full effect of the tower and its surroundings; then cross the pont d'Iéna and head for the base, where you'll find elevators in two of the pillars—expect long lines. (When the tower is open, you can see the 1889 lift machinery in the eastern and western pillars.) You visit the tower in three stages: The first landing provides a view over the rooftops as well as a cinema museum showing films, restaurants, and a bar. The second landing offers a panoramic look at the city. The third landing gives the most spectacular view; Eiffel's office has been re-created on this level, with wax figures depicting the engineer receiving Thomas Edison.

Of course, it's the view most people come for, and this theoretically extends for 65km (40 miles), although weather conditions tend to limit it. Nevertheless, it's fabulous, and the best time for visibility is about an hour before sunset.

We could fill an entire page with tower statistics. (Its plans spanned 6,000 sq. yards of paper, and it contains 2.5 million rivets.) But forget the numbers. Just stand beneath the tower and look straight up. It's like a rocket of steel lacework shooting into the sky.

To get to **Le Jules Verne** (© **01-45-55-61-44**), the second-platform restaurant, take the private south foundation elevator. You can enjoy an aperitif in the piano bar, then take a seat at one of the dining room's tables, all of which provide an inspiring view. The menu changes seasonally, offering fish and meat dishes that range from filet of turbot with seaweed and buttered sea urchins to veal chops with truffled vegetables. Reservations are recommended.

Champ de Mars, 7e. © **01-44-11-23-23**. www.tour-eiffel.fr. Admission to first landing 3.70€ ($4.25), second landing 7€ ($8.05); third landing 10€ ($12); stairs to second floor 3.20€ ($3.70). Sept–May daily 9:30am–11pm; June–Aug daily 9am–midnight. Fall and winter, stairs open only to 6:30pm. Métro: Trocadéro, Ecole Militaire, or Bir-Hakeim. RER: Champ de Mars–Tour Eiffel.

4 The Major Museums

Turn to "The Top Attractions," above, for a comprehensive look at the **Musée du Louvre** and the **Musée d'Orsay.**

If you're a cultural buff, consider a purchase of **Carte Musées et Monuments** (Museum and Monuments Pass), admitting you to some 70 museums in Paris and its environs. It's estimated that if you plan to visit three or four museums, it's worth the investment in this card, which is sold at all major museums and Métro stations. A 1-day pass costs 22€ ($25); 3 consecutive days, 38€ ($44); and 5 consecutive days, 52€ ($60). Information is available at Association InterMusees, 4 rue Brantôme, 3e (© **01-44-61-96-60**). Métro: Rambuteau. See p. 65 for details on the **Paris-Visite** pass, valid for 1 to 5 days on the public transport system, including the Métro, the city buses, the RER (regional express) trains within Paris city limits, and even the funicular to the top of Montmartre.

Centre Pompidou ✸✸✸   Reopened in January 2000 in what was called in the 1970s "the most avant-garde building in the world," the restored Centre Pompidou is packing in the art-loving crowds again. The dream of former president Georges Pompidou, this center for 20th- and 21st-century art, designed by Richard Rogers and Renzo Piano, opened in 1977 and quickly became the focus of controversy. Its bold exoskeletal architecture and the brightly painted pipes and ducts crisscrossing its transparent facade (green for water, red for heat, blue for air, yellow for electricity) were jarring in the old Beaubourg neighborhood. Perhaps the detractors were right all along—within 20 years the building began to deteriorate so badly a major restoration was called for. The renovation added 450 sq. m (4,844 sq. ft.) of exhibit space and a rooftop restaurant, a cafe, and a boutique; in addition, a series of auditoriums was created for film screenings and dance, theater, and musical performances. Access for visitors with disabilities has also been improved.

The Centre Pompidou encompasses five attractions:

Musée National d'Art Moderne (National Museum of Modern Art) ✸✸✸ offers a large collection of 20th- and 21st-century art. With some 40,000 works, this is the big attraction, though only some 850 works can be displayed at one time. If you want to view some real charmers, seek out Calder's 1926 *Josephine Baker,* one of his earlier versions of the mobile, an art form he invented. You'll also find two examples of Duchamps' series of dada-style sculptures he invented in 1936: *Boîte en Valise* (1941) and *Boîte en Valise* (1968). And every time we visit we have to see Dalí's *Hallucination partielle: Six images de Lénine sur un piano* (1931), with Lenin dancing on a piano.

In the **Bibliothèque Information Publique (Public Information Library),** people have free access to a million French and foreign books, periodicals, films, records, slides, and microfilms in nearly every area of knowledge. The **Centre de Création Industriel (Center for Industrial Design)** emphasizes the contributions made in the fields of architecture, visual communications, publishing, and community planning; and the **Institut de Recherche et de Coordination Acoustique-Musique (Institute for Research and Coordination of Acoustics/Music)** brings together musicians and composers interested in furthering the cause of contemporary and traditional music. Finally, you can visit a re-creation of the Jazz Age studio of Romanian sculptor Brancusi, the **Atelier Brancusi** ✸, a minimuseum slightly separate from the rest of the action.

The museum's **forecourt** is a free "entertainment center" featuring mimes, fire-eaters, circus performers, and sometimes musicians. Don't miss the nearby **Stravinsky fountain,** containing mobile sculptures by Tinguely and Saint Phalle.

Place Georges-Pompidou, 4e. ℂ **01-44-78-12-33.** www.centrepompidou.fr. Admission 7€ ($8.05) adults, 5€ ($5.75) students, free for children under 18. Special exhibits 9€ ($10) adults, 7€ ($8.05) students, free for children under 13. Wed–Mon 11am–10pm. Métro: Rambuteau, Hôtel-de-Ville, or Châtelet–Les Halles.

⌒Tips   A Time-Saving Tip

Museums require you to check shopping bags and book bags, and sometimes lines for these can be longer than the ticket lines. If you value your time, leave your bags in your hotel room or don't go shopping before hitting the museums: Some lines can take 30 minutes. Ask if a museum has more than one check line, and, if so, go to the less-frequented ones.

Musée Carnavalet-Histoire de Paris ★★ *Kids* If you enjoy history, but history tomes bore you, spend some time here for insight into Paris's past, which comes alive in details like the chessmen Louis XVI used to distract himself while waiting to go to the guillotine. The comprehensive and lifelike exhibits are great for kids. The building, a Renaissance palace, was built in 1544 by Pierre Lescot and Jean Goujon, and later acquired by Mme de Carnavalet. The great François Mansart transformed it between 1655 and 1661.

The palace is best known because one of history's most famous letter writers, Mme de Sévigné, moved here in 1677. Fanatically devoted to her daughter (she moved in with her because she couldn't bear to be apart), she poured out nearly every detail of her life in her letters, virtually ignoring her son. A native of the Marais district, she died at her daughter's château in 1696. In 1866, the city of Paris acquired the mansion and turned it into a museum. Several salons cover the Revolution, with a bust of Marat, a portrait of Danton, and a model of the Bastille (one painting shows its demolition). Another salon tells the story of the captivity of the royal family at the Conciergerie, including the bed in which Mme Elisabeth (the sister of Louis XVI) slept and the dauphin's exercise book.

Exhibits continue at the **Hôtel le Pelletier de St-Fargeau,** across the courtyard. On display is furniture from the Louis XIV period to the early 20th century, including a replica of Marcel Proust's cork-lined bedroom with his actual furniture, including his brass bed. This section also exhibits artifacts from the museum's archaeological collection, including some Neolithic pirogues, shallow oak boats used for fishing and transport from about 4400 to 2200 B.C.

23 rue de Sévigné, 3e. © **01-44-59-58-58.** Free admission. Tues–Sun 10am–6pm. Métro: St-Paul or Chemin-Vert.

Musée Jacquemart-André ★★ This is the finest museum of its type in Paris, the treasure trove of a couple devoted to 18th-century French paintings and furnishings, 17th-century Dutch and Flemish paintings, and Italian Renaissance works. Edouard André, the last scion of a family that made a fortune in banking and industry in the 19th century, spent most of his life as an army officer stationed abroad; he eventually returned to marry a well-known portraitist of government figures and the aristocracy, Nélie Jacquemart, and they went on to compile a collection of rare decorative art and paintings in this 1850s town house.

In 1912, Mme Jacquemart willed the house and its contents to the Institut de France, which paid for an extensive renovation and enlargement. The salons drip with gilt and the ultimate in *fin-de-siècle* style. Works by Bellini, Carpaccio, Uccello, Van Dyck, Rembrandt *(The Pilgrim of Emmaus),* Tiepolo, Rubens, Watteau, Boucher, Fragonard, and Mantegna are complemented by Houdon busts, Savonnerie carpets, Gobelin tapestries, della Robbia terra cottas, and an awesome collection of antiques. The three 18th-century Tiepolo frescoes of spectators on balconies viewing Henri III's 1574 arrival in Venice are outstanding.

Take a break with a cup of tea in Mme Jacquemart's high-ceilinged dining room, adorned with 18th-century tapestries. Salads, tarts, *tourtes* (pastries filled with meat or fruit), and Viennese pastries are served during museum hours.

158 bd. Haussmann, 8e. © **01-45-62-11-59.** www.musee-jacquemart-andre.com. Admission 8€ ($9.20) adults, 6€ ($6.90) ages 7–17, free for children 6 and under. Daily 10am–6pm. Métro: Miromesnil or St-Philippe-du-Roule.

Musée Marmottan–Claude Monet ★★ In the past, an art historian or two would sometimes venture here to the edge of the Bois de Boulogne to see what Paul Marmottan had donated to the Académie des Beaux-Arts. Hardly anyone else did until 1966, when Claude Monet's son Michel died in a car crash, leaving a then–$10 million bequest of his father's art to the little museum. The Académie suddenly found itself with 130-plus paintings, watercolors, pastels, and drawings. Monet lovers could now trace the evolution of the great man's work in a single museum. The collection includes more than 30 paintings of Monet's house at Giverny and many of waterlilies, his everlasting fancy, plus *Willow* (1918), *House of Parliament* (1905), and a **Renoir portrait** of the 32-year-old Monet. The museum had always owned Monet's *Impression: Sunrise* (1872), from which the Impressionist movement got its name. Paul Marmottan's original collection includes fig-leafed nudes, First Empire antiques, assorted objets d'art, Renaissance tapestries, bucolic paintings, and crystal chandeliers. You can also see countless miniatures donated by Daniel Waldenstein.

2 rue Louis-Boilly, 16e. ☏ **01-44-96-50-33**. www.marmottan.com. Admission 6.50€ ($7.50) adults, 4€ ($4.60) ages 8–24, free for children 7 and under. Tues–Sun 10am–6pm. Métro: La Muette.

Musée National du Moyen Age/Thermes de Cluny (Musée de Cluny) ★★

Along with the Hôtel de Sens in the Marais, the Hôtel de Cluny is all that remains of domestic medieval architecture in Paris. Enter through the cobblestoned **Cour d'Honneur** (Court of Honor), where you can admire the flamboyant Gothic building with its vines, turreted walls, gargoyles, and dormers with seashell motifs. First the Cluny was the mansion of a rich 15th-century abbot, built on top of/next to the ruins of a Roman bath (see below). By 1515, it was the residence of Mary Tudor, widow of Louis XII and daughter of Henry VII and Elizabeth of York. Seized during the Revolution, the Cluny was rented in 1833 to Alexandre du Sommerard, who adorned it with medieval artworks. After his death in 1842, the government bought the building and the collection.

This collection of medieval arts and crafts is superb. Most people come to see *The Lady and the Unicorn Tapestries* ★★★, the most acclaimed tapestries of their kind. All the romance of the age of chivalry—a beautiful princess and her handmaiden, beasts of prey, and house pets—lives on in these remarkable yet mysterious tapestries discovered only a century ago in Limousin's Château de Boussac. Five seem to deal with the

> ⌐ *Finds* **Museum Oasis**
>
> Inaugurated at the Musée de Cluny is a garden that's a return to the Middle Ages. The garden was inspired by the detail of the museum's most fabled treasure, *The Lady and the Unicorn Tapestries*. The garden is small but richly planted and rests under chestnuts and sycamores.

senses (one, for example, depicts a unicorn looking into a mirror held by a dour-faced maiden). The sixth shows a woman under an elaborate tent with jewels, her pet dog resting on an embroidered cushion beside her, with the lovable unicorn and his friendly companion, a lion, holding back the flaps. The background in red and green forms a rich carpet of spring flowers, fruit-laden trees, birds, rabbits, donkeys, dogs, goats, lambs, and monkeys.

The other exhibits range widely: Flemish retables; a 14th-century Sienese John the Baptist and other sculptures; statues from Sainte-Chapelle (1243–48); 12th- and 13th-century crosses, chalices, manuscripts, carvings, vestments, leatherwork, jewelry, and coins; a 13th-century Adam; and recently discovered heads and fragments of statues from Notre-Dame de Paris. In the fan-vaulted medieval chapel hang tapestries depicting scenes from the life of St. Stephen.

Downstairs are the ruins of the **Roman baths,** from around A.D. 200. The best-preserved section is seen in room X, the frigidarium (where one bathed in cold water). Once it measured 21m × 11m (69 ft. × 36 ft.), rising to a height of 15m (49 ft.), with stone walls nearly 1.5m (5 ft.) thick. The ribbed vaulting here rests on consoles evoking ships' prows. Credit for this unusual motif goes to the builders of the baths, Paris's boatmen. During Tiberius's reign, a column to Jupiter was found beneath Notre-Dame's chancel and is now on view in the court—called the "Column of the Boatmen," it's believed to be the oldest sculpture created in Paris.

In the Hôtel de Cluny, 6 place Paul-Painlevé, 5e. © 01-53-73-78-15. Admission 5.50€ ($6.35) adults, 4€ ($4.60) ages 18–25, free for children 17 and under. Wed–Mon 9:15am–5:45pm. Métro: Cluny–La Sorbonne.

Musée National Eugène Delacroix This museum is for Delacroix groupies, among whom we include ourselves. If you want to see where he lived, worked, and died, this is worth at least an hour. Delacroix (1798–1863) is something of an enigma to art historians. Even his parentage is a mystery. Many believe Talleyrand was his father. One biographer saw him "as an isolated and atypical individualist—one who respected traditional values, yet emerged as the embodiment of Romantic revolt." Baudelaire called him "a volcanic crater artistically concealed beneath bouquets of flowers." The museum is on one of the Left Bank's most charming squares, with a romantic garden. A large arch on a courtyard leads to Delacroix's studio—no poor artist's studio, but the creation of a solidly established man. Sketches, lithographs, watercolors, and oils are hung throughout. If you want to see more of Delacroix's work, head to the Chapelle des Anges in St-Sulpice (p. 204).

6 place de Furstenberg, 6e. © 01-44-41-86-50. www.musee-delacroix.fr. Admission 5€ ($5.75) adults, 2.60€ ($3) ages 18–25, free for children 17 and under. Wed–Mon 9:30am–5pm. Métro: St-Germain-des-Prés.

Musée Picasso ✹✹ When it opened at the beautifully restored Hôtel Salé (Salt Mansion, built by a man who made his fortune by controlling the salt distribution in 17th-c. France) in the Marais, the press hailed it as a "museum for Picasso's Picassos." And that's what it is. The state acquired the world's greatest Picasso collection in lieu of $50 million in inheritance taxes: 203 paintings, 158 sculptures, 16 collages, 19 bas-reliefs, 88 ceramics, and more than 1,500 sketches and 1,600 engravings, along with 30 notebooks. These works span some 75 years of the artist's life and ever-changing style.

The range of paintings includes a remarkable 1901 self-portrait; *The Crucifixion* and *Nude in a Red Armchair;* and *Le Baiser (The Kiss), Reclining Nude,* and *Man with a Guitar,* all painted at Mougins on the Riviera in 1969 and 1970. Stroll through the handsome museum seeking your own favorite—perhaps the wicked *Jeune garçon à la langouste (Young Man with a Lobster),* painted in Paris in 1941. There are also several intriguing studies for *Les Demoiselles d'Avignon,* which shocked the establishment and launched cubism in 1907. Because the collection is so vast, temporary exhibits featuring items like his **studies of the Minotaur** are held twice per year. Also here is Picasso's own treasure trove of art, with works by Cézanne, Rousseau, Braque, Derain, and Miró. Picasso was fascinated with African masks, many of which are on view.

In the Hôtel Salé, 5 rue de Thorigny, 3e. © 01-42-71-25-21. www.paris.org/Musees/Picasso. Admission 5.50€ ($6.35) adults, 4€ ($4.60) ages 18–25 and seniors, free for children 17 and under. Apr–Sept Wed–Mon 9:30am–6pm; Oct–Mar Wed–Mon 9:30am–5:30pm. Métro: St-Paul, Filles du Calvaire, or Chemin Vert.

Musée Rodin ✹✹ Today Rodin is acclaimed as the father of modern sculpture, but in a different era his work was labeled obscene. The world's artistic taste

> **Finds** **Looking for a Quick Escape?**
>
> The little alley behind the Musée Rodin winds its way down to a pond with fountains and flowerbeds and even sand pits for children. It's one of the most idyllic hidden spots in Paris.

changed, and in due course in 1911 the French government purchased Rodin's studio in this gray-stone 18th-century mansion in the Faubourg St-Germain. The government restored the rose gardens to their 18th-century splendor, making them a perfect setting for Rodin's most memorable works.

In the courtyard are three world-famous creations. Rodin's first major public commission, *The Burghers of Calais,* commemorated the heroism of six citizens of Calais who in 1347 offered themselves as a ransom to Edward III in return for ending his siege of their port. Perhaps the single best-known work, *The Thinker,* in Rodin's own words, "thinks with every muscle of his arms, back, and legs, with his clenched fist and gripping toes." Not completed when Rodin died, *The Gate of Hell,* as he put it, is "where I lived for a whole year in Dante's *Inferno.*"

Inside, the sculpture, plaster casts, reproductions, originals, and sketches reveal the freshness and vitality of a remarkable artist. You can almost see his works emerging from marble into life. Everybody is attracted to *Le Baiser (The Kiss),* of which one critic wrote, "the passion is timeless." Upstairs are two versions of the celebrated and condemned **nude of Balzac,** his bulky torso rising from a tree trunk (Albert E. Elsen commented on the "glorious bulging" stomach). Included are many versions of his *Monument to Balzac* (a large one stands in the garden), Rodin's last major work. Other significant sculptures are the soaring *Prodigal Son, The Crouching Woman* (the "embodiment of despair"), and *The Age of Bronze,* an 1876 study of a nude man modeled after a Belgian soldier. (Rodin was falsely accused of making a cast from a living model.) Generally overlooked is a room devoted to Rodin's mistress, Camille Claudel, a towering artist in her own right. She was his pupil, model, and lover, and created such works as *Maturity, Clotho,* and the recently donated *The Waltz* and *The Gossips.*

In the Hôtel Biron, 77 rue de Varenne, 7e. (C) **01-44-18-61-10.** www.musee-rodin.fr. Admission 5€ ($5.75) adults, 3€ ($3.45) ages 18–25, free for children 17 and under. Apr–Sept Tues–Sun 9:30am–5:45pm; Oct–Mar Tues–Sun 9:30am–4:45pm. Métro: Varenne.

5 Specialty Museums

Be sure to turn to "The Top Attractions" and "The Major Museums," both earlier in this chapter, for the cream of the crop. "Especially for Kids," later in this chapter, includes museums parents and kids alike will love. The museums below represent the curious, fascinating, and sometimes arcane balance of Paris's offerings.

ART & MUSIC MUSEUMS

Musée Bourdelle ★ *Finds* Here you can see works by Rodin's star pupil, Antoine Bourdelle (1861–1929), who became a celebrated artist in his own right. Along with changed exhibits, the museum displays the artist's drawings, paintings, and sculptures, and lets you wander through his studio, garden, and house. The original plaster casts of some of his greatest works are on display, but what's most notable here are the 21 studies of Beethoven. Though some of the exhibits are badly captioned, you'll still feel the impact of Bourdelle's genius.

16–18 rue Antoine-Bourdelle, 15e. ℂ 01-49-54-73-73. Free admission to the permanent collection. Tues–Sun 10am–5:40pm. Métro: Montparnasse-Bienvenue.

Musée Cognacq-Jay ✮ The founders of La Samaritaine department store, Ernest Cognacq and his wife, Louise Jay, were fabled for their exquisite taste. To see what they accumulated from around the world, head for this museum in the 16th-century Hôtel Denon, with its Louis XV and Louis XVI paneled rooms. Some of the 18th century's most valuable decorative works are exhibited, ranging from ceramics and porcelain to delicate cabinets and paintings by Canaletto, Fragonard, Greuze, Chardin, Boucher, Watteau, and Tiepolo.

In the Hôtel Donon, 8 rue Elzévir, 3e. ℂ 01-40-27-07-21. Free admission. Tues–Sun 10am–5:40pm. Métro: St-Paul or Rambuteau.

Musée d'Art Moderne de la Ville de Paris & Musée des Enfants This museum bordering the Seine has a permanent collection of paintings and sculpture owned by the city, but come here only if visits to the d'Orsay and Louvre haven't satiated you. It presents ever-changing exhibits on individual artists from all over the world or on trends in international art. You'll find works by Chagall, Matisse, Léger, Rothko, Braque, Dufy, Picasso, Utrillo, and Modigliani. Seek out Pierre Tal Coat's *Portrait of Gertrude Stein* and keep Picasso's version of this difficult subject in mind. The Musée des Enfants has exhibits and shows for children.

11 av. du Président-Wilson, 16e. ℂ 01-53-67-40-00. Admission 7.60€ ($8.75) adults, 3.80€ ($4.35) for ages 26 and under. Tues–Fri 10am–5:30pm; Sat–Sun 10am–7pm. Métro: Iéna or Alma-Marceau.

Musée de la Musique In the $120 million stone-and-glass Cité de la Musique, this museum serves as a tribute and testament to music. You can view 4,500 instruments from the 16th century to the present as well as paintings, engravings, and sculptures that relate to musical history. It's all here: cornets disguised as snakes, mandolins, lutes, zithers, music boxes, even an early electric guitar. Models of the world's great concert halls and interactive display areas give you a chance to hear and better understand musical art and technology.

In the Cité de la Musique, 221 av. Jean-Jaurès, 19e. ℂ 01-44-84-45-00. www.cite-musique.fr. Admission 6.50€ ($7.50) adults, 5.20€ ($6) ages 19–25, 3.20€ ($3.70) children 18 and under; visits with commentary 10€ ($12) adults. Tues–Sat noon–6pm; Sun 10am–6pm. Métro: Porte-de-Pantin.

Musée des Arts d'Afrique et d'Océanie In this Art Deco building built for the 1931 French Colonial exhibition, you'll find an extensive collection of central African art that's especially rich in carved masks and statues, aboriginal bark paintings, and some magnificent bronzes from Benin. There are also some art objects from the Pacific islands and a limited collection of woven carpets and gold jewelry from the Magreb region of Arab-speaking North Africa. In the cellars are aquariums and terrariums containing crocodiles, iguanas, and tortoises.

293 av. Daumesnil, 12e. ℂ 01-43-46-51-61. Admission 4€ ($4.60) adults, free for children under 18. Fri–Wed 10am–5:30pm. Métro: Porte Dorée.

Musée des Arts Décoratifs ✮ In the northwest wing of the Louvre's Pavillon de Marsan, this museum boasts furnishings, fabrics, wallpaper, and objets d'art from the Middle Ages to the present—but we recommend it only if you have an abiding interest in the subject. Notable on the first floor are the 1920s Art Deco boudoir, bath, and bedroom of couturier Jeanne Lanvin by Rateau. Decorative art from the Middle Ages to the Renaissance is on the second floor;

collections from the 17th, 18th, and 19th centuries occupy the third and fourth floors. The fifth has centers on wallpaper and drawings and documentary centers detailing fashion, textiles, toys, crafts, and glass trends. The newest addition is a **Musée de la Publicité (Museum of Advertising),** with posters from the 18th century, and film, TV, and radio commercials from the 1930s to today. Architect Jean Nouvel designed a cutting-edge interior that also displays avant-garde video techniques.

In the Union Centrale des Décoratifs, 107 rue de Rivoli, 1e. (*C*) **01-44-55-57-50.** Admission 6€ ($6.90) adults, 4.50€ ($5.20) ages 18–25, free for 17 and under. Tues–Sun 10am–6pm. Métro: Palais Royal or Tuileries.

Musée Edith Piaf *(Finds)*   This privately run museum is filled with Piaf memorabilia such as photos, costumes, and personal possessions. The daughter of an acrobat, Giovanna Gassion grew up in this neighborhood and assumed the name of Piaf ("little sparrow"); her songs, like "La Vie en Rose" and "Non, je ne regrette rien," eventually were heard around the world. You must phone in advance for the security code you need to buzz your way in. Nearby is the **Villa Calte,** a beautiful example of the fine architecture many locals are trying to save (ask for directions at the Piaf museum). Fronted by an intricate wrought-iron fence, the house has a pleasant garden where parts of Truffaut's *Jules et Jim* were filmed.

5 rue Crespin-du-Gast, 11e. (*C*) **01-43-55-52-72.** Free admission but donations appreciated. Mon–Thurs 1–6pm by appointment only. Métro: Ménilmontant.

Musée National des Arts Asiatiques-Guimet ★★   This is one of the most beautiful Asian museums in the world and it houses one of the world's finest collections of Asian art. Some 3,000 pieces of the museum's 45,000 works are on display. The museum was named for its founder, research chemist/industrialist Emile Guimet. The Guimet, opened in Lyon but transferred to Paris in 1889, received the Musée Indochinois du Trocadéro's collections in 1931 and the Louvre's Asian collections after World War II. The most interesting exhibits are Buddhas, serpentine monster heads, funereal figurines, and antiquities from the temple of Angkor Wat. Some galleries are devoted to Tibetan art, including fascinating scenes of the Grand Lamas entwined with serpents and demons.

6 place d'Iéna, 16e. (*C*) **01-47-23-61-65.** www.museeguimet.com. Admission 7€ ($8.05) adults, 5€ ($5.75) ages 18–25, free for 17 and under. Wed–Mon 9:45am–6pm. Métro: Iéna or Alma-Marceau.

Musée Nissim de Camondo ★   Visit this museum for a keen insight into the decorative arts of the 18th century. The pre–World War I town house was donated to the Musée des Arts Décoratifs by Comte Moïse de Camondo in memory of his son, Nissim, a French aviator killed in combat during World War I. The museum is like the home of an aristocrat—rich with needlepoint chairs, tapestries (many from Beauvais or Aubusson), antiques, paintings, bas-reliefs, silver, Chinese vases, crystal chandeliers, Sèvres porcelain, Savonnerie carpets, and even a Houdon bust. The Blue Salon, overlooking Parc Monceau, is most impressive. The kitchen of the original mansion has been reopened in its original format, capable of serving hundreds of dinner guests at one time, with few alterations from its original Belle Epoque origins. Fittings and many of the cooking vessels are in brass or copper, and the walls are tiled.

63 rue de Monceau, 8e. (*C*) **01-53-89-06-40.** Admission 5€ ($5.75) adults, 3.50€ ($4.05) ages 18–25, free for children 17 and under. Wed–Sun 10am–5pm. Closed Jan 1, May 1, Bastille Day (July 14), and Dec 25. Métro: Villiers.

Musée Zadkine   This museum near the Jardin du Luxembourg was once the home of sculptor Ossip Zadkine (1890–1967), and his collection has been turned over to the city for public viewing. Included are some 300 pieces of sculpture, displayed in the museum and the garden. Some drawings and tapestries are also exhibited. At these headquarters where he worked from 1928 until his death, you can see how he moved from "left wing" cubist extremism to a renewed appreciation of the classic era. You can visit his garden for free even if you don't want to go into the museum—in fact it's one of the finest places to relax in Paris on a sunny day, sitting on a bench taking in the two-faced *Woman with the Bird.*

100 bis rue d'Assas, 6e. ✆ **01-55-42-77-20.** www.paris.fr/musees/zadkine. Admission 3.50€ ($4.05) adults, 2.20€ ($2.55) for ages 26 and under. Tues–Sun 10am–5:30pm. Métro: Notre-Dame des Champs or Vavin.

CRAFT & INDUSTRY MUSEUMS

Manufacture Nationale des Gobelins ✰   Did you know a single tapestry can take 4 years to complete, employing as many as three to five full-time weavers? The founder of this dynasty, Jehan Gobelin, came from a family of dyers and clothmakers and in the 15th century discovered a scarlet dye that made him famous. By 1601, Henry IV imported 200 weavers from Flanders to make tapestries full-time. Until this endeavor, the Gobelin family hadn't made any tapestries. Colbert, Louis XIV's minister, bought the works, and under royal patronage the craftsmen set about executing designs by Le Brun. After the Revolution, the industry was reactivated by Napoleon. Les Gobelins is still going strong, and some of the antique high-warp looms are still in use. You can visit the *ateliers* (studios) of the weavers, who sit behind huge screens of thread, patiently inserting stitch after stitch.

42 av. des Gobelins, 13e. ✆ **01-44-54-19-33.** Tours in French (with English pamphlets) 8€ ($9.20) adults, 6€ ($6.90) ages 7–24, free for children under 7. Tues–Thurs 2 and 2:45pm. Métro: Gobelins.

Musée d'Art et Histoire du Judaisme ✰✰   Security is tight, but it's worth the effort. In the Hôtel De St-Aignan, dating from the 1600s, this museum of Jewish history has been handsomely and impressively installed. The development of Jewish culture is traced not only in Paris, but in France itself as well as in Europe. Many of the exhibitions are devoted to religious subjects, including menorahs, torah ornaments, and ark curtains, in both the Ashkenazi and Sephardic traditions. For us, the most interesting documents relate to the notorious Dreyfus case. Also on parade is a collection of illuminated manuscripts, Renaissance torah arks, and paintings from the 18th and 19th centuries, along with Jewish gravestones from the Middle Ages. The best display is of the artwork by leading Jewish painters and artists ranging from Soutine to Zadkine, from Chagall to Modigliani.

Hôtel de St-Aignan, 71 rue du Temple, 3e. ✆ **01-53-01-86-60.** www.mahj.org. Admission 6.10€ ($7) adults, 3.80€ ($4.35) ages 18–26, free for children under 18. Mon–Fri 11am–6pm; Sun 10am–6pm (window closes at 5:15pm). Métro: Rambuteau.

Musée National de Céramique de Sèvres ✰✰   Next door to the Manufacture Nationale de Sèvres (p. 246), this museum boasts one of the world's finest collections of faience and porcelain, some of which belonged to Mme du Barry, Mme de Pompadour's successor as Louis XV's mistress (Mme de Pompadour *loved* Sèvres porcelain). On view is the Pompadour rose (which the English called the rose du Barry), a style much in vogue in the 1750s and 1760s. The painter Boucher made some of the designs used by the factory, as did the sculptor Pajou (he created the bas-reliefs for the Opéra at Versailles). The factory pioneered what became known as the *Louis Seize* (Louis XVI) style—it's all here, plus lots more, including works from Sèvres's arch rival, Meissen.

Place de la Manufacture, Sèvres, 15e. ℂ 01-41-14-04-20. Admission 4€ ($4.60) adults, 2.60€ ($3) ages 18–25, free for children 17 and under. Wed–Mon 10am–5pm. Métro: Pont de Sèvres, then walk across the Seine to the Left Bank.

HISTORY MUSEUMS

Musée de l'Histoire de France (Musée des Archives Nationales) ★   The official home of the archives that reflect the convoluted history of France, this small but noteworthy palace was first built in 1371 as the **Hôtel de Clisson,** and later acquired by the ducs de Guise, who figured prominently in France's bloody wars of religion. In 1705, most of it was demolished by the prince and princesse de Soubise, through their architect, the much-underrated Delamair, and rebuilt with a baroque facade. The princesse de Soubise was once the mistress of Louis XIV, and apparently, the Sun King was very generous, giving her the funds to remodel and redesign the palace into one of the most beautiful buildings in the Marais. *Tip:* Before entering through the building's main entrance, the gracefully colonnaded Cour d'Honneur (Court of Honor), walk around the corner to 58 rue des Archives, where you'll see the few remaining vestiges—a turreted medieval gateway—of the original Hôtel de Clisson.

In the early 1800s, the site was designated by Napoleon as the repository for his archives, and it has served that function ever since. The archives contain documents that predate Charlemagne. But depending on the policies of the curator, only some of them are on display at any given moment, and usually as part of an ongoing series of temporary exhibitions that sometimes spill out into the **Hôtel de Rohan,** just around the corner on the rue Vieille du Temple.

Within these exhibitions, you're likely to see the penmanship of Marie Antoinette in a farewell letter she composed just before her execution; Louis XVI's last will and testament; and documents from Danton, Robespierre, Napoleon I, and Joan of Arc. The Archives have the only known sketch of the Maid of Orléans that was completed during her lifetime. Even the jailers' keys from the long-since-demolished Bastille are here. Despite the undeniable appeal of the documents it shelters, one of the most intriguing aspects of this museum involves the layout and decor of rooms that have changed very little since the 18th century. One of the finest is the **Salon de la Princesse** (aka, the Salon Ovale), an oval-shaped room with sweeping expanses of gilt and crystal and a series of artfully executed ceiling frescoes by Van Loo, Boucher, and Natoire.

In the Hôtel de Soubise, 60 rue des Francs-Bourgeois, 3e. ℂ 01-40-27-60-00. Admission 3.05€ ($3.50) adults, 2.30€ ($2.65) ages 18–25, free for children under 18. Mon and Wed–Fri 10am–5:30pm; Sat–Sun 1:45–5:30pm. Métro: Hôtel-de-Ville or Rambuteau.

Paris-Story (Kids)   This very touristy 45-minute multimedia show retraces the city's history in a state-of-the-art theater. The 2,000 years since Paris's birth unroll to the music of such musicians as Wagner and Piaf. Maps, portraits, and scenes from dramatic times are projected on the large screen as a running commentary (heard through headphones in 1 of 12 languages) gives details about art, architecture, and events. Many visitors come here for a preview of what they want to see; others stop for an in-depth look at what they've already visited.

11 bis rue Scribe, 9e. ℂ 01-42-66-62-06. www.paris-story.com. Admission 8€ ($9.20) adults, 5€ ($5.75) students/under age 18. Daily 9am–7pm. Shows begin every hour on the hour. Métro: Opéra. RER: Auber.

THE OFFBEAT

Fragonard Musée du Parfum (Finds)   This perfume museum is in a 19th-century theater on one of Paris's busiest thoroughfares. As you enter the lobby through a courtyard, the scented air will remind you why you're there—to appreciate perfume enough to buy a bottle in the ground-floor shop. But first, a short visit upstairs introduces you to the rudiments of perfume history. The copper containers with spouts and tubes were used in the distillation of perfume oils, and the exquisite collection of perfume bottles from the 17th century to the 20th century is impressive.

39 bd. des Capucines, 1e. ℂ 01-47-42-93-40. www.fragonard.com. Free admission. Mon–Sat 9am–6pm. Métro: Opéra.

Musée de la Chasse   Near the Musée Carnavalet, this mansion was also designed by Mansart, and its museum is for the specialist who, like Hemingway, hunts for sport. Mounted heads are plentiful, from the antelope to the elephant, from the bushbuck to the waterbuck to the bush pig. You'll find a Rembrandt sketch of a lion, a number of Desportes wild-animal portraits, and rifles (many from the 17th c.) inlaid with pearls or engraved with ivory. The outstanding hunt tapestries are often perversely amusing—one a cannibalistic romp, another showing a helmeted man standing eye to eye with a bear he's stabbing to death. The collection of paintings includes works by Rubens, Breughel, Oudry, Chardin, and Corot.

In the Hôtel Guénégaud, 60 rue des Archives, 3e. ℂ 01-53-01-92-40. Admission 4.60€ ($5.30) adults, 2.30€ ($2.65) students/seniors, 1€ ($1.15) ages 5–16, free for children 4 and under. Tues–Sun 11am–6pm. Métro: Rambuteau or Hôtel-de-Ville.

Musée de l'Erotisme   A tribute to the primal appeal of human sexuality, this art gallery/museum is in a 19th-century town house that had been a raunchy cabaret. It presents a tasteful but risqué collection of art and artifacts, with six floors boasting an array of exhibits like erotic sculptures and drawings. The oldest object is a palm-size Roman *tintinabulum* (bell), a phallus-shaped animal with the likeness of a nude woman riding astride it. Modern objects include resin, wood, and plaster sculptures by French artist Alain Rose and works by American, Dutch, German, and French artists, including the free-form works of Robert Combas. Also look for everyday items with erotic themes from South America (terra-cotta pipes shaped like phalluses) and the States (a 1920s belt buckle that resembles a praying nun when it's fastened and a nude woman when it's open). The gift shop sells Asian amulets, African bronzes, and terra-cotta figurines from South America. There's also a gallery where serious works of art are sold.

72 bd. de Clichy, 18e. ℂ 01-42-58-28-73. Admission 7€ ($8.05) adults, children under 17 not permitted. Daily 10am–2am. Métro: Blanche.

Musée de l'Institut du Monde Arabe   Many factors have contributed to France's preoccupation with the Arab world, but three of the most important include trade links that developed during the Crusades, a large Arab population living today in France, and the still-painful memories of France's lost colonies in North Africa. For insights into the way France has handled its relations with the Arab world, consider making a trek to this bastion of Arab intellect and aesthetics. Designed in 1987 by architect Jean Nouvel, it includes expositions on calligraphy, decorative arts, architecture, and photography produced by the Arab/Islamic world, and insights into its religion, philosophy, and politics. There's a gift shop and bookshop on-site, and archival resources that are usually open only to bona-fide scholars. Views from the windows of the on-site Moroccan restaurant encompass Notre-Dame, l'Ile de la Cité, and Sacré-Coeur.

1 rue des Fossés St-Bernard, 5e. ℂ 01-40-51-38-38. Entrance to permanent exhibitions 4€ ($4.60) adults, 3€ ($3.45) students, free for children under 12. Entrance to temporary exhibits 7€ ($8.05) adults, 5€ ($5.75) students, free for children under 12. Tues–Sun 10am–6pm. Métro: Jussieu.

Musée du Vin This museum is in an ancient stone-and-clay quarry used by 15th-century monks as a wine cellar. It provides an introduction to the art of wine making, displaying various tools, beakers, cauldrons, and bottles in a series of exhibits. The quarry is right below Balzac's house (p. 208), and the ceiling contains a trap door he used to escape from his creditors.

5 rue des Eaux, 16e. (✆) 01-45-25-63-26. www.museeduvinparis.com. Admission 8€ ($9.20) adults, 5.70€ ($6.55) students. Tues–Sun 10am–6pm. Métro: Passy.

6 The Important Churches

Turn to "The Top Attractions" earlier in this chapter for a full look at the **Cathédrale de Notre-Dame, Basilique du Sacré-Coeur,** and **Sainte-Chapelle.**

American Cathedral of the Holy Trinity This cathedral is one of Europe's finest examples of Gothic Revival architecture and a center for the presentation of music and art. It was consecrated in 1886 and George Edmund Street, best known for the London Law Courts, created it. Aside from the architecture, you'll find remarkable pre-Raphaelite stained-glass windows illustrating the *Te Deum,* an early-15th-century triptych by an anonymous painter (probably a monk) known as the Roussillon Master; a needlepoint collection including kneelers depicting the 50 state flowers; and the 50 state flags in the nave. A **Memorial Cloister** commemorates Americans who died in Europe in World War I and all the victims of World War II. Documentation in several languages explains these and other highlights. The cathedral is also a center of worship and community outreach, with a schedule of Sunday and weekday services in English. Les Arts George V, a cultural organization, presents reasonably priced choral concerts, lectures, and art shows.

23 av. George V, 8e. (✆) 01-53-23-84-00. Free admission. Mon–Fri 9am–5pm. Sun Holy Eucharist 9am, 11am, and 12:30pm. Métro: Alma-Marceau or George-V.

Basilique St-Denis ✦✦ In the 12th century, Abbot Suger placed an inscription on the bronze doors here: "Marvel not at the gold and expense, but at the craftsmanship of the work." France's first Gothic building that can be dated precisely, St-Denis was constructed between 1137 and 1281 and was the "spiritual defender of the State" during the reign of Louis VI ("The Fat"). The facade has a rose window and a crenellated parapet on the top similar to the fortifications of a castle. The stained-glass windows—in stunning mauve, purple, blue, and rose—were restored in the 19th century.

The first bishop of Paris, St. Denis became the patron saint of the monarchy, and royal burials began in the 6th century and continued until the Revolution. The sculpture designed for the **tombs**—some two stories high—span French artistic development from the Middle Ages to the Renaissance. (There are guided tours in French of the Carolingean-era crypt.) François I was entombed at St-Denis, and his funeral statue is nude, though he demurely covers himself with his hand. Other kings and queens here include Louis XII and Anne de Bretagne, as well as Henri II and Catherine de Médicis. Revolutionaries stormed through the basilica during the Terror, smashing many marble faces and dumping royal remains in a lime-filled ditch in the garden. (These remains were reburied under the main altar during the 19th c.) Free organ concerts are given Sundays at 11:15am.

Place de l'Hôtel-de-Ville, 2 rue de Strasbourg, St-Denis. (✆) 01-48-09-83-54. Free admission. Apr–Sept Mon–Sat 10am–7pm, Sun noon–7pm; Oct–Mar Mon–Sat 10am–5pm, Sun noon–5pm. Closed Jan 1, Nov 1 and 11, Dec 25. Métro: St-Denis.

La Madeleine ✦✦ La Madeleine is one of Paris's minor landmarks, dominating rue Royale, which culminates in place de la Concorde. Though construction began in 1806, it wasn't consecrated until 1842. Resembling a Roman temple, the building was intended as a monument to the glory of the Grande Armée (Napoleon's idea, of course). Later, several alternative uses were considered: the National Assembly, the Bourse, and the National Library. Climb the 28 steps to the facade and look back: You'll be able to see rue Royale, place de la Concorde and its obelisk, and (across the Seine) the dome of the Hôtel des Invalides. Don't miss Rude's *Le Baptême du Christ,* to the left as you enter.

Place de la Madeleine, 8e. © 01-44-51-63-00. Free admission. Daily 8am–7pm. Métro: Madeleine.

Mosquée de Paris ✶   This beautiful pink marble mosque was built in 1922 to honor the North African countries that had given aid to France during World War I. Today, North Africans living in Paris gather on Friday, the Muslim holy day, and during Ramadan to pray to Allah. Short tours are given of the building, its central courtyard, and its Moorish garden; guides present a brief history of the Islamic faith. However, you may want just to wander around on your own, then join the students from nearby universities for couscous and sweet mint tea at the Muslim **Restaurant de la Mosquée de Paris** (© **01-43-31-18-14**), adjoining the grounds, open daily from noon to 3pm and 7 to 10:30pm.

Place du Puits-de-l'Ermite, 5e. © 01-45-35-97-33. Admission 3€ ($3.45) adults, 2€ ($2.30) students/children. Sat–Thurs 9:30am–5pm. Métro: Monge.

St-Etienne-du-Mont ✶✶   Once there was an abbey here, founded by Clovis and later dedicated to St. Geneviève, the patroness of Paris. Such was the fame of this popular saint that the abbey proved too small to accommodate the pilgrimage crowds. Now part of the Lycée Henri IV, the Tour de Clovis (Tower of Clovis) is all that remains of the ancient abbey—you can see the tower from rue Clovis. Today the task of keeping St. Geneviève's cult alive has fallen on this church, practically adjoining the Panthéon. The interior is Gothic, an unusual style for a 16th-century church. Building began in 1492 and was plagued by delays until the church was finally finished in 1626.

Besides the patroness of Paris, such men as Pascal and Racine were entombed here. St. Geneviève's tomb was destroyed during the Revolution, but the stone on which her coffin rested was discovered later, and her relics were gathered for a place of honor at St-Etienne. The church possesses a remarkable early-16th-century **rood screen:** Crossing the nave, it's unique in Paris—called spurious by some and a masterpiece by others. Another treasure is a wood **pulpit,** held up by Samson, clutching a bone in one hand, with a slain lion at his feet. The fourth chapel on the right when you enter contains impressive 16th-century stained glass.

1 place St-Geneviève, 5e. © 01-43-54-11-79. Free admission. Sept–June Mon–Sat 8:30am–noon and 2–7pm, Sun 9am–noon and 3:30–7:30pm; July–Aug Tues–Sun 10am–noon and 4–7:15pm. Métro: Cardinal Lemoine or Luxembourg.

St-Eustache ✶✶   This Gothic and Renaissance church completed in 1637 is rivaled only by Notre-Dame. Madame de Pompadour and Richelieu were baptized here, and Molière's funeral was held here in 1673. The church has been known for organ recitals ever since Liszt played in 1866. Inside rests the **black-marble tomb** of Jean-Baptiste Colbert, the minister of state under Louis XIV; atop the tomb is his marble effigy flanked by statues of *Abundance* by Coysevox and *Fidelity* by Tuby. The church's most famous painting is Rembrandt's *The Pilgrimage to Emmaus.* There's a side entrance on rue Rambuteau.

2 rue du Jour, 1e. © 01-42-36-31-05. www.st-eustache.org. Free admission. Daily 9am–7pm. Sun Mass 9:30am, 11am, and 6pm; Sun organ recitals 5:30pm. Métro: Les Halles.

Moments **Gregorians Unplugged**

St-Germain-des-Prés stages wonderful concerts on the Left Bank; it boasts fantastic acoustics and a marvelous medieval atmosphere. The church was built to accommodate an age without microphones, and the sound effects will thrill you. For more information, call ℭ **01-43-25-41-71.** Arrive about 45 minutes before the performance if you'd like a front-row seat. Tickets are 25€ to 45€ ($29–$52).

St-Germain-des-Prés ★★   It's one of Paris's oldest churches, from the 6th century, when a Benedictine abbey was founded here by Childebert, son of Clovis. Alas, the marble columns in the triforium are all that remain from then. The Normans nearly destroyed the abbey at least four times. The present building has a Romanesque nave and a Gothic choir with fine capitals. At one time, the abbey was a pantheon for Merovingian kings. Restoration of the site of their tombs, **Chapelle de St-Symphorien,** began in 1981, and unknown Romanesque paintings were discovered on the triumphal arch. Among the others interred here are Descartes (his heart, at least) and Jean-Casimir, the king of Poland who abdicated his throne. The Romanesque tower, topped by a 19th-century spire, is the most enduring landmark in St-Germain-des-Prés. Its church bells, however, are hardly noticed by the patrons of Les Deux Magots across the way.

When you leave the church, turn right on rue de l'Abbaye and have a look at the 17th-century pink **Palais Abbatial.**

3 place St-Germain-des-Prés, 6e. ℭ 01-43-25-41-71. Free admission. Daily 8am–8pm. Métro: St-Germain-des-Prés.

St-Germain l'Auxerrois ★★   Once it was the church for the Palais du Louvre, drawing an assortment of royalty, courtesans, men of art and law, and local artisans. Sharing place du Louvre with Perrault's colonnade, the church contains only the foundation stones of its original 11th-century belfry. The chapel that had stood here was greatly enlarged in the 14th century by the addition of side aisles and became a beautiful church, with 78m (256 ft.) of stained glass, including some rose windows from the Renaissance. The intricately carved **church-wardens' pews** are outstanding, based on 17th-century Le Brun designs. Behind them is a **15th-century triptych** and **Flemish retable,** so badly lit you can hardly appreciate it. The organ was ordered by Louis XVI for Sainte-Chapelle. Many famous men were entombed here, including the sculptor Coysevox and the architect Le Vau. Around the chancel is an intricate **18th-century grille.**

The saddest moment in the church's history was on August 24, 1572, the evening of the St. Bartholomew Massacre. The tower bells rang, signaling the supporters of Catherine de Médicis, Marguerite de Guise, Charles IX, and the future Henri III to launch a slaughter of thousands of Huguenots, who'd been invited to celebrate the marriage of Henri de Navarre to Marguerite de Valois.

2 place du Louvre, 1e. ℭ 01-42-60-13-96. Free admission. Daily 8am–7pm. Métro: Louvre-Rivoli.

St-Sulpice ★★   Pause first outside St-Sulpice. The 1844 fountain by Visconti displays the sculpted likenesses of four bishops of the Louis XIV era: Fenelon, Massillon, Bossuet, and Flechier. Work on the church, at one time Paris's largest, began in 1646. Though laborers built the body by 1745, work on the bell towers continued until 1780, when one was finished and the other left incomplete.

One of the priceless treasures inside is Servandoni's rococo **Chapelle de la Madone (Chapel of the Madonna),** with a Pigalle statue of the Virgin. The church has one of the world's largest organs, comprising 6,700 pipes; it has been played by musicians like Marcel Dupré and Charles-Mari Widor.

The real reason to come here is to see the Delacroix frescoes in the **Chapelle des Anges (Chapel of the Angels),** the first on your right as you enter. Look for his muscular Jacob wrestling (or dancing?) with an effete angel. On the ceiling, St. Michael is having some troubles with the Devil, and yet another mural depicts Heliodorus being driven from the temple. Painted in Delacroix's final years, the frescoes were a high point in his baffling career. If these impress you, pay the painter tribute by visiting the Musée Delacroix (see "The Major Museums").

Rue St-Sulpice, 6e. ✆ 01-46-33-21-78. Free admission. Daily 8:30am–8pm. Métro: St-Sulpice.

Val-de-Grâce ✷✷   According to an old proverb, to understand the French you must like Camembert cheese, the pont Neuf, and the dome of Val-de-Grâce. Its origins go back to 1050, when a Benedictine monastery was built here. In 1619, Louis XIII appointed as abbess Marguerite Veni d'Arbouze, who asked Louis's wife, Anne of Austria, for a new monastery. After 23 years of a childless marriage, Anne gave birth to a boy who went on to be known as the Sun King. To express his gratitude, Louis XIII approved the rebuilding of the church, and at the age of 7, on April 1, 1645, the future Louis XIV laid Val-de-Grâce's first stone. Mansart was the main architect, and to him we owe the facade in the Jesuit style. Le Duc, however, designed the dome, and Mignard added the frescoes. Le Mercier and Le Muet also had a hand in the church's fashioning. The church was turned into a military hospital in 1793 and an army school in 1850.

1 place Alphonse-Laveran, 5e. ✆ 01-40-51-47-28. Admission 4.60€ ($5.30) adults, 2.30€ ($2.65) children, children under 6 free. Daily 9am–5pm. Métro: Port Royal.

7 Architectural & Historic Highlights

Arènes de Lutèce   Discovered and partially destroyed in 1869, this amphitheater is Paris's most important Roman ruin after the baths in the Musée de Cluny (p. 193). Today the site is home to a small arena, not as grand as the original, and gardens. You may feel as if you've discovered a private spot in the heart of the city, but don't be fooled. Your solitude is sure to be interrupted, if not by groups of students playing soccer then by parents pushing strollers down the paths. This is an ideal spot for a picnic—bring a bottle of wine and baguettes to enjoy in this vestige of the ancient city of Lutétia.

At rues Monge and Navarre, 5e. No phone. Free admission. May–Sept daily 8am–10pm; Oct–Apr daily 8am–5:30pm. Métro: Jussieu.

Bibliothèque Nationale de France, Site Tolbiac/François Mitterrand The French National Library opened in 1996 with a futuristic design by Dominique Perrault (a quartet of 24-story towers evoking the look of open books); this is the last of the *grand projets* of the late François Mitterrand. It boasts the same grandiose scale as the Cité de la Musique and houses the nation's literary and historic archives; it's regarded as a repository of the French soul, replacing outmoded facilities on rue des Archives. The library incorporates space for 1,600 readers at a time, many of whom enjoy views over two levels of a garden-style courtyard that seems far removed from Paris's urban congestion.

This is one of Europe's most user-friendly academic facilities, emphasizing computerized documentation and microfiche—a role model that will set academic and literary priorities well into the future. The public has access to as many as 180,000 books plus thousands of periodicals, with an additional 10 million historic (including medieval) documents shown to qualified experts. Though the appeal of this place extends mainly to serious scholars, there's a handful of special exhibits that might interest you, as well as concerts and lectures. Concert tickets rarely exceed 15€ ($17) for adults and 10€ ($12) for students, seniors, and children; a schedule is available at the library.

Quai François-Mauriac, 13e. ℂ 01-53-79-49-49. www.bnf.fr. Admission 3.50€ ($4.05). No one under 16 admitted. Tues–Sat 10am–8pm; Sun noon–7pm. Métro: Bibliothèque François-Mitterrand.

Conciergerie ★★   London has its Bloody Tower and Paris has its Conciergerie. Even though the Conciergerie had a long regal history before the Revolution, it was forever stained by the Reign of Terror and lives as an infamous symbol of the time when carts pulled up constantly to haul off fresh supplies of victims for Dr. Guillotin's wonderful little invention.

Much of the Conciergerie was built in the 14th century as an extension of the Capetian royal Palais de la Cité. You approach through its landmark twin towers, the **Tour d'Argent** (where the crown jewels were stored at one time) and **Tour de César,** but the **Salle des Gardes (Guard Room)** is the actual entrance. Even more interesting is the dark and foreboding Gothic **Salle des Gens d'Armes (Room of People at Arms),** utterly changed from the days when the king used it as a banquet hall. However, architecture plays a secondary role to the list of prisoners who spent their last days here. Few in its history endured tortures as severe as those imposed on Ravaillac, who assassinated Henry IV in 1610. In the Tour de César, he received pincers in the flesh and had hot lead and boiling oil poured on him like bath water before being executed (see the Hôtel de Ville entry below). During the Revolution, the Conciergerie became a symbol of terror to the nobility and enemies of the State. A short walk away, the Revolutionary Tribunal dispensed a skewed, hurried justice—if it's any consolation, the jurists didn't believe in torturing their victims, only in decapitating them.

After being seized by a crowd of peasants who stormed Versailles, Louis XVI and Marie Antoinette were brought here to await their trials. In failing health and shocked beyond grief, *l'Autrichienne* ("the Austrian," as she was called with malice) had only a small screen (sometimes not even that) to protect her modesty from the gaze of guards stationed in her cell. By accounts of the day, she was shy and stupid, though the evidence is that on her death she displayed the nobility of a true queen. (What's more, the famous "Let them eat cake" she supposedly uttered when told the peasants had no bread, is probably apocryphal—besides, at the time, cake flour was less expensive than bread flour, so even if she said this, it wasn't meant cold-heartedly.) It was shortly before noon on the morning of October 16, 1793, when her executioners came for her, grabbing her and cutting her hair, as was the custom for victims marked for the guillotine.

Later, the Conciergerie housed other prisoners, including Mme Elisabeth; Mme du Barry, mistress of Louis XV; Mme Roland ("O Liberty! Liberty! What crimes are committed in thy name!"); and Charlotte Corday, who killed Marat while he was taking a sulphur bath. In time, the Revolution consumed its own leaders, such as Danton and Robespierre. Finally, one of Paris's most hated men, public prosecutor Fouquier-Tinville, faced the guillotine to which he'd sent so many others. Among the few interned here who lived to tell the tale was American Thomas Paine, who reminisced about his chats in English with Danton.

1 quai de l'Horloge, 1e. ℂ 01-53-40-60-93. www.monum.fr. Admission 6.10€ ($7) adults, 4.10€ ($4.70) ages 18–25, free for children under 18. Daily 9:30am–6pm. Métro: Cité, Châtelet, or St-Michel. RER: St-Michel.

Hôtel de Ville ✪   On a large square with fountains and early-1900s lampposts, the 19th-century Hôtel de Ville isn't a hotel but Paris's grandiose City Hall. The medieval structure it replaced had witnessed countless municipally ordered executions. Henry IV's assassin, Ravaillac, was quartered alive on the square in 1610, his body tied to four horses that bolted in opposite directions. On May 24, 1871, the Communards doused the City Hall with petrol, creating a blaze that lasted for 8 days. The Third Republic ordered the structure rebuilt, with many changes, even creating a Hall of Mirrors evocative of that at Versailles. For security reasons, the major splendor of this building is closed to the public. However, the information center sponsors exhibits on Paris in the main lobby.

29 rue de Rivoli, 4e. ✆ 01-42-76-43-43. Free admission. Information center Mon–Sat 9:30am–7pm. Métro: Hôtel–de–Ville.

Institut de France ✪   Designed by Louis Le Vau, this dramatic baroque building with an enormous cupola is the seat of all five Academies that dominate France's intellectual life—Française, Sciences, Inscriptions et Belles Lettres, Beaux-Arts, and Sciences Morales et Politiques. The members of the Academie Française (limited to 40), guardians of the French language referred to as "the immortals," gather here. Many are unfamiliar figures (though Jacques Cousteau and Marshall Pétain were members), and the Academy is remarkable for the great writers and philosophers who have *not* been invited to join—Balzac, Baudelaire, Diderot, Flaubert, Descartes, Proust, Molière, Pascal, Rousseau, and Zola, to name only a few. The cenotaph was designed by Coysevox for Mazarin.

23 quai de Conti, 6e. ✆ 01-44-41-43-40. Free admission (guests can walk into courtyard only). Métro: Louvre.

La Grande Arche de La Défense ✪   Designed as the architectural centerpiece of the sprawling satellite suburb of La Défense, this massive steel-and-masonry arch rises 35 stories. It was built with the blessing of the late François Mitterrand and extends the magnificently engineered straight line linking the Louvre, Arc de Triomphe du Carrousel, Champs-Elysées, Arc de Triomphe, avenue de la Grande Armée, and place du Porte Maillot. The arch is ringed with a circular avenue patterned after the one winding around the Arc de Triomphe. The monument is tall enough to shelter Notre-Dame beneath its heavily trussed canopy. An elevator carries you up to an observation platform, where you get a view of the carefully planned geometry of the surrounding streets.

You'll notice nets rigged along the Grande Arche. When pieces of Mitterrand's *grand projet* started falling to the ground, they were erected to catch the falling fragments. If only such protection existed for all politicians' follies!

1 place du parvis de La Défense, Puteaux, 15e. ✆ 01-49-07-27-57. Admission 7€ ($8.05) adults, 5.50€ ($6.35) for children 4–17. Daily 9am–8pm.

Palais Bourbon/Assemblée Nationale ✪   The French parliament's lower house, the Chamber of Deputies, meets at this 1722 mansion built by the duchesse de Bourbon, a daughter of Louis XIV. You can make reservations for one of two types of visits as early as 6 months in advance. Tours on art, architecture, and basic French government processes are given Monday, Friday, and Saturday. They're in French (in English with advance booking). You may also observe sessions of the National Assembly, held Tuesday afternoon and all day Wednesday and Thursday beginning at 9:30am. Remember, this is a working government building, and all visitors are subject to rigorous security checks.

33 quai d'Orsay, 7e. ✆ 01-40-63-64-08. Free admission. Hours vary, so call ahead. Métro: Assemblée Nationale.

Palais Royal ★★   The Palais Royal was originally known as the Palais Cardinal, for it was the residence of Cardinal Richelieu, Louis XIII's prime minister. Richelieu had it built, and after his death it was inherited by the king, who died soon after. Louis XIV spent part of his childhood here with his mother, Anne of Austria, but later resided at the Louvre and Versailles. The palace was later owned by the duc de Chartres et Orléans (see the entry for Parc Monceau under "Parks & Gardens"), who encouraged the opening of cafes, gambling dens, and other public entertainments. Though government offices occupy the Palais Royal and are not open to the public, do visit the **Jardin du Palais Royal,** an enclosure bordered by arcades. Don't miss the main courtyard, with the controversial 1986 Buren sculpture—280 prison-striped columns, oddly placed.

Rue St-Honoré, 1e. No phone. Free admission. Métro: Palais Royal–Musée du Louvre.

Panthéon ★★   Some of the most famous men in French history (Victor Hugo, for one) are buried here on the crest of the mount of St. Geneviève. In 1744, Louis XV vowed that if he recovered from a mysterious illness, he'd build a church to replace the Abbaye de St. Geneviève. He recovered but took his time fulfilling his promise. It wasn't until 1764 that Mme de Pompadour's brother hired Soufflot to design a church in the form of a Greek cross with a dome reminiscent of St. Paul's in London. When Soufflot died, his pupil Rondelet carried out the work, completing the structure 9 years after his master's death.

After the Revolution, the church was converted into a "Temple of Fame" and became a pantheon for the great men of France. Mirabeau was buried here, though his remains were later removed. Likewise, Marat was only a temporary tenant. Voltaire's body was exhumed and placed here—and allowed to remain. In the 19th century, the building changed roles so many times—a church, a pantheon, a church again—that it was hard to keep its function straight. After Hugo was buried here, it became a pantheon once again. Other notable men entombed within are Rousseau, Soufflot, Zola, and Braille. Only one woman has so far been deemed worthy of placement here: Marie Curie, who joined her husband, Pierre. Most recently, the ashes of André Malraux were transferred to the Panthéon because, according to President Jacques Chirac, he "lived [his] dreams and made them live in us." As Charles de Gaulle's culture minister, Malraux decreed the arts should be part of the lives of all French people, not just Paris's elite.

Before entering the crypt, note the striking frescoes: On the right wall are scenes from Geneviève's life, and on the left are the saint with a white-draped head looking out over medieval Paris, the city whose patron she became, as well as Geneviève relieving victims of famine with supplies.

Place du Panthéon, 5e. © 01-44-32-18-00. Admission 7€ ($8.05) adults, 4.50€ ($5.20) ages 18–25, free for children 17 and under. Daily 10am–6pm (last entrance 45 min. before closing). Métro: Cardinal Lemoine or Maubert-Mutualité.

8 Literary Landmarks

If there's a literary bone in your body, you'll feel a vicarious thrill on discovering the haunts of the writers and artists who've lived, worked, and played in Paris.

Take the Métro to place St-Michel to begin your tour. As you wander away from the Seine, you'll encounter **rue de la Huchette,** one of the Left Bank's most famous streets. Its inhabitants were immortalized in Eliot Paul's *The Last Time I Saw Paris.* Continuing on, you'll enter the territory of the Beat Generation, home to the **Café Gentilhomme** (no longer there) described by Jack Kerouac in *Satori* *in Paris.* Allen Ginsberg's favorite, the **Hôtel du Vieux-Paris,** 9 rue Gît-le-Coeur, 6e, still attracts those in search of the Beats.

Stroll down **rue Monsieur-le-Prince,** the "Yankee alleyway," where Richard Wright, James McNeill Whistler, Henry Wadsworth Longfellow, and Oliver Wendell Holmes lived at one time or another. During a visit in 1959, Martin Luther King Jr. came to call on Richard Wright, the Mississippi-born African-American novelist famous for *Native Son.* King climbed to the third-floor apartment at **no. 14** to find that Wright's opinions on the civil rights movement conflicted with his own. Whistler rented a studio at **no. 22,** and in 1826, Longfellow lived at **no. 49.** Oliver Wendell Holmes Sr. lived at **no. 55.** After strolling along this street, you can dine at the haunts of Kerouac and Hemingway. (See our recommendation of **Crémerie-Restaurant Polidor,** 41 rue Monsieur-le-Prince, 6e, on p. 154.) Or cross back over to the Right Bank for a drink at the famed **Hôtel de Crillon,** 10 place de la Concorde, 8e (p. 88), where heroine Brett Ashley broke her promise to rendezvous with Jake Barnes in Hemingway's *The Sun Also Rises.* Zelda and F. Scott Fitzgerald lifted their glasses here as well.

For details on **Harry's New York Bar,** 5 rue Daunou, 2e, see "Literary Haunts" in chapter 10, "Paris After Dark." For a description of **Les Deux Magots, Le Procope,** and **La Rotonde,** see "The Top Cafes" in chapter 6. And for coverage of the bookstore **Shakespeare and Company,** see "Books" in chapter 9.

Here are two great museums for hard-core literary fans:

Maison de Balzac   In the residential district of Passy, near the Bois de Boulogne, sits this modest house with a courtyard and garden. Honoré de Balzac fled to this house in 1840 after his possessions and furnishings were seized, and lived here for 7 years (to see him, you had to know a password). If a creditor knocked on the rue Raynouard door, Balzac was able to escape through the rue Berton exit. The museum's most notable memento is Balzac's "screech-owl" (his nickname for his tea kettle), which he kept hot throughout the night as he wrote *La Comédie Humaine.* Also enshrined are Balzac's writing desk and chair and a library of special interest to scholars. The little house is filled with caricatures of Balzac. A biographer once wrote: "With his bulky baboon silhouette, his blue suit with gold buttons, his famous cane like a golden crowbar, and his abundant, disheveled hair, Balzac was a sight for caricature."

47 rue Raynouard, 16e. ✆ **01-55-74-41-80.** www.paris.org/Musees/Balzac. Admission 3.30€ ($3.80) adults, 1.60€ ($1.85) 26 and under. Tues–Sun 10am–6pm. Métro: Passy or La Muette.

Maison de Victor Hugo ★   Today, theatergoers who've seen *Les Misérables,* even those who haven't read anything by Paris's 19th-century novelist, come to place des Vosges to see where Hugo lived and wrote. Some thought him a genius, but Cocteau called him a madman, and an American composer discovered that in his old age he was carving furniture with his teeth! From 1832 to 1848, the novelist/poet lived on the second floor of the Hôtel Rohan Guéménée, built in 1610 on what was then place Royale. The museum owns some of Hugo's furniture as well as pieces that once belonged to Juliette Drouet, the mistress with whom he lived in exile on Guernsey, one of the Channel Islands.

Worth the visit are Hugo's drawings, more than 450, illustrating scenes from his own works. Mementos of the great writer abound, including samples of his handwriting, his inkwell, and first editions of his works. A painting of Hugo's 1885 funeral procession at the Arc de Triomphe is on display, as are many portraits and souvenirs of his family. Of the furnishings, a chinoiserie salon stands out. The collection even contains Daumier caricatures and a bust of Hugo by David d'Angers, which, compared to Rodin's, looks saccharine.

6 place des Vosges, 4e. © 01-42-72-10-16. Free admission. Tues–Sun 10am–5:40pm. Closed national holidays. Métro: St-Paul, Bastille, or Chemin-Vert.

9 Parks & Gardens

JARDIN DES TUILERIES

The spectacular statue-studded **Jardin des Tuileries** ✶✶, bordering place de la Concorde, 1e (© **01-44-50-75-01;** Métro: Tuileries or Concorde), is as much a part of Paris as the Seine. Le Nôtre, Louis XIV's gardener and planner of the Versailles grounds, designed the gardens. Some of the gardens' most distinctive statues are the 18 enormous bronzes by Maillol, installed within the Jardin du Carroussel, a subdivision of the Jardin des Tuileries, between 1964 and 1965, under the direction of then-Culture Minister André Malraux.

About 100 years before that, Catherine de Médicis ordered a palace built here, the **Palais des Tuileries;** other occupants have included Louis XVI (after he left Versailles) and Napoleon. Twice attacked by Parisians, it was burned to the ground in 1871 and never rebuilt. The gardens, however, remain. In orderly French manner, the trees are arranged according to designs and even the paths are arrow-straight. Breaking the sense of order and formality are bubbling fountains.

JARDIN DU LUXEMBOURG

Hemingway once told a friend that the **Jardin du Luxembourg** ✶✶ in the 6th arrondissement (Métro: Odéon; RER: Luxembourg) "kept us from starvation." He related that in his poverty-stricken days in Paris, he wheeled a baby carriage (the vehicle was considered luxurious) through the garden because it was known "for the classiness of its pigeons." When the gendarme went across the street for a glass of wine, the writer would eye his victim, preferably a plump one, then lure him with corn and "snatch him, wring his neck," and hide him under the blanket. "We got a little tired of pigeon that year," he confessed, "but they filled many a void."

The Luxembourg has always been associated with artists, though children, students, and tourists predominate nowadays. Watteau came this way, as did Verlaine. Balzac didn't like the gardens at all. In 1905, Gertrude Stein would cross them to catch the Batignolles/Clichy/Odéon omnibus, pulled by three gray mares, to meet Picasso in his studio at Montmartre, where he painted her portrait.

(**Fun Fact** **Did You Know?**

The odd name of the Jardin des Tuileries comes from the clay earth of the land here, once used to make roof tiles called *tuiles.*

Half of Paris can be found in the Tuileries on a warm spring day, listening to the birds and admiring the daffodils and tulips. As you walk toward the Louvre, you'll enter the **Jardin du Carrousel,** dominated by the **Arc de Triomphe du Carrousel,** at the Cour du Carrousel. Pierced with three walkways and supported by marble columns, the monument honors Napoleon's Grande Armée, celebrating its victory at Austerlitz. The arch is surmounted by statuary, a chariot, and four bronze horses.

Marie de Médicis, the wife of Henri IV, ordered the **Palais du Luxembourg** built on this site in 1612, shortly after she was widowed. A Florentine by birth, the regent wanted to create another Pitti Palace, where she could live with her "witch" friend, Leonora Galigal. Architect Salomon de Brossee wasn't entirely successful, though the overall effect is Italianate. Alas, the queen didn't get to enjoy the palace, as her son, Louis XIII, forced her into exile when he discovered she was plotting to overthrow him. She died in poverty in Cologne. For her palace, she'd commissioned from Rubens 21 paintings that glorified her life, but they're now in the Louvre. You can visit the palace only the first Sunday of each month at 10:30am, for 8€ ($9.20). However, you must call ℂ **01-42-34-23-62** to make a reservation.

You don't really come to the Luxembourg to visit the palace; the gardens are the attraction. For the most part, they're in the classic French tradition: well groomed and formally laid out, the trees planted in patterns. Urns and statuary on pedestals—one honoring Paris's patroness, St. Geneviève, with pigtails reaching to her thighs—encircle a central water basin. Another memorial is dedicated to Stendhal. Kids can sail a toy boat, ride a pony, or attend an occasional Grand Guignol puppet show. And you can play *boules* (lawn bowling) with a group of elderly men who wear black berets and have Gauloises dangling from their mouths.

BOIS DE BOULOGNE

One of the most spectacular parks in Europe is the **Bois de Boulogne** 🎕🎕, Porte Dauphine, 16e (ℂ **01-40-67-90-82;** Métro: Les Sablons, Porte Maillot, or Porte Dauphine), often called the "main lung" of Paris. Horse-drawn carriages traverse it, but you can also drive through. You can discover its hidden pathways, however, only by walking. You could spend days in the Bois de Boulogne and still not see everything.

Porte Dauphine is the main entrance, though you can take the Métro to Porte Maillot as well. West of Paris, the park was once a forest kept for royal hunts. It was in vogue in the late 19th century: Along avenue Foch, carriages with elegantly attired and coiffured Parisian damsels would rumble along with their foppish escorts. Nowadays, it's more likely to attract run-of-the-mill picnickers. (Be careful at night, when hookers and muggers proliferate.)

When Napoleon III gave the grounds to the city in 1852, they were developed by Baron Haussmann. Separating Lac Inférieur from Lac Supérieur is the **Carrefour des Cascades** 🎕 (you can stroll under its waterfall). The Lower Lake contains two islands connected by a footbridge. From the east bank, you can take a boat to these idyllically situated grounds, perhaps stopping off at the cafe/restaurant on one of them.

Restaurants in the bois are numerous, elegant, and expensive. The **Pré Catelan** 🎕 contains a deluxe restaurant of the same name (ℂ **01-44-14-41-14**) occupying a gem of a Napoleon III–style château, and also a Shakespearean theater in a garden planted with trees mentioned in the bard's plays. Nearby is **La Grande Cascade** (ℂ **01-45-27-33-51**), once a hunting lodge for Napoleon III.

Jardin d'Acclimatation, at the northern edge of the park, is for children, with a zoo, an amusement park, and a narrow-gauge railway (see "Especially for Kids," later in this chapter, for more details). Two racetracks, the **Hippodrome de Longchamp** 🎕🎕🎕 and the **Hippodrome d'Auteuil,** are in the park (see "A Day at the Races," below). The Grand Prix is run in June at Longchamp (the site of a medieval abbey). Fashionable Parisians always turn out for this, the women in their finest haute couture. To the north of Longchamp is the **Grand Cascade,** an artificial waterfall.

In the western section of the bois, the 24-hectare (59-acre) **Parc de Bagatelle** ⭐ (℃ **01-40-67-97-00**) owes its existence to a bet between the comte d'Artois (later Charles X) and Marie Antoinette, his sister-in-law. The comte wagered he could erect a small palace in less than 3 months, so he hired nearly 1,000 craftsmen (cabinetmakers, painters, Scottish landscape architect Thomas Blaikie, and others) and irritated the locals by requisitioning all shipments of stone and plaster arriving through Paris's west gates. He won his bet. If you're here in late April, it's worth visiting the Bagatelle just for the tulips. In late May, one of the finest rose collections in Europe is in full bloom. For some reason, as the head gardener confides to us, "This is the major rendezvous point in Paris for illicit couples." In September, the light is less harsh than in summer or even in February; when stripped of much of its greenery, the park's true shape can be seen.

Parc de Bagatelle is open daily from 9am to dusk, charging adults 1.50€ ($1.75) and those ages 7 to 26 .75€ (85¢); it's free for children 6 and under.

PARC MONCEAU
Much of **Parc Monceau** ⭐, 8e (℃ **01-42-27-39-56;** Métro: Monceau or Villiers), is ringed with 18th- and 19th-century mansions, some evoking

Proust's *Remembrance of Things Past.* Carmontelle designed it in 1778 as a private hideaway for the duc d'Orléans (who came to be known as Philippe-Egalité), at the time the richest man in France. The duke was noted for his debauchery and pursuit of pleasure, so no ordinary park would do. It was opened to the public in the days of Napoleon III's Second Empire.

Monceau was laid out with an Egyptian-style obelisk, a medieval dungeon, a thatched farmhouse, a Chinese pagoda, a Roman temple, an enchanted grotto, various chinoiseries, and a waterfall. These fairy-tale touches have largely disappeared, except for a pyramid and an oval naumachia fringed by a colonnade. Now the park is filled with solid statuary and monuments, one honoring Chopin. In spring, the red tulips and magnolias are worth the air ticket to Paris.

10 Cemeteries

Sightseers often view Paris's cemeteries as being somewhat like parks, suitable places for strolling. The graves of celebrities are also a major lure. Père-Lachaise, for example, is a major attraction; the other cemeteries are of lesser interest.

Cimetière de Montmartre ★   This cemetery, established in 1795, lies west of Montmartre and north of boulevard de Clichy. Russian dancer **Vaslav Nijinsky,** novelist **Alexandre Dumas *fils,*** impressionist **Edgar Degas,** and composers **Hector Berlioz** and **Jacques Offenbach** are interred here, along with **Stendhal** and lesser literary lights like **Edmond** and **Jules de Goncourt** and **Heinrich Heine.** A more recent tombstone honors **François Truffaut,** film director of the *nouvelle vague* (new wave). We like to pay our respects at the tomb of **Alphonsine Plessis,** heroine of *La Dame aux camélias,* and **Mme Récamier,** who taught the world how to lounge. **Emile Zola** was buried here, but his corpse was exhumed and promoted to the Panthéon in 1908. In 1871, the cemetery was used for mass burials of victims of the Siege and the Commune.

20 av. Rachel, 18e. ℂ **01-53-42-36-30.** Free admission. Mon–Fri 8am–6pm; Sat 8:30am–6pm; Sun 9am–6pm (to 5:30pm in winter). Métro: Blanche or Place Clichy.

Cimetière de Passy   This cemetery runs along Paris's old northern walls, south and southwest of Trocadéro. It's a small graveyard sheltered by chestnut trees, but it contains many gravesites of the famous—a concierge at the gate can guide you. Painters **Edouard Manet** and **Romaine Brooks** and composer **Claude Debussy** are tenants. Many great literary figures since 1850 were interred here, including **Tristan Bernard, Jean Giraudoux,** and **François de Croisset.** Also present are composer **Gabriel Fauré,** aviator **Henry Farman,** actor **Fernandel,** and high priestess of the city's most famous literary salon, **Natalie Barney,** along with **Renée Vivien,** one of her many lovers.

2 rue du Comandant-Schloesing, 16e. ℂ **01-47-27-51-42.** Free admission. Mar–Nov daily 8am–5:30pm; Dec–Feb daily 8:30am–5:15pm. Métro: Trocadéro.

Cimetière du Montparnasse ★   In the shadow of the Tour Montparnasse, this debris-littered cemetery is a burial ground of yesterday's celebrities. A map to the left of the main gateway will direct you to the gravesite of its most famous couple, **Simone de Beauvoir** and **Jean-Paul Sartre.** Others resting here include **Samuel Beckett, Guy de Maupassant, Pierre Larousse** (famous for his dictionary), **Capt. Alfred Dreyfus,** auto tycoon **André Citroën,** sculptors **Ossip Zadkine** and **Constantin Brancusi,** actress **Jean Seberg,** composer **Camille**

Saint-Saëns, photographer **Man Ray,** and **Charles Baudelaire,** who'd already written about "plunging into the abyss, Heaven or Hell."

3 bd. Edgar-Quinet, 14e. ☎ **01-44-10-86-50.** Free admission. Mon–Fri 8am–6pm; Sat 8:30am–6pm; Sun 9am–6pm (to 5:15pm Nov–Mar). Métro: Edgar Quinet.

Cimetière du Père-Lachaise ★★★   When it comes to name-dropping, this cemetery knows no peer; it has been called the "grandest address in Paris." A free map of Père-Lachaise is available at the newsstand across from the main entrance (also see the map on p. 214).

Everybody from Sarah Bernhardt to Oscar Wilde to Richard Wright is here, along with Honoré de Balzac, Jacques-Louis David, Eugène Delacroix, Maria Callas, Max Ernst, and Georges Bizet. Colette was taken here in 1954; her black granite slab always sports flowers, and legend has it that cats replenish the roses. In time, the little sparrow, Edith Piaf, followed. The lover of George Sand, poet Alfred de Musset, was buried under a weeping willow. Napoleon's marshals, Ney and Masséna, lie here, as do Frédéric Chopin and Molière. Marcel Proust's black tombstone rarely lacks a tiny bunch of violets (he wanted to be buried beside his friend/lover, composer Maurice Ravel, but their families wouldn't allow it).

Some tombs are sentimental favorites: Love-torn graffiti radiates 1km (half a mile) from the tomb of Doors singer **Jim Morrison.** The great dancer **Isadora Duncan** came to rest in the Columbarium, where bodies have been cremated and "filed" away. If you search hard enough, you can find the tombs of that star-crossed pair **Abélard** and **Héloïse,** the ill-fated lovers of the 12th century—at Père-Lachaise they've found peace at last. Other famous lovers also rest here: A stone is marked **"Alice B. Toklas"** on one side and **"Gertrude Stein"** on the other, and eventually France's First Couple of film were reunited when **Yves Montand** joined his wife, **Simone Signoret.** (Montand's gravesite attracted much attention in 1998: His corpse was exhumed in the middle of the night for DNA testing in a paternity lawsuit—he wasn't the father.)

Covering more than 44 hectares (109 acres), Père-Lachaise was acquired by the city in 1804. Nineteenth-century sculpture abounds, as each family tried to outdo the other in ostentation. Monuments also honor Frenchmen who died in the Resistance or in Nazi concentration camps. Some French Socialists still pay tribute at the **Mur des Fédérés,** the anonymous gravesite of the Communards who were executed in the cemetery on May 28, 1871. When these last-ditch fighters of the Commune, the world's first anarchist republic, made their final desperate stand against the troops of the French government, they were overwhelmed, lined up against the wall, and shot in groups. A handful survived and lived hidden in the cemetery for years like wild animals, venturing into Paris at night to forage for food.

16 rue du Repos, 20e. ☎ **01-55-25-82-10.** Free admission. Mon–Fri 8am–6pm; Sat 8:30am–6pm; Sun 9am–6pm (to 5:30pm early Nov to early Mar). Métro: Père-Lachaise.

Cimetière St-Vincent   Because of the artists and writers who have their resting places in the modest burial ground of St-Vincent, with a view of Sacré-Coeur on the hill, it's sometimes called "the most intellectual cemetery in Paris"—but that epithet seems more apt for other graveyards. Artists **Maurice Utrillo** and **Théopile-Alexandre Steinien** were buried here, as was musician **Arthur Honegger** and writer **Marcel Aymé.** In theory, the cemetery is open all day, but if you disturb the caretaker's lunch—any time from noon to 2pm—you'll regret it.

6 rue Lucien-Gaulard, 18e. ☎ **01-46-06-29-78.** Free admission. Mar 6–Nov 5 Mon–Sat 8:30am–6pm, Sun 9am–6pm; Nov 6–Mar 5 Mon–Fri 8am–5:15pm, Sat 8:30am–5:15pm, Sun 9am–5:15pm. Métro: Lamarck-Caulaincourt.

Père-Lachaise Cemetery

Abélard & Héloïse **37**
Guillaume Apollinaire **5**
Pierre-Auguste
  Beaumarchais **30**
Hans Bellmer **24**
Sarah Bernhardt **9**
Georges Bizet **17**
Maria Callas **3**

Frédéric Chopin **36**
Colette **23**
Auguste Comte **34**
Jean Baptiste Camille
  Corot **11**
Honoré Daumier **10**
Jacques-Louis David **19**
Honoré de Balzac **16**

Eugène Delacroix **15**
Gustave Doré **14**
Isadora Duncan **6**
Paul Eluard **26**
Max Ernst **2**
Théodore Géricault **20**
Jean-Auguste-Dominique
  Ingres **13**

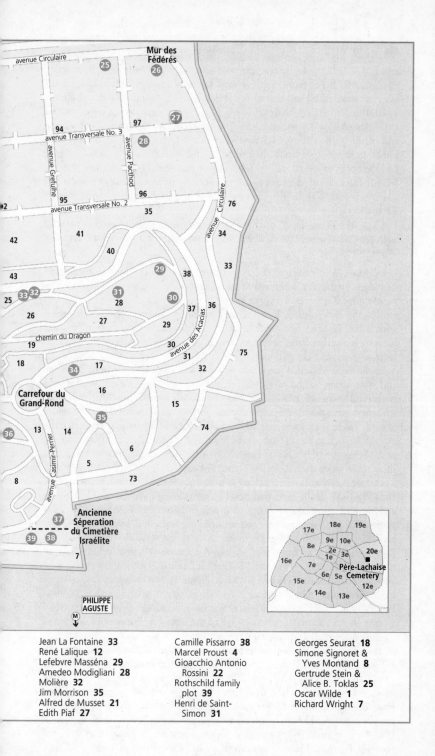

avenue Circulaire

Mur des Fédérés

⑤25   ⑥26

97   ㉗27

94   avenue Transversale No. 3
㉘28

95   avenue Transversale No. 2   76
35

42   41   34

43   40   33

㉙29   38

㉛31   ㉚30   36
28

33 32   37   29
26   27   avenue des Acacias
19   chemin du Dragon   30   31   75

18   17   32

Carrefour du Grand-Rond   16

㉟35   15

36   13   14   74

6

5   73

8

Ancienne Séperation du Cimetière Israélite

㊲37

㊵39 ㊳38

7

PHILIPPE AGUSTE
Ⓜ
↓

Jean La Fontaine **33**	Camille Pissarro **38**	Georges Seurat **18**
René Lalique **12**	Marcel Proust **4**	Simone Signoret &
Lefebvre Masséna **29**	Gioacchio Antonio	Yves Montand **8**
Amedeo Modigliani **28**	Rossini **22**	Gertrude Stein &
Molière **32**	Rothschild family	Alice B. Toklas **25**
Jim Morrison **35**	plot **39**	Oscar Wilde **1**
Alfred de Musset **21**	Henri de Saint-	Richard Wright **7**
Edith Piaf **27**	Simon **31**	

11 Paris Underground

Les Catacombes ✪ Every year an estimated 50,000 visitors explore some 910m (2,985 ft.) of tunnel in these dank catacombs to look at 6 million ghoulishly arranged skull-and-crossbones skeletons. First opened to the public in 1810, this "empire of the dead" is now illuminated with electric lights over its entire length. In the Middle Ages, the catacombs were quarries, but by the end of the 18th century, overcrowded cemeteries were becoming a menace to public health. City officials decided to use the catacombs as a burial ground, and the bones of several million persons were transferred here. In 1830, the prefect of Paris closed the catacombs, considering them obscene and indecent. During World War II, the catacombs were the headquarters of the French Resistance.

1 place Denfert-Rochereau, 14e. ☎ 01-43-22-47-63. www.multimania.com/houze. Admission 5€ ($5.75) adults, 3.30€ ($3.80) seniors, 2.50€ ($2.90) ages 16–25, free for children under 14. Tues–Sun 2–4pm. Métro: Denfert-Rochereau.

Les Egouts ✪ Some sociologists assert that the sophistication of a society can be judged by the way it disposes of waste. If so, Paris receives good marks for its mostly invisible sewer network. Victor Hugo is credited with making them famous in *Les Misérables:* Jean Valjean takes flight through them, "all dripping with slime, his soul filled with a strange light." Hugo also wrote, "Paris has beneath it another Paris, a Paris of sewers, which has its own streets, squares, lanes, arteries, and circulation."

In the early Middle Ages, drinking water was taken directly from the Seine and wastewater poured onto fields or thrown onto the then-unpaved streets, transforming the urban landscape into a sea of rather smelly mud. Around 1200, the streets were paved with cobblestones, and open sewers ran down the center of each. These open sewers helped spread the Black Death, which devastated the city. In 1370, a vaulted sewer was built on rue Montmartre, draining effluents into a Seine tributary. During Louis XIV's reign, improvements were made, but the state of waste disposal in Paris remained deplorable.

During Napoleon's reign, 31km (19 miles) of sewer were constructed beneath Paris. By 1850, as the Industrial Revolution made the manufacture of iron pipe and steam-digging equipment more practical, Baron Haussmann developed a system that used separate channels for drinking water and sewage. By 1878, it was 580km (360 miles) long. Beginning in 1894, the network was enlarged, and laws required that discharge of all waste and storm-water runoff be funneled into the sewers. Between 1914 and 1977, an additional 966km (600 miles) were added. Today, the network of sewers is 2,093km (1,300 miles) long. It contains freshwater mains, compressed air pipes, telephone cables, and pneumatic tubes. Every day, 1.2 million cubic meters of wastewater are collected and processed by a plant in the suburb of Achères. One of the largest in Europe, it's capable of treating more than 2 million cubic meters of sewage per day.

The city's sewers are constructed around four principal tunnels, one 5.5m (18 ft.) wide and 4.5m (15 ft.) high. It's like an underground city, with the street names clearly labeled. Each branch pipe bears the number of the building to which it's connected. These underground passages are truly mammoth. Sewer tours begin at pont de l'Alma on the Left Bank, where a stairway leads into the city's bowels. However, you often have to wait in line as much as half an hour. Visiting times might change during bad weather, as a storm can make the sewers dangerous. The tour consists of a film, a small museum visit, and then a short trip through the maze. *Warning:* The smell is pretty bad, especially in summer.

Pont de l'Alma, 7e. ✆ **01-53-68-27-82.** Admission 3.80€ ($4.35) adults, 3.05€ ($3.50) students, seniors, and children 5–12, free for children under 5. May–Oct Sat–Wed 11am–5pm. Closed Nov–Apr. Métro: Alma-Marceau. RER: Pont de l'Alma.

12 A Day at the Races

Paris boasts an army of avid horse-racing fans who get to the city's eight race-tracks whenever possible. Information on current races is available in newspapers and magazines like *Tierce, Paris-Turf, France-Soir,* and *L'Equipe,* all sold at kiosks throughout the city.

The epicenter of Paris horse racing is the **Hippodrome de Longchamp** ★★★, in the Bois de Boulogne, 16e (✆ **01-44-30-75-00;** RER or Métro: Porte Maillot, then a shuttle bus). Established in 1855, during the autocratic but pleasure-loving reign of Napoleon III, it's the most prestigious, boasts the greatest number of promising thoroughbreds, and awards the largest purse in France. The most important events at Longchamp are the **Grand Prix de Paris** in late June and the **Prix de l'Arc de Triomphe** in early October.

Another racing venue is the **Hippodrome d'Auteuil,** also in the Bois de Boulogne (✆ **01-40-71-47-47;** Métro: Porte Auteuil, and then walk). Known for its steeplechases and obstacle courses, it sometimes attracts more than 50,000 Parisians at a time. Spectators appreciate the park's promenades as much as they do the equestrian events. Races are conducted early March to late November.

13 Neighborhood Highlights

Some of Paris's neighborhoods are attractions unto themselves. The 1st arrondissement probably has a higher concentration of attractions per block than anywhere else. Though all Paris's neighborhoods are worth wandering, some are more interesting than others. This is especially true of Montmartre, the Latin Quarter, and the Marais, so we've featured them as walking tours in chapter 8.

ISLANDS IN THE STREAM: ILE DE LA CITE & ILE ST-LOUIS

ILE DE LA CITE ★★★, **WHERE PARIS WAS BORN**   Medieval Paris, that blend of grotesquerie and Gothic beauty, bloomed on this island in the Seine (Métro: Cité). Ile de la Cité, which the Seine protects like a surrounding moat, has been known as "the cradle" of Paris ever since. As Sauval once observed, "The Island of the City is shaped like a great ship, sunk in the mud, lengthwise in the stream, in about the middle of the Seine."

Few have written more movingly about its heyday than Victor Hugo, who invited the reader "to observe the fantastic display of lights against the darkness of that gloomy labyrinth of buildings; cast upon it a ray of moonlight, showing the city in glimmering vagueness, with its towers lifting their great heads from that foggy sea." Medieval Paris was a city not only of legends and lovers but of blood-curdling tortures and brutalities. No story illustrates this better than the affair of Abélard and his charge Héloïse, whose jealous uncle hired ruffians to castrate her lover. (The attack predictably quelled their ardor; he became a monk, she an abbess.) You can see their graves at Père-Lachaise (see "Cemeteries").

Because you'll want to see all the attractions on Ile de la Cité, begin at the cathedral of Notre-Dame. Proceed next to the Sainte-Chapelle moving west. After a visit there, you can head northeast to the Conciergerie. To cap off your visit, and for the best scenic view, walk to the northwestern end of the island for a view of the bridge, pont Neuf, seen from Square du Vert Galant.

The island's stars, as mentioned, are **Notre-Dame, Sainte-Chapelle,** and the **Conciergerie**—all described earlier. Across from Notre-Dame is the **Hôtel Dieu,** built from 1866 to 1878 in neo-Florentine style. This is central Paris's main hospital, replacing the 12th-century hospital that ran the island's entire width. Go in the main entrance and take a break in the spacious neoclassical courtyard whose small garden and fountain make a quiet oasis.

Don't miss the ironically named **pont Neuf** ("New Bridge") at the tip of the island opposite from Notre-Dame. The span isn't new—it's Paris's oldest bridge, begun in 1578 and finished in 1604. In its day it had two unique features: It was paved and it wasn't flanked with houses and shops. Actually, with 12 arches, it's not one bridge but two (they don't quite line up)—one from the Right Bank to the island and the other from the Left Bank to the island. At the **Musée Carnavalet** (p. 192), a painting called *The Spectacle of Buffoons* shows what the bridge was like between 1665 and 1669. Duels were fought on it, the nobility's great coaches crossed it, peddlers sold their wares, and entertainers like Tabarin went there to seek a few coins from the gawkers. As public facilities were lacking, the bridge also served as a de facto outhouse.

Just past pont Neuf is the "prow" of the island, the **square du Vert Galant.** Pause to look at the equestrian statue of beloved Henri IV, who was assassinated by Ravaillac (see the entry for the Conciergerie). A true king of his people, Henri was also (to judge from accounts) regal in the boudoir—hence the nickname "Vert Galant" (Old Spark). Gabrielle d'Estrées and Henriette d'Entragues were his best-known mistresses, but they had to share him with countless others, some of whom would casually catch his eye as he was riding along the streets. In fond memory of the king, the little triangular park continues to attract lovers. It appears to be a sunken garden because it remains at its natural level—the rest of the Cité has been built up during the centuries.

ILE ST-LOUIS ★★   Cross pont St-Louis, the footbridge behind Notre-Dame, to Ile St-Louis, and you'll find a world of tree-shaded quays, town houses with courtyards, restaurants, and antiques shops. (You can also take the Métro to Sully-Morland or Pont Marie and cross the bridge.) The fraternal twin of Ile de la Cité, Ile St-Louis is primarily residential; nearly all the houses were built from 1618 to 1660, lending the island a remarkable architectural unity. Plaques on the facades identify the former residences of the famous. **Marie Curie** lived at 36 quai de Béthune, near pont de la Tournelle, and sculptor **Camille Claudel** (Rodin's mistress) lived and worked in the Hôtel de Jassaud, 19 quai de Bourbon.

The most exciting mansion—though perhaps with the saddest history—is the 1656–57 **Hôtel de Lauzun,** 17 quai d'Anjou, built for Charles Gruyn des Bordes. He married Geneviève de Mouy and had her initials engraved on much of the interior decor; their happiness was short-lived, because he was convicted of embezzlement and sent to prison in 1662. The next occupant was the duc de Lauzun, who resided there for only 3 years. He had been a favorite of Louis XIV until he asked for the hand of the king's cousin, the duchesse de Montpensier. Louis refused and had Lauzun tossed into the Bastille. Eventually the duchesse pestered Louis into releasing him, and they married secretly and moved here in 1682, but domestic bliss eluded them—they fought often and separated in 1684. Lauzun sold the house to the grandnephew of Cardinal Richelieu and his wife, who had such a grand time throwing parties, they went bankrupt. Baron

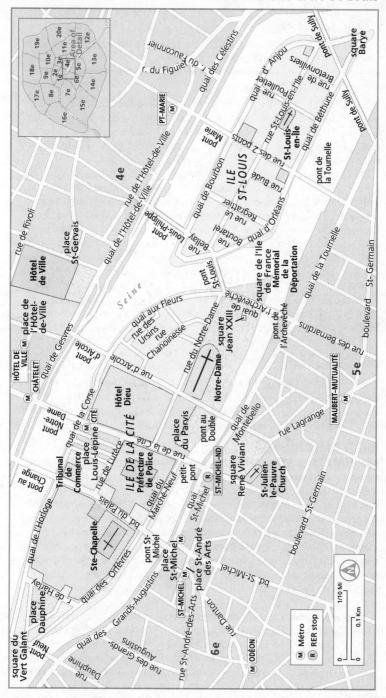

> **Tips Ice Cream**
>
> If you need a refreshment break on Ile St-Louis, head for ice cream at **Berthillon**, 31 rue St-Louis-en-l'Ile.

Pichon bought it in 1842 and rented it out to a hashish club. Tenants Baudelaire and Gaultier regularly held hashish soirees in which Baudelaire did research for his *Les Paradis artificiels* and Gaultier for his *Le Club hes hachichins.* Now the mansion belongs to the city and is used to house official guests. The interior is sometimes open for temporary exhibits, so call the tourist office.

Hôtel Lambert, 2 quai d'Anjou, was built in 1645 for Nicholas Lambert de Thorigny. The portal on rue St-Louis-en-l'Ile gives some idea of the splendor within, but the house's most startling element is the oval gallery extending into the garden. Designed to feature a library or art collection, it's best viewed from the beginning of quai d'Anjou. Voltaire and his mistress, Emilie de Breteuil, lived here—their quarrels were legendary. The mansion also housed the Polish royal family for over a century, before becoming the residence of actress Michèle Morgan. It now belongs to the Rothschild family and isn't open to the public.

Nos. 9, 11, 13, and 15 quai d'Anjou also belonged to the Lamberts. At **no. 9** is the house where painter/sculptor/lithographer Honoré Daumier lived from 1846 to 1863, producing hundreds of caricatures satirizing the bourgeoisie and attacking government corruption. He was imprisoned because of his 1832 cartoon of Louis-Philippe swallowing bags of gold extracted from the people.

Near the Hôtel de Lauzun is the church of **St-Louis-en-l'Ile,** no. 19 bis rue St-Louis-en-l'Ile. Despite a dour exterior, the ornate interior is one of the finest examples of Jesuit baroque. Built between 1664 and 1726, this church is still the site of many weddings—with all the white stone and gilt, you'll feel as if you're inside a wedding cake. Look for the 1926 plaque reading "In grateful memory of St. Louis in whose honor the city of St. Louis, Missouri, USA, is named."

RIGHT BANK HIGHLIGHTS

LES HALLES ✿   For 8 centuries, **Les Halles** (Métro: Les Halles; RER: Châtelet–Les Halles) was the city's major wholesale fruit, meat, and vegetable market. In the 19th century, Zola called it "the underbelly of Paris." The smock-clad vendors, beef carcasses, and baskets of vegetables all belong to the past, for the original market, with zinc-roofed Second Empire "iron umbrellas," has been torn down. Today the action has moved to a steel-and-glass edifice at Rungis, a suburb near Orly. In 1979 the **Forum des Halles,** 1–7 rue Pierre-Lescot, 1e, opened. This large complex, much of it underground, contains shops, restaurants, and movie theaters. Many of the shops are unattractive, but others contain a wide display of merchandise that has made the mall popular with residents and visitors.

For many visitors, a night on the town still ends in the wee hours with a bowl of onion soup at Les Halles, usually at **Au Pied de Cochon (The Pig's Foot),** 6 rue Coquillière, 1e (p. 120), or at **Au Chien Qui Fume (The Smoking Dog),** 33 rue du Pont-Neuf, 1e (© 01-42-36-07-42). One of the classic scenes of old Paris was elegantly dressed Parisians (many fresh from Maxim's) standing at a bar drinking cognac with blood-smeared butchers. Some writers have suggested that 19th-century poet Gérard de Nerval introduced the custom of frequenting Les Halles at such an unearthly hour.

A newspaper correspondent described today's scene: "Les Halles is trying to stay alive as one of the few places where one can eat at any hour of the night."

LEFT BANK HIGHLIGHTS

ST-GERMAIN-DES-PRES ★★

This neighborhood in the 6th arrondissement (Métro: St-Germain-des-Prés) was the postwar home of existentialism, associated with Sartre, de Beauvoir, Camus, and an intellectual bohemian crowd that gathered at **Café de Flore, Brasserie Lipp,** and **Les Deux Magots** (see chapter 6). Among them, black-clad poet and singer Juliette Greco was known as *la muse de St-Germain-des-Prés,* and to Sartre she was the woman who had "millions of poems in her throat." Her long hair, black slacks, black sweater, and black sandals launched a fashion trend adopted by young women everywhere. In the 1950s, new names appeared, like Françoise Sagan, Gore Vidal, and James Baldwin, but by the 1960s, tourists were firmly entrenched.

St-Germain-des-Prés still retains an intellectually stimulating bohemian street life, full of many interesting bookshops, art galleries, *cave* (basement) clubs,

Mother of the Lost Generation

"So Paris was the place that suited those of us that were to create the twentieth century art and literature, naturally enough." Gertrude Stein, who made this pronouncement, wasn't known for her modesty.

In the 1920s, she and her lover, Alice B. Toklas, became the most famous expats in Paris. To get an invitation to call on Lovey and Pussy (nicknames for Gertrude and Alice) at **27 rue de Fleurus,** in the heart of Montparnasse, was to be invited into the innermost circle of expatriate Paris. Though their former residence is in private hands and you can't go inside, literary fans flock to this fabled address to stare at the facade.

Though Gertrude didn't achieve popular success until the 1933 publication of her *Autobiography of Alice B. Toklas,* she was adored by many members of the Lost Generation—all except Ernest Hemingway, who tarred her in his posthumous memoir, *A Moveable Feast.* But to many sensitive young men (often gay) arriving from America in the 1920s, La Stein was "The Mother of Us All." These young fans hung on to her every word, while Alice baked her notorious hash brownies in the kitchen.

At rue de Fleurus, Gertrude and Alice surrounded themselves with modern paintings, including pieces by Vallotton, Toulouse-Lautrec, Picasso, Gauguin, and Matisse. Gertrude paid $1,000 for her first Matisse and $30 for her first Picasso. The Saturday-night soirées became legendary, and one writer said her salon was an international conspiracy to promote modern art. Many denounced Gertrude, however, including avant-garde magazines of the time, which called her a "fraud, egomaniac, and publicity seeking." Braque called her claim to influence art in Paris "nonsense."

In spite of the attacks, jokes, and speculation, Stein, at least in public, kept her ego intact. Bernard Fay once told her he'd met three people in his life who ranked as geniuses: Gide, Picasso, and herself. "Why include Gide?" Stein asked.

bistros, and coffeehouses. But the stars of the area are two churches, **St-Germain-des-Prés,** 3 place St-Germain-des-Prés, and **St-Sulpice,** rue St-Sulpice (for both, see "The Important Churches," earlier in this chapter), and the **Musée National Eugène Delacroix,** 6 place de Furstemburg (p. 194). Nearby, **rue Visconti** was designed for pushcarts and is worth visiting today. At **nos. 20–24** is the residence where dramatist Jean-Baptiste Racine died in 1699. And at **no. 17** is the house where Balzac established his printing press in 1825. (The venture ended in bankruptcy, forcing the author back to his writing desk.) Such celebrated actresses as Champmeslé and Clairon also lived here.

MONTPARNASSE ✯✯   For the "lost generation," life centered around the cafes of Montparnasse, at the border of the 6th and 14th arrondissements (Métro: Montparnasse-Bienvenue). Hangouts like the **Dôme, Coupole, Rotonde,** and **Sélect** became legendary, as artists—especially American expats—turned their backs on touristy Montmartre. Picasso, Modigliani, and Man Ray came this way, and Hemingway was also a popular figure. So was Fitzgerald when he was poor (when he wasn't, you'd find him at the Ritz). Faulkner, MacLeish, Duncan, Miró, Joyce, Ford Madox Ford, and even Trotsky spent time here.

The most notable exception was Gertrude Stein, who never frequented the cafes. To see her, you had to wait for an invitation to her salon at **27 rue de Fleurus.** She bestowed this favor on Sherwood Anderson, Elliot Paul, Ezra Pound, and, for a time, Hemingway. When Pound launched himself into a beloved chair and broke it, he incurred Stein's wrath, and Hemingway decided there wasn't "much future in men being friends with great women."

American expatriate writer Natalie Barney, who moved to Paris as a student in 1909 and stayed for over 60 years, held her grand salons at **20 rue Jacob** (actually in St-Germain-des-Prés). Every Friday, her salon attracted the literati of her day, like Gertrude Stein, Djuna Barnes, Colette, Sherwood Anderson, T. S. Eliot, Janet Flanner, James Joyce, Sylvia Beach, Marcel Proust, and William Carlos Williams. The group met on and off for half a century, interrupted only by two world wars. Near place de Furstemburg, Barney's former residence is landmarked but not open to the public. In the garden you can see a small Doric temple bearing the inscription *A l'Amitié,* "to friendship."

Aside from the literary legends, one of the most notable characters was **Kiki de Montparnasse** (actually named Alice Prin). She was raised by her grandmother in Burgundy until her mother called her to Paris to work. When a sculptor discovered her, she became an artist's model and adopted her new name; soon she became a prostitute, and would bare her breasts to anyone who'd pay her three francs. She sang at **Le Jockey,** 127 bd. du Montparnasse, which no longer exists: In her black hose and garters, she captivated dozens of men, among them Frederick Kohner, who went so far as to entitle his memoirs *Kiki of Montparnasse.* Kiki later wrote her own memoirs, with an introduction by Hemingway. Papa called her "a Queen," noting that was "very different from being a lady."

Completed in 1973 and rising 206m (676 ft.) above the skyline, the **Tour Montparnasse** (☎ 01-45-38-52-56) was denounced by some as "bringing Manhattan to Paris." The city soon passed an ordinance outlawing any further structures of this size in the heart of Paris. Today, the modern tower houses an underground shopping mall as well as much of the infrastructure for the Gare de Montparnasse rail station. You can ride an elevator up to the 56th floor (where you'll find a bar and restaurant), and then climb three flights to the roof

---

Moments Memorial to a Princess

Place de l'Alma (Métro: Alma-Marceau) has been turned into a tribute to the late Diana, princess of Wales, killed in an auto accident August 31, 1997, in a nearby underpass. The bronze flame in the center is a replica of the one in the Statue of Liberty and was a gift from the *International Herald Tribune* to honor Franco-American friendship. Many bouquets and messages (and even graffiti) are still placed around the flame.

Paris has also opened the **Center for Nature Discovery, Garden in Memory of Diana, Princess of Wales,** at 21 rue des Blancs-Manteaux in the Marais. The small park, which you can visit daily during daylight hours, is devoted to teaching children about nature and gardening, and contains flowers, vegetables, and decorative plants.

---

terrace. The view encompasses virtually every important Paris monument, including Sacré-Coeur, Notre-Dame, and La Défense. Admission to the tower costs 7€ ($8.05) for adults, 6€ ($6.90) for seniors, 5.50€ ($6.35) for students, and 4.55€ ($5.25) for children 5 to 14 (4 and under free). April to September, it's open daily from 9:30am to 11:30pm; October to March, hours are Monday to Friday from 9:30am to 10:30pm.

The life of Montparnasse still centers around its cafes and exotic nightclubs, many only a shadow of what they used to be. Its heart is at the crossroads of **boulevard Raspail** and **boulevard du Montparnasse,** one of the settings of *The Sun Also Rises.* Hemingway wrote that "boulevard Raspail always made dull riding." Rodin's controversial statue of Balzac swathed in a large cape stands guard over the prostitutes who cluster around the pedestal. Balzac seems to be the only one in Montparnasse who doesn't feel the weight of time.

14 Especially for Kids

If you're staying on the Right Bank, take the children for a stroll through the **Jardin des Tuileries** (p. 209), where there are donkey rides, ice-cream stands, and a marionette show; at the circular pond, you can rent a toy boat. On the Left Bank, similar treats exist in the **Jardin du Luxembourg** (p. 209). After a visit to the Eiffel Tower, you can take the kids for a donkey ride in the **Champ de Mars.**

A Paris tradition, **puppet shows** are worth seeing for their colorful productions—they're a genuine French child's experience. At the Jardin du Luxembourg, puppets reenact plots set in Gothic castles and Oriental palaces; many critics say the best puppet shows are held in the Champ de Mars.

On Sunday afternoon, French families head to the **Butte Montmartre** to bask in the fiesta atmosphere. You can join in: Take the Métro to Anvers and walk to the *funiculaire* (the cable car that carries you up to Sacré-Coeur). Once up top, follow the crowds to place du Tertre, where a Sergeant Pepper–style band will usually be blasting off-key and you can have the kids' pictures sketched by local artists. You can take in the views of Paris from the various vantage points and treat your children to ice cream. For a walking tour of Montmartre, see chapter 8.

Your kids may want to check out the Gallic versions of Mickey Mouse and his pals, so see chapter 11, "Side Trips from Paris," for **Disneyland Paris.**

Finds The "Beach" of Paris

Relaxing under a palm tree on a chaise longue sounds more Caribbean than Parisian but a nearly 4.8km (3-mile) stretch of sandy shore has opened along the Seine. With the Eiffel Tower looming in the background, visitors and locals can splash in fountains, swing in hammocks, play volleyball, or else enjoy a picnic. Just don't go into the polluted water of the murky Seine. The Paris beach opened in the late summer of 2003, after tons of sand were poured into concrete bases along the river. The beach is free to all.

MUSEUMS

Cité des Sciences et de l'Industrie ★★ *Kids*   A city of science and industry has risen here from unlikely ashes. When a slaughterhouse was built on the site in the 1960s, it was touted as the most modern of its kind. It was abandoned in 1974, and the location on the city's northern edge presented the government with a problem. What could be built in such an unlikely place? In 1986, the converted premises opened as the world's most expensive ($642 million) science complex, designed to "modernize mentalities" in the service of modernizing society.

The place is so vast, with so many exhibits, that a single visit gives only an idea of the scope of the Cité. Busts of Plato, Hippocrates, and a double-faced Janus gaze silently at a tube-filled riot of high-tech girders, glass, and lights. The sheer dimensions pose a challenge to the curators of its constantly changing exhibits. Some exhibits are couched in Gallic humor—imagine using the comic-strip adventures of a jungle explorer to explain seismographic activity. **Explora,** a permanent exhibit, occupies the three upper levels of the building and examines four themes: the universe, life, matter, and communication. The Cité also has a **multimedia library,** a **planetarium,** and an **"inventorium"** for kids. The silver-skinned geodesic dome called **La Géode**—a 34m-high (112-ft.) sphere with a 370-seat theater—projects the closest thing to a 3-D cinema in Europe and has several surprising additions, including a real submarine.

The Cité is in the **Parc de La Villette,** an ultramodern science park surrounding some of Paris's newest housing developments. This is Paris's largest park—twice the size of the Tuileries. The playgrounds, fountains, and sculptures are all innovative. Here you'll find a belvedere, a video workshop for children, and information about exhibits and events, along with a cafe and restaurant.

In the Parc de La Villette, 30 av. Corentine-Cariou, La Villette, 19e. (© 01-40-05-80-00. www.cite-sciences.fr. Cité Pass (entrance to all exhibits) 7.50€ ($8.65) adults, free for children 7 and under. Géode 8.75€ ($10). Tues–Sat 10am–6pm; Sun 10am–7pm. Métro: Porte de La Villette.

Musée de la Marine ★★ *Kids*   If your children have saltwater in their veins, you may want to take them to this museum. Old ship models abound, like the galley *La Réale,* the *Royal-Louis,* the ivory *Ville de Dieppe,* the gorgeous *Valmy,* and a **barge** built in 1811 for Napoleon I that was used to carry Napoleon III and Empress Eugénie on their visit to Brest in 1858. You'll find some souvenirs of explorer Laperouse's wreck on Vanikoro Island in 1788 as well as many documents and artifacts concerning merchant fishing and pleasure fleets, oceanography, and hydrography, with films illustrating the subjects. Thematic exhibits explain ancient wooden shipbuilding and the development of scientific instruments.

In the Palais de Chaillot, place du Trocadéro, 16e. (© 01-53-65-69-69. Admission 7€ ($8.05) adults, 5.40€ ($6.20) ages 8–25 and over 65, free for children 7 and under. Wed–Mon 10am–6pm. Métro: Trocadéro.

Musée Grévin ★ *Kids*   The Grévin is Paris's number-one waxworks. Comparisons to Madame Tussaud's are almost irresistible, but it isn't all blood and gore and doesn't shock as much as Tussaud's. It presents French history in a series of tableaux. Depicted are the 1429 consecration of Charles VII in the Cathédrale de Reims (armored Joan of Arc, carrying her standard, stands behind the king); Marguerite de Valois, first wife of Henri IV, meeting on a secret stairway with La Molle, who was soon to be decapitated; Catherine de Médicis with Florentine alchemist David Ruggieri; Louis XV and Mozart at the home of the marquise de Pompadour; and Napoleon on a rock at St. Helena, reviewing his victories and defeats. There are also displays of contemporary sports and political figures, as well as 50 of the world's best-loved film stars.

Two shows are staged frequently throughout the day. The first, called the **"Palais des Mirages,"** starts off as a sort of Temple of Brahma and, through magically distorting mirrors, changes into an enchanted forest, then a fête at the Alhambra in Granada. A magician is the star of the second show, **"Le Cabinet Fantastique";** he entertains children of all ages.

10 bd. Montmartre, 9e. ☎ 01-47-70-85-05. Admission 16€ ($18) adults, 9€ ($10) children 14 and under. Daily 10am–6pm. Ticket office closes 1 hr. before museum. Métro: Grands Boulevards.

Musée National d'Histoire Naturelle (Museum of Natural History) ★ *Kids*
This museum in the Jardin des Plantes, founded in 1635 as a research center by Guy de la Brosse, physician to Louis XIII, has a range of science and nature exhibits. The museum's **Grande Gallery of Evolution** recently received a $90 million restoration. At the entrance, a 26m (85 ft.) skeleton of a whale greets you. One display containing the skeletons of dinosaurs and mastodons is dedicated to endangered and vanished species, and there are galleries specializing in paleontology, anatomy, mineralogy, and botany. Within the museum's grounds are **tropical hothouses** containing thousands of species of unusual plant life and a **menagerie** with small animals in simulated natural habitats.

57 rue Cuvier, 5e. ☎ 01-40-79-30-00. www.mnhn.fr. Admission 7€ ($8.05) adults, 5€ ($5.75) students/seniors (over 60)/kids 4–16. Wed–Mon 10am–5pm. Métro: Jussieu or Gare d'Austerlitz.

AN AMUSEMENT PARK

Jardin d'Acclimatation ★ *Kids*   Paris's definitive children's park is the 10-hectare (25-acre) Jardin d'Acclimation in the northern part of the Bois de Boulogne. This is the kind of place that amuses tykes and adults, but not teenagers. The visit starts with a ride on a green-and-yellow narrow-gauge train from Porte Maillot to the Jardin entrance, through a stretch of wooded park. The train operates at 30-minute intervals Wednesday, Saturday, and Sunday from 10:30am until the park closes; one-way fare costs 1.25€ ($1.45). En route you'll find a **house of mirrors,** an **archery range,** a **miniature-golf course, zoo animals,** a **bowling alley,** a **puppet theater** (performances Thurs, Sat, Sun, and holidays), a **playground,** a **hurdle-racing course, junior-scale rides, shooting galleries,** and **waffle stalls.** You can trot the kids off on a **pony** or join them in a **boat** on a mill-stirred lagoon. **La Prévention Routière** is a miniature roadway operated by the Paris police: Youngsters drive through in small cars equipped to start and stop, and are required by two genuine gendarmes to obey street signs and light changes. Inside the gate is an easy-to-follow map. The park is circular—follow the road in either direction and it'll take you all the way around and bring you back to the train at the end.

In the Bois de Boulogne, 16e. ☎ 01-40-67-90-82. Admission 2.50€ ($2.90), free for children 3 and under. June–Sept daily 10am–7pm; Oct–May daily 10am–6pm. Métro: Sablons.

A ZOO

Parc Zoologique de Paris *(Kids)*   There's a modest zoo in the Jardin des Plantes, but without a doubt, the best zoo is here on the southeastern outskirts of Paris, quickly reachable by Métro. Many of this modern zoo's animals, which seem happy and are playful, live in settings similar to their natural habitats, hemmed in by rock barriers, not bars or cages. You'll never see an animal in a cage too small for it. The lion has an entire veldt to himself, and you can lock eyes comfortably across a deep protective moat. On a cement mountain like Disneyland's Matterhorn, exotic breeds of mountain goats and sheep leap from ledge to ledge or pose gracefully for hours while watching the penguins in their pools at the mountain's foot. Keep well back from the bear pools or you might get wet.

In the Bois de Vincennes, 53 av. de St-Maurice, 12e. © 01-44-75-20-10. Admission 8€ ($9.20) adults, 5€ ($5.75) children and students 4–25/adults over 60, free for children 3 and under. Daily 9am–5:30pm (to 5pm Dec–Mar). Métro: Porte Dorée.

15 Organized Tours

BY BUS

Tours are offered by **Cityrama,** 149 rue St-Honoré, 1e (© **01-44-55-61-00;** Métro: Palais Royal or Musée du Louvre), which operates double-decker red-and-yellow buses with oversize windows and multilingual recorded commentaries giving an overview of Paris's history and monuments.

By far the most popular is a 2-hour bus ride, with recorded commentary in your choice of 10 languages, through Paris's monumental heart. Departing from place des Pyramides, adjacent to rue de Rivoli, 1e, it's offered eight times a day between May and October, and four times a day between November and April. The cost is 24€ ($28) per person; free for children under 12. Other, more specialized (and detailed) tours include a 3½-hour **"Artistic Tour"** that encompasses the interiors of Notre-Dame and the Louvre (Mon and Wed–Sat, departing at 9:45am), priced at 48€ ($55). Guided tours to the mammoth royal palace at **Versailles** depart twice a day (at 9:30am and 2:45pm) year-round for a price of 58€ ($67) per person. And 5-hour jaunts to the majestic gothic cathedral at **Chartres** depart every Tuesday, Thursday, and Saturday April to October at 1:45pm for a per-person price of 48€ ($55). Tours of **Paris by night** depart at 10pm April to October for a price of 24€ ($28) per person. Any of these night tours can be supplemented—for an additional fee—with add-ons that include river cruises on the Seine and attendance at selected cabaret shows.

Moments **Friday Night "Rando" Fever**

The Paris Roller Rando takes over the city on Friday nights, "rando" being short for *randonnée,* meaning tour or excursion. The starting time is around 10pm at the place de l'Italia (also the name of the Métro stop). Roller folk from Paris and throughout Ile de France amass here to begin their 3-hour weekly journey through the city on rollerblades. Every Friday three motorcycle policemen lead the way with dome lights flashing, signaling moving cars to get out of the way. First-aid wagons follow the "rollers." On an average night in Paris some 20,000 rollers show up. Many visitors like to stay up late that night to watch these "mad, mad Parisians" in all their crazed "rollermania."

CRUISES ON THE SEINE

A Seine boat tour provides sweeping vistas of the riverbanks and some of the best views of Notre-Dame. Many of the boats have open sun decks, bars, and restaurants. **Bateaux-Mouche** cruises (© 01-40-76-99-99; Métro: Alma-Marceau) depart from the Right Bank, next to pont de l'Alma, and last about 75 minutes, costing 7€ ($8.05) for adults and 4€ ($4.60) for children 5 to 15. May to October, tours leave daily at 20- to 30-minute intervals, beginning at 10am and ending at 11:30pm; November to April, there are at least nine departures daily from 11am to 9pm, with a schedule that changes according to demand and the weather. Three-hour **dinner cruises** depart daily at 8:30pm and cost 125€ ($144), depending on which prix fixe menu you order; jackets and ties are required for men. Less formal **lunch cruises,** departing every day at 1pm and returning about 2 hours later, cost 50€ ($58) per person.

Some people prefer longer excursions on the Seine and its canals. The 3-hour **Seine et le Canal St-Martin** tour, offered by **Paris Canal** (© 01-42-40-96-97), requires reservations. The tour begins at 9:30am on the quays in front of the Musée d'Orsay (Métro: Solférino) and at 2:30pm in front of the Cité des Sciences et de l'Industrie at Parc de La Villette (Métro: Porte de La Villette). Excursions negotiate the waterways of Paris, including the Seine, an underground tunnel below place de la Bastille, and the Canal St-Martin. Tours are offered twice daily from mid-March to mid-November; the rest of the year, on Sunday only. The cost is 16€ ($18) for adults, free for children under 4. With the exception of trips on Sundays and holidays, prices are usually reduced to 12€ ($14) for students and seniors, and to 9€ ($10) for children 4 to 11.

BIKE TOURS

The best are offered by **Mike's Bike Tours** (© 01-56-58-10-54), departing from avenue Gustave-Eiffel near the tower (look for a large green flag advertising the tours). From May to August 15, tours leave daily at 11am and 3:30pm, costing 25€ ($29). At other times of the year, departures are only at 11am. Night tours are at 7pm Sunday and Friday. You get an English-speaking look at Paris almost entirely on sidewalks, in parks, and along the Seine, taking in the most famous landmarks, like the Louvre and Notre-Dame.

Strolling Around Paris

The best way to discover Paris is on foot. Our favorite walks are along the Seine and down the Champs-Elysées from the Arc de Triomphe to the Louvre. In this chapter we highlight the attractions of Montmartre, the Latin Quarter, and the Marais.

For more walking tours in the City of Light, see *Frommer's Memorable Walks in Paris.*

WALKING TOUR 1 **MONTMARTRE**

Start:	Place Pigalle (Métro: Pigalle).
Finish:	Place Pigalle.
Time:	5 hours, more if you break for lunch. It's a 4km (2½-mile) trek.
Best Time:	Any day it isn't raining. Set out by 10am at the latest.
Worst Time:	After dark.

There are soft-white three-story houses and slender barren trees sticking up from the ground like giant toothpicks—that's how Utrillo, befogged by absinthe, saw Montmartre. Toulouse-Lautrec painted it as a district of cabarets, circus freaks, and prostitutes. Today Montmartre remains truer to the dwarfish Toulouse-Lautrec's conception than it does to Utrillo's.

Before all this, Montmartre was a sleepy farm community with windmills dotting the landscape. The name has always been the subject of disagreement, some arguing it originated from the "mount of Mars," a Roman temple at the top of the hill, others asserting it's "mount of martyrs," a reference to the martyrdom of St. Denis, who was beheaded here with fellow saints Rusticus and Eleutherius.

Turn right after leaving the Métro station and go down boulevard de Clichy; turn left at the Cirque Medrano, and begin the climb up rue des Martyrs. On reaching rue des Abbesses, turn left and walk along this street, crossing place des Abbesses. Go uphill along rue Ravignan, which leads to tree-studded place Emile-Goudeau, in the middle of rue Ravignan. At no. 13, across from the Timhôtel, is the:

❶ Bateau-Lavoir (Boat Washhouse)

Though gutted by fire in 1970, this building, known as the cradle of cubism, has been reconstructed by the city. While Picasso lived here

(1904–12), he painted one of the world's most famous portraits, *The Third Rose* (of Gertrude Stein), as well as *Les Demoiselles d'Avignon*. Other residents were van Dongen, Jacob, and Gris; Modigliani, Rousseau, and Braque had studios nearby.

Rue Ravignan ends at place Jean-Baptiste-Clément. Go to the end of the street and cross onto rue Norvins (on your right). Here rues Norvins, St-Rustique, and des Saules collide a few steps from rue Poulbot, a scene captured in a famous Utrillo painting. Turn right and go down rue Poulbot. At no. 11 you come to:

Walking Tour 1: Montmartre

1 Bateau-Lavoir (Boat Washhouse)
2 Espace Dalí Montmartre
3 Place du Calvaire
4 Place du Tertre
5 St-Pierre
6 Sacré-Coeur
7 Musée de Vieux Montmartre
8 Cabaret des Assassins
9 Moulin de la Galette
10 Cimetière de Montmartre
11 Moulin Rouge
12 Boulevard de Clichy
13 Place Pigalle

② Espace Dalí Montmartre

The phantasmagoric world of Espace Dalí Montmartre (© **01-42-64-40-10**) features 300 original Dalí works, including his famous 1956 lithograph of Don Quixote.

Rue Poulbot crosses tiny:

③ Place du Calvaire

Here you find a panoramic view of Paris. On this square once lived artist/painter/lithographer Maurice Neumont (a plaque marks the house).

From place du Calvaire, head east along rue Gabrielle, taking the first left north along the tiny rue du Calvaire, which leads to:

④ Place du Tertre

This old town square is tourist central. All around the square are terrace restaurants with dance floors and colored lights, while Sacré-Coeur gleams through the trees. The cafes overflow with people, as do the indoor and outdoor art galleries. Some of the "artists" still wear berets (you'll be asked countless times if you want your portrait sketched). The square is so loaded with local color that it can seem gaudy and inauthentic.

TAKE A BREAK
Many restaurants in Montmartre, especially those around place du Tertre, are unabashed tourist traps. An exception is **La Crémaillère 1900**, 15 place du Tertre, 18e (© **01-46-06-58-59**). As its name suggests, this is a Belle Epoque dining room, retaining much of its original look, including many paintings. You can sit on the terrace opening onto the square or retreat to the courtyard garden. A full menu is served throughout the day, including a standard array of French classics. Go any time daily from noon to 12:30am.

Right off the square fronting rue du Mont-Cenis is:

⑤ St-Pierre

Originally a Benedictine abbey, this church has played many roles: a Temple of Reason during the Revolution, a food depot, a clothing store, and even a munitions factory. These days, one of Paris's oldest churches is back to being a church.

Facing St-Pierre, turn right and follow rue Azais to:

⑥ Sacré-Coeur

The basilica's Byzantine domes and bell tower loom above Paris and present a wide vista (see "The Top Attractions: From the Arc de Triomphe to the Tour Eiffel" in chapter 7). Behind the church, clinging to the hillside, are steep, crooked little streets that have survived the march of progress.

Facing the basilica, take the street on the left (rue du Cardinal-Guibert), then go left onto rue du Chevalier-de-la-Barre and right onto rue du Mont-Cenis. Continue on this street to rue Cortot, then turn left. At no. 12 is the:

⑦ Musée de Vieux Montmartre

Musée de Vieux Montmartre (© **01-46-06-61-11**) presents a collection of mementos of the neighborhood. Luminaries like Dufy, van Gogh, Renoir, and Suzanne Valadon and her son, Utrillo, occupied this 17th-century house, and it was here that Renoir put the final touches on his *Moulin de la Galette* (see below).

From the museum, turn right, heading up rue des Saules past a winery, a reminder of the days when Montmartre was a farming village on the outskirts of Paris. A grape-harvesting festival is held here every October. The intersection of rue des Saules and rue St-Vincent is one of the most visited and photographed corners of the butte. Here, on one corner, sits what was the famous old:

⑧ Cabaret des Assassins

This was long ago renamed **Au Lapin Agile** (see "Chansonniers" in chapter 10). Picasso and Utrillo frequented this little cottage, which numerous artists have patronized and painted. On any given afternoon, French folk tunes, love ballads, army songs, sea chanteys, and music hall ditties stream out of the cafe and onto the street.

Turn left on rue St-Vincent, passing the Cimetière St-Vincent on your right (see "Cemeteries" in chapter 7). Take a left onto rue Girardon and climb the stairs. In a minute or two, you'll spot on your right two of the *moulins* (windmills) that used to dot the butte. One of these, at no. 75, is the:

9 Moulin de la Galette

This windmill (entrance at 1 av. Junot) was built in 1622 and was immortalized in oil by Renoir (the painting is in the Musée d'Orsay). When it was turned into a dance hall in the 1860s, it was named for the *galettes* (cakes made with flour ground inside the mills) that were sold here. Later, Toulouse-Lautrec, van Gogh, and Utrillo visited the dance hall. A few steps away, at the angle of rue Lepic and rue Girardon, is the Moulin Radet, now part of a restaurant.

Turn right onto rue Lepic and walk past no. 54. In 1886, van Gogh lived here with his brother Guillaumin. Take a right turn onto rue Joseph-de-Maistre, then left again on rue Caulaincourt until you reach the:

10 Cimetière de Montmartre

This final resting place is second in fame only to Père-Lachaise and is the haunt of Nijinsky, Dumas fils, Stendhal, Degas, and Truffaut, among others (see "Cemeteries" in chapter 7).

From the cemetery, take avenue Rachel, turn left onto boulevard de Clichy, and go to place Blanche, where stands a windmill even better known than the one in Renoir's painting, the:

11 Moulin Rouge

One of the world's most talked about nightclubs, Toulouse-Lautrec immortalized the Moulin Rouge. The windmill is still here, and so is the cancan, but the rest has become an expensive, slick variety show with an emphasis on undraped females (see "Nightclubs & Cabarets" in chapter 10).

From place Blanche, you can begin a descent on:

12 Boulevard de Clichy

En route, you'll have to fight off the pornographers and hustlers trying to lure you into sex joints. With some rare exceptions, notably the citadels of the *chansonniers* (songwriters), boulevard de Clichy is one gigantic tourist trap. But everyone who comes to Paris invariably winds up here.

The boulevard strips and peels its way down to where you started:

13 Place Pigalle

The center of nudity in Paris was named after a French sculptor, Pigalle, whose closest brush with nudity was a depiction of Voltaire in the buff. Toulouse-Lautrec had his studio right off the square at 5 av. Frochot. Of course, place Pigalle was the notorious "Pig Alley" of World War II. When Edith Piaf was lonely and hungry, she sang in the alleyways, hoping to earn a few francs for the night.

WALKING TOUR 2 THE LATIN QUARTER

Start:	Place St-Michel (Métro: St-Michel).
Finish:	The Panthéon.
Time:	3 hours, not counting stops.
Best Time:	Any weekday from 9am to 4pm.
Worst Time:	Sunday morning, when everybody is asleep.

This is the precinct of the Université de Paris (known for its most famous branch, the Sorbonne), where students meet and fall in love over café crème and croissants. Rabelais named it the Quartier Latin after the students and the professors who spoke Latin in the classroom and on the streets. The sector teems with belly dancers, restaurants, cafes, bookstalls, *caveaux* (basement nightclubs), *clochards* (bums), *chiffonniers* (ragpickers), and *gamins* (kids).

A good starting point for your tour is:

❶ Place St-Michel

Balzac used to draw water from the fountain (Davioud's 1860 sculpture of St. Michel slaying the dragon) when he was a youth. This was the scene of frequent skirmishes between the Germans and the Resistance in the summer of 1944, and the names of those who died here are engraved on plaques around the square.

TAKE A BREAK
Open 24 hours, **Café le Départ St-Michel**, 1 place St-Michel ((*C* **01-43-54-24-55**), lies on the banks of the Seine. The decor is warmly modern, with etched mirrors reflecting the faces of a diversified crowd. If you want to fortify yourself for your walk, opt for one of the warm or cold snacks, including sandwiches.

To the south, you find:

❷ Boulevard St-Michel

Also called by locals Boul' Mich, this is the main street of the Latin Quarter as it heads south. This is a major tourist artery and won't give you a great insight into local life. For that, you can branch off onto any of the streets that feed into the boulevard, and find cafes, bars, gyro counters, ice-cream stands, crepe stands, and bistros like those pictured in movies set in Paris in the 1950s. The Paris Commune began here in 1871, as did the student uprisings of 1968.

From place St-Michel, with your back to the Seine, turn left down:

❸ Rue de la Huchette

This typical street was the setting of Elliot Paul's *The Last Time I Saw Paris* (1942). Paul first wandered here "on a soft summer evening, and entirely by chance," in 1923 and then moved into no. 28, the Hôtel Mont-Blanc. Though much has changed, some of the buildings are so old they have to be propped up by timbers. Paul captured the spirit

of the street more evocatively than anyone, writing of "the delivery wagons, makeshift vehicles propelled by pedaling boys, pushcarts of itinerant vendors, knife-grinders, umbrella menders, a herd of milk goats, and the neighborhood pedestrians." (The local bordello has closed, however.) Today you see lots of Greek restaurants.

Branching off from this street to your left is:

❹ Rue du Chat-qui-Pêche

This is said to be the shortest, narrowest street in the world, containing not one door and only a handful of windows. It's usually filled with garbage or lovers or both. Before the quay was built, the Seine sometimes flooded the cellars of the houses, and legend has it that an enterprising cat took advantage of its good fortune and went fishing in the confines of the cellars— hence the street's name, which means "Street of the Cat Who Fishes."

Now retrace your steps toward place St-Michel and turn left at the intersection with rue de la Harpe, which leads to rue St-Séverin. At the intersection, take a left to see:

❺ St-Séverin

A flamboyant Gothic church named for a 6th-century recluse, St-Séverin was built from 1210 to 1230 and was reconstructed in 1458, over the years adopting many of the features of Notre-Dame, across the river. The tower was completed in 1487 and the chapels from 1498 to 1520; Hardouin-Mansart designed the Chapelle de la Communion in 1673 when he was 27, and it contains some beautiful Rouault etchings from the 1920s. Before entering, walk around the church to examine the gargoyles, birds of prey, and reptilian monsters projecting from its roof. To the right, facing the church is the 15th-century "garden of ossuaries." The stained glass inside St-Séverin, behind the altar, is a stunning adornment using great swaths of color to depict the seven sacraments.

start here

place St-Michel

ST-MICHEL

rue Danton

ILE DE LA CITÉ

Cloître N.Dame

Notre-Dame

pont St-Louis

ILE ST-LOUIS

quai St-Michel

r. de la Huchette

r. St-Severin

rue de la Harpe

CLUNY-LA SORBONNE

Université Paris VI

6e

bd. St-Germain

rue St-Jacques

r. Dante

rue Galande

rue Lagrange

pont de l'Archevêché

Seine

quai de la Tournelle

MAUBERT MUTUALITÉ

rue des Ecoles

rue de Cluny

5e

bd. St-Germain

rue des Bernardins

rue de Poissy

Université Paris VI

bd. St-Michel

rue Monsieur le Prince

r. de la Sorbonne

rue St-Jacques

r. Victor-Cousin

rue Cujas

rue Soufflot

rue des Carmes

rue Monge

St-Etienne du Mont

rue Descartes

LUXEMBOURG

rue Gay Lussac

place du Panthéon

rue Clovis

finish here

rue du Cardinal Lemoine

rue P. & M. Curie

rue d'Ulm

"Take a Break"

1 Place St-Michel
2 Boulevard St-Michel
3 Rue de la Huchette
4 Rue du Chat-qui-Pêche
5 St-Séverin
6 St-Julien-le-Pauvre
7 Musée de Cluny
8 Sorbonne
9 Eglise de la Sorbonne
10 Panthéon

After visiting the church, go back to rue St-Séverin and follow it to rue Galande, then continue on until you reach:

6 St-Julien-le-Pauvre

This church is on the south side of square René-Viviani. First stand at the gateway and look at the beginning of rue Galande, especially the old houses with the steeples of St-Séverin rising across the way; it's one of the most frequently painted scenes on the Left Bank. Enter the courtyard and you'll be in medieval Paris. The garden to the left offers the best view of Notre-Dame. Everyone from Rabelais to Thomas Aquinas has passed through the doors of this church. Before the 6th century, a chapel stood on this spot. The present church goes back to the Longpont monks, who began work on it in 1170 (making it the oldest church in Paris). In 1655, it was given to the Hôtel Dieu and in time became a small warehouse for salt. In 1889, it was presented to the followers of the Melchite Greek rite, a branch of the Byzantine church.

Return to rue Galande and turn left at the intersection with rue St-Séverin. Continue until you reach rue St-Jacques, turn left, and turn right when you reach boulevard St-Germain. Follow this boulevard to rue de Cluny, turn left, and head toward the entrance to the:

7 Musée de Cluny

Even if you're rushed, see *The Lady and the Unicorn* tapestries and the remains of the Roman baths. (See "The Major Museums" in chapter 7.)

After your visit to the Cluny, exit onto boulevard St-Michel, but instead of heading back to place St-Michel, turn left and walk to place de la Sorbonne and the:

⑧ Sorbonne

One of the most famous academic institutions in the world, the Sorbonne was founded in the 13th century by Robert de Sorbon, St. Louis's confessor, for poor students who wished to pursue theological studies. By the next century it had become the most prestigious university in the West, attracting such professors as Thomas Aquinas and Roger Bacon and such students as Dante, Calvin, and Longfellow. Napoleon reorganized it in 1806. The courtyard and galleries are open to the public when the university is in session. In the Cour d'Honneur are statues of Hugo and Pasteur. At first glance from place de la Sorbonne, the Sorbonne seems architecturally undistinguished. In truth, it

was rather indiscriminately reconstructed in the early 1900s. A better fate lay in store for the:

⑨ Eglise de la Sorbonne

Built in 1635 by Le Mercier, this church contains the marble tomb of Cardinal Richelieu, a work by Girardon based on a design by Le Brun. At his feet is the remarkable statue *Learning in Tears.*

From the church, go south on rue Victor-Cousin and turn left at rue Soufflot. At the street's end lies place du Panthéon and the:

⑩ Panthéon

Sitting atop Mont St-Geneviève, this nonreligious temple is the final resting place of such distinguished figures as Hugo, Zola, Rousseau, Voltaire, and Curie. (See "Architectural & Historic Highlights" in chapter 7.)

WALKING TOUR 3	THE MARAIS

Start:	Place de la Bastille (Métro: Bastille).
Finish:	Place de la Bastille.
Time:	4½ hours, with only brief stops en route. The distance is about 4.5km (2¾ miles).
Best Time:	Monday to Saturday, when more buildings and shops are open. If interiors are open, often you can walk into courtyards.
Worst Time:	Toward dusk, when shops and museums are closed, and it's too dark to admire the architectural details.

When Paris began to overflow the confines of Ile de la Cité in the 13th century, the citizenry began to settle in Le Marais, a marsh that used to be flooded by the Seine. By the 17th century, the Marais had become the center of aristocratic Paris and some of its great *hôtels particuliers* (mansions), many now restored or still being spruced up, were built by the finest craftsmen in France. In the 18th and 19th centuries, fashion deserted the Marais for the expanding Faubourg St-Germain and Faubourg St-Honoré. Industry took over, and once-elegant hotels deteriorated into tenements. There was talk of demolishing the neighborhood, but in 1962 the community banded together and saved the historic district.

Today, the 17th-century mansions are fashionable once again. The *International Herald Tribune* called this area the latest refuge for the Paris artisan fleeing the tourist-trampled St-Germain-des-Prés. (However, that doesn't mean the area doesn't get its share of tourist traffic; quite the contrary.) The "marsh" sprawls across the 3rd and 4th arrondissements bounded by the Grands Boulevards, rue du Temple, place des Vosges, and the Seine. It has become Paris's center of gay/lesbian life, particularly on rues St-Croix-de-la-Bretonnerie, des Archives, and Vieille-du-Temple, and is a great place for window-shopping in trendy boutiques, up-and-coming galleries, and more.

10e

M Metro Stop
"Take a Break"

bd. St-Martin

place de la République

rue du Faubourg du Temple

0 ___ 1/5 Mi
0 ___ .2 Km

Conservatoire des Arts et Métiers

TEMPLE

RÉPUBLIQUE

avenue de la République

rue St-Martin

rue de Turbigo

bd. du Temple

ARTS ET MÉTIERS

PARMENTIER M

3e

rue du Temple

rue Beaubourg

rue des Archives

rue de Bretagne

rue de Charlot

OBERKAMPF

bd. Oberkampf

rue Voltaire

RAMBUTEAU

rue Pastourelle

Musée de la Chasse

rue de Poitou

FILLES DU CALVAIRE

ST-AMBROISE

St-Ambroise

Centre Pompidou

Archives Nationales

rue des 4 Fils

rue du Temple

ST-SÉBASTIAN FROISSART

rue Vieille

rue de Thorigny

r. St-Claude

ST-CLAUDE

RICHARD LENOIR

rue Barbette

rue Elzevir

Parc Royal

rue de Turenne

St-Denis

rue Beaumarchais

HÔTEL DE VILLE

rue des Francs

rue Payenne

r. St-Gilles

Chemin Vert

11e

Hôtel de Ville

rue de Rivoli

rue des Rosiers

rue Pavée

rue de Bourgeois

CHEMIN-VERT

rue du Chemin Vert

Théâtre de la Bastille

rue Fr. Miron

rue F. Duval

rue Malher

place des Vosges

BRÉGUET SABIN

rue des Tournelles

bd. Richard Lenoir

St-Gervais

ST-PAUL M

St-Paul

r. de Birague

rue de la Roquette

quai de l'Hôtel de Ville

r. Charlemagne

rue St-Paul

rue St-Antoine

PONT-MARIE M

pont St-Louis

pont Marie

4e

finish here

place de la Bastille

start here

rue du Faubourg St-Antoine

Notre-Dame

ILE ST-LOUIS

BASTILLE

Opéra Bastille

Notre-Dame

St-Louis-en-l'Ile

bd. Henri IV

Seine

rue de Charenton

quai de la Tournelle

pont de la Tournelle

pont de Sully

SULLY MORLAND M

bd. Bourdon

bd. de la Bastille

avenue Daumesnil

bd. St-Germain

quai St-Bernard

Seine

quai Henri IV

12e

Université Paris VI

Begin your tour at the site that spawned one of the most celebrated and abhorred revolutions in human history:

❶ Place de la Bastille

On July 14, 1789, a mob attacked the Bastille prison located here, igniting the French Revolution. Now nothing of this symbol of despotism remains. Built in 1369, its eight huge towers once loomed over Paris. Within them, many prisoners, some sentenced by Louis XIV for "witchcraft," were kept, the best known being the "Man in the Iron Mask." And yet when the revolutionary mob stormed the fortress, only seven prisoners were discovered. (The Marquis de Sade had been shipped to the madhouse 10 days earlier.) The authorities had discussed razing it, so the attack meant little. But what it symbolized and what it unleashed can never be undone, and each July 14 the country celebrates Bastille Day with great festivity. Since the late 1980s, what had been scorned as a grimy-looking traffic circle has become an artistic focal point, thanks to the construction of the Opéra Bastille on its eastern edge.

It was probably easier to storm the Bastille in 1789 than it is now to cross over to the center of the square for a close-up view of the:

❷ Colonne de Juillet

The July Column doesn't commemorate the Revolution but honors the victims of the July Revolution of 1830, which put Louis-Philippe on the throne after the heady but wrenching victories and defeats of Napoleon Bonaparte. The winged God of Liberty, whose forehead bears an emerging star, crowns the tower.

From place de la Bastille, walk west along rue St-Antoine for about a block. Turn right and walk north along rue des Tournelles, noting the:

❸ Statue of Beaumarchais

Erected in 1895, it honors the 18th-century author of *The Barber of Seville* and *The Marriage of Figaro,* set to music by Rossini and Mozart, respectively.

Continue north for a long block along rue des Tournelles, then turn left at medieval-looking rue Pas-de-la-Mule (Footsteps of the Mule), which will open suddenly onto the northeastern corner of enchanting:

❹ Place des Vosges

This is Paris's oldest square and once its most fashionable, boasting 36 brick-and-stone pavilions rising from covered arcades that allowed people to shop no matter what the weather. The buildings were constructed according to a strict plan: The height of the facades is equal to their width and the height of the triangular roofs is half the height of the facades. In 1559, Henri II was killed while jousting on a spot near the Hôtel des Tournelles; his widow, Catherine de Médicis, had the place torn down. The current square was begun in 1605 on Henri IV's orders and called place Royal; the king intended the square to be the scene of businesses and social festivities and even planned to live there, but Ravaillac had other plans and assassinated Henri 2 years before its completion in 1612. By the 17th century, the square was the home of many aristocrats. During the Revolution, it was renamed place de l'Invisibilité, and its statue of Louis XIII was stolen (probably melted down). A replacement now stands in its place.

In 1800, the square was renamed place des Vosges because the Vosges *département* (an administrative unit) was the first in France to pay its taxes to Napoleon. The addition of chestnut trees sparked a controversy; critics say they spoil the perspective. Even though its fortunes waned when the Marais went out of fashion, place des Vosges is back big time. Over the years, the famous often took up residence: Descartes, Pascal, Cardinal Richelieu, courtesan Marion Delorme, Gautier, Daudet, and Mme de Sévigné all lived here. But its best-known occupant was Victor Hugo (his home, now a museum, is the only house open to the public).

Place des Vosges is the centerpiece of many unusual, charming, and/or funky shops. At 20 place des Vosges is one of the best of these:

⑤ Deborah Chock

This shop (☎ **01-48-04-86-86**) sells reproductions of the colorful and contemporary paintings of Deborah Chock, who is noted for the pithy phrases on the background of her paintings that reflect insights from the worlds of poetry, philosophy, and psychoanalysis. Use it as a debut before you explore the many other art galleries in the neighborhood. The staff is English-speaking and well versed in the currents of the Paris art scene.

TAKE A BREAK Two cafes hold court from opposite sides of place des Vosges, both serving café au lait, wine, and *eaux de vie* (brandies); sandwiches; pastries; and tea: **Ma Bourgogne** at no. 19 (☎ **01-42-78-44-64**), on the western edge, and **La Chope des Vosges** at no. 22 (☎ **01-42-72-64-04**).

Near the square's southeastern corner at 6 place des Vosges, commemorating the life and times of a writer whose works were read with passion in the 19th century, is the:

⑥ Maison de Victor Hugo

Hugo's former home is now a museum (☎ **01-42-72-10-16**) and literary shrine (see "Literary Landmarks" in chapter 7). Hugo lived there from 1832 to 1848, when he went into voluntary exile on the Channel Islands after the rise of the despotic Napoleon III.

Exit from place des Vosges from its northwestern corner (opposite the Maison de Victor Hugo) and walk west along rue des Francs-Bourgeois until you reach the intersection with rue de Sévigné, then make a right. At no. 23 is the:

⑦ Musée Carnavalet

This 16th-century mansion is now a museum (☎ **01-44-59-58-32**) devoted to the history of Paris and the French Revolution (see "The Major Museums" in chapter 7).

Continue to a point near the northern terminus of rue de Sévigné, noting no. 29 (now part of the Carnavalet). This is the:

⑧ Hôtel le Peletier de St-Fargeau

The structure bears the name of its former occupant, who was considered responsible for the death sentence of Louis XVI. It's used as offices and can't be visited.

At the end of the street, make a left onto lovely rue du Parc-Royal, lined with 17th-century mansions. It leads to place de Thorigny, where at no. 5 you'll find the:

⑨ Musée Picasso

The museum occupies the **Hôtel Salé,** built by a salt-tax collector (see "The Major Museums" in chapter 7). You can visit the museum either now or come back at the end of the tour.

Walk northeast along rue Thorigny and turn left onto rue Debelleyme. After a block, near the corner of rue Vieille-du-Temple, at 108 rue Vieille-du-Temple, is a particularly worthwhile art gallery (among dozens in this neighborhood):

⑩ Yvon Lambert

This gallery (☎ **01-42-71-09-33**) specializes in contemporary and sometimes radically avant-garde art by international artists. The art is displayed in a cavernous main showroom, spilling over into an annex room. An excellent primer for the local arts scene, it provides an agreeable contrast to the 17th-century trappings all around you.

Continue north for 2 short blocks along rue Debelleyme until you reach rue de Bretagne. Anyone who appreciates a really good deli will want to stop at 14 rue de Bretagne:

⑪ Les Iles Grecques

This deli (☎ **01-42-71-00-56**) is the most popular of the area's ethnic take-out restaurants, a perfect place to buy picnic supplies before heading to square du Temple (up rue de Bretagne) or place des Vosges. You'll find moussaka, stuffed eggplant, stuffed grape leaves, olives, *tarama* (a savory paste made from fish roe), and both meatballs and vegetarian balls. It's open Monday from 4 to 8pm and Tuesday to Sunday from 10am to 2pm and 3:30 to 8pm.

After you fill up on great food, note that at the same address is:

⑫ Hier, Aujourd'hui, et Demain

At this shop (✆ **01-42-77-69-02**) you can appreciate France's love affair with 1930s Art Deco. Michel, the owner, provides an array of bibelots and art objects, with one of the widest selections of colored glass in town. Works by late-19th-century glassmakers such as Daum, Gallé, and Legras are shown. Some items require special packing and great care in transport; others can be carted home as souvenirs.

Now walk southeast along rue Charlot to no. 10 at the corner of rue Pastourelle, where you'll be tempted by the fabrics of:

⑬ Dominique Picquier

Looking to redo your settee? This stylish shop (✆ **01-42-72-39-14**) sells a wide roster of fabric (50% cotton, 50% linen) that stands up to rugged use. Most patterns are based on some botanical inspiration, like ginkgo leaves, vanilla pods and vines, and magnolia branches. Most cost 46€ ($53) per meter (3¼ ft.), although some particularly plush velvets can go as high as 128€ ($147) per meter.

Nearby, at 9 rue Charlot, adjacent to the corner of rue Charlot and rue du Perche, is the Marais's large experimental art gallery, the:

⑭ Passage de Retz

Opened in 1994, this avant-garde gallery (✆ **01-48-04-37-99**) has about 630 sq. m (6,781 sq. ft.) of space to show off its highly amusing exhibits. It has shown Japanese textiles, American abstract expressionist paintings, modern Venetian glass, contemporary Haitian paintings, and selections from affiliated art galleries in Quebec.

Walk 1 block farther along rue Charlot, turn left for a block onto rue des 4 Fils, then go right on rue Vieille-du-Temple to no. 87, where you'll come across Delamair's:

⑮ Hôtel de Rohan

The fourth Cardinal Rohan, the larcenous cardinal of the "diamond necklace scandal" that led to a flood of destructive publicity for Marie Antoinette, once lived here. The first occupant of the hotel was reputed to be the son of Louis XVI. The interior is usually closed to the public, except during an occasional exhibit. If it's open, check out the amusing **Salon des Singes (Monkey Room).** Sometimes you can visit the courtyard, which boasts one of the finest sculptures of 18th-century France, *The Watering of the Horses of the Sun,* with a nude Apollo and four horses against a background of exploding sunbursts. (If you want to see another Delamair work, detour to 60 rue des Francs-Bourgeois to see the extraordinary Hôtel de Soubise, now housing the **Musée de l'Histoire de France** [p. ###].)

Along the same street at no. 47 is the:

⑯ Hôtel des Ambassadeurs de Hollande

Here, Beaumarchais wrote *The Marriage of Figaro.* It's one of the most splendid mansions in the Marais, and despite its name was never occupied by the Dutch embassy.

Continue walking south along rue Vieille-du-Temple until you reach:

⑰ Rue des Rosiers

Rue des Rosiers (Street of the Rosebushes) is one of the most colorful and typical streets remaining from Paris's old Jewish quarter, and you'll find an intriguing blend of living memorials to Ashkenazi and Sephardic traditions. The Star of David shines from some of the shop windows; Hebrew letters appear, sometimes in neon; couscous is sold from shops run by Moroccan, Tunisian, or Algerian Jews; restaurants serve kosher food; and signs appeal for Jewish liberation. You'll come across many delicacies you might've read about but never seen, such as sausage stuffed in a gooseneck, roots of black horseradish, and pickled lemons.

TAKE A BREAK
The street offers a cornucopia of ethnic eateries that remain steadfast to their central European, Ashkenazi origins. **Chez Jo Goldenberg,** 7 rue des Rosiers (⟨ 01-48-87-20-16), has plenty of room to sit down and eat (see chapter 6 for more details).

Take a left onto rue des Rosiers and head down to rue Pavée, which gets its name because it was the first street in Paris, sometime during the 1300s, to have cobblestones placed over its open sewer. At this "Paved Street," turn right and walk south until you reach the St-Paul Métro stop. Make a right along rue François-Miron and check out no. 68, the 17th-century:

⑱ **Hôtel de Beauvais**
Though the facade was damaged in the Revolution, it remains one of Paris's most charming hotels. A plaque announces that Mozart lived there in 1763 and played at the court of Versailles. (He was 7 at the time.) Louis XIV presented the mansion to Catherine Bellier, wife of Pierre de Beauvais and lady-in-waiting to Anne of Austria; she reportedly had the honor of introducing Louis, then 16, to the facts of life. To visit the interior, apply to the **Association du Paris Historique** on the ground floor.

Continue your walk along rue François-Miron until you come to a crossroads, where you take a sharp left along rue de Jouy, cross rue Fourcy, and turn onto rue du Figuier, where at no. 1 you'll see the:

⑲ **Hôtel de Sens**
The structure was built between the 1470s and 1519 for the archbishops of

Sens. Along with the Cluny on the Left Bank, it's the only domestic architecture remaining from the 15th century. Long after the archbishops had departed in 1605, the wife of Henri IV, Queen Margot, lived here. Her new lover, "younger and more virile," slew her old lover as she looked on in amusement. Today, the hotel houses the **Bibliothèque Forney** (⟨ 01-42-78-14-60). Leaded windows and turrets characterize the facade; you can go into the courtyard to see more ornate stone decoration—the gate is open Tuesday to Friday from 1:30 to 8:15pm and Saturday from 10am to 8:15pm.

Retrace your steps to rue de Fourcy, turn right, and walk up the street until you reach the St-Paul Métro stop again. Turn right onto rue St-Antoine and continue to no. 62:

⑳ **Hôtel de Bethune-Sully**
Work began on this mansion in 1625, on the order of Jean Androuet de Cerceau. In 1634, it was acquired by the duc de Sully, once Henri IV's minister of finance. After a straitlaced life as the "accountant of France," Sully broke loose in his declining years, adorning himself with diamonds and garish rings and a young bride, who's said to have had a thing for very young men. The hotel was acquired by the government just after World War II and is now the seat of the National Office of Historical Monuments and Sites, with an information center and a bookshop inside. Recently restored, the relief-studded facade is especially appealing. You can visit the interior with a guide on Saturday or Sunday at 3pm, and can visit the courtyard and the garden any day; chamber music concerts are frequently staged here.

9

Shopping

Shopping is a favorite pastime of Parisians; some would even say it reflects the City of Light's soul. This is one of those rare places where you don't have to go to any special area to shop—opportunities surround you wherever you are. Each walk you take will immerse you in uniquely French styles. The windows, stores, people, and even their dogs brim with energy, creativity, and a sense of visual expression found in few other cities.

You don't have to buy anything to appreciate shopping in Paris—just soak up the art form the French have made of rampant consumerism. Peer in the *vitrines* (display windows), absorb cutting-edge ideas, witness new trends, and take home with you a whole new education in style.

1 The Shopping Scene

BEST BUYS

PERFUMES, MAKEUP & BEAUTY TREATMENTS   A discount of 20% to 30% makes these items a great buy; qualify for a VAT refund (see below) and you'll save 40% to 45% off the Paris retail price, allowing you to bring home goods at half the U.S. price. Duty-free shops abound in Paris and are always less expensive than the ones at the airports.

For bargain cosmetics, try out French dime store and drugstore brands like **Bourjois** (made in the Chanel factories), **Lierac,** and **Galenic. Vichy,** famous for its water, has a skin-care and makeup line. The newest retail trend in Paris is the *parapharmacie,* a type of discount drugstore loaded with inexpensive brands, health cures, beauty regimes, and diet plans. These usually offer a 20% discount.

FOODSTUFFS   Nothing makes a better souvenir than a product of France brought home to savor later. Supermarkets are located in tourist neighborhoods; stock up on coffee, designer chocolates, mustards (try Maille or Meaux brand), and perhaps American products in French packages for the kids. However, to be sure you don't try to bring home a prohibited foodstuff, see "Entry Requirements & Customs" in chapter 3, "Planning Your Trip to Paris."

FUN FASHION   Sure you can buy couture or *prêt-à-porter* (ready to wear), but French teens and trendsetters have their own stores where the latest looks are affordable. Even the dime stores in Paris sell designer copies and hotshot styles. In the stalls in front of the department stores on boulevard Haussmann, you'll find some of the latest accessories, guaranteed for a week's worth of small talk once you get home.

GETTING A VAT REFUND

The French **value-added tax** (**VAT—TVA** in French) is 19.6%, but you can get most of that back if you spend 182€ ($209) or more in any store that participates in the VAT refund program. Most stores participate.

Once you meet your required minimum purchase amount, you qualify for a tax refund. The amount of the refund varies with the way the refund is handled and the fee some stores charge you for processing it. So the refund at a department store may be 13%, whereas at a small shop it may be 15% or even 18%.

You'll receive **VAT refund papers** in the shop; some stores, like Hermès, have their own, while others provide a government form. Fill in the forms before you arrive at the airport and expect to stand in line at the Customs desk for as long as half an hour. You're required to show the goods at the airport, so have them on you or visit the Customs office before you check your luggage. Once the papers have been mailed, a credit will appear, often months later, on your credit card bill. All refunds are processed at the point of departure from the **European Union (EU),** so if you're going to another EU country, don't apply for the refund in France.

Be sure to mark the paperwork to request that your refund be applied to your credit card so you aren't stuck with a check in euros that's hard to cash. This also ensures the best rate of exchange. In some airports, you're offered the opportunity to get your refund back in cash, which is tempting. But if you accept cash in any currency other than euros, you'll lose money on the conversion rate.

To avoid VAT refund hassles, ask for a Global Refund form ("Shopping Checque") at a store where you make a purchase. When leaving an EU country, have it stamped by Customs, after which you take it to a Global Refund counter at one of more than 700 airports and border crossings in Europe. Your money is refunded on the spot. For information, contact **Global Refund,** 707 Summer St., Stamford, CT 06901 (© **800/566-9828;** www.globalrefund.com).

DUTY-FREE BOUTIQUES

The advantage of duty-free shops is that you don't have to pay the VAT, so you avoid the red tape of getting a refund. Both Charles de Gaulle and Orly airports have shopping galore (de Gaulle has a virtual mall with crystal, cutlery, chocolates, luggage, wine, pipes and lighters, lingerie, silk scarves, perfume, knitwear, jewelry, cameras, cheeses, even antiques). You'll also find duty-free shops on the avenues branching out from the Opéra Garnier, in the 1st arrondissement. Sometimes there are bargains, but most often not. Usually these stores jack prices up, so even though there's no duty, you're not getting a good deal. In general, these duty-free shops are best for last-minute buys or the impulse shopper who feels he or she is leaving Paris without having bought enough.

BUSINESS HOURS

Usual shop hours are Monday to Saturday from 10am to 7pm, but hours vary, and Monday mornings don't run at full throttle. Small shops sometimes close

---

Tips **Shopping Etiquette**

When you walk into a French store, it's traditional to greet the owner or sales clerk with a direct address, not a fey smile or even a weak *bonjour.* Only a clear and pleasant *"Bonjour, madame/monsieur"* will do.

And if you plan to enter the rarefied atmospheres of the top designer boutiques (to check out the pricey merchandise, if not to buy anything), be sure to dress the part. You don't need to wear couture, but do leave the sneakers and sweat suit back at your hotel. The sales staff will be much more accommodating if you look as if you belong there.

for a 2-hour lunch break and may not open at all until after lunch on Monday. Thursday is the best day for late-night shopping, with stores open to 9 or 10pm.

Sunday shopping is limited to tourist areas and flea markets, though there's growing demand for full-scale Sunday hours. The department stores are now open on the five Sundays before Christmas. The **Carrousel du Louvre,** a mall adjacent to the Louvre, is hopping on Sunday, but closed on Monday. The tourist shops lining rue de Rivoli across from the Louvre are open on Sunday, as are the antiques villages, flea markets, and specialty events. There are several food markets in the streets on Sunday. For our favorites, see the box, "Food Markets" (p. 255). The **Virgin Megastore** on the Champs-Elysées, a big teen hangout, pays a fine to stay open on Sunday.

SHIPPING IT HOME

Shipping charges will possibly double your cost, and you may have to pay duties on the items (see above). The good news: The VAT refund is automatically applied to all shipped items, so there's no need to worry about the 182€ ($209) minimum. Some stores have a $100 minimum for shipping. You can also walk into any post office and mail home a jiffy bag or box of goodies. French do-it-yourself boxes can't be reopened once closed, so pack carefully. The clerk at the post office will help you assemble the box (it's tricky), seal it, and send it off.

GREAT SHOPPING NEIGHBORHOODS

Here are the best of the shopping arrondissements:

1ST & 8TH ARRONDISSEMENTS   These two arrondissements adjoin each other and form the heart of Paris's best Right Bank shopping strip—they're one big hunting ground. This area includes the **rue du Faubourg St-Honoré,** where the big designer houses are, and the **Champs-Elysées,** with hot mass-market and teen scenes. At one end of the 1st is the **Palais Royal,** one of the best shopping secrets in Paris, where an arcade of boutiques flanks each side of the garden of the former palace.

Also here is **avenue Montaigne,** Paris's most glamorous shopping street, boasting 2 blocks of ultrafancy shops, where you float from big name to big name and in a few hours can see everything from Dior to Caron. Avenue Montaigne is also the address of **Joseph,** a British design firm, and **Porthault,** makers of the poshest sheets in the world.

2ND ARRONDISSEMENT   Right behind the Palais Royal is the **Garment District (Sentier),** as well as a few sophisticated shopping secrets, such as **place des Victoires.**

In the 19th century, this area became known for its *passages,* glass-enclosed shopping streets—in fact, the world's first shopping malls. They were also the city's first buildings to be illuminated by gaslight. Many have been torn down, but a dozen or so have survived. Of them all, we prefer **Passage den Grand Cerf,** between 145 rue St-Denis and 10 rue Dussoubs (Métro: Bourse), lying a few blocks from the Beaubourg. It's a place of wonder, filled with everything from retro-chic boutiques and (increasingly) Asian-themed shops. What's exciting is to come upon a discovery, perhaps a postage-stamp-size shop with a special jeweler who creates unique products such as jewel-toned safety pins.

3RD & 4TH ARRONDISSEMENTS   The border between these two arrondissements gets fuzzy, especially around **place des Vosges,** center stage of the Marais. The districts offer several dramatically different shopping experiences.

On the surface, the shopping includes the "real people stretch" (where all the nonmillionaires shop) of **rue de Rivoli** and **rue St-Antoine,** featuring everything from Gap and a branch of Marks & Spencer to local discount stores and mass merchants. Two "real people" department stores are in this area, **Samaritaine** and **BHV;** there's also **Les Halles** and the **Beaubourg** neighborhood, which is anchored by the Centre Pompidou.

Hidden in the Marais is a medieval warren of twisting streets chockablock with cutting-edge designers and up-to-the-minute fashions and trends. Start by walking around place des Vosges for galleries, designer shops, and special finds, then dive in and lose yourself in the area leading to the Musée Picasso.

Finally, the 4th is the home of the **Bastille,** an up-and-coming area for artists and galleries where you'll find the newest entry on the retail scene, the **Viaduc des Arts** (which actually stretches into the 12th). It's a collection of about 30 stores occupying a series of narrow vaulted niches under what used to be railroad tracks. They run parallel to avenue Daumesnil, centered around boulevard Diderot.

6TH & 7TH ARRONDISSEMENTS   Though the 6th is one of the most famous shopping districts in Paris—it's the soul of the Left Bank—a lot of the good stuff is hidden in the zone that turns into the residential district of the 7th. **Rue du Bac,** stretching from the 6th to the 7th in a few blocks, stands for all that wealth and glamour can buy.

9TH ARRONDISSEMENT   To add to the fun of shopping the Right Bank, the 9th sneaks in behind the 1st, so if you choose not to walk toward the Champs-Elysées and the 8th, you can head to the city's big department stores, all built in a row along **boulevard Haussmann** in the 9th. Department stores include not only the two big French icons, **Au Printemps** and **Galeries Lafayette,** but also a large branch of Britain's **Marks & Spencer** and a branch of the Dutch answer to Kmart, low-priced **C&A.**

2 Shopping A to Z

ANTIQUES

Argenterie de Turenne *Finds*   Inside, you'll find old-fashioned gentility and masses of silver, both secondhand sterling and plated, much made in France during the 19th and early 20th centuries. The array of trays, water pitchers, cutlery, napkin rings, tumblers, and punchbowls is staggering, but what many visitors find amazing is that congenially battered silver-plated forks and spoons are sold by weight, at the rate of 61€ ($70) per kilo (about 2 lb.). The store lies within the Marais, a short walk from place des Vosges, on a block that's lined with purveyors of other old-fashioned grace notes that include antique glassware and porcelain. Open Tuesday to Saturday 10:30am to 7pm. 19 rue de Turenne, 4e. © 01-42-72-04-00. Métro: St-Paul.

Le Louvre des Antiquaires   Across from the Louvre, this store offers three levels of fancy knickknacks and 250 vendors. It's just the place if you're looking for 30 matching Baccarat crystal champagne flutes from the 1930s, a Sèvres tea service from 1773, or a signed Jean Fouquet gold-and-diamond pin. Too stuffy? No problem. There's always the 1940 Rolex with the aubergine crocodile strap. Prices can be high, but a few reasonable items are hidden here. What's more, the Sunday scene is fabulous, and there's a cafe with a variety of lunch menus. Pick up a free map and brochure of the premises from the information desk. Open Tuesday to Sunday 9am to 7pm. Closed Sunday July to Aug. 2 place du Palais-Royal, 1e. © 01-42-97-27-00. Métro: Palais Royal.

Mlinaric, Henry, and Zervudachi David Mlinaric is the British interior designer who redecorated Spencer House (Princess Diana's ancestral home in London) as well as all of Lord Rothschild's private residences. Tino Zervudachi is one of the hot Young Turks of Paris design. Hugh Henry, like Mlinaric, is English. Together, these three musketeers are the chicest antiques dealers on the Right Bank, specializing in museum-quality 18th-century items. Open Monday to Friday 10am to 1pm and 2 to 6pm. 54 Galerie de Montpensier, Palais-Royal, 1e. *©* 01-42-96-08-62. Métro: Palais Royal.

Village St-Paul This isn't an antiques center but a cluster of dealers in their own hole-in-the-wall hideout. It really hops on Sunday. Bring your camera, because inside the courtyards and alleys is a dream vision of hidden Paris: dealers in a courtyard selling furniture and other decorative items in French-country and formal styles. The rest of the street, stretching from the river to the Marais, is also lined with dealers. Open Thursday to Monday 11am to 7pm. 23–27 rue St-Paul, 4e. No phone. Métro: St-Paul.

ART

Artcurial This is the best, most famous, and most prestigious place in Paris for contemporary art. Many art forms are displayed here, from jewelry and design to sculpture and tapestries. Open Monday to Saturday 10:30am to 7pm. Centre d'Art Contemporain, 61 av. Montaigne, 8e. *©* 01-42-99-16-16. Métro: Franklin-D.-Roosevelt.

Galerie Adrien Maeght This art house is among the most famous names, selling contemporary art on a fancy Left Bank street that's far more fashionable than the bohemian Left Bank Picasso knew. Open Monday 10am to 6pm; Tuesday to Saturday 9:30am to 7pm. 42 rue du Bac, 7e. *©* 01-45-48-45-15. Métro: Rue du Bac.

Galerie 27 This tiny closet sells lithographs by famous artists of the early 20th century, including Picasso, Miró, and Léger. Contemporary artists are also represented. Open Tuesday to Saturday 10am to 1pm and 2:30 to 7pm. 27 rue de Seine, 6e. *©* 01-43-54-78-54. Métro: St-Germain-des-Prés or Odéon.

J. C. Martinez In its way, this is one of the most charming and old-fashioned art galleries in Paris. Established in the mid-1970s within a single room that's loaded with at least 400 separate boxes, it specializes in antique prints and engravings, most of them crafted between the late 1700s and around 1910, and some even earlier. You can rummage randomly through the inventories here, depending on how rare they are. But if your parameters are more specialized, the staff will guide you toward whatever subject interests you the most. If you're interested in engravings of birds, botany, fashion, sailing ships, floral arrangements, architectural renderings, or horse races, there's at least one box devoted to that particular subject. And if you're interested in the way the borders of France and its internal regions have been organized and reorganized since the days of the *ancien régime,* there's a wondrous collection of maps crafted at different times of the nation's complicated history. Open Monday to Saturday 10:30am to 12:30pm and 2 to 7pm. 21 rue St-Sulpice, 6e. *©* 01 43-26-34-53. Métro: Odéon or Mabillon.

Viaduc des Arts This complex of boutiques and crafts workshops occupies the vaulted spaces beneath one of the 19th-century railway access routes into the Gare de Lyon. Around 1990, crafts artists, including furniture makers, potters, glassblowers, and weavers, began renting the then-empty niches beneath the viaduct, selling their wares to homeowners and members of Paris's decorating trades. Several trend-setting home-furnishing outfits have rented additional

---

> ⌒Finds   An Open-Air Canvas Gallery
>
> The **Paris Art Market** is "the place to go" on a Sunday. At the foot of
> Montparnasse Tower, this market is like an open-air gallery and has done
> much to restore the reputation of Montparnasse (14e) as a *quartier* for
> artists. Some 100 artists participate, including painters, sculptors, and
> photographers, even jewelers and hat makers. Head for the mall along
> the boulevard Edgar Quinet for the best work. Go any time on Sunday
> between 10am and 7:30pm (Métro: Montparnasse).

---

spaces. Stretching for more than 2 blocks between the Opéra Bastille and the
Gare de Lyon, it allows one to see what Parisians consider chic in terms of home
decorating. Open Monday to Saturday 11am to 7pm. 9–147 av. Daumesnil, 12e.
✆ **01-44-75-80-66.** Métro: Bastille or Gare de Lyon.

BOOKS

If you like rare and unusual books, patronize one of the *bouquinistes,* the owners of those army-green stalls that line the Seine. This is where tourists in the
1920s and 1930s went to buy "dirty" French postcards. You might get lucky and
come across some treasured book, like an original edition of Henry Miller's
Tropic of Cancer, which was banned for decades in the United States. We like to
start with the guy who sells travel posters right off the pont des Arts, and work
our way toward the rest. Some of the *bouquinistes* are noted for giving the
Parisians a reputation for rudeness, but don't let them intimidate you.

See also the **Marché aux Livres** under "Markets" and **FNAC** and **Virgin
Megastore** under "Music."

Brentano's   A block from the Opéra Garnier, Brentano's is a large English-
language bookstore selling guides, maps, novels, and nonfiction as well as greeting cards, postcards, holiday items, and gifts. Open Monday to Saturday 10am
to 7:30pm. 37 av. de l'Opéra, 2e. ✆ **01-42-61-52-50.** Métro: Opéra or Pyramide.

Galignani   Sprawling over a large street level and supplemented by a mezzanine, this venerable wood-paneled bookstore has thrived since 1810. Enormous
numbers of books are available in French and English, with a special emphasis
on French classics, modern fiction, sociology, and fine arts. Looking for English-
language translations of works by Balzac, Flaubert, Zola, or Colette? Most of
them are here; if not, they can be ordered. Open Monday to Saturday 10am to
7pm. 224 rue de Rivoli, 1e. ✆ **01-42-60-76-07.** Métro: Tuileries.

Les Mots à la Bouche   This is Paris's largest, best-stocked gay bookstore. You
can find French- and English-language books as well as gay-info magazines like
Illico, e.m@le, and *Lesbia.* You'll also find lots of free pamphlets advertising
gay/lesbian venues and events. Open Monday to Saturday 11am to 11pm; Sun-
day 2 to 8pm. 6 rue Ste-Croix-la-Bretonnerie, 4e. ✆ **01-42-78-88-30.** Métro: Hôtel-de-Ville.

Librairie la Bail-Weissert   Paris is filled with rare-book shops, but this one
has the best collection of atlases, rare maps, and engravings from the 15th century to the 19th century. The shop sells original topographical maps of European and world cities, along with various regions of Europe. There's also a
superb collection of architectural engravings. Open Monday to Friday 10am to
12:30pm and 2 to 7pm. Saturday only by appointment. 5 rue Lagrange, 5e. ✆ **01-
43-29-72-59.** Métro: Maubert-Mutualité or St-Michel.

Shakespeare and Company The most famous bookstore on the Left Bank was Shakespeare and Company, on rue de l'Odéon, home to Sylvia Beach, "mother confessor to the Lost Generation." Hemingway, Fitzgerald, and Stein were frequent patrons, as was Anaïs Nin, the diarist noted for her description of struggling American artists in 1930s Paris. Nin helped her companion, Henry Miller, publish *Tropic of Cancer,* a book so notorious in its day that returning Americans trying to slip copies through Customs often had them confiscated as pornography. (When times were hard, Nin herself wrote pornography for a dollar a page.) Long ago, the shop moved to rue de la Bûcherie, a musty old place where expatriates still swap books and literary gossip and foreign students work in exchange for modest lodgings. Check out the lending library upstairs. Open daily 11am to midnight. 37 rue de la Bûcherie, 5e. No phone. Métro: St-Michel.

Tea and Tattered Pages At this largely English-language paperback bookshop, you can take a break from browsing to have tea. Though it's out of the way, an extra dose of charm makes it worth the trip. Open Monday to Saturday 11am to 7pm; Sunday noon to 6pm. 24 rue Mayet, 6e. ℭ 01-40-65-94-35. Métro: Duroc.

Village Voice Bookshop This favorite of expatriate Yankees is on a side street in the heart of the best Left Bank shopping district, near some of the gathering places described in Gertrude Stein's *The Autobiography of Alice B. Toklas.* Opened in 1981, the shop is a hangout for literati. Its name has nothing to do with the New York weekly. Open Monday 2 to 8pm; Tuesday to Saturday 10am to 8pm; Sunday 2 to 7pm. 6 rue Princesse, 6e. ℭ 01-46-33-36-47. Métro: Mabillon.

W. H. Smith This store provides books, magazines, and newspapers published in English (most titles are from Britain). You can get the *Times* of London, of course, and the Sunday *New York Times* is available every Monday. There's a fine selection of maps and travel guides, plus a special children's section that includes comics. Open Monday to Saturday 9am to 7:30pm; Sunday 1 to 7:30pm. 248 rue de Rivoli, 1e. ℭ 01-44-77-88-99. Métro: Concorde.

CERAMICS, CHINA & PORCELAIN

La Maison Ivre This charming shop is perfect for country-style ceramics that add authenticity to French-country decor. It carries an excellent selection of handmade pottery from all over France, with an emphasis on Provençal and southern French ceramics, including ovenware, bowls, platters, plates, pitchers, mugs, and vases. Open Monday to Saturday 10:30am to 7pm. 38 rue Jacob, 6e. ℭ 01-42-60-01-85. Métro: St-Germain-des-Prés.

Limoges-Unic/Madronet Housed in two shops on the same street, this store is crammed with crystals like Daum, Baccarat, Lalique, Haviland, and Bernardaud. You'll also find other table items: glass and crystal, silver, whatever your heart desires. They'll ship your purchases, and English is widely spoken. Open Monday to Saturday 10am to 6:30pm. 34 and 58 rue de Paradis, 10e. ℭ 01-47-70-54-49. Métro: Gare de l'Est.

Manufacture Nationale de Sèvres Once endorsed and promoted by the mistresses to the French kings, Sèvres today manufactures only 4,000 to 5,000 pieces of porcelain every year. Of these, many are reserved in advance as replacements for government and historical entities. Open Monday to Friday 11am to 6pm. 4 place André-Malraux, 1e. ℭ 01-47-03-40-20. Métro: Palais Royal.

CHILDREN: FASHION & TOYS

Au Nain Bleu This is the largest, oldest, and most centrally located toy store in Paris. More important, it's probably the fanciest toy store in the world. But don't panic—in addition to the expensive stuff, you'll find rows of cheaper items (like penny candy) on the first floor. Open Monday to Saturday 10am to 6:30pm. 408 rue St-Honoré, 8e. ℂ 01-42-60-39-01. Métro: Concorde or Madeleine.

Bonpoint   Grandparent alert! Bonpoint is part of a well-known almost-haute-couture chain specializing in clothing for children and adolescents ages 1 week to 16 years. The clothing is well tailored, traditional, and expensive. Drool over formal party and confirmation dresses and baptismal robes, embroidered and edged in lace. Open Monday to Saturday 10am to 7pm. 15 rue Royale, 8e. ℂ 01-47-42-52-63. Métro: Concorde.

Natalys   Part of a French chain with a dozen stores in Paris and many else-where, Natalys sells upscale versions of children's (6 and under) and maternity wear. It has just enough French panache without going over the top in design or price. Open Monday to Saturday 10am to 7:45pm. 92 av. des Champs-Elysées, 8e. ℂ 01-43-59-17-65. Métro: George-V.

Orchestra *Finds*   If you prefer clothes that have hip, hot style and color but are wearable, washable, and affordable, forget Bonpoint and try this small shop—it's a representative of a truly sensational French line of clothes for toddlers. And it's only a block from place de la Madeleine. Open Monday to Saturday 10am to 7pm. 18 rue Vignon, 9e. ℂ 01-42-66-24-74. Métro: Madeleine.

COSMETICS

Stephane Marais   Brilliant makeup artist Stephane Marais transformed ordi-nary-looking women into beauties and beautiful women into goddesses during fashion shows at Chanel and Gaultier. In 2002, in collaboration with the Japan-ese cosmetics syndicate Shiseido, he launched his own line of cosmetics, which are sold here within a boutique that's more whimsical and fluid than virtually any other in Paris—it changes radically every 3 months. Depending on when you arrive, the setup might resemble a sushi bar in Nagasaki, a loft space in Manhat-tan, or a thrift store selling amiably battered secondhand furniture from the age of Sputnik. It's fun, funky, and a regular haunt for the likes of Linda Evangelista, Eva Herzigova, and Sophia Coppola. Prices range from 7€ ($8.05) for an eye-brow pencil to 35€ ($40) for a container of foundation. Open Monday to Sat-urday 10:30am to 7:30pm. 217 rue St-Honoré, 1e. ℂ 01-42-61-73-22. Métro: Tuileries.

CRYSTAL

Baccarat   Opened in 1764, Baccarat is one of Europe's leading purveyors of full-lead crystal. You won't be able to comparison shop Baccarat crystal at its var-ious branches—a central organization sets rigid prices. But if you're hunting for bargains, head for the rue de Paradis outlet and check out special sales or pro-motions on discontinued items. These sales are the biggest during 2 weeks in mid-January. Baccarat's more prestigious outlet is on place de la Madeleine, but the 11 place des Etats Unis 16e one is larger and contains the **Musée de Bac-carat.** Open Tuesday to Friday 10am to 7pm; Monday and Saturday 10am to 7:30pm (bis rue de Paradis store open Mon–Fri 10am–6:30pm; Sat 10am–noon and 2–5:30pm). 11 place de la Madeleine, 8e. ℂ 01-42-65-36-26. Métro: Madeleine. Also: 30 bis rue de Paradis, 10e. ℂ 01-47-70-64-30. Métro: Gare de l'Est.

Lalique   Lalique is known for its smoky frosted-glass sculpture, Art Deco crys-tal, and unique perfume bottles. The shop sells a wide range of merchandise, including leather belts with Lalique buckles and silk scarves at about 213€ ($245), designed to compete directly with those sold by Hermès. Open Monday to Wednesday 10am to 6:30pm; Thursday to Friday 9:30am to 6:30pm; Saturday 9:30am to 7pm. 11 rue Royale, 8e. © 01-53-05-12-12. Métro: Concorde.

DEPARTMENT STORES

In addition to the stores below, **La Samaritaine,** 19 rue de la Monnaie, 1e (© **01-40-41-20-20;** Métro: Pont Neuf or Châtelet–Les Halles), and **BHV,** 52 rue de Rivoli, 4e (© **01-42-74-90-00;** Métro: Hôtel-de-Ville), offer the department-store experience at slightly lower prices. La Samaritaine has a fine inexpensive restaurant with a panoramic view on the top floor.

Au Bon Marché   Don't be fooled by the name ("low-budget" or "cheap") of this two-part Left Bank department store—for about 20 years, it has worked hard to position itself in the luxury market, selling fashion for men, women, and children; furniture; upscale gifts; and housewares. Some visitors compare it to Bloomingdale's with a French accent. This is the oldest department store in Paris, dating from 1852. Of course, it can't compete with the grand *magasins* (department stores) like Galeries Lafayette (see below), except in one category: Au Bon Marché has a superior rug department, which it has fine-tuned as its specialty since 1871. It also has one of the largest food halls in Paris. Open Monday to Wednesday and Friday 9:30am to 7pm; Thursday 10am to 9pm; Saturday 9:30am to 8pm. 22–24 rue de Sèvres, 7e. © 01-44-39-80-00. Métro: Sèvres-Babylone.

Au Printemps   Take a look at the facade of this store for a reminder of the Gilded Age. Inside, the merchandise is divided into housewares (**Printemps Maison),** women's fashion (**Printemps de la Mode),** and men's clothes (**Le Printemps de l'Homme).** This is better for women's and children's fashion than Galeries Lafayette. As for the top names in perfume, it's in a dead-heat with Galeries Lafayette. Although visitors feel more pampered in Galeries Lafayette, Au Printemps's customer service is dazzling, putting all major department stores in Paris to shame. Check out the magnificent stained-glass dome, through which turquoise light cascades into the sixth-floor **Café Flo,** where you can have a coffee or a full meal. Interpreters at the Welcome Service in Printemps de la Mode will help you find what you're looking for, claim your VAT refund, and so on. Au Printemps also has a tourist discount card, offering a flat 10% discount. Immediately adjacent to the store and under the same management, but with its own phone and storefront, is **Citadium,** 56 rue Caumartin, 9e (© **01-55-31-74-00),** which specializes in sporting equipment and sports clothes for men, women, and children. Open Monday to Wednesday and Friday to Saturday 9:35am to 7pm; Thursday 9:35am to 9pm. 64 bd. Haussmann, 9e. © 01-42-82-50-00. Métro: Havre-Caumartin. RER: Auber or Haussmann–St-Lazare.

Finds **Spying on Paris as a Shopper**

Everyone knows about the views from the Eiffel Tower and Sacré-Coeur. Here's another. Shoppers can take the elevator and some stairs to the 11th floor at the top of the **La Samaritaine** department store (No. 2) at 19 rue de la Monnaie, 1e (© 01-40-41-20-20; Métro: Pont Neuf or Châtelet–Les Halles). At 74m (243 ft.), a 360-degree panorama sweeps across Paris, including the bridge pont Neuf, the dome of Invalides where Napoleon rests, and the cathedral at Notre-Dame. An enamel frieze on the store's roof identifies the landmarks for you. The platform is open Monday to Saturday from 9:30am to 7pm (until 10pm Thurs).

Colette   Named after the great French writer, Colette is a swank citadel for a la mode fashion. It buzzes with excitement, displaying fashions by some of the city's most promising young talents, including Marni and Lucien Pellat-Finet. This is for the sophisticated shopper who'd never be caught dead shopping the Galeries Lafayette and the like. Not to be overlooked are home furnishings by designers like Tom Dixon and even zany Japanese accessories. Even if you don't plan to buy anything, patronize the tea salon, with its fresh quiches, salads, and cakes, plus three dozen brands of bottled water. Open Monday to Saturday 11am to 7:30pm. 213 rue St-Honoré, 1e. ✆ **01-55-35-33-90.** Métro: Tuileries or Pyramide.

Galeries Lafayette   Opened in 1896, with a lobby capped by an early-1900s stained-glass cupola classified as a historic monument, Galeries Lafayette is Europe's largest department store. If you have time for only one department store, make it this one. This store could provision a small city with everything from perfume to fashion. It is even more user friendly than Au Printemps, and in fashion it places more emphasis on upcoming designers. It also concentrates on an upscale roster of everything you need to furnish and maintain a home; thousands of racks of clothing for men, women, and children; and a staggering array of cosmetics, makeup products, and perfumes. Menswear is concentrated in a section called **Lafayette Hommes;** also in the complex is **Lafayette Gourmet,** one of the fanciest grocery stores in Paris, selling culinary exotica at prices usually lower than those at Fauchon (see "Food: Chocolate, Honey, Pâtés & More," below). A floor above street level is a concentration of high-end semi-independent boutiques, including Cartier, Vuitton, and Prada Sport. A fashion show is held at least once daily, usually in the **Salon Opéra.** At the street-level **Welcome Desk,** you can be told in many languages where you can find this or that in the store, where you can get a taxi back to your hotel, and so on. Open Monday to Wednesday and Friday to Saturday 9:30am to 6:45pm; Thursday 9:30am to 9pm. 40 bd. Haussmann, 9e. ✆ **01-42-82-34-56.** Métro: Chaussée d'Antin. RER: Auber.

Talmaris   This is called the world's smallest department store. Actually, it's a boutique showcase for Alain-Paul Ruzé, who spends 6 months a year traveling the world picking up treasures which he brings back to Paris and sells at this outlet. He's likely to turn up with about anything, perhaps an American flag from the 1700s that he discovered in a Greenwich Village flea market in Manhattan. Both costly and less expensive items are sold. 61 av. Mozart, 16e. ✆ **01-42-88-20-20.** Métro: Ranelagh.

FABRICS

Souleiado   This is the only Paris branch of one of Provence's most successful purveyors of the bright fabrics and thick pottery of France's southern tier. Fabrics are measured out by scissors-wielding saleswomen, then sold by the meter for seamstresses to whip into curtains, tablecloths, or whatever. There's also rack after rack of *prêt-à-poser* (ready to hang) curtains, tablecloths, and bedcovers, each based on historically accurate reproductions of 18th-century prints as discovered in such cities as Avignon, Arles, and Marseille. In a separate shop just around the corner, at 78 rue de Seine (same phone), there are displays of table settings, housewares, and gift items, each reflecting the bright sunshine and colors (usually ochre, cerulean blue, and a strong medium green) of the Midi. Open Monday to Saturday 11:30am to 7pm. 3 rue Lobineau, 6e. ✆ **01-43-54-62-25.** Métro: Odéon or Mabillon.

Finds **A Touch of Africa in the Marais**

A stroll down Rue Elzévir in the Marais is like a trip to Senegal. Valeria Schlumberger, a Frenchwoman who lives for part of the year on Ile de Gorée, off the coast of Dakar, has opened up several storefronts on this street in the Marais, all under the umbrella organization of La Compagnie du Sénégal et de l'Afrique de l'Ouest (www.csao.fr). Madame Schlumberger's aim is to distribute the crafts and products of the craftspeople of West Africa to the Paris market. For example, you can find beautiful hand-woven and hand-dyed bolts of cloth that make fabulous curtains, cushion covers, or quilts. Many decorative items are made of recycled material where metallic bits and pieces are turned into decorative objects from tins, cans, or even aerosol sprays. Multicolored carpets are sold, along with basketwork, and paintings. The leading outlets, all in the 3rd Arrondissement, include **The Boutique,** 1–3 Rue Elzévir (✆ **01-44-54-55-88**); and **La Gallery,** 15 rue Elzévir (✆ **01-44-54-90-50**). **La Jokko,** 5 rue Elzévir (✆ **01-42-74-35-96**), is a languid bar, ideal for drinking between rounds of shopping. At the association's restaurant, **le Petit Dakar,** 6 rue Elzévir (✆ **01-44-59-34-74**), you can order such native specialties as grouper with cassava and rice, topped off by lychee ice cream.

FASHION
CUTTING-EDGE CHIC

Azzedine Alaïa   Alaïa, who became the darling of French fashion in the 1970s, is the man who put body consciousness back into Paris chic. If you can't afford the current collection, try the **stock shop** around the corner at 18 rue de Verrerie, 4e (✆ **01-42-72-19-19**), where last year's leftovers are sold at serious discounts. Both outlets sell leather trench coats, knit dresses, pleated skirts, cigarette pants, belts, purses, and fashion accessories. Open Monday to Saturday 10am to 7pm. 7 rue de Moussy, 4e. ✆ **01-42-72-19-19**. Métro: Hôtel-de-Ville.

Courrèges   Don't look now: André Courrèges is hot again. Even those little white vinyl go-go boots and disco purses in silver metallic cloth are back. Courrèges brings a humorous touch to 1970s retro, with bold color, plastic, and fun. Open Monday to Saturday 10am to 7pm. 40 rue François-Ier, 8e. ✆ **01-53-67-30-00**. Métro: Franklin-D.-Roosevelt.

Hervé Leger   This creator of the Band Aid Dress *(La Robe à bandes),* a tightly wrapped concoction of stretch materials and color, has opened his own shop for those with curves to flaunt and cash to burn. Open Monday to Saturday 10am to 7pm. 29 rue du Faubourg St-Honoré, 8e. ✆ **01-40-20-16-50**. Métro: Concorde or Madeleine.

Jean Paul Gaultier   Supporters of this high-camp, high-fashion mogul describe him as an avant-garde classicist without allegiance to any of the aesthetic restrictions of the bourgeoisie. Detractors call him a glorified punk rocker with a gimmicky allegiance to futurist models as interpreted by *Star Trek.* Whatever your opinion, it's always refreshing and insightful, especially for fashion buffs, to check out France's most iconoclastic designer. There's a franchise branch of his store at 6 rue Vivienne, 2e (✆ **01-42-86-05-05;** Métro: Bourse), but the company's main branch, and site of its biggest inventories, is at avenue George V. Open Monday and Saturday 10:30am to 7pm; Tuesday to Friday 10am to 7pm. 40 av. George V, 8e. ✆ **01-44-43-00-44**. Métro: George-V.

Lolita Lempicka   Her name and reputation as a fashion designer originated in the underground arts scene of the Marais. Since then, she's gone mainstream with a pair of shops, each highly visible and stacked with the kind of long and short dresses a woman can wear at a formal or relaxed-chic cocktail or dinner party. Clothes are inventive and usually very sexy, often in colors that include soft black, varying shades of pink, turquoise, and brownish-maroon. They also stock women's shoes. Open Monday to Saturday 10:30am to 7pm. 46 av. Victor-Hugo, 16e. © 01-45-02-14-46. Métro: Etoile.

DESIGNER BOUTIQUES & FASHION FLAGSHIPS

There are two primary fields of dreams in Paris when it comes to showcasing the international big names: rue du Faubourg St-Honoré and avenue Montaigne. Though the Left Bank is gaining in status with recent additions like Dior, Armani, and Vuitton, the heart of the international designer parade is on the Right Bank.

Rue du Faubourg St-Honoré is so famous and fancy it's simply known as "the Faubourg." It was the traditional miracle mile until recent years, when the really exclusive shops shunned it for the wider and even more deluxe avenue Montaigne at the other end of the arrondissement. (It's a long but pleasant walk from one fashion strip to the other.) **Avenue Montaigne** is filled with almost unspeakably fancy shops, but a few of them have affordable cafes (try Joseph at no. 14) and all have sales help that's almost always cordial to the well dressed.

The mix is quite international—from British (**Joseph**), to German (**Jil Sander**), to Italian (**Krizia**). **Chanel, Lacroix, Porthault, Ricci, Dior,** and **Ungaro** are a few of the big French names. Also check out some of the lesser-known creative powers. And don't miss a visit to **Caron.** Most of the designer shops sell men's and women's clothing. The Faubourg hosts other traditional favorites: **Hermès, Lanvin, Jaeger, Rykiel,** and the upstart **Façonnable,** which sells preppy men's clothing in the United States through a business deal with Nordstroms. Lanvin has its own men's shop (**Lanvin Homme**), which has a cafe that's perfect for a light (and affordable) lunch.

Alain Figaret   Alain Figaret is one of France's foremost designers of men's shirts and women's blouses. Though this store has a broad range of fabrics, 100% cotton is its specialty. Also check out the silk neckties in distinctively designed prints and the silk scarves for women. If you're comparison shopping, Figaret and Charvet (see below) are half a block apart. Open Monday to Saturday 10am to 7:30pm. 21 rue de la Paix, 2e. © 01-42-65-04-99. Métro: Opéra.

Chanel   If you can't have the sun, the moon, and the stars, at least buy something with Coco Chanel's initials on it, either a serious fashion statement (drop-dead chic) or something fun and playful (tongue in chic). Karl Lagerfeld's designs come in all flavors and have added a subtle twist to Chanel's classicism. This store is adjacent to the Chanel couture house and behind the Ritz, where Mlle Chanel once lived. Check out the beautiful staircase of the *maison* before you shop the two-floor boutique—it's well worth a peek. Open Monday to Saturday 10am to 7pm. 31 rue Cambon, 1e. © 01-42-86-26-00. Métro: Concorde or Tuileries.

Charvet   The duke of Windsor made Charvet famous, but Frenchmen of distinction have been buying their shirts here for years. The store offers ties, pocket squares, underwear, and pajamas as well, plus women's shirts, all custom-tailored or straight off the peg. Open Monday to Saturday 10am to 6:30pm. 28 place Vendôme, 1e. © 01-42-60-30-70. Métro: Opéra.

Christian Dior   This fashion house is set up like a small department store, selling men's, women's, and children's clothing, as well as affordable gift items, makeup, and perfume on the street level. For several years, cutting-edge Brit designer John Galliano has been in charge of the collections. Unlike some of the other big-name fashion houses, Dior is very approachable. Open Monday to Saturday 10am to 7pm. 30 av. Montaigne, 8e. ✆ 01-40-73-54-44. Métro: Franklin-D.-Roosevelt.

Givenchy   This deluxe outlet opened in 1962 and is often mentioned in annual lists of best-dressed women. Both branches listed below sell very high-quality ready-to-wear clothing for both men and women, but if you're a woman who's looking for examples of an increasingly rarified art form, head for the branch on the avenue George V, and proceed one floor above street level. Open Monday to Saturday 10am to 7:30pm. 3 av. George V, 8e. ✆ 01-44-31-50-00. Métro: Alma-Marceau. Also: 28 rue du Faubourg St-Honoré, 8e. ✆ 01-42-65-54-54. Métro: Franklin-D.-Roosevelt.

Hermès   France's single most important status item is a scarf or tie from Hermès. Patterns on these illustrious scarves, retailing for about 240€ ($276), have recently included the galaxies, Africa, the sea, the sun, and horse racing and breeding. But the choices don't stop there—this large flagship store has beach towels and accessories, dinner plates, clothing for men and women, a large collection of Hermès fragrances, and even a saddle shop; a package of postcards is the least expensive item sold. Ask to see the private museum upstairs. Outside, note the horseman on the roof with his scarf-flag flying. Open Monday to Saturday 10:30am to 6:30pm. 24 rue du Faubourg St-Honoré, 8e. ✆ 01-40-17-47-17. Métro: Concorde.

Louis Vuitton   Its luggage is among the most famous and prestigious in the world, a standard accessory aboard the first-class cabins of aircraft flying transatlantic and transpacific. Not content to cover the world's luggage with his initials, Vuitton has branched into leather goods, writing instruments, travel products, and publishing. Look for the traditional collection of leather, including Vuitton's monogrammed brown-on-brown bags in printed canvas, on the street level. The mezzanine showcases upscale pens, writing supplies, and stationery. And the top floor carries the company's newest line—women's shoes and bags. Open Monday to Saturday 10am to 7pm. 6 place St-Germain-des-Prés, 6e. ✆ 01-45-49-62-32. Métro: St-Germain-des-Prés.

Yves Saint Laurent   One of France's most creative and interesting designers burst into world fame in the 1970s with his use of rich patterns and textures in women's evening wear, and has been going strong ever since. If you're looking to acquire clothing designed (or inspired) by his precedents, there are several branches. Women's clothing, of all degrees of formality, is sold at 19–21 avenue Victor-Hugo, 16e (✆ 01-45-00-64-64; Métro: Etoile). The only outlet in Paris with clothing for men (in addition to clothing for women) is at 12 place St-Sulpice, 6e (✆ 01-43-26-84-40 for the menswear department; 01-43-29-43-00 for women's wear). If you're looking for custom-tailored haute couture, and a fabulously expensive garment that might end up on the society pages of your local newspaper or in a museum in 20 years, head for Yves Saint Laurent Haute Couture. All stores open Monday 1 to 7pm; Tuesday to Saturday 10:30am to 7pm. 5 av. Marceau, 16e. ✆ 01-44-31-64-00. Métro: Alma-Marceau.

DISCOUNT & RESALE

Anna Lowe   Adjacent to the Bristol Hotel, one of the most expensive addresses in Paris, is one of the city's premier boutiques for women who want to purchase heavily discounted clothing (new, with labels intact) from some of the world's best-known fashion designers. Expect discounts of up to 50% on last year's collections from such artists as Valentino, Thierry Mugler, John Galliano,

Chanel, Versace, and many more. Your find might be what a model wore down the runway at last year's fashion show, excess inventories from factories that— for whatever reason—never got paid, or overstock from boutiques looking to make room for new inventories. Prices are reasonable and the labels, in many cases, still retain their old magic and sense of chic. Open Monday to Saturday 10am to 7pm. 104 rue du Faubourg St-Honoré, 8e. © 01-42-66-11-32. Métro: Miromesnil.

Annexe des Créateurs   Few stores in Paris have received as much publicity recently as this high-end, very glamorous discount outlet, where the collections of top-drawer designers are discounted by between 30% and 70%. Charming owner and founder Edwige Meister inventories the slightly out-of-date women's wear of Mügler, Versace, Moschino, Gaulthier, Vivienne Westwood, and more. The staff insists that garments are in "perfect or near-perfect condition," and usually derive from terribly wealthy, obsessively stylish women who refuse to wear any garment more than once. It "isn't inconceivable," according to Mlle Meister, for a client to sell (on consignment) a garment in one of these two boutiques, then immediately pass through the interconnecting door to buy a used (but unworn) garment in the boutique's counterpart a few steps away. *Note:* Plans for this organization's future involve selling used garments via the Web at www.annexedescreateurs.com. Open Tuesday to Saturday 11am to 7pm. 19 rue Godot de Mauroy, 9e. © 01-42-65-46-40. Métro: Madeleine.

Au Gré du Vent   This is where the wives of diplomats and millionaires and self-made women from all arenas of Parisian life arrive, discreetly, with plastic shopping bags loaded with occasionally worn couture, which Au Gré du Vent sells on consignment. Hanging enticingly in this cheerful store—depending on that day's inventory—might be garments from Chanel, Hermès, Prada, Gucci, Dolce & Gabbana, or Gaulthier. You won't always find the size or style you're looking for, but a woman with a sense of adventure can have a lot of fun here. Open Monday 3 to 7pm; Tuesday to Saturday 11am to 7pm. 10 rue des Quatre Vents, 6e. © 01-44-07-28-73. Métro: Odéon.

Défilé des Marques   French TV stars often shop here, picking up St. Laurent, Dior, Lacroix, Prada, Chanel, Versace, Hermès, and others at a fraction of the price. Yes, they sell discounted Hermès scarves as well. Low prices here derive from the skill of the owners at picking up used clothing in good condition from last year's collections, and in some cases, retro-chic clothing from collections of many years ago, sometimes from estate sales. Open Tuesday to Saturday 11am to 7:30pm. 171 rue de Grenelles, 7e. © 01-45-55-63-47. Métro: Latour-Maubourg.

Le Depot-Vente de Buci-Bourbon   This is one of the best consignment shops in the 6th arrondissement, with a wide array of merchandise for both men and women. Who knows what you'll find? Perhaps marked-down Hermès scarves, Valentino skirts, Chanel shoes, and Givenchy blouses. Open Tuesday to Saturday 10am to 7pm. 4–6 rue de Bourbon-de-Château, 6e. © 01-46-34-45-05. Métro: Mabillon.

L'Une et L'Autre *Finds*   Hidden in an apartment on the second floor of a building, this shop has amazing discounts on the big brand names sold in expensive 16th arrondissement boutiques. An item that might sell for 535€ ($615) in a boutique is sold here for 230€ ($265). Open Monday to Friday and first Saturday of the month 11am to 6pm. 24 rue Feydeau, 2e. © 01-44-76-03-03. Métro: St-Paul.

Réciproque   Forget about serious bargains, but celebrate what could be your only opportunity to own designer clothing of this caliber. Within a series of seven storefronts side by side along the same avenue, you'll find used clothing from every major name in fashion, along with shoes, accessories, menswear, and wedding gifts. Everything has been worn, but some items only on fashion runways or during photo shoots. Open Tuesday to Friday 11am to 7:30pm; Saturday 10:30am to 7:30pm. 88–123 rue de la Pompe, 16e. ℭ **01-47-04-30-28.** Métro: Pompe.

SR Store   This is where great designer Sonia Rykiel dumps all that good stuff she didn't move in main-line boutiques. Everything is half price. Open Tuesday to Saturday 10am to 7pm. 64 rue d'Alésia, 14e. ℭ **01-43-95-06-13.** Métro: Alésia.

Tati Galerie Gaité   Some of its fans define this place as a low-end version of Galeries Lafayette (see above), with lower prices and a lot less class. What you'll find is crowded display racks, relatively indifferent service, and absolutely no emphasis on architectural finesse. Despite that, the place does a roaring business in, among others, sales of wedding dresses that range from bouffant to sleek. The displays sprawl over several floors of jumbled-up housewares, clothing, sportswear and sporting-goods equipment, and kitchenware. Genuine bargains can sometimes be culled from the maze. Open Monday to Saturday 9:30am to 7:30pm. 68 rue du Maine, 14e. ℭ **01-56-80-06-80.** Métro: Gaité. Also: 4 bd. Rochechouart, 18e. ℭ **01-55-29-50-00.** Métro: Barbés.

VINTAGE COUTURE

Didier Ludot   Fashion historians salivate when they're confronted with an inventory of vintage haute couture. In this frenetically stylish shop, albeit at prices that rival what you'd expect to pay for a serious antique, you'll find a selection of gowns and dresses created between 1900 and 1980 for designing women who looked *faaabulous* at Maxim's, at chic cocktail parties on the avenue Foch, in Deauville, or wherever. Open Monday to Saturday 11am to 7pm. 24 Galerie de Montpensier, in the arcades surrounding the courtyard of the Palais-Royal, 1e. ℭ **01-42-96-06-56.** Métro: Palais-Royal.

FOOD: CHOCOLATE, HONEY, PATES & MORE

Albert Ménès   One of Paris's most prestigious small-scale purveyors of foodstuffs prides itself on selling only goods that have been picked, processed, and packaged by hand. The 45 producers represented offer sugared almonds, Breton sardines, exotic honeys, terrines, jams, pâtés, baked goods, and more. It's all esoteric, even by French standards. Ménès prides itself, strangely enough, on being the first food store in France to import both Heinz Ketchup and Kellogg's Corn Flakes, both of which appeared on shelves for the first time here in the 1920s. Open Monday 2 to 7pm; Tuesday to Friday 11am to 7pm. 41 bd. Malesherbes, 8e. ℭ **01-42-66-95-63.** Métro: St-Augustin or Madeleine.

Christian Constant   Opened in 1970, Christian Constant sells some of Paris's most delectable chocolates by the kilo. Each is a blend of ingredients from Ecuador, Colombia, or Venezuela, usually mingled with scents of spices and flowers like orange blossoms, jasmine, the Asian blossom *ylang,* and *vetiver* and *verveine* (herbs usually used to brew tea). Open Monday to Friday 8:30am to 9pm; Saturday to Sunday 8am to 8:30pm. 37 rue d'Assas, 6e. ℭ **01-53-63-15-15.** Métro: St-Placide.

Fauchon   At place de la Madeleine stands one of the city's most popular sights—not the church, but Fauchon, a hyperupscale megadelicatessen that thrives within a city famous for its finicky eaters. It's divided into three divisions that include an *épicerie* (for jams, crackers, pastas, and exotic canned goods); a *pâtissier* (for breads, pastries, and chocolates); and a *traiteur* (for cheeses, terrines, pâtés, caviar, and fruits). Prices are steep, but the inventories—at least to serious foodies—are fascinating. At some (but not all) of the counters, you'll indicate to attendants what you want from behind glass display cases, and get an electronic ticket, which you'll carry to a *caisse* (cash register). Surrender your tickets, pay the tally, then return to the counter to pick up your groceries. In other cases, you simply load up your shopping basket with whatever you want and pay for your purchases at a cash register, just as you would at any grocery store.

On the same premises, Fauchon has a restaurant, **Brasserie Fauchon,** and a tea salon, which showcases the pastry-making talents of its chefs. Among the many offerings is a *Paris-Brest,* a ring in the shape of a bicycle wheel that's loaded with pastry cream, almond praline, buttercream, and hazelnut paste capped with almonds. Open Monday to Saturday 9:30am to 7pm. 26–30 place de la Madeleine, 8e. ℂ 01-47-42-60-11. Métro: Madeleine.

Hédiard   This 1850 temple of *haute gastronomie* has recently been renovated, perhaps to woo tourists away from Fauchon. The decor is a series of salons filled with almost Disneyesque displays meant to give the store the look of an early-1900s spice emporium. Hédiard is rich in coffees, teas, jams, and spices. The decor changes with whatever holiday (Halloween, Easter, Bastille Day) or special promotion (the coffees of Brazil, the teas of Ceylon) are in effect at the time. Upstairs, you can eat at the Restaurant de l'Epicerie. Open Monday to Saturday 9am to 11pm. 21 place de la Madeleine, 8e. ℂ 01-43-12-88-77. Métro: Madeleine.

Jadis et Gourmande   This chain of chocolatiers has a less lofty rep than Christian Constant and more reasonable prices. They're best known for their alphabetical chocolate blocks, which allow you to spell out any message (well . . . almost), in any language. *"Merci"* comes prepackaged. Open Monday 1 to 7pm; Tuesday to Saturday 10am to 7pm. 27 rue Boissy d'Anglas, 8e. ℂ 01-42-65-23-23. Métro: Madeleine.

La Maison du Chocolat   At its five Paris locations, this shop offers racks of marvelous chocolates priced individually or by the kilo, at around 92€ ($106) per kilo (about 2 lb.). These stores offer a variety of chocolate-based products,

Food Markets

Outdoor markets are plentiful in Paris. Some of the better-known are the **Marché Buci** (see "Markets" below); the **rue Mouffetard market,** open Tuesday to Sunday from 9:30am to 1pm and Tuesday to Saturday from 4 to 7pm (6e; Métro: Monge or Censier-Daubenton); and the **rue Montorgueil market,** behind the St-Eustache church, open Monday to Saturday from 9am to 7pm (1e; Métro: Les Halles). The trendiest market is **Marché Biologique,** along boulevard Raspail, a tree-lined stretch lying between rue de Rennes and rue du Cherche-Midi, 6e. It's open Sunday 8:30am to 6:30pm (Métro: Montparnasse). Even Parisian celebrities can be spotted shopping under brightly colored awnings among the stacks of organic dairy products, fish, seafood, and fresh fruits and vegetables. You can also eat here, perhaps lured to a vendor from Brittany making whole-grain crepes or one selling algae bread. Nonfood items are also for sale. Do you own a doormat made from recycled tires? You could if you shop here.

including chocolate pastries, usually more affordable than the candy, and even chocolate milk! All locations open Monday to Saturday, May to October 10am to 7pm; November to April 10am to 7:30pm. 225 rue du Faubourg St-Honoré, 8e. © 01-42-27-39-44. Métro: Ternes. Also: 52 rue François-Ier, 8e. © 01-47-23-38-25. Métro: Alma-Marceau. 8 bd. de la Madeleine, 8e. © 01-47-42-86-52. Métro: Madeleine. 19 rue de Sèvres, 6e. © 01-45-44-20-40. Métro: Rue de Sèvres. 89 av. Raymond-Poincaré, 16e. © 01-40-67-77-83. Métro: Victor-Hugo.

Le Maison du Miel   "The House of Honey" has been a family tradition since before World War I. The entire store is devoted to products made from honey: honey oil, honey soap, and various honeys to eat, including one made from heather. This store owes a tremendous debt to the busy bee. Monday to Saturday 9:15am to 7pm. 24 rue Vignon, 9e. © 01-47-42-26-70. Métro: Madeleine, Havre-Caumartin, or Opéra.

Les Abeilles *Finds*   This store inventories a greater supply of French honey than we've ever seen in one place. Test your understanding of France's geography by asking for honey that's culled from flowers in whatever region of the country you specify. And for a scented reminder of your trip to the City of Light, ask for "urban honey" from beehives within Paris and its suburbs. Because of the wide variety of flowers and shrubs from which urban bees gather their nectar, this honey may be among the most desirable of all. Open Tuesday to Saturday 11am to 7pm. 21 rue de la Butte-aux-Cailles, 13e. © 01-45-81-43-48. Métro: Place d'Italie or Corvisart.

Maison de la Truffe   Cramped and convivial, the layout of this shop was modeled after a Parisian's fantasy of an affable, cluttered, old-fashioned butcher shop in Lyon. It's an excellent source for foie gras, caviar, black and white truffles, and other high-end foodstuffs. Artfully assembled gift baskets are a house specialty. One corner is devoted to a restaurant where many (but not all) of the dishes contain the costly items (especially truffles) sold in the shop. Examples include noodles or risottos with truffles, and caviar with all the fixings. A prix fixe menu costs 19€ ($22) without truffles, 60€ ($69) with truffles. Most main courses cost 16€ to 98€ ($18–$113), except for caviar, which begins at 135€ to 240€ ($155–$276) per person. The restaurant is open during the open hours of the shop, although the last food order is accepted 45 minutes prior to closing. Open Monday 9:30am to 8pm; Tuesday to Saturday 9:30am to 9pm. 19 place de la Madeleine, 8e. © 01-42-65-53-22. Métro: Madeleine or Auber.

Poilâne   One of Paris's best-loved bakeries, Poilâne hasn't changed much since it opened in 1932. Come here to taste and admire the beautiful loaves of bread decorated with simple designs of leaves and flowers that'll make you yearn for an all-but-vanished Paris. Specialties include apple tarts, butter cookies, and a chewy sourdough loaf cooked in a wood-burning oven. Breads can be specially wrapped to stay fresh during your journey home. Cash only. *Note:* Cherche-Midi location open Monday to Saturday 7:15am to 8pm; Grenelle location Tuesday to Sunday 7:15am to 8:15pm. 8 rue du Cherche-Midi, 6e. © 01-45-48-42-59. Métro: St-Sulpice. Also: 49 bd. de Grenelle, 15e. © 01-45-79-11-49. Métro: Dupleix.

JEWELRY

Bijoux Burma   If you can't afford any of the spectacular and expensive bijoux at the city's world-famous jewelers, come here to console yourself with some of the best fakes anywhere. This quality costume jewelry is the secret weapon of many a Parisian woman. Open Monday to Saturday 10am to 6:30pm. 50 rue François-Ier, 8e. © 01-47-23-70-93. Métro: Franklin-D.-Roosevelt.

The City's Most Historic Shopping Arcade

When one of history's greatest shoppers, Thomas Jefferson, wanted, say, an ivory-handled knife or a timepiece, he headed for the **Palais Royal,** 1e (Métro: Louvre–Palais Royal), just across rue de Rivoli from the Louvre. Even before the Revolution, the arcades of the Palais Royal were known for their sheltered shops and cafes.

Paris is rich in iron-and-glass galleries, the first "shopping malls" of the Western world, but some are a bit seedy. In our view, none has the charm of the Palais Royal. You can enter, among other choices, the arcades from the **rue de Montpensier** behind the Comédie-Française.

Following in the footsteps of Colette or Jean Cocteau, former residents, you can spend a lovely afternoon. The merchandise? Almost anything. As you wander, here's a sampling of what might await you: military medals, traditional lead-made French toy soldiers, vintage clothes from any number of fashionistas (perhaps creations of Patou or Balenciaga), silk vests, wooden toys, music boxes, accessories for women, bronze sculptures, china, cobalt glass, perfumes, antiques (mainly neoclassical), autographs of famous French celebrities, hand-crafted shoes—you name it.

Expensive **Le Grand Véfour,** one of the greatest restaurants of Paris, is recommended in chapter 6. You can dine much more modestly at **restaurant du Palais Royal,** 110 galerie de Valois (✆ **01-40-20-00-27**), which is closed Sunday. In summer the restaurant's tables spread out into the garden. Or you can order tea at **La Muscade,** 67 galerie de Montpensier (✆ **01-42-97-51-36**), with its restored garden. Treat yourself to the orange-and-chocolate tart. Closed Monday.

Cartier   One of the most famous jewelers in the world, Cartier has prohibitive prices to match its glamorous image. Go to gawk, and if your pockets are deep enough, pick up an expensive trinket. Open Monday to Saturday 10:30am to 7pm. 23 place Vendôme, 1e. ✆ **01-44-55-32-50**. Métro: Opéra or Tuileries.

Van Cleef & Arpels   Years ago, Van Cleef's designers came up with an intricate technique that remains a vital part of its allure—the invisible setting, wherein a band of sparkling gemstones, each cut to interlock with its neighbor, creates an uninterrupted flash of brilliance. Come browse with the rich and famous. Open Monday to Saturday 10am to 7pm. 22 place Vendôme, 1e. ✆ **01-53-45-45-45**. Métro: Opéra or Tuileries.

KITCHENWARE

A. Simon   Established in 1884, this large kitchenware shop supplies restaurants and professional kitchens. But it will also cover your table with everything from menu cards and wine tags to knives, copper pots, and pans—not to mention white paper doilies and those funny little paper things they put on top of the tablecloth at bistros. Open Monday 2 to 6:30pm; Tuesday to Saturday 9am to 6pm. 48 rue Montmartre, 2e. ✆ **01-42-33-71-65**. Métro: Les Halles.

Dehillerin   Dehillerin is Paris's most famous cookware shop, in the "kitchen corridor," alongside A. Simon (see above) and several other kitchenware stores.

The shop has more of a professional feel to it than beginner-friendly A. Simon, but don't be intimidated. Equipped with the right tools from Dehillerin, you, too, can learn to cook like a master chef. Open Monday 9am to 12:30pm and 2 to 6pm; Tuesday to Saturday 9am to 6pm. 18 rue Coquillière, 1e. ✆ 01-42-36-53-13. Métro: Les Halles.

LEATHER GOODS

Morabito   This glamorous leather purveyor was originally established by an Italian entrepreneur on the place Vendôme in 1905. In the 1990s, it was partially acquired by an organization in Tokyo. Today, from a site on the very glamorous rue François Ier, it sells chicer-than-thou handbags that begin at a bare minimum of 200€ ($230) and quickly climb to 9,120€ ($10,488) and more. There are also suitcases—some of the best in Paris—for men and women. Open Monday to Friday 10am to 6:45pm; Saturday 11am to 6:30pm. 55 rue François Ier, 1e. ✆ 01-53-23-90-40. Métro: George-V.

LINENS

Vis a Vis   Vis a Vis sells what some connoisseurs have described as the most beautiful sheets, pillowcases, and table linens in the world. Most are designed by Danielle Postel-Vinay, whose factory in the 12th arrondissement employs 150 professional embroiderers who labor at the depictions of flowers, tendrils, vines, clover blossoms, dragonflies, birds, and butterflies that grace the products sold here. At its most extravagant and indulgent, a single lace-trimmed, linen bedsheet with two pillowcases might require 6 months to weave, and sell for 4,500€ ($5,175). Not everything here is so costly. The most frequently used fabrics include Egyptian cotton, and to a lesser degree, cotton, satin, linen, and silk. Also sold are baby clothes, any of which would be appropriate for a christening or a baptism in front of thousands. Open Monday to Saturday 10:30am to 7pm. 25 rue Royale, 8e. ✆ 01-43-12-55-40. Métro: Madeleine.

LINGERIE

Cadolle   Herminie Cadolle invented the brassiere in 1889. Today her family manages the store she founded, and they still make specialty brassieres for the Crazy Horse Saloon. This is the place to go if you want made-to-order items or are hard to fit. Open Monday to Saturday 9:30am to 1pm and 2 to 6:30pm. 14 rue Cambon, 1e. ✆ 01-42-60-38-37. Métro: Concorde.

Nikita   This is the discount sales outlet for all the big names in lingerie, including Bolero, Lise Charmel, Lejaby, Simone Pérèle, and Aubade. Most of the lingerie sold here is half the price of its counterparts in Right Bank boutiques. Open Monday to Saturday 9:30am to 7:30pm; Sunday 9:30am to 1pm. 22 rue Levis, 7e. ✆ 01-42-12-01-30. Métro: Villiers.

Sabbia Rosa   Everything here is filmy, silky, and sexy. Look for undergarments (slips, brassieres, and panties) and the kind of negligees that might've been favored by Brigitte Bardot in *And God Created Woman*. Madonna has been spotted shopping for panties that can go as high as 520€ ($598). Open Monday to Saturday 10am to 7pm. 73 rue des Sts-Pères, 6e. ✆ 01-45-48-88-37. Métro: Sèvres-Babylone or St-Germain.

MALLS

Carrousel du Louvre   If you want to combine an accessible location, a fun food court, boutiques, and plenty of museum gift shops with a touch of culture, don't miss the Carrousel. Always mobbed, this is one of the few venues allowed to open on Sunday. There's a Virgin Megastore, a branch of The Body Shop, and several other emporiums for conspicuous consumption. Check out Diane Claire for the fanciest souvenirs of Paris you've ever seen. Open Tuesday to Sunday 10am to 8pm. 99 rue de Rivoli, 1e. No phone. Métro: Palais Royal or Musée du Louvre.

Forum des Halles   Once the site of Paris's great produce market, Les Halles is now a vast crater of modern metal with layers of boutiques built around a courtyard. There's one of everything here, but the feel is very sterile, without a hint of Parisian *joie de vivre*. Open Monday to Saturday 10am to 7:30pm. 1-7 rue Pierre-Lescot, 1e. No phone. Métro: Etienne-Marcel or Châtelet–Les Halles.

Les Trois Quartiers   Named after the junction of the three neighborhoods (Madeleine, Opéra, and Concorde) where it sits, this is a mall of at least 19 upscale boutiques specializing in clothing, perfume, and cosmetics for men and women. The largest is Madelios, a menswear store that stocks Yves Saint Laurent, Ralph Lauren, and Hugo Boss, among others. Open Monday to Saturday 10am to 6pm. 21 bd. de la Madeleine, 1e. ✆ 01-42-97-80-06. Métro: Madeleine.

Marché St-Germain   The Marché St-Germain used to be an open-air food market until it was transformed into a modern shopping mall. Now only a few food and vegetable stalls remain in one corner; low ceilings, neon lights, and mostly American and British chain stores like Kitchen Bazaar and Kenzo dominate the rest of the market. Open Monday to Saturday 10am to 8pm. 14 rue Lobineau, 6e. ✆ 01-43-26-01-44. Métro: Mabillon.

Montparnasse Shopping Centre   This shopping center is sort of a quick-fix minimall in a business center and hotel (Le Meredien) complex, with a small branch of Galeries Lafayette and some inexpensive boutiques. Visiting it is really worthwhile only if you also take a trip across the street to Inno, with its deluxe supermarket in the basement. Open Monday to Saturday 8:30am to 10pm. Between rue de l'Arrivée and 22 rue du Départ, 14e. No phone. Métro: Montparnasse-Bienvenue.

Palais des Congrès de Paris Boutiques   A shopping center for convention-goers inside the Palais des Congrès, this mall offers some 50 shops, including branch stores of many French big names. You'll also find a Japanese department store and hairdresser. Its anonymity and distance from most of touristy Paris has taken its toll on some of the shops, but if you happen to be in the neighborhood, it might be useful. Open Monday to Saturday 10am to 7pm. 2 place de la Porte-Maillot, 17e. No phone. Métro: Porte Maillot.

MARKETS

Marché aux Fleurs   Artists and photographers love to capture the Flower Market on canvas or film. The stalls are ablaze with color, and each is a showcase of flowers, most of which escaped the perfume factories of Grasse on the French Riviera. The Flower Market is along the Seine, behind the Tribunal de Commerce. On Sunday it becomes the **Marché aux Oiseaux (Bird Market).** Open daily 8:30am to 4pm. Place Louis-Lépine, Ile de la Cité, 4e. No phone. Métro: Cité.

Marché aux Livres Ancien et d'Occasion   This charming two-building market for used books, old books, rare books, and ephemera is in the middle of nowhere but thronged by serious collectors. The market is covered but open, and doesn't close on a rainy day—the valuable texts are draped in plastic. (For more books, don't forget the *bouquinistes* along the left bank of the Seine, on quai de Montebello.) Open Sunday 10am to 4pm in winter; 10am to 6pm in summer. Parc Georges-Brassens, rue Brancion, 15e. ✆ 01-45-32-12-17. Métro: Porte de Vanves.

Marché aux Puces de la Porte de Vanves This weekend event sprawls along two streets and is the best flea market in Paris—dealers swear by it. There's little in terms of formal antiques and furniture. It's better for old linens, used Hermès scarves, toys, ephemera, costume jewelry, perfume bottles, and bad art. Asking prices tend to be high, as dealers prefer to sell to nontourists. On Sunday there's a food market one street over. Open Saturday to Monday 6:30am to 4:30pm. Av. Georges-Lafenestre, 14e. No phone. Métro: Porte de Vanves.

Marché aux Puces St-Ouen de Clignancourt Paris's most famous flea market is a grouping of more than a dozen flea markets—a complex of 2,500 to 3,000 open stalls and shops on the northern fringe of the city, selling everything from antiques to junk, from new to vintage clothing. The market begins with stalls of cheap clothing along avenue de la Porte de Clignancourt. As you proceed, various streets will tempt you. Hold on until you get to rue des Rosiers, then turn left. Vendors start bringing out their offerings around 9am and start taking them in around 6pm, but hours are flexible depending on weather and crowds. Monday is traditionally the best day for bargain seekers, because the market is more sparsely attended and the merchants are more eager to sell.

First-timers always want to know two things: "Will I get any real bargains?" and "Will I get fleeced?" It's all relative. Obviously, dealers (who often have a prearrangement to have items held for them) have already skimmed the best buys. And it's true that the same merchandise displayed here will sell for less in the provinces. But for the visitor who has only a few days to spend in Paris—and only half a day for shopping—the flea market is worth the experience. Vintage French postcards, old buttons, and bistro ware are affordable. Each market has its own personality and an aura of Parisian glamour you can't find elsewhere.

Dress casually and show your knowledge if you're a collector. Most dealers are serious and get into the spirit of things only if you speak French or make it clear you know what you're doing. The longer you stay, the more you chat, the more you show your respect for the goods, the more room you'll have for negotiating. Most of the markets have restroom facilities; some have central offices to arrange shipping. Cafes, pizza joints, and even a few restaurants are scattered around. Almost without exception, they are bad. The exception is **Le Soleil,** 109 av. Michelet, St-Ouen (© **01-40-10-08-08**), which was converted from a cafe into a family-run restaurant by Louis-Jacques Vannucci. Catering to flea market shoppers, the restaurant looks as though it was flea market–decorated as well. The French food is excellent, especially the sautéed chicken in a light cream sauce, the green-bean salad tossed with tomato cubes, and the fresh Norman cod and the tiny mussels cooked in a rich broth. Open daily for lunch and Thursday to Saturday for dinner. *Note:* Beware of pickpockets and teenage troublemakers while shopping the market. Open Saturday to Monday 9am to 7pm. Av. de la Porte de Clignancourt, 18e. No phone. Métro: Porte de Clignancourt (turn left and cross bd. Ney, then walk north on av. de la Porte Montmartre). Bus: 56, 85, 155, or 166.

Marché aux Timbres This is where Audrey Hepburn figured it out in *Charade,* remember? At this stamp collector's paradise, nearly two dozen stalls are set up on a permanent basis under shady trees on the eastern edge of the Rond-Point. The variety of stamps is almost limitless—some common, some quite rare. Generally open Thursday to Sunday 10am to 7pm. Av. Matignon, off the Champs-Elysées at Rond-Point, 8e. No phone. Métro: Franklin-D.-Roosevelt or Champs-Elysées–Clémenceau.

Marché Buci This traditional French food market is held at the intersection of two streets and is only a block long, but what a block it is! Seasonal fruits and vegetables cover tabletops and chickens spin on the rotisserie. One stall is entirely devoted to big bouquets of fresh flowers. Monday mornings are light. Open daily 9am to 7pm. Rue de Buci, 6e. No phone. Métro: St-Germain-des-Prés.

MUSEUM SHOPS

Boutiques des Musées de France (Réunion des Musées Nationaux/ RMN)   This shop contains a selection of reproductions of originals contained in France's 20 Musées Nationaux, including the Louvre, the Musée d'Orsay, the Grand Palais, and the Musée Picasso. Prices range from 15€ ($17) for a pair of ear clips to as much as 456€ ($524) for a reproduction of an object from Greek, Assyrian, or Roman antiquity. There are two branches of this organization, one beneath the glass pyramid of the Louvre. Open Wednesday to Monday 9am to 8pm (Forum des Halles, Mon–Sat 10:30am–7:30pm). 99 rue de Rivoli, 1e. ℭ 01-40-20-50-50. Métro: Louvre. Also: Level 2 of the Forum des Halles, Porte-Berger Niveau, 2e. ℭ 01-40-39-92-21. Métro: Halles.

La Boutique de la Comédie Française   This is the official gift/souvenir shop of France's most historic and prestigious theater. The plays commemorated inside have elicited in the French as much emotion and loyalty as Shakespeare has in the British. Look for plates and cups depicting 18th-century misers, maidens, and faithful servants, as well as scarves, pens, drinking glasses, and napkins honoring the French theater. You might appreciate *les chopes* (beer mugs) emblazoned with the frontispiece of Molière's original folio for *Le Bourgeois Gentilhomme*. The gift shop remains open in August, when the theater is closed. Open Monday to Saturday 11am to 8:30pm; Sunday 1 to 8:30pm. 2 rue de Richelieu, 1e. ℭ 01-44-58-14-30. Métro: Palais Royal.

La Boutique du Musée de la Monnaie   Jewelry made from coins and/or semiprecious stones, reproductions of antique coins, and medallions of every imaginable sort are sold here. If your tastes and interests involve small, cunning, valuable objects, this might be the place for you. Open Tuesday to Sunday 11am to 5pm. 11 quai de Conti (entrance at 2 rue Guénégaud), 6e. ℭ 01-40-46-55-35. Métro: Pont Neuf or Odéon.

La Boutique du Musée des Arts Décoratifs   This two-part boutique is divided by the entryway to the museum. On the right as you enter is a fabulous bookstore. On the left is a boutique selling reproductions of museum items: gifts, knickknacks, and even a custom-made Hermès scarf. Open daily 10am to 7pm. In the Palais du Louvre, 105 rue de Rivoli, 1e. ℭ 01-42-61-04-02. Métro: Palais Royal or Tuileries.

Printemps Design   This shop's designers liken its merchandise to what's in the MOMA gift shop in New York City. Loosely associated with Le Printemps department store (but without the clothing), it features a frequently changing roster of stylish art objects and gift items. Many of the pieces are the work of well-known masters of their craft, like Phillippe Starck, Ron Arad, and the four-woman French design team known as Tse-Tse. Open Wednesday to Monday 11am to 10pm. Centre Pompidou, 19 rue Beaubourg, 4e. ℭ 01-44-78-15-78. Métro: Hôtel-de-Ville.

MUSIC

FNAC   This is a large chain of music and bookstores known for its wide selection and discounted prices. There are eight branches in Paris, with the largest being at 136 rue de Rennes, Montparnasse. Other locations include: rue St-Lazare, avenue des Champs-Elysées, Forum des Halles, avenue des Ternes, and

The Scent of a Parisian

If there's one reason international shoppers come to Paris, it's cosmetics—after all, the City of Light is the world capital of fragrances and beauty supplies. These are a few of our favorite perfume and makeup shops:

While you can buy **Parfums Caron** scents in any duty-free or discount *parfumerie*, it's worth visiting the source of some of the world's most famous perfumes. The tiny shop is at 34 av. Montaigne, 8e (✆ **01-47-23-40-82**; Métro: Franklin-D.-Roosevelt), boasting old-fashioned glass beakers filled with fragrances and a hint of yesteryear. Fleur de Rocaille, a Caron scent, was the featured perfume in the movie *Scent of a Woman*. Store hours are Monday to Saturday from 10am to 6:30pm.

While there are other branches and you can test Goutal bathroom amenities at many upscale hotels, the sidewalk mosaic tile and the unique scents make the **Annick Goutal**, at 14 rue Castiglione, 1e (✆ **01-42-60-52-82**; Métro: Concorde), worth stopping by. Try Eau d'Hadrien for a unisex splash of citrus and summer. Store hours are Monday to Saturday from 10am to 7pm.

Shiseido, the world's fourth-largest maker of cosmetics and skin-care goods, has become more prominent thanks to the efforts of the **Salons du Palais Royal Shiseido**, 142 Galerie de Valois, Palais Royal, 1e (✆ **01-49-27-09-09**; Métro: Palais Royal). In addition to an awesome array of skin-care products and makeup, it stocks 18 exclusive fragrances created by the company's artistic director, Serge Lutens. Don't be afraid to wander in and ask for some scent strips. Open Monday to Saturday from 10am to 7pm.

avenue d'Italie. All are open Monday to Saturday 10am to 7:30pm except Champs-Elysées, open daily noon to midnight. 136 rue de Rennes, 6e. ✆ **01-49-54-30-00**. Métro: St-Placide.

Virgin Megastore Paris has three branches of Europe's biggest, most widely publicized CD and record store. The Champs-Elysées branch is the city's largest music store; a bookstore and cafe are downstairs. The store's opening in a landmark building helped rejuvenate the avenue. You'll find a Virgin Megastore at each airport. Open Monday to Saturday 10am to midnight; Sunday noon to midnight (other locations: Carrousel du Louvre, Sun–Tues 10am–8pm, Wed–Sat 10am–10pm; Gare Montparnasse, Mon–Thurs 7am–8pm, Fri 7am–9pm, Sat 7am–8pm). 52–60 av. des Champs-Elysées, 8e. ✆ **01-49-53-50-00**. Métro: Franklin-D.-Roosevelt.

PERFUME & MAKEUP (DISCOUNT)

Catherine *Finds* This family-owned shop sells an impressive stock of all the big-name perfumes and cosmetics at discounts of 20% to 25%. In addition, its paperwork is usually extremely well organized, allowing refunds of the value-added tax (VAT) to be cleared quickly through Customs. Many on the staff speak English. Open Tuesday to Saturday 9am to 7pm; Monday 10:30am to 7pm. 7 rue Castiglione, 1e. ✆ **01-42-61-02-89**. Métro: Concorde.

Editions de Parfums Fréderic Malle If you're jaded and bored with the big-brand name perfumes that are sold at every duty-free airport in Europe, consider a visit to this boutique where brands are more personalized. This is the only outlet of an organization that was founded in 2000 by master perfumer Fréderic Malle, whose nose is as sensitive as that of any wine expert. Each of the scents sold here comes in a standardized bottle (they call it a flacon) in either a 50ml (priced at 54€–95€/$62–$109), depending on the scent) or a 100ml (priced at 68€–115€/$78–$132) size. Scents are designed for either men or women, come in varying intensities of floral, spice, or "Oriental" motifs, and carry names that include Iris Poudre, Noir Épices, En Passant, and one of the bestsellers, Musc Ravageur. There's a lot of elegant chichi about this place (the paneled decor was designed by super-decorators Andrée Putnam and Olivier Lempereur), but the scents inside are often lovely. One of the things we like best about the place is the framed photographic portraits of each of the men and women who created the original scents sold within the boutique. Open Monday to Saturday 11am to 7pm. 37 rue de Grenelle, 7e. ✆ 01-42-22-77-22. Métro: Rue du Bac.

Freddy Parfums The discounts here are fabulous: up to 40% on perfumes, handbags, cosmetics, silk scarves, and neckties. Freddy of Paris is near American Express and the Opéra. Open Monday to Saturday 9:30am to 7pm. 3 rue Scribe, 9e. ✆ 01-47-42-63-41. Métro: Opéra.

Maki You get some of the best deals in cosmetics and makeup here. In fact, it's the place where French actors and many models come for quality makeup products at discounted prices. The shop lies in the middle of a theater area. The staff will often give you advice about makeup. Open Tuesday to Saturday 11am to 1pm and 2:30 to 6:30pm. 9 rue Mansart, 9e. ✆ 01-42-81-33-76. Métro: Blanche.

Parfumerie Générale With cosmetics and makeup from at least 40 different manufacturers from around the world, this place will impress you with its encyclopedic knowledge of what makes women look good. The decor includes stark white walls with splashes of lollipop colors and a Mondrian-inspired carpet in a vivid design of interconnected rectangles. Cosmetics and makeup from manufacturers in England, the U.S., Greece, Japan, Australia, and France are displayed, applied, and hawked by an army of saleswomen at a long "cosmetics bar." There's also a collection of perfume and a separate room with a macho-looking barbershop where a guy can get a really good shave or trim. Open Monday to Saturday 11am to 7pm. 6 rue Robert Estienne (a narrow dead-end street funneling into the rue Marbeuf), 8e. ✆ 01-43-59-10-62. Métro: Franklin-D.-Roosevelt.

SHOES

Rodolphe Menudier This is a boutique that elevates shoe buying into an artistic experience akin to a visit to a high-tech, postmodern museum. The black-lacquer and brushed stainless steel decor includes one wall that's sheathed in silver-painted leather and another entirely faced in slate. These high-glam grace notes provide a backdrop for a small collection of stylish but relatively conservative men's shoes, and a large collection of both standard and fetishistic shoes for ladies. Expect an inventory with footwear designed either for the office or, say, a prolonged schlep through the streets and museums of Paris. But if you're in the market for frighteningly high spike heels, in colors that include gold, silver, or outrageously patterned fabric, or the kind of high-altitude platform shoes that are definitely not for anyone with vertigo, this shop might be for you. Open Monday 11am to 7pm; Tuesday to Saturday 10am to 7pm. 14 rue Castiglione, 1e. ✆ 01-42-60-86-27. Métro: Tuileries.

SOUVENIRS & GIFTS

Au Nom de la Rose   Tasteful and frilly, this shop is divided into two distinct parts, one selling flowers, the other gift items. The flower shop sells many of the arrangements that decorate local hotels and restaurants, while the gift shop specializes in anything that's scented, emblazoned, or permeated with "the spirit or scent of the rose." Expect rose-hip jams and marmalades, scented soaps and candles, rose water–based perfumes, decorative items for the home and kitchen, and handbags, makeup kits, and scarves, each decorated in a floral (usually rose-patterned) motif. Flower shop open daily 9am to 9pm. Gift shop daily 10am to 7:30pm. 46 rue du Bac, 7e. ℂ 01-42-22-22-12. Métro: Rue du Bac.

Galerie Architecture Miniature Gault   This store features Lilliputian town models of French villages and Parisian neighborhoods complete with houses, stores, and fountains, all built to scale. A hand-painted ceramic depiction of a house or national monument ranges from 15€ to 700€ ($17–$805), depending on its size and intricacy. Open Monday to Saturday 10am to 7pm; Sunday 11am to 7pm. 206 rue de Rivoli, 1e. ℂ 01-42-60-51-17. Métro: Tuileries.

La Tuile à Loup   This emporium has been selling authentic examples of all-French handcrafts since around 1975, making a name through its concentration of hand-produced woven baskets, cutlery, and woodcarvings. Especially appealing are the hand-painted crockery and charming stoneware from traditional manufacturers like Quimper and Malicorne and from small-scale producers in the Savoie Alps and Alsace. Open Monday 1 to 7pm; Tuesday to Saturday 10:30am to 7pm. 35 rue Daubenton, 5e. ℂ 01-47-07-28-90. Métro: Censier-Daubenton.

Finds **Sign of the Times**

A shop like **Manufacture Plaques Emaillées** stands in sharp contrast to the mass-merchandise in most department stores. Established in 1908 when the Art Nouveau craze swept Paris, they have done a respectable business promoting turn-of-the-20th-century Parisian charm ever since. Their specialty is the custom manufacture of cast-iron plaques, enameled and baked, commemorating virtually any event, person (including yourself), or piece of real estate that appeals to you. Charles and Denis, the long-time owners, offer a variety of shapes, sizes, and colors for the finished product. The most endearing, in our opinion, are the street signs, *"style ville de Paris,"* that can bear the name of your home, your child, the street you live on (or would like to live on), or the fictitious boulevard of your choice: AVENUE JOHN WAYNE, LAS VEGAS, for example. Colors run the spectrum of the rainbow, although Charles warns in advance that gilding or silver-plating is not an option. Expect to pay from around 135€ ($155) for a street sign–size plaque, and much more for plaques that can measure up to about 2m (6½ ft.) wide, suitable perhaps for a storefront. It will take 3 to 4 weeks for your plaque to be manufactured, after which it can be shipped. Shipping can be expensive, and in our opinion (because of the cast-iron nature of what's in the package), complicated. Much smaller plaques, some ready-made, are also available. It's located at 18 bd. des Filles-du-Calvaire, 11e (ℂ 01-47-00-50-95; Métro: St-Sébastien). Credit cards are not accepted.

STATIONERY

Cassegrain   Nothing says elegance more than thick French stationery and notecards. Cassegrain offers beautifully engraved stationery, most often in traditional patterns, and business cards engraved to order. Several other items for the desk, many suitable for gifts, are for sale as well; there are even affordable pencils and small desktop accessories. Open Monday to Saturday 10am to 7pm. 422 rue St-Honoré, 8e. ℭ **01-42-60-20-08**. Métro: Concorde.

TABLEWARE

Conran Shop   This shop might remind you of an outpost of the British Empire, valiantly imposing Brit aesthetics and standards on the French-speaking world. Inside, you'll find articles for the kitchen and dining room, glass and crystal vases, fountain pens and stationery, reading material and postcards, and even a selection of chocolates, teas, and coffees to help warm up a foggy English day. Open Monday to Friday 10am to 7pm; Saturday 10am to 7:30pm. 117 rue du Bac, 7e. ℭ **01-42-84-10-01**. Métro: Sèvres-Babylone.

Geneviève Lethu   This Provençal designer has shops all over France, with 19 others in and around Paris, all selling her clever and colorful Pottery Barn–meets–French Mediterranean tableware. The rue de Rennes branch is the largest. Newer designs stress influences from India, South America, and Africa as well. Energy, style, and verve are rampant and the prices are moderate. Open Monday to Saturday 10:15am to 7pm. 95 rue de Rennes, 6e. ℭ **01-45-44-40-35**. Métro: St-Sulpice.

WINES

Lavinia   This is the largest wine-and-spirits store in Europe, opening in 2002 to great acclaim in Paris. Spread over three floors near place de la Madeleine, it stocks more than 3,000 bottles of French wines along with 2,000 bottles from all over the world. There is a lunch-only restaurant on-site, as well as a tasting bar. Champagnes and foreign wines are found on the ground floor. It's the only place in Paris where you can buy a good bottle of South Dakota wine. Open Monday to Saturday 10am to 8pm. 3–5 bd. de la Madeleine, 1e. ℭ **01-42-97-20-20**. Métro: Madeleine.

Les Caves Taillevent   This is a temple to the art of making fine French wine. Associated with one of Paris's grandest restaurants, Taillevent, it occupies the street level and cellar of an antique building. Stored here are more than 25,000 bottles of wine, with easy access in nearby warehouses to almost a million more. Open Monday 2 to 8pm; Tuesday to Friday 9am to 8pm; Saturday 9am to 7:30pm. 199 rue du Faubourg St-Honoré, 8e. ℭ **01-45-61-14-09**. Métro: Charles de Gaulle–Etoile.

Nicholas *(Finds*   The flagship store of this boutique chain, with more than 110 branches around Paris plus another 380 branches in France, offers fair prices for bottles you might not be able to find in the States. Aside from the usual Bordeaux and Burgundies, look for some of the rarer regional wines, like Gewürztraminer from Alsace, Collioure from Languedoc-Rousillon, and the pricey but sublime Côte Rotie from the Côtes du Rhône outside Lyon. Open Monday to Saturday 9:30am to 8pm. 31 place de la Madeleine, 8e. ℭ **01-42-68-00-16**. Métro: Madeleine.

10

Paris After Dark

When darkness falls, the City of Light lives up to its name—the monuments and bridges are illuminated, and the glow of old-fashioned and modern street lamps, the blaze of sidewalk-cafe windows, and the glare of neon signs flood the avenues and boulevards. Parisians start the serious part of their evenings as Anglos stretch, yawn, and announce it's time for bed. Once the workday is over, most people go to a cafe to meet with friends over a drink and perhaps a

meal (see "The Top Cafes" in chapter 6); then they may head home or proceed to a restaurant or the theater; and much later they may show up at a bar or a dance club.

In this chapter, we describe Paris's after-dark diversions—from attending a Molière play at the Comédie-Française to catching a cancan show at the Moulin Rouge to sipping a sidecar at Harry's New York Bar to partying at Le Queen with all the boys.

1 The Performing Arts

LISTINGS   Announcements of shows, concerts, and operas are plastered on kiosks all over town. You'll find listings in the weekly *Pariscope,* an entertainment guide with a section in English, or the English-language bimonthly *Boulevard.* Performances start later in Paris than in London or New York—from 8 to 9pm—and Parisians tend to dine after the theater. You may not want to do the same, because many of the less expensive restaurants close as early as 9pm.

TICKETS   There are many ticket agencies in Paris, most near the Right Bank hotels. *Avoid them if possible.* You can buy the cheapest tickets at the box office of the theater or at discount agencies that sell tickets at discounts of up to 50%. One is the **Kiosque Théâtre,** 15 place de la Madeleine, 8e (no phone; Métro: Madeleine), offering leftover tickets for about half price on the performance day. Tickets for evening shows are sold Tuesday to Friday from 12:30 to 8pm and Saturday from 2 to 8pm. Tickets for matinees are sold Saturday from 12:30 to 2pm and Sunday from 12:30 to 4pm. Other branches are in the basement of the Châtelet–Les Halles Métro station and in front of Gare Montparnasse.

Students with ID can often get last-minute tickets by applying at the box office an hour before curtain time.

The easiest (and most expensive) way to get tickets, especially if you're staying in a first-class or deluxe hotel, is to ask your concierge to arrange for them. A service fee is added, but it's a lot easier if you don't want to waste precious hours in Paris trying to secure often hard-to-get tickets.

Tickets for festivals, concerts, and the theater are easy to obtain through one of these locations of the **FNAC** record store chain: 136 rue de Rennes, 6e (© **01-49-54-30-00;** Métro: St. Placide), or in the Forum des Halles, 1–7 rue Pierre-Lescot, 1e (© **01-40-41-40-00;** Métro: Châtelet–Les Halles).

Tips **A Stateside Ticket Agency**

Selling tickets to cultural events throughout Europe, **Keith Prowse** maintains headquarters in the United States at 234 W. 44th St., Suite 1000, New York, NY 10036 (*©* **800/223-6108**; www.keithprowse.com). Its Paris office is at 7 rue de Clichy, 9e (*©* **01-42-81-88-88**; Métro: Place Clichy). The company will mail tickets (usually in the form of a voucher) to you, or they'll fax you a confirmation, and leave tickets at the box office for pickup prior to the performance. There's a markup of about 25% over box-office prices on each ticket, which includes the handling charges. The organization is particularly good at acquiring tickets to either of the Paris opera houses, to any of the big-league cabarets (including the Moulin Rouge, Crazy Horse, and Chez Michou), and to any of the sightseeing tours or cruises recommended within this guidebook. Hotel packages are also available.

THEATER

Comédie-Française ★★ Those with even a modest understanding of French can delight in a sparkling production of Molière at this national theater, established to keep the classics alive and promote important contemporary authors. Nowhere else will you see the works of Molière and Racine so beautifully staged. The box office is open daily from 11am to 6pm, but the hall is dark from mid-July to early September. In 1993 a Left Bank annex was launched, the **Comédie Française-Théâtre du Vieux-Colombier,** 21 rue du Vieux-Colombier, 4e (*©* **01-44-39-87-00**). Though its repertoire varies, it's known for presenting serious French dramas. Discounts are available if you reserve in advance. 2 rue de Richelieu, 1e. *©* **01-44-58-15-15.** Tickets 27€ ($31) adults, 16€–($18) 26 and under. Métro: Palais Royal or Musée du Louvre.

OPERA, DANCE & CLASSICAL CONCERTS

Cité de la Musique ★★★ This testimony to the power of music has been the most widely applauded, the least criticized, and the most innovative of the late François Mitterrand's *grands projets*. At the city's northeastern edge in what used to be a run-down and depressing neighborhood, this $120-million stone-and-glass structure incorporates a network of concert halls, a library and research center for the study of all kinds of music, and a museum (see "Specialty Museums" in chapter 7). The complex hosts a rich variety of concerts, ranging from Renaissance music through 19th- and 20th-century works, including jazz and traditional music from nations around the world. 221 av. Jean-Jaurès, 19e. *©* **01-44-84-45-00,** or 01-44-84-44-84 for tickets. Tickets 6.50€–12€ ($7.50–$14) for 4:30 and 8pm concerts. Métro: Porte de Pantin.

Maison de Radio France This is the site of many of the performances of the **Orchestre Philharmonique de Radio France** and the somewhat more conservative **Orchestre National de France.** The concert hall's box office is open Monday to Saturday from 11am to 6pm. 116 av. du Président-Kennedy, 16e. *©* **01-56-40-15-16.** Tickets 7.50€–55€ ($8.65–$63). Métro: Passy-Ranelagh.

Opéra Bastille ★★★ This controversial building—it has been called a "beached whale"—was designed by Canadian architect Carlos Ott, with curtains by Japanese designer Issey Miyake. Since the house's grand opening in July

1989, the Opera National de Paris has presented works like Mozart's *Marriage of Figaro* and Tchaikovsky's *Queen of Spades*. The main hall is the largest of any French opera house, with 2,700 seats, but music critics have lambasted the acoustics. The building contains two other concert halls, including an intimate 250-seat room that usually hosts chamber music. Both traditional opera performances and symphony concerts are presented here, as well as both classical and modern dance. Several concerts are given for free in honor of certain French holidays. Write ahead for tickets. 2 place de la Bastille, 4e. ℂ **01-40-01-17-89**. Tickets 20€–114€ ($23–$131) opera, 20€–80€ ($23–$92) dance. Métro: Bastille.

Opéra Comique   This is a charming venue for light opera, on a smaller scale than Paris's major opera houses. Built in the late 1890s in an ornate style that might remind you of the Opéra Garnier, it's the site of small productions of operas like *Carmen, Don Giovanni, Tosca,* and *Palleas & Melisande*. There are no performances from mid-July to late August. The box office, however, is open year-round Monday to Saturday from 11am to 7pm. 5 rue Favart, 2e. ℂ **08-25-00-00-58**. Tickets 15€–100€ ($17–$115). Métro: Richelieu-Drouot.

Opéra Garnier ★★★   Once the haunt of the Phantom, this is the premier venue for dance and once again for opera. Charles Garnier designed this 1875 rococo wonder during the heyday of the French Empire; the facade is adorned with marble and sculpture, including *The Dance* by Carpeaux. Following a year-long renovation, during which the Chagall ceiling was cleaned and air-conditioning was added, the facade is gleaming as it did for Napoleon III. You can see the original gilded busts and statues, the rainbow-hued marble pillars, and the mosaics. The Opéra Garnier combines ballet and opera, and offers one of the most elegant evenings you can spend in the City of Light. Because of the competition from the Bastille, the Garnier has made great efforts to present more up-to-date dance works, like choreography by Twyla Tharp, Agnes de Mille, and George Balanchine. The box office is open Monday to Saturday from 11am to 6:30pm. Place de l'Opéra, 9e. ℂ **01-40-01-17-89**. Tickets 23€–114€ ($26–$131) opera, 9€–70€ ($10–$81) dance. Métro: Opéra.

Théâtre des Champs-Elysées   This Art Deco theater, attracting the haute couture crowd, hosts both national and international orchestras (such as the

---

Moments The Music of Angels

Some of the most moving music in Paris echoes through its churches, with sounds that can take you back to the Middle Ages. At **Eglise de St-Eustache,** rue Rambuteau (ℂ **01-42-36-31-05**; Métro: Les Halles), High Mass with the organ playing and the choir singing is at 11am on Sunday. In summer, concerts are played on the organ, marking the church's role in holding the premiere of Berlioz's *Te Deum* and Liszt's *Messiah*. Tickets to these special concerts sell for 12€ to 26€ ($14–$30).

The **American Church in Paris,** 65 quai d'Orsay, 7e (ℂ **01-40-62-05-00**; Métro: Invalides or Alma-Marceau), sponsors free concerts from September to June on Sundays at 5pm. You can also attend free concerts at **Eglise St-Merri,** 78 rue St-Martin, 4e (ℂ **01-42-74-59-39**; Métro: Hôtel-de-Ville). These performances are staged with variables based on the availability of the performers, from September to July on Saturdays at 9pm, and again on Sundays at 4pm.

Vienna Philharmonic) as well as opera and ballet. The box office is open Monday to Saturday from 1 to 7pm. There are no performances in August. 15 av. Montaigne, 8e. ✆ **01-49-52-50-50**, or 01-49-52-07-41 for box office. Tickets 9.10€–114€ ($10–$131). Métro: Alma-Marceau.

Théâtre National de Chaillot   Part of the architectural complex facing the Eiffel Tower, this is one of the city's largest concert halls, hosting cultural events that are announced on billboards in front. Sometimes (rarely) dance is staged here, or you might see a brilliantly performed play by Marguerite Duras. The box office is open Monday to Saturday from 11am to 7pm, Sunday 1 to 5pm. 1 place du Trocadéro, 16e. ✆ **01-53-65-30-00**. www.theatre-chaillot.fr. Tickets 25€–31€ ($29–$36) adults, 20€–26€ ($22–$29) seniors over 60, 12€–19€ ($13–$22) under age 25. Métro: Trocadéro.

2 The Club & Music Scene

Paris is still a late-night mecca, and both the quantity and the variety of nightlife exceed that of other cities. Nowhere else will you find such a huge, mixed array of nightclubs, bars, dance clubs, cabarets, jazz dives, music halls, and honky-tonks.

A MUSIC HALL

Olympia   Charles Aznavour and other big names appear in this cavernous hall. The late Yves Montand appeared once, and the performance was sold out 4 months in advance. Today you're more likely to catch Gloria Estefan. A typical lineup might include an English rock group, Italian acrobats, a French singer, a dance troupe, juggling American comedians (doing much of their work in English), and the featured star. A witty MC and an onstage band provide a smooth transition. Performances usually begin at 8:30pm Tuesday to Sunday, with Saturday matinees at 5pm. 28 bd. des Capucines, 9e. ✆ **08-92-68-33-68**. Tickets 30€–60€ ($35–$69). Métro: Opéra or Madeleine.

CHANSONNIERS

Chansonniers (literally "songwriters") provide a bombastic musical satire of the day's events. This combination of parody and burlesque is a time-honored Gallic amusement and a Parisian institution. Songs are often created on the spot, inspired by the "disaster of the day."

Au Caveau de la Bolée   To enter this bawdy *boîte* (small nightclub), you descend into the catacombs of the early-14th-century Abbaye de St-André, once a cafe that attracted Verlaine, who slowly snuffed out his life with absinthe here. The singing is loud and smutty, the way the predominantly student audience likes it. Occasionally, the audience sings along. You'll enjoy this place a lot more if you can follow the thread of the French-language jokes and satire, but even if you can't, there are enough visuals (magic acts and singers) to amuse. The prix fixe dinner is followed by a series of at least four entertainers, usually comedians. In lieu of paying admission for the cabaret, you can order dinner. If you've already had dinner, you can order just a drink. Open Monday through Saturday; dinners 8:30 to 10:30pm, shows 10:30pm to 1:30am. 25 rue de l'Hirondelle, 6e. ✆ **01-43-54-62-20**. Admission to show, including a prix fixe dinner, 50€ ($58). Admission to show only, including 1 drink, 25€. Métro: St-Michel.

Au Lapin Agile ⋆   Picasso and Utrillo patronized this little cottage near the top of Montmartre, then known as the Cabaret des Assassins, and it has been painted by many artists, including Utrillo. You'll sit at carved wooden tables in a dimly lit room with walls covered by bohemian memorabilia and listen to French folk tunes, love ballads, army songs, sea chanteys, and music-hall ditties. You're encouraged to sing along, even if it's only the *"oui, oui, oui—non, non, non"* the refrain of "Les Chevaliers de la Table Ronde." Open Tuesday to Sunday 9pm to 2am. 22 rue des Saules, 18e. ✆ 01-46-06-85-87. Cover, including 1st drink, 24€ ($28). Métro: Lamarck-Caulaincourt.

Théâtre des Deux Anes   Since 1920, this theater has staged satires of the foibles, excesses, and stupidities of French governments. Favorite targets are President Jacques Chirac and other mandarins of the *hexagone française.* Cultural icons, French and foreign, receive a grilling that's very funny and sometimes caustic. The place considers itself more of a theater than a cabaret and doesn't serve drinks or refreshments. The 2½-hour show is conducted in rapid-fire French slang, so if your syntax isn't up to par, you won't appreciate its charms. Performances are given Tuesday through Saturday at 8:30pm, with matinees offered Saturday at 4:30pm and Sunday at 3:30pm; closed July to September. 100 bd. de Clichy, 18e. ✆ 01-46-06-10-26. Tickets 36€–40€ ($41–$46). Métro: Place de Clichy.

NIGHTCLUBS & CABARETS

Decidedly expensive, these places give you your money's worth by providing lavishly spectacular floorshows. With the exception of Café Concert Ailleurs, they generally attract an older crowd. They are definitely not youth-oriented.

Chez Michou   The setting is blue, the MC wears blue, and the spotlights bathe performers in yet another shade of blue. The creative force behind the color coordination and a dollop of cross-genderism is Michou, veteran impresario whose 20-odd cross-dressing belles bear names like Hortensia and DuDuche; they lip-sync in costumes from haute couture to haute concierge, paying tribute to Americans like Whitney Houston and Tina Turner, and French stars like Mireille Mathieu, Sylvie Vartan, and Brigitte Bardot. If you don't want dinner, you'll have to stand at the bar, paying a compulsory 31€ ($36) for the first drink. Dinner is served nightly at 8:30pm (reservations required); shows begin nightly at 10:30pm. 80 rue des Martyrs, 18e. ✆ 01-46-06-16-04. Cover (including dinner, aperitif, wine, coffee, and show) 95€ ($109). Métro: Pigalle.

Crazy Horse Saloon   Since 1951, this sophisticated strip joint has thrived thanks to good choreography and a sly, coquettish celebration of the female form. The theme binding each of the 5-minute numbers (featuring gorgeous dancers in erotic costumes) is La Femme in her various states: temperamental, sad, dancing/bouncy, or joyful. Dance numbers that endure season after season include "Le Laser" and "The Erotic Lesson." Dinner, costing 125€ to 155€ ($144–$178), is a tasteful event served at Chez Francis, a restaurant under separate management a few steps away. Shows last just under 2 hours. You'll find a small number of women among the audience of mainly businessmen. Shows Sunday to Friday 8:30 and 11pm; Saturday at 7:30, 9:45, and 11:50pm. 12 av. George V, 8e. ✆ 01-47-23-32-32. Reservations recommended. Cover 69€–90€ ($79–$104), including 2 drinks at a table. Métro: George-V or Alma-Marceau.

Folies-Bergère   The Folies-Bergère has been an institution since 1869. Josephine Baker, the African-American singer who danced in a banana skirt and threw bananas into the audience became "the toast of Paris" here. According to legend, the first GI to reach Paris at the 1944 Liberation asked for directions to the club. Don't expect the naughty and slyly permissive skin-and-glitter revue that used to be the trademark of this place. In 1993, that all ended with a radical restoration of the theater and a reopening under new management. Today, it's a conventional 1,600-seat theater devoted to a frequently changing roster of big-stage performances in French, many of which are adaptations of Broadway blockbusters. Recent examples have included restagings of *Fame* and *Saturday Night Fever,* and a revue of male strippers inspired by America's Chippendales. There's even been a relatively highbrow reenactment of one of the classics of the French-language repertory, *L'Arlésienne,* by 19th-century playwright Alphonse Daudet. True, there's always an acknowledgment of the nostalgia value of the old-time, much naughtier Folies-Bergère, and endless nods to the stars of yesterday (especially Josephine Baker and her topless act with bananas), but if you're looking for artful nudity presented with unabashed Parisian permissiveness, head for the Crazy Horse Saloon or the Lido. There's an on-site restaurant serving dinners in one of the theater's salons, but most spectators opt just for the show, and not the meal. Shows are usually given Tuesday through Saturday at 9pm and Sunday at 3pm. 34 rue Richer, 9e. ℂ 01-44-79-98-98. Tickets 32€–52€ ($37–$60); dinner and show 90€ ($104). Métro: Grands-Boulevards or Cadet.

L'Ane Rouge   This red-and-black minitheater has been a showcase for French satire and humor since it opened shortly after World War II. You'll enjoy a well-flavored dinner of French specialties, followed by a 2-hour medley of French-language standup comedy, ribald stories, and politicized jokes. If your knowledge of French is zero, you won't enjoy this place; ditto if you hate being singled out by a comedian in front of a crowd. Dinner served nightly at 8pm; shows nightly 10pm to midnight. 3 rue Laugier, 17e. ℂ 01-43-80-79-97. Reservations recommended. Métro: Ternes.

Le Canotier du Pied de la Butte   The worst thing you can say about this place is that it's touristy, but the visitors share a genuine appreciation of the nuances, lyricism, and poetry of popular French songs. Each performance includes appearances by two men and two women, who interact with their own versions of the hits made famous by Piaf, Montand, Brel, and Chevalier. Nostalgia is unleashed by the bucketful in a cozy red, black, and white theater with room for no more than 70. 62 bd. Rochechouart, 18e. ℂ 01-46-06-02-86. Reservations required. Cover 38€ ($44) including 1st drink. Performances daily 7:30–9pm. Métro: Anvers.

Le Paradis Latin   Built in 1889 by Alexandre-Gustave Eiffel, with the same metallic skeleton as the famous tower, Le Paradis Latin represents the architect's only venture into theater design. The place is credited with introducing vaudeville and musical theater to Paris. In 1903 the building was a warehouse, but in the 1970s it was transformed into a successful cabaret whose singers, dancers, and special effects extol the fun, frivolity, and permissiveness of the City of Light. The show includes tasteful nudity (they contrast their more dignified nudity—breasts only—with the more blatant and unabashed nudity at Crazy Horse), a ventriloquist, and a trapeze artist. The MC speaks in French and English. Dinner Wednesday to Monday 8pm; reviews at 9:30pm. 28 rue Cardinal-Lemoine, 5e. ℂ 01-43-25-28-28. Cover 75€ ($86) including half a bottle of champagne; dinner and show 109€–200€ ($125–$230). Métro: Jussieu or Cardinal Lemoine.

Lido de Paris ★   The Lido's $15-million current production, *C'est Magique,* is a dramatic reworking of the classic Parisian cabaret show, with eye-popping special effects and new themes, both nostalgic and contemporary, including aerial and aquatic ballets using more than 60,000 gallons of water. The show, the most expensive ever in Europe, uses 80 performers, $4 million in costumes, and a $2 million lighting design with lasers. There's even an ice rink that magically appears and disappears. The legendary topless Bluebell Girls are still here, how-ever. Now that celebrated chef Paul Bocuse is a consultant, the cuisine is better than ever. Dinner served nightly 9pm; shows 11:30pm. 116 bis av. des Champs-Elysées, 8e. ℂ 800/227-4884 in the U.S., or 01-40-76-56-10. Dinner dance 140€–200€ ($161–$230); show only 100€ ($115). Prices include half a bottle of champagne per person. Métro: George V.

Moulin Rouge   This is a camp classic. Toulouse-Lautrec immortalized the Moulin Rouge and its habitués in his works, but he'd probably have a hard time recognizing it today. Colette created a scandal by giving an onstage kiss to Mme de Morny, but it's harder to shock today's audiences. Try to get a table, as the view is much better on the main floor than from the bar. The emphasis on the strip routines and sexiness of the Belle Epoque and Paris between the wars keeps drawing crowds. Handsome men and women, virtually all topless, contribute to the appeal. The finale usually includes two dozen of the belles ripping loose with a topless cancan. Dinner and show nightly 7pm. Place Blanche, 18e. ℂ 01-53-09-82-82. Cover including champagne 82€–92€ ($94–$106); dinner and show 130€–160€ ($150–$184); for seats at the bar, cover (including 2 drinks) 63€ ($72). Métro: Blanche.

Villa d'Este   In the past, this club booked Amalia Rodrigues, Portugal's lead-ing *fadista* (singer of traditional Portuguese music), and French chanteuse Juli-ette Greco. Today you're more likely to hear French singer François de Guelte or other top talent from Europe and America. Villa d'Este has been around for a long time, and the quality of its offerings remains high. You'll probably hear some of the greatest hits of beloved French performers like Piaf, Aznavour, Brassens, and Brel. 4 rue Arsène-Houssaye, 8e. ℂ 01-42-56-14-65. Cover (including 1st drink) 30€ ($35); dinner (including wine) and show 42€–115€ ($48–$132). Métro: Charles-de-Gaulle-Etoile.

JAZZ, SALSA, ROCK & MORE

The great jazz revival that long ago swept America is still going strong here, with Dixieland, Chicago, bop, and free jazz rhythms being pounded out in dozens of jazz cellars, mostly called *caveaux*. Most clubs are between rue Bonaparte and rue St-Jacques on the Left Bank. The crowds attending clubs to hear rock, salsa, and the like are definitely young, often in their late teens, 20s, or early 30s. The exception to that is in the clubs offering jazz nights—lovers of jazz span all ages.

Au Duc des Lombards   Comfortable and appealing, this jazz club replaced an earlier club several years ago and has thrived ever since. Artists begin playing at 9pm and continue (with breaks) for 5 hours, touching on everything from "free jazz" to more traditional forms like "hard bop." Unlike many of its com-petitors, tables here can be reserved and will usually be held until 10:30pm. Daily 9pm to 3am. 42 rue des Lombards, 1e. ℂ 01-42-33-22-88. Cover 19€ ($22). Métro: Châtelet.

Baiser Salé   This musically varied cellar club is lined with jazz-related paint-ings and has a large central bar and an ongoing roster of videos showing great jazz moments from the past. There's no food or even any particular glamour—everything is very mellow and laid-back. Genres featured include Afro-Caribbean, Afro-Latino, salsa, merengue, R&B, and sometimes fusion. Daily 6pm to 6am; music 10pm to 3am. 58 rue des Lombards, 1e. ℂ 01-42-33-37-71. Cover 8€ ($9.20) Wed–Sun. Métro: Châtelet.

Bus Palladium   In a single room with a long bar, this rock temple has var-nished hardwoods and fabric-covered walls that barely absorb the reverberations of nonstop recorded music. You won't find techno, punk rock, jazz, blues, or soul. It's rock for hard-core rockers ages 18 to 35. Tuesday through Saturday 11pm to 6am. 6 rue Fontaine, 9e. ℂ **01-53-21-07-33.** Cover 20€ ($23) all the time for men, and Fri–Sat for women (includes 1st drink). Métro: Blanche or Pigalle.

Caveau de la Huchette ⊛ This celebrated jazz *caveaux*, reached by a winding staircase, draws a young crowd, mostly students, who dance to the music of well-known jazz combos. In prejazz days, Robespierre and Marat frequented the place. Sunday to Thursday 9:30pm to 2:30am; Friday to Saturday and holidays 9:30pm to 4am. 5 rue de la Huchette, 5e. ℂ **01-43-26-65-05.** Cover 11€ ($12) Sun–Thurs, 13€ ($15) Fri–Sat; students 9€ ($10). Métro/RER: St-Michel.

La Chapelle des Lombards *Finds* The club's proximity to the Opéra Bastille seems incongruous, considering the African/Caribbean jazz and Brazilian samba that's the norm. It's a magnet for South American and African expatriates, and the rhythms and fire of the music propel everyone onto the dance floor. Thursday to Saturday 10:30pm to 1am. 19 rue de Lappe, 11e. ℂ **01-43-57-24-24.** Cover 12€–20€ ($14–$23) including 1st drink. Women free Thurs before midnight. Métro: Bastille.

L'Arbuci Smoky, dimly lit, and artfully chaotic, this basement-level establishment functions primarily as a restaurant offering jazz 5 nights a week. Don't be put off by the way it looks from the outside—once you enter and have a drink or two, you're likely to have fun, enjoying the jazz produced by players from the Philippines, Southeast Asia, Africa, and virtually everywhere else in between. If you don't want dinner, you'll pay between 2.80€ and 10€ ($3.20–$12) per drink, depending on what you order. 25 rue de Buci, 6e. ℂ **01-44-32-16-00.** No cover. Prix fixe menus 15€–30€ ($17–$35). Restaurant open daily noon–1am. Live music is presented Thurs–Sat at midnight. Bar remains open till 3am nightly. Métro: Mabillon or St-Germain-des-Prés.

Le Bilboquet This restaurant/jazz club/piano bar, where the film *Paris Blues* was shot, offers some of the best music in Paris. Jazz is played on the upper level in the restaurant, **Le Bilboquet,** a wood-paneled room with a copper ceiling, brass-trimmed and red-painted sunken bar, and Victorian candelabra. The menu is limited but classic French, specializing in lamb, fish, and beef. Dinner is 55€ ($63). The club is open nightly 8:30pm to 2am, with music beginning at 9:30pm. 13 rue St-Benoît, 6e. ℂ **01-45-48-81-84.** Métro: St-Germain-des-Prés.

Les Etoiles Since 1856, this red-swabbed music hall has shaken with the sound of performers at work and patrons at play. Its newest incarnation is as a restaurant/dance club where the music is exclusively salsa and merengue and the food South American. Expect hearty portions of fried fish, shredded pork or beef, white rice, beans, and flan, with meals costing 20€ ($23). Open Thursday to Saturday 9pm to 4:30am. 61 rue du Château d'Eau, 10e. ℂ **01-47-70-60-56.** Cover for nondiners 10€ ($12), including 1st drink. Métro: Château d'Eau.

Le Sunset/Le Sunside A staple on the Parisian jazz circuit since 1976, Le Sunset/Le Sunside maintains two separate bar areas, one on street level and one in the cellar, where separate jazz shows—each 3 hours in duration—begin at 9:30pm and 10:30pm, respectively. Expect a decor that (in the cellar) emulates a Métro station, thanks to a sheath of gloss-white tiles, and a roster of French, Italian, and U.S.-derived artists that have included Roy Haynes, Aldo Romano, Richard Galliano, and, more recently, Steve Grossman, Mark Turner, and Simon Goubert. Whereas Le Sunset is dedicated to electric jazz and world music, Le Sunside is a temple of more conservative and classic jazz. Doors open nightly at 8:30pm. 60 rue des Lombards, 1e. ℂ **01-40-26-46-60.** Cover 15€–20€ ($17–$23). Métro: Châtelet.

New Morning   Jazz maniacs come to drink, talk, and dance at this long-enduring club. It remains on the see-and-be-seen circuit, so you might spy Spike Lee or Prince. The high-ceilinged loft was turned into a nightclub in 1981. Many styles of music are performed, and the club is popular with jazz groups from Central and South Africa. Call to find out what's going on the night you plan to visit. Sometimes it's open on Sunday. Hours are generally Monday to Saturday 8pm to 1:30am. 7–9 rue des Petites-Ecuries, 10e. © 01-45-23-51-41. www.new morning.com. Cover 16€–25€ ($18–$29). Métro: Château d'Eau.

Slow Club ✦   One of the most famous jazz cellars in Europe, capped with medieval ceiling vaults that give a marvelous acoustic intimacy, Slow Club presents a revolving set of artists who tend to focus on New Orleans jazz. Patrons, mostly in their 30s and early 40s, appreciate the music's cross-cultural diversity. There's live music every night but Wednesday, when recorded dance music, everything from swing to rock, is featured. Wednesday to Saturday 10pm to 3:30am. 130 rue de Rivoli, 1e. © 01-42-33-84-30. Cover 13€ ($15). Métro: Châtelet.

DANCE CLUBS

The nightspots below are among hundreds of places where people in their 20s or early 30s go to dance—distinct from others where the main attraction is the music. The area around the church of **St-Germain-des-Prés** is full of dance clubs, but they come and go so quickly you could arrive to find a hardware store in the place of last year's white-hot club—but, like all things in nature, the new spring up to take the place of the old. Check *Time Out: Paris* or *Pariscope* to get a sense of the current trends. Most of these clubs don't really get going until well after 10pm.

Batofar   Self-consciously proud of its status as a club that virtually everybody views as hip, Batofar sits within a converted barge that floats beside an embankment on the Seine, sometimes with hundreds of gyrating dancers, most of whom are in their 20s and 30s. House, garage, techno, and live jazz from groups that hail from (among other places) Morocco, Senegal, and Germany sometimes add to the creative mix. Come here for an insight into late-night Paris at its most raffish and countercultural, and don't even try to categorize many of the after-dark denizens you're likely to meet. Tapas can be ordered beginning at 4€ ($4.60) a plate, and beer costs around 7€ ($8) a bottle. Open Tuesday to Saturday from 6pm to 3 or 4am, depending on business. Facing 11 quai François Mauriac, 13e. © 01-56-29-10-33. Cover 8€–15€ ($9.20–$17). Closed Nov–Mar. Métro: Quai de la Gare.

Club Zed *Finds*   Hip, breezy, and very French, this popular nightspot in a former bakery with a vaulted masonry ceiling may surprise you with its mix of musical offerings, including samba, rock 'n' roll, 1960s pop, and jazz. There are also specific theme parties, such as the one at Halloween, where virtually everyone comes in costume. Open Thursday 10:30pm to 3am; Friday to Saturday 11pm to 5:30am. 2 rue des Anglais, 5e. © 01-43-54-93-78. Cover 8€–16€ ($9.20–$18) including 1st drink. Métro: Maubert-Mutualité.

Favela Chic   No other nightclub in Paris succeeds at satirizing and respecting Brazilian-ness as effectively as this one. Set in the grungy-trendy Oberkampf nightclub district, it attracts good-looking, trendy men and women who come to dance, flirt, and chat in any of at least a dozen languages. There's definitely a fashionable slant to this place, but as regards the specific style, that's anybody's guess. Live music alternates with recorded music, and there are even some afternoon samba workshops for teenagers. Open Tuesday to Friday 7:30pm to 2am,

A Bar Crawl in Trendy Ménilmontant

If **rue Oberkampf** were any hotter, it would melt. How did it happen so fast? Longtime residents shake their heads and worry that the quirky authenticity of the neighborhood may disappear under the swarms of night crawlers who've migrated north from the Bastille. "Too many *banlieusards* (suburbanites) go to the Bastille," the owner of Café Cannibale told us, referring to the reluctance of trendy Parisians to socialize with the suburban crowd.

The success of ultrahip **Café Charbon,** 109 rue Oberkampf, 11e (© **01-43-57-55-13**), open daily from 9am to 2am (until 4am on weekends) and set within what was built around 1900 as a dance hall, encouraged entrepreneurs to renovate abandoned factories and bars for the artists flowing into the neighborhood and for the crowd that was tiring of the Bastille. Some of the new spots are intentionally dilapidated, while others evoke the elegance of 19th-century watering holes. The walls often exhibit the work of local artists, the music is fairly low key, and the drinks are reasonably priced (a glass of mint tea makes a refreshing alternative to alcohol). You can have a salad, snack, or hot *plat du jour,* but the food is secondary to the ambience.

Start from the Ménilmontant Métro stop and head down rue Oberkampf. Your first stop should be the divey **Le Scherkhan** at no. 144 (© **01-43-57-29-34**), where you can sink into an easy chair under the fangs of a stuffed tiger, inhale the incense, and dream of equatorial Africa. It's open daily from 5pm to 2am. Stop in at the live-music club **Le Cithéa** at no. 114 (© **01-40-21-70-95**), open daily from 7pm to 4am. Here you get a show ranging from funk or reggae to jazz fusion and house. Later, continue on to **Café Mercerie** at no. 98 (© **01-43-38-81-30**), open Monday to Friday from 5pm to 2am and Saturday and Sunday from 3pm to 2am. At the end of the grungy bar is a tiny back room lined with long sofas. Farther down on the same side of the street at no. 99 is the plush **Mecano Bar** (© **01-40-21-35-28**), open daily from 9am to 2am. Mysterious old implements on the wall are left over from its days as a tool factory. The spacious back room has a palm tree, a skylight, and murals of seminude ladies lounging about in *fin-de-siècle* naughtiness.

Backtrack a few steps and turn left onto rue St-Maur to nos. 111–113, the **Blue Billard** (© **01-43-55-87-21**), open daily from 11am to 2am. This camera-factory-turned-upscale-bar/pool hall has 18 billiard tables under a mezzanine and skylight. A few steps farther on at no. 117 is a local favorite, **Les Couleurs** (© **01-43-57-95-61**), open daily from 4pm to 2am. It's outfitted with tacky posters, chrome-and-plastic chairs, and kitschy rec-room lamps. Live bands regularly play "free jazz," alternative rock, and anything experimental. Turn right at rue Jean-Pierre-Timbaud and at no. 93 you'll find **Café Cannibale** (© **01-49-29-95-59**), open daily from 8am to 2am. This softly lit beauty shimmers with candles, mirrors, and chandeliers. Prix fixe menus, usually priced at between 5.50€ and 8.90€ ($6.35 and $10), include a good-value Sunday brunch for 17€ ($20).

More After-Dark Diversions

On a Paris night, the cheapest entertainment, especially if you're young, is **"the show"** staged at the southeastern tip of Ile de la Cité, behind Notre-Dame. A sort of Gallic version of the Sundowner Festival in Key West, it attracts just about everyone who ever wanted to try his or her hand at performance art. The entertainment is spontaneous and usually includes magicians, fire-eaters, jugglers, mimes, and music makers from all over, performing against the backdrop of the illuminated cathedral. This is one of the greatest places in Paris to meet other young people in a sometimes moderately euphoric setting.

Also popular is a **stroll along the Seine** after 10pm. Take a graveled pathway down to the river from the Left Bank side of pont de Sully, close to the Institut du Monde Arabe, and walk to the right, away from Notre-Dame. This walk, which ends near place Valhubert, is the best place to see spontaneous Paris in action at night. Joggers and saxophone players come here, and many Parisians show up to take part in impromptu dance parties.

To quench your thirst, wander onto Ile St-Louis and head for the **Café-Brasserie St-Regis,** 6 rue Jean-du-Bellay, 4e, across from pont St-Louis (© **01-43-54-59-41;** Métro: Pont-Marie). If you want to linger, you can order a *plat du jour* or a coffee at the bar. But try doing as the Parisians do: get *une bière à emporter,* a 3€ ($3.45) beer to go in a cup and take it with you on a stroll around the island. The cafe is open daily until 2am.

If you're caught waiting for the Métro to start running again at 5am, try the **Sous-Bock Tavern,** 49 rue St-Honoré, 1e (© **01-40-26-46-61;** Métro: Les Halles), open daily from 11am to 5am. Young drinkers gather here to sample 400 varieties of beer. If you want a shot of whiskey, there's a choice of 60 varieties. The dish to order is a platter of mussels—curried, with white wine, or with cream sauce; they go well with the brasserie-style fries.

Saturday until 4am. 18 rue du Faubourg du Temple, 11e. © **01-40-03-02-66.** www.favelachic. com. Cover (Sat only) 10€ ($12). Métro: République.

La Balajo   Opened in 1936, this dance club is best remembered as the venue where Edith Piaf first won the hearts of thousands of Parisians. Today it's easy to compare Le Balajo to New York City's Roseland—an old-fashioned venue steeped in nostalgia that sometimes manages to shake the dust out for special parties and events to become hip and cutting-edge. Sessions held 3 afternoons a week focus on tangos, *paso dobles,* and waltzes, and are a lot more staid than their late-night counterparts. Then you get a younger crowd, lots of hot merengue and salsa (Tues–Thurs nights) and disco (Fri–Sat nights). Monday, Thursday, and Sunday 2:30 to 6:30pm; Tuesday through Saturday 10:30pm to 5am. 9 rue de Lappe, 11e. © **01-47-00-07-87.** Cover 8€–9.10€ ($9.20–$10) for afternoon sessions; 17€ ($20) for nighttime sessions. Entrance includes the first drink. Métro: Bastille.

La Coupole   This landmark cafe has a basement ballroom that's a popular place to waltz and tango to orchestra music as well as bump and grind to "disco retro" (the best tunes of the 1960s, 1970s, and 1980s). Usually, the venue is house,

If you're looking for the most flamboyant drag in Paris, head to **Madame Arthur,** 75 bis rue des Martyrs, 18e (✆ 01-42-54-40-21; Métro: Abbesses or Pigalle). It's the longest-running show in town, attracting both straights and gays. The creative force behind the affair is Mme Arthur, who's no lady and whose stage name during her shticks as emcee is Chantaline. The performances include 9 to 11 artists with names like Vungala, Lady Lune, and Miss Badabou. You can visit just to drink or dine from a prix fixe menu (reservations required). The club is open daily from 8:30 to 10:30pm for dinner, with the show beginning at 10:30pm. Additional shows, according to demand, are held Friday and Saturday at 7pm, with dinner beginning at 6pm. After the last show, around 12:30am, the place becomes a disco. Cover (including the first drink) is 26€ ($30); dinner and the show is 47€ ($54) Sunday through Thursday; and 63€ ($72) Friday and Saturday.

If drag shows aren't your cup of tea, how about *Last Tango in Paris?* At **Le Tango,** 13 rue au Maire, 3e (✆ 01-42-72-17-78; Métro: Arts et Métiers), memories of Evita and Argentina live on. This dive with a bordello decor features *zouk* music from the French Caribbean and Africa, as well as house, garage, and virtually every form of high-energy music known. Most patrons are gay and lesbian and in their 20s and 30s. The cover is 8€ ($9.20). It's open Friday and Saturday from midnight to 5am.

If you're looking for a sophisticated, laid-back venue, consider the **Sanz-Sans,** 49 rue du Faubourg St-Antoine, 4e (✆ 01-44-75-78-78; Métro: Bastille or ledrue Rollin). It's a multiethnic playground where the children of prominent Parisians mingle, testifying to the unifying power of jazz. In this red-velvet duplex, the most important conversations seem to occur over margaritas on the stairway or the back room couches. The later it gets, the sexier the scene becomes. There's no cover.

garage, and rock 'n' roll music, but Tuesday nights the focus is on salsa. The upstairs cafe is covered in "The Top Cafes" in chapter 6. Open Tuesday 9pm to 5am, Friday to Saturday 3 to 7pm and 10pm to 5am. 102 bd. Montparnasse, 14e. ✆ 01-43-20-14-20. Ballroom cover 12€–18€ ($14–$21) for evening sessions. Métro: Vavin.

La Flèche d'Or ★ *Finds* The setting for this hip nightclub is a small railway station adjacent to the Père-Lachaise cemetery built in the 1890s and decommissioned by the SNCF in the 1950s. You're likely to have a radically different experience here depending on the night. Tuesday features whatever amateur group wants to volunteer; as many as 20 different bands—some talented, others less so—perform. Wednesday has electronic live and recorded music, Thursday reggae, Friday ska, Saturday focuses on live bands from everywhere, especially Africa, and Sunday has salsa and merengue. The walls are often hung with paintings from temporary art exhibitions (they're for sale), and every Sunday morning, beginning at 11am, there's some kind of political forum and debate. Open Tuesday to Sunday 7pm to 2am. 102 bis rue de Bagnolet, 20e. ✆ 01-43-72-04-23. Cover free to 5.50€ ($6.35). Métro: Alexandre Dumas.

La Java   This dance hall used to be one of the most frequented in Paris, and the great Piaf and Chevalier made their names here. Today, you can still waltz and perhaps even tango on a Sunday afternoon. Brazilian and Latin themes predominate on some nights. Open Wednesday to Saturday 11pm to 5am; Sunday 8pm to 2am. 105 rue du Faubourg du Temple, 10e. ✆ 01-42-02-20-52. Cover 10€–15€ ($12–$17). Métro: Belleville.

Le Saint   Occupying three medieval cellars deep in Paris's university area, this place lures 20- and 30-somethings who dance and drink and generally enjoy being in a Left Bank student dive. The music melds New York, Los Angeles, and Europe and often leads to episodes of "Young Love Beside the Seine." Open Tuesday to Saturday 10pm to 6am. 7 rue St-Severin, 5e. ✆ 01-43-25-50-04. Cover 8€–15€ ($9.20–$17) including 1st drink. Métro: St-Michel.

Les Bains ★   The name, "The Baths," comes from this hot spot's former function as a Turkish bath, once attracting gay clients, none more notable than Marcel Proust. It may be hard to get in if the doorman doesn't think you're trendy and chic. (Yes, that was Jennifer Lopez we saw whirling around the floor.) Dancing begins at midnight, and a supper club–like restaurant lies upstairs. Meals cost 38€ to 46€ ($44–$53). On certain nights this is the hottest party in Paris. Mondays are increasingly gay, although sexual preference is hardly an issue. "We all walk the waterfront," one DJ enigmatically told us as he played soul, house music, or whatever. 7 rue du Bourg-l'Abbae, 3e. ✆ 01-48-87-01-80. Cover 20€ ($23). Daily midnight–6am. Métro: Etience Marcel.

Les Coulisses   Its premises combine a cellar-level dance club with a street-level restaurant that bears two names. During the day, from 7:30am to around 8pm, it's known as La Bohème; from 8pm to 5:30am, it becomes a bit more formal and is called Les Coulisses. The food remains the same, with a prix fixe menu at 32€ ($37). Most nighttime patrons eventually filter down to the dance club, where the decor is a cross between a feudal château and a scene from the Italian *Commedia dell'Arte*. The crowd ranges in age from 20 to around 45. Restaurants open Tuesday to Saturday 9pm to midnight; dance club open Tuesday to Saturday 11pm to 5am. 5 rue St-Rustique, 18e. ✆ 01-42-62-89-99. Cover 30€ ($35) Fri–Sat, but free for patrons of either restaurant. Métro: Abbesses or Funiculaire.

New Riverside   If thoughts of Woodstock fill you with nostalgia and you want to meet Parisians between 25 and 40 who feel the same, this is the place for you. The Left Bank cellar club attracts droves of people who appreciate the indestructible premises and nostalgic music. You'll hear a range of 1970s rock and pop, especially the Doors. Open nightly 8:30pm until dawn. 7 rue Grégoire-de-Tours, 6e. ✆ 01-43-54-46-33. Cover for men 15€ ($17) including 1st drink, but women pay cover only after midnight Fri–Sat. Métro: St-Michel or Odéon.

Nouveau Casino   Some Paris-watchers consider this the epitome of the counterculture and hyperhip context that blossoms along the rue Oberkampf, beginning around 8pm every night. Positioned within what used to be a movie theater, immediately adjacent to the Café Charbon, it's a large, drafty space sheathed with metal panels and columns, centered on a dance floor and an enormous and bizarre-looking bar that resembles an iceberg. Every night of the week there are live concerts between 8pm and 1am, and every Friday and Saturday the party continues from 1am till dawn with a DJ who spins some of the most avant-garde dance music in Paris. Celebrities spotted here include Prince Albert of Monaco and French film stars Vincent Cassel and Matthieu Kassovitz. 109 rue

Oberkampf, 9e. 📞 **01-43-57-57-40.** www.nouveaucasino.net. Concerts 12€–13€ ($14–$15); dance club 5€–16€ ($5.75–$18). Métro: St-Maur, Parmentier, or Menimontant.

Rex Club   This echoing blue-and-orange space emulates the techno-grunge clubs of London, complete with an international mood-altered crowd enjoying the kind of music only someone 18 to 28 could love. A host of DJs, including techno-circuit celeb Laurent Garnier, is on hand. Open Wednesday to Saturday 11:30pm to 6am. 5 bd. Poissonnière, 2e. 📞 **01-42-36-83-98.** Cover 8€–13€ ($9.20–$15). Métro: Bonne Nouvelle.

3 Bars, Pubs & Clubs

WINE BARS

Many Parisians now prefer wine bars to traditional cafes or bistros. The food is often better and the ambience more inviting. For cafes, see "The Top Cafes" in chapter 6.

Au Sauvignon   This tiny place, with ceramic tiles and frescoes done by Left Bank artists, has tables overflowing onto a covered terrace where wines range from the cheapest Beaujolais to the most expensive St-Emilion Grand Cru. A glass is 4.50€ to 5.50€ ($5.20–$6.35), and it costs an extra .50€ (60¢) to consume it at a table. To accompany your wine, choose an Auvergne specialty, like goat cheese or a terrine. The Poilâne bread is ideal with ham, pâté, or goat cheese. Open daily 8:30am to 10pm. 80 rue des Sts-Pères, 7e. 📞 **01-45-48-49-02.** Métro: Sèvres-Babylone.

Aux Négociants   Ten minutes downhill from the north facade of Sacré-Coeur, this *bistro à vins* has flourished since 1980 as an outlet for wines produced in the Loire Valley. Artists, vendors, and office workers come here, linked by an appreciation of wine, costing 3€ to 5€ ($3.45–$5.75) per glass, and the *plats du jour,* costing 12€ to 15€ ($14–$17). Open Monday noon to 2:30pm, Tuesday through Friday noon to 10:30pm. 27 rue Lambert, 18e. 📞 **01-46-06-15-11.** Métro: Lamarck-Caulincourt or Château Rouge.

Juveniles   This is a British-owned spin-off of one of Paris's most successful wine bars, nearby Willi's. Louder, less formal, less restrained, and (at least to wine lovers) more daring than its older sibling, it prides itself on experimenting with a wide roster of wines from "everywhere." High-quality but lesser-known wines from Spain, France, California, and Australia decant for 3€ to 11€ ($3.45–$13) per glass. Anything you like, including the "wine of the week," can be hauled away uncorked from the wine boutique here. There's also an assortment of tapas-inspired platters for 7€ ($8.05). Bar open Monday through Saturday noon to 1am; restaurant open Monday through Saturday noon to 3pm and 6 to 11:30pm. 47 rue de Richelieu, 1e. 📞 **01-42-97-46-49.** Métro: Palais Royal.

La Tartine   Mirrors, brass detail, and frosted-globe chandeliers make La Tartine look like a movie set of old Paris. At least 60 wines are offered at reasonable prices, including seven kinds of Beaujolais and a large selection of Bordeaux by the glass. Glasses of wine cost 3€ to 8€ ($3.45–$9.20), and the charcuterie platter costs 8€ ($9.20). We recommend the light Sancerre wine and goat cheese from the Loire Valley. Open Tuesday through Saturday 8am to 2am, Sunday and Monday 10am to 10pm. 24 rue de Rivoli, 4e. 📞 **01-42-72-76-85.** Métro: St-Paul.

Le Sancerre   Engagingly old-fashioned, with an agreeable staff and food prepared fresh every day, this wine bar specializes in vintages from the Loire Valley and Sancerre. The latter, produced in red, rosé, and white, is known for its not-too-dry fruity aroma and legions of fans who believe it should be more celebrated. Other wine choices include Chinon and Saumur wine (both from the Loire Valley) as well as Pinot de Bourgogne (from Burgundy) and Gamet (from the Ardèche Valley in France's southwest). Food items usually include *andouillette* (chitterling sausages), omelets with flap mushrooms, fresh oysters, and quiche. Glasses of wine cost 2.85€ to 4.45€ ($3.30–$5.10); simple platters of food cost 9€ to 11€ ($10–$13) each. Open Monday through Friday 8am to 9:30pm; Saturday 8:30am to 4pm. 22 av. Rapp, 7e. © 01-45-51-75-91. Métro: Alma-Marceau.

Les Bacchantes   Les Bacchantes prides itself on offering more wines by the glass (at least 50) than any other wine bar in Paris, and also does a hefty restaurant trade serving well-prepared *cuisine bourgeoise* (comfort food). Amid exposed beams, Belle Epoque posters, and old-fashioned paneling, chalkboards announce a great list of vintages and platters. The wines, at 2.60€ to 6€ ($3–$6.90) per glass, are mainly French. Platters of food cost 9.10€ to 15€ ($10–$17). Open Monday through Saturday noon to midnight. 21 rue Caumartin, 9e. © 01-42-65-25-35. Métro: Opéra or Madeleine.

Willi's Wine Bar ⭐   Journalists and stockbrokers patronize this increasingly popular wine bar in the center of the financial district, run by Englishman Mark Williamson. About 250 kinds of wine are offered, including a dozen specials you can taste by the glass for 3€ to 19€ ($3.45–$22). Lunch is the busiest time—on quiet evenings you can better enjoy the warm ambience and admire the 16th-century beams. Daily specials are likely to include lamb brochette with cumin and Lyonnaise sausage in truffled vinaigrette, plus spectacular desserts like chocolate terrine. A prix fixe lunch costs 28€ ($32), with a prix fixe dinner going for 35€ ($40). Bar open Monday through Saturday noon to 11pm; meals served Monday through Saturday noon to 2:30pm and 7 to 11pm. 13 rue des Petits-Champs, 1e. © 01-42-61-05-09. Métro: Bourse, Pyramide, or Palais Royal.

BARS, PUBS & CLUBS

These "imported" places trying to imitate American cocktail bars or British pubs mostly strike an alien chord. But that doesn't prevent fashionable Parisians from barhopping (not to be confused with cafe-sitting). Many bars in Paris are youth-oriented. But if you're an older traveler who prefers to take your expensive drink in one of the grand luxe bars of the world, Paris has those as well. The bars at the **Plaza Athénée, Crillon,** and **Ritz,** for example, are among the grandest in the world and provide a uniquely Parisian experience to those who want to don their finest apparel and take along a gold-plated credit card. In general, bars and pubs are open daily from 11am to 1:30am.

Académie de la Bière *Value*   The decor is paneled and rustic, an appropriate foil for an "academy" whose curriculum includes more than 150 kinds of beer from microbreweries. More than half of the dozen beers on tap are from small-scale breweries in Belgium that deserve to be better known that that country's bestseller, Stella Artois. Snack-style food is available, including platters of mussels, assorted cheeses, and sausages with mustard. Open daily 11am to 2am. 88 bis bd. du Port-Royal, 5e. © 01-43-54-66-65. Métro: Port Royal.

Bar du Crillon   Though some visitors consider the Bar du Crillon too stiff and elegant to allow anyone to have a good time, its social and literary history is remarkable. Hemingway set a climactic scene of *The Sun Also Rises* here, and over the years it has attracted practically every upper-level staff member of the nearby American embassy, as well as heiresses, stars, starlets, and wannabes. Under its new owner, the Concorde Group, designer Sonia Rykiel has redecorated the bar. Down the hall is the Edwardian **Jardin d'Hiver,** where, amid potted palms and upscale accessories, you can order tea, cocktails, or coffee; it's open daily from noon to 9pm. In the Hôtel du Crillon, 10 place de la Concorde, 8e. © **01-44-71-15-00.** Métro: Concorde.

Barfly   Catering to a cool, fashionable, international crowd, this is an artfully decorated, busy bar and supper club that is hip, stylish, and a lot of fun. Set in the heart of one of Paris's most expensive residential and commercial neighborhoods (real-estate brokers refer to it as "the Golden Triangle"), it's laid out in one enormous street-floor area that boasts hardwood floors, riveting and large photo-realistic paintings, a surreal and postmodern interpretation of Winged Victory, and a blue stone bar said to be the longest in Paris. Cutting-edge music plays, deep armchairs are scattered artfully throughout, and a restaurant, specializing in Asian/French/Pacific Rim cuisine, including sushi, serves late suppers for between 35€ and 50€ ($40–$58) per person. Open daily noon to 2am. 49–51 av. George V, 8e. © **01-53-67-84-60.** Métro: George-V.

Bar Hemingway/Bar Vendôme   In 1944, during Paris's liberation, Ernest Hemingway and a group of Allied soldiers made history by "freeing" the Ritz from the Nazis and ordering a round of martinis. The Ritz commemorates this event in the **Bar Hemingway** with bookish memorabilia, rows of newspapers, and stiff drinks served in a woodsy English-club setting. Look for its entrance, and homage to other writers, close to the hotel's rue Cambon entrance. More fun than the Bar Vendôme, the Hemingway is virtually a singles bar—unfussy, chic, and often filled with newly single, attractive women, many taking classes at the on-site cooking school. The Vendôme, in contrast, retains its old-world stateliness. Between 5:30 and 8:30pm, it's wise to reserve a table. Bar Hemingway is open Tuesday through Saturday 6:30pm to 2am; Bar Vendôme is open daily noon to 3pm for lunch, 4 to 6pm for tea, and 6pm to 1am for drinks. In the Hôtel Ritz, 15 place Vendôme, 1e. © **01-43-16-30-30.** Métro: Opéra.

Barrio Latino   It would be easy to spend an entire evening at this multistoried emporium of good times, Gallic flair, and Latino charm. Here's what you can expect: Tapas bars and dance floors on *rez-de-chausée* (street level) and *2eme étage* (third floor); a Latino restaurant on *1er étage* (second floor); and a private club on *dernière étage* (top floor). Staff members roll glass-covered carts loaded with tapas around the floors, selling them like hot dogs at an American baseball game. The restaurant (open daily noon–3pm and 7:30pm–12:30am) serves main courses that range from 8.50€ to 26€ ($9.80–$30) and include Argentinean steaks, Brazilian *feijoada,* and Mexican chili con carne, all of which taste wonderful with beer, caipirinhas, Cuba Libres, and rum punches. Marvelous recorded Latino music surrounds you everywhere you go. Clientele is very mixed: mostly straight, partly gay, and 100% blasé about such matters. The bar is open daily 11am to 2am. 46 rue du Faubourg St-Antoine, 12e. © **01-55-78-84-75.** Cover 8€ ($9.20) but only for nondiners, non-VIPs, and only on Fri–Sat after 9pm. Métro: Bastille.

Bob Cool   A hot Parisian Left Bank bar, this rendezvous point attracts a hip and rather laid-back coterie of friends to its precincts not far from the famous street, rue St-André-des-Arts. Tables and chairs are found in the front room, with banquettes in the back. Writers and artists, ranging in age from 18 to 60, are drawn here, especially during the happy hour from 5 to 9pm when you buy one drink and get the second libation free. The bartender selects the music. On our last visit, Dominican Republic merengue was the rage. Open Monday through Saturday 5pm to 2am. 15 rue des Grands Augustins, 6e. (C) **01-46-33-33-77**. Métro: Odéon or St-Michel.

Chez Richard   This is our favorite bar in the 4th arrondissement, and a great place for people-watching, lying inside a courtyard off rue Vieille-du-Temple. The interior is lined with stone, and the ceiling fans and palm leaves evoke old Algiers (once a French colony). The action is on two levels, and hip music is played in the background. Happy hour daily from 6 to 8pm is very popular with Left Bank young people. The bartenders are among the hippest in town. Open Tuesday through Saturday 6pm to 2am (closed 2 weeks in Aug). 37 rue Vieille-du-Temple, 4e. (C) **01-42-74-31-65**. Métro: Hotel-de-Ville.

China Club   Designed to recall France's 19th-century colonies in Asia or a bordello in 1930s Shanghai (on the ground floor) and England's empire-building zeal in India (upstairs), the China Club will allow you to chitchat or flirt with the singles who crowd into the street-level bar, then escape to calmer, more contemplative climes upstairs. You'll see regulars from the worlds of fashion and the arts, along with a pack of postshow celebrants from the nearby Opéra Bastille. A street-level Chinese restaurant serves dinner daily from 7pm to 12:30am, and in the more animated (and occasionally raucous) cellar bar, live music is presented every Friday and Saturday from 10pm to 3am. 50 rue de Charenton, 12e. (C) **01-43-43-82-02**. Daily 7pm–2am. Métro: Bastille or Ledru Rollin.

La Belle Hortense   There are dozens of other bars and cafes near this one, but none maintains a bookstore in back, and few seem so self-consciously aware of their roles as ersatz literary salons. Come for a glass of wine and participation in a discussion within what's defined as "a literary bar." It's named after a pulpy 19th-century romance (*La Belle Hortense*) set within the surrounding neighborhood. Glasses of wine cost 3.50€ to 6€ ($4.05–$6.90). Open daily 5pm to 2am. 31 rue Vieille du Temple, 4e. (C) **01-48-04-71-60**. Métro: Hôtel de Ville.

Le Bar   Because of the crush of wannabes who scheme, maneuver, and manipulate their way into the bar of this ultraprestigious hotel, there's absolutely no guarantee that you'll get in, so make sure you have an alternative plan. Should you get inside, you'll find a street-level location of rich-looking paneling, high tables, barrel-shaped armchairs, glossy bar tops, and the kind of lighting that makes almost anyone look fabulous. Chat here can get bitchy, and it's anyone's guess how rich the pampered crowd really is. Be prepared for theme cocktails that in many cases are too pink, too cloying, and certainly too expensive. Open daily 6pm to 1:30am. In the Hotel Plaza-Athénée, 25 av. Montaigne, 8e. (C) **01-53-67-66-65**. Cocktails 20€–23€ ($23–$26). Métro: Alma-Marceau.

Le Bar de L'Hôtel   This is the hyperartsy and theatrically decorated bar of a hotel that has wooed film-industry types who want to avoid the more mainstream luxury of Paris's palatial hotels. The rose-filter cheeriness is deceptive: This is the hotel where Oscar Wilde died, disgraced and impoverished. In 2000, the bar, along with the rest of the hotel, was renovated by decorating bigwig Jacques Garcia. Expect a high-Victorian color scheme of terra cotta and dark green, marble columns, an imposing marble-topped bar, and an appealing sense of baroque (or Byzantine) intrigue. Drinks here sometimes segue into the nearby on-site restaurant, which is open Tuesday through Saturday from noon to 3pm and 8 to 10:30pm. Bar open daily 4pm to 1am. In L'Hôtel, 13 rue des Beaux-Arts, 6e. (C) **01-44-41-99-00**. Métro: St-Germain-des-Prés.

Le Forum   Patrons, who include frequent business travelers, compare this place to a private club in London. The comparison is due partly to the polished oak paneling and ornate stucco, and partly to the selection of single-malt whiskeys. You can also try 250 cocktails, including many that haven't been popular since the Jazz Age. Champagne by the glass is common, as is that social lubricant, the martini. Open Monday through Friday 11:30am to 2am, Saturday 5pm to 2am. 4 bd. Malesherbes, 8e. ✆ 01-42-65-37-86. Métro: Madeleine.

Le Fumoir   At Le Fumoir, the well-traveled crowd that lives or works in the district provides a kind of classy raucousness. The decor is a lot like that of an English library, with about 6,000 books providing an aesthetic backdrop to the schmoozing. A Danish chef prepares an international menu featuring meal-size salads (the one with scallops and lobster is great), roasted codfish with zucchini, and roasted beef in red-wine sauce. More popular are the stiff mixed drinks, the wines and beers, and the dozen or so types of cigars for sale. Open daily 11am to 2am. 6 rue de l'Amiral-de-Coligny, 1e. ✆ 01-42-92-00-24. Métro: Louvre-Rivoli.

Maito Habana   The macho brown-and-green decor evokes a men's club. You can drink Cuba Libres, cognac, or coffee, or eat platters of food, with main courses costing 13€ to 18€ ($15–$21). You can also puff away at any of the cigars stocked for the pleasure of the patrons (regulars sometimes store their cigars in a safe originally designed as a safety-deposit vault). Live music is presented at 11pm Tuesday to Saturday. Cafe and cigar service Monday 9am to 8pm, Tuesday through Friday 9am to 5pm, and Saturday 8pm to 5am; meals served Monday noon to 3:30pm, Tuesday through Saturday 8pm to midnight. 19 rue de Presbourg, 16e. ✆ 01-45-00-84-84. Métro: Etoile.

Man Ray   This chic rendezvous off the Champs-Elysées is dedicated to Man Ray, the famous photographer and American Dadaist, who usually felt more comfortable roaming Montparnasse than the 8th. Many of Man Ray's photos decorate the club. The club is a media favorite, mainly because some of its owners are Johnny Depp, Sean Penn, and John Malkovich. Entry is discreet, through large wrought-iron doors, and there's virtually no sign. In the basement is a bustling restaurant presided over by two winged Indonesian goddesses. Main courses begin at 23€ ($26). The bar upstairs is big and bustling. Jazz is presented Monday to Thursday from 7 to 9pm in the bar, and every night after 11pm a DJ provides music. On Fridays the place is transformed into a dance club after 11pm, with an entrance cost of 15€ ($17), including the first drink. Restaurant open Monday through Friday noon to 2:30pm, daily 7:30pm to 12:30am; bar open daily 6pm to 2am. 34 rue Marbeuf, 8e. ✆ 01-56-88-36-36. Métro: Franklin-D.-Roosevelt.

Moosehead   Throughout this very Left Bank place, you'll be surrounded by the restaurant's primary decorative theme: anything and everything to do with ice hockey. As such, the walls are lined with framed photographs of hockey players in action, and jerseys and memorabilia that reflect the favorite sport, and some of the favorite teams, of the owners, and many of the staff. Expect a rough and ready sports-loving crowd that includes lots of Canadian, British, Irish, French, and U.S. sports fans. Theme nights here include, depending on the weather and the mood of the organizers, beach parties (where some of the less inhibited clients might strip to their underpants within sightlines of whimsically useless beach parasols) and country-western bashes. Open Monday to Friday 4pm to 2am, Saturday to Sunday 11am to 2am. 16 rue des Quatre Vents, 6e. ✆ 01-46-33-77-00. Métro: Odéon.

4 Gay & Lesbian Bars & Clubs

Gay life is centered around **Les Halles** and **Le Marais,** with the greatest concentration of gay and lesbian clubs, restaurants, bars, and shops between the Hôtel de Ville and Rambuteau Métro stops. Gay dance clubs come and go so fast that even the magazines devoted to them, like *Illico*—distributed free in the gay bars and bookstores—have a hard time keeping up. For lesbians, there is *Lesbian Magazine.* Also look for Gai Pied's *Guide Gai* and *Pariscope*'s regularly featured English-language section, "A Week of Gay Outings." Also important for both men and women is *Têtu Magazine,* sold at most newsstands.

For more on Paris's gay and lesbian scene, try *Frommer's Gay & Lesbian Europe.*

Café Cox, 15 rue des Archives, 4e (℃ **01-42-72-08-00**), gets so busy in the early evening that the crowd stands on the sidewalk. This is where you'll find the most mixed gay crowd in Paris—from hunky American tourists to sexy Parisian men. A hot new place in Les Halles is **Le Tropic Café,** 56 rue des Lombards, 1e (℃ **01-40-13-92-62;** Métro: Châtelet–Les Halles), where the trendy, good-looking crowd parties until dawn. **Le Gibus,** 18 rue du Faubourg du Temple, 11e (℃ **01-47-00-78-88;** Métro: République), opens every night as a late-night dance club, entertaining diverse collections of counterculture Parisians. But Friday and Saturday nights are deliberately and exclusively gay, attracting some of the most drop-dead gorgeous men in the city. Drag shows, at least on weekends, form part of the entertainment. It's open nightly from midnight to 6am. Weeknight entrance costs from 5€ to 20€ ($5.75–$23), depending on the venue, but on gay nights the charge is 18€ ($21), including the first drink.

A restaurant with a bar popular with women is **Okawa,** 40 rue Vieille-du-Temple, 4e (℃ **01-48-04-30-69;** Métro: Hôtel de Ville), where trendy lesbians (and some gay men) enjoy happy hour. **Les Scandaleuses,** 6 rue des Ecouffes, 3e (℃ **01-48-87-39-26;** Métro: St-Paul), is a bar for gay women where an unattached female can usually find a drinking buddy to tell her troubles to.

Amnesia Café The Amnesia's function and crowd may change during the day, but you'll always find a cadre of local gays. This cafe/tearoom/bistro/bar includes two bar areas, a mezzanine, and a cellar bar, **Amni-Club,** open in the evening. The drinks of choice are beer, cocktails, and *café amnesia,* a specialty coffee with cognac and Chantilly cream. Deep armchairs, soft pillows, and 1930s accents create an ambience conducive to talk and laughter—it's not as sexually charged as the nearby bars. Open daily noon to 2am. 42 rue Vieille-du-Temple, 4e. ℃ **01-42-72-16-94.** Métro: Hôtel de Ville.

Banana Café This popular bar is a stop for gays visiting or doing business in Paris. Occupying two floors of a 19th-century building, it has walls the color of an overripe banana, dim lighting, and a policy of raising the drink prices after 10pm, when things become really interesting. There's a street-level bar and a cellar dance floor that features a live pianist and recorded music—sometimes with dancing. On many nights, go-go dancers perform from spotlit platforms in the cellar. Open daily from 5pm to 4 or 5am. 13 rue de la Ferronnerie, 1e. ℃ **01-42-33-35-31.** Métro: Châtelet–Les Halles.

La Champmeslé La Champmeslé—with dim lighting, background music, and comfortable banquettes—is a cozy meeting place for lesbians (and even for "well-behaved" gay men). It's housed in a 300-year-old building with exposed stone and ceiling beams and 1950s-style furnishings. On Thursday and Saturday, one of the premier lesbian events of Paris, a cabaret, begins at 10pm; every month there's a well-attended exhibit of paintings by mostly lesbian artists. The bar honors a celebrated 17th-century actress, La Champmeslé, who was instrumental in interpreting the fledgling dramatic efforts of celebrated playwright Racine. Open Monday through Wednesday from 2pm to 2am, Thursday through Saturday until 5am. 4 rue Chabanais, 2e. ℂ **01-42-96-85-20**. Métro: Pyramides or Bourse.

Le Central Established in 1980 in a 300-year-old town house, Le Central is a staple of gay men's life in the Marais. Outfitted with an indestructible decor of battered paneling and windows that wrap around on two sides, it attracts local residents who make the place their hangout, and goodly numbers of attractive male tourists and the Parisians who appreciate them. Don't be surprised if the friendships you forge here are with other Yanks, Aussies, or Brits. A small gay hotel is upstairs. Open Monday to Friday from 4pm to 2am, Saturday to Sunday from 2pm to 2am. 33 rue Vieille-du-Temple, 4e. ℂ **01-48-87-99-33**. Métro: Hôtel de Ville.

Le Depot This gay pleasure palace stages everything from Queer Mother Nights to Putas at Work. Wander the rooms downstairs with your companion for the night. The pick-up area and best cruising grounds is in the section where porno flicks are being shown on television sets mounted on the walls. There are backrooms downstairs if you'd like to get better acquainted with your catch of the evening. Lesbians after 11pm patronize the upstairs dance floor. The age range here is from 18 to 50. The post Sunday brunch gay tea dance is one of the happening events of Paris. Open daily from 2pm to 8am. 10 rue aux Ours, 3e. ℂ **01-44-54-96-96**. Cover 7.50€–10€ ($8.65–$12). Métro: Etienne-Marcel.

Le Pulp This is one of the most popular lesbian dance clubs, looking like a burgundy-colored 19th-century French music hall. It's best to show up before midnight. The venue, as the French like to say, is *très cool,* with cutting-edge music played in a setting that just happens to discourage the presence of men. Open Thursday through Saturday from 11:30pm until dawn. 25 bd. Poissonière, 2e. ℂ **01-40-26-01-93**. Cover 8€–12€ ($9.20–$14). Métro: Grands Boulevards.

Le Queen Should you miss gay life a la New York, follow the flashing purple sign on the "main street" of Paris, near the corner of avenue George V. The place is often mobbed, primarily with gay men and (to a lesser degree) models, actresses, and the like. Look for go-go boys, drag shows, muscle shows, and everything from 1970s-style disco nights (Mon) to Tuesday-night foam parties in summer, when cascades of mousse descend onto the dance floor. Go very late. Open daily from 11pm to 4 or 5am. 102 av. des Champs-Elysées, 8e. ℂ **01-53-89-08-90**. Cover 10€–20€ ($12–$23), including 1st drink, Fri–Sat. Métro: Franklin-D.-Roosevelt.

Open Café/Café Cox Although technically this side-by-side pair of gay men's bars are independent, their clienteles are so interconnected, and there's such traffic between them, that we—like many other residents of this neighborhood—usually jumble them together. Both define themselves as bars rather than dance clubs, but on particularly busy nights, one or another couple might actually begin to dance. Simple cafe-style food is served throughout the day. Don't come here with preconceptions about what type of guy you're likely to find—patrons can include just about every type of male that roams the streets of gay Europe today. Open Sunday to Thursday from 11am to 2am, Friday to Saturday to 4am. 15 and 17 rue des Archives, 4e (ℂ **01-42-72-26-18** and 01-42-72-08-00). Métro: Hôtel de Ville.

Sundays at La Scala At least within the gay vocabulary, Sunday nights in Paris could be dull until a group of nightlife entrepreneurs gained access to the sleek basement-level interior of an otherwise mostly straight nightclub in the shadow of City Hall. Beginning at 6pm every Sunday, the venue becomes flamboyantly extroverted, even defiantly so, thanks to a clientele of mostly gay men who flirt, dance, and cavort on a glossy-looking dance floor till around 2am, theoretically in time to recover for a productive work week. 188 rue de Rivoli, 1e. ℭ 01-42-61-64-00. Cover 22€ ($25) per person, with first drink included. Métro: Hôtel de Ville.

5 Literary Haunts

Harry's New York Bar   The ads tell you to instruct your cab driver, "Sank roo doe Noo." Opened on Thanksgiving Day in 1911 by a bearded Hemingway precursor by the name of MacElhone, Harry's New York Bar is sacred to Papa disciples as the spot where members of the ambulance corps drank themselves silly during World War I. White Lady and sidecar cocktails were invented here in 1919 and 1931, respectively, and it's the alleged birthplace of the Bloody Mary and the headquarters of a fraternity of drinkers known as the International Bar Flies (IBF). In the street-level bar, daytime crowds draw from the area's insurance, banking, and travel industries; evening crowds include pre- and post-theater groupies and night owls. In the cellar, a pianist plays daily from 10pm to 2am. Open daily 10am to 4am. 5 rue Daunou, 2e. ℭ 01-42-61-71-14. Métro: Opéra or Pyramides.

Rosebud   The popularity of this place, known for a bemused and indulgent attitude toward anyone looking for a drink and some talk, hasn't diminished since the 1950s, when it attained its fame. The name refers to the beloved sled of Orson Welles' great *Citizen Kane*. Around the corner from Montparnasse's famous cafes, and thick in associations with Sartre and de Beauvoir, Ionesco, and Duras, Rosebud draws a crowd aged 35 to 65, though the staff has recently remarked on the appearance of students. Drop in at night for a glass of wine, a shot of whiskey, or a hamburger or chili con carne. Open daily 7pm to 2am. 11 bis rue Delambre, 14e. ℭ 01-43-35-38-54. Métro: Vavin.

11

Side Trips from Paris

Paris is the center of a curious land-locked island known as the **Ile de France.** Shaped roughly like a saucer, it's encircled by a thin ribbon of rivers: the **Epte, Aisne, Marne,** and **Yonne.** Fringing these rivers are forests with famous names—**Rambouillet, St-Germain, Compiègne,** and **Fontainebleau.** These forests are said to be responsible for Paris's clear gentle air and the unusual length of its spring and fall. This may be debatable, but there's no argument they provide the

capital with a fine series of day trips, all within easy reach.

The forests surrounding Paris were once the domain of royalty and the aristocracy, and they're still sprinkled with the magnificent châteaux of their former masters. Together with ancient villages, glorious cathedrals, and cozy country inns, they make the Ile de France irresistible. In this chapter, we offer only a handful of the possibilities for day jaunts. For a more extensive list, see Frommer's France 2005.

1 Versailles ⭐

21km (13 miles) SW of Paris, 71km (44 miles) NE of Chartres

For centuries, the name of the Parisian suburb of Versailles resounded through the consciousness of every aristocratic family in Europe. The palace here out-dazzled every other kingly residence in Europe—it was a horrendously expensive scandal and a symbol to later generations of a regime obsessed with prestige above all else.

Back in the *grand siècle* (the 17th century), all you needed was a sword, a hat, and a bribe for the guard at the gate. Provided you didn't look as if you had smallpox, you'd be admitted to the **Château de Versailles,** where you could stroll through salon after glittering salon—watching the Sun King rise—and dress and dine and do even more intimate things while you gossiped, danced, plotted, flirted, and trysted.

Today, Versailles needs the return of Louis XIV and his treasury. You wouldn't believe it when looking at the glittering Hall of Mirrors, but Versailles is down at the heels. It suffers from a lack of funds, which translates into a shortage of security; this budget crunch was made even worse in 1999 when a windstorm wreaked havoc here.

You get to see only half of the palace's treasures; the rest are closed to the public. Some 3.2 million visitors arrive annually; on average they spend 2 hours.

ESSENTIALS
GETTING THERE To get to Versailles catch the **RER** line C at the Gare d'Austerlitz, St-Michel, Musée d'Orsay, Invalides, Ponte de l'Alma, Champ de Mars, or Javel stop and take it to the Versailles Rive Gauche station, from which there's a shuttle bus to the château. Priced at 5.20€ ($6) round-trip, the transit takes 35 to 40 minutes; Eurailpass holders travel free on the RER, but they'll

A Weekend in London

Of course, Paris offers a seemingly endless list of wonderful things to see and do, but now that transit between the French capital and the British capital is easier than ever, why not take a weekend jaunt to London?

The **Eurostar** (© 08-92-35-35-39) train roars through the **Channel Tunnel (Chunnel),** reducing the travel time between Paris's Gare du Nord and London's Waterloo Station to 3 hours. With some restrictions, fares between London and Paris begin at 139€ ($160) or 224€ ($258) for one-way transport (depending on day and time) and at 415€ ($477) for round-trip in second class. First-class transit begins at 315€ ($362) one-way and 565€ ($650) round-trip, per person. Additional discounts, in many cases, are offered to holders of Eurail and Britrail passes, youths under 26, students, and persons over 60. And for passengers looking for additional perks to first-class transport, packages can be bought beginning at 399€ ($459) per person each way that allow access to first-class waiting lounges in Paris and London, enhanced cuisine onboard, and taxi service between the station of your final destination and your hotel. If you need a hotel in London or Paris, the staff at one of Eurostar's affiliates can set up a rail/hotel package at a discounted rate. For round-trip transport plus a night in a hotel in London or Paris, plus a sightseeing package, rates begin at 625€ ($719) per person in first class and 475€ ($546) per person in second class. Ask Eurostar about special promotions and you may discover some surprising discounts. Examples include a departure from and a return to either city on the same day at round-trip rates that can be about the same as a one-way ticket.

From North America, call the **Eurostar** division of Rail Europe at © 800/EUROSTAR. For details about hotel packages, contact **Euro-Vacations** at © 877/387-6822. If you're already in Paris, contact any travel agency, talk to your concierge, or check www.raileurope.com.

need to show their Eurailpass at the kiosk near any RER entrance to receive a ticket that will open the turnstile leading onto the RER platforms.

An alternate method of reaching Versailles from central Paris involves regular **SNCF trains,** which make frequent runs from two railway stations (Gare St-Lazare and Gare Montparnasse) to Versailles. Trains departing from Gare St-Lazare arrive at the Versailles Rive Droite railway station; trains departing from Gare Montparnasse arrive at Versailles Chantiers. Both stations lie within a 10-minute walk from the château, and we highly recommend the walk as a means of orienting yourself with the town, its geography, its scale, and its architecture. If you can't or don't want to walk, you can take bus B, bus H, or (in midsummer) a shuttle bus marked CHATEAU from any of the three stations directly to the château for a fee of 2.50€ ($2.90) each way per person. Again, because of the vagaries of each of the bus schedules, we highly recommend the walk. Directions to the château are clearly signposted from each of the three railway stations.

As a last resort—and frankly, we do not recommend it—you can use a combination of **Métro** and **city bus.** Travel to the Pont de Sèvres stop by Métro, then transfer to bus no. 171 for a westward trek that'll take 35 to 60 minutes, depending on traffic. The bus will cost you three Métro tickets and deposit you near the château gates.

If you have a **car,** take N-10, following the signs to Versailles, and then proceed along avenue de Général-Leclerc. Park on place d'Armes in front of the château.

VISITOR INFORMATION   Three main avenues radiate from place d'Armes in front of the palace. The **tourist office** is on one of them, at 2 bis av. de Paris (✆ **01-39-24-88-88**).

TOURING VERSAILLES

Château de Versailles ✦✦✦   Within 50 years, this residence was transformed from Louis XIII's simple hunting lodge into an extravagant palace. Begun in 1661, the construction of the château involved 32,000 to 45,000 workmen, some of whom had to drain marshes—often at the cost of their lives—and move forests. Louis XIV set out to build a palace that would be the envy of all Europe, and he created a symbol of pomp and opulence that was to be copied, yet never quite duplicated, all over Europe and even in America.

So he could keep an eye on the nobles of France (and with good reason), Louis XIV summoned them to live at his court. He amused them with constant entertainment and banquets and balls, and amused himself with a roster of mistresses, the most important of whom was Mme de Maintenon (he secretly married her after his queen, Marie-Thérèse of Spain, died). To some he awarded such vital tasks as holding the hem of his ermine-lined robe. While the aristocrats played away their lives, often in silly intrigues and games, the peasants on the estates, angered by their absentee landlords, sowed the seeds of the Revolution.

When Louis XIV died in 1715, he was succeeded by his great-grandson, Louis XV, who continued the outrageous pomp, though he's said to have predicted the outcome: *"Après mois le déluge"* (After me, the deluge). His wife, Marie Leszczynska of Poland, was shocked by the court's blatant immorality. When her husband tired of her, she lived as a nun, and the king's attention turned to Mme de Pompadour, who was accused of running up a debt far beyond that of a full-scale war. Mme de Pompadour handpicked her successor, Mme du Barry, who was just about as foolhardy with the nation's treasury.

Louis XVI found his grandfather's and father's behavior scandalous—in fact, on gaining the throne in 1774 he ordered the "stairway of indiscretion" (secret stairs leading up to the king's bedchamber) be removed. This dull, weak king (who was virtuous and did have good intentions) and his Austrian-born queen, Marie Antoinette, were well liked at first, but the queen's excessive frivolity and wild spending soon led to her downfall. Louis and Marie Antoinette were at Versailles on October 6, 1789, when they were notified that mobs were marching on the palace. As predicted, *le déluge* had arrived.

Napoleon stayed at Versailles but never seemed fond of it. Louis-Philippe prevented the destruction of the palace by converting it into a museum dedicated to the glory of France. To do that, he had to surrender some of his own not-so-hard-earned currency. Many years later, John D. Rockefeller contributed heavily toward the restoration of Versailles and work continues to this day.

The six magnificent **Grands Appartements** ✦✦✦, each of them suites of rooms outfitted by various potentates and their entourages during the palace's heyday, are in the Louis XIV style, each named after the allegorical painting on their ceilings. The largest is the **Hercules Salon,** with a ceiling painted by François Lemoine depicting the Apotheosis of Hercules. In the **Mercury Salon** (with a ceiling by Jean-Baptiste Champaigne), the body of Louis XIV was put on display in 1715; his 72-year reign was one of the longest in history.

The most famous room at Versailles is the 71m-long (233 ft.) **Hall of Mirrors** ✦✦✦, built to link the north and south *appartements* (apartments). Begun in 1678 by Mansart in the Louis XIV style, it was decorated by Le Brun and his team with 17 large arched windows matched by corresponding beveled mirrors in simulated arcades, plus amazing chandeliers and gilded lamp bearers. The vaulted ceiling is covered with paintings in classic allegorical style depicting key episodes (some of them lavishly embellished) from the life and career of Louis XIV. On June 28, 1919, the treaty ending World War I was signed in this corridor. Ironically, the German Empire was also proclaimed here in 1871.

The royal *appartements* were for show, but Louis XV and Louis XVI retired to the **Petits Appartements** ✦✦ to escape the demands of court etiquette. Louis XV died in his bedchamber in 1774, a victim of smallpox. In the second-floor **King's Appartements,** he stashed away first Mme de Pompadour and then Mme du Barry. Attempts have been made to return the **Queen's Appartements** to their appearance in the days of Marie Antoinette, when she played her harpsichord for audiences of specially invited guests.

Her king, Louis XVI, had an impressive **Library,** designed by Gabriel. Its panels are delicately carved, and the room has been restored and refurnished. The **Clock Room** contains Passement's astronomical clock, encased in gilded bronze. Twenty years in the making, it was completed in 1753 and is supposed to keep time until the year 9999. At the age of 7, Mozart played for the court in this room.

Gabriel designed the **Opéra** ✸✸ for Louis XV in 1748, though it wasn't completed until 1770. In its heyday, it took 3,000 candles to light the place. Using harmonies of gold and white, Hardouin-Mansart built the **Royal Chapel** ✸✸✸ in 1699, dying before its completion. Louis XVI, when still the dauphin, married

Marie Antoinette here in 1770. Both the bride and the groom in this arranged marriage between rival empires (France and Austria) were teenagers.

You'll be confronted with three alternatives in how to experience the main palace at Versailles. An unguided visit, where you can tour the Grands Appartements at your own speed, costs 7.50€ ($8.65) per person (free for persons under 18). If this is your interest, address yourself to Porte (Entranceway) A.

If you prefer a group tour, with guided commentary in English and French, of the same terrain plus some additional areas of the château, including the Opera House and the Chapel, expect to pay the 7.50€ ($8.65) entrance noted above, plus a supplement of either 4€ or 8€ ($4.60 or $9.20), depending on whether you opt for a 60-minute or a 90-minute tour. If the guided group tour of either duration appeals to you, go to Porte D. The final option involves renting a portable cassette player with a recorded tour in English or French, which will allow you to tour the Grands Appartements plus the Opera and Chapel, for a fee of 11€ to 13€ ($13–$15). Visitors with ample amounts of time may prefer this method of touring the château. Depending on how quickly you move through the château's vast labyrinth, the prerecorded option will take between 1 and 4 hours. If the prerecorded option appeals to you, go to Porte C.

Your visit will include access to the **Musée de l'Histoire de France** (℗ 01-39-25-70-70), a suite of rooms containing mostly framed historical paintings and engravings. Accessible via Porte D in the château, it traces the history of the parliamentary process in France following the collapse of the monarchy in 1789, with exhibits on how laws are made and enforced.

Place d'Armes. ℗ 01-30-83-78-00. Fax 01-30-83-77-90. Admission to the château 7.50€ ($8.65) adults; 5€ ($5.75) adults after 3:30pm, children 17–18, and seniors over 60; free for children under 17. May 2–Sept 30 Tues–Sun 9am–6pm (to 5:30pm the rest of the year). Closed Dec 25 and Jan 1.

Gardens of Versailles ★★★   The Gardens of Versailles were laid out by the landscape artist Le Nôtre, who created a Garden of Eden using ornamental lakes and canals, geometrically designed flower beds, and avenues bordered with statuary. At the peak of their glory, 1,400 fountains spewed forth. *The Buffet* is exceptional, having been designed by Mansart. One fountain depicts Apollo in his chariot pulled by four horses, surrounded by tritons emerging from the water to light the world. On the 1.5km-long (1 mile) Grand Canal, Louis XV—imagining he was in Venice—used to take gondola rides with his favorite of the moment.

On Christmas Day 1999, the most violent windstorm in France's history thundered through Paris, causing extensive damage to parks and gardens in the Ile de France. At Versailles, the wind toppled 10,000 trees and blew out some windows at the magnificent château. The palace has now reopened, but the difficult task of replanting the thousands of trees will take some time, and it'll be years before they return to their lush grandeur. Nonetheless, there is still much that remains to enchant, and the gardens get better and better every month.

Place d'Armes (behind the Palace of Versailles). ℗ 01-30-83-78-88. Admission 3€ ($3.45) Mon–Fri, 6€ ($6.90) Sat–Sun, free for children 17 and under. May–Oct daily 7am–sundown; Nov–Apr daily 8am–sundown.

The Trianons & The Hamlet   A long walk across the park will take you to the **Grand Trianon (Grand Pavilion)** ★★, in pink-and-white marble. Le Vau built a Porcelain Trianon here in 1670, covered with blue and white china tiles, but it was fragile and soon fell into ruin. So, in 1687, Louis XIV commissioned Hardouin-Mansart to build the Grand Trianon. Traditionally, it has been a place where France has lodged important guests, though de Gaulle wanted to turn it

---

---

into a weekend retreat. Nixon once slept here in the room where Mme de Pompadour died. Mme de Maintenon also slept here, as did Napoleon. The original furnishings are gone, of course, with mostly Empire pieces there today.

Gabriel, the designer of place de la Concorde in Paris, built the **Petit Trianon** ★★ in 1768 for Louis XV. Louis used it for his trysts with Mme du Barry. When he died, Louis XVI presented it to his wife, and Marie Antoinette adopted it as her favorite residence, a place to escape the rigid life and oppressive scrutiny at the main palace. Many of the current furnishings, including a few in her rather modest bedchamber, belonged to the ill-fated queen.

Rousseau's theories about recapturing the natural beauty and noble simplicity of life were much in favor in the late 18th century, and they prompted Marie Antoinette to have Mique build her the 12-house **Le Hameau (Hamlet)** on the banks of the Grand Trianon Lake in 1783. She wanted a chance to experience the simplicity of peasant life—or at least peasant life as seen through the eyes of a frivolous queen. Dressed as a shepherdess, she would come here to watch sheep being tended and cows being milked, men fishing, washerwomen beating their laundry in the lake, and donkey carts bringing corn to be ground at the mill. The interiors of the hamlets cannot be visited, but the surrounding informal landscaping—in obvious contrast to the formality of the other gardens at Versailles—and bizarre origins make views of their exteriors one of the most popular attractions here.

Follow the signs from the place d'Armes (to the immediate right after entering the Palace of Versailles). ☎ 01-30-83-78-00. Entrance to both Trianons 5€ ($5.75) for adults, free for children under 17; after 3:30pm, entrance to both Trianons reduced to 3€ ($3.45) for adults. May–Sept daily noon–6pm; Oct–Apr daily noon–5pm.

Grande Écurie ★ *(Finds)*   The latest attraction at Versailles is the newly reopened stables of Louis XIV. For 2 centuries, these historic stables were closed to the public. Constructed by the famed architect Jules Hardouin-Mansart, these stables once housed more than 600 horses of the king. The line of horses owned by the king are long gone, of course, and today the stables are home to 20 cream-colored Lusitanian horses from Portugal. Visitors to the stables are taken on a brief guided tour and can then witness morning dressage demonstrations. Ten advanced equestrian students direct the horses, and costumed riders demonstrate equestrian choreography performed to music.

The Gardens of Versailles. ☎ 01-39-02-07-14. Admission 7.50€ ($8.65) adults, 3€ ($3.45) 17 and under. Tues–Fri 9am–1pm; Sat–Sun 11am–3pm.

SEASONAL EVENTS

SUMMER EVENING SPECTACLES   The **Fêtes de Nuit de Versailles (Rêve de Roi)** is a government-sponsored summer program of evening fireworks and illuminated fountains. These always capture the heightened sense of the glory of France's *ancien régime*. At randomly scattered Saturday evenings in August and September, 200 actors in period costume portray Louis XVI and members of his court against a backdrop of exploding fireworks. You sit on bleachers clustered at the château's boulevard de la Reine entrance, adjacent to the Fountain of Neptune. Depending on the location of your seat, tickets cost between 13€ and 43€ ($15–$49) each. Gates that admit you into the bleacher area open 90 minutes before show time, and the show itself lasts 90 minutes.

You can buy tickets in advance at the **tourist office** in Versailles (see above)—inquire by phone, fax, or mail—or in Paris at any of the **FNAC** stores (p. 261). You can also take your chances and buy tickets an hour prior to the event from a kiosk adjacent to the boulevard de la Reine entrance. Call ℭ **01-30-83-78-88** for general information about any of the nighttime or afternoon spectacles on the grounds.

AFTERNOON PROMENADES IN THE PARK (Moments)   Every Sunday between early April and mid-October, and every Saturday between July and September between 11am and noon and between 3:30 and 5:30pm, classical music is broadcast through the park and the fountains are turned on. (Virtually every fountain in the park is turned on in stages. The most charming displays occur between 3:30 and 5:30pm.) These **Grandes Eaux Musicales** duplicate the aesthetic vision of the 18th-century architects who designed Versailles. During these sessions, hundreds of visitors walk freely around the park, enjoying the grand architecture, lavish waterworks, and recorded music of the same period as the palace's construction. The cost of admission to the park during these events is 6€ ($6.90) for adults, free for children under 18. Call ℭ **01-30-83-78-88** for more information.

WHERE TO DINE

Le Potager du Roy (★) FRENCH   Philippe Letourneur cooks from the heart, specializing in a simple cuisine with robust flavors. His restaurant occupies an 18th-century building in a neighborhood known as the Parc des Cerfs ("Stag Park," where courtiers could find paid companionship with B- and C-list courtesans). The skillfully prepared menu is reinvented with the seasons and may include foie gras with vegetable-flavored vinaigrette, roasted duck with a navarin of vegetables, macaroni ragout with a *persillade* (a mixture of chopped parsley and garlic) of snails, and roasted codfish with roasted peppers in the style of Provence. For something unusual, order the fondant of pork jowls with a confit of fresh vegetables. Try to save room for the chocolate cake, flavored with orange and served with coconut ice cream.

1 rue du Maréchal-Joffre. ℭ **01-39-50-35-34.** Reservations required. Prix fixe menu 32€–47€ ($37–$54). AE, V. Tues–Fri noon–2:30pm; Tues–Sat 7:30–10:30pm.

Le Quai No. 1 (Value) FRENCH/SEAFOOD   This informal bistro occupies an 18th-century building overlooking the château's western facade. Lithographs and wood paneling spangle the dining room, and outside is a terrace. Though the cuisine isn't as opulent or expensive as what's served in chef Gérard Vié's grander Les Trois Marches (below), it's charming and dependable in presentation. The prix fixe menus make Le Quai a bargain. Specialties are stuffed baby mullet with sweet-basil sauce, filet of seawolf grilled with caramelized onions, and sautéed scallops with a vinegar crafted from aged banyuls dessert wine. Care and imagination go into the food, and the service is professional and polite.

1 av. de St-Cloud. ℂ 01-39-50-42-26. Reservations required. Main courses 15€–16€ ($17–$18); prix fixe lunch 16€ ($18), dinner 21€–32€ ($24–$37). MC, V. Tues–Sat noon–2:30pm and 7:30–11:30pm.

Les Trois Marches ★★★ FRENCH   This is one of the best restaurants in the Ile de France. The Hôtel Trianon Palace became famous in 1919 when it served as headquarters for signatories to the Treaty of Versailles, and the dining room retains an old-world splendor. Gérard Vié is the most talented and creative chef in town, attracting a discerning crowd that doesn't mind paying the high prices. His *la cuisine de la gastronomie française* is subtle, often daring, and the service is smooth: a warm *parmentier* (potato preparation) of crayfish and oysters, both ingredients *en tartare* and both of them "salted" with caviar; a tartare of lobster that's minced, then poached, then fried, and served with aromatic herbs; scallops cooked on their shell with a covering of braised endives and exotic mushrooms; and rack of suckling veal pierced with truffles and served with a reduction of artichokes and salsify. In autumn, you might find pennelike pasta, tossed with morels, mushrooms, and Parmesan and blended in a butter sauce with white Alba truffles. Dessert might include a deliberately undercooked coffee-flavored chocolate cake served with a chicory-flavored ice cream.

In the Hôtel Trianon Palace, 1 bd. de la Reine. ℂ 01-39-50-13-21. Reservations required far in advance. Prix fixe menu 58€–160€ ($67–$184). AE, DC, MC, V. Tues–Sat 12:30–2pm and 7:30–10pm. Closed Aug.

2 The Forest & Château of Rambouillet ★

55km (34 miles) SW of Paris, 42km (26 miles) NE of Chartres

Once known as La Forêt d'Yveline, the **Forest of Rambouillet** ★ is one of the loveliest forests in France. More than 19,000 hectares (46,930 acres) of greenery stretch from the valley of the Eure to the high valley of Chevreuse, the latter rich in medieval and royal abbeys. Lakes, copses of deer, and even wild boar are some of the attractions of this "green lung." Most people, however, come here to see the château, which you can visit when it's not in use as a "Camp David" for French presidents.

ESSENTIALS

GETTING THERE   **Trains** depart from Paris's Gare Montparnasse every 20 minutes throughout the day. One-way passage costs 7€ ($8.05) for about a 35-minute ride. Information and train schedules can be obtained by contacting **La Gare de Rambouillet,** place Prud'homme (ℂ 08-91-36-20-20). By **car,** take N-10 southwest from Paris, passing Versailles along the way.

VISITOR INFORMATION   The **tourist office** is at the Hôtel de Ville, place de la Libération (ℂ 01-34-83-21-21).

SEEING THE CHATEAU

Château de Rambouillet ★   Dating from 1375, the château is surrounded by a park in one of the most famous forests in France. Superb woodwork is used throughout, and the walls are adorned with tapestries, many from the era of Louis XV. Before it became a royal residence, the marquise de Rambouillet kept a house here; it's said she taught Paris's cultured ladies and gentlemen how to talk, introducing them to poets and painters. François I, the Chevalier king, died of a fever here in 1547 at age 52. When the château was later occupied by the comte de Toulouse, Rambouillet was often visited by Louis XV, who was amused (in more ways than one) by the comte's high-spirited wife. Louis XVI eventually acquired the château, but Marie Antoinette found it boring and called it "the toad." In his surprisingly modest boudoir are four panels representing the continents.

In 1814, Napoleon's second wife, Marie-Louise (daughter of Francis II, emperor of Austria), met at Rambouillet with her father, who convinced her to abandon Napoleon and France after her husband's defeats at Moscow and Leipzig. Afterward, she fled to her original home, the royal court in Vienna, with Napoleon's 3-year-old son, François-Charles-Joseph Bonaparte (also known as l'Aiglon—the Young Eagle—and, at least in title, the King of Rome). Before his death in Vienna at age 21, his claim on the Napoleonic legacy was rejected by France's enemies, despite the fact that his father had had a special annex to the château at Rambouillet built especially for his use. Before his final exile to the remote island of St. Helena, Napoleon insisted on spending a final night at Rambouillet, where he secluded himself with his meditations and memories.

In 1830, the elderly Charles X, Louis XVI's brother, abdicated the throne at Rambouillet as a mob marched on the château and his troops began to desert him. From Rambouillet, he embarked for a safe but controversial haven in England. Afterward, Rambouillet fell into private hands. At one time it was a fashionable restaurant attracting Parisians by offering gondola rides. Napoleon III returned it to the Crown. In 1897, it was designated a residence for the presidents of the Republic. In 1944, Charles de Gaulle lived here briefly before giving the order for what was left of the French army to join the Americans in liberating Paris.

It takes about 2 hours to see the château at Rambouillet.

Parc du Château. © **01-34-83-00-25.** Admission 6.10€ ($7) adults, 4.10€ ($4.70) students 18–25, 2.30€ ($2.65) ages 12–17, free for children under 12. Apr–Sept Wed–Mon 10–11:45am and 2–5pm; Oct–Mar Wed–Mon 10–11:45am and 2–4pm.

WHERE TO DINE

La Poste TRADITIONAL FRENCH   On a street corner in the town's historic center, this restaurant dates from the mid–19th century, when it provided meals and shelter for the region's mail carriers. The two dining rooms have rustic beams and old-fashioned accents that complement the flavorful old-fashioned food.

Moments **Through an Enchanted Forest**

Rambouillet and its forests can provide a verdant interlude. If you've exhausted the idea of a ramble through the gardens that surround the château (or if they're closed because of a visit from the president of France), consider a visit to the **Rochers d'Angennes,** rocky hillocks that remain as leftovers from the Ice Age. To reach them, park your car on the D107, where you'll see a sign pointing to the **Rochers et Etang d'Angennes,** about 4km (2½ miles) north of the hamlet of Epernon. Walk along a clearly marked trail, through a pine forest, before you eventually reach a rocky plateau overlooking the hills and a pond (*l'Etang d'Angennes*) nestled into the surrounding countryside. Roundtrip, from the site of your parked car to the plateau and back, your promenade should take between 30 and 45 minutes.

Good-tasting menu items include a fricassee of chicken and crayfish; noisettes of lamb "prepared in the style of a roebuck," with a *Grand Veneur* sauce (that's made with red wine, autumn berries, a touch of vinegar "to make it acidic," and crème fraîche). Also popular are civets of both *une bîche* (female venison) and rabbit.

101 rue de Général-de-Gaulle. (℃ **01-34-83-03-01.** Reservations recommended Sat–Sun. Main courses 15€–20€ ($17–$23); prix fixe menu 21€–31€ ($24–$36). AE, MC, V. Tues–Thurs and Sat noon–2pm; Tues–Sat 7–10pm.

3 The Cathedral at Chartres ★★★

97km (60 miles) SW of Paris, 76km (47 miles) NW of Orléans

Many observers feel the architectural aspirations of the Middle Ages reached their highest expression in the glorious Cathédrale de Chartres. Come to see its soaring architecture, highly wrought sculpture, and, above all, its stained glass, which gave the world a new color: Chartres blue. It takes a full day to see Chartres.

ESSENTIALS

GETTING THERE   From Paris's Gare Montparnasse, **trains** run directly to Chartres, taking less than an hour and passing through a sea of wheat fields. Tickets cost 24€ ($28) round trip. Call **La Gare de Rambouillet** at (℃ **08-91-36-20-20.** By **car,** take A10/A11 southwest from the *périphérique* and follow the signs to Le Mans and Chartres.

VISITOR INFORMATION   The **tourist office** is on place de la Cathédrale ((℃ **02-37-18-26-26**).

SEEING THE CATHEDRAL

Cathédrale Notre-Dame de Chartres ★★★   Reportedly, Rodin once sat for hours on the sidewalk, admiring this cathedral's Romanesque sculpture. His opinion: Chartres is the French Acropolis. When it began to rain, a kind soul offered him an umbrella, which he declined, so transfixed was he by this place.

The cathedral's origins are uncertain; some have suggested it grew up over an ancient Druid site that later became a Roman temple. As early as the 4th century, there was a Christian basilica here. An 1194 fire destroyed most of what had by then become a Romanesque cathedral but spared the western facade and crypt. The cathedral you see today dates principally from the 13th century, when it was rebuilt with the efforts and contributions of kings, princes, churchmen, and pilgrims from all over Europe. One of the world's greatest high Gothic cathedrals, it was the first to use flying buttresses to support the soaring dimensions within.

French sculpture in the 12th century broke into full bloom when the **Royal Portal** ★★★ was added. A landmark in Romanesque art, the sculptured bodies are elongated, often stylized, in their long flowing robes. But the faces are amazingly (for the time) lifelike, occasionally winking or smiling. In the central tympanum, Christ is shown at the Second Coming, with his descent depicted on the right, his ascent on the left. Before entering, walk around to both the **North Portal** and the **South Portal,** each from the 13th century. They depict such biblical scenes as the expulsion of Adam and Eve from the Garden of Eden.

Inside is a celebrated **choir screen;** work on it began in the 16th century and lasted until 1714. The niches, 40 in all, contain statues illustrating scenes from the life of the Madonna and Christ—everything from the *Massacre of the Innocents* to the *Coronation of the Virgin.*

Moments **Music of the Spheres**

If you're visiting Chartres on a Sunday afternoon, the cathedral features a free 1-hour organ concert at 4:45pm, when the filtered light of the Ile de France sunset makes the western windows come thrillingly alive.

But few rushed visitors ever notice the screen: They're too transfixed by the light from the **stained glass** ★★★. Covering an expanse of more than 3,000 square yards, the glass is unlike anything else in the world. The stained glass, most of which dates from the 12th and 13th centuries, was spared in both world wars by painstakingly removing it piece by piece. See the windows in the morning, at noon, in the afternoon, at sunset—as often as you can. Like the petals of a kaleidoscope, they constantly change. It's difficult to single out one panel or window above the others, but an exceptional one is the 12th-century *Vierge de la belle verrière* (**Our Lady of the Beautiful Window**) on the south side. Of course, there are three fiery rose windows, but you couldn't miss those if you tried.

The **nave,** the widest in France, still contains its ancient floor labyrinth, which formed a mobile channel of contemplation for monks. The wooden *Notre-Dame du piller* (**Virgin of the Pillar**), to the left of the choir, dates from the 14th century. The crypt was built over 2 centuries, beginning in the 9th. Enshrined within is *Our Lady of the Crypt,* a 1976 Madonna that replaced one destroyed during the Revolution.

Try to take a tour conducted by **Malcolm Miller** (© 02-37-28-15-58; fax 02-37-28-33-03), an Englishman who has spent 3 decades studying the cathedral; his tours in English offer a rare blend of scholarship, enthusiasm, and humor. He usually conducts 75-minute tours at noon and 2:45pm Monday to Saturday for 10€ ($12). Tours are canceled in the event of pilgrimages, religious celebrations, and large funerals. French-language tours at 6€ ($6.90) are conducted by other guides from Easter to late October at 10:30am and 3pm and the rest of the year at 2:30pm.

If you feel fit enough, don't miss the opportunity, especially in summer, to climb to the top of the **New Bell Tower.** Open the same hours as the cathedral, except for a closing between noon and 2pm, it costs 4€ ($4.60) for adults and 3€ ($3.45) for students. The **crypt,** gloomy and somber but rich with a sense of medieval history, can be visited only as part of a French-speaking tour conducted whenever there's enough demand. The cost is 1.65€ ($1.90).

After your visit, stroll through the **Episcopal Gardens** and enjoy yet another view of this remarkable cathedral.

16 Cloître Notre-Dame. © 02-37-21-59-08. Free admission. Daily 8:30am–7:30pm.

EXPLORING THE OLD TOWN

If time remains, you may want to explore the medieval cobbled streets of the **Vieux Quartier** ★ (Old Town). At the foot of the cathedral are lanes containing gabled houses and humped bridges spanning the Eure River. From the pont de Bouju, you can see the lofty spires in the background. Try to find **rue Chantault,** which boasts houses with colorful facades, one 8 centuries old.

A highlight of your visit will be **Musée des Beaux-Arts de Chartres** ★, 29 Cloître Notre-Dame (© 02-37-36-41-39), next to the cathedral. A former Episcopal palace, the building at times competes with its exhibitions—one part dates from the 15th century and encompasses a courtyard. This museum of fine arts boasts a collection covering the 16th to the 20th centuries, including the work of masters like Zurbarán, Watteau, and Brósamer. Of particular interest is David Ténier's *Le Concert*. From October 1 to May 2, it's open Wednesday to Monday from 10am to noon and 2 to 5pm (closed Sun mornings); from May 3 to September 30 hours are 10:30am to 6pm. Admission is 2.50€ ($2.90) for adults and free for children under 12.

WHERE TO STAY

Hotel Châtelet   This modern hotel has many traditional touches. The rustic guest rooms are inviting, with reproductions of Louis XV and Louis XVI furniture. The larger, more expensive rooms face a garden and avoid street noise. Many windows along the back garden side of the hotel open onto a view of the cathedral. The bathrooms come with shower and tub and don't have a lot of shelf space. In chilly weather, there's a log-burning fire in one of the salons. Breakfast is the only meal served, but there are numerous restaurants close by.

6–8 av. Jehan-de-Beauce, 28000 Chartres. ℂ **02-37-21-78-00.** Fax 02-37-36-23-01. www.hotelchatelet. com. 48 units. 61€–83€ ($70–$95) double, 3rd person 9.15€ ($11) extra. AE, DC, MC, V. Parking 6€ ($6.90). **Amenities:** Bar; limited room service; rooms for those with limited mobility. *In room:* TV, minibar, hair dryer.

Le Grand Monarque Best Western Chartres's leading hotel, a Best Western, occupies a mid-19th-century building around a courtyard. It attracts people who enjoy its old-world charm, with its Art Nouveau stained glass and Louis XV chairs in the dining room. The guest rooms are decorated with reproductions of antiques, and most have sitting areas. The baths are motel standard. The hotel also has an anachronistic restaurant (a local critic found the kitchen trapped in an "*ancien régime* time warp").

22 place des Epars, 28005 Chartres. ℂ **800/528-1234** in the U.S., or 02-37-21-00-72. Fax 02-37-36-34-18. www.bw-grand-monarque.com. 55 units. 105€–155€ ($121–$178) double; 210€ ($242) suite. AE, DC, MC, V. Parking 8€ ($9.20). **Amenities:** 2 restaurants; brasserie; bar; 24-hr. room service; laundry service/dry cleaning; nonsmoking rooms. *In room:* A/C (in suites), TV, dataport, minibar, hair dryer, safe (in suites).

WHERE TO DINE

La Vieille Maison ★★ MODERN FRENCH Even if the food here wasn't superb, the 14th-century building that contains it could be visited for its historic value. The dining room, outfitted in the Louis XIII style and tones of deep reds and soft green, is centered around a narrow ceiling vault, less than 2m (6½ ft.) across, crafted of chiseled white stone blocks during the 800s. Cuisine is supervised by Bruno Letartre, who is the only *maître cuisinier de France* (awarded by the Association of Maître Cuisinier of France) in Chartres. The menu changes between four and five times a year, reflecting the seasonality of the Ile de France and its produce. Recent examples that have impressed local critics include foie gras of duckling; roasted crayfish with Indian spices; profiteroles stuffed with a mixture of snails and frogs' legs served with a parsley-flavored cream sauce; crisp-roasted sea bass with a confit of tomatoes and rice; supreme of turbot with saffron, baby vegetables, and saffron; and noisettes of venison fried with both Jamaican and Szechuan pepper and wild mushrooms. Dessert raves go to an apple-and-fig tart served with walnut-flavored ice cream.

5 rue au Lait. ℂ **02-37-34-10-67.** Reservations recommended. Main courses 45€–65€ ($52–$75); prix fixe menus 29€ and 46€ ($33 and $53). AE, MC, V. Tues–Sun noon–2:15pm; Tues–Sat 7–9:15pm. Closed 1 week in Aug.

Le Buisson Ardent ★ *Value* TRADITIONAL FRENCH Housed in a charming 16th-century house in the most historic section of town, this restaurant is one floor above street level in the shadow of the cathedral. The prix fixe menus change with the seasons. The least expensive is one of the town's best luncheon values, and an excellent break on your day trip. Everything is made with fresh meats, produce, and fish. The most popular dishes are escalope of foie gras with apples and Calvados, and *émincé* (thin slices) of roasted pigeon with sweetbreads and honey sauce. Other dishes are simpler, like codfish flavored with coriander and served with parsley flan. A dessert specialty is crispy hot pineapples with orange and passion fruit salad.

10 rue au Lait. ℂ **02-37-34-04-66.** Reservations recommended. Main courses 13€–22€ ($15–$25); prix fixe meals 18€ and 23€ ($21 and $26). MC, V. Thurs–Tues noon–2pm and 7–9:30pm.

4 Giverny ★

80km (50 miles) NW of Paris

On the border between Normandy and the Ile de France, Giverny—now the home of the Claude Monet Foundation—is where the great painter lived for 43 years. The restored house and its gardens are open to the public. Budget 2 hours to spend at Giverny.

ESSENTIALS

GETTING THERE   It takes a full morning to get to Giverny and to see its sights. Take the Paris-Rouen **train** from Paris's Gare St-Lazare to the Vernon station, where a taxi can take you the 3 miles to Giverny. Perhaps the easiest way to enjoy Giverny is on a full-day **bus tour,** costing 60€ ($69) per person, whose focal point is Monet's house and garden. These summer tours depart at 1:45pm Tuesday to Saturday. In summer you can arrange this through **Cityrama,** 4 place des Pyramides, 1e (© **01-44-55-61-00;** Métro: Palais Royal), or year-round by contacting **American Express,** 11 rue Scribe, 9e (© **01-47-14-50-00;** Métro: Opéra).

If you're **driving,** take the Autoroute de l'Ouest (Port de St-Cloud) toward Rouen. Leave the autoroute at Bonnières, then cross the Seine on the Bonnières Bridge. From here, a direct road with signs will bring you to Giverny. Expect it to take about an hour; try to avoid weekends. Another way is to leave the highway at the Bonnières exit and go toward Vernon. Once here, cross the bridge over the Seine and follow the signs to Giverny or Gasny (Giverny is before Gasny). This is easier than going through Bonnières, where there aren't many signs.

SHOW ME THE MONET

Claude Monet Foundation ★★★   Born in 1840, the French Impressionist was a brilliant innovator, excelling in presenting the effects of light at different times of the day. Some critics claim that he "invented light." His paintings of the Rouen cathedral and of waterlilies, which one critic called "vertical interpretations of horizontal lines," are just a few of his masterpieces.

Monet first came to Giverny in 1883. Many of his friends used to visit him here at Le Pressoir, including Clemenceau, Cézanne, Rodin, Renoir, Degas, and Sisley. When Monet died in 1926, his son, Michel, inherited the house, but left it abandoned until it decayed. The gardens became almost a jungle, inhabited by river rats. In 1966, Michel died and left it to the Académie des Beaux-Arts. It wasn't until 1977 that Gerald van der Kemp, who restored Versailles, decided to work on Giverny. A large part of it was restored with gifts from U.S. benefactors, especially the late Lila Acheson Wallace, former head of *Reader's Digest.*

You can stroll the garden and view the thousands of flowers, including the *nymphéas.* The Japanese bridge, hung with wisteria, leads to a setting of weeping willows and rhododendrons. Monet's studio barge was installed on the pond.

Rue Claude-Monet Parc Gasny. © **02-32-51-28-21.** Admission 5.50€ ($6.35) adults, 4€ ($4.60) children 7–18, free for children under 7. Apr–Oct Tues–Sun 9:30am–6pm.

Musée d'Art Americain Giverny ★ *Finds*   Lying about 90m (295 ft.) from Monet's former house and gardens, this museum showcases the U.S.-born artists, mainly Impressionists, who were influenced by Monet and lived at Giverny. Among the more famous painters were John Singer Sargent and William Metcalf, who often summered at Giverny, writing about its glories to other artists. The American painters came from 1887 onward, drawn more by the charm of the village than by the presence of Monet himself. It is estimated that some 100 artists came to live in Giverny, although they did not have much contact, if any, with Monet. He considered these American painters "a nuisance."

99 rue Claude Monet. © **02-32-51-94-65.** Admission 5.50€ ($6.35) adults, 4€ ($4.60) seniors and students, 3€ ($3.45) children 12–18, free for children under 12. Free admission 1st Sun of each month. Apr–Nov daily 10am–6pm.

WHERE TO STAY

La Musardiere   Giverny has become so popular with visitors that many local homes are opening as B&Bs to accommodate the overnight flow. We find this small inn to be the best of the lot. Just a short walk from Monet's museum and gardens, it is a former manor house opening onto a scenic park filled with ancient trees. The building with its Mansard roof dates from 1880 and was around in Monet's time. Many of the antique features and architectural adornments are still in place. Bedrooms are medium in size, each attractively and comfortably furnished, each with a small bathroom with tub or shower. The hotel also operates its own restaurant and crêperie.

Rue Claude-Monet 27620 Giverny. ℂ **02-32-21-03-18.** Fax 02-32-21-60-00. 11 units. 54€–72€ ($62–$83) double, 84€ ($97) suite. AE, DC, MC, V. Free parking. **Amenities:** Restaurant, bar. *In room:* TV, dataport, hair dryer.

WHERE TO DINE

Auberge du Vieux Moulin TRADITIONAL FRENCH   The Boudeau family maintains a series of dining rooms filled with original Impressionist paintings in a stone building with a pair of flowering terraces. Since you can walk here from the museum in about 5 minutes, leave your car in the museum lot. Specialties range from escalope of salmon with sorrel sauce to aiguillettes of duckling with peaches. The food is good country fare, and the staff is charming.

21 rue de la Falaise. ℂ **02-32-51-46-15.** Main courses 15€–18€ ($17–$21); prix fixe menu 23€–29€ ($26–$33). MC, V. Tues–Sun noon–3pm and 7:30–10pm. Closed Nov Sat–Sun only (same hours Tues–Fri).

Baudy FRENCH *(Finds)*   We hesitate to recommend this place because of the never-ending buses arriving from Paris, but it's a local legend and deserves a look. Formerly it was the pink villa used by the American painters as their lodging in the 19th century heyday of this town. It was called an *epicerie-buvette* (a small hangout with a few tables) and was run by Monet's friends, Angelina and Gaston Baudy. Metcalf was the first artist to arrive on Madame Baudy's doorstep, and he was followed by a string of other painters. In time artists such as Cézanne could be found wandering around the rose garden here. The place no longer has its "legendary two tables," at which Madame Baudy fed the artists, but it now hosts most visitors to Giverny, feeding them a simply prepared, traditional French cuisine. Big, freshly made salads, and a changing array of hot food is served daily.

81 rue Claude Monet. ℂ **02-32-21-10-03.** Reservations recommended. Main courses 10€–14€ ($12–$16). MC, V. Tues–Sat 10am–9pm; Sun 10am–3pm. Closed Nov–Mar.

Les Jardins de Giverny ★★ FRENCH/NORMAN   This is the best restaurant in town and a favorite of Monet's most devoted fans, many of whom make frequent visits here. The restaurant lies just a short stroll away from Monet's gardens. In summer you can dine with your table opening onto a rose garden. The decor is smart and sophisticated, and the menu is carefully planned, based on market-fresh ingredients.

On our most recent visit, our party ordered some delightful dishes: veal kidneys in a *beurre blanc* (a foamy lemon-butter sauce), duckling with both fresh and dried fruit, and some top-quality scallops in a tarragon and white wine sauce. Many of the dishes are spiked with the "beverages of the land"—that is, the foie gras which comes flavored with Calvados. In autumn, duck in Norman cider is a perennial favorite.

Rue du Roy. ℂ **02-32-21-60-80.** Reservations essential. Main courses 17€–24€ ($20–$28); prix fixe menu 26€–37€ ($30–$43). AE, MC, V. Tues–Sun noon–3pm and 7:30–10pm. Closed Nov–Mar.

Restaurant Les Fleurs ✦ FRENCH   Capably managed by Michel and Annie Graux, this pleasant and sought-after restaurant does a large percentage of its business with art lovers either before or after their visit to the Monet Museum in nearby Giverny, just across the river. Set on the main street of Vernon, 5km (3 miles) southwest of the museum, it is outfitted in tones of "caviar gray" and white. Chef Michel completed an apprenticeship with culinary megastar Alain Ducasse; his restaurant focuses on flavorful, tried-and-true *cuisine bourgeoise* (comfort food) that many diners remember fondly from their childhoods. Menu items include fresh fish such as sea bass, served with a saffron sauce that might be accompanied by a flavorful risotto of the day. Other dishes include an array of homemade terrines and pâtés; fresh scallops with a lobster-flavored cream sauce; a platter that's entirely devoted to different preparations of duckling, and a variety of meats grilled simply and flavorfully, *à la plancha* (on an iron skillet).

71 rue Sadie-Carnot, Vernon. ✆ **02-32-51-16-80.** Reservations recommended. Main courses 19€–23€ ($22–$26); prix fixe menus 21€–40€ ($24–$46). AE, MC, V. Tues–Sun noon–2:30pm; Tues–Sat 7:30–9:30pm. Closed Aug. From the Monet Museum in Giverny, drive 5km (3 miles) SW, crossing the Seine, and following the signs to Vernon.

5 Disneyland Paris

32km (20 miles) E of Paris

After provoking some of the most controversial reactions in recent French history, the multimillion-dollar Euro Disney Resort opened in 1992 as one of the world's most lavish theme parks, situated on a site about one-fifth the size of Paris in the suburb of Marne-la-Vallée. In 1994, it unofficially changed its name to Disneyland Paris. In its early days, European journalists delighted in belittling it and accusing it of everything from cultural imperialism to the death knell of French culture. But after a rough start, the resort is on track.

In fact, it's now the number-one attraction in France, with 50 million annual visitors. "MONSIEUR MICKEY TRIUMPHS!" the French press headlined. Disney surpasses the Eiffel Tower and the Louvre in numbers of visitors and accounts for 4% of the tourism industry's foreign currency sales. Disneyland Paris looks, tastes, and feels like its parents in California and Florida, except for certain touches of European flair—the use of pastel colors rather than primary colors, and the $10 cheeseburgers *avec pommes frites* (with french fries). Allow a full day to see the park.

ESSENTIALS

GETTING THERE   The resort is linked to the **RER** commuter express rail network (Line A), which maintains a stop within walking distance of the park. Board the RER at such Paris stops as Charles de Gaulle-Etoile, Châtelet-Les Halles, or Nation. Get off at Line A's last stop, Marne-la-Vallée/Chessy, 45 minutes from

Sizing Up Monsieur Mickey

In terms of how Disneyland Paris compares to Disney's parks in the United States, it's in the middle of the pack, with top honors going to Florida's Walt Disney World and California's Disneyland running a distant third. The layout of Disneyland Paris resembles the Orlando Magic Kingdom, but the French property is smaller and has fewer attractions and rides. Disneyland Paris expanded in 2002 with the addition of Walt Disney Studios (see below).

central Paris. The round-trip fare from central Paris is 12€ ($14). Trains run every 10 to 20 minutes, depending on the time of day.

Each of the hotels in the resort connects by **shuttle bus** to both Orly and Charles de Gaulle. Buses depart from both airports at intervals of 45 minutes. One-way transportation to the park from either airport costs 14€ ($16) for adults and 12€ ($14) children 3 to 11 years old.

If you're coming by **car,** take A-4 east from Paris, getting off at exit 14, marked DISNEYLAND PARIS. Guest parking at any of the thousands of parking spaces is 8€ ($9.20) per day. An interconnected series of moving sidewalks speeds up pedestrian transit from the parking areas to the theme park's entrance. Parking for guests at any of the resort's hotels is free.

SPENDING THE DAY AT DISNEY

Disneyland Paris ★★★   The resort was designed as a total vacation destination: Included within one enormous unit are the Disneyland Park with its five entertainment "lands," six hotels, a campground, an entertainment center (Village Disney), a 27-hole golf course, and dozens of restaurants, shows, and shops. Peak season is mid-June to mid-September, as well as Christmas and Easter weeks. Entrance to Village Disney is free, though there's usually a cover charge for the dance clubs.

In the park, **Main Street, U.S.A.** features horse-drawn carriages and street-corner barbershop quartets. From the Main Street Station, steam-powered trains leave for a trip through a Grand Canyon Diorama to **Frontierland,** with paddle-wheel steamers reminiscent of the Mississippi Valley described by Mark Twain. The park's steam trains chug past **Adventureland**—with swashbuckling 18th-century pirates, the tree house of the Swiss Family Robinson, and a roller coaster called Indiana Jones and the Temple of Peril . . . Backwards! that travels in reverse—to **Fantasyland.** Here you can see the symbol of the park, *Le Château de la belle au bois dormant* (the Sleeping Beauty Castle), whose soaring pinnacles and turrets are a spectacular idealized interpretation of the châteaux of France.

Visions of the future are displayed at **Discoveryland,** whose tributes to human invention and imagination are drawn from the works of Leonardo da Vinci, Jules Verne, H. G. Wells, the modern masters of science fiction, and the *Star Wars* series. Discoveryland has proven among the most popular of all the areas and is one of the few that was enlarged (in 1995) after the park's inauguration. A noteworthy addition was a roller coaster called **Space Mountain,** which emulates an earth-to-moon transit as conceived by Jules Verne. Another popular attraction here is an in-theater experience, **Honey, I Shrunk the Kids,** where 3-D and animation gives the illusion that the audience has been shrunk.

As Disney continues to churn out animated blockbusters, look for its newest stars to appear in the park. The fact that the characters from such films as *Aladdin, The Lion King,* and *Pocahontas* are actually made of celluloid hasn't kept them out of the Ice Capades, and it certainly won't keep them out of Disneyland Paris.

Disney also maintains an entertainment center, **Village Disney,** whose indoor/outdoor layout is a cross between a California mall and the Coney Island boardwalk. Scattered on either side of a pedestrian walkway, illuminated by overhead spotlights, it's just outside the boundaries of the fenced-in acreage containing the bulk of Disneyland's attractions. The complex accommodates dance clubs, snack bars, restaurants, souvenir shops, and bars for adults who want to escape from the children for a while. Unlike the rest of the park, admission to **Village Disney** is free, so it attracts night owls from Paris and its suburbs who wouldn't otherwise be particularly interested in the park itself.

Disneyland Paris recognizes that long lines tend to frustrate families. In 2000 the park inaugurated the **Fast Pass** system, where participants go to various popular rides and receive a reservation for a 1-hour time block within which they should return. Within that 1-hour period, waiting times are usually no more than 8 minutes. This system is presently used for five of the most popular rides: Space Mountain (Discoveryland), Indiana Jones and the Temple of Peril . . . Backwards! (Adventureland), Big Thunder Mountain (Frontierland), Star Tours (Discoveryland), and Peter Pan's Flight (Fantasyland).

The park places height restrictions on only three rides. Riders of Big Thunder Mountain roller coaster must be at least 1m (3 ft., 3 in.) tall; and riders of both Space Mountain and Indiana Jones and the Temple of Peril . . . Backwards! must be at least 1m, 40 centimeters (4 ft., 7 in.) tall.

Other than that, age suggestions for individual rides become meaningless, because many adults seem to adore rides that are safe for even the youngest children, like Peter Pan's Flight and Snow White's Ride. The official guide to the park, distributed free at the resort's hotels and at City Hall on Main Street U.S.A., gives subtle suggestions, but it's anything but dictatorial (in fact, it's deliberately vague) about delineating which rides are suitable for which age groups.

Guided 3-hour tours for 20 or more people can be arranged for 29€ to 33€ ($33–$38) and 23€ ($26) for children 3 to 11. In view of the well-marked paths leading through the park and the availability of printed information in numerous languages, the guided tours aren't really necessary. You can no longer rent coin-operated lockers, however, you can store baggage for 2.50€ ($2.90) per day. Wheelchairs and children's strollers rent for 6€ ($6.90) per day, with a 150€ ($173) deposit for the wheelchair and 70€ ($81) deposit for the stroller. Babysitting is available at any of the hotels if 24-hour advance notice is given.

Marne-la-Vallée. ℂ **01-60-30-60-53** (Disneyland Paris Guest Relations office, in City Hall on Main Street, U.S.A.). www.disneylandparis.com. Admission to park for 1 day, depending on season, 39€ ($45) adults, 29€ ($33) children 3–12, free for children under 3; a 2-day ticket 69€ ($79) adults, 49€ ($56) children 3–12; and a 3-day ticket 105€ ($121) adults, 78€ ($90) children 3–12. July–Aug daily 9am–8pm; Sept–June daily 9am–6pm, depending on school and public holidays.

FOR THOSE WITH AN EXTRA DAY: WALT DISNEY STUDIOS

Next to Disneyland, **Walt Disney Studios** opened in the spring of 2002, offering a full day's experience; it takes guests on a behind-the-scenes interactive discovery of film, animation, and television. The audience is put right in the heart of the action. The four production areas of the studio are based on the real thing, and the park offers guests the chance to step through the screen and experience a world of attractions, entertainment, special effects, and never-seen-before shows.

The main entrance to the studios, called the Front Lot, consists of "Sunset Boulevard," which is an elaborate soundstage complete with hundreds of film props. The Animation Courtyard allows visitors to learn the trade secrets of Disney animators, and the Production Courtyard lets guests take a look behind the scenes of film and TV production. At Catastrophe Canyon guests are plunged into the heart of a film shoot. Finally, the Back Lot is home to special-effects and stunt workshops. A live stunt show features cars, motorbikes, and jet skis.

Marne-la-Vallée. ℂ **01-60-30-60-53**. Admission 39€ ($45) adults, 29€ ($33) children 3–12. Open daily 10am–6pm.

WHERE TO STAY

The only reason it's necessary to spend the night here is if you didn't get enough of Mickey Mouse the first day and want to hang out for another Disney adventure the following morning. Otherwise, you can easily make Disney a day trip from Paris because the transportation links are excellent.

The resort's six hotels share a reservation service. In North America, call © **407/W-DISNEY.** In France, contact the **Central Reservations Office,** Euro Disney Resort, S.C.A., B.P. 105, F-77777 Marne-la-Vallée Cedex 4 (© **01-60-30-60-30**).

VERY EXPENSIVE

Disneyland Hotel ★★ Mouseketeers with rich daddies and mommies check in here at Disney's poshest hotel, charging Paris Ritz tariffs. At the park entrance, this flagship four-story hotel is Victorian, with red-tile turrets and jutting balconies. The spacious guest rooms are plush, but use Disney images, with cartoon depictions and a candy-stripe decor. The beds are king, double, or twin; in some rooms armchairs convert to day beds. Paneled closets, large mirrors, and safes are found in some units. Accommodations in the rear overlook Sleeping Beauty's Castle and Big Thunder Mountain. Some less desirable units open onto a parking lot. The luxurious combination baths have marble vanities, tubs, and twin basins. On the Castle Club floor, you get free newspapers, all-day beverages, and access to a well-equipped private lounge.

Disneyland Paris, B.P. 105, F-77777 Marne-la-Vallée Cedex 4. © **01-60-45-65-00.** Fax 01-60-45-65-33. www.disneylandparis.com. 496 units. 340€–536€ ($391–$616) double; from 715€ ($822) suite. Rates include breakfast. AE, DC, MC, V. **Amenities:** 2 restaurants; bar; health club with indoor pool; whirlpool; sauna; 24-hr. room service; babysitting; laundry service/dry cleaning; nonsmoking rooms; rooms for those with limited mobility. *In room:* A/C, TV, dataport, minibar, hair dryer, safe.

EXPENSIVE

Hotel New York ★ Picture an Art Deco New York of the '30s. Inspired by the Big Apple, this hotel is designed around a nine-story central "skyscraper" flanked by the Gramercy Park Wing and the Brownstones Wing. (The exteriors of both wings resemble row houses.) More interested in convention bookings, this hotel is less family friendly than the others in the park. Guest rooms are comfortable, with Art Deco accessories, New York–inspired memorabilia, and roomy combination baths with twin basins and tub-and-shower combos. Try for one of the units fronting Lake Buena Vista instead of those facing the parking lot.

Disneyland Paris, B.P. 100, F-77777 Marne-la-Vallée Cedex 4. © **01-60-45-75-92.** Fax 01-60-45-73-33. www.disneylandparis.com. 565 units. 214€–321€ ($246–$369) double, from 530€ ($610) suite. Rates include breakfast. AE, DC, MC, V. **Amenities:** 2 restaurants; bar; indoor and outdoor pool; exercise room; sauna; 24-hr. room service; babysitting; nonsmoking rooms; rooms for those with limited mobility. *In room:* A/C, TV, dataport, minibar, hair dryer, safe.

Newport Bay Club ★★ You expect to see the reincarnation of old Joe Kennedy walking along the large veranda with its slated roofs, awnings, and pergolas. It's very Hyannis Port here, and it's also the biggest hotel in France. This hotel is designed with a central cupola, jutting balconies, and a blue-and-cream color scheme, reminiscent of a harbor-front New England hotel around 1900. The layout is irregular, with nautically decorated guest rooms in various shapes and sizes. The most spacious rooms are the corner units. The combination baths are roomy, with deluxe toiletries and tub and shower. The upscale Yacht Club and the less formal Cape Cod are the dining choices.

Disneyland Paris, B.P. 105, F-77777 Marne-la-Vallée Cedex 4. © **01-60-45-56-55.** Fax 01-60-45-55-33. www.disneylandparis.com. 1,093 units. 175€–277€ ($201–$319) double, from 375€ ($431) suite. Rates include breakfast. AE, DC, MC, V. **Amenities:** 2 restaurants; bar; indoor and outdoor pool; health club; sauna; 24-hr. room service; nonsmoking rooms; rooms for those with limited mobility. *In room:* A/C, TV, dataport, minibar, safe.

Sequoia Lodge   Built of gray stone and roughly textured planking and capped by a gently sloping green copper roof, this hotel resembles a lodge in the Rockies. The design, with parquet floors and giant chimneys, evokes the Prairie Houses of architect Frank Lloyd Wright. The hotel consists of a large central building with six chalets nearby, each housing 100 rooms. The guest rooms are comfortably rustic, with tiled baths with tub and shower. The Hunter's Grill serves spit-roasted meats carved on your plate. Less formal is the Beaver Creek Tavern.

Disneyland Paris, B.P. 100, F-77777 Marne-la-Vallée Cedex 4. © 01-60-45-52-48. Fax 01-60-45-51-33. www.disneylandparis.com. 1,011 units. 149€–249€ ($171–$286) double, from 395€ ($454) suite. Rates include breakfast. AE, DC, MC, V. **Amenities:** 2 restaurants; 2 bars; indoor/outdoor pool; health club; sauna; laundry service/dry cleaning; nonsmoking rooms; rooms for those with limited mobility. *In room:* A/C, TV, dataport, minibar, hair dryer.

MODERATE

Hotel Cheyenne/Hotel Santa Fe *(Kids)*   Next door to each other near a recreation of Texas's Rio Grande are the resort's least expensive hotels. Both evoke the Old West: The Cheyenne accommodates visitors in 14 two-story buildings along Desperado Street; the Santa Fe, sporting a desert theme, encompasses four "nature trails" winding among 42 adobe-style pueblos. The Cheyenne is a particular favorite among families, offering a double bed and bunk beds. An array of activities are offered for children, including a play area in a log cabin with a lookout tower and a section where you can explore the "ruins" of an ancient Anasazi village. There's a mariachi atmosphere in the Rio Grande Bar, and country music in the Red Garter Saloon Bar. The only disadvantage, according to some parents with children, is the absence of a pool. Tex-Mex specialties are offered at La Cantina (Santa Fe), and barbecue and smokehouse specialties predominate at the Chuck Wagon Cafe (Cheyenne).

Disneyland Paris, B.P. 115, F-77777 Marne-la-Vallée Cedex 4. © 01-60-45-63-12 (Cheyenne) or 01-60-45-79-22 (Santa Fe). Fax 01-60-45-62-33 (Cheyenne) or 01-60-45-78-33 (Santa Fe). www.disneylandparis. com. 2,000 units. Hotel Cheyenne 107€–212€ ($123–$244) double; Hotel Santa Fe 92€–186€ ($106–$214) double. Rates include breakfast. AE, DC, MC, V. **Amenities:** Restaurant; bar; room service; massage; babysitting; laundry service/dry cleaning; nonsmoking rooms; rooms for those with limited mobility. *In room:* A/C, TV, dataport.

WHERE TO DINE

Disneyland Paris offers a gamut of cuisine in no less than 45 restaurants and snack bars. You can live on burgers and fries at this place, or you can experiment with vaunted cuisine that's best appreciated at the following upscale restaurants.

Auberge de Cendrillon TRADITIONAL FRENCH   This is a fairy-tale version of Cinderella's sumptuous country inn, with a glass couch in the center. A master of ceremonies, in a plumed tri-corner hat and wearing an embroidered tunic and lace ruffles, welcomes you. Yes, there are corny elements, but the chefs do go out of their way to make a big deal out of French cuisine. For the most part, they succeed admirably. Our favorite appetizers are their warm-goat-cheese salad with lardons or their smoked-salmon platter. Either choice will put you in the mood for some of the classics of the French table, especially loin of lamb roasted under a zesty mustard coating or tender sautéed veal medallions that are like nuggets of flavor. An aromatic chicken is also perfectly roasted in puff pastry. Because the restaurant follows the park's seasonal schedules, lunches are usually easier to arrange than dinners.

In Fantasyland. © 01-64-74-24-02. Reservations recommended. Main courses 20€–27€ ($23–$31); prix fixe menu 33€ ($38) for adults, 13€ ($14) for children 3–12. AE, DC, MC, V. Wed–Fri 11:30am–4pm; Sat 11:30am–7pm; Sun 11:30am–5pm.

California Grill ★★ *Kids* CALIFORNIAN/FRENCH   This is Disneyland Paris's showcase eatery with cuisine that's equivalent to a one-Michelin-star restaurant. Focusing on the lighter specialties for which the Golden State is famous, with many concessions to French palates, this elegant restaurant manages to accommodate both adults and children gracefully. Even French food critics are impressed with the chef's oysters prepared with leeks and salmon. We also embrace the appetizer of foie gras with roasted red peppers, and the entree of roasted pigeon with braised Chinese cabbage and black-rice vinegar. Another winning selection is fresh salmon roasted over beech wood and served with a sprinkling of walnut oil, sage sauce, asparagus, and fricassee of forest mushrooms. Many items are specifically for children. If you want a quiet, mostly adult venue, go here as late as your hunger pangs will allow.

In the Disneyland Hotel. © 01-60-45-65-00. Reservations required. Main courses 35€–40€ ($40–$46); children's menu 24€ ($28). AE, DC, MC, V. Apr–Oct daily 6:30–11pm; Nov–Mar daily 6:30–10:30pm.

Inventions *Kids* *Value* INTERNATIONAL   This might be the only buffet restaurant in Europe where animated characters like Mickey and Minnie go table-hopping. With views over a park, the restaurant contains both smoking and nonsmoking sections, and four enormous buffet tables devoted, respectively, to starters, shellfish, main courses, and desserts. Selections are wide, portions can be copious, and absolutely no one leaves this place hungry. Don't expect *grande cuisine*—that's the domain of the more upscale (also-recommended) California Grill, within the same hotel. What you'll get is a sense of American bounty and culinary generosity, with ample doses of cartoon fantasy thrown in.

In the Disneyland Hotel. © 01-60-45-65-83. Reservations not necessary. Lunch buffet 32€ ($37) adults, 18€ ($21) children 7–11, 16€ ($18) children 3–6, free for children under 3; dinner buffet 43€ ($49) adults, 24€ ($28) children 7–11, 18€ ($21) children 3–6, free for children under 3. AE, DC, MC, V. Daily 12:30–3pm and 6–10:30pm.

DISNEYLAND AFTER DARK

The premier theatrical venue of Disneyland Paris is **Le Legende de Buffalo Bill** in the Disney Village (© **01-60-45-71-00**). This twice-per-night stampede of entertainment recalls the show that once traveled the West with Buffalo Bill and Annie Oakley. You'll dine at tables arranged amphitheater-style around a rink where sharpshooters, runaway stagecoaches, and dozens of horses and Indians ride fast and perform alarmingly realistic acrobatics. A Texas-style barbecue, served assembly-line by waiters in 10-gallon hats, is part of the experience. Despite its corny elements, it's not without its charm and an almost mournful nostalgia for a way of life of another continent and another century. Wild Bill himself is dignified and the Indians suitably brave. Two shows are staged at 6:30 and 9:30pm costing (with dinner included) 53€ ($61) for adults, 33€ ($38) ages 3 to 11.

6 Fontainebleau ⌒★

60km (37 miles) S of Paris, 74km (46 miles) NE of Orléans

Within the vestiges of a forest that bears its name (the Forêt de Fontainebleau), this suburb of Paris has offered refuge to French monarchs throughout the country's history. Kings from the Renaissance valued it because of its nearness to rich hunting grounds and its distance from the slums and smells of the city. Napoleon referred to the Palais de Fontainebleau, which he embellished with his distinctive monogram and decorative style, as "the house of the centuries." Many pivotal and decisive events have occurred inside, perhaps none more

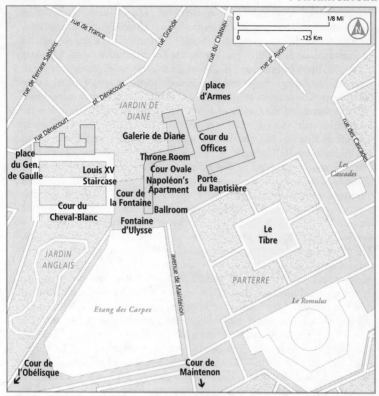

memorable than when Napoleon stood on the horseshoe-shaped exterior stairway and bade farewell to his shattered army before departing for Elba.

After the glories of Versailles, a visit to Fontainebleau can be a bit of a letdown, especially if followed immediately on the day after you saw Versailles. Fontainebleau, although a grand château, actually looks like a place a king could live, whereas Versailles is more of a production. If you stay for lunch, a trip to Fontainebleau should last a half-day.

ESSENTIALS

GETTING THERE **Trains** depart from Paris's Gare de Lyon. The trip takes between 45 and 60 minutes and costs 7.50€ ($8.65) each way. Fontainebleau's rail station is 2km (1¼ miles) from the château, in Avon. A local bus (it's marked simply A/B CHATEAU) makes the trip to the château at 15-minute intervals Monday to Friday, and at 30-minute intervals every Saturday, for 1.50€ ($1.75) each way. By **car,** take A-6 south from Paris, exit onto N-191, and follow the signs.

VISITOR INFORMATION The **tourist office** is at 4 rue Royale (© 01-60-74-99-99).

SEEING THE PALACE

Palais de Fontainebleau ✹✹✹ Napoleon's affection for this palace was understandable. He followed the pattern of a succession of French kings in the pre-Versailles days who used Fontainebleau as a resort and hunted in its forests.

François I tried to turn the hunting lodge into a royal palace in the Italian Renaissance style, bringing artists, including Benvenuto Cellini, there to work for him. Under this patronage, the School of Fontainebleau gained prestige, led by painters Rosso Fiorentino and Primaticcio. The artists adorned the 63m-long (206-ft.) **Gallery of François I** ✫✫✫, where stucco-framed panels depict such scenes as *The Rape of Europa* and the monarch holding a pomegranate, a symbol of unity. The salamander, the symbol of the Chevalier king, is everywhere.

Sometimes called the Gallery of Henri II, the **Ballroom** ✫✫✫ displays the interlaced initials "H&D," referring to Henri and his mistress, Diane de Poitiers. Competing with this illicit tandem are the initials "H&C," symbolizing Henri and his ho-hum wife, Catherine de Médicis. At one end of the room is a monumental fireplace supported by two bronze satyrs, made in 1966 (the originals were melted down during the Revolution). At the other side is the balcony of the musicians, with sculptured garlands. The ceiling displays octagonal coffering adorned with rosettes. Above the wainscoting is a series of frescoes, painted between 1550 and 1558, which depict mythological subjects such as *The Feast of Bacchus*. An architectural curiosity is the richly adorned **Louis XV Staircase** ✫✫. The room above it was originally decorated by Primaticcio for the bedroom of the duchesse d'Etampes, but when an architect was designing the stairway, he simply ripped out her floor. Of the Italian frescoes that were preserved, one depicts the queen of the Amazons climbing into Alexander the Great's bed.

When Louis XIV ascended to the throne, he neglected Fontainebleau because of his preoccupation with Versailles. However, he wasn't opposed to using the palace for houseguests, specifically such unwanted ones as Queen Christina, who had abdicated the throne of Sweden in a fit of religious fervor. Under the assumption that she still had "divine right," she ordered the brutal murder of her companion Monaldeschi, who had ceased to please her. Though Louis XV and then Marie Antoinette took an interest in Fontainebleau, the château found its renewed glory under Napoleon. You can wander around much of the palace on your own, visiting sites evoking the Corsican's 19th-century imperial heyday. They include the **throne room** where he abdicated his rulership of France, his **offices,** his monumental **bedroom,** and his **bathroom.** Some of the smaller Napoleonic Rooms contain his personal mementos and artifacts.

After your trek through the palace, visit the **gardens** and, especially, the **carp pond;** the gardens, however, are only a prelude to the Forest of Fontainebleau.

Place du Général-de-Gaulle. ✆ 01-60-71-50-70. Combination ticket for *grands appartements* 5.50€ ($6.35) adults, 4€ ($4.60) students 18–25, free for children under 18; ticket to *petits appartements* and Napoleonic Rooms 3€ ($3.45) adults, 2.30€ ($2.65) students 18–25, free for children under 18. June–Sept Wed–Mon 9:30am–6pm; Oct–May Wed–Mon 9:30am–5pm.

WHERE TO STAY

Grand Hotel de l'Aigle-Noir ✫   Once the home of Cardinal de Retz, this mansion stands opposite the château. It was built with a formal courtyard entrance, using a high iron grille and pillars crowned by black eagles. It was converted into a hotel in 1720 and has recently been remodeled, making it the finest lodgings in town. The guest rooms are decorated with Louis XVI, Empire, or Restoration antiques or reproductions with plush mattresses and elegant bathroom amenities. All but four units have tub-shower combinations. The remaining four units have showers only. Have a drink in the Napoleon III–style piano bar. Later, you can dine on elegant French cuisine with formalized service in the grand dining room, **Le Beauharnais.**

27 place Napoléon-Bonaparte, 77300 Fontainebleau. ✆ **01-60-74-60-00.** Fax 01-60-74-60-01. www.hotel aiglenoir.fr. 53 units. 205€–236€ ($236–$271) double; from 390€ ($449) suite. AE, DC, MC, V. Parking 9€ ($10). **Amenities:** Restaurant; bar; indoor pool; sauna; 24-hr. room service; laundry service/dry cleaning; nonsmoking rooms; rooms for those with limited mobility. *In room:* A/C, TV, dataport, minibar, hair dryer.

WHERE TO DINE

Le Caveau des Ducs TRADITIONAL FRENCH   Beneath a series of 17th-century stone vaults, this restaurant occupies what was once a storage cellar for the château. Wood and flickering candles preserve the illusion. In terms of grandeur, it's not in the same league as Le Beauharnais at Grand Hotel de l'Aigle-Noir, but it offers somewhat less pretentious food in a dramatic setting. Menu items are supervised by owner/chef André Murith, a longtime resident of Fontainebleau who's noted for his sense of humor. Examples include an excellent version of onion soup with a cheesy crust; marinated salmon with olive oil; a fried combination of foie gras with apples; a sweet and salty magret of duckling with caramelized apples; and a filet of rump steak served with Brie sauce. Desserts might include frozen nougat with red berries, or apple tart flambéed in Calvados and served with vanilla ice cream.

24 rue de Ferrare. ✆ **01-64-22-05-05.** Reservations recommended. Main courses 16€–22€ ($18–$25); prix fixe menu 22€–39€ ($25–$45). AE, MC, V. Daily noon–2pm and 7–10pm.

Le François-Ier ✮ TRADITIONAL FRENCH   The top dining choice attracts with a Louis XIII decor, wine-making memorabilia, and walls the owners think are about 200 years old. If weather permits, sit on the terrace overlooking the château and the Cour des Adieux. In game season, the menu includes hare, roebuck, duck liver, and partridge. Other choices may be cold salmon with *cèpes* (flap mushrooms), *rognon de veau* (veal kidneys) with mustard sauce, and a salad of baby scallops with crayfish. The cuisine is meticulous, with an undeniable flair. The *magrêt de canard* (duck) flavored with cassis is delicious.

3 rue Royale. ✆ **01-64-22-24-68.** Reservations required. Main courses 14€–23€ ($16–$26); prix fixe menu 15€ ($17) at lunch Mon–Fri, 28€ ($32) available anytime. AE, MC, V. Mon–Sat noon–2:30pm and 7:30–9pm.

Appendix A:
Paris History 101

IN THE BEGINNING

Paris emerged at the crossroads of three major traffic arteries on the muddy island in the Seine that today is known as Ile de la Cité.

By around 2000 B.C., the island served as the fortified headquarters of the Parisii tribe, who called it Lutétia. The two wooden bridges connecting the island to the river's left and right banks were among the region's most strategically important, and the settlement attracted the attention of the Roman Empire. In his *Commentaries,* Julius Caesar described his conquest of Lutétia, recounting how its bridges were burned during the Gallic War of 52 B.C. and how the town on the island was pillaged, sacked, and transformed into a Roman-controlled stronghold.

Within a century, Lutétia became a full-fledged Roman town, and some of the inhabitants abandoned the frequently flooded island in favor of higher ground on what is today the Left Bank. By A.D. 200, barbarian invasions threatened the stability of Roman Gaul, and the populace from the surrounding hills flocked to the island's fortified safety. Over the next 50 years, a Christian community gained a foothold there. According to legend, St. Denis served as the city's first bishop (around 250). By this time the Roman Empire's political power had begun to wane in the region, and the cultural and religious attachment of the community to the Christian bishops of Rome grew even stronger.

During the 400s, with the decline of the Roman armies, Germanic tribes from the east (the Salian Franks) were able to invade the island, founding a

Dateline

- 2000 B.C. Lutétia thrives along a strategic crossing of the Seine, the headquarters of the Parisii tribe.
- 52 B.C. Julius Caesar conquers Lutétia during the Gallic Wars.
- A.D. 150 Lutétia flourishes as a Roman colony, expanding to the Left Bank.
- 200 Barbarian Gauls force the Romans to retreat to the fortifications on Ile de la Cité.
- 300 Lutétia is renamed Paris; Roman power weakens in northern France.
- 350 Paris's Christianization begins.
- 400s The Franks invade Paris, with social transformation from the Roman to the Gallo-Roman culture.
- 466 Clovis, founder of the Merovingian dynasty and first non-Roman ruler of Paris since the Parisii, is born.
- 800 Charlemagne, founder of the Carolingian dynasty, is crowned Holy Roman Emperor and rules from Aachen in modern Germany.
- 987 Hugh Capet, founder of France's foremost early medieval dynasty, rises to power; his family rules from Paris.
- 1100 The Université de Paris attracts scholars from throughout Europe.
- 1200s Paris's population and power grow, though it is often unsettled by plagues and feudal battles.
- 1422 England invades Paris during the Hundred Years' War.
- 1429 Joan of Arc tries to regain Paris for the French; the Burgundians later capture and sell her to the English, who burn her at the stake in Rouen.
- 1500s François I, first of the French Renaissance kings, embellishes Paris but chooses to maintain his court in the Loire Valley.
- 1549 Henri II rules from Paris; construction of public and private residences begins, many in the Marais.

Frankish dynasty and prompting a Frankish-Latin fusion in the burgeoning town. The first of these Frankish kings, Clovis (466–511), founder of the Merovingian dynasty, embraced Christianity as his tribe's religion and spearheaded an explicit rejection of Roman cultural imperialism by encouraging the adoption of Parisii place names like "Paris," which came into common usage during this time.

The Merovingians were replaced by the Carolingians, whose heyday began with Charlemagne's coronation in 800. The Carolingian Empire sprawled over western Germany and eastern France, but Paris was never its capital. The city remained a commercial and religious center, sacred to the memory of St. Geneviève, who reputedly protected Paris when the Huns attacked it in the final days of the Roman Empire. The Carolingians came to an end in 987, when the empire fragmented because of the growing regional, political, and linguistic divisions between what would become modern France and modern Germany. Paris became the seat of a new dynasty, the Capetians, whose kings ruled France throughout the Middle Ages. Hugh Capet (938–996), the first of this line, ruled as comte de Paris and duc de France from 987 to 996.

THE MIDDLE AGES

Around 1100, Paris began to emerge as a great city, boasting on its Left Bank a university that attracted scholars from all over Europe. Meanwhile, kings and bishops began building the towering Gothic cathedrals of France, one of the greatest of which became Paris's Notre-Dame, a monument rising from the beating heart of the city. Paris's population increased greatly, as did the city's mercantile activity. During the 1200s, a frenzy of building transformed the skyline with convents and churches (including the jewel-like Sainte-Chapelle, completed

1564 Construction begins on Catherine de Médicis's Palais des Tuileries; building facades in Paris move from half-timbered to more durable chiseled stonework.

1572 The Wars of Religion reach their climax with the St. Bartholomew's Day massacre of Protestants.

1598 Henri IV, the most eccentric and enlightened monarch of his era, endorses the Edict of Nantes, granting tolerance to Protestants; a crazed monk fatally stabs him 12 years later.

1615 Construction begins on the Palais du Luxembourg for Henri IV's widow, Marie de Médicis.

1636 The Palais Royal is launched by Cardinal Richelieu; soon two marshy islands in the Seine are interconnected and filled in to create Ile St-Louis.

1643 Louis XIV, the "Sun King" and the most powerful ruler since the Caesars, rises to power; he moves his court to the newly built Versailles.

1776 The American Declaration of Independence strikes a revolutionary chord in France.

1789 The French Revolution begins.

1793 Louis XVI and his Austrian-born queen, Marie Antoinette, are publicly guillotined.

1799 Napoleon Bonaparte crowns himself Master of France and embellishes Paris further with neoclassical splendor.

1803 Napoleon abandons French overseas expansion and sells Louisiana to America.

1812 Napoleon is defeated in the Russian winter campaign.

1814 Aided by a coalition of France's enemies, especially England, the Bourbon monarchy under Louis XVIII is restored.

1821 Napoleon Bonaparte dies.

1824 Louis XVIII dies and Charles X succeeds him.

1830 Charles X is deposed and the more liberal Louis-Philippe is elected king; Paris prospers as it industrializes.

1848 A violent working-class revolution deposes Louis-Philippe, who's replaced by autocratic Napoleon III.

continues

in 1248 after just 2 years). During the next century, the increasingly powerful French kings added dozens of monuments of their own.

As time passed, Paris's fortunes became closely linked to the power struggles between the French monarchs in Paris and the various highly competitive feudal lords of the provinces. Because of this tug of war, Paris was dogged by civil unrest, takeovers by one warring faction after another, and a dangerous alliance between the English and the powerful rulers of Burgundy during the Hundred Years' War. Around the same time, the city suffered a series of plagues, including the Black Death. To the humiliation of the French monarchs, the English army invaded the city in 1422. Joan of Arc (ca. 1412–31) tried unsuccessfully to reconquer Paris in 1429, and 2 years later the English, supported by a tribunal of French ecclesiastics, burned her at the stake in Rouen. Paris was reduced to poverty and economic stagnation, and its embittered and greatly reduced population turned to banditry and street crime to survive.

Despite Joan's tragic end, the revolution she inspired continued until Paris was finally taken from the English in 1436. During the following several decades, the English retreated to the port of Calais, abandoning their once-mighty French territories. France, under the leadership of Louis XI (1423–83), witnessed an accelerating rate of change that included the transformation of a feudal and medieval social system into the nascent beginnings of a modern state.

THE RENAISSANCE & THE REFORMATION

The first of the Renaissance monarchs, François I (1494–1547), began an enlargement of Paris's Louvre (which had begun as a warehouse storing the archives of Philippe Auguste before being transformed into a Gothic

- 1853–70 On Napoleon III's orders, Baron Haussmann redesigns Paris's landscapes and creates the Grands Boulevards.
- 1860s The Impressionist style of painting emerges.
- 1870 The Franco-Prussian War ends in the defeat of France; Paris is threatened by Prussian cannons placed on the outskirts of the city; a revolution in the aftermath of this defeat destroys the Palais des Tuileries and overthrows the government; the Third Republic rises with its elected president, Marshal MacMahon.
- 1878–1937 Several international expositions add monuments to the Paris skyline, including the Tour Eiffel and Sacré-Coeur.
- 1895 Capt. Alfred Dreyfus, a Jew, is wrongfully charged with treason and sentenced to life on Devil's Island. The incident will lead to one of the major French political scandals of the 19th century.
- 1898 Emile Zola publishes *J' Accuse* in defense of Dreyfus and flees into exile in England.
- 1906 Dreyfus is finally exonerated and his rank restored.
- 1914–18 World War I rips apart Europe.
- 1940 German troops invade Paris; the French government, under Marshal Pétain, evacuates to Vichy, while the French Resistance under Gen. Charles de Gaulle maintains symbolic headquarters in London.
- 1944 U.S. troops liberate Paris; de Gaulle returns in triumph.
- 1948 The revolt in the French colony of Madagascar costs 80,000 French lives; France's empire continues to collapse in Southeast Asia and equatorial Africa.
- 1954–62 War begins in Algeria and is eventually lost; refugees flood Paris, and the nation becomes divided over its North African policies.
- 1958 France's Fourth Republic collapses; General de Gaulle is called out of retirement to head the Fifth Republic.
- 1968 Paris's students and factory workers engage in a general revolt; the French government is overhauled in the aftermath.

fortress by Louis IX in the 1100s) to make it suitable as a royal residence. Despite the building's embellishment and the designation of Paris as the French capital, he spent much of his time at other châteaux amid the hunting grounds of the Loire Valley. Many later monarchs came to share his opinion that Paris's narrow streets and teeming commercialism were unhealthy, and chose to reside elsewhere.

In 1549, however, Henri II (1519–59) triumphantly established his court in Paris and successfully ruled France from within its borders, solidifying the city's role as the nation's undisputed capital. Following their ruler's lead, fashionable aristocrats quickly began to build *hôtels particuliers* (private residences) on the Right Bank, in a marshy low-lying area known as Le Marais (the swamp).

It was during this period that the Paris we know today came into existence. The expansion of the Louvre continued, and Catherine de Médicis (1518–89) began building her Palais des Tuileries in 1564. From the shelter of dozens of elegant urban residences, France's aristocracy imbued Paris with its sense of architectural and social

- 1981 François Mitterrand is elected France's first Socialist president since the 1940s; he's reelected in 1988.
- 1989 Paris celebrates the bicentennial of the French Revolution.
- 1992 Euro Disney opens on the outskirts of Paris.
- 1994 François Mitterrand and Queen Elizabeth II ride under the English Channel in the new Chunnel.
- 1995 Jacques Chirac is elected over Mitterrand, who dies the following year; Paris is crippled by a general strike; terrorists bomb the subway.
- 1997 Authorities enforce strict immigration laws, causing strife for African and Arab immigrants and dividing the country; French voters elect Socialist Lionel Jospin as Chirac's new prime minister.
- 1998 Socialists triumph in local elections across France.
- 1999 The euro is introduced; on Christmas Day a violent storm assaults Paris and the Ile de France, damaging buildings and toppling thousands of trees.
- 2002 France replaces its national currency, the franc, and switches to the euro, the new European currency.
- 2003 Attacks on French Jews mark the rise of anti-Semitism, the worst since WWII.

style, as well as the Renaissance's mores and manners. Stone quays were added to the Seine's banks, defining their limits and preventing future flood damage, and royal decrees established a series of building codes. To an increasing degree, Paris adopted the planned perspectives and visual grace worthy of the residence of a monarch.

During the late 1500s and 1600s, the French kings persecuted Protestants. The bloodletting reached a high point under Henri III (1551–89) during the St. Bartholomew's Day massacre of 1572. Henri III's tragic and eccentric successor, Henri IV (1553–1610), ended the Wars of Religion in 1598 by endorsing the Edict of Nantes, offering religious freedom to the Protestants of France. Henry IV also laid out the lines for one of Paris's memorable squares: place des Vosges. A deranged monk infuriated by the king's support of religious tolerance stabbed him in 1610.

After Henri IV's death, his second wife, Marie de Médicis (1573–1642), acting as regent, planned the Palais du Luxembourg (1615), whose gardens have functioned ever since as a rendezvous point for Parisians. In 1636, Cardinal Richelieu (1585–1642), who virtually ruled France during the minority of Louis XIII, built the sprawling premises of the Palais Royal. Under Louis XIII (1601–43), two uninhabited islands in the Seine were joined together with landfill, connected to Ile de la Cité and to the mainland with bridges, and renamed

Ile St-Louis. Also laid out were the Jardin des Plantes, whose flowers and medicinal herbs were arranged according to their scientific and medical category.

THE SUN KING & THE FRENCH REVOLUTION

Louis XIV (1638–1715) was crowned king of France when he was only 9 years old. Cardinal Mazarin (1602–61), Louis's Sicilian-born chief minister, dominated the government in Paris during the Sun King's minority. This era marked the emergence of the French kings as absolute monarchs. As if to concretize their power, they embellished Paris with many of the monuments that still serve as symbols of the city. These included new alterations to the Louvre and the construction of the pont Royal, quai Peletier, place des Victoires, place Vendôme, Champs-Elysées, and Hôtel des Invalides. Meanwhile, Louis XIV absented himself from the city, constructing, at a staggering expense, the Château de Versailles, 21km (13 miles) southwest. Today the palace stands as the single most visible monument to the most flamboyant era of French history.

Meanwhile, the rising power of England, particularly its navy, represented a serious threat to France, otherwise the world's most powerful nation. One of the many theaters of the Anglo-French conflict was the American Revolution, during which the French kings supported the Americans in their struggle against the Crown. Ironically, within 15 years, the fervor the monarchs had nurtured crossed the Atlantic and destroyed them. The spark that kindled the fire came from Paris itself. For years before the outbreak of hostilities between the Americans and the British, the Enlightenment and its philosophers had fostered a new generation of thinkers who opposed absolutism, religious fanaticism, and superstition. Revolution had been brewing for almost 50 years, and after the French Revolution's explosive events, Europe was completely changed.

Though it began with moderate aims, the Revolution had soon turned the radical Jacobins into overlords, led by Robespierre (1758–94). On August 10, 1792, troops from Marseilles, aided by a Parisian mob, threw Louis XVI (1754–93) and his Austrian-born queen, Marie Antoinette (1755–93), into prison. Several months later, after countless humiliations and a bogus trial, they were guillotined at place de la Révolution (later renamed place de la Concorde) on January 21, 1793. The Reign of Terror continued for another 18 months, with Parisians of all political persuasions fearing for their lives.

THE RISE OF NAPOLEON

It required the militaristic fervor of Napoleon Bonaparte (1769–1821) to unite France once again. Considered then and today a strategic genius with almost limitless ambition, he restored to Paris and France a national pride that had diminished during the Revolution's horror. After many impressive political and military victories, he entered Paris in 1799, at the age of 30, and crowned himself "First Consul and Master of France." In 1804, he named himself Emperor of France.

A brilliant politician, Napoleon moderated the atheistic rigidity of the early adherents of the Revolution by establishing peace with the Vatican. Soon thereafter, the legendary love of Parisians for their amusements began to revive; boulevard des Italiens became the rendezvous point of the fashionable, while boulevard du Temple, which housed many of the capital's theaters, became the favorite watering hole of the working class. In his self-appointed role as a French Caesar, Napoleon continued to alter Paris's face with the construction of the neoclassical arcades of rue de Rivoli (1801), the Arc du Carrousel and Arc de Triomphe, and the neoclassical grandeur of La Madeleine. On a less grandiose scale, the city's slaughterhouses and cemeteries were sanitized and moved away from the center of town, and new industries began to crowd workers from the countryside into the cramped slums of a newly industrialized Paris.

Napoleon's victories had made him the envy of Europe, but his infamous retreat from Moscow during the winter of 1812 reduced his formerly invincible army to tatters as 400,000 Frenchmen lost their lives. After a complicated series of events that included his return from exile, Napoleon was defeated at Waterloo by the armies of the English, the Dutch, and the Prussians. Exiled to the British-held island of St. Helena in the remote South Atlantic, he died in 1821, possibly the victim of an unknown poisoner. Sometime later, his body was returned to Paris and interred in a massive porphyry sarcophagus in the Hôtel des Invalides, Louis XIV's monument to the ailing and fallen warriors of France.

In the power vacuum that followed Napoleon's expulsion and death, Paris became the scene of intense lobbying over France's future. The Bourbon monarchy was soon reestablished, but with reduced powers. In 1830, the regime was overthrown. Louis-Philippe (1773–1850), duc d'Orléans and the son of a duke who had voted in 1793 for the death of Louis XVI, was elected king under a liberalized constitution. His prosperous reign lasted for 18 years, during which England and France more or less collaborated on matters of foreign policy.

Paris reveled in its prosperity, grateful for the money and glamour that had elevated it to one of the world's top cultural and commercial centers. Paris opened its first railway line in 1837 and its first gas-fed streetlights shortly after. It was a time of wealth, grace, culture, and expansion, though the industrialization of certain working-class districts produced great poverty. The era also witnessed the development of French cuisine to the high form that still prevails, while a newly empowered bourgeoisie reveled in its attempts to create the good life.

THE SECOND EMPIRE

In 1848, a series of revolutions spread from one European capital to the next. The violent upheaval in Paris revealed the dissatisfaction of members of the working class. Fueled by a financial crash and scandals in the government, the revolt forced Louis-Philippe out. That year, Emperor Napoleon's nephew, Napoleon III (1808–73), was elected president by moderate and conservative elements. Appealing to the property-owning instinct of a nation that hadn't forgotten the violent revolution of less than a century before, he established a right-wing government and assumed complete power as emperor in 1851.

In 1853, Napoleon III undertook Europe's largest urban redevelopment project by commissioning Baron Eugène-Georges Haussmann (1809–91) to redesign Paris. Haussmann created a vast network of boulevards interconnected with a series of squares that cut across old neighborhoods. While this reorganization gave the capital the look for which it's now famous, screams of outrage sounded throughout the neighborhoods that the construction split apart. By 1866, the entrepreneurs of an increasingly industrialized Paris began to regard the Second Empire as a hindrance. In 1870, during the Franco-Prussian War, the Prussians defeated Napoleon III at Sedan and held him prisoner along with 100,000 of his soldiers. Paris was threatened with bombardments from German cannons, by far the most advanced of their age, set up on the city's eastern periphery.

Although agitated diplomacy gained a Prussian withdrawal, international humiliation and perceived military incompetence sparked a revolt in Paris. One of the immediate effects was the burning of one of Paris's historic landmarks, the Palais des Tuileries. Today, only the gardens of this once-great palace remain. The events of 1870 ushered in the Third Republic and its elected president, Marshal Marie Edme Patrice Maurice de MacMahon (1808–93), in 1873.

Under the Third Republic, peace and prosperity gradually returned, and Paris regained its glamour. Universal expositions held in 1878, 1889, 1900, and 1937 were the catalyst for the construction of such enduring monuments as the Trocadéro, the Palais de Chaillot, the Tour Eiffel, the Grand Palais and the Petit Palais, and the neo-Byzantine Sacré-Coeur. The *réseau métropolitain* (the Métro) was constructed, providing a model for subway systems throughout Europe.

WORLD WAR I

International rivalries and conflicting alliances led to World War I, which, after decisive German victories for 2 years, degenerated into the mud-slogged horror of trench warfare. Industrialization during and after the war transformed Paris and its environs into one of the largest metropolitan areas in Europe and undisputed ever since as the center of France's intellectual and commercial life.

Immediately after the Allied victory, grave economic problems, coupled with a populace demoralized from years of fighting, encouraged the rise of Socialism and the formation of a Communist party, both movements centered in Paris. Also from Paris, the French government, led by the vindictive Georges Clemenceau (1841–1929), occupied Germany's Ruhr Valley, then and now one of that country's most profitable and industrialized regions, and demanded every centime of reparations it could wring from its humiliated neighbor, a policy that contributed to the outbreak of World War II.

THE 1920s—AMERICANS IN PARIS

The so-called Lost Generation, led by American expatriates Gertrude Stein and Alice B. Toklas, topped the list of celebrities who "occupied" Paris after World War I, ushering in one of its most glamorous eras. The living was cheap in Paris. Two people could manage for about a year on a $1,000 scholarship, provided they could scrape up another $500 or so in extra earnings. Paris attracted the littérateur, bon viveur, and drifter. Writers like Henry Miller, Ernest Hemingway, and F. Scott Fitzgerald all lived here. Even Cole Porter came, living first at the Ritz, then at 13 rue de Monsieur. James Joyce, half blind and led around by Ezra Pound, arrived in Paris and went to the salon of Natalie Barney. She became famous for pulling off stunts like inviting Mata Hari to perform a Javanese dance completely nude at one of her parties, labeled "for women only, a lesbian orgy." Novelist Colette was barred, though she begged her husband to let her go.

With the collapse of Wall Street, many Americans returned home, except hard-core artists like Henry Miller, who wandered around smoking Gauloises and writing *Tropic of Cancer,* which was banned in America. "I have no money, no resources, no hopes. I am the happiest man alive," Miller said. Eventually, he met diarist Anaïs Nin, and they began to live a life that gave both of them material for their prose. But even such die-hards as Miller and Nin eventually realized 1930s Paris was collapsing as war clouds loomed. Gertrude and Alice remained in France, as other American expats fled to safer shores.

THE WINDS OF WAR

Thanks to an array of alliances, when Germany invaded Poland in 1939, France had no choice but to declare war. Within a few months, on June 14, 1940, Nazi armies marched down the Champs-Elysées and passed beneath the Arc de Triomphe. Newsreel cameras recorded the French openly weeping at the sight. The city suffered little from the war materially, but for 4 years it survived in a kind of half-life—cold, dull, and drab—fostering scattered pockets of fighters who resisted sometimes passively and sometimes with active sabotage.

During the Nazi occupation of Paris, the French government, under Marshal Henri Pétain (1856–1951), moved to the isolated resort of Vichy and cooperated (or collaborated, depending on your point of view) with the Nazis. Tremendous internal dissension, the memory of which still simmers today, pitted many factions against one another. The Free French Resistance fled for its own safety to London, where it was headed by Charles de Gaulle (1880–1970). On September 9, 1945, a government of national unity was formed under de Gaulle's presidency. A constituent National Assembly was then elected. De Gaulle's disagreement with the National Assembly led in January of 1946 to the tendering of his resignation.

POSTWAR PARIS

Despite gains in prestige and prosperity after the end of World War II, Paris was rocked many times by internal dissent as domestic and international events embroiled the government in controversy. In 1951, Paris celebrated the 2,000th anniversary of the city's founding and poured much energy into rebuilding its image as a center of fashion, lifestyle, and glamour. Paris became internationally recognized as both a staple in the travel diets of many North Americans and as a beacon for art and artists.

The War of Algerian Independence (1954–58), in which Algeria sought to go from being a French *département* (an integral extension of the French nation) to an independent country, was an anguishing event, more devastating than the earlier loss of France's colonies. The population of France (Paris in particular) ballooned as French citizens fled Algeria and returned with few possessions and much bitterness. In 1958, as a result of the enormous loss of lives, money, and prestige in the Algerian affair, France's Fourth Republic collapsed, and de Gaulle was called out of retirement to form a new government, the Fifth Republic. In 1962, the Algerian war ended with victory for Algeria, as France's colonies in central and equatorial Africa became independent one by one. The sun had finally set on the French Empire.

In 1968, a general revolt by Parisian students, whose activism mirrored that of their counterparts in the United States, turned the capital into an armed camp, causing a near-collapse of the national government and the very real possibility of total civil war. Though the crisis was averted, for several weeks it seemed as if French society was on the brink of anarchy.

CONTEMPORARY PARIS

In 1981, François Mitterrand (1916–96) was elected the first Socialist president of France since before World War II by a very close vote. Massive amounts of capital were taken out of the country, and though the drain slowed after initial jitters, many wealthy Parisians still prefer to invest their money elsewhere.

Paris today still struggles with social unrest in Corsica and from Muslim fundamentalists both inside and outside of France. In the mid-1990s, racial tensions continued to nag at France, as the debate over immigration raged. Many right-wing political parties have created a racial backlash against North Africans and against "corruptive foreign influences" in general.

On his third try, Jacques Chirac (b. 1932), a longtime mayor of Paris, won the presidency of France in 1995 with 52% of the vote. Mitterrand turned over the reins on May 17 and died shortly thereafter. France embarked on a new era, but Chirac's popularity faded in the wake of unrest caused by an 11.5% unemployment rate. In the spring of 1998, France ousted its Conservative parties in an endorsement of Prime Minister Lionel Jospin (b. 1937) and his Socialist-led government. The triumph of Jospin and his Communist and Green Party allies represented a disavowal of the center-right Conservatives. This was a stunning blow to Chirac's neo-Gaullists and the center-right parties led by François Leotard, and certainly to Jean-Marie Le Pen's often-fanatical National Front.

By putting the Left back in charge, the French had voted against all the new ideas proposed for pushing their country into competitiveness and out of its economic doldrums. But Jospin's popularity gradually diminished, and in the elections of 2002, he was voted out of office and announced his retirement from politics. Jacques Chirac came back into power and became one of the most powerful leaders opposing the United State's war in Iraq.

In 1999, France joined with 11 other European Union countries in adopting the euro as its standard of currency, though the French franc remained in circulation until March 2002. The new currency, it is hoped, will accelerate the creation of a single economy, comprising nearly 300 million Europeans, with a combined gross national product approaching, by some estimates, $9 trillion, larger than that of the United States.

On an ominous note, attacks against Jews in France reached their highest level since World War II. An increase in anti-Semitic acts coincided with heightened tensions in the Middle East. In 2003, Jewish schools, temples, and cemeteries were attacked. Slogans denouncing Jews were regularly spray-painted on school walls and over Jewish cemeteries. The same year witnessed a stabbing of a rabbi in Paris and the beating of Jewish youths with metal bars at an antiwar protest in Paris.

Appendix B:
Glossary of Useful Terms

I t is often amazing how a word or two of halting French will change your hosts' disposition in their home country. At the very least, try to learn a few numbers, basic greetings, and—above all—the life-raft phrase, *Parlez-vous anglais?* ("Do you speak English?"). As it turns out, many people do speak a passable English and will use it liberally, if you demonstrate the basic courtesy of greeting them in their language. Go out, try our glossary, and don't be bashful. *Bonne chance!*

1 Useful French Words & Phrases

English	French	Pronunciation
Yes/No	**Oui/Non**	wee/noh
Okay	**D'accord**	*dah*-core
Please	**S'il vous plaît**	seel voo *play*
Thank you	**Merci**	*mair*-see
You're welcome	**De rien**	duh ree-*ehn*
Hello (during daylight)	**Bonjour**	bohn-*jhoor*
Good evening	**Bonsoir**	bohn-*swahr*
Goodbye	**Au revoir**	o ruh-*vwahr*
What's your name?	**Comment vous appellez-vous?**	kuh-*mahn* voo za-pell-ay-voo?
My name is	**Je m'appelle**	*jhuh* ma-pell
How are you?	**Comment allez-vous?**	kuh-*mahn* tahl-ay-voo?
So-so	**Comme ci, comme ça**	kum-*see*, kum-*sah*
I'm sorry/excuse me	**Pardon**	pahr-*dohn*

GETTING AROUND & STREET SMARTS

English	French	Pronunciation
Do you speak English?	**Parlez-vous anglais?**	par-lay-voo zahn-*glay*?
I don't speak French	**Je ne parle pas français**	jhuh ne parl pah frahn-*say*
I don't understand	**Je ne comprends pas**	jhuh ne kohm-*prahn* pas
Could you speak more loudly/ more slowly?	**Pouvez-vous parler plus fort/ plus lentement?**	Poo-*vay* voo par-lay ploo for/ ploo lan-te-*ment*?
What is it?	**Qu'est-ce que c'est?**	kess kuh *say*?
What time is it?	**Qu'elle heure est-il?**	kel uhr eh-*teel*?
What?	**Quoi?**	kwah?
How? or What did you say?	**Comment?**	ko-*mahn*?
When?	**Quand?**	kahn?

English	French	Pronunciation
Where is?	Où est?	ooh eh?
Who?	Qui?	kee?
Why?	Pourquoi?	poor-*kwah?*
here/there	ici/là	ee-*see*/lah
left/right	à gauche/à droite	a goash/a drwaht
straight ahead	tout droit	too drwah
Fill the tank (of a car), please	Le plein, s'il vous plaît	luh plan, seel-voo-*play*
I want to get off at	Je voudrais descendre à	jhe voo-*dray* day-son drah-ah
airport	l'aéroport	lair-o-*por*
bank	la banque	lah bahnk
bridge	pont	pohn
bus station	la gare routière	lah gar roo-tee-*air*
bus stop	l'arrêt de bus	lah-*ray* duh boohss
by means of a car	en voiture	ahn vwa-*toor*
cashier	la caisse	lah *kess*
cathedral	cathedral	ka-tay-*dral*
church	église	ay-*gleez*
driver's license	permis de conduire	per-*mee* duh con-*dweer*
elevator	l'ascenseur	lah sahn *seuhr*
entrance (to a building or a city)	une porte	ewn port
exit (from a building or a freeway)	une sortie	ewn sor-*tee*
gasoline	du pétrol/ de l'essence	duh pay-*troll*/ de lay-*sahns*
hospital	l'hôpital	low-pee-*tahl*
luggage storage	consigne	kohn-*seen*-yuh
museum	le musée	luh mew-*zay*
no smoking	défense de fumer	day-*fahns* de fu-may
one-day pass	ticket journalier	tee-kay jhoor-nall-ee-*ay*
one-way ticket	aller simple	ah-*lay sam*-pluh
police	la police	lah po-*lees*
round-trip ticket	aller-retour	ah-*lay* re-*toor*
second floor	premier étage	prem-ee-*ehr* ay-*taj*
slow down	ralentir	rah-lahn-*teer*
store	le magasin	luh ma-ga-*zehn*
street	rue	roo
subway	le métro	le *máy*-tro
telephone	le téléphone	luh tay-lay-*phone*
ticket	un billet	uh *bee*-yay
toilets	les toilettes/les WC	lay twa-*lets*/les vay-*say*

NECESSITIES

English	French	Pronunciation
I'd like	Je voudrais	jhe voo-*dray*
a room	une chambre	ewn *shahm*-bruh
the key	la clé (la clef)	la clay

English	French	Pronunciation
How much does it cost?	**C'est combien?/ Ça coûte combien?**	say comb-bee-*ehn?/* sah coot comb-bee-*ehn?*
That's expensive	**C'est cher/chère**	say share
Do you take credit cards?	**Est-ce que vous acceptez les cartes de credit?**	es-kuh voo zaksep-*tay* lay kart duh creh-*dee?*
I'd like to buy	**Je voudrais acheter**	jhe voo-dray ahsh-*tay*
aspirin	des aspirines/ des aspros	deyz ahs-peer-*een/* deyz ahs-*proh*
condoms	**des préservatifs**	day pray-ser-va-*teef*
dress	**une robe**	ewn robe
envelopes	**des envelopes**	days ahn-veh-*lope*
gift	**un cadeau**	uh kah-*doe*
handbag	**un sac**	uh sahk
hat	**un chapeau**	uh shah-*poh*
map of the city	**un plan de ville**	unh plahn de *veel*
newspaper	**un journal**	uh zhoor-*nahl*
phone card	**une carte téléphonique**	uh cart tay-lay-fone-*eek*
postcard	**une carte postale**	ewn carte pos-*tahl*
road map	**une carte routière**	ewn cart roo-tee-*air*
shoes	**des chaussures**	day show-*suhr*
soap	**du savon**	dew sah-*vohn*
stamp	**un timbre**	uh *tam*-bruh
writing paper	**du papier è lettres**	dew pap-pee-*ay* a *let*-ruh

IN YOUR HOTEL

English	French	Pronunciation
Are taxes included?	**Est-ce que les taxes sont comprises?**	ess-keh lay taks son com-*preez?*
balcony	**un balcon**	uh bahl-cohn
bathtub	**une baignoire**	ewn bayn-*nwar*
hot and cold water	**l'eau chaude et froide**	low showed ay fwad
Is breakfast included?	**Petit déjeuner inclus?**	peh-*tee* day-jheun-*ay* ehn-*klu?*
room	**une chambre**	ewn *shawm*-bruh
shower	**une douche**	ewn dooch
sink	**un lavabo**	uh la-va-*bow*
suite	**une suite**	ewn sweet
We're staying for . . . days	**On reste pour . . . jours**	ohn rest poor . . . jhoor

NUMBERS & ORDINALS

English	French	Pronunciation
zero	**zéro**	*zare*-oh
one	**un**	oon
two	**deux**	duh
three	**trois**	twah
four	**quatre**	*kaht*-ruh
five	**cinq**	sank

English	French	Pronunciation
six	**six**	seess
seven	**sept**	set
eight	**huit**	wheat
nine	**neuf**	noof
ten	**dix**	deess
eleven	**onze**	ohnz
twelve	**douze**	dooz
thirteen	**treize**	trehz
fourteen	**quatorze**	kah-*torz*
fifteen	**quinze**	kanz
sixteen	**seize**	sez
seventeen	**dix-sept**	deez-*set*
eighteen	**dix-huit**	deez-*wheat*
nineteen	**dix-neuf**	deez-*noof*
twenty	**vingt**	vehn
thirty	**trente**	trahnt
forty	**quarante**	ka-*rahnt*
fifty	**cinquante**	sang-*kahnt*
one hundred	**cent**	sahn
one thousand	**mille**	meel
first	**premier**	*preh*-mee-ay
second	**deuxième**	*duhz*-zee-em
third	**troisième**	*twa*-zee-em
fourth	**quatrième**	*kaht*-ree-em
fifth	**cinquième**	*sank*-ee-em
sixth	**sixième**	*sees*-ee-em
seventh	**septième**	*set*-ee-em
eighth	**huitième**	*wheat*-ee-em
ninth	**neuvième**	*neuv*-ee-em
tenth	**dixième**	*dees*-ee-em

THE CALENDAR

English	French	Pronunciation
Sunday	**dimanche**	dee-*mahnsh*
Monday	**lundi**	luhn-*dee*
Tuesday	**mardi**	mahr-*dee*
Wednesday	**mercredi**	mair-kruh-*dee*
Thursday	**jeudi**	jheu-*dee*
Friday	**vendredi**	vawn-druh-*dee*
Saturday	**samedi**	sahm-*dee*
yesterday	**hier**	ee-*air*
today	**aujourd'hui**	o-jhord-*dwee*
this morning/ this afternoon	**ce matin/ cet après-midi**	suh ma-*tan*/ set ah-preh mee-*dee*
tonight	**ce soir**	suh *swahr*
tomorrow	**demain**	de-*man*

2 Food, Menu & Cooking Terms

English	French	Pronunciation
I would like	**Je voudrais**	jhe voo-*dray*
to eat	**manger**	mahn-*jhay*
Please give me	**Donnez-moi,**	doe-nay-*mwah,*
	s'il vous plaît	seel voo play
a bottle of	**une bouteille de**	ewn boo-*tay* duh
a cup of	**une tasse de**	ewn tass duh
a glass of	**un verre de**	uh vair duh
a plate of breakfast	**une assiette de**	ewn ass-ee-*et* duh
	le petit-déjeuner	luh puh-*tee* day-zhuh-*nay*
a cocktail	**un apéritif**	uh ah-pay-ree-*teef*
the check/bill	**l'addition/la note**	la-dee-see-*ohn*/la noat
dinner	**le dîner**	luh dee-*nay*
a knife	**un couteau**	uh koo-*toe*
a napkin	**une serviette**	ewn sair-vee-*et*
a spoon	**une cuillère**	ewn kwee-*air*
Cheers!	**A votre santé!**	ah vo-truh sahn-*tay!*
fixed-price menu	**un menu**	uh may-*new*
fork	**une fourchette**	ewn four-*shet*
Is the tip/service	**Est-ce que le service**	ess-ke luh ser-*vees*
included?	**est compris?**	eh com-*pree?*
Waiter!/	**Monsieur!/**	mun-*syuh*/
Waitress!	**Mademoiselle!**	mad-mwa-*zel*
wine list	**une carte des vins**	ewn cart day *van*
appetizer	**une entrée**	ewn en-*tray*
main course	**un plat principal**	uh plah pran-see-*pahl*
tip included	**service compris**	sehr-*vees* cohm-*pree*
wide-ranging	**menu dégustation**	may-*new* day-gus-ta-see-*on*
sampling of the		
chef's best efforts		

MEATS

English	French	Pronunciation
beef stew	**du pot-au-feu**	dew poht o *fhe*
marinated beef	**du boeuf à la mode**	dew bewf ah lah *mhowd*
braised with		
red wine and		
served with		
vegetables		
chicken	**du poulet**	*dew poo*-lay
rolls of pounded	**des quenelles**	day ke-*nelle*
and baked		
chicken, veal,		
or fish, often		
pike, usually		
served warm		
chicken, stewed	**du coq au vin**	dew cock o vhin
with mushrooms		
and wine		

English	French	Pronunciation
frogs' legs	des cuisses de grenouilles	day cweess duh gre-*noo*-yuh
ham	du jambon	dew jahm-*bohn*
lamb	de l'agneau	duh lahn-*nyo*
rabbit	du lapin	dew lah-pan
sirloin	de l'aloyau	duh lahl-why-*yo*
steak	du bifteck	dew beef-*tek*
filet steak, embedded with fresh green or black peppercorns, flambéed and served with a cognac sauce	un steak au poivre	uh stake o *pwah*-vruh
double tenderloin, a long muscle from which filet steaks are cut	du chateaubriand	dew *sha*-tow-bree-ahn
stewed meat with white sauce, enriched with cream and eggs	de la blanquette	duh lah blon-*kette*
veal	du veau	dew *voh*

FISH

English	French	Pronunciation
fish (freshwater)	du poisson de rivière/du poisson d'eau douce	dew pwah-sson duh ree-vee-*aire*/dew pwah-sson d'o *dooss*
fish (saltwater)	du poisson de mer	dew pwah-sson duh *mehr*
Mediterranean fish soup or stew made with tomatoes, garlic, saffron, and olive oil	de la bouillabaisse	duh lah booh-ya-*besse*
herring	du hareng	dew ahr-*rahn*
lobster	du homard	dew oh-*mahr*
mussels	des moules	day *moohl*
mussels in herb-flavored white wine with shallots	des moules marinières	day moohl mar-ee-nee-*air*
oysters	des huîtres	dayz hoo-*ee*-truhs
shrimp	des crevettes	day kreh-*vette*
smoked salmon	du saumon fumé	dew sow-mohn fu-*may*
tuna	du thon	dew tohn
trout	de la truite	duh lah tru-*eet*

SIDES & APPETIZERS

English	French	Pronunciation
butter	du beurre	dew bhuhr
bread	du pain	dew pan
goose liver	du foie gras	dew fwah grah
potted and minced pork and pork byproducts, prepared as a roughly chopped pâté	des rillettes	day ree-*yett*
rice	du riz	dew ree
snails	des escargots	dayz ess-car-*goh*

FRUITS & VEGETABLES

English	French	Pronunciation
cabbage	du choux	dew *shoe*
eggplant	de l'aubergine	duh loh-ber-*jheen*
grapes	du raisin	dew ray-*zhan*
green beans	des haricots verts	day ahr-ee-coh *vaire*
lemon/lime	du citron/ du citron vert	dew cee-*tron*/ dew cee-tron *vaire*
pineapple	de l'ananas	duh lah-na-*nas*
potatoes	des pommes de terre	day puhm duh *tehr*
potatoes au gratin	des pommes de terre dauphinois	day puhm duh tehr doh-feen-wah
french-fried potatoes	des pommes frites	day puhm *freet*
spinach	des épinards	dayz ay-pin-*ards*
strawberries	des fraises	day *frez*

SOUPS & SALADS

English	French	Pronunciation
fruit salad	une salade de fruit/ une macédoine de fruits	ewn sah-lahd duh *fwee*/ ewn mah-say-doine duh fwee
green salad	une salade verte	ewn sah-lahd *vairt*
lettuce salad	une salade de laitue	ewn sah-lahd duh lay-tew
onion soup	de la soupe à l'oignon	duh lah soop ah low-*nyon*
salad, native to Nice, composed of lettuce, tuna, anchovies, capers, tomatoes, olives, olive oil, wine vinegar, and herbs	une salade niçoise	ewn sah-lahd nee-*swaz*
sauerkraut	de la choucroute	duh lah chew-*kroot*
vegetable soup with basil	de la soupe au pistou	duh lah soop oh pees-tou

BEVERAGES

English	French	Pronunciation
beer	**de la bière**	duh lah bee-*aire*
milk	**du lait**	dew *lay*
orange juice	**du jus d'orange**	dew joo d'or-*ahn*-jhe
water	**de l'eau**	duh lo
red wine	**du vin rouge**	dew vhin *rooj*
white wine	**du vin blanc**	dew vhin *blahn*
coffee (black)	**un café noir**	uh ka-fay *nwahr*
coffee (with cream)	**un café crème**	uh ka-fay *krem*
coffee (with milk)	**un café au lait**	uh ka-fay o *lay*
coffee (decaf)	**un café décaféiné** (slang: **un déca**)	un ka-fay day-kah-fay-*nay* (uh *day*-kah)
coffee (espresso)	**un café espresso** (**un express**)	uh ka-fay e-*sprehss*-o (un ek-*sprehss*)
tea	**du thé**	dew *tay*
herbal tea	**une tisane**	ewn tee-*zahn*

DESSERTS

English	French	Pronunciation
cake	**du gâteau**	dew gha-tow
cheese	**du fromage**	dew fro-*mahj*
thick custard dessert with a caramelized topping	**de la crème brulée**	duh lah krem bruh-*lay*
caramelized upside-down apple pie	**une tarte tatin**	ewn tart tah-*tihn*
tart	**une tarte**	ewn tart
vanilla ice cream	**de la glace à la vanille**	duh lah glass a lah vah-*nee*-yuh
fruit, especially cherries, cooked in batter	**du clafoutis**	dew kla-foo-*tee*

SPICES & CONDIMENTS

English	French	Pronunciation
mustard	**de la moutarde**	duh lah moo-*tard*-uh
pepper	**du poivre**	dew *pwah*-vruh
salt	**du sel**	dew *sel*
sugar	**du sucre**	dew *sooh*-kruh

COOKING METHODS

English	French	Pronunciation
cooked in parchment paper	**en papillotte**	ehn pah-pee-*yott*
puff pastry shell	**vol-au-vent**	vhol-o-*vhen*

English	French	Pronunciation
a method of food preparation native to Lyon and its region that usually includes wine sauce accented with shredded and sautéed onions	à la lyonnaise	ah lah lee-ohn-*nehz*
method of cooking whereby anything (including fish, meat, fruits, or vegetables) is simmered in a reduction of its own fat or juices	un confit	uh khon-*feeh*

Index

See also Accommodations and Restaurant indexes, below.

FROMMER'S® NATIONAL PARK GUIDES

Algonquin Provincial Park
Banff & Jasper
Family Vacations in the National
    Parks

Grand Canyon
National Parks of the American
    West
Rocky Mountain

Yellowstone & Grand Teton
Yosemite & Sequoia/Kings
    Canyon
Zion & Bryce Canyon

FROMMER'S® MEMORABLE WALKS

Chicago
London

New York
Paris

San Francisco

FROMMER'S® WITH KIDS GUIDES

Chicago
Las Vegas
New York City

Ottawa
San Francisco
Toronto

Vancouver
Walt Disney World® & Orlando
Washington, D.C.

SUZY GERSHMAN'S BORN TO SHOP GUIDES

Born to Shop: France
Born to Shop: Hong Kong,
    Shanghai & Beijing

Born to Shop: Italy
Born to Shop: London

Born to Shop: New York
Born to Shop: Paris

FROMMER'S® IRREVERENT GUIDES

Amsterdam
Boston
Chicago
Las Vegas
London

Los Angeles
Manhattan
New Orleans
Paris
Rome

San Francisco
Seattle & Portland
Vancouver
Walt Disney World®
Washington, D.C.

FROMMER'S® BEST-LOVED DRIVING TOURS

Austria
Britain
California
France

Germany
Ireland
Italy
New England

Northern Italy
Scotland
Spain
Tuscany & Umbria

THE UNOFFICIAL GUIDES®

Beyond Disney
Central Italy
Chicago
Cruises
Disneyland®
England
Florida
Florida with Kids
Inside Disney

Hawaii
Las Vegas
London
Maui
Mexico's Best Beach Resorts
Mini Las Vegas
Mini-Mickey
New Orleans
New York City

Paris
San Francisco
Skiing & Snowboarding in the
    West
Walt Disney World®
Walt Disney World® for
    Grown-ups
Walt Disney World® with Kids
Washington, D.C.

SPECIAL-INTEREST TITLES

Athens Past & Present
Cities Ranked & Rated
Frommer's Best Day Trips from London
Frommer's Caribbean Hideaways
Frommer's China: The 50 Most Memorable Trips
Frommer's Exploring America by RV
Frommer's Gay & Lesbian Europe
Frommer's Best RV and Tent Campgrounds
    in the U.S.A.

Frommer's Road Atlas Europe
Frommer's Road Atlas France
Frommer's Road Atlas Ireland
Frommer's Wonderful Weekends from
    New York City
The New York Times' Guide to Unforgettable
    Weekends
Retirement Places Rated
Rome Past & Present